the "SMART goals Book"

Turn Your Dreams and Wants into Achievable SMART Goals!

A comprehensive manual of effective Goal-Setting for entrepreneurs, managers, and parents

by Anna Stevens

Contact us at *www.SMARTgoalsBook.info*

This publication is designed to provide accurate and authoritative information in regards to the subject matter covered. It is sold with the understanding that the publisher is not engaged in rendering legal, accounting, or other professional service. If legal advice or other expert assistance is required, the services of a competent professional person should be sought. The publisher and the author make no representations or warranties with respect to the accuracy or completeness of the contents of this work and specifically disclaim all warranties, including, without limitation, warranties of fitness for a particular purpose. No warranty may be created or extended by sales or promotional materials. Neither the publisher nor the author shall be liable for damage arising here from. Moreover, the fact that an organization or a website referred to in this work as a citation and/or a potential source of further information does not mean that the author or the publisher endorse the information the organization or the website may provide or a recommendation it may make. Further, readers should be aware that websites may have changed or disappeared between when this work was written and when it is read.

Foreword by **Alvin C. Miles**
Images for the cover by **Anna Rumiantseva**
Cover design by **Vanessa Lowry**
Interior design by **Aleksandar Pers**
Illustrations for interior by **Muhammad Hammad** and **Simaar Charms**

ISBN-13: 978-0615773674
ISBN-10: 0615773672
LCCN: 2013905025

In the effort to support abused women and children and to raise awareness of domestic violence as well as to contribute funds, Anna Stevens donates one percent of all book sales to Women's Resource Center to End Domestic Violence. You, too, can get involved, make a difference, and change someone's life. Visit www.wrcdv.org

This book is dedicated to my mother, Lyudmila, who - I now finally know - loves me, and whom I love, too.

Praise for the "SMART Goals Book" by Anna Stevens

Anna's approach is succinct and to the point. I manage a small diverse group of individuals scattered across an entire GA state, and their time is at a premium. I plan to introduce them to Anna's book and methods of developing SMART goals as a way to make the most of their time while doing their primary job and advancing their position and value to the company.

— **Bill Markesteyn**, Field Services Manager, *Hewlett-Packard Company*

This book is great for anyone who is not afraid to make their dreams come true, regardless of where they are in personal or professional life. Anna Stevens openly shares the recipes for success through valuable goal-setting principles, which derive from her personal experiences. This book is a must read for any up and coming entrepreneur who is just starting out. It is also a valuable resource for all professionals seeking to achieve their dreams.

— **Jason J. Oliver**, Human Resources Director, *AT&T Mobility*

Anna has taken a key business and personal concept, goal-setting, and has provided an action-oriented tool that individuals can actually use each and every day at work and at home. Great job!!!

— **Bernadette Boas,** Coach, Author, Speaker, Radio Personality, Creator of the movement *Shedding the Bitch*®

This chic has got it GOing! Not letting the hand she was dealt keep her dreams from becoming reality, Anna took control of her life's journey and now challenges you by asking "are you in control of your life's journey or do you let life's circumstances control you?" Packed with essential keys, motivational guidance and action oriented, step-by-step game plans, The SMART goals book is a must have for every 'go get 'em' entrepreneur's library.

— **Coach Jenn Lee**, Motivational Speaker, Small Business Strategist, Corporate Trainer and Life Coach, *Coach Jenn Lee*

Anna was a star MBA student in my class, but in SMART Goals Book, she reverses roles and becomes the teacher. Her easy-to-follow roadmap to success in the face of seemingly hopeless personal and professional dilemmas are motivational, inspirational, and universal for all.
— **Perry Binder, J.D.**, Legal studies professor, *Author of 99 Motivators for College Success*

This book is like a conversation with a coach. I found the personal anecdotes weaved around other people's stories uplifting. Most of all, this book offers common sense exercises that, if done periodically, will keep our goals in clear sight. Great job, Anna!
— **Rita Izaguirre**, Former Senior Vice President of Talent Acquisition, Diversity and Compliance for SunTrust Banks Inc., Principal, *IDEIAS*

Few people have Anna's outlook on life, and even fewer have the ability to get others to see things in a positive and practical way. Anna is an amazing woman with positive energy and a genuine desire to help people attain their life-goals, sharing her proven strategies that one can apply in life and in business. Anna is a powerful example of a woman's capacity for resilience. This book is very touching and will make one stand up and say "Yes, I can". It is not only a manual or a "how-to" book, but it is more of a "how-I-did-it" book, which will inspire you as it did me. Go, Anna!
— **Laurie Sossa**, President, *Southern Barter Club and Eco-Trade Global*

I met Anna when she participated in volunteer training for the Women's Resource Center to End Domestic Violence. She introduced herself during a break and offered to help in any way she could. Over the years, Anna has helped in countless ways. Perhaps most importantly, she has helped as a powerful example for other survivors. Many are surprised when they hear how quickly Anna learned English or how recently she was in a shelter herself. Anna is a reminder of what is possible when accountability and commitment drive realistic goals. Now with her book, Anna shares her own strategies for setting goals. Readers will learn how to overcome obstacles, avoid self-doubt, and develop as well as accomplish realistic goals. Read her book today for relatable examples and easy-to-use ideas for planning and achieving success in any aspect of your life.

— **Barbara Gibson,** Safehouse Director, *Women's Resource Center to End Domestic Violence*

Anna! Thank you, thank you, thank you for helping me simplify my life by using SMART goals! I'm no stranger to setting goals, but fall short at times due to the everyday hustle and bustle of life. Your book did a great job at explaining how the fine details help make the goal more obtainable and reachable. As a working single parent of a very busy young lady, I sometimes get my goals put on the back burner. I feel that Turn Your Dreams and Wants into Achievable SMART Goals! will not only help me professionally, but also as a parent. After reading your book, my daughter and I both have set some goals and the detailed steps on how we wish to achieve them. We have also decided to write five things each evening that we are thankful for. Thanks so much for sharing your life experiences and letting us know that despite what circumstances you deal in life with, good or bad, you can always come out a winner!

— **Lynn Lopes**, Super Mom, Program Manager, *Central Atlanta Progress*

I am a mother of five children and found Anna's book to be so helpful and inspiring! Since I have read Anna's book, my children and I are working on our own mission statement that will help us reach our personal and family goals. It is a must-read!

— **Lorynn Hollie**, *Mother of Five*

Turn Your Dreams and Wants into Achievable SMART Goals! isn't just about setting goals; it's about reaching them. Reaching amazing goals may seem like magic or luck to some people, but it is a skill that can be developed. This book is more than a riveting story of a woman's triumph over adversity. It's a practical toolkit for applying Anna Stevens' hard-won insights on planning and achievement to your own personal or business challenges.

— **Joe M. Turner,** America's Chief Impossibility Officer, Speaker, Entertainer, Author of High JOEltage – 101 JOElts for Becoming Amazingly Effective, *Turner Magic Entertainment*

Why do I love Anna Stevens and her new SMART goals Book? It could be because of our mutual love for Frank Sinatra and how we each studied his purposeful craft. It could also be because Anna epitomizes my life's work of freeing struggling men, women, and youth from the curse of homelessness. And yet, after reading SMART goals Book, I am convinced it is because Anna courageously forged her every dream-achieving step, from the deepest part of her character, and without the many resources and lifelines we often take for granted. By knitting together her remarkable journey with actionable insight, Anna Stevens has provided us with a manual for quickly setting and achieving goals, while also helping us rewrite our own "life scripts" so they no longer dissuade or derail us.
— **Tiger Todd**, Founder, CEO and Chief Change Strategist, *Heroes Incorporated*

In my opinion, Anna Stevens' book hopes to provide assistance on how to organize your career-goals and your life in general. Many people forget to first balance all aspects of life, and then career success will naturally follow.
— **Solange Warner**, Founder, *World Chamber of Commerce*

Anna's book is relevant to every person who reads it - business professionals, entrepreneurs, parents, managers, students, and the list goes on! Her directions and worksheets are simple yet impactful. She provides an easy system for anyone to find out who they really are. Anna's book provides intimate details about her life, making you feel as though she is sitting in the room with you and helping you through every step. Her story is powerful and inspiring.
— **Logan Hooks**, Director of Communication, *RAISE Global Services*

A highly motivating, simple, clear, logical system, which helps with self-analysis and self-development. Deep analysis of the self-development process will help the reader achieve measurable goals in no time. Personal stories reveal different angles of life and solutions to it. I strongly recommend this book, especially for families with children of any age. Inspirational, empowering and strong!!! Easy and enjoyable to read.
— **Lilia Postolachi**, Director of Membership and International Service, *World Trade Center*

Anna's book is full of very practical information, wonderful stories, and first-hand knowledge. Anna walks us through how to properly set and achieve goals and how to avoid the traps that hold us back. I recommend it for anyone who is struggling to accomplish all of those things they want to accomplish.

— **Brent Darnell**, International Best-Selling Author of The People-Profit Connection, *Brent Darnell International*

As author Anna Stevens points out in her new book, Turn Your Dreams and Wants Into Achievable SMART Goals, the idea of SMART goals has been around for decades. However, I have never seen anyone apply the process with such relevance to so many areas of life. Anna's personal application of the lessons she teaches the reader is, perhaps, the most inspirational reason to follow her lead. I thought at first that there would be little new that I would learn from Anna's book, but find myself now studying how to apply her directions to more than one neglected dream and want of my own. Thanks to Anna Stevens for her down-to-earth approach and incredible inspiration!

— **Dr. Don Osborne**, Author of The Probable Future: You Can Predict it & You Can Change it, *Think Then Lead*

Turn Your Dreams and Wants into Achievable SMART Goals! is a must-read! Anna provides practical information in a format that is easy to follow. Her willingness to share her personal and professional journeys is truly inspirational and provides solid evidence that her methods truly work. This is a book that will remain in my toolbox for many years to come. I'm already making a list of the people who will be getting it as a gift!

— **Bambi S. Bellflowers**, MSHRM, SPHR, Human Resources Professional

Anna has written a very provocative and hard-hitting book that tells us exactly what we need to do if we want to succeed in any aspect of our life. The challenge for all of us is whether or not we are willing to put in the effort, as described in the book, to achieve our goals. The fear of failure is what prevents us from being specific about our goals, which is what SMART goals concept requires.

— **S. Jeffrey Ackerman, M.D.,** Senior Healthcare Executive

I congratulate Anna Stevens for bringing SMART goals system to a new level of understanding. I have used SMART goals for years, and Anna has provided a rich resource for all of us. Her practical and user-friendly SMART guidelines will help countless people to get better control of their life-problems. I cannot think of a more helpful book for people who want to achieve greatness in their personal and professional life.
— **Donald Booz**, Executive Coach, Former District Executive Minister at Brethren Disaster Ministries

The SMART goals Book is absolutely wonderful for those wanting to achieve optimal success. Anna gives you easy ways to set goals and achieve them. This step-by-step guide allows you to measure your achievements along the way. It's definitely the perfect guide in achieving your dreams. As an author, coach and speaker, Anna Stevens has proven that she has the key to success!
— **Felicia Phillips**, Sustainability Guru, Publisher, *H3O Eco Magazine*

You may ask yourself: "What do I need with another goal setting book?" That is the wrong question to ask in relationship to Anna Stevens' book, Turn Your Dreams and Wants into Achievable SMART Goals! You should be asking yourself: "How quickly can I get my copy, start reading, and start changing my life?" and "Why didn't I have this book years ago?" This book may not have hit the book store shelves when you felt that you needed it years ago, but that is because it was being orchestrated by Anna's experiences. Anna has the unbelievable gift of taking her personal experiences and the experiences of others and compiling them into a thoughtful, well-choreographed plan of action to enable you to lead the life you desire, to the tune of your own music. When Anna says "The books is full of practical and motivational content and includes both theory and examples or relevant experiences," she does not under-deliver. I especially like her use of practical examples from her life and that of others to demonstrate her points and to guide you through the process. It is easy to quote the experts, the super-achievers. However, Anna has been able to demonstrate her points with the "living reality": real-life examples. In addition, Anna does not lead you to believe that your life-long negative scripts are not there. In fact, she acknowledges the negative voice that may be sounding off in your head and gives you the tools to dim and silence that darker side which impedes your success and happiness. Although it is hard to pinpoint one thing in Anna's SMART goals Book that was the most helpful to me, one of my favorite and most powerful exercises was the development of my own personal mission statement. This has enabled me to look at the big picture and set goals using my resources that supported my own personal mission and not that someone else. Anna has shared with the world her system so that we can each achieve our greatest potential. It is one of the greatest gifts you will ever receive, and for that I am eternally grateful.

— **BevAnn Bonds**, Entrepreneur, SMART Goals Enthusiast, *Business Support Solutions*

I've had the pleasure of personally knowing Anna for some time now. Seeing her publish a masterpiece such as this is not shocking. Turn Your Dreams and Wants into Achievable SMART Goals! captured every essence of what is needed in today's world. The personalized approach to writing of this book brings a sense of being in a one-on-one conversation with Anna. Opening the pages of this book will change your life! Given the user-friendly templates and step-by-step guidance, putting the book down will be extremely difficult. Anna refused to let the challenges of life hold her back. Today, she shares with the world how she did it. Turn Your Dreams and Wants into Achievable SMART Goals! is a timely and resourceful book that every person who desires to change their life must have. Get your highlighters, notebooks and pens out, because things are about to shift!

— **Natasha Davis-Bowen**, RN-BSN, MBA-M, Author, Speaker, Trainer, Radio and Television Host, CEO and Senior Business & Marketing Strategist, *Visionary People LLC*

With so many books previously written about goal-setting, when Anna asked for feedback on hers, frankly I was looking for something "different". I was not disappointed. This book is a powerhouse of strategies, reflections, and quotes. Regardless of where someone is in their life, they can significantly benefit both personally and professionally. One unique feature is Anna's sharing of rich content followed by her personal experiences. This is definitely a must-read for anyone wanting to significantly step up their game. Eloquently written, Anna's book is a masterpiece.

— **Bonnie Ross Parker**, America's Connection Diva, *The Joy of Connecting*

I wanted to make sure you realize that you are making a difference in the world. Reading your book helped me break through and there was almost a physical sensation as if a weight was lifted from my shoulders. It was as if my brain had rebooted and came back online functioning at 100%. Thanks! Our pasts are very different but we both have had to overcome daunting obstacles and personal challenges to reach where we are today. We will have to sit down some evening with a glass of wine and I'll tell you some of my experiences. Thanks again for helping me break through. I'll be re-reading it over the next few days and working on updating my goals.

— **Don Cross, DC, FIAMA, FABDA**

Anna Stevens' book is so much more than a stuffy book explaining how to correctly complete each letter of the acronym. Anna writes with passion as she convinces us that if she can do it, so can we! Anna provides not only motivation, but also a step-by-step method of setting and achieving seemingly impossible goals. This book will definitely go in my consulting toolkit!

— **Cindy Jacoby**, Chief Engagement Officer, *BizHelp Consulting*

As a passionate motivational speaker and the daughter of a longtime community activist, I have instilled in me to follow the biblical instruction to be "our brothers' and sisters' keeper." So, through my philosophy of "Each one who reaches one, that agrees to teach one, who then empowers and encourages one, who then lifts one..." we become part of the group of many that started with the awesome power of one. That is what Anna Stevens has done with this book! I pride myself on being innovative and creative in my own approach to issues and goal-setting, but Anna has surpassed me in my methods! This book should be the "standard in classroom teaching" in the minds of our children, starting in middle school. Outstanding job, Anna!

— **Stacy Witherspoon**, Managing Partner, *SOTH LLC*

Without a question, Anna is one of the most dynamic women I've encountered. I admire greatly her determination and perseverance to overcome all of the hardships she has faced in life in order to succeed. I have witnessed first hand that Anna is quite gifted at being able to discern clear paths for long term vision and direction. She also has a keen ability to hone in on the action steps to facilitate bringing the vision to the forefront to become a reality. I personally enjoyed the exercises she provides in her book that allow people to get a lock in on interacting with dreams which they may have been holding at arms length. No matter what stage you are at in the pursuit of your goals, this book will provide insight and practical tools to move you closer to achieving them.

— **Ashley Feagin**, Director of Corporate Development, *RAISE Global Services*

In her own unique style demonstrating passion and grace under pressure, Anna Stevens has written her story in a compelling and inspirational way that will appeal to anyone wanting to improve their life for the better. Anna's accomplishments are testament to her own goal-setting process. If you have goals you want to achieve, use Anna's methods to increase your own efficiency and effectiveness.

— **David Cory, M.A.**, President, *The Emotional Intelligence Training Company Inc.*

Upon reading the book, my aha-moment was that you wrote the book that I had been wanting to write. Your SMART goals Book is definitely for me and other entrepreneurs, managers, and parents who desire to set specific, measurable, action-oriented, realistic, and time-bound goals and achieve them. Your personal experiences were a great way to show how SMART goals were used in action to help you overcome numerous obstacles. I enjoyed the exercises, tips and, of course, your personal experience anecdotes. I am so pleased to have been touched by your story! May you be blessed with loads of love, happiness and continued success!

— **Kevin Mills**, Marketing Manager, *Mills And Associates Inc.*

Anna's book, Turn Your Dreams And Wants Into Achievable SMART Goals!, is a must-read for anyone wanting to put structure around achieving a set of specific goals for your life. I especially enjoyed seeing Anna integrate her personal story as examples of how someone can overcome adversity, come with nothing, and through a series of strategies meet success levels most people only dream about. Her story is inspiring and shows how through perseverance and a systematic approach many achievements are possible. One part I found fascinating was the chapter on applying her principles to children. In today's society, where children are pampered and tied to parents through constant contact, her suggestions and tools to create independence and responsibility in children are right on target. People who embrace this strategy will no doubt see their young children grow up strong and confident. Congratulations, Anna, on a job well done.

— **Carol McKown**, Chief Solutions Officer, *RAISE Global Services*

Acknowledgements

This book is about how to set and achieve goals that guarantee success. The techniques, strategies, systems, and solutions I share here were created and tested in my own personal experience through overcoming very significant and often times tragic challenges on my own personal journey.

When you learn the way I have, you have many people to thank for many great things. I would like to say a word of appreciation to the director of Kursk Higher Teacher's Training School, where during 1998-2002 I worked on obtaining my Elementary School Teacher Certificate. She believed in me and she gave me my first ticket to the life I dreamed of.

A special thank-you is going to all my professors at The State All-Russian Financial and Economical Institute, where during 2002-2008 I worked on my B.B.A. in Management. They challenged me to grow and believed in me so much that I always cared to do my best to justify their faith in me.

My gratitude extends to the Women's Resource Center to End Domestic Violence, Atlanta Legal Aid Society, Catholic Charities' Immigration Legal Services, Rachel Gedrich, Greg Goodwin, Elena Bowser, Adrienne Fagler, Tricia Siaso, Oleg Chernov, Yaslynn Mack, and Rick Craddock for giving me a hand when I was going through many difficulties trying to survive after my escape from domestic violence. They are the reason why I am still here, in this country, stronger than ever and successful as they always believed I could be. Without them this book would have been impossible.

I would like to express my appreciation to those who contributed to the production of this book; particularly Alvin C. Miles for writing the thoughtful Foreword and encouraging me, W. Frank Blount for creating a statement of support that is now published on the cover of the book, Katharine Pike for producing outstanding content for the About the Author section, as well as Logan Hooks and Stacy Witherspoon for helping with edits.

I wish to sincerely thank my mother who after so many years of difficulties in the relationship with me has found courage and strength to reconnect again, and who shed a great deal of so needed light on many questions I had about what had actually happened between the two of us in this life. What had always appeared to be painful and terrifying, now, thanks to her, is more understandable and justifiable. I have recently realized that my mother does actually love me, and I do love her, too. My heart is peaceful now.

Last but not least, my gratitude is endless and I have no right words to express it when it comes to my loving husband, Dr. Philip Day, who magically found me on Facebook and surrounded me with tender love, strong respect, ardent support, and unlimited encouragement - exactly what I always wanted and needed. I love you, Philip!

Contents

Foreword 18

Introduction: Homeless, Hopeless, and Helpless. 19

The Concepts of Accountability and Commitment. 28

Five Critical Exercises to Help You Figure Out
What You Really Want. 32

Look at the Big Picture of Your Life Overall. 38

A Special Mindset for Designing Your SMART Goals 41

Creating Your Ten Year Plan. 45

The What, the Why, and the How of SMART Goals. 48

Importance of Both Substance and Process of SMART Goals. 52

The SMART Goals Template 55

When Self-Doubt and Negative Self-Talk Get in the Way 59

An Accountability Partner as a Source of Support 69

Self-Accountability, Self-Discipline, and Self-Leadership 76

Common Sense and Flexibility with SMART Goals 78

SMART Goals for Entrepreneurs. 83

SMART Goals for Managers. 96

SMART Goals for Parents. 99

How to Choose a Measure of Your Progress 104

How and When I used My Comprehensive
SMART Goals System 106

Next Steps for You After Reading This Book 114

Thirty-Five Great Quotes to Get You Motivated 116

About the Author. 120

Connect with the Author 123

Foreword

When I was invited to write the foreword for Turn Your Dreams and Wants Into Achievable SMART Goals!, I reflected on my thirty-one year career in telecommunications. Over that span, I've mentored and coached many smart people who initially didn't have concrete goals or a plan for their achievement. I've transitioned my career to academia and over the past several years, I've mentored, coached and interviewed hundreds of mid-career professionals who desire to earn an MBA to move forward in their personal and professional lives. Many of them have a good idea of their goals and a path forward, but the majority are uncertain. Since MBA graduates represent a small percentage of the general population in America, one can assume there are millions more people with uncertainty about their goals and future. I accepted the invitation to encourage you to read this book because I know it fills a vital need!

Anna Stevens has written this book to help fill the void millions of people feel about their future and how to manifest it. She's qualified to write this book because she's used the power of its principles to lift herself from homelessness to happiness; from a battered wife to a happy wife; from joblessness to entrepreneurship, social activist for change and now - successful author! What Anna has done here is to put together a thoughtful, personal, and thorough guide to help you take control of your existence by empowering your future. She does so in a way that you would expect from a person who practices what she preaches; by letting you into her past and the dramatic experiences that shaped her beliefs about the abundance life has to offer.

Empowering people to realize they determine the outcome of their own lives is not always easy. I've personally benefitted from these principles as I've transitioned to my dream career and I continue to manifest the life I envision, so recommending this book is very easy. If digested, this comprehensive manual offers entrepreneurs, managers and parents the opportunity to meet their responsibility to be effective leaders in both their personal and professional lives.

If your goal is to thrive and not just survive – it's time to dream again because you're holding a powerful tool to help you convert those dreams and wants into achievable SMART goals!

—**Alvin C. Miles,** Director, Graduate Faculty, Host of Global Leader Radio!™, *Executive MBA Programs, Kennesaw State University*

CHAPTER 1

Introduction: Homeless, Hopeless, and Helpless

Life is 10 percent what happens to you and 90 percent how you react to it.
- Charles Swindoll

In April of 2009, I escaped from my abusive ex-husband and was placed in a shelter for victims of domestic violence. I felt alone in a foreign country, unable to speak the native language. I was incapable of asking for even simple things and, what's worse, unable to understand what people around me were saying. Four short years ago, that was me in America: deaf, blind, and dumb.

There are many goal-setting books and concepts out there. Is this book any different? If so, what makes it so special? I know you are asking such questions, and I think it's fair. Undoubtedly, this book is very unique, and here's why. Many authors write books about a single terrible event that happened in their life and caused them to have a breakthrough moment that changed the way they lived their life or viewed it. Some authors write about their illness or, perhaps, that of a loved one; others share how they went broke and then became rich. There wasn't a disastrous or tragic event that caused me to write this book. Rather, there was a tragic and disastrous journey, full of such events.

It started with my birth: my mother couldn't have an abortion due to health-related issues. Thus, she agreed to have a baby; however, she wanted a boy. As a result, when I was born and discovered to be a girl, my mother dressed me as a boy and called me Anton, a boy's name. I was abandoned by my father and raised by a single mother, learning the feeling of rejection at a very young age. I felt rejected not only by the community I lived in, but also by my very own grandmother who has never forgiven my mother for getting pregnant out of wedlock. I started smoking when I was eleven years old, and when I was thirteen my friends and I drank straight liquor in the woods. I've been abused and raped. I tried to commit suicide twice when I was a teen. I lived in a shelter when I was twenty-six: homeless, hopeless, and helpless - in a foreign country, where I knew nobody, no culture, and no language. Yet, I am a women with three college degrees and a great deal of diverse international professional experience; I'm an entrepreneur and a beloved wife, who will soon graduate with an

My mother and I in 1984.
I'm 6 months old.

"It started with my birth: my mother couldn't have an abortion due to health-related issues. She agreed to have me, but wanted a boy, so when a girl was born, my mother dressed me as a boy and called me a boy's name Anton instead of my own name"

MBA from one of the best business schools in the United States. I am also a happy person overall and possess a strong desire for life and an endless drive for success. That is what makes this book so special: here I share my systematic approach to life challenges, and I know that this approach works. It worked hundreds and hundreds of times for me on my own journey and also for my clients on their personal and professional journeys. I see this book as my way of giving back to humanity and helping you. Because I've witnessed too many individuals face problems and give up on their goals right away, or even worse, let go of their life by turning to drugs or alcohol for help, my heart had been calling me for years to share with you the tools that helped me survive and succeed.

FROM MY PERSONAL EXPERIENCE...

During my workshops, I usually ask how many people have goals already set. Interestingly, many people say that they do. Yet, when I ask them to share their goals, they say something like this: "I want to be healthy", "I want to run my business successfully", "I want to be a better parent", and the like. Out of the many people, there was only one person in my experience who showed me her written plan, which she carried with her all the time. It contained a detailed description not only of what she wanted and desired, but also of how she was going to achieve that.

Suppose you want to go to Moscow, Russia. Is that enough for getting to your destination? Do you think that it would help you accomplish this goal faster if you had a detailed plan? Suppose you write down where you want to stay, places you want to visit, so now you know how long you need to be there and how much money it will take, which now enables you to come up with ideas on how you will save up and what you need to prepare to go on such a trip. Would it make a difference in your expenses if you decided to go there during Winter? Of course, because you would need to buy snow boots, a warm jacket, wool pants, and so forth. Would all these details help you become more clear and focused on your goal, if you ever decide that it is realistic at all for you? It's the same with everything else in your life. Just to come up with an idea of what you want or desire is not enough for achieving it. You need a detailed step-by-step plan that will guide you, help you evaluate your progress, and allow you to adjust accordingly.

I now want to ask you one question: are you in control of your life's circumstances or do you let life's circumstances control you?

WHAT THIS BOOK IS ABOUT

Do you know where you're going in life? That will make a great deal of difference in deciding which way you should go. Are you familiar with any people who live their best day every day? They seem to be so accomplished, happy, successful... Their life is meaningful, their relationships are fulfilling, their health is excellent, their businesses are prospering, their finances are blooming... And you wonder: what is their secret? The secret is that they know who they are, what they want, and how to get it. They set thoughtful, ambitious yet realistic goals and - the biggest secret - they follow through. No matter what others think of their chances for success, these people believe in themselves. They don't make excuses; rather, they find support and resources to make good things happen for themselves, their families, their businesses, their communities, and the world. If you're interested in the theory behind the above statement of mine, please refer to a study called "Building a Practically Useful Theory of Goal Setting and Task Motivation: A 35-Year Odyssey" by Edwin A. Locke and Gary P. Latham (R. H. Smith School of Business, University of Maryland).

In this book I will share with you my clear, simple, and complete step-by-step system that will help you set and achieve significant and meaningful goals. The book is full of practical and motivational content and includes both theory and examples of relevant experiences. Discover each step of the process I describe here and apply the skills you learn as you go. Do not miss or skip chapters - go one step at a time to achieve the best results. Using this simple yet powerful approach, you're guaranteed to turn your dreams and wants into achievable SMART goals.

The first known use of the term "SMART goals" occurred in the November 1981 issue of Management Review by George T. Doran. What do we actually mean when say "SMART goals"? SMART stands for Specific, Measurable, Action-oriented, Realistic and Time-bound.

You see, there are many people in your life who can influence your decisions, your evaluation of reality, and even your own sense of self-worth. Your boss has a great idea about what you want and should do in your career. Your spouse has many thoughtful beliefs about what's best for you and what you're capable of accomplishing. Your mother is persuaded that she knows best where you really should be at this point of your life... Everyone has a unique understanding of who you are, what you're capable of, and what your future should look like. Yet, the only one whose ideas and beliefs about you and your life really matter is you. You are the very person who determines what you will and will not do, what you like and dislike, what motivates and what discourages you. Consequently, all the answers to your questions about what your goals can and should be lie within, so does your power to accomplish those goals. This book has been written to help you discover your very own standards for success and find purpose in your work, life, and relationships.

WHY YOU SHOULD READ THIS BOOK

This book is a comprehensive manual and a detailed guide to effective goal-setting for entrepreneurs, managers, and parents. I have worn all of these hats in my life and career, and am very familiar with the challenges these roles carry along. Having overcome many of the obstacles associated with those roles, I developed a methodology that is proven to work well. So, one day I thought to myself: "How wonderful it would be to share my strategic system to help others gain clarity and focus with their goals!" And here it is - you're reading it right now.

My book offers practical strategies to identify the goals that are meaningful and matter most to you. It teaches you to objectively evaluate your goals and eliminate the ones that are not realistic. It provides solutions for overcoming challenges that arise as you're moving along the way to your success. It coaches you how to face fears rather than to avoid them. It arms you with useful tools and know-hows to empower you to take actions that will ensure the results you desire. Finally, this book supplies you with questions that are meaningful and significant and are aimed to help you through your self-discovery process.

Despite what you already know about goals, this book is a must-read as it offers a practical step-by-step strategy that is proven to produce positive long-lasting results.

WHOM THIS BOOK IS FOR

This book is for you, if you seek to advance to the next level in your life, career, relationships, health, and wealth. If you are tired of meaningless new year's resolutions, if you are sick of making promises to your wonderful self and breaking them, if you lack interest and motivation and are stuck in your comfort-zone, realizing that laziness has become your worst enemy, if you get distracted easily and get off track, and if you just want some fresh thoughts on how to discover and achieve what you really want - this is your book! Read it, share it, and keep it on your desk to refer to it often.

THIS BOOK FOR ENTREPRENEURS

Everyone needs something to aim for. You can call it a challenge, or you can call it a goal. It is what makes us humans. It was challenges that took us from being cavemen to reaching for the stars.
- Richard Branson

During the Summer of 2011, I established my own small consulting company out of a strong desire to finally be my own boss, to live in accordance with my own values, and to set my own schedule. I was driven by the idea of helping people build their happily-ever-after, create their own success, and find meaning in their life. Frankly speaking, that was all I had - just those two things: the desire to achieve independence and the idea of helping others. I had no funds, no experience, no network, and no clue where to even start. Today my business is growing, my network is expanding, and my so-hardly-gained entrepreneurial skills and experiences are serving me well in assisting other business owners with their start-ups.

Without a doubt, there was a lot of struggle on my journey; yet, there was a great deal of learning, long sleepless nights of endless but inspiring work, and many-many fears. Fears of success, fears of failure, fears of responsibility, fears of criticism, fears of competition, fears of the unknown, and many more fears that forced me to often get in my own way. I faced, acknowledged them, and turned them into motivation, energy, and confidence to help me get where I wanted to be.

How did I make it happen? With my proven methods of setting and achieving SMART goals. I applied them again and again, step after step, and they always worked perfectly. Just keep reading this book to discover my secret-methods. Learn them, practice them, embed them in your daily routine, and, I promise, you will build strong success for your entrepreneurial business.

THIS BOOK FOR MANAGERS

Management is all about managing in the short-term while developing the plans for the long-term.
- Jack Welch

Managers' responsibility is to ensure that people deliver the expected results, which are the company's strategy. The company's strategy, in turn, determines its competitive advantage. So, if a manager does a poor job of motivating employees' productivity, the enterprise is a weak competitor.

For a business to strengthen its position on the market, its managers should become skillful at helping their subordinates to set and achieve specific and measurable goals with realistic deadlines and clear expectations. Managers should also mentor employees through challenges, helping them grow and develop new skills.

In this book, managers will find a wealth of practical information about SMART goals (Specific, Measurable, Action-oriented, Realistic and Time-bound) and will also get familiarized with unique worksheets and templates, which they can use to assist their subordinates with setting and achieving goals on a regular basis.

To ensure that employees develop and demonstrate accountability and commitment, there is a special chapter on how to work with a mentor, how to qualify one for such a role, and what benefits an accountability partner provides for education, motivation, inspiration, and ideation in the business environment.

THIS BOOK FOR PARENTS

Where parents do too much for their children, the children will not do much for themselves.
- Elbert Hubbard

I have learned the true meaning of this quote through my own parenting experience. We all know many people who come from hardworking families, where they had to grow up with a bare minimum and become self-sufficient and independent at a very young age. We look at them now and see responsible citizens, self-reliant adults, successful members of the business community, outstanding performers, and just happy people. Yes, they're happy, because they know the meaning of labor, they appreciate the pleasure of leisure, they value relationships with others, and they respect themselves.

In contrast, there are people who come from wealthy families, had nannies to do everything for them, went to private schools where they were surrounded with special attention, never did their own laundry, never learned how to cook an omelet for themselves, never even gained the essential skills of unwinding on their own before bedtime, and of course, never did anything for anyone else either. You look at their adult life and see how dependent they are on others and how unhappy they are because of that. They need someone to constantly take care of them. They may see no meaning in their life as little things don't satisfy them, because they were spoiled at a very young age. They may suffer a variety of eating disorders, use drugs, alcohol and other extremes in search of satisfaction and comfort. And, above all, in search of themselves.

My friend Casey Horan once said: "We don't raise children - we raise people." I agree with his statement with all my heart. Our responsibility as a parent is to teach our children habits for success, embed responsibility in them, encourage them to exercise accountability, direct them to discover the power of independent thinking, coach them through challenges with meaningful questions rather than to give them bold answers, guide them to practice healthy lifestyle to prolong their life rather than to surround them with a digital world of electronic devices and virtual relationships, while they sit on a couch all day long and shorten their lifetime.

This book is full of practical, real-life parenting ideas that come from my own experience as a parent. The book also contains a chapter specifically dedicated to SMART goals for parents.

The walk I talk in this book comes from my daily life with my two stepsons and also from my five years of experience as a teacher with a diverse group of children, whose ages ranged from seven to seventeen. In the United States, while going through some difficult times in my life as a victim of domestic violence, I also worked as a nanny in several families with different cultural backgrounds. I observed their parenting skills, I learned them, evaluated them, and I witnessed and assessed the results of the strategies that those people applied. This combination of all the knowledge and experiences I've gained throughout the years is shared with you in this book to help you guide your children to success, wellness, and happiness in life.

Overall, this book is a comprehensive manual for entrepreneurs, managers, and parents who want to learn how to set specific, measurable, action-oriented, realistic and time-bound goals and achieve them promptly. Here you will find theoretical concepts about goals and practical examples that support those concepts. You will learn that often it's not the big things, but rather the small things that matter most in achieving success: your mindset, your attitude, your habits, your daily routine, the choices you make, and the people you surround yourself with.

The system I share here will help you achieve superior performance in each area of your life to which it's applied. Utilize this methodology for exceptional success and enjoy the rewards!

WHY AND HOW THIS BOOK WAS BORN

Since establishing my private consulting and coaching company, EQ for Success, LLC, I have worked with a diversity of professionals from all walks of life. Even more interesting is the fact that my clients have different cultural backgrounds as many of them are international people. They are representatives of both genders and different ages. Nevertheless, the majority of my clients have struggled to set their goals. One main reason why is that they don't really know what they want. Some of them also report as their reason the lack of time to think things through. Others say they don't need written goals, seeing that they may lose flexibility in decision-making. Yet, all these people benefited significantly from my SMART goals system that they had to apply, and those who followed through achieved impressive results. That is why I decided to write this book and make my powerful solutions available to the public, so that everyone who desires success can learn how to overcome challenges of goal-setting and become a greater achiever.

CHAPTER 2

The Concepts of Accountability and Commitment

Let today be the day you stop having conflict between your actions and your goals and finally align your greatest intent with your purposeful actions, creating a universal symphony serenading your success!
- Steve Maraboli

The difference between successful people and unsuccessful people is that successful people do all the things unsuccessful people don't want to do. Hence, successful people demonstrate accountability and commitment.

Before we talk about accountability, let's define it. Accountability is an ability to accept responsibility for own actions, decisions, and behaviors as well as the impact and consequences of those. It is your capacity to fulfill your obligations. Simply put, it means "you can be count upon." Whom do you have to be accountable to? Well, it depends. Yourself first and, maybe, your children, parents, spouse, boss, colleagues, bank that provided you with a mortgage, friends who let you stay with them until you got back on your feet after being laid off, your fitness instructor who helps you get back in shape, your doctor who works with you through your healing journey, your brother who looks up to you, and the list can go on and on.

There are two types of accountability, or leadership. Personal leadership, which is the accountability you demonstrate toward your own self and your own personal life, health and any goals you establish for yourself. There is also accountability to others - the leadership you

INTERESTING TO KNOW...

Consider the example of Barb Guerra, a woman with no arms who can do everything with her feet. Born in 1976, she became a victim of an electrical accident while living in Pasadena, Texas, when she was two years old. Barb has lost both of her arms. Despite the tragedy, she does not consider herself handicapped by any means. Contrariwise, today Barb is a wife, a mother, a business owner, a model, a dancer, a swimmer, and a professional health coach. Despite the fact that after the accident and the surgery the doctors predicted that Barb would not even survive, she saw a purpose in her life: "I believe God had a plan for me. I am here to serve a purpose. I believe I am here, on earth, to be an example and inspiration." Through demonstrating accountability to others whom she is encouraged to serve and through fulfilling her commitment to the purpose of her life, Barb has been able to achieve very significant goals, year after year.

If the story of succeeding without arms is not persuading enough, here's the story of succeeding with neither arms nor legs. This is a true proof that accountability and commitment can take you wherever you want to go. Born in 1982 in Melbourne, Australia, without any medical explanation or warning, Nick Vujicic arrived into this world without arms or legs... Imagine the shock of his parents, Dushka Vujicic and Boris Vujicic! They were so concerned about their son and his ability to live a normal life... Many would wonder: "What could one ever do or become with such an extreme disability?" Well, let's see: Nick is a swimmer, a golfer, a well-respected around the globe motivational speaker, an author of multiple books; he travels around the world changing the lives of millions of people, he is happily married, and he just recently became a daddy of a baby boy, Kiyoshi James Vujicic. Nick has told his story of success and happiness on various television and radio programs, and here's what he believes: "If God can use a man without arms and legs to be His hands and feet, then He will certainly use any willing heart!"

Stories of Nick and Barb demonstrate the true power of the following formula:

Accountability + Commitment = Success

FROM MY PERSONAL EXPERIENCE...

In my fourth semester at Robinson College of Business, where I work on obtaining my MBA, I had to take another "numbers-subject", Corporate Finance. I am not a "numbers-person" at all. Numbers are hard for me. Well, let me be honest - numbers annoy me to death. Given that the subject was taught in English and I learned English on my own at home, I was not at all excited about the semester, knowing how difficult it would be for me to make good grades. But like it or not, I had to take the course.

From the first class, I had realized how lucky we were to have a great instructor. Whenever I would face difficulties working on my class projects, I would e-mail my professor with the pictures of my notes, explaining my solutions and my way of thinking and asking him to point out to me where I needed to think differently and why. And my professor would always reply with a detailed, thoughtful feedback. Seeing how much he cared for the quality of my learning and my grades, being thankful for the time he invested into helping me, I set the SMART goal of earning the best grade I could and committed to getting as much as possible out of that class. I did a lot of research online on the concepts that were hard to understand, I watched numerous videos on YouTube to learn how to use an HP financial calculator to solve a variety of homework problems, I invested many hours into taking and retaking quizzes to get all hundred points on as many of them as possible, I spent days and nights preparing for the final exam, and I practiced and practiced, again and again. Indeed, my commitment to excellence along with my accountability to myself and my professor helped me achieve amazing results: I got an "A" for the course!

Nothing is as fulfilling and joyful as the realization of your own strength and power to make a difference when you successfully overcome a significant challenge. I was very excited when received the following e-mail from my professor after our last exam: "I know that you worked very hard and invested much effort into this class. Obviously, it paid off, because you had the fourth highest final exam score in the class... I am proud of your work. You should be proud..."

demonstrate to achieve mutual, common goals, jointly with others.

What about commitment? Commitment is what transforms a promise into reality. It is the likelihood of your taking actions which you promised to take. It is your determination to accomplishing the desired results.

Accountability and commitment are essential keys to successful goal achieving. Accountability empowers you not to wait to be reminded or told what to do next, but rather keep up with your promises on your own doing what's necessary to succeed. Commitment allows you to stay strong and not to give up when times are tough.

To make it easier for you to understand the two concepts and to differentiate between them, let's assume your goal is to lose thirty pounds by running every morning for thirty minutes. Accountability will be demonstrated here by setting an alarm clock early, getting up, brushing your teeth, filling a bottle with water, putting your sports outfit on, and getting out of your house. Commitment here will be demonstrated by actually starting to run and doing it for thirty minutes, despite the rain, wind or pain in your left shoulder.

Remember what Dr. Stephen Covey once said: "Accountability breeds response-ability." That resonates well with Vince Lombardi's statement: "The quality of a person's life is in direct proportion with their commitment to excellence, regardless of their chosen field of endeavor." Remember those words any time you're thinking of giving up!

Accountability enables you to take charge. Commitment empowers you to follow through. Together these two can help you move a mountain!

CHAPTER 3

Five Critical Exercises to Help You Figure Out What You Really Want

Life is not a matter of chance...it is a matter of choice.
- Ka

It is often very comfortable for people to just go with the flow in life, career, and relationships - just simply let someone else take charge, make decisions, provide guidance, and literally do all the hard work of thinking and planning. But is that really all there's in life for you? Is this going to lead you to the destination you'd like to end up at? Do you know what you want and do you pursue it, or do you live simply on auto-pilot? Let me help you figure out what you really want in each area of your life.

EXERCISE ONE. What is your ideal future? One week from now? A month from now? A year, five and ten years from today? Where would you like to end up in your life?

The Old You Exercise.

Imagine yourself being ninety-eight years old. You are sitting in a rocking chair in a quiet room and thinking about the life you've lived to this day. You look back and realize that you had a very good life, and it gives you a feeling of fulfillment. You have no regrets and think to yourself: "If I had to do it again, I wouldn't change anything in my wonderful life." Now, get a pen and some paper and write down the definition and the details of that "very good life" you were just thinking about.

EXERCISE TWO. During my workshops, I usually offer the exercise that activates the mindset of happiness. Here's what I recommend to do.

The Happiest Day in Your Life.

Get a pen and a piece of paper and describe in all the details what the happiest day in your life would look like. Where would it be? Whom would it be with? What would the circumstances be? What would your health conditions be? What would you be wearing, saying, and doing? Just let your imagination flow freely! Once you're done, you should have some breakthrough ideas about what you really want and what matters most to you in life.

EXERCISE THREE. It is also highly desirable that you go through the simple questionnaire below and rate each statement on a scale from one to ten.

The Ten Essential Statements that Help You Discover Yourself.

- *I am satisfied with myself*
- *I am happy with the way I look*
- *I am pleased with my relationships*
- *I am open to and acceptive of constructive criticism*
- *I am positive and persistent when times get tough*
- *I am excited about the successes of other people*
- *I am fine asking for help or an advice*
- *I am open-minded and adaptable to change*
- *I am delighted to meet new people and make connections*
- *I am aware of myself and guided by my own goals, standards, and values*

How many statements got a ten from you? This exercise should have helped you discover what it is that you really want and need to work toward.

EXERCISE FOUR. All the best ideas come and go very quickly, and that is the reason why I always recommend to do all exercises with a pen and paper in hand. This time you will write a letter to your very own but much younger self.

The Young You Exercise.

Write a letter to your younger self (choose the age at which you were the most aspiring and had ambitious expectations of life). Explain to that young person how you have gotten to where you are at right now. Describe what has been motivating and what has been discouraging you. Reveal the details of what you've done with the dreams and desires of that young you. Expound where you're going now and where you see yourself ending up. How does it feel to that young and inspired you to hear what you're saying on paper now?

After this exercise you should be able to say without a doubt what it is that you really want in life.

EXERCISE FIVE. If you want more exercises to assist you, please continue with the one below.

The Five Essential Questions that Lead You to Self-Discovery.

- *What kind of a person are you? Just go ahead and describe yourself as "tall", "smart", "kind", "procrastinator", "complainer", "lazy", "independent", "compassionate", and so on.*

- *What do you value most? Be honest! Is it "beer and TV", "money and career", "family and children", "freedom and flexibility", or what is it, really?*

- *What would you like to be remembered for? Get it out, be true to yourself! Is it "crazy hair and funny jokes", "always perfect attire and strong work ethic", "skinny waist and healthy eating habits", "volunteering and making a difference in the community", or ...?*

- *What are the three adjectives you'd like people to use when describing you? If you experience any difficulties finding the right words, you may want to research a list of positive and negative adjectives to help you express yourself.*

- *What positive difference have you made or plan to make? Examples here may include "helped a friend to stop smoking", "volunteered at a non-profit", "participated in a fundraiser for a meaningful cause", "donated blood to a blood bank", "helped a sick neighbor walk the dog", "inspired someone to go back to school", and the like.*

It has always interested me how some people know what they want from a very early age while others can never figure it out. Hopefully, having completed all the five exercises you will know exactly what you want at this point.

INTERESTING TO KNOW...

Consider the mermaid girl Shiloh Pepin who was for nearly ten years known as the world's only living mermaid. Shiloh Pepin was born with "mermaid syndrome" known as sirenomelia. The condition fused her legs together to look like a mermaid's tail. Due to the illness, the little mermaid had only one working kidney, no lower colon, and no genital organs, which forced her to always wear a special bag for her needs, preventing her from being allowed at a public pool. Despite the fact that the little mermaid was expected to die a few days after her birth, according to the doctors' expectations, Shiloh Pepin lived over ten years of a joyful and happy life. I learned from the stories about that amazing little girl that she knew exactly what she wanted - to be able to swim and to play on a playground with other children one day. Unfortunately, the fused together blood vessels in her legs prevented her from having the legs separated.

However, that didn't stop courageous Shiloh Pepin from achieving her goals. Thanks to her supportive family, loving friends, wonderful community, as well as her own determination, motivation, confidence, and willingness to work hard, one day she was able to be on a playground with other children. Most significantly, at the end of her ninth year of life, she was even able to go to a summer camp and be away from home and her parents for more than one night, independent and self-sufficient, committed to living each day of her life to the fullest. Finally, for her last, tenth birthday, Shiloh Pepin was swimming in her very own swimming pool in the back yard of her house, with many other children, just like she always dreamed. The little mermaid was an amazing example of a person who knew exactly what she wanted, whether it was in regards to the future in one day, one week, or one year. What touched me most about the little mermaid is how much love she had for life and for people and how adventurous and fearless she was, despite her condition. "You will never know unless you try" said Shiloh Pepin once, expressing her attitude toward life. She was a true inspiration!

FROM MY PERSONAL EXPERIENCE...

After I had rescued myself from an abusive marriage and when I was already living in a shelter for victims of domestic violence, I realized that I had no goals of my own, not even my own thoughts or opinions. It was so sad yet explainable: for many months my ex-husband was influencing my life, literally telling me what to do, think, want, and so on. My caseworker at the shelter had informed me that for her to be able to help me, I had to figure out my next steps. So, I started by exploring what it was that I really wanted. I remember creating a list of meaningful reasons that explained exactly why I was happy to be alive. I listed ten of them. This was my little breakthrough moment. Furthermore, by asking myself the questions I shared with you earlier in this chapter, I realized that there were three things I wanted most: freedom to make my own choices, acceptance in the new community, and success. I was already free physically, so next steps for me were to get a divorce, obtain a job, and find a place to live. In order to be accepted by people in America, I knew I had to somehow learn English very fast, adjust to the new culture as soon as possible, and get out there, despite my fears. Lastly, while success was yet undefined at that time, I already felt deeply in my heart that if I stayed strong and kept working on myself, I would figure it all out very soon. And I did.

After having been rejected many times while searching for a job, I faced the reality: I had to obtain a graduate degree in this country in other to get what I wanted here. I knew nothing about the school system in the US and I spoke very limited English when my friend came to visit me at my new apartment and recommended that I enroll in an MBA program. Thinking back, I am amazed now how clueless I was and how fast I put it all together, thanks to my research skills, strong learning ability, and boundless drive to succeed. The conversation with the friend took place in October of 2010, and just a few weeks later I had already explored the three MBA programs in Atlanta, made up my mind as to which one I wanted to join, and started preparing for the Academic English Test I had to take as my first step. On January 24th of 2011, I passed the test with a high enough score, which allowed me to apply for Professional MBA at Georgia State University, J. Mack Robinson College of Business. Practicing English every morning at 4 am before work and every night ▶

▶ *before bed-time, I had written all the essays required, obtained essential recommendations, and that very Spring I was already sitting in a small room in Downtown Atlanta, being interviewed for the MBA program I had dreamed to join. My graduation is coming in a few months as of the day I'm writing this story. That is the power of the self-discovery process I'm sharing with you in this book!*

CHAPTER 4

Look at the Big Picture of Your Life Overall

I work really hard at trying to see the big picture and not getting stuck in ego. I believe we're all put on this planet for a purpose, and we all have a different purpose... When you connect with that love and that compassion, that's when everything unfolds.
- Ellen DeGeneres

Life happens, and often daily events, problems we face, decisions we have to make on the go, and our own moods distract us, make us forget our goals, and force us to lose sight of what matters most. In order to help you stay aware and conscious throughout each day of your life, I recommend you develop a *personal mission statement*. Additionally, I suggest that you create a list of *values* that will guide you in relationships, in business, in your family life, and in your decision-making overall.

Fundamental principles of mission statement production and values creation process are honesty with your own self and thoughtfulness about your life purpose, which we discovered in the previous chapter.

Seven Important Steps to Help You Create a Personal Mission Statement

• *Identify what is already good about your life and what worked for you so far overall. Try to outline common themes. Write everything down.*

• *Develop a list of attributes that have served as the foundation of the suc-*

cesses and accomplishments you had written above.

• *Specify what didn't work well for you so far in life, career or relationships.*

• *Indicate the qualities that contributed to those downfalls.*

• *Name the good things you would like to see happen in your life and to yourself. This can be in regards to your career, family, health, or life in general.*

• *Create a list of attributes you think you will need to possess to turn these things into your reality.*

• *Finally, based on the above self-discoveries, produce a paragraph with a few memorable sentences that will serve as a promise to your own self and will help you navigate through your journey.*

Note that the process of composing a mission statement may take several hours, days or maybe even weeks. Do not rush through it - take your time. Moreover, make sure you keep all the drafts and review them whenever you have a clear and focused state of mind. Even more importantly, remember to perform all the steps outlined in this chapter without consulting with others. It is *your* mission statement, and it has to come from *your* heart. Last but not least, *record your final version of the mission statement, print it out, and place it where you will see it every day*. You may also decide to carry a copy of it in your wallet. Another option to consider is inserting the statement into your e-mail signature. No matter what you decide, the purpose remains unchanged: to help you be mindful no matter what the circumstances. A thoughtful and thorough mission statement will assist you in making faster and more effective tactical decisions in each area of your life and provide guidance through adversity.

Personal values recorded in writing are aimed to echo your mission statement. To create a list of values for yourself, follow the steps below.

Five Essential Steps to Help You Create a List of Personal Values

• *Start by answering these questions. What drives you crazy? What will you absolutely not be able to tolerate? Demonstration of what personal characteristics will for sure cause you to walk away? Write those down.*

• *In contrast, who are the people you admire? Why do you look up to them?*

What values do they demonstrate with their actions? Write those down as well.

• *Now it's time to reflect on yourself. Do you hold the same values you admire in others? On a blank page of paper make two separate columns. In the first column write down the values you admire in people and already carry yourself. In the second one list those you admire yet are still to acquire.*

• *As you draft your table of values, remember to ask yourself from time to time: "Is this particular value supporting or diminishing my mission?"*

• *After a few drafts, you should have the final document that contains somewhere between five and seven core values you can stick to and use as your guidance in daily life.*

Both mission statement and list of values require that you look at the big picture of your life overall. Doing so will force you to get out of your comfort zone and think outside the box. Pursuing your mission statement and living up to your identified values will help you deal effectively with avoidance, procrastination, victim mentality, as well as control your impulses and sacrifice short-term pleasure for long-term sustainable success.

Remember what Jim Rohn once said: "Be careful of what you give up in pursuit of what it is that you want."

FROM MY PERSONAL EXPERIENCE...

My personal mission statement: "I believe that each individual is unique and has a great potential for growth. I admire the differences in people and keep my mind free of prejudgments or prejudices. I aim to listen to others with a true desire to understand their points of view and respect their values. I believe in the power of mind. I am committed to inspiring people to be proactive about their life success in order to achieve their highest goals."

My values: honesty, proactivity, openmindness, thoughtfulness, and enthusiasm.

CHAPTER 5

A Special Mindset for Designing Your SMART Goals

By failing to prepare, you are preparing to fail.
- Benjamin Franklin

Setting SMART goals takes a very special mindset. You need to feel grateful for what you already have accomplished or accumulated in life. Your goals have to come from a good, peaceful place of abundance. You need to be purpose-centered, verbally-expressive, and ready to do the required work step-by-step. Above all, you have to be enthusiastic, inspired, and ready to commit.

Five Crucial Steps to Prepare Your Mind for Setting SMART Goals

• *Let's first call up your gratitude! Start by thanking yourself and the higher being you believe in for everything you already have: your life (many people don't make it to your age at all), your health (there are many people who are suffering from a deadly disease this very moment), your family (many people feel lonely and abandoned), your job (many people today suffer from unemployment and are unable to survive), your home (there are millions of less fortunate and homeless people in this world), your talents, creativity, and the like.*

• *Now, when we activated your gratitude, let's mobilize your self-apprecia-tion! List a few ways in which you already contribute to the world, make a positive difference, and create a strong impact. This doesn't necessarily have to be earning a billion of dollars, coming up with the next Apple-like idea, or establishing a Red-Cross-like non-profit. You may very likely already be the next Steve Jobs, but even if not, you are significant in your own way. Think about the time when you helped your next-door neighbor take the trash out while she was sick. Think about the when time you volunteered and made a positive difference in someone's life. Or, perhaps, you gave a compliment to a cashier at Walmart and that made her day. Or, maybe, you taught yourself English in just a few months like I did. Write it all down and thank yourself for it. Working with people, I sometimes face a difficult situation when people can't think of anything significant they've done. If you are experiencing such a problem, I recommend that you ask a trusted friend or colleague what it is that he or she appreciates in you, admires or respects you for. Tell your friend that it's important to be serious and honest. Write down what the friend says. Remember that you matter and you are very significant: you actually just heard it from your friend.*

- *At this moment, when you are thankful and appreciative, let's get you happy! What are your default-settings: happiness or unhappiness? Do you wake up excited about a new day or do you hate waking up at all? Do you feel good for no reason or do you need a special reason to feel good? To the question "Are you happy?" would you answer "Yes" or do you need a particular condition, such as winning a lottery, buying a private island, and more, in order for you to feel happy? Check your default-settings and write down your findings. If you discover that you are unhappy by default, repeat step number one and two above.*

- *Now when you feel worthy, significant, magnificent, and happy, you are ready to set goals for success. Your final step is to realize in your mind that not only developing a detailed strategy, but mainly taking the necessary actions on a consistent basis - that is the secret of great achievers. If your mind starts sabotaging you by asking "Why would you want this change?", ask back "Why not?"; If your mind will doubt you by asking "Why today? You can wait to start next Monday or on the first of next year...", you reply "Why would I be waiting any longer to start living a better life?" Implementation of your strategy is as important as the strategy itself.*

- *Your mind is all set now. Go to a quiet room, where you can have some private, uninterrupted time. You are ready to start creating your SMART goals.*

As we move forward and you are challenged with my questions, make sure you keep all your notes in order. Confirm that all your information and thoughts are in writing and in a place that is easily-accessible by you. While answering questions, remember to write in complete sentences, so that you can actually review and understand your notes in two or five years from now, without having to guess about what you had written. Also remember: when making a choice of words, especially verbs, select positive forms rather than negative. For example, instead of saying "I don't want to become overweight", write "I want to lose ten pounds and keep that unwanted weight off my beautiful body." Be as detailed and as specific as possible in describing your goals and answering the questions I share with you here. Moreover, remember that you are your only judge. You are the one, who has to be persuaded that your goal is meaningful enough, so that you will commit. You are the only one who can determine whether or not your goal is realistic. Thus, be honest and don't rush - it's important that you take your time to think, write, assess, criticize, and rewrite.

FROM MY PERSONAL EXPERIENCE...

In May of 2009, when I was brought to a shelter for victims of domestic violence by a police officer, I didn't even know who I was anymore. I couldn't even think on my own after eight months of abuse, emotional pressure, and diverse violence that I had experienced. I was crying for days, asking myself why it all has happened to me... One day in April I found myself at a park and, to my own surprise, I had no idea where I was and how I got there. With some help of ambassadors from Downtown Atlanta, I got back to the shelter, walked straight into my room, locked myself in the bathroom, looked myself in the eye, and promised that I will move forward with my life and focus on the bright future rather than my dark past. As I did so, I felt in my heart that I wasn't honest. I confessed it to myself. Right away, I felt ashamed. I looked in the mirror again and repeated that promise with all my courage, stated it, embedded it in my soul and my mind, and only then did I feel that I really meant what I said. I knew at that point that if I were to cry, look back, and feel sad again, I would break a promise to my own self. I wasn't going to let it happen! That very day my life had started to change. And here I am, three and a half years later, sharing that amazing experience with you in my very own book!

Writing goals requires you to be mentally present. Your mind has to be clear and focused. Your heart has to be calm. You need to be as much of yourself as possible when you start working on your goals. I usually recommend to my clients to have a mirror in front of them as it helps people ensure that they won't trick themselves. Often, when you look at yourself in the mirror and make a promise, your eyes will tell you the truth about whether or not you will follow through. Use this method to communicate with yourself.

CHAPTER 6

Creating Your Ten Year Plan

Without goals and plans to reach them you are like a ship
that has set sail with no destination.
- Fitzhugh Dodson

You have already done some great work of discovering and exploring what it is that you really want. You have also prepared your mind. Now it is time to move to the next step. Below is the template for you to create your ten year plan. It is crucial that you dig deep inside yourself and find out what your plans, expectations, wants, desires, and dreams may be. Please start by filling out this template.

Envision your life in six months from today and visualize yourself. Think about where you will be in your career, what health conditions you will have, what kind of relationships will surround you, what your family and money situation will be, and what meaning you will have in life overall, which usually comes from the difference you make.

Think about the same areas of your life in terms of one, five, and ten years from now. Be as realistic as possible. It is very important that you take this self-discovery exercise seriously. These questions are thought-provoking and can lead you to some very significant aha-moments.

This process will help you become clear and focused on what you want for yourself long-term. Clarity and focus are what separates those who do achieve their goals from those who don't.

DISCOVER AND EXPLORE YOUR TEN YEAR PLAN

	Your Career	Your Health	Your Relationships	Your Family	Your Money	Difference You Make
Six Months						
One Year						
Five Year						
Ten Year						

FROM MY PERSONAL EXPERIENCE...

I personally don't set goals of having a huge house, an expensive car, or a private boat within ten years; yet I would like to gain more stability in my life, I want my future to be less unpredictable, and I wish to have more certainty in my business. To support these three wishes of mine, I set a goal of purchasing different types of insurance, saving money in several different ways, and diversifying the revenue stream for my business. I'd also like to remain a size zero as I have been for the last thirteen years and I would like to be healthy in general. For that, I exercise daily and just set a goal of running at least three times around the neighborhood every other day. All these indicators on the ten year plan determine what goals you set. For example, I personally, instead of setting a goal of purchasing a TV, set a goal of purchasing workout equipment that will improve my health and help me cope with stress in a more effective way. Another example is that, instead of buying a new car to replace my old worn-out SUV, I decided to invest money in publishing this book to support my business and the goal of diversifying its revenue streams. Similarly, your ten year plan will determine the SMART goals you set for yourself.

CHAPTER 7

The What, the Why, and the How of SMART Goals

He who has a why to live can bear almost any how.
- Friedrich Nietzsche

After having done all the exercise, you are ready to dive into SMART goals' specifics. As was mentioned before, SMART stands for Specific, Measurable, Action-oriented, Realistic and Time-bound. Let's explore this together.

Specific answers the questions What? Why? and How?
The <u>What </u>is your head - it identifies WHAT it is that you need to accomplish.
The <u>Why</u> is your soul - it specifies WHY you should accomplish it, it gives meaning to your goal, it outlines the purpose and the benefit of achieving that goal.
The <u>How</u> is your hands - it focuses on the tools and strategies needed for achieving your goal.

Example: "Schedule a lunch-and-learn with the Chamber of Commerce to promote our company's business services through an educational workshop that uncovers the importance of our value proposition."

In this example, you see the following three parts:
"Schedule a lunch-and-learn with the Chamber of Commerce..." - the What.

"...to promote our company's business services..." - the Why.
"...through an educational workshop that uncovers the importance of our value proposition." - the How.

Answering all three of these questions is essential for motivating you, helping you stay on the right track, and keeping you accountable for the progress as well as the overall results.

Measurable answers the questions How much? How many? or How will I know when I progress? It identifies what tangible evidence you will measure your success by. Remember: if you can't measure it, you can't manage it! So, set some criteria that you can use to determine whether or not you've made any progress toward your success at a particular point in time. This selected criteria has to enable you to evaluate how far you have come and how long you have until your goal is considered accomplished.

Compare the two examples below.

Example 1: "Lose weight by Christmas"
Example 2: "Lose fifteen pounds by Christmas to fit in a size four dress by exercising every Monday, Wednesday and Friday from 6 p.m. to 7 p.m. and eating healthy."

As you can see, example one's goal is too vague and is hard to measure at a specific point in time as it does not indicate how to measure the progress. The goal in the second example meets the requirements of answering the What, Why and How questions and provides a clear criteria for measurement of success - a size four dress for which specific fifteen pounds have to be lost.

Action-oriented. Every time you set a goal, it has to start with a verb that identifies the specific action that's needed to be taken in order to successfully achieve that goal. "It is not only what we do, but also what we don't do, for which we are accountable" - Moliere, a French Playwrite once said.

Compare the two examples below.

Example 1: "I want to get a salary raise."
Example 2: "Set up a meeting with my manager for November 3rd at 9 a.m. to discuss my performance and accomplishments and request a $1,500 raise."

It is evident from these examples that in example two the goal starts with a powerful verb which identifies exactly what has to be done. In example one the "I want" phrase is meaningless as it only identifies a wish and not the readiness to make a commitment.

Realistic. When you set your goal, remember to check your reality testing. The goal "Lose 25 lb in two days to fit the wedding dress" is very specific, measurable, action-oriented and time-bound, however, it is not realistic. If a goal fails to be realistic, there is no chance it will be achieved. Furthermore, if you set unrealistic goals too often, that creates disappointment and frustration and discourages you from trying. Thus, it is essential for your goal to be realistic yet challenging and inspiring.

Ask yourself the following questions.

- Is it possible for anyone to accomplish this goal under similar circumstances?
- Is it probable for me to accomplish this goal under my particular circumstances?
- Will accomplishing this goal challenge me without defeating?

Time-bound. You have to set the time frame for accomplishing your goal. If you don't, it may take forever to reach your destination and you may get tired and change your focus. Consequently, to help you obtain and keep the sense of urgency that will help you stay focused, you have to set a deadline by which the goal has to be achieved. If you haven't achieved it by that deadline, don't give up - be flexible and adjust your deadline in accordance with the progress you make.

It's ok to not meet every deadline, but at least you know that you are moving toward the goal. Also, it helps you figure out what it is that you need to do every day to contribute to achieving your success.

Compare the following examples.

Example 1: "Learn social media next Summer."
Example 2: "Create a Facebook profile and page as well as establish Twitter and Pinterest accounts by July 15 next year and schedule updates every day at 10 am to engage potential customers in a dialogue and generate business buzz for higher SEO rankings."

When you compare the two examples, you will understand that the word "Summer" is too vague for establishing a time frame. It cannot serve as a deadline for a goal. Instead, time should be identified as a specific date by which you will check the progress you will have made and assess what else will have to be done to complete your goal. However, statements like "Christmas", "Thanksgiving", and the like can be used for the purpose of a deadline, without a doubt, as they are specific enough.

Utilize the above system to set SMART goals that emphasizes what you want to happen, by when, how it can be made possible, and who can, perhaps, help you overcome potential challenges along the way.

CHAPTER 8

Importance of Both Substance and Process of SMART Goals

This trend of reporting process over substance is unfortunate...
- Eric Alterman

As this book was being written, I was encouraging people on my e-mail list to contribute to the book by asking questions about setting and achieving goals. One of such questions was this: "Should I focus more

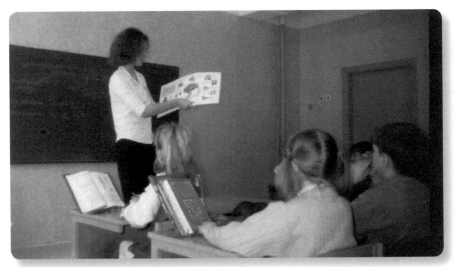

I am explaining the details of Central Nervous System to 9-year-olds. Winter of 1998.

"All of a sudden, I felt in my heart that I wanted to become something great. Perhaps, a great teacher..."

FROM MY PERSONAL EXPERIENCE...

I remember being an eighteen year old young woman in college, working on becoming an elementary school teacher. I was busy partying, going to a night club a few times a week, getting drunk, and doing crazy things that most teens usually do. One sunny day, after classes, for whatever godly reason, my Literature instructor, whom I loved and admired a great deal, took me to her home, which was in a very good neighborhood in the small city of Kursk where we lived. When I saw her nice, clean, comfortable, and modern home, the pictures of her family's traveling experiences, and her awards and recognitions for making a positive difference in the field of Education, I realized that life can be more for me than just fights of drunk relatives at my home and parties with my friends at a night club. All of a sudden, I felt in my heart that I wanted to become something great. Perhaps, a great teacher and a strong woman like her. I had finally woken up to the importance of the journey itself, not just the destination. I had also realized that, even though I was focusing on the substance of my goal of obtaining a degree in Education, I totally disregarded the process of becoming a good person to be qualified for the role of a good teacher. After that, I radically changed my lifestyle: replaced my regular teen-type activities with regular great-teacher-type activities, such as going to libraries, doing research, reading books at home, watching interesting educational TV programs, connecting and networking with great teachers, and learning from them. Similarly, I want you, too, to reflect on yourself and assess whether or not you focus enough on both substance and process, in other words, both journey and destination of your SMART goals.

on the substance or on the process of my SMART goals?"

I believe that both are equally important: by setting a high-quality SMART goal you will enable yourself to be conscious and your actions will carry more meaning; meanwhile, it is the execution of the SMART goals strategy that separates achievers from the rest of the people. Thus, I recommend that you focus on both substance and process of your goals.

Three Necessary Steps to Help You Focus on Both Substance and Process of SMART Goals

- *When you set a SMART goal, make sure you look outside of your comfort zone and challenge your current conditions.*

- *When you execute the SMART strategy, check your impulse control, which enables you to sacrifice short-term pleasures for the long-term sustainable results you desire to achieve.*

- *When your confidence is shaking and your faith in yourself is weak, remember that self-discipline is the key tool of those who have succeeded.*

Furthermore, you need to learn how to consciously distinguish between doing your business and doing your business productively. You may often be busy working on many different things, but at the same time feel like you make no progress. Look at what you are usually busy with and answer this question: are the things that you focus on and busy with really the ones that contribute most to achieving your SMART goal?

CHAPTER 9

The SMART Goals Template

Although goals are important, having a plan of action is vital to the success of those goals. Having a goal with no plan of action is like wanting to travel to a new destination without having a map.
- Steve Maraboli, Life, the Truth, and Being Free

Here is the big moment: you are now fully prepared and ready to write down your SMART goals. Please allow me to share with you the SMART goals template I use with my clients! This template is very powerful as long as you follow the step-by-step instructions offered below. Once you thoughtfully fill out this template, you then may place it somewhere where you will notice it all the time to be reminded of your SMART goals and to keep the commitment. You may use a separate copy of this template for your career goal, your health goal, and any other goal you may come up with.

A LIST OF MEANINGFUL QUESTIONS TO GUIDE YOU THROUGH THE PROCESS

To help you through the above template, here's a list of questions you may ask yourself to ensure that your goal meets the requirements and will be inspiring for you yet attainable.

As you start working on YOUR GOAL section of the above template, remember to ask yourself:

• On a scale from one to ten, how committed am I to achieving this goal?

USE THIS TEMPLATE TO SET SMART GOALS FOR YOURSELF

Your Goal	Time Frame	Positive Outcomes	Measure of Progress	Required Support and Resources	Challenges to Overcome

If the answer is lower than eight, you need a different goal, with a different WHY - perhaps, a more meaningful WHY.

Also examine yourself with the following:

• What can I do every day that will contribute to my success?

Remember: start with the end in mind.

As you're working on your template, in the YOUR GOAL section, remember: this is your WHAT, and it starts with a verb that identifies the action that's needed to be taken in order to achieve success.

As you continue working on your template, in the TIME FRAME section, keep in mind that this is your deadline by which you will check on your progress of accomplishing your goal.

As you move to the POSITIVE OUTCOMES section of the template, which reflects your WHY, challenge yourself with the following questions:

• What are the specific strengths of this goal?

• What opportunities would it open up for me?

• What could it make possible for me?

• What would it be like, if I achieved this goal?

As you advance to the REQUIRED SUPPORT AND RESOURCES and CHALLENGES TO OVERCOME, search within yourself for the answers to these questions:

• What are the challenges I may face in achieving this goal?

• What is stopping me?

• What are my concerns about it?

• Do I have any fears related to my goal?

• Who or what could help me overcome those challenges and fears and how?

• Who may be the one already achieved a similar to this goal and to whom I could reach out for an advice?

• To what extent can I influence the process of achieving my goal?

• Am I ready to do my best? Am I 100% committed?

FROM MY PERSONAL EXPERIENCE...

When in April of 2009 I escaped from my ex-husband and was placed in a shelter for victims of domestic violence, in addition to many of my tragic problems, I didn't speak any English. Imagine yourself in a foreign country, deaf, blind, and dumb. That was me in America in 2009. I was unable to read even names of street signs, incapable to say or ask for even simple things, and, worst of all, unskillful in understanding what the people around me were saying. When I had set a SMART goal of teaching myself English, I only had a few strategies in place: listen to others, ask people to repeat their words and phrases, try to guess the meaning of those, and don't feel embarrassed, but rather try, try and try every day; watch kids' cartoons and research words you want to learn; find articles on Google that you have already read in Russian, translate them to English with Google's tool, and memorize the phrases you need; print out and learn the songs of Frank Sinatra as he sings slowly and his pronunciation is clear; and practice, practice, practice...

I did not have the exact time frame for achieving my goal, because I had no idea how to even do what I was going to do, but I was very committed to trying. My time frame was identified as "As soon as possible". No need to describe the challenges on my list - everything was a challenge. Yet, the benefits were so much greater and so much more important: freedom, opportunity, and ability to be myself and be seen as an equal member of the community. Committed to excellence and determined to succeed, I taught myself English in just a few months, and on January 24th of 2011 I passed the Academic English Test with a score of seven out of nine, which was as high as I needed it to be in order for me to be considered for the MBA program I wanted to join. This is an inspiring example of the endless power that the SMART goals approach brings to you to help you achieve the impossible.

CHAPTER 10

When Self-Doubt and Negative Self-Talk Get in the Way

Our way of thinking creates either good or bad outcomes.
- Stephen Richards

THE BIGGEST ENEMY OF VICTORY IS SELF-DOUBT

Setting your goals is just the first step on your way to success. The next step is to commit, follow through, and remain accountable for the outcome of the journey. You have got to be ready to own your rewards and your errors. The biggest enemy of victory here is self-doubt. Below are some examples of thoughts that may spoil your motivation and discourage you from even trying to fulfill your ambitions.

- I'm not good enough.
- I don't have enough information.
- I've never done anything like this before.
- If my brother/sister/father/boss can't do it, I definitely will fail.
- I always try and then quit, this is no different.
- Nobody believes in me.
- No one cares anyway.
- And many more similar negative statements that kill your good spirit.

Your thoughts can either work for you or against you. You make the choice. One day I saw the below quote being passed around on Facebook (unfortunately, the author was not mentioned, so it is unknown), and I was amazed with it's deep meaning. Let me share it with you.

Watch your thoughts - they become words.
Watch your words - they become actions.
Watch your actions - they become habits.
Watch your habits - they become your character.
Watch your character - it becomes your destiny.

I'd like for you to become aware of your own inner talk. This will be your first step on the journey of adopting positive self-talk. Here's how you can do it.

Five Vital Steps to Help You Change Your Negative Self-Talk to Positive

- *Think about yourself driving your car. What's on your mind? What are you thinking to yourself right before entering a very important meeting? What thoughts occupy you when you have to make an important decision?*

- *Write these down - spend two to three days in observation, take notes and, finally, create the list of your self-talk. Fill it with your discoveries.*

- *Now I want you to circle those thoughts that are positive and I want you to praise yourself for the good thoughts.*

- *Then, underline the thoughts that are negative, damaging to your self-image, and I want you to come up with a list of good, positive, empowering, inspiring, and motivational thoughts that will fill you with drive to succeed.*

- *Repeat these good thoughts, memorize them, and any time you feel down or catch yourself thinking negatively, bring the positive thoughts to work and see how your attitude, environment, and your circumstances will improve. You will notice the difference!*

FROM MY PERSONAL EXPERIENCE...

On January 15th of 2013, three days before my 30th birthday, there was a lot of excitement up in the air about my upcoming birthday party. My husband was calling me every hour saying "I love you" and hanging up, which we both considered a very funny thing to do. I received a missed call and a voicemail from him at 3:17 p.m. He usually takes lunch from 1 p.m. to 3 p.m. at his chiropractic clinic. I was confident that the voicemail was another "I love you" for me, so I hurried to listen to it.

The recording started with a bunch of noise and music, so it became obvious to me that my husband has called me accidentally (as he had done many times before) and that he did not intentionally leave me that voicemail. In fact, he was not even aware of the fact that his phone was calling me on its own. One little detail before we go any further: by then, I already moved back to Atlanta to finish my MBA at GA State University, and my husband stayed in Savannah, where his practice is located.

Anyway, after about a minute of music and noise, I heard that he said to somebody in the room these exact words: "I just want to find out what the heck is going on with you. I thought you didn't want to see me anymore. I kept calling and calling, saying "I love you", I wanted to make sure you knew it, but it screwed up"... It was a total of twenty-six seconds, but it changed my entire reality. I at first remained paralyzed. Then, I listened to the whole voicemail again, and again, and again, until I started feeling a fever. My hands were shaking as my mind was picturing my husband with another woman as he was telling her the words I heard on the voicemail... I called my husband.

I asked nicely where he spent his lunch. During our friendly conversation he admitted that he did not call me after 3 p.m. at all. He quickly realized that I was fishing for something, so he asked me upfront. I told him about the voicemail, word-by-word. My husband said that it was, perhaps, not him, or, maybe, it was radio. He asked me how sure I was that it was his voice. He said he couldn't recall anything like that and the only person he talked to was the server at a restaurant, where he went for lunch. A server? I asked what her name was, hung up on him, and called the restaurant ask- ▶

▶*ing for her. Nothing mattered to me at that point, because I already let my mind accuse my husband of cheating. I pictured it very clearly in my mind, so whatever he was saying appeared to be a lie, no matter what it was.*

I talked to the server. Then, I went to my neighbor Charlie and let him listen to the voicemail. Interestingly, Charlie said this: "It may not be what you think it is"... I was crying, and it was evident to me that it was exactly what I thought it was. After several unpleasant calls to the server and some other people, and after taking all my anger, disappointment, and frustration out on my husband, I finally discovered what had happened. My husband went to the restaurant for lunch. There he talked to a server, who happened to go through a custody battle with her husband. The guy took her son out of state and did not let her see the child.

Philip and I, December of 2010. Image by Ken Jacobs.

"My husband was calling me every hour saying "I love you" and hanging up, which we both considered a very funny thing to do."

A little detail: my husband and I are currently raising two boys from his previous marriage, but he also has another son, who is much older and was raised away from my husband, which is a tragic and a very painful experience of his past. I knew that my husband spent years trying to reach out to his oldest son, but with no success. I even once hired a private investigator to obtain the boy's information, but we never got our calls returned and eventually had to give up on the idea of reconnecting with him. So, that day, on January 15th of 2013, in the conversation with the server, my husband happened to share about the situation with his oldest son and how he was calling him for years and wanted to "find out what the heck was going on", but the son apparently never responded, which was, as my husband thought, a "total screwup"...

Wow! Have I learned a lesson? Oh yes, I have! ▶

> ▶ *After my husband and I settled down from this weird situation, I realized something important: some people spend their time hoping for the better, and others spend their time fearing the worst. I discovered that I belong to the second category of people... Remember, my neighbor Charlie said: "It may not be what you think it is"? And he was right! No matter what, I had to believe my husband's word. But instead, I was destroying years of a wonderful relationship with my hurtful, doubtful thoughts: "Here we go again, I can never find a loyal man!" and "Of course, he's a cheater! I'm under a spell forever as my mother was telling me years ago...", and the like.*
>
> *The lesson I have learned is that it's time to take control over my self-doubt and negative self-talk and replace it with faithful and veracious thoughts before it's too late.*

BOOST YOUR SENSE OF SELF-WORTH

At this point you may be wondering: how in the world can I just change my thoughts like this? Frankly, there is no magic. It is not an event. It is rather a process. The good news is that it's free to try, and the sooner you start, the better. From the time I was a little girl, my mother placed a great deal of guilt on my shoulders: for being born, for being a girl, for my father's absence in her life, for lack of money, for lack of a better opportunity for her, and for many other things. Needless to say, my self-worth was very minimal. Below I will share with you several exercises that I have used to boost my sense of self-worth and become a strong goal achiever.

Three Exceptional Techniques Proven to Boost Your Sense of Self-Worth

 This technique is very simple for starters. Begin your practicing when you are by yourself, in a private environment, such as your bathroom, for example. It may feel extremely weird at first, but I promise, as long as you keep practicing, you will be amazed how your appreciation of your own great self will grow. Look at yourself in the mirror and say: "I love

you. I love you for who you are. I love you for being unique. I love you for your strengths, even though I know you have some weaknesses and faults like any other human being does. I love you for your accomplishments. I love you for your courage to try this exercise and for your desire to better yourself. You are very special! Great things are ahead!" Trying to do this for the first time, you may laugh at yourself or think it's crazy. It happens to almost everyone when people just get exposed to this unusual yet powerful exercise. What I recommend is that you write down what strengths you love yourself for - simply make a list, so it becomes tangible and real, instead of creating a feeling as if you were just saying something you don't believe in. List your uniquenesses as well, for the similar reason. And just keep practicing, with only one condition: look yourself in the eye as you say your words out loud. Self-talk is a skill. Similarly to how you would teach a baby to sit, stand, crawl, walk, and talk, you have to patiently teach yourself the skill of a loving self-talk.

"Tell me about myself" We are often asked during job interviews: "Tell me about yourself." This time, you will be an interviewer rather than an interviewee. You will ask your family members and friends who they think you are. What words would they use to describe you? What do they love you for? What is so special about you? As always, you write down the answers and return to your list for inspiration when you doubt yourself next time.

"A Happiness Journal" When I was in my first year of teaching school, I remember ironing my freshly-washed clothes in my grandfather's room when, all of a sudden, I heard on the radio that doctors in the UK became concerned about the level of happiness nationwide. It was decided that children there from now on would be taught how to be happy. I was so curious! I myself had already started working with young children back then, so I wanted to know everything about this revolutionary idea. I kept listening. They explained the details of their method: the children were asked to write daily, before bedtime, about any five things that they are thankful for or that made them happy that day. It was also announced that this new methodology had already been tested and proved to enhance children's performance, better their health, and refine their behavior by cultivating positive attitude. Wow! How cool was that! Free tool for my toolkit!

I sure needed to try it right away myself. And I did. I bought a beautiful pink journal and was daily writing down a few things that I was thankful for or that made me happy. These were acts of kindness I've noticed, a nice word said to me by someone, my health, sunny weather, the bus that came on time, and the like. I soon realized what a wonderful world we live in! Then, I started a journal like this for my own self - literally thanking myself for different things

FROM MY PERSONAL EXPERIENCE...

If you have read the "About the Author" section of this book, you know I had dealt with a lot of self-doubt in my life: not only as an adult, but also as a child. Even though I performed very strongly at school, my family treated me very poorly, so I was always unsure of myself, until I invented one powerful positive affirmation, or you can call it a mantra. I started practicing this simple yet very inspiring statement every time I'd experience negative thoughts or self-doubt, and it would help me deal effectively with the problem. When you feel down, discouraged, unsure, or insecure, just say these three magic statements to yourself repeatedly and you will boost your confidence almost instantly - your whole attitude will change! Here's my mantra: I'm worth, I can, I matter. No negative thoughts allowed!

My mother and I in 2001, Kursk, Russia.
Image by Victor Gridasov.

"Even though I performed very strongly at school, my family treated me very poorly, so I was always unsure of myself."

every day. As was expected, it made a significant difference in the way I viewed myself from that point on.

Thus, I suggest that you, too, start and keep a Happiness Journal for your own self: write about yourself there as if you were somebody else. Did you do a random act of kindness today? Did you say something nice to someone? How did you help a colleague? How did you cheer up a stranger? How did you make a cashier at a grocery store smile? How did you give a next-door neighbor such needed hand? Praise your wonderful self with thanks every time you do something good! Describe in details how great you are. Remember to always mention why. You deserve it after all.

This exercise will boost your sense of self-worth, enhance your self-confidence, improve your self-love, and overall make you feel good about your amazing self. Try it today and see what happens!

To inspire you, let me share a poem that a Facebook friend of mine passed to me (unfortunately, the author wasn't mentioned, so it is unknown).

> **When you arise in the morning,**
> **Give thanks for the morning light,**
> **Give thanks for your life and strength,**
> **Give thanks for your food,**
> **And give thanks for the joy of living!**

Collect all the good thoughts and feelings you've gathered during the exercises described above. Use these positive thoughts to replace your negative self-talk. Do it on a consistent basis as you would develop the skill of drawing or dancing. You will see that the positive change will occur very soon. I'd love to hear from you about your progress! Share it on my Twitter @SMARTgoalsBook.

"IF ONLY", "I CAN'T", AND "WHEN THE TIME IS RIGHT"

Your attitude determines your altitude. Are you aware of it? Is your default-setting happiness or unhappiness? How do you see the world around you? Is it a welcoming or a scary place to be in? How do you see yourself in it? Are you appreciated and wanted by people or do you feel neglected? Are you excited about tomorrow or is your tomorrow boring or full of the unexpected? Did you know that you see the reality you're in not as it really is, but as you really are? Sounds crazy? Not at all.

I know many people who have been born with one totally normal head, two healthy legs, hands, eyes, ability to speak, learn, and do well in life, but, because they view this very world differently, they consciously decide to make a damage to their originally healthy body with their unstoppable unhealthy eating habits, smoking, or drugs. They consciously limit their own possibilities.

Are you keeping yourself a prisoner of your own limitations? Do you discourage yourself by procrastinating and waiting for "when the time is right"? Do you see yourself as a victim of circumstances, justifying your own laziness with the "If only" type of excuses? Does your lack of actions come from the "I can't" type of place? It is time for you to get rid of your "If only" and to start creating the success you deserve! Remember what Henry Ford once said: "Whether you think you can, or you think you can't - you're right."

To inspire you, let me share this poem that was passed to me by a Facebook friend of mine (unfortunately, the author wasn't mentioned, so it is unknown).

Don't wait until everything is just right.
It will never be perfect.
There will always be challenges,
Obstacles,
And less than perfect conditions.
So what?
Get started now!
With each step you take, you will grow stronger and stronger,
More and more skilled,
More and more self-confident,
And more and more successful.

INTERESTING TO KNOW...

Consider conjoined twins Abby and Brittany Hensel. The girls were born with a genetically-damaged body. Yes, only one body for the two of them. What's special about the twins is that, despite their genetic uniqueness, they view themselves as a powerful human being, with endless strength and double-opportunities. That enabled them to live a meaningful and active life, have friends, party with other kids, receive great education, and even obtain driver's license. In fact, two of those: one for each of the girls. They are now twenty-two years old, seeking a job after their graduation. The girls look with a great hope into the future as they believe that, even though the two of them only have one body, having two heads, two brains, and two different professional perspectives will allow them to make double in salary! The girls have always viewed the world as a friendly, welcoming place with numerous possibilities. That allowed them to have a high quality of life and be surrounded with love of family and support of many of their friends. They are a true inspiration!

CHAPTER 11

An Accountability Partner as a Source of Support

Your accountability partner keeps you on track and moving forward in all aspects of your development.
- Mike Staver

Setting SMART goals is essential as we've learned from the previous chapters. You need to identify the areas that may hold some obstacles and challenges and you have to create a plan on how to deal with those. However, sometimes you are unaware of such areas, simply because you just don't know what it is that you don't know. Thus, you can't build a SMART goal. It's similar to my example of how I taught myself English - you just have to explore your strategies for overcoming obstacles as you go. To solve this type of challenges, you need an accountability partner.

THE DEFINITION AND BENEFITS OF AN ACCOUNTABILITY PARTNER

Earlier in this book we defined accountability and discussed why it matters. From my experience as a coach and consultant, I know that adults are skillful at rationalizing almost any excuse to avoid achieving their goal. To increase your chances for success, find an accountability partner. Having an accountability partner skyrockets the likelihood that you will do what you say when you say you'll do it. Why? Because of the following five benefits your accountability partner provides.

Attention. When you get an accountability partner, you receive the essential attention to your goal. It's like making a public commitment to something - you're now not alone in your desire to succeed anymore (your accountability partner wants your success as well; just make sure this person really keeps your best interest in mind). Making a public commitment to achieving a goal is a very powerful way to stay on the right track.

Motivation. This is that extra push you need to get started. It is also that extra push you need when daily life pulls you down and tries to take you back to the same old routine. You can reach out to your accountability partner for that essential encouragement, so you can start and keep moving forward in the right direction.

Information. An accountability partner can be a source of information for you when you lack knowledge or experience in some areas. Hard and wise questions from your accountability partner can help you figure out what it is that you don't know. Obtaining that extra information will help you stay clear, focused, and relevant.

The Five Benefits of an Accountability Partner.

"Having an accountability partner skyrockets the likelihood that you will do what you say, when you say you'll do it."

Ideation. It's nice to have an accountability partner when you're stuck and not sure how to proceed further. Brainstorming together can take your success in achieving your SMART goal to the next level.

Inspiration. When you've made a huge progress and are excited about the results you've achieved, your accountability partner is a perfect person to share that excitement with, which in turn will help you create even more inspiration for even greater future accomplishments.

HOW TO FIND AN ACCOUNTABILITY PARTNER

The best way to find an accountability partner is through networking with like-minded industry professionals and colleagues at work and through joining clubs and associations that meet your interests. Searching for a mentor is similar to searching for a spouse: you two need to share common values, concerns, experiences, communication style, and, of course, have time to invest into meaningful conversations with one another.

First, make a list of the qualities you're looking for in a potential accountability partner. What kind of person would it be in a perfect situation? What sort of experiences would this person have? What contributions would you expect this person to make to help you achieve your SMART goal?

Second, think through and write down what time commitment you would expect to make and to receive in order for this accountability partnership to be successful.

Third, and most important, create a detailed description of the traits, attributes, qualities, and experiences you can offer to benefit your potential accountability partner. Try to answer the question "What's in It for Him/Her?", which will help you gain confidence for when you decide to ask that person to be your mentor.

Below are some other ways to come across a perfect accountability partner.

• Find like-minded people among friends, family, or online (for exam-

FROM MY PERSONAL EXPERIENCE...

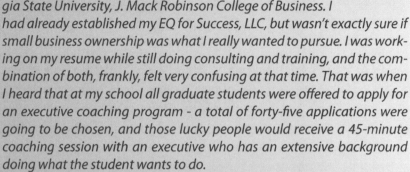

The toughest time for me in terms of business decisions was when I was in my first year of graduate school at Georgia State University, J. Mack Robinson College of Business. I had already established my EQ for Success, LLC, but wasn't exactly sure if small business ownership was what I really wanted to pursue. I was working on my resume while still doing consulting and training, and the combination of both, frankly, felt very confusing at that time. That was when I heard that at my school all graduate students were offered to apply for an executive coaching program - a total of forty-five applications were going to be chosen, and those lucky people would receive a 45-minute coaching session with an executive who has an extensive background doing what the student wants to do.

I was excited and submitted my resume and a 500-word essay, which explained why I thought I deserved to be accepted to this exclusive program. Luckily, I was in! When I came to that coaching session, I met an executive who not only was willing to help me identify what I wanted to do in the future, but also was a consultant who owned a business and also previously had worked for a corporation in the past. He had a great deal of knowledge to share with me and to compare being an employee to working for own self. Notwithstanding my desire to talk about working in corporate world, he told me upfront that he recognized a great deal of potential in me and thinks that I will be better off working as a consultant and owning my own business. Frankly speaking, at that time I wasn't even thinking about mentors or accountability partners for myself, but looking back now, I realize that the conversation that day was a very significant point in my success.

A few weeks later, I was having a similar coaching session with an executive career coach at one of the world's famous career management agencies. When I walked in with my resume, he, too, was trying to talk me into pursuing my own business. Those were two people who had never even talked to one another, yet they were both giving me the same advice. Because of that, all my thoughts from that point on were dedicated to making my own business a success.

▶

> ▶ *Some time later, during a networking event at school, I overheard that the school offers mentorship programs to students. That's when I started thinking to myself: "If I were to have a mentor, what would that person be like?" After several honest conversations with myself, I came up with a list of traits I'd be looking for in a potential accountability partner. After all, I realized that the gentleman whom I met during the executive coaching session at school was the only perfect candidate for such a role. I immediately contacted him on LinkedIn, letting him know that it would be a great honor for me, if he'd agree to be my mentor. Luckily, he replied some time later, stating that he would do so, but that his time was limited, so he would only be able to meet me once every two months. It worked well for me given the fact that I was a solopreneur and an MBA student with multiple responsibilities. For our first meeting, I prepared an agenda - the questions I had about my business. He shared many valuable how-tos with me. After that initial meeting, I realized that I, too, should do something to make the relationship mutually-beneficial. I had to contribute. I am very good at branding and social media, and he needed that type of professional advice for his business, so our meetings became mutually-beneficial and very fulfilling for me, because I was not just receiving, but giving as well. Essentially, with my accountability partner I was able to accomplish my relevant business goals much faster than I had ever expected.*

ple, you may use Facebook groups, LinkedIn groups, Google hangouts, forums, etc. to reach out for support and motivation).
• Take advantage of iPhone and iPad apps for goal-tracking, some of which enable you to allow other users to monitor your progress, while you're monitoring their progress yourself, thus creating mutual accountability.

The stronger is your public commitment to the SMART goal, the higher is your chance to succeed in achieving it.

THE LIST OF TWENTY WORLD'S FAMOUS ACCOUNTABILITY PARTNERS

To demonstrate the popularity of an accountability-partner concept among famous people and great achievers, I am sharing with you a list of successful visionaries who have or had an accountability partner (mentor) on their journey to excellence.

- American educator, author, businessman, and keynote speaker Dr. Stephen Covey mentored a popular self-help author, motivational speaker, entrepreneur, and business coach Brian Tracy.

- American entrepreneur, author, and motivational speaker Jim Rohn mentored the serial entrepreneur, venture capitalist, and publisher of SUCCESS magazine, Darren Hardy.

- World's famous self-help author, and motivational speaker Anthony Robbins mentored world's biggest inspiration, therapist, and motivational speaker Dr. Sean Stephenson.

- The inventor of management consulting, Peter Drucker, mentored an American business consultant, author, and lecturer on the subject of corporate sustainability and growth Jim Collins.

- Flickr's cofounders, Stewart Butterfield and Catarina Fake, mentored the creator of Etsy, Rob Kalin.

- Serial tech entrepreneurs Ali and Hadi Partovi mentored Drew Houston and Arash Ferdowsi of Dropbox.

- Adam D'Angelo of Quora mentored Kevin Systrom of Instagram.

- An international financier and major player in the junior mining industry Robert Friedland mentored Apple's founder, Steve Jobs.

- Steve Jobs of Apple was a mentor to Larry Page of Google, Marc Benioff of Salesforce, and Mark Zuckerberg of Facebook.

- Mark Zuckerberg of Facebook mentored Reid Hoffman of LinkedIn.

- PC inventor, Ed Roberts, mentored Bill Gates of Microsoft.

- Stanford Professor Frederick Terman mentored the HP founders, Bill Hewlett and David Packard.

- The CEO of National Cash Register, Robert Patterson, mentored the founder of IBM, Thomas Watson.

- World's famous investor and financier Warren Buffet mentored the publisher of Washington Post, Donald Graham.

- Famous Russian scientist Leonid Isaakovich Mandelshtam mentored Nobel Laureate in Physics of 1958 Igor Yevgenyevich Tamm.

- An American famous professional basketball player and entrepreneur Michael Jordan mentored Kwame Brown, NBA #1 draft pick in 2001.

- Duke University basketball coach Mike Krzyzewski mentored NCAA basketball champion player Shane Battier.

- Famous Russian poet, novelist, and literary translator Boris Pasternak mentored Andrei Voznesensky, a Russian poet and writer, who had been referred to by Robert Lowell as "one of the greatest living poets in any language."

- American famous author and poet Maya Angelou mentored an Ameriacan media star Oprah Winfrey.

- An American high school band director Virgil Spurlin mentored the 42nd President of the United States, Bill Clinton.

CHAPTER 12

Self-Accountability, Self-Discipline, and Self-Leadership

The most important quality I look for in a player is accountability. You've got to be accountable for who you are. It's too easy to blame things on someone else.
- Lenny Wilkens, Former NBA Basketball Coach

By now you have already set your SMART goal and found an accountability partner. A thoughtful accountability partner will add a great deal of value to your journey. However, no accountability partner will do the work for you. You are the one who must demonstrate a strong commitment to your own goal. Only you can establish self-discipline and stick with it. And, without a doubt, you have got to be your own leader to make decisions, provide guidance, evaluate your progress, search for resources, and adjust accordingly.

Many leaders acknowledge that the most difficult leadership task is to lead one's own self. Whether you are an entrepreneur, manager, or parent, you, first of all, have to walk your own talk. Whatever it is that you would teach your subordinates or preach to your children, you have got to do it, too.

When times get tough and you feel like giving up, remember: between what happens to us and what we do with it lies the power of our choice. Planning to start a new great initiative on Monday? Why not start it today? Wish you could have some extra time to become more successful? Ask yourself: "Do successful people have more hours in each day?" Write down where and when you procrastinate and acknowledge what's holding you back. Exercise your discipline and power of choice to overcome those challenges. Also, discover where you focus most of your attention: on the things that are within your influence or on the things that are out of your control. The weather is bad? The pollution is too high? The coworker is too annoying? Are you concerned too much about such things and can't concentrate on getting important tasks done? Are these things something you can change? Why be so concerned about them? Concentrate your mind, energy, and effort on what is within your control and influence and let go of the things that you cannot change.

Powerful, isn't it? Here's the formula I've discovered through my own life experience and that of other people:

Discipline + Consistency = Success

Remember what Abraham Lincoln once said: "The best way to predict your future is to create it."

INTERESTING TO KNOW...

Consider the teen behavior expert, Youth Speaker Josh Shipp, who is working on a global scale to help troubled teens wake up to reality of success and great achievement. He was abandoned by both parents right at birth at the hospital. He was then accepted by a foster family, but only for six months. Then, another foster family welcomed Josh, only to teach him that a promise means nothing in this world. Thanks to the help of the next foster family, Josh has concluded that people deserve no trust. After that, the following foster family abused Josh, and so on and on - he moved from one foster family to another. You're likely to think to yourself now: "Poor child..." Ironically, Josh himself, despite life's numerous tragedies and misfortunes, is happy, proud, and very successful now. Moreover, he has no regrets whatsoever about his childhood and even says that he would change nothing in his past. And here's what else Josh says: "Whether your relationship with your parents is awesome or awful, you and only you are in control of one thing - you."

CHAPTER 13

Common Sense and Flexibility with SMART Goals

Common sense is seeing things as they are and doing things as they ought to be.
- Harriet Beecher Stowe

During my workshops, I always ask who in the audience has goals set already. I was very surprised one time to hear from one gentleman that goals written on a piece of paper constrain his flexibility, forcing him to miss out on opportunities. By no means do I want you to feel this way about goals.

Consider this example. There are at least two ways of getting to Miami, FL, from Atlanta, GA, where I live. You can choose either I-75 or I-95. You can still be flexible with whether to take your car or that of your wife, how many stops to make, which rest area to choose, and what restaurant to go to while on your way; yet unless you do make that initial choice in regards to which highway you will take, you are highly unlikely to get to Miami at all, no matter how much you dream of reaching your destination. Do you see where I'm going with this? Your SMART goal is aimed to serve as your GPS to help you reach your destination faster and with a higher probability. Of course, after you choose the highway to take and as you're driving to Miami already, there may be rain, a car-accident, or heavy traffic that will force you to adjust your plans and be flexible, but you still need to have your GPS to pursue your goal of getting to Miami.

Here's another example. Suppose you set a goal of putting aside

$120,000 in the next three years to buy a house. Suppose you plan to save by cutting on shopping, travel, and going-out expenses. Suppose also that your mother gets very ill and passes away in another state. Don't think that this book suggests that accountability and commitment to your SMART goal should keep you from going to your mother's funeral, which involves spending the money you were saving for the house. Without a doubt should you use your common sense when faced with such a choice. In this situation, of course, the choice should be your mother and not the house. In contrast, given the same goal, suppose you had promised to yourself not to go out and rather eat at home, so you can save money for the same house. Suppose your friends are begging you to meet up at a restaurant this coming Friday. In this situation, you should know exactly what to choose: a house or a dinner at a restaurant. In fact, there's always an option of inviting your friends over and having them bring snacks or food for dinner. After all, remember to differentiate objectively between flexibility and irresponsibility.

As I already mentioned, often circumstances that arise on our journey to the desired destination make us change our plans. Too many times in my life have I seen people give up on their goals simply because of some challenges or obstacles that get in their way. Tell me frankly: would you turn around and go back or just remain on the side of the road, if during your trip to Miami from Atlanta it started raining heavily? Would you change your plans, if your headlight went out? Probably not. You would wait for the rain to stop and proceed. Similarly, you would find a place to fix your headlight and continue the trip.

Below I will share with you some strategies on how to deal with the obstacles and challenges that may get in your way as you start and continue the journey to achieving your SMART goals.

DEALING WITH REJECTION

Rejection is something each of us may experience many times throughout life. There's a story that was told at a church last Christmas: two people are fired the same day in the same way. One person packs personal belongings, walks around, says good-bye to peers, gets in the car, and drives home to meet a better opportunity. Another person gets in

INTERESTING TO KNOW...

Consider the story of Sean Stephenson, actually, Dr. Stephenson as he just recently obtained his PhD. Expected to die at birth, Dr. Sean Stephenson has faced numerous reasons to hate his life and to give up. Why? He suffered more than two hundred bone fractures by the age of eighteen. He is in constant pain every day of his incredible journey. He is almost thirty-five years old and has only reached the height of three feet. He is permanently confined to a wheelchair. His job application was rejected thousands of times by the employers who were fearful of Sean's disability. Enough reasons to give up, right? Disability, pain, rejection... Well, not for this man, who's been named by the media as the "Three Foot Giant." After all, Sean established his own company, became a motivational speaker, changed the lives of millions of people worldwide, got married just recently, makes a great deal of money, gained incredible popularity, and is as happy as a man can be! Lesson learned about rejection? As we say in Russia: "God only does what's best for you."

If that's not enough to inspire you, here's a story of Lizzie Velasquez, the skinniest woman in the world. At the age of twenty-four she never weighted over sixty pounds due to her undiagnosed illness, which only three people in the entire world suffer from. Every year Lizzie runs genetic tests, and every year those come back with the same puzzling answer: she is healthy and normal. But the reality is that she was labeled by the on-line bullies as the "World's Ugliest Woman." I am now embarrassed to confess that when I first saw Lizzie on YouTube I was shocked. I hope it's ok that I'm honest with you like this. And let me tell you this: the more I learned about this incredible young woman, the more I fell in love with her - for who she is. Lizzie's journey is a true story of rejection - even children would never play with her when she was little. What's more is that these days Lizzie receives ugly e-mails from angry bullies who advice that she kills herself. Guess what? Instead of feeling sorry for herself, Lizzie started speaking up on the issue of bullying. Today she motivates the audiences of thousands of people, appears on TV on a regular basis, she authored two books, and she is full of life and confidence. When you have a problem dealing with rejection, go search YouTube for Lizzie's videos - she will inspire the best in you!

the car, drives home, gets a gun, comes back to the office, and shoots the boss... Which one of these characters best reflects your attitude toward rejection?

HOW TO ACCEPT A FAILURE

Besides rejection, we often struggle from a failure. What is a failure? In my opinion, a failure is a *perception* of an event, a project, a thing, or a person, made in comparison with the general public's definition of success. Simply put, if you do not meet the society's paradigm of success, you are a failure. Do you agree with this? Just for a minute recall Steve Jobs and his career path! Remember Jim Rohn, who was broke at the age of twenty-five, yet he finished his life a popular, successful, and wealthy man! Consider Michael Jordan's professional experience, expressed in his own words as the following: "I've missed more than nine thousand shots in my career. I've lost almost three hundred games. Twenty-six times I've been trusted to take the game-winning shot, but I missed. I've failed over and over and over again in my life. And that is why I succeeded." Think also about Muhammad Ali and his comments on the issue of failure: "A champion has got to be able to take a good punch, and then another punch, and then another good punch, and still keep on going."

You have to know how to fail, bounce back, and return a stronger achiever. You have got to face rejection, find strength within yourself, go change the world, and prove that you are worth the best.

Here are the five steps I've developed that will help you deal with a failure or rejection in a more effective way.

Five Necessary Steps to Take When Faced with Failure or Rejection

- *Keep your cool. Ask yourself: "Is what I feel like doing or saying right now going to contribute to achieving my goal or is it going to delay it?" Be in control of your future!*

- *Be the person you admire. How would someone whom you admire act in the similar circumstances? Pretend as if you were that person and act at your best!*

FROM MY PERSONAL EXPERIENCE...

The hardest experience of rejection I've ever had in my life was when I got kicked out of the shelter for victims of domestic violence, where I lived after escaping from my abusive ex-husband. The reason was that they thought I was dating my ex-husband... Yes, you are right thinking that that's the guy whom I was hiding from, suffering every day. No, of course, I wasn't dating him, and that situation was very sad, because I had nowhere to go and I spoke no English. I had to clean houses, worked as a dog nanny, babysitter, hostess, driver, and took many other cash job opportunities to survive. In the meantime, I had multiple court cases to deal with. I also was sick and had lost ten pounds. My life was a disaster! But now, when I see where I was able to get myself, I am happy that I was rejected back in 2009 by the staff of that shelter. The circumstances they put me under forced me to teach myself English very fast, call attorneys three hundred times a day looking for pro bono help, which is exactly how I took care of my legal circumstances, work out at the Stone Mountain Park, which is exactly how I kept my sanity, adjust to the culture in almost no time, which is exactly how I became independent, and more. I now know that God, indeed, only does what's best for us. Spiritual gifts come wrapped in adversity.

• *Get busy. Take a look at your alternatives. Go explore them! Success may be waiting right around the corner!*

• *Stay positive. A night is always the darkest right before the sunrise... Best things are ahead!*

• *Set a new SMART goal and go for it! You are the one who can make your dreams come true!*

Utilize these strategies and you will soon be far beyond your own expectations of success. Remember what Henry Ford once said: "Failure is simply an opportunity to begin again, this time more intelligently."

CHAPTER 14

SMART Goals for Entrepreneurs

You read a book from beginning to end. You run a business the opposite way. You start with the end, and then you do everything you must to reach it.
- Harold S. Geneen

As an entrepreneur, you have many goals from coming up with the next best idea to obtaining capital for funding it through investors and gaining visibility and brand recognition through PR and marketing. George Burns once said: "Define your business goals clearly, so that others can see them as you do."

I know many entrepreneurs who go out there and start a business without figuring out first who they really are and what their business is actually going to be about. Once you came up with a big idea, your number one step is to set a big goal called "vision". As in any other area of life, in business, too, you must *start with the end in mind*. Below is a combination of questions you may want to begin your self-discovery process with.

STEPS FOR DISCOVERING BUSINESS SELF-IDENTITY FOR AN ENTREPRENEUR

Create a strong vision. Ask yourself: "What do I want to be when I grow up?" That means that you visualize exactly what you want your company to become five years from now. How do you want people to speak about your business? What do you want New York Times to say about your now start-up in the breaking news article, released on December 31st ten years from now?

Develop a list of values. When you start and continue your business, you have to be aware of what is desirable and what is unacceptable for you as a business person. For that, you need a list of values. How to develop one is explained step-by-step in this book. You need about five or seven quality-based statements that will determine how you make your business decisions, who your ideal client is, whom you want to attract as an investor or a business partner, and so forth. A great example of a value-driven business is Fabienne Fredrickson, a woman entrepreneur who very straightforwardly announces all over the place, including her website, what type of a person you have to be in order to qualify for becoming her client. You'd think: "I can't eliminate clients just because they don't match my list of values! I need clients, because they bring money!" Guess what? Fabienne Fredrickson's business is doing just fine, because by developing a list of business values and sticking to it, she commits to only working with those clients whom she can make happy. Happy clients go and tell more people about how great Fabienne is; those people have to qualify to become Fabienne's client; she makes them happy; and they go and tell more people about her awesome services. And so on and on - Fabienne became very successful using this method of following her own list of values in business.

Design a mission statement. A mission statement for your business will be a sort of extension of its vision, only stating how exactly you will comply with it on a daily basis. In other words, it will explain how you will work toward your business vision. Constructing your mission statement, you need to ask yourself: "How do I add value with my business?" Just keep in mind that it has to be a statement that can be understood by *a person of average intelligence with no background in your field.* Thus, the language you use for your mission statement should be simple, and the statement itself should be memorable. To help you out with that, here's my advice: imagine that you meet your ideal client in an elevator and have a very limited time to tell him about your company. How would you answer the following question, addressed to you by that ideal client: "What's in it for me?" This method should enable you to create a 30-second elevator-pitch for your business.

Now, when you have discovered your identity as an entrepreneur, you need to think how you can elevate your brand. It will take a development of a long-term and a short-term strategies. In order to be recognized as a brand of a particular quality tomorrow, you have to start with the right foot today. I suggest that you look into becoming a socially-responsible enterprise.

THE WHAT, WHY, AND HOW OF BECOMING A SOCIALLY-RESPONSIBLE BUSINESS

As a business owner, you have the number one goal for your company of becoming and remaining profitable to survive and succeed. To achieve profitability and success, you need *quality capital* and *talented people.*

To attract quality capital, you need to differentiate yourself from your competitors and demonstrate to your investors that your ideas and business model are worth their money. In other words, you have to prove that you deliver a great value and create a win-win success.

To attract talented people, especially millennials (the representatives of the Generation Y who are very advanced in technology, digital media, and communications and who can bring this value to grow your bottom-line), you need to also differentiate yourself from competitors and develop a value proposition to high-potential talent that will meet their expectations and motivate their creativity and innovation, so that they can produce more effectively and efficiently to ensure your business' vitality.

How do you do all that? What steps can you take as the decision-maker to get your company more attractive for potential investors, talented professionals, and other stake holders? My answer for you is corporate social responsibility, which reflects your triple bottom-line. The substance of the triple bottom-line concept is explained below.

People. How much does your company care for human rights? Do you hire people with disabilities? How do you ensure healthy work environment? How do implement best labor practices to improve your employees' well-being? What is your level of performance on product

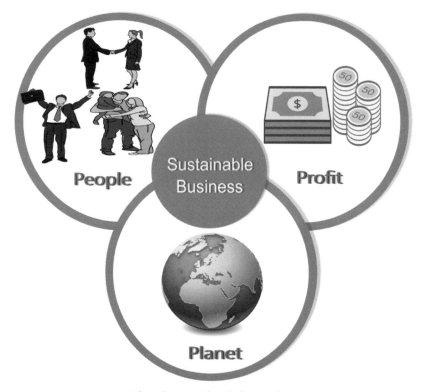

The substance of triple bottom-line.

"By becoming a socially-responsible business, you will demonstrate your organization's authenticity and commitment to transparency, which will allow you to stand out from the competition and attract the desired capital and talent to grow your business and ensure its success."

responsibility: does your product help people or does it hurt them?

Profit. What is the positive impact that your company makes on the economy as a whole? How many jobs do you create? How do you provide capital and investments for the community to build roads and schools?

Planet. Where does your waste go? What steps do you take to reduce your waste and improve your enterprise's efficiency? How do you contribute to bettering the environment and saving the planet?

These three components of your triple bottom-line are being measured by Key performance Indicators (KpIs) that are a part of Global Reporting Initiative (GRI). You may have heard of that document referred to as the G3 report, also known as "Ecological Footprint Reporting", "Environmental Social Governance (ESG) Reporting", "Triple Bottom-Line (TBL) Reporting", and "Corporate Social Responsibility (CSR) Reporting". Experts believe that by 2020 all businesses will be reporting not only on their financial performance, but also on their sustainability performance. Today, well-known companies like Coca-Cola, Ford, Volkswagen, Citigroup, Barclays, Nike, Adidas, and many other global businesses use the GRI framework not only to showcase their contribution to the community, but also to prove to the shareholders that their companies are forward-looking and ready to fulfill the highest expectations.

Corporate Social Responsibility starts with you - the entrepreneur, the business owner, the decision-maker. By becoming a socially-responsible business, you will demonstrate your organization's authenticity and commitment to transparency, which will allow you to stand out from the competition and attract the desired capital and talent to grow your business and ensure its success.

SETTING SMART GOALS FOR YOUR ENTREPRENEURIAL COMPANY

Becoming an entrepreneur requires a great idea. Starting and running an entrepreneurial business takes a lot of guts. It also commands you to often be a do-it-yourself type of person. That is exactly what I am right now in my business. I do my own everything: from funding my company to developing products, creating and executing marketing and media strategies, designing and performing workshops, finding clients, creating interactive websites, writing and publishing articles and this very book - I do it all.

Below is a guide to your SMART entrepreneurial goals that I've invented to help starters take off successfully. Once you have established your business identity, following the above described methodology of mine, and once you have decided how you plan to add value by becoming a socially-responsible enterprise, it's time for you to get started and let the world know about your extraordinary business.

Your SMART strategy for funding. You have to figure out what type of funding you will use, because each type has its own pros and cons. Your choice may be an angel investor, a venture capitalist, a bank loan, or you may choose to use friends and family as providers of the capital. Outline the positive outcomes and potential negative consequences of each method of obtaining the needed funding. After that, choose the one that suits your standards and expectations best. Write a SMART strategy in regards to whom you will approach, when and how, what preparation is required on your side, who can refer you to the investor, what challenges may arise in your way, and so on, until you are crystal-clear on what has to be done within what timeframe.

Your SMART strategy for complying with laws and regulations. Suppose your entrepreneurial business is based on a special technology that requires particular licensing; or perhaps, you plan to do business with the Government and need to obtain special permissions or follow certain regulations. There may be a variety of requirements you will have to meet before you can actually start doing business. Ironically, this may very likely be that situation in which you simply don't know what it is that you don't know. So, do your research, find every type of information related to the business and the regulations as well as potential authorities you will have to deal with. Visit their websites, call them, and do what it takes to eliminate as much "I didn't know it" as possible. Write a SMART strategy in regards to how and when you will move toward your goal, one step at a time. There may be deadlines to meet - everything has to be noted on your SMART goals worksheet. Hire an expert who can become your accountability partner. Once you have a clear detailed plan and feel focused, go for it!

Your SMART strategy for attracting partners and building a team. When you complete the process of self-discovery, which is explained in this book, you are ready to ask yourself the following business-related questions. What am I already good at in my business? What gaps do I still need to close? What do I already do well? What else can I do to achieve my entrepreneurial aspirations? Who of my competitors does well in the area where I'm still looking to improve? What kind of people does that company have in charge in that area? Answering these questions will lead you to identifying the kind of people you need on your team to succeed. Set your SMART goal establishing time-frame and strategy in regards to how, when, and where you will look for, find, attract, and retain those people.

Your SMART strategy for developing a website. Developing a website can take one day, one year, or it can be an ongoing process of constant improvement. I built the website for this book myself, except for the banner. You can check it out at www.SMARTgoalsBook.info. I also developed a website for my husband's chiropractic clinic having only spent one day on it. Take a look at it at www.DayChiropracticSavannah.com.

The first step is the most important one: you always start with a domain name. What combination of words will represent the core of your business while also being easy to remember for the general public?

The second step is to determine whether you want your website to provide a one-way communication opportunity, meaning that you will speak through it to your visitors, or a two-way communication opportunity, allowing your visitors to comment on your posts, like and share them, and so on. Keep in mind that a business-card type of a website, where you are the only one who can speak, post, and share information, is like going to a networking event and not caring to learn about the people you meet. Thus, I recommend having an engaging website with many social share tools integrated into it.

The third step requires you to consider what devices your potential client may access your website from. This will make sense when you try to choose the platform for your website. For instance, flash websites that allow pictures and background music to be played will likely show as a blank page on any Apple device. Conversely, a Wordpress-based website will appear well, regardless of what device it is viewed on. Make sure the widgets you include and the plugins you install are mobile-friendly, so that your website will appear correctly on all devices. Pay particular attention to videos; secure a video player that is mobile-friendly as well.

The fourth step is to ideate in regards to what you want your banner to look like. A website banner is like your smile at a networking event: people will notice and remember you based on your smile. Make sure the colors you use are appropriate for your audience and the combination of fonts you choose is easy to read. Let's say you won't use black fonts on an orange banner - you will choose white fonts instead, because they are more comfortable for a human eye, especially when you look at the website from a mobile device.

Finally, you have to design a site map, create high-quality content for pages and subpages, produce attention-catching videos, and establish a blog, so your website is relevant and up to date, given that you will actually keep up with the blog.

My general advice is this: when you're trying to choose a theme for your website, keep your main target customer in mind. Is it a C-level executive? Choose a plain white background and calm colors as well as business-like images and videos. Don't have pictures flashing as you invite people to read the content - it's very distracting.

Research by Forbes Insight reveals that 59 percent of executives prefer watching short videos over reading the text when they visit a website. Some other interesting facts that may encourage you to look into creating great videos for your website are listed below.

• According to the Internet Retailer, 52 percent of consumers say that watching product videos makes them more confident in their online purchase decisions.

• When a video is information-intensive, 66 percent of consumers will watch the video two or more times, according to the Internet Retailer.

• More than three out of five consumers will spend at least two minutes watching a video that educates them about a product or service they plan to purchase, and 37 percent will watch videos for more than three minutes, according to MarketingCharts.com.

Overall, make the information on your website easy to find for your visitors. In other words, your job is to reduce their learning curve and help them understand who you are and what you can do for them, in the least amount of time. *Place yourself in the shoes of your ideal client and develop a concept for your engaging website from that perspective.*

For each of the steps outlined above you will need to establish milestones on your SMART goals worksheet. You will also need to do research to overcome challenges that may arise as you work on your website's design and content. You may even need an accountability partner to consult with, unless, of course, you hire someone to do everything for you. Even if you choose to do so, you will have to create some of the concepts, review and critique projects, and I suggest that you refer to this chapter for guiding questions. I'd love to see your entrepreneurial website. Post the link to it on my Facebook page or blog. You can find those at www.SMARTgoalsBook.info.

Your SMART strategy for creating on-line presence. Building on-line presence includes a Blog, Facebook profile and pages, LinkedIn profile and pages, Pinterest, Twitter, YouTube, Google Plus, events on social networks, articles on Forbes and Huffington Post as well as other professional well-known websites. I have already explained the concepts of website design and development. Now, let's talk about social networks. I often hear from entrepreneurs: "Social media is too time-consuming. I don't have energy for this!" You will need to ask yourself this questions: "Are my clients on Facebook? Are they on Twitter? Are they on Pinterest, YouTube, LinkedIn...?" If so, *how can you afford to dismiss your clients?* You've got to be where they are! LinkedIn profile is a must-have for any serious entrepreneur today. Not only does it give you an opportunity to showcase your accomplishments, but it also allows you to gain and expand credibility by obtaining endorsements from people. Complete your LinkedIn profile up to one hundred percent. After you have already indicated your former and current places of employment as well as your education and awards, use the following questions to determine what impression you'd like your profile to make.

Five Thought-Provoking Questions to Answer When Developing a Comprehensive LinkedIn Profile

- *What is the tagline you'd like to see and hear after your name when being introduced on Fox News?*

- *Imagine that you are invited to be featured in a magazine. You're asked to provide a bio of 200 words. Using professional language, in ten complete sentences answer the following question: who are you and how do you add value?*

- *What are the ten key words you'd like to be found on-line for when your potential clients, who don't yet know you, search for someone like you?*

- *If you accidentally happened to hear two people talk about you at an event, what would you like to hear them say? Write five adjectives.*

- *How many people know you as a professional? Who of them could recommend you on LinkedIn and for what kind of work? Make a list.*

Once you complete this short questionnaire, you are ready to write your LinkedIn tagline and summary based on your answers. Then, start connecting with your current and former colleagues, partners, and bosses. Ask these people to endorse you. Never send them a generic message though; tailor it for each individual. Make sure your request is very clear. What do you want to be endorsed for? What position? What skills or qualities? Be very professional in the language you use and also be polite. LinkedIn recommendations can actually be embedded into your website and add credibility and recognition that way as well. I used embedded LinkedIn recommendations for myself on my website www.SMARTgoalsBook.info.

Develop a LinkedIn company page. It is a free tool to market your business and products or services. Remember to update it on a regular basis.

Create a Facebook profile. It's a necessity, if you want to be able to build a page for your business. When you build the page, make sure that all the attributes look professional and are the same as you used for your website and LinkedIn: colors, logos, content, and so on. It's important for your on-line outlets to send the same message and to have the same theme, so that your brand is recognizable by people and easy to remember.

Repeat the same process with all of your social networks. Definitely utilize the power of YouTube and don't dismiss a free opportunity to produce, publish, and promote short and simple videos that can help you gain credibility and recognition and promote yourself and your company.

Keep in mind that social media is a relationship-management tool, so you've got to be responsive in order to establish and maintain relationships. Share news, behind-the-scenes types of photos, and value-added content. In other words, share something that people can only get if they follow you or are connected to you. Just having a page out there is noting; engaging with your community is everything!

Your SMART strategy for marketing. Marketing includes creation and production of business cards, e-news letters, adds in magazines, on radio and TV, brochures that will explain the value of what you offer to people, educational videos on YouTube to establish your credibility, testimonials from clients on your website, connecting all your social media to your website and integrating them all together, so that people can easily navigate from your Facebook to Twitter, from your LinkedIn to your website, and so on.

You may also have to schedule some speaking engagements to gain more visibility and promote your message. You may host webinars, either by yourself or jointly with other experts, so that both of you can attract more attention and get a better exposure. There are also adds on social networks to consider. And all of these should lead to a high-quality website page, where you gather e-mails of the visitors, propose your products and services, have your contact information, upcoming events, and social media.

there must be an irresistible offer on your website, in exchange to which you will ask people to give you their name and e-mail address, so you can then send them regular e-mail updates about your products and services or your new projects. You may offer an e-book, an audio-file with your interview, a test, an assessment, a white paper, a special report, and anything else that may be considered value-added by your ideal client. A mere "Sign up for our news letter" button doesn't work today in such rapidly-changing, highly-competitive business environment. You have to stand out of the crowd. Thus, your give-away has to be relevant and value-added. Once you convert your visitors into members of your community, you will have pre-qualified customers to market to.

Finally, as a part of your marketing strategy, you may decide to write a book to demonstrate your knowledge and expertise. Every one of these marketing activities has to have a SMART strategy and be aligned with your business' overall goals, standards, and values.

Your SMART strategy for PR. You cannot spell "profit" without PR. This includes writing and distributing press releases, pitching and preparing for media appearances, such as TV and radio, creating quality content and publishing articles, pitching to other popular people and blogs, encouraging them to write about you and your business, and so on. When you set your SMART strategy for PR, make sure it supports all your other SMART strategies for overall marketing, networking, and business development: the same message, the same content, the same promise to your audience, and the same perspective on the topic of your expertise. If you have a radio interview scheduled, make sure you are promoted there using appropriate key words, determined by you for your business. This will increase your visibility on search engines. Also, ensure that your bio for media appearances matches the bio on your website, Facebook, LinkedIn, and in all other places: consistency is the key. Furthermore, arrange having a give-away to the listeners during your interview: maybe, a free e-book, for which the audience has to go to your website and enter their name and e-mail address there to receive your gift. You will add value to people, gain credibility as an expert, and increase traffic to your website. When you think about entrepreneurial projects like this, ask yourself: "What else can I use this one media appearance for?" Execute accordingly.

Your SMART strategy for networking. I have already explained the value and the essence of networking for an entrepreneur. I just want to remind you of the following questions you need to answer: "Who is your ideal client?" and "Where can you find that person?" You've got to be where your client is in order to get the business! This rule of thumb is applicable to live events with face-to-face interactions and to professional social networks, such as LinkedIn. Develop a SMART strategy that will help you add value to your ideal client's experience: you may share some valuable information, such as an article or a white paper; you may send out e-cards for holidays; whatever it is that you choose to do to stay in touch, have a SMART strategy in place, so that you are always ready to present your best side when the time is right.

Your SMART strategy for product development and diversifying your revenue stream. Creating products can help you diversify your revenue stream. Books, e-books, apps for mobile devices, CDs, DVDs, podcasts, worksheets, toolkits, magazines, audio and video download-able instantly from your website - all or any of these options can ensure that you have some source of passive income, which is highly desirable for entrepreneurs and allows to stop trading time for money and, instead, start creating and delivering more value.

Find out what your clients really want, what needs are currently unsatisfied, and think how you may be able to solve such problems. Establish a SMART strategy and describe in details what obstacles people who already produced that or similar to that type of product faced, how they overcame those obstacles, and how you can possibly avoid problems using current technology. You may find an accountability partner anywhere in the world now, thanks to the Internet. Remember that the more products you offer, especially on-line, the more revenue you can generate while in your sleep.

You are now all set and know exactly how to think in terms of your entrepreneurial SMART goals. Definitely print out several copies of the templates I provide in this book and use those templates for every type of goal you need to achieve. It will help you gain clarity and focus in fulfilling your entrepreneurial ambitions.

CHAPTER 15

SMART Goals for Managers

Good business leaders create a vision, articulate the vision, passionately own the vision, and relentlessly drive it to completion.
- Jack Welch

As a manager, you have a purpose of maximizing shareholders' wealth. That means that you have to accomplish goals established for you by your company's shareholders. Additionally, being a manager, you don't work in a vacuum - you have a team. Thus, you also have your team's goals you need to achieve. Moreover, you are in charge of many people, whom you usually have to help to set and reach their goals for performance. Ultimately, you have your personal career goals that need to be attained as well. The common trait for all of the above goals of a manager is that they also have to be multiplied by two: short-term goals and long-term goals for each category. Sounds overwhelming? No worries! There's a way to deal with this problem effectively - simply use the template for SMART goals that I share in this book.

When you develop the SMART goal that will satisfy your shareholders, think about the market and where your company is currently positioned. Figure out what's working well and what's not. Compare it to the overall company's vision and mission. Research your competitors and see who of them is way beyond your company now. Take a close look at what the competitor is doing and assess what of this your company isn't currently doing. How can you model after your competitor and do even better? What will it take? How can you help your company to catch up? Build your SMART goal upon your findings.

When you develop a SMART goal for your team, remember that it's a great tool to increase your team's motivation. To help your subordinates own the goal and feel responsible for achieving it, include them in the process of developing the SMART goal. Of course, for your team to be effective, it may likely require team members to collaborate with other teams or departments. This would be a good topic to discuss when you work on the SUPPORT AND RESOURCES REQUIRED section of the SMART goals template offered in this book. Your team members may serve as accountability partners for one another. They may also find accountability partners within departments they have to collaborate with. Together, you may come up with great ideas on how to diversify your team's competencies. You should also consider how each of you can add more value and make a note on your SMART goals worksheet.

When you help your employees set their goals, look beyond their job description. Encourage them to think about where each of them personally wants to be five years from now. Have them consider how they can add great value to advancing your company's position in the marketplace, while also progressing rapidly toward their own career goals and obtaining the desired skills and knowledge. The popular saying suggests that eighty percent of productivity comes from twenty percent of activity. That means that your employees are very likely to show up for work to do just as much as required to receive their paycheck. Yet, I know for a fact that, if you ensure that professional SMART goals of your employees are aligned with their personal SMART goals for their career overall, you will get the most out of them in terms of productivity and commitment to excellence.

As you work on developing the SMART career goal for yourself, make sure you first go through all the exercises that I shared in this book. Once you know what you want and where you're going as well as where you plan to end up, use the template to set your SMART goal that is aligned with your self-discoveries.

Finally, you have to realize that you are the one to execute upon these goals and strategies. It may require you to help people stop second-guessing themselves. It may take your courage to lead them toward some essential mind-shifts. And it is your direct responsibility to ensure that your team is wholeheartedly into achieving the best and greatest results. When all of you are on board, your strategy is clear and your minds are focused, you will be able to achieve the desired goals in the shortest time.

CHAPTER 16

SMART Goals for Parents

If you raise your children to feel that they can accomplish any goal or task they decide upon, you will have succeeded as a parent and you will have given your children the greatest of all blessings.
- Brian Tracy

Being a parent means constantly setting goals for your family overall, for yourself as a parent, and for each of your children. Of course, as they grow, your job will become to assist and guide them, but in the beginning you are responsible for laying the groundwork for success.

The goals for your family can be set using the template I share in this book. Before you start working on the development of the actual SMART goal, you have to go through the process of discovering your family's identity. Are all of you on the same page? Do you share the same values? Do you endorse the same positive behaviors while prohibiting the unacceptable behaviors that all of you consider as such?

Why is it so important to be like-minded in terms of expectations, united in terms of standards, and harmonious in terms of values in a family? Let me answer this question with the following personal story.

I was raised by a single mother who lived with her parents and two other sisters, each of whom had a daughter as well. I was the youngest out of all the girls. Everyone in the family had a personal opinion in regards to how the children were supposed to be raised. We were expected to obey not only our mothers, but also our grandparents and teachers. I was going through a great deal of confusion, questioning, and objection. When my mother would discipline me in accordance with *her* standards, grandma would come into the room and tell me not to listen to my mom, because she is a nobody. Instantly, my mother would shift her focus to arguing with grandma in front of me about the authority problems, while I would stand there, puzzled, and deny both of them as I was losing my respect. Then, my grandfather or my aunts would join, and here comes a fight! The result that they had achieved was this: I disregarded all of them due to their multi-standard, bias, unauthentic approach to parenting, and I substituted the lack of harmonious standards with my own ideas and paradigms. I ran away from my home and stayed with friends quite often. I drank, smoked, you name it... And that is the reason why I strongly recommend now that you ensure that all members of your family are clear and in agreement in regards to what is considered good moral, norms, values, and rules.

My grandmother in 2005. Kursk, Russia.

"When my mother would discipline me in accordance with her standards, grandma would come into the room and tell me not to listen to my mom, because she is a nobody."

Once you as a family have gone through the steps needed to develop your family's mission statement and once all of you have defined your common values, you can start setting your SMART goals. Suppose you intent to have a healthy lifestyle and establish healthy eating habits. You will use the SMART goals template to identify this as your goal. You will establish a timeframe: if your family members seek to lose some weight, there will be a realistic deadline. It may be specified that you eat certain things every day, once a week, twice a month, or however your diet goes.

FROM MY PERSONAL EXPERIENCE...

As I had mentioned before, when I left my abusive ex-husband and was trying to restore myself and rebuild my life, while in a foreign country, I worked with many families as a nanny. One of them was a Jewish family with three children.

The family was extremely wealthy. They lived in a huge house that even had an elevator in it. They were committed to raising their children as independent and grateful as possible. They were the ones whom I learned from that anything can be accomplished with children, if only you're committed as a family to a mutual goal. Let's start with this: their six-month-old daughter was admitted to a dancing school, where she, along with seven or eight other six-month-olds, was dancing and singing twice a week. No it wasn't a typo: yes, six m-o-n-t-h-s old! That's what I thought to myself, too: "Impossible!", until I saw those babies with my very own eyes.

How did they achieve something like this? With a system, a SMART goal, and a wholehearted commitment to it. In fact, they ensured that anyone who was dealing with their children was also committed to the same goal. Their morning always started with a schedule. The schedule and the entire routine for each child were outlined and described in details in a special manual for nannies created by the mother. Each of the children made their own breakfast. I'm talking about a six-month-old girl, a four-year-old boy, and a six-year-old boy. The mother was giving the baby girl some choices, while pulling food for her out of the refrigerator, but the rest the baby girl did herself. The rule for the boys was to make their beds by themselves, dress by themselves, play by themselves, and clean up by themselves, too. Each of the three children had a separate bedroom. The bedrooms were always in order.

No food was ever thrown away in that house: if something wasn't eaten during a meal, it went straight to a small plastic container with a dark-blue lid, and it was eaten by the family next time. Most shockingly, the rule of thumb was that, no matter how loudly or for how long the baby girl would cry, when she had to climb the stairs, no one was allowed to pick her up. She had to do it on her own. It seemed to be inhumane to me at first, but then I realized that the children were so independent, self-sufficient, polite, smart, and simply incredible, because of the goals and rules their parents established and followed. ▶

▶ *Another family was an Indian couple. Very good, sweet people. They had a two-year-old boy and were almost due for a baby when I started working for them. Their goal was to make sure that the oldest child knew his routine and was used to following it, so that there would be less drama with the new baby around. They had a videocamera installed in the toddler's room. He was supposed to go to bed at 7 p.m. and also take a nap during the day. The mother had taught me that when he'd go to bed, no matter how hard he'd cry, I was not allowed to go in and, instead, was supposed to wait for five minutes. Then, I had to open the door and with a strict voice say: "It is sleepy time now. If you don't want to do sleepy time, do quiet time!" I was supposed to close the door. If he would cry, I was now ordered to wait fifteen minutes instead of five. And so on and on, until he would learn and follow the routine. I was amazed with the results! That little boy was very good at everything, very independent, and very smart!*

I will also tell you about a Russian-American family I worked with. Their goal was to teach their son how to love books. Every morning and every afternoon, after his sleepy time, he was taught to crawl to his rocking chair and snuggle with his various books. I was impressed seeing how much that love for reading grew as he grew!

Suppose your family's goal is to also learn how to appreciate diversity and cultural differences. The details of your SMART plan in that case will include going to a theater, visiting museums, scheduling play-dates in different communities in your city, attending music festivals, and other similar activities. The challenges and obstacles to overcome may include a long commute, if you don't live in the heart of your city, or financial commitment required to fulfill your joint ambitions, finding people who represent diversity, and reaching out to them. Whatever goal your family chooses, you have to ensure that everyone participates in its SMART strategy creation and is committed to it.

As you can see, being a parent requires many responsibilities, including loving your children genuinely while disciplining them rigidly. Your job is to teach them habits for success. Your chore is to ensure that they obtain the skills that will serve them well for life. You need to challenge them to pass their own fears and limitations to expand their horizons. You are in the position to advise them of how to love life, be tolerant of people, and be acceptive of own self. Your task is also to ensure that they are able to build social relationships and appreciate the meaning of those. Your role as a parent is invaluable, please do not underestimate it. To be a good parent, set SMART goals to ensure successful future for your youngsters!

CHAPTER 17

How to Choose a Measure of Your Progress

If you focus on results, you will never change. If you focus on change,
you will get results.
- Jack Dixon

How to choose a measure for the progress you achieve with your SMART goal is a question I'm asked very frequently. There are three general mistakes people make in regards to the measure. You already saw two of the examples that I presented here before; however, I wanted to make sure I separate these three mistakes and bring them to your attention. Review them and reflect on yourself.

Mistake One. Sometimes, when we set our goals, we make them too broad. Compare the two examples below.

Example 1: "Lose weight by Christmas."
Example 2: "Lose 15 pounds by Christmas to fit a size 4 dress by exercising every Monday, Wednesday, and Friday from 6 p.m. to 7 p.m. and eating healthy."

As you can see, example one's goal is too vague and is hard to measure at a specific point of time as it does not indicate how to measure the progress. The goal in the other example meets the requirements of answering the What, Why, and How questions and provides a clear criteria for measuring success - a size 4 dress, for which specific 15 pounds have to be lost in a specific way.

Mistake Two. Often, we set unrealistic standards that, we know in advance, are impossible to be met, at least under our current circumstances. Ask yourself:

• Is it possible for anyone to accomplish this goal under similar circumstances?

• Is it probable for me to accomplish this goal under my particular circumstances?

• Will accomplishing this goal challenge me without defeating?

Mistake Three. Frequently, while setting standards for our goals, we look at ourselves from a prism of someone else's perspective of us. Sounds crazy? Let me clarify. Consider the following example. I was raised in Russia, where at the time it was a norm to have children at the age of eighteen and nineteen. My mother told me every day: "When you become a mother, you will...." or "Just wait until you have children, then..." So, I was taught from a very early age to look at myself through that prism my mom created - "Anna with children", "Anna as a mother". Guess what? I was very unhappy for years, unable to achieve my goal of having children, until I just recently realized that I wasn't accepting me as I am - "Anna without children". Once I finally got rid of that prism I inherited from my mother, I accepted myself without comparing the actual me to my mother's norms and standards that she created for me.

I have a question for you: "Do you compare yourself to your own standards, progress, and expectations or do you look at yourself through someone else's prism of what your life should be like?" Answer this question honestly and from your heart, and, if needed, go back to the beginning of this book to search inside yourself.

CHAPTER 18

How and When I used My Comprehensive SMART Goals System

Become the leader of your life. Lead yourself to where you want to be.
Breathe life back into your ambitions, your desires, your goals,
your relationships.
- Steve Maraboli

As you've learned already, I was born in a single-mother family and lived with many siblings in a 3-bedroom, one-bathroom condo in the city of Kursk, Russia. There were ten of us: six adults and four kids. My relatives were alcoholics, so were my neighbors. Because of that, drinking, smoking, and fighting were regular and normal events at my home. Obviously, I didn't have much love, support, or encouragement in my childhood.

While in middle school, I was jealous of confident girls. So, I decided to participate in some after-school activities, one of which was a comedy club. To start performing on stage, I had to motivate and empower myself, which I did through my SMART goals system. What I had to do was obvious to me. The benefits of taking the required actions were clear, too: increased self-confidence, enhanced popularity, more friends, and improved self-worth. For many years I participated in acting, singing, comedy, and other forms of public performance. I loved it, and it served me well for life through the skills I've obtained and good habits I've developed.

After the ninth grade, I wanted to go to college, because a few other peers of mine did so. Back then in Russia, you had to have either connections or money. My friends were supported by parents and their cash, but I was on my own. I had to prepare myself for college at the age of fifteen: apply for admission, pass the exams, and do all that alone. Well, thanks to my proven SMART goals system, I did it. For four years at that college I was one of the top students and graduated with high honors.

A picture of me in May of 1984.

"...drinking, smoking, and fighting were regular and normal events at my home."

Likewise, in 2002, I wanted to enroll in a business school. While friends of mine had support of either connections or cash of their families, I again was on my own. And I did it again! As always, using my powerful SMART approach to goals. For six years I was a head of my cohort in that business school, wrote several research papers, won prizes, received multiple awards, presented on numerous local, regional, national, and international conferences on the topic of Importance of Human Capital for Organizational Success, and graduated with high honors again.

In July of 2008, I moved to the United States and a real tragedy happened to me, which I shared with you throughout this book. To restore myself and rebuild my life, I applied these very SMART goals strategies for success that I presented to you here. And they worked. I am free, happy, healthy, and successful!

My SMART goals process works anywhere, anytime, for anyone who is willing to do the work that success requires, demonstrates accountability, and exhibits commitment.

AS AN ENTREPRENEUR.

Being an entrepreneur, I utilize my comprehensive approach to SMART goals every day. Business, especially when you run it solo, requires you to perform multiple tasks, develop multiple strategies, and literally be a multiple-role person. From business development to networking, marketing, PR, web design and video production - I do it all in my business. The main challenge for me was to get out there and start meeting people and spreading the word about my business. Let me share with you a few quick notes I found written on my own SMART worksheet. I came up with these tips to grow and expand my business network, and you can use them to grow yours.

Increase Your Likability. Networking means growing the number of your connections. Think now about a networking event you attended just recently. How many people do you remember out of all the people you met? Why do you remember those lucky ones? What stood out about them? What stands out about you? That's the questions I asked myself many times. And that led me to creating a list of qualities I admired in other people. I suggest you do it now as we go. Circle the qualities you like in others. Think now about how you could develop the same qualities in your own self, so you can enhance your likability in the business community. That was what I did time and time again to establish my business image.

Create a Business Card that Speaks for You. I created a business card with all my information. I included all my social media links to allow people to reach out to me in a convenient for them way. I developed a brochure to outline the benefits of my services to several categories of people and shared my short bio and picture to allow people to put together a name and a face. I was giving those away everywhere, while talking to people and learning more about them. I also asked some of my friends to place the brochures at their offices.

Develop an Elevator-Pitch. I developed a 30-second elevator-pitch about who I am and what I do. I suggest you do it, too. Just ask yourself as you're creating your pitch: "What's in it for that other person I'm approaching and pitching to?" and "Why should that person listen to me?" When you come to an event, be prepared to present your elevator-pitch in a very casual way.

Research People in Advance. I recommend that you research people in advance and learn about them as much as you can. When you meet them, you can impress them with what you know about them already. People appreciate the fact that you took some time to look them up: it makes them feel important.

I want you to remember this: you will never have a second chance to make the first impression. That is exactly why you need a detailed SMART goals plan for networking.

The rule I've unveiled was this: people judge you - it's the law of life. The only difference is that they may judge you based on what they've learned about you from you or they may do so based on what others say about you. Consequently, your goal is to make sure people have a first-hand experience with you and learn about you from you.

Remember what John Kehoe once said: "Like it or not, you're either an asset or a liability to your success."

AS A MANAGER.

When I worked as a manager in the telecommunications industry, my goal was to mainly ensure a great customer service experience. I interacted face-to-face with so-called difficult clients, or unsatisfied customers. At first, it was exhausting to hear people constantly complain or even yell at you. However, after I had set a SMART goal of turning one hundred percent of those unsatisfied customers into loyal company advocates, my daily interactions became very meaningful. The obstacle for me was people's anger. I committed to overcoming it by hearing every person out. I would invite customers to sit down with me and would listen with all my heart, trying to understand the core of their problem, rather than mentally formulating my next response to their complaint. My sincerity led to an increase in brand loyalty. Formerly unsatisfied customers were now very happy and went to tell their friends about their outstanding customer service experience with the company I worked for.

Accomplishing my SMART goal was not a one-day event. It was rather a process that involved my daily practice of facial expression in front of a mirror, training of my pose to send a message of compassion rather then arrogance, and also working to suit my own tone of voice to communicate humanity and kindness. As a result, even after I left the company, I remember many of the clients I had worked with would meet me somewhere at a store or on a street, greet me, and thank for their great customer service experience.

I also remember how I was appointed to open a telecom retail store at a new location in my city. It was exciting, yet required a great deal of work: from logistics and stocking the inventory to ensuring the proper preparation of employees and readiness of the facility. It was a cold Winter, and the place was far away from my home. The worst part was that there wasn't a restroom in that building. In spite of all the obstacles though, with detailed SMART strategies in place and a deep commitment to the goal, the store was opened on time and became a success.

Another time I applied the SMART approach to goals was when a local bank started offering loans to the customers of our telecom company. I had to go and learn how their software worked, what documents had to be processed and how, what requirements people had to meet, how to check their credibility and income, and much more. There wasn't a credit agency like the one in the US now. I had to do everything by myself, using a phone to talk to the borrower's employer, neighbors, and other people who could testify for his or her credibility and income. I know it sounds silly now, when I am in America building websites, businesses, and social networks... But back then in Russia I didn't even have a computer. I remember setting a SMART goal with all the details, procedures, documents, laws, regulations, and rules outlined on my worksheet. To learn everything from the opposite side, I even borrowed from that bank myself. A few weeks later, I was an expert, issuing loans to people in line on almost auto-pilot.

AS A PARENT.

As long as I remember myself, I always wanted to have at least four children. Two of them appeared in my life out of the blue when their daddy befriended me on Facebook and some time later asked me to marry him.

When I met the boys they were five and six years old. They had been mainly raised by my husband's mother. Because of that, their daily life mostly included just school and TV-watching. I remember asking my boyfriend at the time to bring some dress-up clothes for the boys, to which his answer was that they didn't have any, because they never went anywhere, except for school. This lifestyle was shocking to me. I wanted to help.

I started by having long and often unpleasant conversations with my now husband about what kind of future he was preparing the children for. They were weak: I remember taking them for a walk around the neighborhood and how they complained that their legs were hurting. They had no social skills: I remember one family dinner with many adults being present when my oldest stepson took a fork, ate one bite of food with it, went back to the kitchen, took another fork, ate one bite of food, went back for another fork, and so on. I was disturbed by such behavior, yet it was considered a norm by the rest of the family. The boys also knew no responsibility: they had never made their own beds, tied their own shoes, or picked their plates after dinner. They played no sports, had no bikes, had never had a sleepover in their entire life, and had never been to a museum or a theater. When one day I took them to the school library and got a book for them, I was almost instantly asked to return the book, which was justified by the fact that the boys always lose things.

I was determined to help my husband come up with a strategy for raising these children, for teaching them essential social and self-care skills, for encouraging them to take responsibility, and for helping them grow out of their baby blankets and sippy cups that they still were using at their age.

Today, the boys are eight and nine. They play basketball, ride bikes, have friends, and already had two sleepovers: one in Atlanta and another one in Savannah, which they hosted by themselves. They have been to the museums numerous times, played at the famous Leggo Land in Atlanta, visited the GA Aquarium on multiple occasions, and even went behind the scenes there to explore the life of sharks and other sea creatures. The Atlanta Zoo, the Museum of Natural History, the Wild Animal Safari - I took them everywhere I could to help them gain unforgettable hands-on experiences that they can never receive through watching TV. They now read books from a library and actually take care of those on their own. They have their own bedroom and are fully responsible for making beds every morning and keeping the room in order.

The boys have matured so much! My husband was very acceptive of change and our new goals of preparing the boys for success and helping them grow into independent and self-sufficient young men. It is very fulfilling to see the positive improvements in the lives and performance!

Let me ask you now this one very important question: for what kind of future do you prepare your children? Answer this question with dignity and make notes in your journal. If your findings are disappointing to you, go back to the beginning of this book, were we talked about self-discovery, values, and the big picture of your life. Take a look at the exercises I offer there. Perhaps, you need to go through that process once again to gain clarity and focus, so that you can achieve what you really want and help your children succeed.

CHAPTER 19

Next Steps for You After Reading This Book

All personal achievements start in your mind. The first step is to know exactly what your problem, goal or desire is.
- W. Clement Stone

Very often we find a good book, read it, have an aha-moment, and then get busy with our daily routines and forget about everything we've learned from the book. I would like for you to not miss an opportunity to make a real positive change in your life, career, relationships, and health. I would like for you to uncover your gaps and start working on them today. I know how convenient it can often be to remain undisturbed in your nice comfort-zone. I also know that questioning yourself can be very difficult, unpleasant, disruptive, or even painful. That being said, I also know for sure that the change you decide to make and actually do make can be the most rewarding and can expand your horizons like you would have never dreamed before. No matter what the obstacle, I believe you can overcome it!

Consider this amazing story I heard from a Facebook friend of mine (unfortunately, the author wasn't mentioned, so it is unknown):

One day a farmer's donkey fell down into a well. The animal cried piteously for hours as the farmer tried to figure out what to do. Finally, he decided the animal was old, and the well needed to be covered up anyway; it just wasn't worth it to retrieve the donkey.

He invited all his neighbors to come over and help him to cover up the well. They all grabbed a shovel and began to shovel dirt into the well. At first, the donkey realized what was happening and cried horribly. Then, to everyone's amazement he quieted down. A few shovel loads later, the farmer finally looked down the well. He was astonished at what he saw. With each shovel of dirt that hit his back, the donkey was doing something amazing. He would shake it off and take a step up.

As the farmer's neighbors continued to shovel dirt on top of the animal, he would shake it off and take a step up. Pretty soon, everyone was amazed as the donkey stepped up over the edge of the well and happily trotted off!

Life is a journey, and it may often feel as if it were going to shovel dirt on you. Despite the difficulties that arise on your path to achieving your SMART goals, keep your destination in mind, shake off "the dirt", and take a step up to move toward your desired success.

You have read my book, learned a great deal of useful information, prepared your mind, developed an action plan, and now all you need to do is take the steps described below.

THE SEVEN-STEP PLAN OF ACTIONS TO TAKE AFTER READING THE SMART GOALS BOOK

- Figure out what you really want, using the system I shared with you in chapter two.

- Prepare your mind for setting goals, following the steps I suggested in chapter four.

- Fill out the ten year plan template.

- Complete the SMART goals template, using my thought-provoking questions.

- Find an accountability partner to motivate, energize, inspire you, and help you stay clear and focused on achieving success in the area of your desire.

- Take actions with consistency and remember: actions you take are as important as those you don't take.

- Stay focused on what matters most, yet be flexible to recognize opportunities and be present in every moment of your daily life by remembering your mission and following your values.

Apply my comprehensive methodology and enjoy the rewards! Remember to recommend this book to friends, family, and colleagues, so that they, too, can turn their dreams and wants into achievable SMART goals.

CHAPTER 20

Thirty-Five Great Quotes to Get You Motivated

"The shortest distance between two points assumes you know where you're going." – Robert Brault

"The road leading to a goal does not separate you from the destination; it is essentially a part of it." – Charles DeLint

"Goals allow you to control the direction of change in your favor." – Brian Tracy

"The goal you set must be challenging. At the same time, it should be realistic and attainable, not impossible to reach. It should be challenging enough to make you stretch, but not so far that you break." – Rick Hansen

"If I've got correct goals, and if I keep pursuing them the best way I know how, everything falls into line. If I do the right thing right, I'm going to succeed." – Dan Dierdorf

"Discipline is the bridge between goals and accomplishment." – Jim Rohn

"The critical ingredient is getting off your butt and doing something. It's as simple as that. A lot of people have ideas, but there are few who decide to do something about them now. Not tomorrow. Not next week. But today. The true entrepreneur is a doer, not a dreamer." – Nolan Bushnell

"The tragedy in life doesn't lie in not reaching your goal. The tragedy lies in having no goal to reach." – Benjamin Mays

"By recording your dreams and goals on paper, you set in motion the process of becoming the person you most want to be. Put your future in good hands – your own." – Mark Victor Hansen

"Desire is the key to motivation, but it's determination and commitment to an unrelenting pursuit of your goal – a commitment to excellence – that will enable you to attain the success you seek." – Mario Andretti

"Your goals are the road maps that guide you and show you what is possible for your life." – Les Brown

"A goal is a dream with a deadline." – Napoleon Hill

"If you don't know where you are going, you'll end up someplace else." – Yogi Berra

"Nothing can stop the man with the right mental attitude from achieving his goal; nothing on earth can help the man with the wrong mental attitude." – Thomas Jefferson

"If you want to live a happy life, tie it to a goal, not to people or things." – Albert Einstein

"My interest in life comes from setting myself huge, apparently unachievable challenges and trying to rise above them." – Richard Branson

"People are not lazy, they simply have impotent goals. That is goals that do not inspire them." – Anthony Robbins

"Goals are the fuel in the furnace of achievement." – Brian Tracy

"Obstacles are those frightful things you see, when you take your eyes off your goal." – Henry Ford

"You must have long-range goals to keep you from being frustrated by short-range failures." – Charles C. Noble

"Arriving at one goal is the starting point to another." – John Dewey

"Our tradition calls for a commitment to accountability. This is not an assumption – this is a promise that I will be there for you; and I can count on you being there for me." – Bob Ladouceur, De La Salle High School Football Coach

"This one step – choosing a goal and sticking to it – changes everything." – Scott Reed

"People with goals succeed because they know where they're going." – Earl Nightingale

"A good goal is like a strenuous exercise – it makes you stretch." – Mary Kay Ash

"The key to success is to focus our conscious mind on things we desire, not things we fear." – Brian Tracy

"Success equals goals; all else is commentary." – Brian Tracy

"What keeps me going is goals." – Muhammad Ali

"We do believe in setting goals. We live by goals. In athletics we always have a goal. When we go to school, we have the goal of graduation and degrees. Our total existence is goal-oriented. We must have goals to make progress, encouraged by keeping records . . . as the swimmer or the jumper or the runner does . . . Progress is easier when it is timed, checked, and measured. . . . Goals are good. Laboring with a distant aim sets the mind in a higher key and puts us at our best. Goals should always be made to a point that will make us reach and strain." – Spencer W. Kimbal

"The winners in life think constantly in terms of I can, I will, and I am. Losers, on the other hand, concentrate their waking thoughts on what they should have or would have done, or what they can't do." – Dennis Waitley

"The good and the ill of a man lies within his own will." – Epictetus

"Your goal as an entrepreneur should be to use strategic planning to achieve and sustain superior performance over time." – Dr. Sebora

"If you're trying to be miserable, it's important you don't have any goals. No school goals, personal goals, family goals. Your only objective each day should be to inhale and exhale for sixteen hours before you go to bed again. Don't read anything informative, don't listen to anything useful, don't do anything productive. If you start achieving goals, you might start to feel a sense of excitement, then you might want to set another goal, and then your miserable mornings are through. To maintain your misery, the idea of crossing off your goals should never cross your mind." – John Bytheway, How to Be Totally Miserable

"Some of the world's greatest feats were accomplished by people not smart enough to know they were impossible." – Doug Larson

"An invincible determination can accomplish almost anything and in this lies the great distinction between great men and little men." – Thomas Fuller

About the Author

What keeps me going is goals.
- Muhammad Ali

Anna Stevens is the emotional intelligence maven and the founder of EQ for Success, LLC - an Atlanta-based consulting, training, and coaching company, where she helps people understand how emotions affect their behaviors, actions, relationships, productivity, and success. A Russia native, Anna lives and works in the United States. Using her seventeen years of international experience in personal development, Anna helps professionals reach their highest potential.

Talented and ambitious

Many find it remarkable that Anna taught herself to speak and write in English in less than 1.5 years. Others are amazed with Anna's extraordinary educational background - she graduated from a teaching school with a teacher's certificate, business school with a Bachelor's degree in Business Administration, and law school with a Juris Doctor degree - all with high honors. She will soon be adding an MBA from Georgia State University, J. Mack Robinson College of Business to the strong list of her credentials; and she accomplishes that while successfully running her own business as a solopreneur and being married with two stepchildren. Perhaps, you find Anna's life remarkable now, but it wasn't always this way...

Homeless, hopeless, and helpless

Just a few short years ago, Anna became a victim of domestic violence and was living in one of Atlanta's shelters for abused women and children. Confused, frightened, and not speaking one word of English, Anna was homeless, hopeless, and helpless in a foreign country. She had no social connections, no family within 5,000 miles, was sick and at the very edge of her strength.

From a victim to a victor

Having realized that a victim mentality wasn't a good fit for her, Anna used her own know-how of mind power and emotional intelligence to restore herself and rebuild her life. Starting from zero, she has chosen a proactive approach to solving her numerous problems. Despite her educational credentials and great professional experience, she set out to make a living cleaning houses and being a dog nanny while learning English, making connections, and volunteering at a local courthouse, where she was within a short time hired to work. Applying the tools she developed over the years, Anna overcame significant obstacles she had been forced to face and became free, successful, and happy. With her outstanding self-coaching program, Anna turned herself from a victim to a victor!

Happily-ever-after

Today, Anna uses her proven strategies for success to help business

Anna with her husband and their dog.
March of 2013.

professionals elevate their performance and boost their bottom-line. Since she established her own small consulting company, Anna has helped many people, appeared on TV, multiple radio programs and magazines, and presented for a variety of audiences, sharing her insightful solutions to help others build success, happiness, and wellness.

Anna is married to a GA chiropractor Dr. Philip Day, has two steps-ons, Philip and Alan, and a dog name Bruno, whom she rescued from an animal shelter. In her spare time, Anna enjoys networking in the Atlanta's business community, ice-skating with her stepchildren, swimming, exercising, biking, cooking, hiking, traveling, and volunteering at Women's Resource Center to End Domestic Violence to support abused women and children.

- **Katharine Pike,** Natural Weight Loss Expert, Certified Coach and Speaker, *Lighter Body Solution*

Connect with the Author

For consulting opportunities, media inquiries, interviews, speaking engagements, workshops, or to schedule your personal one-on-one coaching session with Anna Stevens, use the following information to contact her.

EQ for Success, LLC

P.O. Box 20424 , Atlanta, Georgia 30325

Email: Anna@EQforSuccess.com

To post your testimonials, comments or to ask a question, please use our social media:

The SMART Goals Book's Facebook Page

www.Facebook.com/TurnYourDreamsAndWantsIntoAchievableSMART-goals

The SMART Goals Book's Twitter

www.Twitter.com/SMARTgoalsBook

EQ for Success' Facebook Page

www.Facebook.com/EQforSuccess

EQ for Success' Twitter

www.Twitter.com/EQforSuccess

EQ for Success' YouTube

www.YouTube.com/EQforSuccess

EQ for Success' Pinterest

www.Pinterest.com/EQforSuccess

EQ for Success' Blog

www.EQforSuccess.wordpress.com

Anna Stevens on LinkedIn

http://www.linkedin.com/in/StevensAnna

If you enjoyed this book, please submit your review on Goodreads.com and Amazon.com

Making Pilgrimages

Making Pilgrimages

Meaning
and
Practice
in Shikoku

Ian Reader

 University of Hawai'i Press
Honolulu

Printed in the United States of America

13 12 11 10 09 08   7 6 5 4 3 2

Library of Congress Cataloging-in-Publication Data

Reader, Ian.
  Making pilgrimages : meaning and practice in Shikoku / Ian Reader.
    p. cm.
  Includes bibliographical references and index.
  ISBN 978-0-8248-2907-0 (pbk. : alk. paper)
  1. Buddhist pilgrims and pilgrimages—Japan—Shikoku Region.
2. Shikoku Region (Japan)—Religious life and customs. I. Title.
  BQ6450.J32S48627 2005
  294.3'435'09523—dc22

                                        2004017278

University of Hawai'i Press books are printed on acid-free
paper and meet the guidelines for permanence and durability
of the Council on Library Resources

Based on design by Josie Herr

Printed by The Maple-Vail Book Manufacturing Group

For Dorothy

Contents

Acknowledgments   ix

Conventions   xiii

Introduction   1

1   Pilgrimage, Practice, Meanings: Making Pilgrimages
    in Shikoku   9

2   Making Landscapes: Geography, Symbol, Legend, and Traces   39

3   Making Pilgrimages: Pilgrims, Motives, and Meanings   75

4   History, Footsteps, and Customs: Making the
    Premodern Pilgrimage   107

5   Shaping the Pilgrimage: From Poverty to the Package Tour
    in Postwar Japan   150

6   Walking Pilgrimages: Meaning and Experience on
    the Pilgrim's Way   187

7   Making Bus Pilgrimages: Practice and Experience
    on the Package Tour   217

8   A Way of Life: Pilgrimage, Transformation, and Permanence   249

Conclusion   267

*Appendix 1. The Eighty-Eight Temples on the Shikoku
Pilgrimage (in Numerical Order)*   273

Appendix 2. Explanations for the Number of Temples on the Henro   277

Appendix 3. Ways of Doing the Pilgrimage: Average Duration and Costs   279

Notes   281

Glossary   317

References   323

Index   337

Acknowledgments

This book has taken far longer to be written than I could have imagined, and I start with an apology to everyone over the past two decades who has heard me talk about the Shikoku pilgrimage and about the "book in progress"—a book that constantly got put aside as other topics, various job and house moves, and other duties got in the way—and has had to wait forever for it to actually be written. Along the way the number of people who have helped me in a variety of ways has been legion, and it would take a book in itself to mention them all. Some are obvious: the many pilgrims and other participants in the Shikoku pilgrimage—temple priests, their families, local innkeepers, officials and workers in bus companies, and Shikoku residents—are thanked collectively for their help and patience and for almost invariably kindly taking the time to answer my questions and help me understand what was going on. Many temple priests went out of their way to provide information, often doing so on the understanding that their anonymity would be preserved when passing on details that they felt I ought to know but that were not in the public domain. A number of temple priests frequently offered me hospitality in my research visits to Shikoku, and these, again without proffering names, are deeply thanked. Officials from various transport companies in Shikoku, notably Iyo Tetsu, have been helpful and willing to answer all manner of questions. Members of a number of pilgrimage associations that are mentioned in this book, notably the Shiga Shingyōkai and the Arita Settaikō, were generous with their time and hospitality. The general warmth and hospitality of the people I have met in Shikoku have been immensely important in helping this project develop; I thank all I have met through the pilgrimage and through my visits to the island.

In academic terms, I have benefited from numerous discussions and help from a host of interested parties across the globe. As ever, George and Willa Tanabe have been great friends and colleagues whose help has enriched my work. Hoshino Eiki has been generous with advice and materials, and his work on the Shikoku pilgrimage has been a source of inspiration and challenge for me, as has the work of other Japanese scholars such as Shinjō Tsunezō and Shinno Toshikazu, scholars whom I have not met but whose pioneering work has made my journey far easier. Osada Kōichi and Sakata Masaaki of Waseda University have helped my work immensely through the studies they have carried out among pilgrims and through their continuing support, friendship, and assistance in getting hold of materials relating to the pilgrimage. During a visit to Japan in 1990–1991 to conduct research on this topic, Professor Kashioka Tomihide, then of the International Research Center for Japanese Studies in Kyoto and later of Kyoto Women's University, provided great support for my research. In Shikoku, Kiyoyoshi Eitoku, a Shingon priest and pilgrimage historian whose knowledge of pilgrimage stones *(henro ishi)* is unsurpassed, provided much help and hospitality on my visit to Shikoku in 2000. Nathalie Kouamé, too, has helped me significantly in understanding the role of local society and of almsgiving in Tokugawa-era Shikoku. Other Western scholars who have been kind with their assistance and support include David Moreton and Fiona MacGregor, both of whom sent me copies of master's dissertations they had written on the subject.

Friends and colleagues at the Nanzan Institute of Religion and Culture in Nagoya, Japan, have always been welcoming during the numerous times I visited Japan claiming to be on one last trip to Shikoku before writing the book. Specific thanks go to Paul Swanson for his interest in the study of pilgrimage and for the ideas that emerged when we guest edited a special edition of the *Japanese Journal of Religious Studies* together in 1997 on this topic. Clark Chilson and Jay Sakashita, too, have been of great help, support, and encouragement over the past few years.

At various stages during this research I have received assistance in the form of grants to support short periods of fieldwork in Japan from the following: The Japan Foundation Endowment Committee, the Leverhulme Trust, the British Academy, and the Nordic Institute for Asian Studies. I thank all these organizations for their support and patience. Colleagues at the various institutions at which I have worked over the years, notably Tessa Carroll and Val Hamilton, who were colleagues at the University of Stirling and who constantly encouraged my work and provided support and useful information, and Ian Gow, now at Nottingham University, who helped me get some research time in Japan whilst he was head of department while I was at Stirling, deserve my thanks. So, too, do colleagues at the Nordic Institute for Asian Studies in Copenhagen, where I spent three happy years from 1995–1998 and where some of the research that went into this book was done. All my colleagues in the Department of Religious Studies at Lancaster University over the past four or so years merit thanks for providing a warm and intellectually lively setting in which to work, and here let me thank particularly

Chakravarthi Ram-Prasad for his intellectual stimulus and discussions over issues of pilgrimage and Asian religions in general and Deborah Sawyer for first suggesting I teach a course on pilgrimage when I moved to Lancaster and for her support ever since. Thanks, too, to my colleagues Paul Fletcher, Gavin Hyman, and David Waines at Lancaster for our "Meaning of Life" evening seminars at the Water Witch, which have often helped put all manner of things into perspective as I was writing the manuscript. At Lancaster, too, I have enjoyed teaching a course on pilgrimage, and I would like to thank the students who have taken that course for their enthusiasm and interest, which helped keep me on my toes and confirmed what I what I have felt all along: that this is a really fascinating topic worthy of extended study. I realize that there are many others who have helped, through kind words, invitations to give papers and talks on aspects of my research, pieces of advice, and helpful comments and clarifications on questions I have raised with them; thanks here go to Elizabeth Harrison, Robert Sharf, Karen Smyers, Jackie Stone, Timothy Barrett, Ryūichi Abe, and many more.

Patricia Crosby of the University of Hawai'i Press is thanked (1) for her patience over the many years during which I promised that the book would certainly be finished "next year"; (2) for listening to all my wonderfully inventive excuses created over the course of many years in which I failed to write the book, still buying me lunch and remaining confident I would finish the book; (3) making me feel so guilty that I eventually did finish it; and (4) ensuring its smooth production into a real book.

My final thanks as ever go to my family, my wife Dorothy and my children Rosie (fourteen as this book is completed) and Philip (eleven). Rosie and Philip have tolerated my obsession with my work with general good humor and have helped provide the warm environment in which I have been able to write this book. Dorothy has, in a very real sense, been with me on every step of the journey that has led to this book. Together, on a freezing day in February 1984, we took the ferry from Osaka to Tokushima to set out on the Shikoku pilgrimage—a walk that took us forty days in often harsh conditions. It was her interest and readiness to allow me to indulge in my own that made the journey possible, and over the years since then she has continued to support my work, visiting Shikoku with me several times and helping with various interviews that are included in this book. Through the whole period during which I have carried out this research and written this book, she has been tolerant of my obsessions, helped me through the downs that inevitably accompany such projects, and been of more support than anyone could imagine. Without her this book would never have been written, and it is to her that it is dedicated, with all my love and gratitude.

Conventions

Throughout this book I draw on testimonies and interviews with hundreds, perhaps in the context of my fieldwork overall, thousands, of informants, some of whom have been willing to talk to me as long as they are not directly identified by name or who have been concerned (as were the pilgrims in the tour party in chapter 7) with preserving their anonymity. Whenever an informant has either requested anonymity or where s/he has not done anything else to put him/herself into the public domain I have always used pseudonyms for them. I have also sought to ensure the anonymity of people who gave me information that was not directly in the public domain or that might cause embarrassment if its source could be identified. At times, for example, information about the workings of, and issues related to, the Shikoku Reijōkai (The Shikoku Pilgrimage Temples' Association, which coordinates the activities of the eighty-eight temples on the Shikoku pilgrimage) came to me from sources inside the temples, with the understanding that I would not identify where it came from, and hence at times I have had to conceal my sources to some degree.

It is a different matter, however, if those I have talked to or interviewed have elsewhere "gone public" in the context of the pilgrimage, whether by publishing something on their experiences or by speaking in an official capacity in which they have made publicly known their positions. Several of the pilgrims and priests whom I interviewed have also published accounts of their experiences, and they were willing to talk to me because they were happy for their experiences and opinions to be further recorded in the public domain. Tsujita Shōyū, cited in chapter 8, who contacted me because he wanted me to hear and report on his lifetime of pilgrimage experience and who had also published short accounts in Japanese books, is a good example. In such cases I have used their real names, as I have for leaders and members of organizations active in the public domain, ranging from the Shikoku Reijōkai to pilgrimage associations such as the Shiga Shingyōkai.

In this book I use a number of Japanese terms that have particular significance in the context of Shikoku, and these are generally explained both in the text and (with their ideograms) in the glossary. I use the standard Hepburn system for romanizing Japanese terms, with the exception that I do not use the long vowels (macron) sign for words and places (e.g., Tokyo, Kyushu, Honshu) that are nowadays widely recognized in the West without them. Japanese names are given in normal Japanese order (family names followed by given names). Buddhist temples names end usually with "-ji" (or occasionally "-dera"), and I have given them as they occur in Japanese (e.g., Ryūkōji, the first pilgrimage temple mentioned in the book) rather than translate the suffixes (e.g., "Ryūkō temple"), since the former always sounds right to my ear and the latter distinctly awkward.

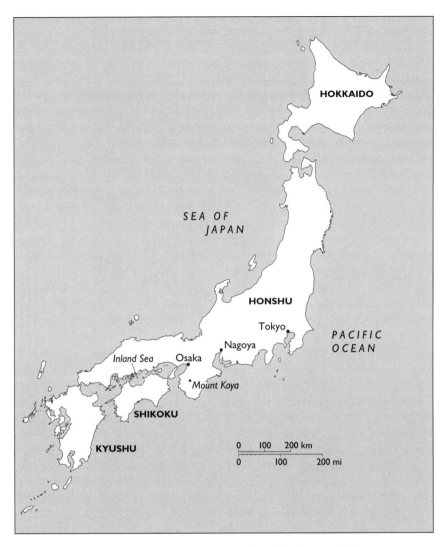

Map of Japan showing the location of Shikoku, the Inland Sea, and the main cities mentioned in the text.

Introduction

There is a Japanese saying that in spring Shikoku comes alive with the sound of pilgrims' bells; that saying seemed particularly appropriate in April 2000 when I returned, after three years' absence, to Shikoku, the fourth largest island in the Japanese archipelago. I was there to continue my research into the Shikoku *henro*, the fourteen-hundred-kilometer-long pilgrimage route that circles the island and in which pilgrims visit eighty-eight temples in a journey that takes at least ten days by bus or car, and several weeks on foot. Spring—the period between mid-March and early May—has traditionally been the peak time for pilgrims to travel in Shikoku, and whereas people may nowadays visit the pilgrimage temples throughout the year, it remains the most conducive and pleasant time for travel there.[1] It is a time when the island's temples are thronged with pilgrims clad in the traditional pilgrim's garb of white shirts, hats (traditionally made of bamboo, although often, nowadays, replaced by white sun hats), and a wooden staff, usually with a small bell attached either to the clothing or to the staff.

I had been conducting research on the pilgrimage for over a decade and a half, had visited Shikoku many times in this period, and had become accustomed to the sound of bells as groups of pilgrims walked up the steps leading to the temples. Their sounds, too, always seemed especially resonant in spring, as if I had always associated Shikoku and spring—the time, indeed, when I have visited it most often. And yet the sounds of bells seemed louder and more vibrant in April 2000 than I remembered from before and the crowds of pilgrims more numerous. On my first full day back in Shikoku, as I alighted from a one-car local train at the tiny station of Iyo Miyanoshita, a couple of stops beyond the town of Uwajima in southwest Shikoku, and headed toward Ryūkōji, one of the pilgrimage temples situated not far away, I was struck by the sheer numbers of pilgrims on the road, and this impression remained with me throughout the rest of my visit.

Pilgrim in full pilgrimage regalia, on the second day of his pilgrimage in April 2000 near Temple 6.

Ryukōji—the name means "temple of the shining dragon"—is known to pilgrims as Dai yonjūichiban, Temple 41; all eighty-eight temples have both a name and a number, though generally pilgrims refer to them by number rather than name. Temple 41 is situated in one of the most pleasant rural parts of Shikoku, of which I had fond memories from my first visit to the island in 1984, when my wife Dorothy and I walked the pilgrimage at the start of an academic and personal journey that just may have come to completion with this book. Because of those memories I had decided to make the area around Ryūkōji the focus of my first day back in Shikoku and planned to walk from Ryūkōji to Temple 42 (Butsumokuji) and Temple 43 (Meisekiji)—a distance of around fifteen kilometers mostly on quiet paths through forests and hills. My intentions were twofold: to unwind from the long journey from England to Shikoku by walking in the warm April weather, and to get back into my pilgrimage studies by spending time on the route and at these temples observing what the pilgrims were doing and to prepare myself for a short period of intensive fieldwork.

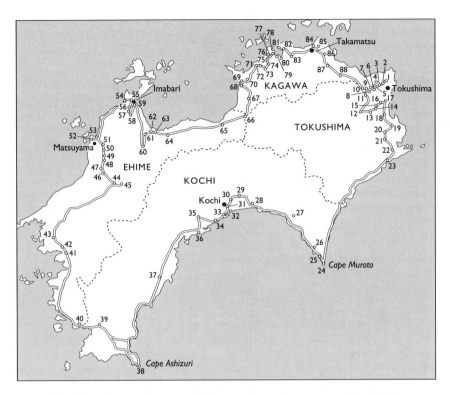

Map of Shikoku showing the four prefectures, the main towns, and the pilgrimage route and temples.

As I walked up the narrow road to Ryūkōji I was passed by numerous buses and microbuses full of pilgrims, and on entering its courtyard I was engulfed by crowds of pilgrims, often in large groups led by a pilgrimage guide or leader *(sendatsu)*. The pilgrims—mostly in groups—chanted prayers, mantras, and pilgrimage songs, lit sticks of incense and candles, threw coins into offertory boxes, and generally milled about, talking to each other, discussing their schedules, the attributes of the temple being visited, and much else besides. The cacophony and chaos[2] of the temple were overwhelming, and so, rather than lingering, I made a quick escape along the quiet path heading to the next temple, along with a female Japanese pilgrim (who will appear again in chapter 3) who felt equally ready to leave behind the noise of the temple.

My immediate impression about pilgrim numbers was confirmed by visits to other temples and by discussions with temple priests, people running pilgrims' lodges, and the officials of transport companies on the island, all of whom considered that pilgrim numbers had risen sharply since around 1998.

Spring in Shikoku: crowds of pilgrims going up and down the steps of one of the pilgrimage temples.

An official of the Iyo Tetsu Company based in Matsuyama, Shikoku, the biggest single carrier of pilgrims in Shikoku, told me that people using its organized pilgrimage tour services had risen by around 30 percent over the last three or so years and that well in excess of one hundred thousand people were now doing the pilgrimage each year.[3]

The reasons for this current rise in numbers will be explored later in this book. Such changes are nothing new in Shikoku, where pilgrim numbers have fluctuated depending on circumstances such as economic conditions and the political attitudes of regional authorities over the ages and from decade to decade. They illustrate that pilgrimage is rarely something that remains static or stable from age to age and that change and development are common characteristics within it. Such issues will be central to this book, which examines the Shikoku pilgrimage in the context of, and as a process of, change. As pilgrimages are made, so too are meanings in the eyes of pilgrims and other participants in the pilgrimage process. As I will discuss in subsequent chapters, pilgrimages are not just "made" by pilgrims who set out to travel along a pilgrimage route but by many other actors as well—from priests and others who look after the sites, to local people who support and interact with pilgrims, to those who provide services for pilgrims. The things these participants do—their acts, the stories they tell, the things they leave at sites—add to the landscape of pilgrimage, which in turn influences those who are involved with the pilgrimage process, who thereby create and make meanings for themselves. As such, the landscape of pilgrimage—a term that, as will be discussed in chapter 2, refers not just to the physical but to the emotional terrain that frames pilgrimage—is, through such meanings, itself constantly (re)made anew.

The purpose and structure of this book

In examining the Shikoku pilgrimage as something that is made and remade through continuing performance and practice, I am primarily concerned with the activities of a variety of actors and forces that have influenced its development and nature, with the landscape and framework that shapes it, and with the meanings that are thereby constructed in the eyes of participants. My focus is primarily on the present day—a term I use to mean, by and large, the latter part of the twentieth and the turn of the twenty-first centuries, the period in which I have conducted fieldwork in the region. My approach is predominantly synchronic, and one of its aims is to show how all manner of themes and participants are linked and operate together within the contemporary structure and process of pilgrimage. However, one cannot understand or properly analyze a phenomenon as rich and diverse as pilgrimage just through observing it, and its participants, synchronically. The traces and influences of the past (including the imagined and legendary past) are, as will be seen in later chapters, vital parts of the emotional landscape that infuses and influences the consciousness of its participants. Thus in order to understand the pilgrimage in the present one needs to understand its past and how this impacts on and colors that present.

This book broadly divides into three sections. The first (chapters 1–3) presents a general overview of the pilgrimage in terms of how it is structured, what it involves, the landscape that frames it, and the motives and general orientations of its pilgrims. In chapter 1 I describe the pilgrimage and its main focus of worship before discussing some theoretical issues relating to pilgrimage in general and outlining the parameters of my study and expanding on the themes outlined above. From there I move on, in chapter 2, to examine the background that frames and shapes the activities of its participants. This background is what I call the emotional landscape of pilgrimage—a term that incorporates not just the geographical features and structures that provide a setting for the pilgrimage, but also nonphysical matters that shape the emotional terrain in which pilgrims voyage, such as the pilgrimage's various legends, symbolic meanings, and miraculous tales, all of which help create the mental landscape framing the pilgrimage and influencing its participants. As I show in chapter 2, this emotional landscape has been shaped and framed by the pilgrims and others in numerous ways and is being constantly reshaped as successive generations of pilgrims pass along the way and as new interpretations of the landscape are formed. In chapter 3 I then turn to a general account of the pilgrims themselves, based mainly on cameo accounts of a number of pilgrims I have met, interviewed, and traveled with. I use their stories to draw out representative aspects of pilgrim practice and experience and to illustrate the variety of motivations and attitudes pilgrims may have, their levels of engagement with the pilgrimage, and the ways in which such pilgrimage practices may be embedded in their daily lives.

I then turn, in the second section, comprising chapters 4 and 5, to the ways in which the pilgrimage has developed and been shaped historically. Some of the issues central to this process will have been touched on in chapter 2, which recounts some of the legends that have become part of the "historical" record of pilgrimage, but in chapters 4 and 5 I turn more specifically to the history of the pilgrimage. In chapter 4 I outline the origins of the pilgrimage, the development of certain important legends and stories, the beginnings of an organized route and the first guidebooks, as well as wayside markers and pilgrims' lodges, all of which indicate the gradual development of a formalized pilgrimage structure. As the pilgrimage developed, too, a number of influential pilgrims began to appear, including people who performed the route numerous times, thereby establishing a custom and practice that remains prevalent in the present—that of making multiple circuits of the island. In chapter 4, also, I discuss the attitude of the local feudal authorities to the pilgrimage and highlight the extent to which the pilgrims themselves in the premodern era, especially the eighteenth and nineteenth centuries (and well into the twentieth century), were widely seen as outsiders and disruptive elements who needed to be kept in check—and yet how they were also surrounded by beliefs associating them with the sacred and hence were seen as specially holy figures worthy of support and help. These dualistic views of the pilgrimage have not entirely disappeared in the present either—and indeed, questions of ambivalence, for example in terms of the nature of the pilgrims and of attitudes to them, recur throughout the book as a continuing theme within the pilgrimage.

The modern era—by which I mean the postwar period, and particularly since the 1950s, when mass transportation effectively altered the way in which most pilgrims travel—has brought numerous developments that have altered the face of the pilgrimage. These include the rapid growth of commercial pilgrimage companies and organized pilgrimage tours, the development of the Shikoku Reijōkai (Shikoku Pilgrimage Temples' Association), which represents the eighty-eight temples, an organized system of ranks bestowed by this association to give status to pilgrims who do the pilgrimage many times, and successful publicity campaigns that have portrayed the pilgrimage as a symbol and image of Japanese cultural tradition. All these are connected, and in chapter 5, in examining how the pilgrimage infrastructure has developed in the age of mass transport, I will look at these connections, as well as the agents (including the bus companies whose activities have changed the ways in which pilgrims travel) that have affected the ways pilgrims make their pilgrimages in the present day.

In the last section of the book I look primarily at experience and practice in the pilgrim community, focusing on the largest and most visible part of the pilgrimage community: the pilgrims themselves. In chapters 6 and 7 I focus, in turn, on the two widely used means of doing the pilgrimage historically and in the present—foot and bus package tours. In chapter 6 my focus is on those who walk the pilgrimage. While nowadays numerically fewer than those who go by bus, pilgrims who travel on foot remain perhaps the most vocal—in terms of written journals and published accounts of their pilgrimages and experiences—and historically enduring section of the pilgrimage community. Since, too, I have retained an interest in foot pilgrimage since my first visit to Shikoku in 1984, and since much of my research has been carried out on the pilgrimage paths of Shikoku, the experiences and attitudes of foot pilgrims remain a central part of my interest. While space (as well as personal experience) does not permit extended discussion of every form or means of doing the pilgrimage, I do, in chapter 7, examine in some detail the most common form of modern pilgrimage by looking at organized pilgrimage tours by bus. The chapter is largely framed around a pilgrimage tour I undertook during my research, through which I attempt to show what goes on in organized group pilgrimage tours, how such pilgrims view and experience the Shikoku pilgrimage, and how they may interact with other pilgrims.

My account of pilgrim activities on the road, as set out in chapters 6 and 7, shows the extent to which pilgrims, whilst in the process of traveling, are largely focused on goals such as getting to the next temple or completing the route, and this perception of pilgrimage as a goal-centered activity is certainly one that has been prevalent in standard academic (and especially anthropological) discussions of the subject. Yet, as I discuss in chapter 8, there are problems with such goal-centered approaches, which generally do not consider what occurs after pilgrims have reached their apparent goals at the end of their journeys. Pilgrimages are not, as chapter 8 shows, just transitory performances carried out at specific locations and directed at particular spatial and temporal goals, but may be points of departure for their participants, impacting on and influencing their lives thereafter and even, as the cases outlined in the chapter indicate, becoming recurrent features in them.

Thus while chapters 6 and 7 primarily follow normative patterns within the anthropological study of pilgrimage by concentrating on pilgrims as they travel and at pilgrimage sites, chapter 8 seeks to show how such apparently transitory performances may be life-transforming events and central features in the identities and lives of participants. It looks at one of the most distinctive features of the Shikoku pilgrimage: the tendency of many of its pilgrims to do it over and over again. A high proportion of pilgrims do the *henro* not just once but several times or more, and examples will be given throughout the book of people who have made dozens and even hundreds of circuits of the island. Chapter 8 focuses on such pilgrims and shows how, for such people, the pilgrimage is a life-transforming event, one that causes them to devote much if not all of their time to making pilgrimages, effectively turning pilgrimage into a way of life so that they sometimes even become "permanent pilgrims" on the road in Shikoku. As such, chapter 8 asserts that pilgrimage is by no means a one-off or marginal phenomenon located somewhere on the fringes of religious life, nor something associated specifically with goals, ends, and going to and from specific sacred places. Rather, it can be a central pillar in the lives of participants, a "way of life" central to their social and religious being. After this section on practice and experience, I briefly, in my conclusion, comment on some of the prevailing themes and issues that have surfaced in my account of the pilgrimage and consider what can be gleaned from this excursus into the world of a specific and prominent Japanese pilgrimage about concepts and theories of pilgrimage in general.

1 PilgRimAge, PRActice, MeANiNgs

MakiNg PilgRimAges iN Shikoku

The Shikoku pilgrimage is one of the most prominent, evocative, and photogenic pilgrimages in a country with a highly developed pilgrimage culture that, as the Japanese scholar Shinno Toshikazu has stated, is one of the most prominent elements in Japanese religious structure.[1] The two Japanese terms most commonly used to refer to the pilgrimage are *"Shikoku hachijūhakkasho"* (eighty-eight sacred places of Shikoku) and *"Shikoku henro"* (Shikoku pilgrimage). The ideograms 遍路 used to write *henro*, one of many Japanese words normally translated in English as "pilgrimage," indicate a "linking route." The significance of the word *"henro"* and its meaning will be discussed later. The two terms indicate an ambivalence in the pilgrimage's structure in that the first (speaking of eighty-eight sacred places, all Buddhist temples) emphasizes the specific places the pilgrim visits, while the second indicates the route that links them. This ambivalence can be found in the different perceptions of pilgrims, often dependent on the ways in which they travel, and other actors (such as the priests who run the temples). As will be seen in later chapters, one can make a rough generalization that those who travel by bus and other modes of motorized transport tend to focus more on the specific points on the route (the temples, i.e., the *hachijūhakksho*), while those who walk find that the "route" (i.e., the *henro*, including the spaces in between the temples) is the prime focus of their attention.

In either case, the pilgrimage involves a fourteen hundred-kilometer journey around Shikoku in which the pilgrim visits the eighty-eight Buddhist temples that are official stages on the route (see appendix 1 for a list of the temples). As such, it represents one of the most prevalent types of pilgrimage found in Japan: a linked circuit in which participants focus not just on one sacred goal, but on a specified number of sites, which collectively form the pilgrimage, and all of which must be visited to complete it.[2] While one finds multiple-site pilgrimages in other parts of the world, they are perhaps more prevalent in Japan than elsewhere, and Japanese dictionaries and compendia of pilgrimage routes list several hundred such routes throughout the country, many of them small and local, but others, like Shikoku, covering whole geographical regions.[3] While such pilgrimages are normally, like Shikoku, centered on Buddhist temples, they are not exclusively so; some of the Shikoku sites were, until the second half of the nineteenth century, Shinto shrines, while some multiple-site Japanese pilgrimages focus on Shinto shrines or a combination of Buddhist and Shinto sites.[4]

Sometimes there are clear canonical reasons for these numbers. The thirty-three-stage Saikoku pilgrimage in western Japan, which, with the Shikoku pilgrimage, is the most prominent multiple-site pilgrimage in Japan,[5] links thirty-three Buddhist temples housing sacred images of Kannon, the bodhisattva of compassion, because in the popular Buddhist text the Lotus Sutra, Kannon declares her mission to save anyone in distress and vows to assume thirty-three different forms to this end.[6] In Shikoku, however, there are no such clear canonical reasons to account for the eighty-eight sacred sites. While a number of popular explanations (the most common of which are centered on numerology, folk beliefs, or interpretations of Buddhist thought that suggest the pilgrimage was so constructed to replicate esoteric Buddhist concepts and are outlined in appendix 2) are commonly referred to in pilgrimage folklore and guidebooks, all are speculative, and none has any substantive historical underpinning. Early pilgrimage guidebooks from the seventeenth century are as unclear on these numerical origins as are modern historians.[7] There may, indeed, be no particular significance to the number save that, as will be discussed in later chapters, as the pilgrimage evolved over time, it incorporated and assimilated a variety of local sacred places and temples associated with all aspects of the island's geography, history, religion, and culture, along with various local pilgrimage routes, with the result that by the time it had coalesced as a fixed pilgrimage, it had come to include eighty-eight places.

Kōbō Daishi and pilgrimage in Shikoku

In pilgrimage typologies developed by Japanese scholars, Shikoku is classified as a *seiseki* pilgrimage—one associated with the sacred traces or presence of a holy person.[8] In Shikoku this figure is Kōbō Daishi, a miracle-working figure with origins in the Japanese Buddhist tradition whose presence permeates the pilgrimage and binds it to the island of Shikoku. Kōbō Daishi is the posthumous title granted by imperial decree in 921 CE to the Buddhist teacher Kūkai (774–835 CE), who was born at Zentsūji in Shikoku and went on to establish the Shingon Buddhist tradition in Japan and to found its main religious center at Kōyasan in the hills of Wakayama Prefecture south of Osaka. In this posthumous guise, Kōbō Daishi was portrayed as transcending death and traveling as a wandering holy figure who dispensed miracles. As such, a cult of devotion grew around him, spreading throughout Japan and flourishing in Shikoku, the island of Kūkai's birth. In the next chapter I will provide more details about Kūkai and the cult of Kōbō Daishi. Here I simply introduce him as a holy figure and note that the Shikoku pilgrimage is one of the most prominent features of Kōbō Daishi veneration *(Daishi shinkō)* in Japan.

Each of the eighty-eight temples has two major halls of worship, one enshrining a main Buddhist image of worship *(honzon)*, which varies from temple to temple but which, indicative of the encompassing nature of the *henro*, includes virtually every important figure from the Japanese Buddhist pantheon of worship, and the other a hall of worship *(daishidō)* dedicated to Kōbō Daishi. Kōbō Daishi's presence is thus found at every temple (and often, too, in their foundation legends). It also permeates the route and island, for Kōbō Daishi is a constant presence accompanying and guarding over pilgrims as they travel. There are parallels here with St. James in the Santiago de Compostela pilgrimage, who not only awaits pilgrims at his cathedral in

Statue of Kōbō Daishi as a wandering pilgrim with begging bowl at Butsumokuji (Temple 42).

Santiago, but also may appear to them on the route. Like St. James, too, whose miracles tend to occur more commonly along the route to Santiago than at his sanctuary,[9] miraculous accounts of Kōbō Daishi's intercession also are associated with pilgrims not just at the temples but along the route they travel.

In some respects Kōbō Daishi is an ambivalent figure, associated both with the established orders of Japanese Buddhism as a founder-figure in Shingon Buddhism and with the popular folk religious traditions of that country in his guise as a wandering miracle worker. This ambivalence and dual association can at times be a source of tension in which the Shikoku Reijōkai and the temple priests—the majority of whom belong to the Shingon Buddhist tradition—and the pilgrims—the majority of whom of whom are not affiliated with Shingon—may have different perceptions of the pilgrimage and the holy figure at its heart. This tension is indicative of how different participants in the pilgrimage process—for example, those who care for holy sites and those who visit them—may have differing views of and attitudes toward a practice in which they have a shared interest.

In pilgrimage lore Kōbō Daishi is forever guarding and accompanying pilgrims on their journeys, and this unity between pilgrim and holy figure marks pilgrims out and gives them a sense of individual power in which they exist in a special and direct relationship with the holy figure. The pilgrim traditionally identifies with Kōbō Daishi through the pilgrim's garb s/he wears —a bamboo hat (often nowadays replaced by the more convenient white sun hat), a *hakui* (white pilgrim's shirt) and staff—which not only mirrors the attire of the wandering monk but also symbolically reflects the presence of Kōbō Daishi with the pilgrim. The pilgrim's staff, for instance, is considered to represent the body of Kōbō Daishi, while the white pilgrim's shirt usually bears a pictorial representation of the holy figure and also the ideograms *dōgyōninin* 同行二人 (two people, one practice), implying that the pilgrim always carries out his/her pilgrimage in the company of the Daishi, as he is familiarly known. This also implies a sense of belonging and community, since the notion of being together with the holy figure is one shared by all pilgrims, who are all involved in the act of *dōgyō*, performing the same practice of following the path Kōbō Daishi is said to have trodden around the island of his birth. This image of following in the footsteps of, and being accompanied by, Kōbō Daishi remains constant no matter how the pilgrim travels.

The pilgrim's attire appears to have undergone relatively little change over the centuries, which helps create an image of tradition that adds to the pilgrimage's modern appeal. Seventeenth-century Shikoku woodblock prints show pilgrims similarly wearing sedge or bamboo hats, with white robes, straw sandals, and wooden staffs.[10] The main changes in modern times have been those of convenience. For example, modern pilgrims rarely wear straw sandals, due to the availability of trainers and modern walking shoes, while tracksuit trousers or jeans frequently take the place of white leggings. Modern pilgrims, especially those who travel in cars and buses, may find the bamboo hat inconvenient and hence replace it with a white sun hat or, sadly popular among male walkers, the appalling baseball cap. Priests who travel as pilgrims usually wear a black priest's robe rather than the *hakui* and often have a grander version of the bamboo hat and staff. Occasionally, too, one encounters pilgrims who, while not priests, are dressed in this manner, indicating that they have taken a priestly vow or temporary ordination for the duration of their journeys.[11]

The attire, besides emphasizing the unity of sacred figure and pilgrim, also marks the pilgrim out as apart from the rest of humankind, traveling in a sacred realm and symbolically "dead to the world."[12] The objects mentioned above—the hat, staff, and pilgrim's shirt—represent items connected with death and funerals and thus manifest the notion that the pilgrim is ready for death at any stage of the journey. I will discuss this symbolism further in the next chapter. As subsequent chapters will show, however, such symbolic meanings are rarely uppermost in the minds of pilgrims. More commonly, pilgrims express pragmatic wishes as the primary reasons behind their pilgrimages, while the modern means of conveyance used by most pilgrims, along with the comfortable circumstances in which they travel and the carefully constructed schedules that are followed, suggest that the modern pilgrim is more intent on arriving at his or her destination at the designated time than in facing death along the way.[13] Such symbolic meanings, however, are important in the emotional framework of the pilgrimage and play a major part in the construction of meaning for pilgrims.

The pilgrim's journey takes him/her on a circuit of the island, normally in a clockwise direction,[14] during which every one of the eighty-eight temples will be visited. The numbers given to each temple indicate not an obligatory route, but one of convenience that developed in the eighteenth century based on the order in which the temples would normally be visited by pilgrims traveling clockwise and starting from near the port of Naruto in eastern Shikoku —the main place where, in the Tokugawa (1600–1868) era, pilgrims entered Shikoku from the Japanese mainland. In this order, Ryōzenji, a relatively short walk from Naruto, came to be known as Temple 1 (*daiichiban*). By starting at Ryōzenji and going in numerical order clockwise around the island, the pilgrim eventually ends up at Ōkuboji (Temple 88), which is located in the mountains less than a day's walk from Ryōzenji. At Ōkuboji there is a stone inscribed with the term *"kechiganjo"* (place of the completion of the vow) to denote that this is where pilgrims' vows to complete the entire circuit are realized. It is customary, although not obligatory, for pilgrims to make an *orei mairi* (return/thanksgiving visit) to the temple where they started their journey, to give thanks for safe completion. Some pilgrims visit Kōyasan, the Shingon Buddhist center in Wakayama founded by Kūkai, either before or after their pilgrimages to pay homage at Kōbō Daishi's mausoleum there as a form of *orei mairi*—a practice that is encouraged by Shingon Buddhist authorities as a way of establishing closer ties between the sect and the pilgrims. Like the *orei mairi*, this is not so much part of the pilgrimage as an addition that appears, in the days of organized tours, to be increasingly normative. Indeed, the scrolls and books that pilgrims carry and that are stamped at each temple visited nowadays usually have a space for a Kōyasan and/or *orei mairi* visit. By contrast, the chronicles of pilgrims in earlier centuries show little evidence of a need to "complete the circle" by returning to this first temple.[15]

Reijō: Pilgrimage temples in Shikoku

The pilgrimage temples are referred to as *reijō* 霊場 (spirit place, also "place where the spirits gather," a term that has associations with death—a recurrent theme in Shikoku—but is also a shortened form of *reigenjō*, or places where miracles occur)[16] or as *fudasho* 札所 ("places where one leaves one's *fuda*"—*fuda* being the pilgrim's calling card, which will be discussed later). The eighty-eight *reijō* encompass multiple aspects of the island's geography and religious traditions. In sectarian terms, they comprise a variety of affiliations: eighty are Shingon Buddhist, representing eleven sects of Shingon, while the other eight belong to the Tendai Buddhist sect (four temples), Rinzai Zen Buddhism (two), and Sōtō Zen and Jishū (one each). The main images of worship at the temples include many of the most popular Buddhist figures venerated in Japan, such as Kannon, Jizō, Amida, and Yakushi. Many of these main images may themselves be the focus of miracle stories relating to pilgrims.

The pilgrimage incorporates a variety of sites, ranging from those associated with Kūkai's life (e.g., his birthplace Zentsūji, Temple 75) and his documented travels (e.g., Tairyūji, Temple 21, and Higashidera, Temple 24), along with sites where he is reputed to have undergone austerities (e.g., Iwayaji, Temple 45) or that have founding legends associated with him (e.g., Gokurakuji, Temple 2). It draws in prominent temples linked to Shugendō, the Japanese mountain ascetic religious tradition that was prominent in Shikoku, and to local cultic practices associated with the spirits of the dead. Sites such as Yokomineji (Temple 60), Unpenji (Temple 66), and Iyataniji (Temple 71) all fall into these categories. It includes temples in prominent areas of agricultural production, which gave rise to important centers of population. Thus the line of temples now numbered from 1 to 10 along the Yoshino River valley outside Tokushima incorporates a local pilgrimage route and an important area of premodern economic production. Other local routes centered on or around important population centers—such as a cluster of temples (numbers 54–59) around the castle town of Imabari in northwest Shikoku, which formed another local pilgrimage route, and a series of temples (46–53) around the castle town of Matsuyama—also indicate the ways in which the pilgrimage has incorporated local practices and centers of political strength. The pilgrimage includes large and powerful temples that have become the focal points around which towns have grown, such as Tatsueji (Temple 19), and temples on the coast, such as the southernmost temple, Kongōfukuji (Temple 38), at Cape Ashizuri facing out over the Pacific Ocean, and Yashimaji (Temple 84) on a hill outside Takamatsu with commanding views over the Inland Sea. Some temples are centers of popular prayer cults that have a prominence beyond their status as pilgrimage temples and may well have been incorporated into the route for such reasons; thus Yakuōji (Temple 23) is widely visited because of its reputation for providing spiritual protection for people in their "unlucky year" *(yakudoshi),* a prominent concept in Japanese folk beliefs.[17] Yet many of the temples are neither striking in terms of physical setting nor in terms of the local religious culture. Unlike, for example, the temples on the Saikoku route, the Shikoku temples are rarely renowned for their cultural assets or treasures or for being important architecturally; their significance comes from being parts of the circuit dedicated to Kōbō Daishi.

The temples are not evenly spaced apart; they often are found in clusters, such as the aforementioned temples along the Yoshino River valley, and sometimes may be only a few hundred meters apart. In one case, two temples (68 and 69 at Kannonji in Kagawa Prefecture) stand in the same courtyard. Some, though, are far apart: one hundred kilometers separates Iwamotoji (Temple 37) and Kongōfukuji (Temple 38), and several others are almost as distant. Thus walkers may sometimes find themselves visiting several temples in a day, yet at other times may walk all day without visiting a single one. By bus it is possible at times to visit ten or more temples in a day, but elsewhere it may take many hours to get between temples, especially on the often narrow and winding roads of the island's interior and when temples are situated in remote mountainous places. Perhaps the least accessible is Yokomineji (Temple 60), which was until 1984 accessible only by foot and even now may reached only by a small forest road inaccessible to buses, and where pilgrims have to transfer to microbuses and then walk some distance.

Theoretically all the temples are equal, since one has to visit them all to complete the pilgrimage. In the eyes of the pilgrims, however, some may be more equal than others. Temples with dramatic physical settings or with powerful historical connections tend to have a greater effect on pilgrims, to be remembered more clearly by them, and to be considered as more appropriate settings for reverence than are smaller temples in unprepossessing locations. For example, Zentsūji, the birthplace of Kūkai/Kōbō Daishi and the headquarters of a Shingon Buddhist sect, is an extensive temple at the heart of the town that has grown around it in the plains of northern Shikoku, and its association with Kōbō Daishi and its splendid courtyard and buildings, including a five-story pagoda, are often commented on in the journals of pilgrims.[18]

When I visited it in 1990 with a party of pilgrims (see chapter 7), they exclaimed that this was truly a splendid place, worthy of special reverence as the birthplace of the Daishi. By contrast, they were somewhat disparaging about the previous temple we had visited, which they later compared unfavorably to Zentsūji, since it was rather small and in a less than striking position, jammed between a hillside and several houses and adjacent to a noisy road along which lorries bound for a nearby quarry hurtled. That temple, they felt, had barely seemed worthy of the status of a pilgrimage temple. I later checked my 1984 Shikoku pilgrimage diary and found that I, too, had made similar comments and compared it unfavorably to Zentsūji. Mountain temples such as Iyataniji, which extends up numerous steep sets of steps, incorporates a number of caves, appears to be tenuously clinging to the mountainside as if perched midway between this world and other realms, and is the setting for numerous miracle tales, or Iwayaji, another mountain temple that is described in the next chapter, also frequently inspire reverence and are remembered by many pilgrims well after some of the less striking temples have faded from memory.

As was noted above, the numerical order of the temples indicates a convenient, not an obligatory, route. Pilgrims may start and finish at whichever temple they wish. Those entering from regions north or west of Shikoku, for example, have generally been more likely to start their journeys at the nearest temple to their point of entry, rather than journeying across to Temple 1. Thus the writer Takamure Itsue, in 1918, traveled across to Shikoku from Kyushu in southern Japan and began her journey at the nearest convenient temple, Meisekiji (Temple 43). In very recent times, as new bridges and new highways have opened between Shikoku and the main island of Honshu, however, it has become easier for those traveling by car or bus to get quickly to Temple 1 and to start from there, as a result of which it appears that more pilgrims nowadays are following the numerical structure of the pilgrimage than in earlier times.[19] Nonetheless, the order in which the *henro* is performed remains the prerogative of each pilgrim. So, too, is the direction in which pilgrims travel: while most travel clockwise, some—and Takamure was one such —go round anticlockwise, a practice known as *gyaku uchi* (visiting in reverse order) that is regarded as more difficult than the normal clockwise manner.[20] According to a survey carried out by a group of researchers from Waseda University led by Osada Kōichi and Sakata Masaaki, Temple 1 is the most common starting place for pilgrims, with 37.4 percent of those surveyed beginning there, and Ōkuboji (Temple 88) was, at 35.2 percent, the most common place to finish. However, virtually every temple was chosen by some pilgrims as their starting or finishing place.[21]

Pilgrims may also visit and worship at sites other than the official eighty-eight. There are many sites known as *bangai* 番外 ("[places of worship] outside the [official] number") that may be visited by pilgrims. As Hoshino Eiki has commented, it was common in premodern Japan for pilgrims to worship at the various shrines and temples they passed,[22] and frequently these came to be considered *bangai,* or places with a link to the pilgrimage route. This custom has continued in the present, and pilgrims may be encouraged by pilgrimage guidebooks to visit at least some *bangai.* Sometimes, guidebooks may mention just a few *bangai,* but others may include large numbers, as was the case with a recent guidebook for walkers that lists 160 additional sites, from wayside statues to large temples and Shinto shrines, where the pilgrim is encouraged to worship.[23]

Among the best-known *bangai* are Kaiganji in Kagawa Prefecture, the place where Kūkai's mother came from and claimed by some as his actual birthplace, and Saba Daishi, a temple midway between Temples 23 and 24 that is often visited by bus pilgrimage tours. This latter provides an example of how circumstance, convenience, and enterprise can turn a small wayside hall of worship (which Saba Daishi was until after World War II) into a thriving temple with a large pilgrims' lodge and strong connections to the Shikoku pilgrimage community. Shortly after the war, a pilgrim who had decided to stay in Shikoku and take the Buddhist tonsure took up residence at Saba Daishi, then a small, unmanned hall of worship with a miracle story linking it to Kōbō Daishi. The pilgrim managed thereafter to build it up into a flourishing temple, chiefly by appealing to the passing pilgrimage trade; Saba Daishi's location between Temples 23 and 24 on the eastern coast of Shikoku provided a convenient place for buses to stop either for lunch or overnight. This priest—and later his son, Yanagimoto Myōzen, who took over the temple—over many years developed close contacts with pilgrimage associations and groups. In so doing they have turned Saba Daishi into one of the best-known and most popular *bangai* on the island.[24] Pilgrims may also visit Shinto shrines in their itineraries, particularly Konpira Shrine at Kotohira, just a few minutes by bus or train from Zentsūji, which appears also in some premodern pilgrimage maps as part of the route.[25]

Making the pilgrimage: Modes, choices, patterns

Pilgrims travel by whatever means they find most convenient or relevant to their purposes, and in time scales and ways suited to their needs—an issue discussed more fully in chapter 3. There are no obligatory rules about how pilgrims should do the pilgrimage. The pilgrimage temples emphasize the importance of a correct spiritual attitude *(kokoroe)* that pilgrims should have, and they provide a printed list of ten rules (often reproduced in guidebooks and including things such as abstinence from alcohol, licentious behavior, swearing, theft, and other criminal acts) that should be followed.[26] However, while these rules shape the moral landscape of the pilgrimage, they are recommendations, not regulations, and, as will be seen in later chapters, some (notably the alcohol rule) may be flexibly interpreted.

Nor is there are any obligation to do the pilgrimage in an ascetic manner, returning "thinner and poorer," as is widely expected in, for example, Hindu pilgrimages.[27] There are some who assert that the only genuine way to do the *henro* is by foot, and it is fairly widely felt, even among those who travel by other means, that this may be the most "authentic" way to do it if possible.[28] However, this view is not universally held, and I have met many who think that going in organized tours by bus is as worthwhile, if not more so, than walking. Thus a temple priest I knew said that it was better to travel with a party of pilgrims on an organized tour led by a good pilgrimage guide *(sendatsu)* because on such tours the pilgrims are continually involved in prayer and worship and spend much of their time listening to stories of miracles and explanations of the significance of various landmarks along the way. Thus in his view, tour groups were where one experienced the most devout elements of pilgrim behavior and practice.

The fact that there are no set rules as to how one should travel may be because the *henro* developed in an era when there were no viable alternatives to walking, and hence it was simply assumed that everyone would walk. However, it is characteristic of pilgrimage in general that whenever developments have occurred to make it more convenient and to make pilgrimage locations more accessible, they have been readily assimilated. This ready adoption of more convenient modes of travel is not just a product of modern times, for, like pilgrims in medieval Europe who took advantage of the development of sea routes that could get them more quickly (and hence safely and cheaply) to major pilgrimage centers,[29] Shikoku pilgrims have made use of improvements in transport infrastructures as and when they have occurred. Thus they readily embraced the development of boat and ferry services in the Tokugawa era, which enabled them to cross rivers and coastal inlets rather than having to walk around them, thereby significantly cutting down the time they needed to spend on their journeys. Developments in later eras, too, have increased the options for pilgrims in terms of the way they can travel.

The crucial element in the pilgrimage is to visit all the temples, and how and in what way this is done is up to the individual pilgrim. Pilgrims may start at whichever temple is most convenient for them, go in whatever order suits them best, use whatever methods of transport they find appropriate or that fit their time schedules, and may break the journey up if they wish into a number of shorter sections, doing the pilgrimage in stages over an extended period. Modern pilgrims can choose to go not only by foot, but via bicycle, bus, car, taxi, and train. In the most recent innovation in Shikoku pilgrimage practice, one can—for a hefty price—even make use of a helicopter pilgrimage service that was inaugurated by a local air transport firm in 1998.[30]

Pilgrims often use several forms of transport, perhaps walking parts of the route and taking buses and trains when this is more convenient. Whichever way one travels involves a considerable investment of time, effort, and money (see appendix 3 for further details). It takes around six weeks to walk the whole route (although some hasty pilgrims have managed to cut this to around thirty days), around ten to twelve days by package bus tour or public transport, and about seven or eight days by private car or taxi. The helicopter pilgrimage takes in all around three days. Apart from the helicopter tours, going by foot is generally the most expensive way, since it involves the longest period and the most nights spent on the road.

One need not perform the pilgrimage in one go. Because of the rapid transportation facilities of modern Japan, which enable them to get to and from Shikoku quickly from anywhere in the country, and because of the country's pressurized work system, which allows little extended time off, many pilgrims choose to break the route down into a number of shorter sections and to complete their pilgrimages over several visits and even over a number of years.[31] Shikoku is divided administratively into four prefectures, and many pilgrims split the journey into four sections via a series of *ikkoku mairi* (one-

Pilgrimage bus, with pilgrims' staffs ready for their use as they descend from the bus at Temple 51. The bus belongs to the Iyo Tetsu Company, the largest carrier of pilgrims in Shikoku.

province pilgrimages), in which they visit the temples of one prefecture at a time. Bus tours often also follow this pattern. Nowadays, too, some people, especially if they live in or near Shikoku, may even do it in a series of very short and even day trip *(higaeri)* visits.

Walkers often break their journeys up. I have met many people who have done, or are doing, the *henro* in a series of walks, punctuated by breaks to return home for work, for family reasons, or to recuperate before embarking on the next stage. Such ways of doing extended pilgrimages are not limited only to Shikoku. Nancy Frey's study of the pilgrimage to Santiago shows that many pilgrims break that route up into a number of manageable sections, returning each time to the place where they left off previously.[32] In such fragmented pilgrimages, the notional boundaries between, and the apparent disjunction of, pilgrimage and everyday life appear to erode, at least until the pilgrimage is completed.

There is no single, fixed route. Different guidebooks provide a variety of paths and potential road routes to follow, with bus pilgrimages naturally following a different route from those taken by walkers.[33] As such, the pilgrimage is a moving landscape whose route has constantly changed over the ages—and continues to do so as transport infrastructures change, as new roads develop, as others fall into disrepair, and as new modes of conveyance (including ropeways and cable cars that now provide alternative ways of getting to some of the mountain temples) appear. All of this offers pilgrims a variety of possibilities and choices as to how they will to get from temple to temple: they can choose to ascend to mountain temples by quiet, steep paths on foot, go by narrow and winding mountain roads (which can be intimidating if one meets a bus on a bend overlooking a sharp precipice, a fate that befell one pilgrim whose miracle story appears in the next chapter), or, in some cases, go by cable cars and ropeways that have been built up to temples such as Unpenji (Temple 66), the highest temple on the route at an elevation of over one thousand meters.

Leaving and taking away: *Osamefuda*, books, and scrolls

The main focus of pilgrim activity, in terms of prayers and rituals, centers on the temples themselves. There are no set routines or practices that pilgrims are obliged to follow at them, although there are some normative patterns, such as praying and making offerings at the main hall of worship and the *daishidō*. Such offerings may include coins, incense, and candles, as well as copies of Buddhist sutras *(shakyō)* that pilgrims have copied by hand as an act of devotion and supplication. Pilgrims may also chant a variety of prayers and mantras, such as the invocation in praise of Kōbō Daishi, "*Namu daishi henjō kongō*" (hail to Daishi, the universally resplendent diamond)—"*henjō kongō"* (the universally resplendent diamond) being the consecration name given to Kūkai by his Chinese Buddhist master, Hui-kuo (746–805), before Kūkai returned to spread the word of esoteric Buddhism in Japan.[34] Another common chant is the *Hannya Shingyō* (shorter Heart Sutra), one of the most popular Buddhist sutras in Japan, which takes only a few minutes to recite and is often accompanied by the rhythmic striking of wooden clappers or bells to mark its rhythm. Some pilgrims (especially those in groups) may also chant the temple's *go-eika* (pilgrimage song); each temple has its own *go-eika,* which relates to some aspect of the temple's history and legends.[35] Such ritual chanting adds to the atmosphere and noise of the sites.

Pilgrims normally also leave, at a special offertory box at the temple, their *osamefuda* (often referred to by pilgrims just as *fuda* or *o-fuda*). In earlier times these used to be made out of wood or metal and pilgrims used to affix or nail them to the wooden pillars of the temples they visited. Nowadays, temples discourage this practice, and *osamefuda* are usually slips of paper that bear a picture of, and invocation to, Kōbō Daishi. Such *fuda* can be purchased in batches at the temples. Pilgrims may write their names and other details on them and use them as name cards, handed out to fellow pilgrims and to donors who give them alms *(settai);* they may also leave them as offerings at the temples. In the latter case, pilgrims may also write on the *fuda* various supplications and requests that they seek from their pilgrimages. They come in a variety of colors relating to the number of times one has done the pilgrimage, as follows.

> White: used by those doing the pilgrimage from the first to fourth time
> Green: five to seven times
> Red: eight to twenty-four times
> Silver: twenty-five to forty-nine times
> Gold: above fifty times

Some pilgrims may also have special brocade *(nishiki) fuda* made if they have done it more than one hundred times. This variety of forms of *fuda* not only indicates that people may perform the *henro* again and again, but it also points to an implicit hierarchy in which status may be acquired through repeated performance and be revealed to fellow pilgrims through the color of one's *fuda.*

In the next chapter, when I discuss the landscape and visual settings of the pilgrimage, I will discuss further these and other things that pilgrims may carry or leave behind. The point to note here is that pilgrims engage with the temples and sites in an active way, not only by praying but also by leaving numerous objects that signify their presence at the temples. They may also take things away with them, for example, lucky charms and amulets bought at the temples,[36] souvenirs purchased at the shops often located at or inside temple gates, and, especially, books and scrolls that are stamped by the temples to mark the visit of the pilgrim.

The practice of *nōkyō*—getting the temple seal *(shuin)* imprinted or stamped into a special pilgrim's book *(nōkyōchō)*, onto a scroll *(kakejiku)*, or onto a pilgrim's shirt—is one of the most common and popular of all pilgrimage acts, and such books, scrolls, and shirts form a common part of the pilgrim's accoutrements. Until recently, it was most common for pilgrims to carry just the book, and this remains the most normal item for walkers to carry, since it is light and fits into a backpack, unlike the scroll. The advent of bus and car transport has led to more pilgrims using scrolls as well as, or in place of, books. Each temple has an office *(nōkyōjo)* where temple officials will—for a small fee (five hundred yen, as of 2000, in the case of a scroll; three hundred for shirts and books)—stamp the temple's seal, in red ink, onto the book or scroll and adorn it with ink-brush calligraphy.

Initially, the reason for getting the stamps was practical. In the Tokugawa era, permission to go beyond one's own feudal region was usually granted only for reasons such as making a pilgrimage.[37] The aspirant pilgrim thus needed to show that s/he had used his/her travel permit appropriately, and

Inscribing the temple's calligraphy on a pilgrim's scroll.

the stamp served as proof of that, showing one had visited the stipulated temples and shrines.[38] From this, a popular belief developed that having a pilgrim's book laden with stamps was a sign of one's spiritual merit and devotion, rather than merely a record of having fulfilled the requirements of a travel permit. Thus the completed book, scroll, or shirt came to be seen as a passport to the Pure Land after death—a notion that readily fitted with general beliefs that one could attain salvation at death or a better rebirth through the pilgrimage (see later chapters). It is also manifest in the practice, found still in Japan, of placing completed pilgrimage books in the casket of the deceased to indicate, as s/he makes a final journey/pilgrimage to other realms, that the deceased is worthy of entry into the Buddhist Pure Land.[39]

Pilgrims may also carry books and scrolls on behalf of others. Doing pilgrimages on behalf of, or as a representative for, someone else is not uncommon in pilgrimage contexts and is widespread in Shikoku, where many pilgrims act as representatives (*daisan*) for others by carrying extra books and/or scrolls for people (e.g., family members, friends) unable to travel with them. I have on occasion met pilgrims carrying stacks of books and scrolls—in one case, a party of half a dozen pilgrims with some twenty books and a dozen scrolls that, they told me, were for absent friends and family members. The notion of getting someone else to do the pilgrimage on one's behalf briefly even became a commercial venture. During the 1980s I came across advertisements in the Japanese media offering for sale completed scrolls and stating that, through their purchase, one could avoid the hardship of pilgrimage yet acquire its merits. This idea, however, met with the disapproval of the Shikoku Reijōkai, which announced that buying such scrolls was not a valid way of "doing" the pilgrimage, thereby blocking this attempt at establishing a commercial practice in this area.[40]

Nowadays, the scroll, normally with a depiction of Kōbō Daishi at its center, is the favored item to carry, despite being far more expensive than the book. It costs several thousand yen to purchase and more than the book to get stamped. In addition, when completed, it has to be mounted and embossed, an expensive business costing tens of thousands of yen. Indeed, a small industry exists around the scrolls, with several small firms and craftsmen in Shikoku and elsewhere making a living out of making, mounting, and embossing scrolls. However, many pilgrims feel the expense is worthwhile, for, when completed, the scroll is a strikingly beautiful object that can be placed on display in one's home. Indeed, many see getting the scroll as a major motivation for doing the pilgrimage, a point made by pilgrims who have said to me that, after seeing such a scroll at someone else's house, they wanted one themselves. Scrolls, like the *nōkyōchō*, can also serve as commemorative reminders of the pilgrimage, "memory aids" (to borrow Frey's term)[41] enabling pilgrims to recall and relive their pilgrimages later. They may also be brought out during funeral ceremonies as relatives of the deceased chant the pilgrimage songs of the temples, thus taking the spirit of the dead once again around the pilgrimage and providing them with additional spiritual merit.

The imagery of tradition

The Shikoku pilgrimage has, especially in the present day, been one of the most—if not the most—widely performed of all pilgrimages in Japan.[42] It has also, in recent years, been Japan's most prominent pilgrimage in terms of media interest, particularly because of the large number of pilgrims who still wear traditional pilgrims' clothing, the numbers who walk and maintain its ascetic traditions, and the endurance of many pilgrimage customs that have declined in other parts of Japan.[43] As such, it has come to be regarded as a striking manifestation of "traditional" Japanese culture and has attracted much publicity, thereby benefiting from the widespread, often nostalgic, tide of interest in traditional customs and practices in contemporary Japan that is

Completed Shikoku pilgrimage scroll, with Kōbō Daishi at its center, hanging up at a pilgrims' lodge in Shikoku. Next to it is a completed Saikoku pilgrimage scroll depicting Kannon.

connected with a continuing search for the reaffirmation of identity in a rapidly changing, modernizing world increasingly open to cultural intrusions from outside.[44]

This dynamic, along with the publicity afforded to the pilgrimage as a symbol of cultural identity, has been a major influence in the recent growth in pilgrim numbers, a point affirmed by many pilgrims I interviewed in April 2000 who told me that their interest in the pilgrimage had been awakened by the attractive depictions of it in the mass media. They especially cited a striking series of television programs made by NHK, Japan's national public television network, broadcast from April 1998 to March 2000. The series, *Kesa no Reijō* (Today's pilgrimage temple), produced a highly photogenic and colorful depiction of both island and pilgrimage, emphasizing the pilgrimage's importance as a manifestation of Japanese cultural tradition and highlighting the beauties of the Shikoku scenery, along with images of pilgrims dressed in white and juxtaposed against a background of ancient temples and mountain paths, and of friendly priests who told interviewers about the history of the sites.[45]

Priests at the Shikoku temples and people working for commercial enterprises associated with the pilgrimage infrastructure have emphasized to me how the NHK series has stimulated interest in the pilgrimage in recent times. The images inherent in NHK's portrayal of the *henro*—as a manifestation of Japanese cultural tradition through which Japanese people can discover their spiritual roots—are important in the modern depiction and construction of the pilgrimage and will be discussed further in chapter 5. So, too, will the activities of the various interest groups, including the temples as well as transport companies that benefit from the rising numbers of pilgrims, that have cooperated in producing these images and popularizing the pilgrimage in the modern day. Such interest groups have naturally welcomed this NHK-inspired rise in pilgrim numbers, as have local and regional authorities and businesses, which have benefited economically as a result, for the pilgrims are a good source of revenue for the local economy. As regional government economic reports emphasize, pilgrims help support a variety of businesses and concerns such as inns, restaurants, souvenir shops, scroll-mounting firms, and the like that are ranged along the route and are intrinsic parts of the pilgrimage infrastructure.[46]

(Inter)national pilgrimage, local pilgrimage, local customs

Detailed contemporary sociological studies of the pilgrimage by researchers from Waseda University in Tokyo led by Osada Kōichi and Sakata Masaaki show that pilgrims come to Shikoku from every part of Japan,[47] a pattern seen rarely even in other widely known Japanese pilgrimages such as Saikoku.[48] The pilgrimage is thus clearly what Surinder Bhardwaj, using his typology based on Indian pilgrimages, would term a "national pilgrimage"—one that draws on a clientele from across the country and one closely associated with symbols of cultural identity, heritage, and belonging.[49] It also attracts a small number of overseas pilgrims—mostly people of Japanese descent from Hawai'i, the mainland United States of America, and South America, but also a small number of Western pilgrims fascinated by Japanese culture.[50]

Yet, while nationally and internationally significant, the *henro* is also a *local* pilgrimage, with many pilgrims coming from Shikoku. It has been often assumed, in studies of pilgrimage, that locals do not visit major sacred sites within their regions but instead prefer to travel farther afield to distant pilgrimage sites that require greater efforts to visit.[51] This assumption does not work for Shikoku. Hoshino's study of the records of pilgrims' lodges from the 1930s and early 1940s shows that 56 percent of the pilgrims who stayed there were from the island.[52] Surveys by Satō Hisamitsu in the 1980s showed that around 40 percent of the pilgrims were either from Shikoku or had their roots there,[53] while research I conducted into *osamefuda* that pilgrims had left at one of the temples in 1991 indicated that many pilgrims were either present or former residents of the island. According to the 1996 Waseda University survey led by Osada and Sakata, over 20 percent of pilgrims were from Shikoku itself—a percentage that may have declined from earlier surveys more because of the rise of pilgrim numbers from outside Shikoku than due to a fall in those from inside.[54]

This localized dimension is highly significant in the construction and development of the pilgrimage. Not only does a large segment of the Shikoku pilgrimage community consist of local residents who are active pilgrims in their own island, but the pilgrimage itself, along with the cult of veneration of Kōbō Daishi, are, as a detailed study by Kaneko Satoru among Shikoku residents has shown, deeply rooted elements in the island's religious culture.[55] The people of Shikoku have played a seminal role in the development of the pilgrimage, assisting in the formation and maintenance of customs and practices central to it and playing a key role in the creation of an infrastructure ranging from pilgrims' lodges to island-based commercial firms (see chapters 4 and 5). As if to emphasize this point, a recent publication on the pilgrimage's history produced under the auspices of one of Shikoku's four prefectural governments states that the island has given rise to a "pilgrimage culture" *(henro bunka)* that is special to, and a product of, Shikoku and its people.[56]

The influences of local culture, however, do not mean that people in Shikoku have universally supported the pilgrimage or that its place in the island's culture and sense of identity is not without contest. As John Eade and Michael Sallnow have observed in other contexts, local populations often harbor ambivalent attitudes toward important pilgrimage locations in their vicinity.[57] Frey has made similar observations in noting that people who live close to the pilgrimage center of Santiago de Compostela in Spain may resent the pilgrims as intruders seeking a cheap form of tourism and ignorant of local religious sentiments.[58]

In Shikoku, too, one finds similarly ambivalent feelings. In many interviews with residents I have heard complaints about the speed of modern pilgrimage and criticisms that bus pilgrims are primarily tourists. On my first visit in 1984 a lady running a tea shop at one temple gave me an extended diatribe about the poor manners of modern pilgrims who, she claimed, rushed madly from place to place, paid no consideration to local customs, and always demanded rapid service rather than waiting their turns patiently. On every subsequent visit I have heard similar complaints from people working at the temples and from residents living along the route. Historically the ambivalence was even more marked. In chapter 4, when I outline the history of the pilgrimage, I will show how pilgrims in the Tokugawa period and beyond were often unwelcome, especially in the eyes of the island's feudal authorities. While modern pilgrims are by and large well-off, their predecessors were often impoverished outsiders who were seen not as symbols of national heritage or as representatives of local tradition, but as probable miscreants and carriers of diseases who begged for alms, were a drain on the local economy, and a threat to public order who needed to be strictly controlled by law.

Growth, unemployed walkers, and ambivalence

While the pilgrimage is now widely regarded as part of the country's cultural heritage, it has not lost all its earlier associations with marginality and ambivalence. The pilgrimage still serves as a means of escape from society, providing those in the present, as in the past, with a means of stepping aside from their ordinary lives and the often restrictive patterns of everyday life in Japan. This has been given particular resonance since the economic recession starting in the 1990s led to widespread unemployment. Many people have responded to the shock of losing their jobs—always a mark of status and of normative belonging in Japan's work-oriented culture—by becoming pilgrims in Shikoku. During my visit to Shikoku in April 2000, I was struck by a clear upsurge in the numbers of people, mostly middle-aged men, walking the route. I probably saw more people on foot each day than I did during the whole forty days I spent on the pilgrimage with my wife in 1984, and far more than on any previous visit to the island. Estimates suggest that as many as two thousand to three thousand pilgrims were annually walking the route at the turn of the millennium—a sharp rise from the mid-1980s and early 1990s when walkers were few and far between.[59]

When I discussed this growth with people in Shikoku, the term they constantly used was *"risutora,"* the Japanese loan word for "restructuring," one of those weasel words of modern capitalism that effectively means reducing workforces and making people unemployed. As Japan's recession worsened through the 1990s, "restructuring" threw large numbers of people—many of them middle-aged males who had spent much of their lives working for a single company—out of work and left them unable to find new employment in a contracting economy. As a result, many have been left feeling estranged from society and keen to search out alternative modes of being.

Some of them have found, in the pilgrimage, a source of solace and meaning.[60] Many have simply wanted to take a break from the day-to-day rigors of society and have used some of their redundancy money to "find themselves anew." Often, for those whose normal status-support structures have been destroyed with their loss of work, the pilgrimage has represented a way of challenging themselves in order to regain a sense of self-respect lost after they had been discarded by their employers.[61] Sometimes the impact of *risutora* has led to life-changing decisions. I met pilgrims in April 2000 who had lost their jobs, become estranged from their families as a result, and had eventually left home to seek peace of mind and a new life through becoming pilgrims. Sometimes they had dropped out of society completely to become beggar pilgrims like those who caused such annoyance to feudal authorities in earlier ages; indeed, complaints have started to appear in Shikoku about this new wave of "drop-out" pilgrims who have taken to begging along the route and trying to subsist on the donations of others.[62]

None of the impulses, motives, and sentiments that have contributed to the growth in pilgrim numbers or to the attitudes of contemporary pilgrims is explicitly modern, of course, nor have they been produced solely by unemployment and recession—or, indeed, by a search for, or pride in, cultural heritage. While the image of the pilgrimage may have undergone a transformation in modern times, there also remains much continuity from the past in terms of the motivations of the pilgrims, with the wish to find new meanings, to search for their roots, to escape, change, or remake their world, or to get away from, or seek solutions to, misfortunes and such unhappy events impelling pilgrims both in premodern and contemporary times. Such continuities are as much part of the pilgrimage (and of this book) as are the changes wrought by modern times. Therefore, while recognizing the potential for the pilgrimage to encompass both strands of continuity and of change, this book also pays attention to the ways in which it can also incorporate diverse and often apparently contradictory themes and messages within its rubric. This point is illustrated by the apparent contradictions between the themes I have just mentioned as central to recent pilgrimage growth—the one celebrating national culture and tradition and facilitated by modern developments, the other reacting to the negative repercussions of modern change—and by the ways in which very different modes of travel, from helicopter tours to ascetic mendicancy, may be incorporated within and be seen as legitimate ways of doing the pilgrimage.

Multiple meanings: Pilgrimage and diversity

The capacity of pilgrimages such as Shikoku to incorporate such diverse themes—and the ways in which they all add to and make the pilgrimage what it is—are primary themes of this book. In this chapter thus far I have particularly alluded to some of the tensions and ambivalence inherent in the pilgrimage: as a local phenomenon *and* a national pilgrimage, as a symbol of cultural tradition *and* of marginalization, as a source of local participation *and* of antipathy toward pilgrims. As this book develops, further areas of diversity and ambivalence—for example, the ways in which pilgrims may find themselves drawn together in a sense of shared enterprise and status-free equality, and yet may also be conscious of, or strive to create, hierarchic differences (indicated, e.g., by different-colored *o-fuda*) between themselves—will emerge.

Such tensions suggest that the Shikoku pilgrimage might fit into the theoretical model proposed by Eade and Sallnow when they argued that pilgrimage should be seen

> as a *realm of competing discourses.* . . . . It is these varied discourses with their multiple meanings and understandings, brought to the shrine by different categories of pilgrims, by residents, and by religious specialists, that are constitutive of the cult itself.[63]

Eade and Sallnow in effect argue that pilgrimage not only provides the setting for contest but also effectively reinforces existing social divisions and tensions between (for example) different ethnic or social groups.[64] There are times when such themes will be evident in Shikoku, as the above comments indicate. However, this is far from suggesting that the pilgrimage is most readily understood or analyzed through the prism of contest or that it is primarily an arena for competing discourses. Often, as will be seen, various discourses may exist side by side, with participants espousing different (rather than necessarily *competing*) understandings of the pilgrimage, and yet remaining able to cooperate and interact with each other even while articulating such differences.

Indeed, while participants may have differing views and understandings, and while there might be various tensions between them, there is much also that is common and shared; for example, the image of Kōbō Daishi being with each pilgrim provides a binding focal point and underpins a sense of shared endeavor and community among those involved in the *henro*. It is a feeling that often surfaces in the accounts of pilgrims. Takamure Itsue, writing about her experiences as a young woman on pilgrimage in 1918, spoke of the sense of "pilgrim's love" *(henro ai)* that dissolved all barriers, drew all pilgrims together, and made everyone on the pilgrimage equal.[65] The aforementioned term "*dōgyō*," which is widely used by pilgrims to refer to other pilgrims doing the same practice (see, e.g., chapter 3), also indicates how they see themselves as sharing a common bond with others.

Such comments about common bonds, equality, and the dissolution of differences appear to suggest that there is much in the *henro* that does not just contradict Eade and Sallnow's theory but reinforces the theoretical arguments of the anthropologist Victor Turner, who argued that pilgrimage frees people of their normal positions within the social hierarchy and thus enables them to experience a state of egalitarian association with their fellow pilgrims. This liminal and antistructural state of escape from normal social constraints produces, according to Turner, a transient and spontaneous state of egalitarian bonding between pilgrims in which all ordinary barriers and social differences evaporate. This temporary and transient state, which he termed "*communitas*," contained the essence of pilgrimage.[66]

However, while there is much in Shikoku to indicate common themes and a sense of togetherness among pilgrims, there is also much, as my earlier comments on tension, ambivalence, and hierarchic themes have implied, to counteract Turner's arguments. This has been the case in most contexts in which pilgrimage has been analyzed, with various studies showing that the capacity of pilgrimage to dissolve barriers between pilgrims (as envisioned in Turner's theories) is generally less pronounced than its aforementioned tendency to intensify differences and divisions.[67] Indeed, Eade and Sallnow's formulation of a theory that emphasizes contest rather than *communitas* as the dominant theme in pilgrimage is founded on a critique of Turner's theories for just such reasons.

As such, neither contest nor *communitas* on their own provide an adequate means of analyzing the *henro*. A further problem with such theories is that they focus on participants in the context of social groupings that either merge together in *communitas* or engage in contests, and largely neglect or downplay the importance of individual understandings of pilgrimage, reducing individual participants, as Barbara Aziz has complained, to an "undifferentiated swirling mass." Aziz, in her account of pilgrims in India and Nepal, argues that every pilgrim has his/her individual motivations and interpretations of their activities and is not necessarily bound by what their fellow travelers think or even by the dynamics of the groups they may travel with.[68] Aoki Tamotsu has also made similar points in his study of the mountain pilgrimage cult of Ontake in central Japan. As Aoki demonstrates, pilgrims to

Ontake generally make the ascent in organized groups (often under the rubric of a particular religious association), but every person involved in the ascent expresses his or her own motivations and expresses individual requests to the deities there, while their journeys, and the struggles they have in making the ascent, are highly individual.[69] Similar themes will emerge in chapter 7, where I examine package pilgrimage tours and illustrate how every pilgrim who participates in them (and who might, from an external perspective, appear to be just one person in an organized group, each performing the same chants and going at the same pace) is undertaking, within their organized, group pilgrimage, an individual journey that relates directly to their personal needs, attitudes, and interpretations.

Encompassing dimensions: Pilgrimage, cacophony, terminology

The problem is that the theoretical models that have developed around the study of pilgrimage emphasize only some of the enormous range of activities and themes that are encompassed within the nature of pilgrimage. I have already noted in the introduction to this book that normative anthropological approaches to pilgrimage have tended to focus on goals and the practices that occur at pilgrimage sites and to not take account of how pilgrimage may be more than a transitory affair and often may become a core element in the lives of participants. Hence any study of pilgrimage needs to take account of what pilgrims take from their pilgrimages and how they may continue, after completing their initial journeys, to remain involved in the pilgrimage—an issue that will surface throughout the book but that will be especially central to chapter 8.

Moreover, if one focuses on or privileges one particular dynamic that can be found within pilgrimage, one may neglect others, reducing, for instance, every pilgrim to a member of an idealistic antistructural community, or to a member of a competing group. This is the point made by Susan Naquin and Chün Fang Yü in their study of pilgrimages in China, in which they seek to go beyond the limiting tendencies of existing theoretical models by arguing for the need "to reconsider the chaos of pilgrimage and to listen again to the cacophony."[70] Thus they emphasize the need to look anew at all aspects of pilgrimage in order to see how all the practices, attitudes, and themes associated with pilgrimage may operate together (even when seemingly disparate and contradictory) to add to what they term the "cumulative effect" of pilgrimage.[71] Eade has recently also recognized this problem in his comment (in a new edition of *Contesting the Sacred*) that "[p]ilgrimage is an unruly process whose regularities cannot be contained within the universalistic structures of integrative analysis."[72]

I have already alluded to this unruliness, to the seeming chaos and cacophony I encountered at Shikoku pilgrimage sites, and to the ambivalence of pilgrimage in Shikoku. All of these are integral elements in the overall makeup of the pilgrimage, and all need to be taken into account in order to understand, and make sense of, its cacophonous, multivalent manifestations. In this context it is relevant to discuss my use of the term "pilgrimage" in relation to Shikoku. I am using the English word "pilgrimage" as a translation of the Japanese term *"henro."* The word *"henro"* refers not just to the route and the temples included in it, but also to participants; the people (i.e., pilgrims) who go around the circuit visiting the temples are also called *henro*. *Henro* is specific in meaning, referring to eighty-eight-stage pilgrimages associated with Kōbō Daishi, of which there are many in Japan, with the Shikoku *henro* being the most prominent and the model on which all other *henro* are based.[73] *Henro* is normally translated in English as "pilgrimage" as much as anything because there are no other words in English that could fulfill an adequate function of rendering the Japanese term. Moreover, it is by no means the only Japanese word to be so translated, for there are several other terms in Japan's complex culture of travel to sites and areas of religious significance that are similarly translated in English as "pilgrimage" but that retain, in Japanese, differences of nuance and meaning signifying a particular type of route or practice. Thus the Saikoku pilgrimage is not a *henro* but a *junrei,* a term that literally means "going around and worshiping" and is sometimes also used in Shikoku.[74]

This raises questions about the validity of using "pilgrimage" as a translation for a Japanese term that has quite specific meanings within Japanese culture. This is an issue not solely related to Japanese, for there are many other languages and cultures in which different terms may be used for different types of travel or visits to sacred locations, but that are implicitly all pushed into the same category through being translated by the English "pilgrimage." Some scholars, indeed, arguing that "pilgrimage" is a term deriving from a particular cultural setting based in a Christian form of worship, think it highly problematic to export it to other cultures.[75] Aware that using this term may have the effect of treating a variety of phenomena through the single lens of one Western category, Jill Dubisch has questioned whether "pilgrimage" as a broad, general category can or should be used across cultures— rather than, say, the plural "pilgrimages," which could imply a multiple phenomenon with various manifestations that cannot be fitted into one broad category and that may vary across cultures. In her study of pilgrimage on a Greek island, for example, Dubisch comments on the problematic blurring of what may or may not be (in terms of Western usage) a "pilgrimage" in the Greek context, where a variety of terms exist relating to different types of visits and travel to sacred places.[76]

Yet, even while questioning whether it is appropriate to impose a term from one cultural setting onto another, Dubisch finds herself reluctant to abandon "pilgrimage," which, she feels, has the potential to allow for cross-cultural comparisons. Moreover, Dubisch remains "struck by the similarities in the practice of journeys to sacred places, even among quite different traditions," and, as such, considers that while studies of pilgrimage show how diverse it can be and how pilgrim behavior may differ from culture to culture, there also is much that is similar, to the extent that the term provides grounds for moderating the "otherness" and the apparent difference of other cultures by showing the similarities that also exist across them.[77]

I, too, recognize the problems involved with imposing meanings and terms across cultures. In Japanese contexts, as in the Greek case, a multiplicity of terms signifying different categories of travel and processes of visiting shrines and temples have become subsumed within the wider category "pilgrimage" through the translation process. Yet, even though, like Dubisch, I am aware of the problems that may arise as a result, I still find the term "pilgrimage" to be a viable, and indeed valuable, term that allows for comparisons and analogies across cultures, that enables us to see how practices in different cultures might share common ground, and that allows us to use analyses of "pilgrimage" in one culture, such as Japan, to develop insights into pilgrimage in other cultural settings. In such terms, I contend, getting locked into the notion that "pilgrimage" is solely a phenomenon or term related to Christian worship and practice is a narrow and restricting position. Rather, one should recognize the potential for it to be used as a term that has resonance outside of Western contexts. Thus I use the term "pilgrimage" throughout this book, both as a viable translation of the Japanese term *"henro"* and as a wider phenomenon and category to which activities such as the Shikoku *henro* can be related and about which it can inform us.

I also use the Japanese term *"henro"* frequently because of its particular resonance in the Japanese context and because it says something important about how I interpret "pilgrimage" as a phenomenon. The word *"henro"* derives from an earlier term used in Shikoku, *"heji"* (going around the region [i.e. island]), and is made up of two ideograms, *"hen"* meaning "widely, everywhere," and *"ro"* meaning "route" or "road." The *henro* is thus a route that extends widely or everywhere and that (drawing on the earlier term *"heji"*) goes around and encompasses (the island). In other words, *henro* indicates something more than just a place-to-place linear route; it is, rather, something that encompasses.

Pilgrimage, in such terms, as the Japanese term implies, is "encompassing." In geographical terms, as will be seen in the next chapter, the *henro* encompasses the island of Shikoku, incorporating its physical features and important religious sites. It also encompasses a variety of themes, issues, and participants, from the pilgrims themselves, the routes they follow, and the temples they visit, to other participants in the pilgrimage process such as those who run the sites and those who cater to and provide services for the pilgrims in various ways, to the landscape, legends, miracle tales, customs, practices, and historical consciousness associated with, and which add to, the institution of pilgrimage in Shikoku. It also, as my comments in the introduction on the tendency of many participants to do the pilgrimage again and again indicate, can encompass the lives of participants. In these terms I do not see pilgrimage simply as related to the process of "going out and returning home" done by pilgrims, or even the travel and acts of worship that they perform, but as a multifaceted, encompassing institution and process that, to use the words of N. Ross Crumrine and Alan Morinis, "incorporates geographical, social, cultural, historical, literary, architectural, artistic and other dimensions" as well as a "wide variety of actors, places, behaviors, times, and specialists."[78] Moreover, it is an encompassing institution that extends beyond the simple processes of visiting sacred places, praying, and playing into providing core meanings in the lives of those who engage in it and whose engagement with the pilgrimage does not end after they have completed their visits to Shikoku's eighty-eight temples.

Unbounded structures, multidisciplinary dimensions

Studying such a multifaceted institution naturally requires a multidisciplinary approach. As I noted in the introduction, any understanding of the *henro* and of Shikoku pilgrims in the contemporary era cannot rely solely on synchronic studies or on the disciplinary approaches and methodological tools of anthropology and sociology, disciplines that are normally prioritized in the study of contemporary phenomena and practices. Understanding the contemporary nature of the *henro* requires awareness also of the pilgrimage's historical roots and of the ways in which the traces of the past have shaped the pilgrimage—and continue to do so in the modern day. Equally, just as pilgrimage needs to be studied in a multidisciplinary way, so, too, does it need to be examined in a variety of settings, rather than being limited to one location or set of locations. Pilgrimage is not just about sites and the locations to which pilgrims travel, a point also made by Dubisch, who emphasizes the importance of "unbounding" the pilgrimage site. By this she means that no study of pilgrimage can be just about its site(s), which

> can be understood only as a setting for a wide range of behaviors, embodying multiple meanings and goals, and as both a part and a manifestation of many other aspects of a society—historical, social, political, economic, and religious.[79]

Thus Dubisch notes that what goes on at sites and in pilgrimages occurs

> within a particular local context, but also within the context of a national—and international—religious tradition, and in a political

environment that is both reflected in and shaped by events that occur at the place of pilgrimage.[80]

I have already alluded to such issues by noting how the *henro* is linked to both local religious culture and to national and sectarian Buddhist traditions, and how a variety of factors, including contemporary concerns about Japanese identity and cultural heritage, as well as economic problems and social malaise, may affect and shape it. Because of this unbounded nature, too, it is hard, if not impossible, to draw boundaries around the "field" of pilgrimage either in disciplinary terms or in the context of one's fieldwork, which is thus not restricted to specific pilgrimage sites alone. As Dubisch found, her research into the pilgrimage on the Greek island of Tinos necessitated the use not just of a variety of approaches and sources in order to grasp the wider meanings of the pilgrimage within the context of Greek culture, history, and gender relations, but also engagement in fieldwork beyond Tinos. There were times when, elsewhere in Greece, she encountered people who had done the pilgrimage there and who wanted or needed to be interviewed, so that almost anywhere—even bars in Athens—became fieldwork locations.[81] This very much resonates with my research into the *henro*, which has necessitated travel to places outside Shikoku that have active pilgrimage associations, visits to tour companies both inside and outside Shikoku that are involved in the pilgrimage business, interviews in the homes of people after they had returned from their pilgrimages—and also the occasional conversations in bars in and outside the island when Japanese people I met, on hearing I was studying the Shikoku *henro*, have told me—sometimes in the liberated mode that comes from what they were consuming—that they, too, had done the pilgrimage and wanted to tell me about their experiences.

This recognition that pilgrimage is unbounded, and hence that the study of a pilgrimage should not be carried out only at the specific sites pilgrims visit, or only through studying pilgrims at such locations, is manifest in Anne Gold's study of the ways of Rajasthani pilgrims in India. As Gold's work vividly indicates, pilgrims start (and usually finish) their journeys within their local communities, they prepare for them within those communities, the practices and beliefs associated with their pilgrimages are very often embedded in the religious and social structures of their communities, and both leaving and returning to their home communities are thus intrinsic parts of their pilgrimages.[82] Far from just being journeys separated or dissociated from home, they may well be very much about home, innately tied to wider patterns of life and social belonging within home communities, and central elements in the social and religious lives of their participants. Again, these are issues integral also to the Shikoku pilgrimage and its participants: in later chapters I will show, for example, how practices associated with the *henro* may be nurtured and supported by communities and pilgrimage associations outside Shikoku, how pilgrimage may be deeply rooted in and be central to the religious lives of participants—to the point, at times, of turning them into what I call "permanent pilgrims"—and how Shikoku can become a second or alternative "home" for pilgrims.

Making pilgrimages

In looking at the pilgrimage as a totality incorporating a variety of interwoven themes and strands, and in talking of the community of people interested and involved with the pilgrimage, my focus extends beyond just those who visit the Shikoku temples as pilgrims. Enough has been said thus far to indicate that there are many people in a variety of settings and occupations who contribute in some way or other to the pilgrimage as it functions and as it is perceived. The most obvious and visible actors in this process are, of course, the pilgrims themselves, and naturally a large part of this book focuses on them, on their experiences, motivations and practices, and the like. Yet others, too, have helped shape the pilgrimage historically and in the present, from the local populace and regional authorities, to temple priests, innkeepers, and commercial and media concerns; all of these are intrinsically part of, and hence need to be considered as active participants in, the pilgrimage process.

Furthermore, I do not differentiate between categories of pilgrim. There have been extensive discussions in the context of pilgrimage as to whether all who visit pilgrimage sites can be considered pilgrims, and one finds frequent references to the notion that certain forms of travel are more authentic than others. As Frey shows in her study of the pilgrim's way to Santiago, those who walk that route clearly regard themselves as "real" pilgrims, while disparagingly referring to those who use motor transport or planes to reach the sacred destination as "inauthentic" and "tourists."[83] Yet, even though there are evident differences in Shikoku in the manner in which pilgrims on foot and those on organized bus package tours behave and in terms of their circumstances of travel and the resultant states of ease and unease they might experience, I do not find it useful to describe one form of travel and performance as more "genuine" or "authentic" than another. I have already noted that in Shikoku there are no stipulated rules as to how one should do the *henro*; hence there can be no single "authentic" way of doing it. While some may emphasize foot pilgrimage as the only "real" way to do the *henro*, there are also others, as I mentioned earlier, who suggest that organized tours may be a better way of enabling the pilgrim to engage more deeply in the faith and worship aspects of the pilgrimage. Dismissing bus and other motorized modes of travel as lesser or less authentic forms of pilgrimage also ignores the equality of opportunity that modernity and modern transport have brought to the pilgrimage. I have discussed this point elsewhere, showing that bus tours have enabled many people who would not otherwise have been able to get around what is a long and difficult pilgrimage route to become pilgrims in Shikoku (see also chapter 7).[84]

As such, too, I regard any attempt to differentiate between "pilgrims" and "tourists" to be unsound, especially when (as seems to be the attitude of the walkers to Santiago cited by Frey) it implies that people who use motorized transport and the like are less genuine in their intentions than those on foot, and more inclined toward play and sightseeing. I am not convinced that this perspective holds true anywhere, and it is by no means so in Shikoku. I have already noted that bus tour groups generally engage in extensive worship at the sites. Indeed, they usually spend longer at the temples than walkers, who often spend little time at the temples and may engage only in cursory prayers (a criticism leveled at walkers by some temple priests—see chapter 6).[85] Nor have I found any evidence that some types of pilgrim (e.g., walkers performing ascetic devotions or people in organized bus groups) engage in any more or less "tourist" activity (e.g., stopping off to see a famous nonpilgrimage sight along the way, dropping in at hot spring resorts such as Dōgo Onsen, located between Temples 51 and 52 and a popular calling place for all types of pilgrim, buying souvenirs at the numerous shops that are found outside temples such as Ōkuboji) than any other.

"Praying and playing" are activities that frequently operate hand in hand. Shinno Toshikazu has written of the "inextricable conjoining of faith and pleasure" in Japanese pilgrimages,[86] and plentiful evidence exists to show how closely the two have been interwoven whether in Japan or elsewhere. Indeed, as has been widely observed, the roots of tourism are closely associated with the practice of pilgrimage.[87] In Western European contexts Victor and Edith Turner have commented on how those who travel in order to pray together also play together, while Horton and Marie-Hèlene Davies have discussed how pilgrimages were promoted through the use of holy days (i.e., holidays), with fairs being held on saints' days so as to attract visitors/pilgrims to holy centers.[88] Studies in Japan, too, emphasize how shrines, temples, and pilgrimage centers operate in similar ways, with prayer, worship, play, and entertainment being part and parcel of the same process.[89]

As such, it would appear methodologically problematic to separate out the "tourist" from the "pilgrim" or to attempt, when discussing pilgrimages such as Shikoku, to distinguish and hence privilege certain types of participant from others. Naquin and Yü have similarly found attempts to differentiate between pilgrims and tourists unhelpful, arguing that pilgrimages and pilgrimage sites are developed and shaped by the accumulated influence and presence of every individual participant who visited them. Thus, referring to the "cumulative effect" (see above) of those who go to pilgrimage centers, they treat "each person who wrote about or went to a pilgrimage site as someone who helped build it" and argue that everyone who goes to a site, in whatever capacity, adds to it and thus helps makes it into what it is at any given time.[90] Alphonse Dupront, in his study of the construction of popular religious phenomena and traditions, makes similar points when he speaks of pilgrimage and pilgrimage sites as being shaped and characterized by the actions of the ordinary people who visit them. Pilgrimages—and pilgrimage sites—are thus "made" into what they are through the accumulated experiences and faith of those who visit them. According to Dupront, pilgrimage sites are consecrated by the presence and faith of pilgrims who add to their sanctity, which is disseminated back to the pilgrims, thereby stimulating further the processes of pilgrimage and sanctification.[91]

While I follow Dupront and Naquin and Yü here, I do not, as I noted earlier, limit my focus to only those who visit the Shikoku sites in the guise of pilgrims but to everyone—from priests officiating at the temples, to those involved in organizing pilgrimage tours, to local people who support (or at times oppose) pilgrimage customs—who has been or is involved in the pilgrimage in any way and who thus helps shape and make it into what it is at any given point. It is not people alone who make the pilgrimage, however; as the next chapter shows, the pilgrimage is framed by its landscape, which is both physical and symbolic, a construction of emotions and legends as well as of physical features. This landscape is thus itself made through the actions of pilgrimage participants, and it in turn reflects back on and influences the participants and shapes their attitudes and journeys. This aspect of the pilgrimage—the landscape in its physical, emotional, and symbolic contexts—is a vital component in the framework of the pilgrimage, central to the understandings of its participants, and it is to this that I turn in the following chapter.

2 Making Landscapes

Geography, Symbol, Legend, and Traces

In this chapter I examine the Shikoku pilgrimage in terms of its landscape, which I see as including not just the geographical terrain and the sacred sites that provide the *henro* with a "visual ideology"[1] that shapes the consciousness of participants, but other elements besides that add to and constitute its emotional terrain. Among the elements that provide the pilgrimage with an atmospheric or emotional power that permeates and enhances the meanings of the physical terrain are the sacred figure of Kōbō Daishi, who is simultaneously a focus of worship, the model for all pilgrims to follow, and the architect (in legend) of the route; the narratives—the legends, miracle tales, and symbolic messages—that suffuse and give meaning to the physical landscape of pilgrimage; and the material objects, signs, and traces that pilgrims have left along the route to mark their presence and influence later pilgrims. All of these are central to the ways that the pilgrimage is seen and experienced. In such terms, one cannot differentiate the performance of the pilgrimage from the landscape (physical and emotional) in which it occurs; the performance itself is part of the moving, changing text[2] of pilgrimage and landscape, shaped and given meaning by the emotional terrain of symbols and legends and influenced by the geographical environment in which it occurs. These produce a constantly developing sense of meaning for those involved in the pilgrimage and indicate how the real and symbolic, and the physical and the emotional, are linked together.

Landscape, narrative, moving text

The importance of the landscape and the material and visual culture it gives rise to is an issue that has not, until comparatively recently, been at the forefront of the agenda in Western academic studies of pilgrimage. As Simon Coleman and John Elsner have argued, there has been a general tendency, especially in anthropological studies of pilgrimage, to focus almost exclusively on the activities of the pilgrims. As a result, they contend, the visual and material culture of pilgrimage sites has been neglected, with sites being treated virtually as empty spaces serving mainly as locales of contest into which competing groups can inscribe their own meanings. As Coleman and Elsner argue, however, this approach overlooks the importance of physical settings and of architecture in giving sites a particular resonance and producing a sense of the sacred that shapes the ways pilgrims feel about them and the experiences they have there.[3]

Coleman and Elsner contend that the physical landscape and the material culture of pilgrimage sites (e.g., their architecture and buildings) frame, shape, and give meaning to pilgrims' experiences and that pilgrimage landscapes can be shaped and transformed through and in the light of pilgrim activities. They discuss, for example, how the physical terrain of the Christian Holy Land was visualized and shaped by early Christian pilgrims in the light of what they had read in the Bible, which served as the sacred text for their pilgrimages. Early Christian pilgrims expected the landscape of the Holy Land to fit with the narrative account they knew—and when it did not, they wanted something done about it, to make terrain accord with narrative. Hence the Holy Land was transformed by early Christian pilgrims so that it would conform to the contours of the sacred text, with churches and holy buildings erected in places where, according to the Bible, events in the life of Jesus and the Apostles occurred. The Bible as text thus provided the blueprint for shaping and modifying the landscape so that pilgrimage conformed to text—and hence became a text mirroring the images narrated in the Bible.[4]

Such visions of the landscape, in which physical terrain is infused with images of sanctity and in which textual narratives enliven the landscape and give life to pilgrimage cults, are widely found in Asia. In Shikoku, for example, there is evident correlation between the physical landscape and sacred narratives, in which the sites and settings of the *henro* are locations richly layered with complex weavings of meaning and textual representation. This richness of meaning inherent in the locales of pilgrimage provides a moving text for the pilgrimage and allows scope for different participants to pursue their agendas and follow their own pilgrimage paths, which are themselves influenced by the settings and landscapes in which they are enacted.

This moving pilgrimage text, however, relates not just to material culture and the physical terrain, for, as Frey comments,

> landscape . . . is not just a neutral backdrop but a multidimensional concept related to the understanding of space and movement and the creation of stories meaningful to the pilgrim.[5]

Frey's reading of landscape (and pilgrimage) as including nonvisible phenomena such as stories is implicit also in Candace Slater's description of the pilgrimage to the northeastern Brazilian city of Juazerio do Norte, centered around the miracle-working Catholic priest Padro Cicero, as a "trail of miracles,"[6] a phrase that conjures up images of how legends and miracle stories play a role in the definition and formation of (physical) pilgrimage routes. It comes through also in Toni Huber's study of the pilgrimage to Pure Crystal Mountain in Tibet, which demonstrates how, for Tibetans, the map of pilgrimage is constructed through stories and sacred narratives, which provide a lens through which to see the landscape.[7]

In Shikoku, sacred narratives such as the legends and miracle tales associated with Kōbō Daishi, along, in the present day, with a growing literature of pilgrimage journals and accounts, as well as visual portrayals such as TV documentaries and photographic essays, provide an emotional map for those involved in the pilgrimage process. They create a trail of images formed of legendary footsteps, miraculous events, and symbolic meanings that infuse the landscape and provide the emotional framework within which the physical manifestations of pilgrimage are played out. It is in and through this interweaving of the emotional and the physical that the pilgrimage and its meanings are shaped, made and remade over time, and through which structure, story, symbol, and practice combine to form an overarching text and narrative.

Sacred Footprints: Kōbō Daishi and the *henro*

Kōbō Daishi is central to the pilgrimage landscape and its narrative. Kōbō Daishi is a title meaning "the great teacher who spread the law (of Buddhism in Japan)," which, as was noted in chapter 1, was posthumously granted by the Imperial Court in 921 to the monk Kūkai.[8] The scion of a minor aristocratic family from Shikoku, Kūkai is generally assumed to have been born at Zentsūji. Through his noble connections, Kūkai initially went to the capital at the time, Heiankyō (Kyoto), to study for a career in government but then turned to the Buddhist path before returning to Shikoku to engage in religious austerities. According to his writings, he visited Cape Muroto in southeast Shikoku and Mount Tairyū in central-eastern Shikoku, both of which were centers for mendicant ascetics, where he performed austerities and gained some of his earliest spiritual experiences.[9] These places, along with his birthplace, subsequently became incorporated into the pilgrimage, with Zentsūji now being Temple 75, while Cape Muroto is the location of Higashidera (Temple 24) and Mount Tairyū the location of Tairyūji (Temple 21).

Later, he returned to Kyoto, assumed Buddhist orders, and, in 804, went to China to study esoteric Buddhism. He returned to Japan in 806, claiming to have mastered and been recognized as an adept in esoteric Buddhist rituals and texts and bringing to Japan the esoteric Shingon (True Word) Buddhism he had studied in China. Eventually acclaimed for his mastery of Buddhist texts and rituals previously unknown in Japan, Kūkai established himself as an influential figure in the religious and political elite of the day. Epitomizing the close relationships between religion, magic, and politics in early Japan, he performed rain rituals and other magico-religious rites at the behest of the Imperial Court and served as a spiritual adviser to emperors and court officials. He also had good organizational abilities, establishing important religious institutions such as the temple Tōji in Kyoto while developing a textual and canonical system for Shingon. In 816 he acquired permission from the Imperial Court to establish the mountain religious center of Kōyasan (Mount Kōya) in Wakayama Prefecture. Kōyasan remains, to this day, the headquarters of Shingon Buddhism.

While operating at elite levels in society, Kūkai also sought to improve the worldly circumstances of the populace in ways that established his credentials as a "man of the people" and as a folk religious hero. In Japan it is widely assumed that inspirational religious leaders should combine spiritual practices and teachings with practical activities designed to bring social benefits and improvements in the lives of ordinary people,[10] and Kūkai very much fitted into this category. In 821, for example, he was responsible for overseeing the reconstruction of the Mannō pond, a major irrigation work in northern Shikoku that is still in use; it was because of Kūkai's popularity and ability to mobilize people that the regional governor petitioned the court for him to be entrusted with this task. He was also a committed educator who, in 828, established the Shugei shuchi-in (School of Arts and Sciences) in Kyoto—the first scholastic institution in Japan open to all regardless of social status and means—and compiled a dictionary (the oldest extant in Japan) for its students. Beyond all this he was a famed and accomplished calligrapher and artist.

Kūkai was clearly one of the great figures of Japanese Buddhism, someone who bridged the gap between the Imperial Court and the ordinary people and between monasticism and the needs of the general populace. His fame and legend have gone far beyond verifiable historical achievements, however, and many other deeds, such as the invention of kana, the Japanese written syllabary, have been attributed to him, as have numerous legends and miraculous deeds. His status in life, great as it was, was transformed afterward through legends that turned him from a great priest and sect founder into a transcendent figure at the center of one of Japan's most powerful and enduring cults of devotion. This transformation began after his death at Mount Kōya in 835 and is closely associated with his posthumous title and with a series of legends proclaiming that he had not died but had transcended death, entering into a state of eternal meditation and enlightenment in which he awaited the coming of Maitreya (Japanese: Miroku), the Future Buddha who would bring salvation to humanity in the distant future.

The legends and the cult that formed around Kōbō Daishi appear to have been originally developed by priests at Mount Kōya in order to shore up the declining fortunes of the sect in the decades after the death of their founder. After Kūkai died, the Shingon sect began to lose influence at the Imperial Court and fragment into factions; it appears to have been the idea of a later head priest, Kangen (853–925), in the early tenth century to revitalize the sect by using the image of its founder as a symbol of unity and source of inspiration.[11] The Imperial Court was successfully petitioned to grant Kūkai a posthumous title—a custom that has been bestowed on many of the great figures and sect founders of Japanese Buddhism—and in 921 Kūkai was given the title Kōbō Daishi.

The legends of Kōbō Daishi began in earnest with the arrival of the Imperial decree bestowing this title. Senior priests at Kōyasan led by Kangen placed the decree in Kūkai's mausoleum, and when they did so, they reported, they found him seated there in meditation, his body still warm.[12] This miraculous story, suggesting Kūkai remained alive and in eternal meditation awaiting the coming of Maitreya, was later embellished and popularized by priests and mendicants from Kōyasan. It helped revive the fortunes of Shingon, turning Kōyasan into a place where people could encounter the "living" holy figure through whom, it came to be believed, they could attain future salvation when Maitreya came to this realm.[13] Thus the cult of Kōbō Daishi became associated with the promise of future salvation—a promise that motivates many pilgrims to do the *henro*.

The cult conflated a historical figure and a legendary one, with the historical Kūkai becoming overlaid with the image of Kōbō Daishi. As mendicants from Kōyasan spread stories of Kūkai/Kōbō Daishi's power around the country, they effectively transformed him into a ubiquitous role model for themselves, as a wandering figure who traveled through the land spreading the message of Buddhism.[14] Thus Kōbō Daishi metamorphosed from a sedentary figure in eternal meditation into a holy wanderer, mendicant priest, and pilgrim, wearing a bamboo hat and robes, clutching a staff and with begging bowl in hand. In this guise Kōbō Daishi became a figure of popular devotion appearing in thousands of stories and temple legends, attributed with founding numerous temples and carving countless statues throughout Japan, even in areas never visited by the historical Kūkai. Similarly, thousands of legends exist throughout the country linking Kōbō Daishi to particular places and miraculous deeds in which he either rewards the virtuous or punishes the mean and greedy and in which he cures the sick and dispenses all manner of worldly and spiritual benefits.[15]

Such legends helped create an extensive cult of worship in which Kōbō Daishi appears to be simultaneously human and divine, with a status akin to a savior and a saint.[16] Indeed, the cult and the compendium of legends have become so extensive that, while posthumous titles containing the epithet "Daishi" (great teacher) have been granted to other Japanese Buddhist leaders, a popular Japanese saying states that "Kōbō stole the title of Daishi";

when Japanese people talk of Daishi (or, using polite terms, o-Daishi-sama), it is Kōbō Daishi to whom they refer.

Kōbō Daishi and the Daishi cult together form a central organizing principle in the pilgrimage and a legendary framing device in its landscape. He is not, however, the only such holy figure whose traces are linked to, and help sanctify, Shikoku. For example, Gyōgi, the influential eighth-century Buddhist priest who traveled around Japan proselytizing a popular Buddhism for the masses and who is the source of numerous temple-foundation legends and miracle tales throughout Japan, also features in the legendary landscape of Shikoku. Gyōgi appears as a temple founder or the carver of temple images in several pilgrimage temple-foundation legends *(engi)*—even though there is no evidence that he was ever on the island.[17] His presence, though, adds to the constructed sanctity of the landscape, associating yet another important figure from the history of popular religion with the pilgrimage. Numerous other mendicant monks known as *hijiri*—Buddhist mendicants who helped spread folk Buddhism in Japan[18]—were also active in Shikoku, and they, too, added to its landscape of stories.

Generally, such stories and legends were given added valence by being attributed to Kōbō Daishi. As Yamamoto Wakako comments, Kōbō Daishi became, in Shikoku, an amalgam of all the mendicant ascetic figures who traveled around the island or were associated with the route.[19] In this process, too, his cult absorbed numerous legends and stories formerly associated with other figures, as can be seen, for example, with the miraculous tale that provides the name for the *bangai* Saba Daishi mentioned in chapter 1. This refers to a tale in which Kōbō Daishi, seeking to teach a lesson to a merchant who was taking a load of dried mackerel *(saba)* to market but who refused to give him even one fish as alms, brought one of the fish back to life. As a result the merchant, stunned by the miraculous deed, repented of his sins and became a believer. In the seventeenth century, however, this tale was attributed not to Kōbō Daishi but to Gyōgi, and the site bore the name Saba Gyōgi; in the eighteenth century, the deed was assimilated into the Daishi cult, and the place name changed to Saba Daishi (see chapter 4).

The Daishi cult is not just assimilative but also transcends sectarian affiliations. While the Shingon sect has assiduously promoted Kōbō Daishi as a living savior and figure of worship,[20] he has gone beyond sectarian boundaries to be venerated virtually across the board in Japan. Pilgrims in Shikoku come from all manner of religious backgrounds (and none), as do those affiliated with faith associations dedicated to Kōbō Daishi and the pilgrimage.[21] The sect-transcending status of Kōbō Daishi is aptly summed up by Ōzeki Gyōō, a Rinzai Zen Buddhist priest who wrote an account of the pilgrimage he made in Shikoku in 1936, in which he explained why, as a Zen priest, he was demonstrating devotion to Kōbō Daishi. According to Ōzeki, Kōbō Daishi was not a sectarian figure associated with a rival sect but a great Japanese Buddhist who brought benefits to all the Japanese people and who should therefore be venerated as such.[22]

Founding the pilgrimage? Meanings, traces, legends

Among the numerous feats attributed to the wandering saint and miracle worker is the founding of the Shikoku pilgrimage. According to Shikoku lore, Kūkai established the pilgrimage on the island of his birth in 815, when he was forty-two—in Japanese terms, his *yakudoshi* (unlucky year), when, according to folk belief, males are especially prone to misfortune and hence should make special efforts to acquire divine protection.[23] In popular legend, Kūkai/Kōbō Daishi's spiritual journey to enlightenment involved him in a real pilgrimage around the island of his birth during his forty-second year, in which he established the *henro* and selected its eighty-eight sites so that others could follow in his footsteps.

The foundation legend is replete with meanings for the pilgrimage. It posits that Kōbō Daishi, on his journey to enlightenment, established the *henro* so pilgrims could walk in his footsteps and reenact his inspirational journey, becoming one with him and attaining their own liberation. Equally, it suggests that the pilgrimage is a means of acquiring practical benefits, such as protection from misfortune, achieved by Kūkai through making the pilgrimage in his unlucky year.

Meaningful as the foundation story might be, however, it lacks historical basis. There is scant evidence that Kūkai (or Kōbō Daishi) founded any of the Shikoku temples, nor, in a well-documented life, is there any evidence that Kūkai visited the island of his birth in 815, a time when he was extremely active around the capital.[24] Moreover, the earliest indications of any form of organized pilgrimage around Shikoku date to the twelfth century, and these speak not of an eighty-eight-stage route but of an "austerity"; the earliest mention of an eighty-eight-stage pilgrimage is not until some centuries later (see chapter 4). The historical evidence thus tells us that the pilgrimage could not have been founded by the historical Kūkai and that he could not have selected the eighty-eight temples on it.

Nevertheless, this foundation story is central to the construction of the pilgrimage landscape in Shikoku and is a recurrent theme in the stories, consciousness, and understanding of priests and pilgrims alike. It is also widely cited as if true by many associated with the *henro*. Thus Hasuo Kanzen, former head priest of Zentsūji and an influential figure in the Shingon Buddhist hierarchy, wrote in 1931 that Kōbō Daishi had founded and walked the pilgrimage in 815.[25] Hatada Zenpō, the now deceased but formerly influential head priest of Anrakuji (Temple 6) and former head of the Shikoku Reijōkai, affirmed in an interview with me that Kōbō Daishi had founded the pilgrimage in 815—a point that appears also in pamphlets published by his temple.[26] In a modern guidebook Yamashita Hirotaka treats the 815 founding as a real, not legendary, event, stating that Kōbō Daishi made the pilgrimage in 815, establishing the eighty-eight sites as he did so. Prior to setting out, he performed austerities for twenty-one days at the site of Temple 1, where he visualized innumerable buddhas and bodhisattvas, which led him to realize that he had a sacred mission to transplant the sacred land of Shakyamuni (the historical Buddha) to Japan. Thus he carved a statue of the Buddha and placed it at Ryōzenji, which he then determined would be the first temple on the route.[27] Yamashita's account contains many elements of poetic invention, including the designation of Ryōzenji as the official starting place of the *henro*. As will be seen in chapter 4, it came to be known as Temple 1 only for reasons of convenience during the early eighteenth century.

Yet poetic invention remains a vital element in the figurative construction of the historical landscape—and so central to it that the 815 foundation story is often presented as authentic even by those who cognitively recognize its legendary nature. I remember a conversation with the priest at one temple in which we laughed together about the historical inaccuracies in books about the *henro*, including several by temple priests he knew. He took some of these from his shelves and pointed out their inaccuracy in treating the 815 foundation story as fact. The next morning, in a sermon to pilgrims who had stayed at the temple, he spoke eloquently of how, in 815, Kōbō Daishi had selected this very place as the site of one of the eighty-eight temples of the pilgrimage he was creating. The temple pamphlet he gave me (which he had written) said the same.

The pilgrims were clearly enthused after the service, chattering excitedly as they filed out of the temple, ready to start that day's travel, their spirits vitalized after having stayed at one of the very places at which the Daishi had stopped and that, a millennium before, he had designated as a pilgrimage site. For them the legend was living fact, brought to life by the priest's narrative. The sermon showed how the priests at pilgrimage sites can play an energizing role by infusing pilgrims with faith and shaping their perceptions. It also indicated just how central such (historically invalid) stories are in the construction of pilgrimage beliefs, how they are vital parts of the emotional landscape of the pilgrimage, helping shape the legendary terrain through which pilgrims travel, and how, even for those aware of their historical invalidity, they serve as vitally enhancing stories that become "real" within the context and framework of the pilgrimage.

Such legends, by speaking of the Daishi as a wanderer around the island, emphasize the importance not just of the sites but of the route that links them together. Kōbō Daishi is not just venerated at the temples; he is a wandering mendicant whose presence permeates the entire route and who is—again like St. James in the pilgrimage to Santiago—depicted in pilgrimage iconography dressed as a pilgrim to his own sacred places.[28] According to pilgrimage lore,

Kōbō Daishi continually walks the pilgrimage dispensing blessings and aiding others, and countless miracle tales have circulated amongst pilgrims over the centuries to this effect, affirming that he may be met anywhere on the route.[29] As such, while the temples form the nodal points of the route, it is the route as a whole, and the island, too, that is suffused with his sacred grace.

Pilgrimage, marginality, otherness

Shikoku and the *henro* have become virtually synonymous in the popular imagination, as is shown by the comment of the popular Japanese religious writer Kino Kazuyoshi that one cannot talk about Shikoku without thinking of the pilgrimage.[30] The (legendary) path around the island taken by Kōbō Daishi was etched, according to pilgrimage lore, into the landscape of Shikoku in the form of the *henro*, which passes through all the four administrative regions of the island and takes in its main geographical features, from its numerous mountains, to its promontories and rugged coastlines, to its river valleys, main agricultural regions, and population centers. It also incorporates local sights and hot-spring resorts, notably the Dōgo hot springs in Matsuyama, which has long been popular with pilgrims. As was noted in chapter 1, too, the pilgrimage includes temples from a variety of affiliations and local religious traditions and with a variety of figures from the Buddhist pantheon of worship.

Yet, while the route encapsulates and encompasses the island, it is also, simultaneously, highly marginal, for the route clings to the edges of Shikoku for much of its duration, circles its sacred mountains, and goes around the fringes rather than through the middle of its main towns.[31] This sense of marginality is also crucial to the *henro*—as, indeed, it is in the construction of many pilgrimages. Shikoku, in such respects, shares similarities with the pilgrimage island of Tinos in Greece, which, as Dubisch shows, is "over there," separate from and marginal to the Greek mainland and hence, for its pilgrims, a "different place."[32] Shikoku's marginality, too, rests in its physical separation. Situated on the southern shore of the Inland Sea, across the water and on the "other shore"—an image of some significance since it conjures up Buddhist notions of death and passing over to "other realms"[33]—from the main population, economic, and political centers of Japan, it has long been seen as a political and economic backwater. In medieval times it was used as a place of exile for those who fell out of favor or who were punished by the Imperial Court: former Emperor Sutoku, for example, who was exiled and died there in the twelfth century, saw his isolation there as being tantamount to dying to the real world. In the modern day, too, the concept of distance and separation remain important themes in pilgrim consciousness, with the journey across to Shikoku signifying a voyage to another realm—and return hence implying rebirth and renewal.

This marginality, which enhances Shikoku's image as a sacred island,[34] is also economic in nature. Long seen as economically backward and poor by the standards of the mainland, it has, in modern times, suffered from the decline of its major industries such as shipbuilding, from depopulation, and, specially, from the migration of younger people to the urban centers and cities of Honshu.[35] This decline and marginality has led to a search for alternative sources of economic sustenance and development—a factor that has been important in the modern development of the pilgrimage industry in Shikoku, in which local and regional authorities have been keen to promote the pilgrimage as a means of bringing people and hence revenue to Shikoku (see chapter 5).

This sense of marginality, separation, and difference was a factor in shaping the consciousness of pilgrims of earlier eras and in making the island appear to be a place apart. It is found still today in the attitudes of many pilgrims I have interviewed, especially those who come to Shikoku from cities such as Tokyo, who have commented that Shikoku represents, for them, a different world from the modern cities they live in. Even though modern communications and transport systems, including the new bridges that have linked Shikoku to the Japanese mainland, may nowadays have physically reduced Shikoku's geographical separation and marginality, it remains, in such terms, associated with notions of difference, marked out as a "a different place" empowered and endowed with (to use James J. Preston's term) "spiritual magnetism."[36]

Landscape, difference, familiarity

This magnetic sense of otherness is mirrored by the physical landscape: apart from a small area of plains in the northwest of the island, Shikoku is a mountainous island with a rugged coastline. The dramatic physical features of the island—notably its mountains but also the two striking promontories of Capes Muroto and Ashizuri—have long been seen as places for ascetic practice, and they contribute to the image of a terrain at the intersection between this and other realms. The promontories, for instance, were seen as mediating spaces between realms and as gateways from which ascetics in medieval times embarked in boats (in what was effectively a form of ritualized suicide) in their attempts to reach Fudaraku—the Pure Land of the bodhisattva Kannon.[37] Cape Ashizuri's reputation as a bridge between this and other worlds and its associations with death and suicide remain strong to this day, especially after Tamiya Torahiko's 1949 novel *Ashizuri Misato* (Cape Ashizuri), which narrates the story of a disillusioned young man who travels among the pilgrims and then commits suicide at Ashizuri. The popularity of the novel thus enhanced the associations between the pilgrimage, death, and the attempt to leave this present life behind: since the publication of Tamiya's novel, the cape has become a well-known place for suicides. Besides the two promontories and its temples, the presence of the sea as a framing device implying connections with other realms is evident at many other points in the pilgrimage landscape: sections of the route follow along the shore, several temples are located either on or close to the shore, and around one-quarter of all the temples have aspects out over the sea.[38]

The island's mountainous terrain also conveys the sense of an "other" place. Mountains in Japan have traditionally been associated with the transcendent and been seen as settings for ascetic practices aimed at attaining enlightenment.[39] They have also been closely associated with the realms of death: the notion—especially strong in premodern times—that the spirits of the recently departed congregate at certain prominent mountains, known as *reizan* 霊山 (spirit mountains), for a period before passing on to other realms was an important element in Japanese folk belief. Thus *reizan*, associated with the realms of death and the presence of the spirits of the dead, were fearful and dangerously "other" places in and yet beyond this world. Several *reizan* are found in Shikoku, including the island's highest peak, Ishizuchisan, around which five pilgrimage temples are located.[40] In all, according to the Shikoku folklorist Takeda Akira, ten *reizan* on the island have become settings for *henro* temples, and together they form a central axis of the pilgrimage route.[41] Perhaps the most striking of these visually is Iyataniji (Temple 71), whose graves and death memorials spread across its mountainside combine to produce what Maeda Takashi terms a "sombre atmosphere" *(yuan no funiki).*[42] Iyataniji, which has been the focus of a cult centered on the spirits of the dead since at least the seventeenth century, is still seen as a place where the spirits of the dead gather and is widely visited as such by local people when their kin die.[43]

While the physical terrain of Shikoku is infused with images of difference, transcendence, and the other, one should caution against visualizing the Shikoku landscape only in such terms, for the landscape can also be seen as something familiar and comforting. This is not only because a large number of the pilgrims come from the island—and hence are traveling in and through their home landscape and to places that may be both pilgrimage centers and local places of worship[44]—but also because the very elements of the landscape that stand for Shikoku's connection to the other are also perceived as manifestations of the "natural" that, in Japanese cultural discourse, is associated with Japanese identity and heritage. I alluded to this point in chapter 1 when speaking of how the *henro* in the modern day is perceived and portrayed as a symbol of tradition and cultural heritage. This point (which will be further illustrated in subsequent chapters) comes through in the popular guidebooks and contemporary promotional literature produced by the Shikoku Reijōkai and other interest groups (and is evident in the NHK broadcasts mentioned in chapter 1). Such literature largely depicts traditionally clad pilgrims amidst the "natural" settings of Shikoku, such as its mountains, coastlines, forests, and the rice fields and moss-covered Buddha images that line the route. All of these are features commonly associated in Japan with the *furusato*—a term that translates as "one's native village" but that in Japanese cultural discourse refers to notions of an idealized homeland unspoiled by modern incursions and redolent with the emotional power of tradition, heritage, and cultural belonging.[45] Thus in popular discourse, the *henro* manifests and indeed typifies the emotionally conceived and imagined landscape of Japanese heritage and cultural belonging.

Thus Shikoku and its landscape simultaneously signify a "different place" that is "over there," a sacred realm that is marginal and associated with the "other," and somewhere that is traditional, familiar, a place of spiritual belonging. This juxtaposition of the different and the familiar is found in other pilgrimage sites, too, as Simon Coleman shows with regard to Walsingham in Norfolk, England, which has been transformed into a sacred realm due to visions and manifestations of the Virgin Mary that gave it an aura of transcendence and exoticism and placed it beyond the normal parameters of this world. Yet it has also acquired an aura of familiarity for the many pilgrims who journey there repeatedly, perhaps several times a year. As Coleman shows, such pilgrims are effectively "arriving at a second home" and hence are encountering and experiencing a place that is "both 'exceptional' and an embodiment of the familiar."[46] As will be seen in subsequent chapters, many pilgrims return to Shikoku again and again so that it becomes virtually their second home, a place that is both different and set apart, a sacred terrain yet close at hand, a familiar spiritual home. The Shikoku pilgrimage landscape is thus ambivalent, simultaneously set apart, marginal, transcendent, other— yet familiar and redolent of identity, home, and belonging.

Envisioned landscapes: Mandalas and cosmic maps

The envisioning of the physical landscape as, and its transformation into, a spiritual arena is a recurrent phenomenon in Japanese religious history. It may be seen, for instance, in Shinto mythological conceptualizations of Japan as the product of the gods *(kami)* who are present in and thus enliven the landscape and its features, and in the actions and visions of Buddhist priests and itinerants who, as they spread their creed throughout the country from around the eighth century, visualized the physical landscape in the light of sacred cosmologies and saw, in the landscape, manifestations and replications of the spiritual domain. Allan Grapard has discussed this issue, showing how mountainous areas were envisioned by Buddhist monks as Buddha realms and as sacred representations of the cosmos.[47] In his study of the Kunisaki Peninsula in Kyushu, Grapard shows how Buddhist monks visualized the landscape of this world in the form of a sacred geography that became the "transcendental abode of buddhas and bodhisattvas *in this world.*"[48] The natural landscape could thus be discovered as the abode of the sacred.

> These landscapes were in geographical areas of great beauty and were viewed by monks who, from the summit of the mountains, thought they were confronted in their ecstatic discovery by a manifestation of the combined *kami* and buddhas to which they had dedicated their arduous ascent.[49]

This process often developed beyond ascetic ascent and visualization to the inscription of the sacred onto the physical terrain, with the erection of temples, the enshrining of deities, and pilgrimages made by the faithful who came to "see" this sacred landscape. As Grapard shows, the inscription process could be highly detailed: at Kunisaki the mountain was transformed into an embodiment of the Lotus Sutra, with the twenty-eight temples and 69,380 statues said to have been placed on it representing the precise number of chapters and the ideograms of the sutra itself.[50] Thus "walking through" the landscape of Kunisaki involved a journey through the sutra, with sutra and landscape and physical and spiritual realms becoming one. As with the case of the Christian Holy Land and the Bible cited earlier, landscape became text, and text was engraved into the landscape as pilgrimage.

Grapard has also discussed how, through such processes, "the site of practice became a natural mandala and a landscape endowed with metaphysical qualities."[51] Similar envisioning processes can be found elsewhere in Japan, notably the mountainous Kumano region south of the ancient capital of Nara, which was "seen" as the manifestation in this realm of Kannon's Pure Land, Fudaraku, and at Kōyasan itself, where Kūkai, seeing in the eight peaks that surrounded it the petals of the lotus, visualized Kōya as a sacred mandala, or map of the cosmos. The envisioning process is also found in the construction of pilgrimage routes that brought together a linked number of sites that encompassed a region (as with the eighty-eight sites of Shikoku). This, Shinno argues, is a means of constructing sacred geographies in the mode of a mandala that features prominent geographical features such as the sea, sky, and mountains.[52]

This vision of the *henro* as being a sacred mandala that encapsulates the cosmos and whose framework is inscribed into the island is one found widely in pilgrimage literature. In his study of Shikoku pilgrimage maps from the Hōreki (1751–1762) era onward, Iwamura Takeo notes that they often described the *henro* as a mandala encapsulating the buddhas of all realms,[53] while Hoshino draws attention to the ways in which the Shikoku *henro* was depicted, particularly in Shingon Buddhist sources from the Meiji (1868–1912) period onward, as representing the Taizō, or womb world, mandala of Shingon Buddhism.[54] Such mandala imagery occurs frequently in modern accounts too, especially those of Shingon priests influential in the Reijōkai. Hatada Zenpō, for instance, described the pilgrimage to me as a mandala and as a map for human life, and these images are used widely in the publications produced by his temple.[55] Gokurakuji (Temple 2) has two splendid mandalas in its main hall of worship, and on the several occasions when I have stayed there the head priest has focused on them during the sermons he delivers to pilgrims who stay overnight. In explaining that the mandalas are effectively spiritual and ritual maps of the cosmos, the priest, Aki Shōgen, emphasizes that the *henro* itself is just such a mandala and cosmic map and that the pilgrims are therefore journeying through the realms of the buddhas and enacting the workings of the cosmos.[56] The image has been widely assimilated by the pilgrim community: Murakami Mamoru's descriptive guidebook of the pilgrimage is entitled *Henro mandara*,[57] while Hirota Mio's account of his 1998 pilgrimage speaks of the promontories of Muroto and Ashizuri as representing the two mandala worlds (the Taizō [womb] and the Kongō [diamond], respectively) of Shingon Buddhism.[58]

Symbolic structures, maps of enlightenment

Mandalas in Buddhist terms are symbolic representations of the cosmos and maps of enlightenment. The depiction of Shikoku as a mandala and, hence, as a map of enlightenment is reinforced by the view that pilgrims who are performing the "same practice" (*dōgyō*) as Kōbō Daishi are symbolically following his path to enlightenment in a journey mapped onto the landscape of Shikoku. In former times Shikoku (the name itself means Four Provinces) was divided administratively into four feudal provinces, Awa, Tosa, Iyo, and Sanuki. With the end of feudalism and the emergence of Japan as a modern nation-state in the nineteenth century, these four became prefectures called, respectively, Tokushima, Kōchi, Ehime, and Kagawa, each with its own regional government. The eighty-eight temples are spread through these four regions (which, in pilgrimage contexts, are often referred to by their premodern names), and this fourfold division is used to represent the four stages of the path to total enlightenment as conceived in Shingon Buddhist thought as follows.

- Temples 1–23 in Awa, now known as Tokushima Prefecture, represent the idea of *hosshin* (awakening the Buddha mind)—the first step necessary for setting out on the spiritual path.
- Temples 24–39 (Tosa, now known as Kōchi) represent *shugyō* (austerities or religious practice), which is necessary in order to hone the spirit and thus attain higher states of consciousness.
- Temples 40–65 (formerly Iyo, now Ehime) stand for *bodai* (the opening of the Buddhist mind).

- Temples 66–88 (Sanuki, now Kagawa) stand for *nehan* (full, unending enlightenment).

The pilgrim's journey, therefore, is one that follows a path to enlightenment in which Kōbō Daishi is both a companion *(dōgyō)* and guide in the pilgrimage, while the island is envisioned as a sacred terrain, mandala, and map for enlightenment.

The notion of pilgrimage as a (symbolic) journey to enlightenment and transcendence is not, of course, uncommon in pilgrimages. In medieval Europe, for example, the pilgrimage to Jerusalem, while involving a journey to a physical place, was widely seen also as a metaphorical journey of the soul—a veritable pilgrim's progress—to higher spiritual realms.[59] Such, indeed, is the potency of the image of a journey to higher realms that scholars such as Alan Morinis have argued that the idea of the pilgrimage as spiritual journey and as an allegory of the journey of the soul is central to the concept of pilgrimage.[60]

In Shikoku this is very much a symbolic and idealized image rather than a structural reality, for, as has already been noted, pilgrims do not always follow the numerical order upon which this symbolic map of enlightenment is based. Indeed, the idea of the pilgrimage as a structured journey to enlightenment may be a modern invention. Hoshino, for instance, states that he has been unable to find convincing evidence that the *hosshin* to *nehan* structure was widely known in prewar times. It is not found in the earliest Shikoku pilgrimage guidebooks from the late seventeenth century, nor in the diaries of later pilgrims such as Nakatsuka Mōhei, who walked around Shikoku for over five decades as a pilgrim between 1865 and 1922 and who was well aware of the predominant pilgrimage customs and ideas of the era. Nor does it appear to occur in prewar pilgrims' journals. However, it has become normative in modern, postwar pilgrimage guidebooks and pilgrims' journals, and Hoshino suggests that this is because of the exertions of temple priests associated with the Reijōkai and Shingon Buddhism who have sought to impose onto the *henro* a particular set of images and views emanating from their tradition.[61]

Here one finds a good example of how the landscape of pilgrimage can be (re)shaped, emotionally and symbolically, by particular interest groups—in this case, the pilgrimage temples, whose envisioning of the pilgrimage landscape has been widely assimilated and is now an element in present-day pilgrimage consciousness. Many contemporary pilgrims' journals, for instance, are framed around the idea of a journey from *hosshin* to *nehan*,[62] a structure that is also used in the NHK television series and its accompanying guidebooks and spin-off publications—which have been produced with the assistance and cooperation of the Reijōkai.[63] Hoshino shows how this imagery can impact on pilgrims by reporting how a female pilgrim he interviewed related her journey through the four prefectures of the island in such terms:

for her, Tokushima Prefecture (Awa) epitomized *hosshin* because it was as she walked through it that she learned how to be a pilgrim, while in Kōchi (Tosa) she suffered from sore feet and hence had to endure the ascetic hardships *(shugyō)* of that province and stage.[64]

Sacred architect and the landscape of miracles

The architect of this mandala and map of enlightenment is, of course, Kōbō Daishi, through his legendary journey that engraved the *henro* onto the Shikoku landscape and his (legendary) founding of temples, whose foundation stories provide narratives through which the physical is transformed into the spiritually transcendent. A case in point is Iwayaji (Temple 45), set in the mountains of central Shikoku. The temple's setting is dramatic. Its main hall of worship is built into the mountainside, which effectively becomes part of the temple's architecture, while pilgrims climb to the temple up steep staircases hewn into the rock, with the mountain towering above them. The place, in other words, uses the natural features of the mountain to create an aura of power, transcendence, and ascent to higher realms.

The temple's foundation story states that Kōbō Daishi encountered a female ascetic performing spiritual training at this spot during his founding pilgrimage in 815. Recognizing his spiritual prowess, she immediately became his devotee and gave him the mountain as a site for spiritual practice.[65] This selfless donation enabled her to attain liberation and ascent into the Pure Land; it also of course affirms the benefit of giving alms to pilgrims. Kōbō Daishi then carved two statues of the fiery Buddhist figure Fudō, one of wood, the other of rock from the mountainside, making the wooden one the main image of the temple and burying the other in the mountain. Through this act the mountain was transformed into and became Fudō. Thus through the miraculous powers of Kōbō Daishi the holy terrain was turned into a living manifestation of buddhahood and an emblematic sign in the sacred geography of the island.

The resonance of the story and what it can mean to pilgrims was evident to me on a visit in April 2000. A young female pilgrim I met there decided to guide me around the temple complex, telling me as she did so about the temple's foundation legend and insisting that the mountain itself *was* Fudō. Later, as I walked down the steps to the road below I fell into conversation with several others who spoke similarly. Two middle-aged female pilgrims from Shikoku who were doing the pilgrimage by car in a series of day trips and praying for good health for a young relative who was sick offered me a lift to the nearest large town, Matsuyama, where I was staying overnight. As we drove along they regaled me with stories about Kōbō Daishi's deeds in the area, linking them to various features of the landscape. In that hillside over there,

One of the halls of worship at Iwayaji, set into the mountainside.

for example, he had performed austerities; over there, he had carved a statue that had given life to the landscape, and so on. Their narrative, in effect, depicted a landscape shaped and given life by the hand of Kōbō Daishi.

Similar images occur in *henro* literature. A popular guidebook written by Hirahata Ryōyū, a Buddhist priest and leader of a nationally prominent pilgrimage society, the Junrei no Kai, states that many of the Shikoku temples are located in the mountains or high on hillsides in places that, even today, cannot be wholly accessed by bus or modern transportation. Thus pilgrims still often have to climb large numbers of steps and walk some distance to get to many of the temples. This, Hirahata informs readers, is something we should be grateful to Kōbō Daishi for, for he (seemingly with the foresight to recognize that modernity would eventually enable pilgrims to make use of motorized transport) has shaped the pilgrimage and placed the temples in such places in order to enable us to perform some austerities and hence acquire heightened spiritual merit from the pilgrimage.[66]

In shaping and sacralizing the landscape, Kōbō Daishi has created an arena in which the miraculous becomes normative. Numerous miracle tales abound in Shikoku to illustrate this point: pilgrims repeatedly talk with each other about the *fushigi* (wonderful, extraordinary) events and the miracles *(reigen)* that they have experienced or have heard about. Many collections of miracle tales, too, have been produced in Shikoku since the late seventeenth century to affirm this point.[67] A recurrent theme of such stories is how Kōbō Daishi has healed the sick and brought benefits to those who help pilgrims. Stories (found throughout Japan but prominent in Shikoku) of how a thirsty Kōbō Daishi had been given water by a woman even though it was scarce in the area and she needed what she had for her own family, and how he struck his staff in the ground to create a gushing spring as a reward feature in early collections of pilgrimage miracle tales. Equally, tales of retribution when he is refused alms (see below) form a counterpart to this framework of miracles while contributing to the notion of a landscape in which extraordinary events occur.

The following story, taken from a collection of miracle tales published by the Shikoku Reijōkai in 1984 and told by a pilgrim, Ogasawara Shōichi, illustrates how pilgrims associate events that happen to them with the presence of Kōbō Daishi. The incident Ogasawara relates happened on his fourth pilgrimage, as he was traveling on a motorbike. As he came round a corner on a steep and narrow mountain road, he relates, he met a bus and, in trying to avoid it, was sent headlong over a steep precipice. His body struck a lone tree just a few feet down the slope, breaking his fall, and he was able to clamber back up, unscathed apart from a few marks on his clothes, much to the amazement of the bus driver and passengers. Later, as he looked down again, he realized that had he fallen to either side of the tree, he would have plunged a long way to certain death; the tree had saved him. He was saved, he realized, because Kōbō Daishi was with him, and he was in Kōbō Daishi's sacred realm.[68]

Ogasawara's story—and his understanding of what happened—is founded in the notion that events that occur on pilgrimage are grounded in the miraculous, that pilgrims are protected by Kōbō Daishi, and that, hence, anything that happens to them occurs under his auspices. Thus Ogasawara was able to interpret this seemingly fortunate event as a miracle of Kōbō Daishi's. The following story—from the same miracle collection—further illustrates and reinforces the notion that the terrain of Shikoku is sacred because of the presence of Kōbō Daishi. In it, Sada Itsue, a female pilgrim in her sixties, speaks of how she suffered so badly from arthritis that she could barely walk. However, since she and her husband were devotees of Kōbō Daishi, they resolved to do the pilgrimage in Shikoku and pray that her health might improve. During the journey to Shikoku, however, Sada records that she was in great pain and feared that she might not cope. Yet, as their ferry docked in Shikoku and as she set foot on the sacred land of Kōbō Daishi, her pain dissolved: Daishi, she recorded, seemed to lift her up, support her, and lead her around the island. She was cured of her pains by the very act of setting foot on the sacred terrain and holy realm of Kōbō Daishi and through being there with him.[69]

Dōgyō: Together with Daishi

Such Shikoku miracle tales emphasize the protective bond between the pilgrim and Kōbō Daishi, and hence the importance of "being together" (dōgyō) with Kōbō Daishi, whose presence is signified and symbolized by items worn or carried by the pilgrim, notably the bamboo hat (kasa), pilgrimage shirt (hakui), and staff (tsue)—all items indicating that the pilgrim is involved, like the wandering Daishi and the ascetics who followed in his footsteps, in a similar endeavor.[70] His presence is especially manifest in the pilgrim's staff, which, besides serving as a mode of support when walking, represents Kōbō Daishi's body. Because the staff is the body of the Daishi, it should, according to pilgrim lore, be treated as a person and therefore be taken into one's lodgings at the end of the day rather than being left outside. This gives rise to a fascinating practice with roots in the Japanese custom of removing one's shoes when entering indoors: since shoes touch the ground and hence are in contact with the dirt of the outside, they are removed upon entering indoors. When pilgrims enter their lodgings at night, they therefore naturally take off their own shoes, but they need to ensure that Kōbō Daishi, who, in the guise of the staff, has been in contact with the ground, also enters into a state of cleanliness. Thus it is customary to wash the base of the staff (Kōbō Daishi's feet) with water prior to bringing it in to one's lodgings.

There is clearly a utilitarian element to this custom in the eyes of those running pilgrims' lodges, for it ensures that pilgrims do not bring in dirt from the outside on the tips of their staffs. Certainly, lodge owners have, in my awareness, been assiduous in ensuring the maintenance of the custom, as is illustrated by the photograph below, which was taken at a pilgrims' lodge in Tokushima Prefecture. The man washing the pilgrims' staffs is the lodge owner and the fourth generation of his family to run the inn, which was established over a century ago. As he explained to me, he is very conscious of a duty to maintain the pilgrimage traditions that have been passed down in his family. The custom of washing Kōbō Daishi's feet was one such—one that the pilgrims in the photograph were unaware of. It had been their first full day on the *henro*, and they were surprised, on arriving at the lodge, to be asked to wait outside rather than be invited straight in. Their surprise was compounded when the owner brought out a bucket of water with which he washed their staffs, informing them as he did so of the meaning of this act and encouraging them to do it wherever they stayed. It was a lesson that, as they commented afterward, they were unlikely to forget. My awareness of the custom came in similar circumstances in 1984 from the lodge owner where we spent our first night in Shikoku. Whether the roots of the custom are primarily pragmatic (and they remain useful means of helping lodge owners keep their inns clean) is perhaps of less significance to pilgrims than their feelings—as evidenced by the couple mentioned here—of being part of a pilgrimage custom that had

Lodge owner in Tokushima Prefecture preparing to wash Kōbō Daishi's feet.

been handed down through the generations in which they, too, were sharing, and which emphasized the significance, in spiritual terms, of the staff they were carrying.

The presence of Kōbō Daishi and the symbolic meanings inherent in the term "dōgyō" are the same no matter how pilgrims travel: all pilgrims, whether going on foot and performing austerities, or traveling on comfortable bus tours or by private car, are together (dōgyō) with Kōbō Daishi. This, at least in theory, provides a universalizing, leveling dynamic to the pilgrimage in which all pilgrims are equal. I use the words "in theory" because there are many ways in which status and hierarchic differences may be created among and expressed between pilgrims (the different colors of fuda, indicative of levels of experience and times of performance, are one such), with the result that the idealized notion that all are equal does not always translate into actuality. What dōgyō means is that each pilgrim has a special personal relationship with Kōbō Daishi, one that gives his/her journey a personal, individual dimension even when s/he is traveling in a group. Yet while dōgyō has individualized meanings, it also helps instill a sense of community among pilgrims, encouraging them to think of other pilgrims as fellow beings who equally share in a special relationship with Kōbō Daishi. I will return to this point in subsequent chapters, where I note how pilgrims and other participants such as temple priests refer to others involved in the pilgrimage as dōgyōsha or dōgyōsan (people doing the same practice—the suffixes being standard Japanese honorific terms), thereby indicating a shared sense of community among those engaged in the henro.

Legends, alms, retribution, salvation

This identification with Kōbō Daishi marks out the pilgrim as being beyond the ordinary, an empowered figure who, by walking with the saint and wearing his symbols, becomes the saint. This image is emphasized in numerous miracle stories in which Kōbō Daishi intervenes to save pilgrims or that affirm the identification of Kōbō Daishi with the pilgrim. This also underpins the custom of settai (alms giving), in which pilgrims either solicit or are voluntarily given alms to assist them in their journeys. The custom of settai is closely linked to the notion that every pilgrim is with—and thus might be—Kōbō Daishi and to miraculous tales of reward and retribution that occur to those who either give or refuse to give alms. The first published collection of Shikoku miracles tales, Shikoku henro kudokuki, collected and published by the ascetic Yūben Shinnen in 1690, is based on such stories and on the injunction that one should give alms to pilgrims because they represent or are the saint. In Shinnen's tales, those who do so gain rewards—and those who refuse suffer retribution that is drastic and immediate.[71]

The most prominent of such legends, first mentioned in a temple inscription from 1567 but repeated in Shinnen's collection, is that of Emon Saburō, whose story also provides an alternative foundation story for the *henro*.[72] In this legend, a mendicant visits the home of the richest man in Shikoku, Emon Saburō, seeking alms. Emon, however, is not just rich, but a miser who refuses, breaking the pilgrim's begging bowl and chasing him away. Shortly after, Emon's eight sons fall ill and die one after another. In his grief Emon realizes that he has sinned grievously: the pilgrim he insulted was Kōbō Daishi, and the deaths are retribution for his avarice and violence. (One might note, too, that the retribution is indicative of an alternative and dangerous side to Kōbō Daishi the pilgrim in Shikoku lore, able to punish and harm as well as reward and save, a facet that conditioned the behavior of some pilgrims in premodern times, as will be seen in chapter 4.) Repenting, Emon sets out as a pilgrim seeking Kōbō Daishi's forgiveness and absolution and, in so doing, travels around Shikoku twenty times clockwise. The paths he walked and the places he stopped thus became the pilgrimage route—which, in this legend, is thus created by the footsteps of Emon Saburō seeking after Kōbō Daishi. Despairing of ever reaching his goal, Emon finally turns around and walks the other way, thereby doing the pilgrimage anticlockwise and giving rise to the idea of *gyaku uchi*, mentioned in chapter 1.

Worn out, Emon eventually sank to the ground, dying. As he did so, Kōbō Daishi appeared before him to grant him absolution, at which point Emon sought a boon, asking that he be reborn into a particular well-off family in his hometown of Matsuyama so that he could then grow up and take over a temple there that was in disrepair. The wish was granted, and as Emon drew his last breath he clutched a stone lying on the ground beside him. Shortly after, a baby was born to the family in Matsuyama; when the baby came out of the womb, the legend states, he was clutching a stone inscribed with the words "Emon Saburō reborn." The baby grew up to take over and use his family's wealth to transform the fortunes of the temple, which became one of the largest on the island, Temple 51 (Ishiteji, "stone-hand temple"), a name that recalls the Emon Saburō legend.

The legend is highly manipulative, designed to encourage the donation of alms and to suggest that the best use of wealth is to support temples. It sets out a number of motifs in the pilgrimage's emotional and moral landscape and creates, via Emon's travels, a further set of (legendary) footsteps in the physical terrain. It promises the possibility of absolution and forgiveness to pilgrims, suggesting that any deed can be forgiven (even the heinous act of insulting a saint) should the person repent and become a pilgrim. It provides moral injunctions for people not to be greedy and mean and to give alms and help pilgrims—and threatens retribution for those who do not.

It creates a bond and helps define the relationship between pilgrims and locals by emphasizing the custom of *settai*. Pilgrims are thus portrayed as dependent on the locals, and yet they also are able to provide them with benefits or retribution—and hence act as moral arbiters of their behavior—while locals are informed of their moral duties to pilgrims, of the moral framework within which they should live, and of their importance as benefactors and supporters of the pilgrimage. The custom sanctifies pilgrims and elevates their status by indicating that all pilgrims should be seen as Kōbō Daishi: just as the humble pilgrim at Emon's door turned out to be Kōbō Daishi, so, too, the legend implies, could any other pilgrim. And, with the image of Emon finally meeting Kōbō Daishi on his final circuit—when, it would appear, he had accumulated enough merit through his travels to deserve salvation—it affirms a widely held pilgrimage belief that anyone doing the pilgrimage can or will encounter the Daishi and achieve salvation.

The Emon Saburō legend also has acquired a physical presence. On the path between Temples 11 and 12, the place where Emon is said to have fallen is marked with the grave where he is said to be interred, while near Temple 46, on the outskirts of Matsuyama, there is a burial mound said to contain his eight sons. At Ishiteji there is a casket that, it is claimed, contains the very stone clutched by Emon Saburō reborn. The priest and writer Hashimoto Tetsuma saw this stone when making the *henro* in 1941, and he noted that it was over two inches long, certainly too large for a baby, in or out of the womb, while even an adult, he thought, would break a bone in trying to grasp it.[73] The stone nevertheless serves as "proof" of the legitimacy of the story in the eyes of participants: Hashimoto writes that when he commented on the size of the stone a temple priest told him that miraculous events transcend everyday understandings.[74] Similarly, an official of the Iyo Tetsu Company, who showed me around the temple in 1990, assured me, as we stood before the casket at Ishiteji, that it contained the very stone Emon had died, and was reborn, clutching.[75]

Thus the physical landscape may be engraved with markers that make real the legends of pilgrimage. While Kōbō Daishi may not, historically, have established the Shikoku pilgrimage and selected its eighty-eight sites in 815, and while Emon Saburō may not have founded the *henro* through his painful wanderings, their legends are central to the accumulated memory, belief structure, and emotional and physical landscape of the pilgrimage. The legends provide meanings relevant to the pilgrims and shape the ways in which the pilgrimage is understood and experienced. They strike a chord, too, I would suggest, because they provide ready models that the pilgrim can either aspire to or identify with—the holy figure in the realms of enlightenment and the penitent seeking forgiveness for his failures—and readily understood moral meanings about the virtues and powers of pilgrimage. As such, they have become part of the accepted wisdom and worldview of participants in the Shikoku pilgrimage, integral elements in its emotional landscape that have become "historical" facts and "legendary realities," narrated as such by priests who rationally can tell researchers that these are legends, yet, with equal assurance, tell pilgrims that their temple was founded by Kōbō Daishi on his founding pilgrimage in 815. Indeed, such "legendary realities" are more relevant to the worldviews and mindsets of the pilgrims who visit the temples and trade pilgrimage miracle tales with each other than is the verifiable history of the pilgrimage.

The empowered pilgrim

The pilgrim is empowered through being with the saint, and this has led some in Shikoku to view pilgrims as potential miracle workers and healers and to seek their help. The journalist Tosa Fumio, walking the pilgrimage in 1971, relates how he was asked to pass his pilgrimage book over the body of a bedridden girl who informed him that her grandmother regularly brought pilgrims in to pray for her. Tosa (a native of Shikoku) recalled, too, that when he was young his grandmother used to do something similar whenever he became sick.[76] The American writer Oliver Statler writes of his discomfort when a similar request was put to him to pray over a sick girl when he was doing the *henro* in 1971.[77]

The *fuda* handed out by pilgrims in return for receiving *settai* have traditionally been regarded as powerful talismanic representations of this spiritual power. In the pre-1945 era it was common for communities in Shikoku to collect together such *fuda* and use them in purification rituals or place them in the corners of rice fields as charms to ward off insects and beckon good harvests.[78] An elderly lady who was our neighbor when we lived near Osaka in the late 1980s told us that she had grown up in prewar Shikoku and that people in her village used to make an archway out of the pilgrims' *fuda* they had received; at the New Year everyone would walk beneath this in a purification ritual. Such customs may not have altogether disappeared, for I have on occasion seen clusters of *fuda* in the corners of rice fields. Also, during my visit in April 2000, I came across a local woman who was going through the offertory box at one temple, picking out gold and silver *fuda*, which she intended to take away as lucky talismans, because, she said, they were imbued with the power of pilgrims who had done the *henro* many times. The Arita Settaikō, a pilgrimage association based in Wakayama Prefecture that organizes donations of *settai* to pilgrims in Shikoku, collects *fuda* from the pilgrims to whom it gives alms. Association members told me that these used to be taken back to their villages in Wakayama, distributed to the households who assisted in the collection of alms, and used as protective charms. Nowadays, however, the association stores the *fuda* at the hall of worship it has built and maintains at Temple 1 (and from which it distributes alms each year to pilgrims). It receives protective amulets from the temple in return and takes them back to Wakayama to distribute to members of its community who have contributed to the *settai* it gives out.[79]

Dead to the world: Pilgrims and the symbols of death

The empowered pilgrim is also special because s/he is in the margins of death, symbolically dead to the world and journeying in death's realms. The very act of becoming a pilgrim and leaving one's home, as Emon Saburō did when he dressed as a pilgrim and left everything behind, is a symbolic act of renunciation, separation, and dying that all pilgrims perform at least temporarily. In Shikoku this act, and its death associations, are expressed through the pilgrim's clothing, which, as well as signifying the presence of Kōbō Daishi, is full of the symbolism of death. The pilgrim's shirt *(hakui)* is white—the color of purity and death in Japan—and is tied in reverse order from normal clothing, an act normally done only when dressing a corpse. As such, it represents the pilgrim's burial shroud. The traditional bamboo hat *(kasa)* bears a Buddhist poem about transience commonly inscribed on coffins in Japan; hence it symbolizes the pilgrim's coffin. The staff *(tsue)* represents not only the body of Kōbō Daishi, but also the pilgrim's gravestone: on it, pilgrims may carve their *kaimyō*—the posthumous name that they will be known by after death and that represents their identity as an ancestor in the next realm[80]—just as it would be on an actual gravestone. Thus symbolically dressed for death, wearing their shroud and carrying their gravestone and coffin, pilgrims are symbolically in the realms of death as they travel. Such death imagery, and hence the idea of the pilgrimage as a journey to another realm, may also be manifest when death actually occurs. In some parts of Japan (including Shikoku) the deceased may be dressed as a pilgrim, shrouded in a *hakui* and placed in the casket with a pilgrim's staff and pilgrim's book (which, as was noted in chapter 1, is seen as a "passport" to the next realm), ready for his/her final journey/pilgrimage.[81]

The imagery of death is thus an important feature of the Shikoku landscape, a point alluded to earlier when I spoke of the *reizan* associated with the *henro*. In premodern times, the association with death was not just symbolic: in an age without the benefits of modern medicine and when many made the pilgrimage seeking Kōbō Daishi's grace and hoping for miraculous cures from illness, death was a recurrent and visible feature of the route. Pilgrims' journals from earlier eras mention seeing corpses of deceased pilgrims along the way or of hearing about deaths in the pilgrim community,[82] while pilgrims who died on the island were often buried by their fellow pilgrims where they fell, so that the route itself was marked by the graves of the departed. I will further discuss the prevalence of death in premodern Shikoku in chapter 4. The point to note here is that in earlier eras the symbolism of death was reinforced by its actuality. As such, Shikoku was a place where the reality of death was present for pilgrims—a point illustrated by an alternative premodern rendition of the name "Shikoku." "Shikoku" is made up of the ideograms *shi* 四 (four) and *koku* 国 (province/country) to indicate the four provinces of the island; by replacing the *shi* (four) with another ideogram also pronounced *shi* 死 but meaning "death," one gets Shikoku, the "country of death."[83]

In modern times, death is rarely an actual occurrence for pilgrims, but it remains a visual element in the pilgrimage landscape, visible in the graves and memorials to the spirits of the dead that are found along the route and around the temples. Praying and performing memorial services for the dead, too, is an important element in the motivations of many pilgrims—some of whom may even carry signs or markers representing the dead or their spirits—to the extent that the journey becomes a voyage with the spirits of the dead (an issue that will be discussed in the next chapter). The importance of death images for Shikoku pilgrims has been noted by the scholar Araki Michio in his account of how a student of his did the pilgrimage as a memorial service for her deceased grandfather and became so totally immersed in the idea of Shikoku as an "other" world and a realm of death that she found it extremely difficult to reintegrate into the mundane world on her return.[84] The emotional connotations of the pilgrimage as a journey in other realms may also be brought home to pilgrims when they put on their pilgrims' clothing: the writer and historian Yamamoto Wakako, for example, on donning pilgrim's attire at the start of her 1988 pilgrimage, commented on her sense of transformation and of feeling she was entering a new realm.[85]

The association between the pilgrimage and death is widely found in contemporary pilgrimage narratives. The volume of miracle stories produced in 1984 by the Shikoku Reijōkai, from which the previously cited Ogasawara miracle story comes, refers to the *henro* as a journey in the borderlands of death, one that oscillates between (symbolic) death and dramatic rebirth and renewal. The miracle stories in the collection affirm this theme, narrating tales in which pilgrims such as Ogasawara face danger, despair, illness, and problems, yet, in the depths of their troubles, experience dramatic transformations or salvation through the grace of Kōbō Daishi. Their journeys thus take them from the depths of darkness to the realms of hope—a fitting metaphor, the book notes, for the pilgrimage and for the Shikoku landscape, whose mountains and valleys provide the physical framework for a metaphorical journey through the valleys of death and the mountains of life.[86]

Sharing the journey, making traces

Pilgrims who follow in the symbolic footsteps of Kōbō Daishi help engrave the pilgrimage onto the landscape of Shikoku, thereby constantly rewriting the textual narrative of pilgrimage through their actions and the traces they leave behind. These serve as signs that inform later pilgrims of those who have gone before them. Being conscious of the impact of the past, of course, enables pilgrims in the present to recognize that their own footsteps and imprints may also influence those who come afterward.

This sense of a shared pilgrimage consciousness passing down through the ages can be found in accounts of pilgrimages such as the Camino to Santiago de Compostela, along which pilgrims have traveled (and died) for over a millennium. Walter Starkie acknowledges the presence of the past and the traces of earlier pilgrims when he speaks of how every step the pilgrim takes along the road to Santiago "evokes memories of those who passed that way century after century."[87] Lee Hoinacki, too, walking the same pilgrimage, states that he felt in touch with the pilgrims of the past who had died on the Camino.[88] The result, according to Frey, is that pilgrims acquire a "sense of shared journey" with those who have gone before them and in whose community they have entered in performing the pilgrimage.[89]

One can readily see—in the images of "doing the same practice together" *(dōgyō)*—how concepts of a shared journey in which the pilgrims of the present travel in the footsteps of pilgrims past may be felt by, and influence, pilgrims in Shikoku. Pilgrims such as Kagita Chūsaburō, who walked the *henro* in 1961, and Takamure Itsue (1918) have written about their awareness of the traces of earlier pilgrims who helped carve out the *henro* route.[90] Harada Nobuo, who walked the pilgrimage in the late 1990s, writes about how he became conscious, as he struggled along the *henro* path, of the presence of past pilgrims who also sweated, cried, and, at times, as the wayside graves reminded him, died while doing the same practice.[91]

Hoshino's interviews with present-day pilgrims show how conscious they were of engaging with the past and of participating in an event deeply rooted in Japanese history.[92] My interviewees, too, reflect similar views, perhaps none more clearly than Miyazaki Tateki, a retired futon maker who runs an organization known as the Henro Michi Hozon Kyōryokukai (Pilgrimage Path Preservation Society) from his home in Matsuyama. Miyazaki, whose activities and story will be discussed at greater length in chapter 8, has dedicated much of his life to the pilgrimage, in particular to restoring old sections of the pilgrimage path that had become overgrown, putting up signs to help pilgrims find their way, and publishing guidebooks designed specifically for walkers. Miyazaki, as a resident of Shikoku, is deeply conscious of the importance of the *henro* in the island's culture and history, and he is also very much aware of the acts of earlier pilgrims who helped develop the route by, for instance, erecting wayside markers for pilgrims. In interviews with me he has spoken about the imprint made on the *henro* by pilgrims such as Shinnen, the seventeenth-century ascetic mentioned earlier in this chapter. For Miyazaki this imprint was vitally important to his own consciousness of the *henro*, inspiring him in his contribution to the route so that future generations would be aware of his presence.[93]

The moving text: What pilgrims leave behind

This sense of shared historical consciousness and of the presence of past pilgrims is enhanced by the objects pilgrims leave behind along the route and at the temples to mark their presence. These objects—such as stones marking the way, inscriptions, talismans, and photographs left by pilgrims at the temples, and signs hung up along the pilgrimage paths—are important visual features in the pilgrimage landscape. Through them pilgrims can leave something of themselves behind on the route, thereby sharing in the process of shaping the pilgrimage landscape for later generations. As such, both temples and route are moving visual texts shaped and reshaped by the activities of the pilgrims who pass through.

One prominent object left by pilgrims is the *osamefuda* (or *fuda*) first mentioned in chapter 1. In earlier eras, *fuda* were generally made of wood and were nailed or otherwise fixed to a temple to announce the pilgrims' visit, and at some temples the *fuda* of past ages may still be seen fixed to pillars and walls, thereby creating an impression of age and tradition. Nowadays temples normally ask pilgrims not to affix *fuda* to the temples, instead providing offertory boxes for them. However, sometimes one finds them stuck to temple walls and pillars, along with various other objects—notably pictures, copies of sutras, prayer requests, and calling cards—that pilgrims wish to leave behind.

Sometimes pilgrims leave business name cards *(meishi)* with their profession, business number, and so on, at the sites, the cards serving both as a calling card to the buddhas and also as a deliberate display of public piety. I have seen many such cards from businessmen, company chairmen, and the like—sometimes with a prayer request that mentions the company name and business. The most striking such display I have seen was the name card (complete with sincere-looking picture) of a politician and member of a regional parliament who appeared to be making the pilgrimage either to seek Kōbō Daishi's help in getting reelected and/or in order to convince fellow temple-goers of his probity and spiritual devotion, and hence of his worthiness for reelection.

It is not uncommon for pilgrims to leave photographs of themselves at the temples, and I have come across many examples with inscriptions detailing aspects of the lives, requests, and experiences of those who put them up. On one of my early visits to Shikoku, in March 1986, I noticed photographs of a priest, aged ninety-five, and his wife, aged eighty-seven, from Kashima in Kyushu affixed to several temples, with an inscription announcing that this was their fifty-third pilgrimage in Shikoku and giving details of other pilgrimages they had done. At the same temples I also noted photographs of a man who wrote that he was seeking relief from illness, and of a couple in their fifties praying for family safety. The inscriptions accompanying such photographs can be highly detailed: one pilgrim, for example, had left a long hand-written and photocopied account at the temples in October and November 1990 detailing his numerous pilgrimages around Shikoku and other routes, along with visits to many mountain pilgrimage centers as well as to Buddhist sites in China. It also told of how he had once walked the Shikoku route barefoot and outlined other ascetic experiences he had had, while providing his address and phone number. I was able to contact and interview him as a result and found that, as expected, since he had been so ready to put his experiences on public display, he was keen to talk to me about his pilgrimage experiences. He lived on the island of Kyushu and claimed he had acquired, through his constant asceticism and pilgrimage activities, the spiritual power to heal people, to exorcise evil spirits, and to divine the future. As a result, he had built up a local clientele of devotees and ran a pilgrimage association.[94] Sometimes the photographs left are of loved ones (sometimes deceased) on behalf of whom the pilgrimage is being done. At times, too, I have seen photographs of loved ones that have been placed at temples by distraught family members, with messages stating plaintively that so-and-so set out on the pilgrimage on such-and-such a date but has not been heard of for some months: has anyone seen him/her?

The offerings left behind are indicative of the immense amount of prior preparation and dedication that may be put into a pilgrimage. An example of this involves *shakyō* (copying Buddhist sutras), normally done by hand. This practice, considered to be a merit-making activity as well as a form of meditation, has a long history in Japan: when one makes a sutra copy in this way, it is common to offer it at a temple along with a request.[95] The *Hannya Shingyō* is the most commonly copied such sutra, since it is only 262 ideograms long and can be copied in under an hour. Many pilgrims will spend time prior to setting out on their pilgrimages, making sutra copies for this purpose—often as many as 176 copies (or more) so that they can leave two copies (one at the main hall of worship and one at the *daishidō*) at each temple they visit. Some of the pilgrims I traveled with in the tour group described in chapter 7, for example, left two copies of the *Hannya Shingyō* at each temple we visited. Sometimes, making such copies may involve more than just calligraphy. I have on occasion come across transcriptions of the sutra with each of the sutra's ideograms carefully inscribed on a separate grain of rice or small stone, which have then been glued to a piece of card or paper in sequence.

Several temples possess items that they claim to have been left behind by pilgrims as a result of miraculous events. At Iyataniji, which has a corpus of miracle tales that narrate how previously infirm pilgrims who made the ascent up to the temple have been able to cast off the symbols of their disabilities and walk thereafter unaided, numerous leg braces, corsets, and body supports line the steps before the main hall of worship. According to temple priests, they have been left by pilgrims who had experienced miraculous cures there.[96] None of these looks less than several decades old, yet their presence still can cause comment and excitement among pilgrims: the party I visited Iyataniji with in 1990 (see chapter 7) were excited as we climbed the steps past them.

Pilgrims may also leave items of their pilgrimage attire behind, particularly when they finish their journey. Several temples have collections of such items, particularly Temple 88, which has a large collection of staffs, shirts, and hats left behind by pilgrims. In this way pilgrims effectively leave something of themselves behind at the temple, ensuring that even after returning home, they remain present on, and represented in, the *henro*.

Pilgrimage groups also may leave signs of their presence by placing banners announcing the name of their group or pilgrimage association (and sometimes, too, its address), the names of those who are leading or traveling with the party, and perhaps also the date of their visit, as well as prayers and petitions addressed to Kōbō Daishi, at the temples. These may also include the names of people who, while not physically in the party, are members of their community or have donated money to assist the group in their pilgrimage and hence are included as members of the party. Nowadays, too, it is not uncommon to see such group lists produced by computer or word processor

Discarded leg braces and other objects left behind by pilgrims after visiting temple 71 (Iyataniji). The pilgrims' staffs have been left here temporarily while pilgrims visit the main hall of the temple upstairs.

printout. Few such items remain on display for very long, for the temples generally clear them away periodically, but they are soon replaced by new offerings, new *fuda,* and the like. It is not uncommon, also, for pilgrimage associations to donate or leave at the temples various items that signify their continuing presence at the sites. The aforementioned hall of worship built by the Arita Settaikō in the precincts of Temple 1, and at where members of the association stay during their almsgiving visits to Shikoku, are one such example through which the association's continuing presence on and engagement with the *henro* are manifest.

Route as text: Stones, markers, and inscriptions

Another important material object in the pilgrimage landscape is the *michi-shirube* (pilgrimage route marker)—most commonly in earlier times the *henro*

Pilgrimage banners left by pilgrimage groups at one of the temples. To the left are a number of old *osamefuda* that have been pasted to the temple pillars.

ishi (pilgrimage stone), many of which have been erected along the route since the late seventeenth century.[97] These have commonly been put up by pilgrims who raised donations for the purpose through begging for or soliciting alms. *Henro ishi* have commonly been engraved with stone hands pointing the way to the next temple or landmark, with inscriptions indicating the distances involved and also the names of donors and the dates they were put up. They serve a number of purposes and express a number of meanings. Pragmatically, they have helped other pilgrims find the way while acting as a testament to the faith of those who put them up and to those who provided the funds for them, and also at times serving as a means of commemorating or celebrating the achievements of those responsible for them.

I will discuss *henro ishi* further in chapter 4, when I look at the historical developments of the pilgrimage. Here I will just draw attention to some prominent pilgrims who, over the centuries, have put up *henro ishi* and whose influence thus remains physically present on the route. The first of these is the ascetic Shinnen, mentioned earlier for his collection of miracle tales but believed to be the first person to erect pilgrimage stones as markers, soliciting alms to this end in the late seventeenth century and putting up numerous stones, several of which can still be seen today.[98] Later pilgrims who followed Shinnen's example include Takeda Tokuemon, a resident of Shikoku who, during the late eighteenth and early nineteenth centuries, regularly went round the pilgrimage three times a year and who is known to have erected around seventy stones between 1794 and 1807, each bearing depictions of Kōbō Daishi and information about distances to the next site, and Shōren, who was active at roughly the same time as Takeda and whose stones similarly featured Kōbō Daishi and route directions. About eighty of Shōren's stones can still be found, mostly in Tokushima Prefecture, all erected between 1804 and 1818.[99] The most active of all in this respect was Nakatsuka Mōhei, the pilgrim mentioned earlier as having walked the *henro* over 280 times between 1865–1922 and who, during his travels, put up or had erected 237 such *henro ishi*.[100] Nakatsuka, as Kiyoyoshi Eitoku indicates, was particularly concerned with marking what were, for him, significant landmarks in his incessant pilgrimage. Thus while he might go several circuits without putting up any stones at all, on some other circuits he put up many stones. For example, his eighty-eighth pilgrimage circuit (done in his forty-second, i.e., *yaku-doshi*, year) was the occasion for putting up nineteen stones, after which he did eleven circuits without a single stone. The next circuit, however—his one hundredth—was commemorated with twenty-eight stones. On his 137th circuit, when Nakatsuka surpassed the number of circuits by Tada Emon (d. 1862), whose 136 circuits were assumed to be the most of any pilgrim at the time, he marked the event with fifteen stones.[101]

Many of these stones can still be seen along the route, and some still serve as useful guideposts for those on foot. However, some, less helpfully for walkers, have been moved to temple courtyards and displayed as historical artifacts, where they serve as a reminder to modern pilgrims of the historical legacy of the *henro*. On one occasion, for example, when walking in 1984, our guidebook informed us that we would find a *henro ishi* at a certain point to indicate which path we should take. The stone was missing, and we briefly lost our way. Later, at the next temple, we found the stone in the temple court-yard, to which it had been moved because the temple authorities considered it to be an important historical object of interest to pilgrims who, traveling by bus, would not otherwise have seen it. Its initial purpose of helping walkers find their way had, of course, been lost in the process.

The tradition of putting up *michishirube* for the benefit of others contin-ues in the present: I have already mentioned the work of Miyazaki Tateki and the Henro Michi Hozon Kyōryokukai in erecting signs and markers for pil-grims, and his traces, in the form of such signposts, can be readily seen throughout the route. There are also other individuals and groups who have erected markers in recent times to help others and to commemorate their own activities. Two examples will suffice here: outside Anrakuji (Temple 6) there is a large stone marker commemorating the activities of the Toho no Kai, a pilgrimage association dedicated to organizing walking pilgrimage tours, on which are engraved the names of hundreds of members who contributed to the stone and to the continuing activities of the society, while at the gates of Temple 18, there is a stone erected on February 5, 1980, by a man named Toyozawa Yoshihiro to commemorate his attainment of the status of *sendatsu* (pilgrimage guide).

Besides these permanent—and often costly—objects, pilgrims put many smaller markers along the route, especially on paths used by foot pilgrims. Here it is common to come across numerous tags, signs, and small plaques hanging from branches and trees or tied to bushes, indicating the presence of past pilgrims and offering prayers and words of encouragement for those who follow in their footsteps. They are often thin strips of metal, sometimes bear-ing the pilgrim's name along with various words and exhortations ranging from the ubiquitous *henro michi* (pilgrimage path), to more complex state-ments informing one that this is the path walked by Kōbō Daishi *("Daishi sama ga aruita michi")*, to simple exhortations of encouragement such as *"ganbatte kudasai"* (keep going/keep at it!) and invocations of praise such as *"Namu daishi henjō kongō."*

These signs—like the *henro ishi*—can certainly provide encouragement to pilgrims as they travel, a point emphasized by the priest Takada Shinkai, who comments on how he was frequently given a mental boost by seeing such signs as he walked the pilgrimage in the late 1970s.[102] They also create a link and sense of empathy between pilgrims in the present day and those who have gone before them. In April 2000, for example, Kiyoyoshi Eitoku, a leading authority on *henro ishi*, took me around northern Shikoku teaching me about the different styles of *henro ishi* put up by pilgrims such as Shinnen, Takeda, and Nakatsuka. When we came across such stones he spoke about the people who had erected them in terms of familiarity, as if a continuing connection existed between him and the historical figures that had put them up. That sense of familiarity had come through to me a couple of days earlier, when I was walking along a quiet, forested path between Temples 41 and 42 and came across a number of *fuda* hanging from the trees exhorting me to "keep going" and telling me this was the path Daishi walked. The *fuda* bore the name of Yanagimoto Myōzen, the priest from Saba Daishi mentioned in chapter 1 whom I had interviewed a decade before, and they reminded me of how he had helped me in my research, taking time out of a busy schedule to answer my questions and provide me with books and materials from his temple. Since the *fuda* bore a quite recent date, they told me that he was still well and actively engaged with the pilgrimage. On the same day I came across several signs put up by Miyazaki Tateki, and these, too, made me feel a sense of familiarity and empathy, since I had interviewed him ten years earlier and had seen his signposts on a number of occasions since. The markers I saw

Commemorative pillar with statue of Kōbō Daishi erected by a pilgrimage association (the Toho no Kai) outside Anrakuji (Temple 6).

on this occasion reminded me that he was still active and encouraged me to phone him and arrange another interview. The Japanese pilgrim I was walking with at the time (and who will feature in the next chapter) also commented on Miyazaki, saying that she felt she somehow "knew" him because she had seen so many of his signs, through which she had come to appreciate the help he provided for walkers such as herself. Her pilgrimage, in other words, was also influenced by Miyazaki's traces.[103]

Moving text, shifting landscape

The Shikoku pilgrimage is thus a moving text that is constantly being rewritten by its participants, who inscribe themselves onto the route through the objects and signs they leave behind and endow it with meanings that are encountered, experienced, and imbibed by subsequent pilgrims. These signs and objects are constantly changing as new pilgrims come along, as temples clear away old *fuda,* and as new objects take their place. Yet even these temporary, shifting signs—and those who leave them—are not simply forgotten,

Wayside marker hung by a pilgrim from a branch along a mountainous section of the pilgrimage path to encourage fellow pilgrims. The inscription gives the date and name of the pilgrim (the priest of Saba Daishi mentioned in this chapter) plus the invocation "Namu daishi henjō kongō."

temporary, and transient elements in the enduring history of the sites, for they are seen by—and hence influence and shape the experiences of—the pilgrims who tread in their footsteps. They thus join and become part of the accumulated landscape of the pilgrimage, parts of its moving, changing text.

This moving text maps out an emotional landscape wedded to a physical terrain that expresses themes of marginality, familiarity, and otherness and of death, salvation, and enlightenment that is shaped by the legendary hand of Kōbō Daishi and by the actual deeds of pilgrims. Both text and landscape are continually changing as new pilgrims make their mark and as modern developments occur. I will discuss these issues further in chapter 5, when I look at the modern history of the *henro* and show how new developments in the transport infrastructure have impacted on the pilgrimage and reshaped the ways in which pilgrims pass through and see the landscape. The point is that the landscape of pilgrimage is not constant but changing and is constantly being made and remade through a continuous interweaving of the physical and the emotional and of past and present, and as pilgrims pass through and leave their traces, thereby making meanings for themselves and for those who come in their wake. They thus help create a "historical" consciousness founded in the combined influences of symbolic imagery, miraculous tales, and the footsteps of past pilgrims and etched into the geography and landscape (real and emotional) of the island and pilgrimage. It is to a closer consideration of these people—the pilgrims who make the pilgrimage, individually and in groups—and their deeds and what makes them into pilgrims that I next turn.

3 Making
Pilgrimages

Pilgrims, Motives, and Meanings

This chapter looks at the motives, attitudes, and practices of pilgrims in Shikoku. My account is necessarily selective because the sheer number of pilgrims (probably over one hundred thousand a year and cumulatively, over the centuries, several millions) makes it impossible to fully categorize or list their every motivation and intention. However, there are some broad themes that recur frequently enough to be considered illustrative of general pilgrim motivations and attitudes, and it is these that I highlight here through a series of cameo portraits of pilgrims I have encountered during my research. Clearly the portraits I draw here are illustrative of the materials I have accumulated in my research and that have shaped my understandings of the *henro*; hence their selection may have been shaped by my own readings and interpretations of the *henro*. I have, however, sought to temper any possible selectivity by drawing on studies and surveys by Japanese scholars.

Walking with Tomoko: Travels with a Japanese pilgrim

My first cameo involves a Japanese woman in her mid-sixties whom I met in April 2000, when, as I mentioned in the introduction, I alighted at Iyo Miyanoshita Station and walked to Temple 41. On the train I had noticed three people whose clothing, staffs, and bells indicated they were pilgrims, and while the seemingly exotic sight of traditionally clad pilgrims on a train captured my attention, it barely seemed to register with the local passengers, who hardly gave the white-clad pilgrims a second glance. It was an indication of how pilgrims can be both "exotic" and familiar; the pilgrims in Shikoku whose white clothes have become such a sign of tradition and difference are also so much a part of the everyday local landscape, visible on local buses and express trains, in airports and coffee shops as well as at the temples, that local people seem to hardly notice them.

As I checked my map outside the station, one of these pilgrims asked me if I were headed for Ryūkōji. When I answered yes, she suggested that we walk together. Pleased at the chance to talk to a pilgrim, I agreed, and so we set off, talking as we went. Tomoko, the lady in question, lived just outside Tokyo and had come to Shikoku by train five days earlier to do a section of the pilgrimage. On this day her plans were, like mine, to walk the fifteen or so kilometers to Temple 43 and then take a train to Matsuyama, the nearest sizable town, to stay overnight. Rather than being fazed by walking with a foreign researcher, she found the idea rather interesting, with the result that we walked together all day, during which time she spoke at length about her life and her reasons for doing the pilgrimage.

One does not always find such ready camaraderie among pilgrims on foot, who can sometimes become so absorbed in their own journeys that they do not appear to take much notice even of their own companions—a point I will discuss further in chapter 6. This is why it is not always easy to talk to pilgrims along the way; some are too absorbed in their personal journeys to want to talk with others. Yet by contrast, some pilgrims are, like Tomoko, willing to talk at length and are quick to join in conversation with others, to share experiences, and to pass on stories—especially those containing rumors of miracles—that they have heard along the way. This impression is affirmed in other accounts written by those walking the *henro* that frequently comment on such camaraderie and story sharing among pilgrims.[1] Many pilgrims, too, appear ready to enter into temporary travel friendships with others met en route who, since they are performing the same practice, are referred to as *dōgyōsan*. This again points to another significant aspect of "doing the pilgrimage together" *(dōgyō)*, in which pilgrims may be conscious not just of an identification between themselves and Kōbō Daishi, but also with other pilgrims. Tomoko certainly regarded other pilgrims as companions in the same enterprise, talking about them as *dōgyōsan*, and she seemed happy to enter into temporary relationships with those she met. To her I was such a person; she was content that we were going the same way and that we could therefore spend time together on the pilgrimage route, sharing information and talking about ourselves and what we were doing.

Tomoko was doing her pilgrimage in short stages, visiting Shikoku for about a week at a time and going to ten or so temples each time. She walked when the distances between temples were relatively short and where the pilgrimage path afforded an opportunity to get off the highways and onto peaceful paths and back roads, but she used buses and trains when temples were far apart or when there was no choice but to go along major roads. Thus she planned to walk from Temple 41 to Temple 43 but intended to get from Temple 43 to Temple 44, over eighty kilometers distant, by public transport.

She stayed in various types of accommodations depending on circumstance. On the night we met, she, like me, stayed at a cheap hotel in Matsuyama. However, she said, she felt it was particularly appropriate for pilgrims to stay at the temples whenever possible, and so, when she could, she ended her day's travels at a temple with a *shukubō* (temple lodge). Such views are held by many pilgrims; over half the temples on the route operate *shukubō*, and there is a general feeling among pilgrims that these are the most appropriate and authentic places for pilgrims to stay at. According to the Waseda University survey, around 90 percent of pilgrims stay at least one night in a temple lodge—a far greater percentage than any other form of accommodation.[2] Yet such views and practices are a shade ironic, since *shukubō* are a relatively recent, twentieth-century development in Shikoku (see chapters 4 and 5) rather than something with deep historical roots.

Tomoko's clothing was a mixture of the traditional and the comfortable modern. She wore a white pilgrim's shirt, a white sun hat, tracksuit trousers, and trainers, and she carried a pilgrim's staff and a small backpack. She wore a Buddhist rosary *(juzu)* around her wrist, which she rubbed when she prayed. At the temples her routine lasted around fifteen minutes or so as she burned incense and lit candles, prayed, recited the Heart Sutra, and made offerings of coins at each hall of worship before getting her pilgrim's book stamped. In her style of travel, too—visiting Shikoku on a number of occasions, usually for around one week to do part of the route before returning home and then starting again where she had left off on her next visit—Tomoko followed a pattern that has become increasingly common. According to the previously mentioned Waseda University survey, little more than a quarter—27.7 percent in all—nowadays perform the *henro* in one go. The large majority—71.1 percent—do it in a series of shorter journeys, with the majority (around 76 percent of those surveyed) spending less than ten days on the road in any one visit.[3] Tomoko thought it would take around two years for her to do the pilgrimage in this way, over half a dozen visits. This, as I mentioned in chapter 1, is not uncommon, and it indicates a form of fragmentation in the pilgrimage and a blurring of any clear-cut dividing lines between everyday and pilgrimage life.

In terms of age, gender, and occupation, too, Tomoko was representative. The *henro* has undergone a marked gender shift in modern times. In the Tokugawa period male pilgrims were more numerous than females, while studies of the 1930s and 1940s show that a majority (around 65 percent in all) were male.[4] This has changed in the present day, with the Waseda survey showing that just over half of pilgrims are female.[5] This itself may be an underestimate, for a survey sponsored by the Himeji Bank in 1985 has suggested that around two-thirds were female,[6] while Satō Hisamitsu's surveys, conducted in the mid-1980s, found that 58 percent of pilgrims were female.[7] Temple priests I have spoken to estimate that around 60 percent or so of the pilgrims are female. My general observations are that this figure could be still higher, while bus company officials have regularly commented to me that considerably more females than males use their bus tours.

Tomoko belonged to the single largest age group of contemporary pilgrims. Thirty-six percent of all pilgrims, according to the Waseda survey, are in their sixties, while those in their seventies comprise around 20 percent.[8] As a retired person, too, she represented another marked trend, with the Waseda survey indicating a recent leap in the numbers of retired people doing the *henro*. Such retirees have, in recent decades, become the single largest group of pilgrims in occupational terms, a trend also noted in the 1985 Himeji Bank survey.[9] As many as half those walking the route in one go, according to the Waseda survey, describe themselves as "unemployed," a term often used by those who have retired as well as by those who are out of work.[10] Given the time necessary to do the *henro*—especially by foot—these are perhaps not unsurprising figures; making pilgrimages, after all, is time consuming and hence is more readily done by those unconstrained by the demands of regular employment.

Pilgrimage activities; ringing the temple bell at Temple 10.

The growing number of older, especially female, pilgrims is clearly linked to economic and social factors in the postwar era. The development of a pensions system has enabled older people to retire and have some time to travel later in life, while greater wealth in general, allied to a highly efficient mass transport system and the development of organized pilgrimage tours, has made pilgrimage increasingly accessible to those who, in earlier times, would simply have been unable to withstand the rigors of the *henro*. Even Tomoko, a sprightly and fit woman who had no difficulty in managing sixteen or so kilometers in a day, thought she would not be able to manage the entire pilgrimage on foot, and certainly not in one go, which is why she sometimes made use of buses and trains.

Modern transportation has also opened up the pilgrimage in geographical terms. In chapter 1 I noted that a sizable number of pilgrims came from Shikoku itself, while studies have shown that throughout the Tokugawa era and well into the postwar period the bulk of pilgrims from outside the island have come from regions surrounding Shikoku—such as the Kansai region around Osaka and the areas facing Shikoku across the Inland Sea.[11] In recent times, however, this geographical spread has become much broader, with growing numbers coming from the Tokyo and Kantō areas as well as from northern Japan—regions that, until comparatively recently, produced few pilgrims because of the distance involved. Now, priests and bus company officials inform me, these are major growth areas as aeroplanes and high-speed trains have reduced the time needed to get to and from the island. Tomoko was representative of this trend, someone who could visit the previously distant island quickly and regularly because of modern high-speed transport—and hence who could readily do her pilgrimage in a series of shorter journeys. Modern transport developments, in other words, have helped make the pilgrimage into a truly national one, with pilgrims from all over Japan rather than, as in the era when everyone walked, a clientele largely drawn from the regions closer to Shikoku.[12]

Good transport facilities have also given pilgrims such as Tomoko real flexibility in timing their visits. Being retired meant she could choose when to travel, and, like most pilgrims, she made sure to avoid the rainy season of June–July, the extremely hot and sticky summer months from July to early September, and the cold winter months from late November to early March, instead timing her visits for spring and early autumn. This was not just because the climate is at its most pleasant and most conducive to walking then, but because of the seasonal attractions—the cherry blossoms of spring and the resplendent hues of the autumn leaves—which made things more aesthetically pleasurable. On this occasion Tomoko was enamored (as I was) with the magnificent flowering cherry blossoms that lined the paths and roads leading to several of the temples. She also enthused about the beauty of Shikoku and about how good and refreshing it was to be amidst forests and hills and away from the tensions and the rush of everyday urban life.

Motives and purposes: Death, memorialization, and overcoming grief

Being able to get away from everyday life and enjoy such surroundings were important motivating elements for Tomoko. Other factors—all of which sounded familiar from my years of talking with Shikoku pilgrims—also played their part. She was doing the pilgrimage as a memorial service *(kuyō)* for the spirit of her recently deceased father, and her intention was to complete her journey around the third anniversary of his death. Memorializing the dead through extended rituals that transform the spirit of the deceased into an ancestor who is venerated as a protector of the family is important in Japan, and it features as a common motivation amongst pilgrims in Shikoku and elsewhere.[13] There is a strong belief among pilgrims that the merit created through their pilgrimages can be transferred to the spirits of their deceased kin and assist them in their journey to ancestorhood and to the Buddhist Pure Land. Equally, too, it is believed that the accumulated merit can assist the living in the journeys their spirits will make, after death, to other realms. One frequently meets pilgrims who are doing the *henro* for this reason.

As with Tomoko, the wish to memorialize the dead is perhaps the most common of all pilgrim motivations in Shikoku, cited as such by around half the pilgrims in the Waseda survey.[14] This is unsurprising given the deep-seated associations between Shikoku, death, and other realms discussed in the previous chapter. It has been a recurrent theme in my interviews with pilgrims; most of the party of pilgrims I describe in chapter 7, for instance, mentioned their ancestors and the wish to memorialize the dead as a major reason for undertaking the *henro*. Other observers have commented similarly. Imai Misako, a journalist who did the pilgrimage with her husband and son in the 1980s, has written about the numbers of pilgrims they met who were doing the *henro* as a memorial for dead spouses and/or children, and she even cites one woman who was prompted to go to Shikoku after her deceased husband appeared in a dream and asked her to do the *henro* with him.[15]

This idea of the deceased being "with" the pilgrim provides another meaning to the term *"dōgyōninin,"* with the person "doing the same practice" referring not just to Kōbō Daishi but also to an accompanying spirit of the dead. Indeed, Miyazaki Ninshō has suggested, albeit based more on speculation than substantive evidence, that this might be the original meaning of the terms *"dōgyō"* and *"dōgyōninin."*[16] It is not uncommon to see Shikoku pilgrims traveling "with" the dead, carrying funeral portraits of their kin or other items that signify the presence of the departed, such as the memorial tablet *(ihai)* that represents the spirit of the ancestor and is normally kept in the family Buddhist altar in Japan, or even an urn containing the ashes of the dead.[17] An illustrated pilgrimage guidebook from 1956 shows this practice in action through photographs of a man carrying the *ihai* of his son, and of a woman, aged (as far as I could judge) around thirty, performing the pilgrimage "with" the spirits of the dead of her household, whose ashes she carried in a box strapped to her breast.[18] The monthly newsletter *Henro* often has accounts of similar practices, and the following are just a number of the reports in it from the mid-1980s onward: a woman aged forty-nine from Kōchi in Shikoku doing the pilgrimage by taxi with friends on her days off and on behalf of her mother and father, whose memorial tablets she was carrying;[19] a man walking, sleeping out, and doing the pilgrimage as a memorial on the first anniversary of his father's, and seventeenth anniversary of his mother's, death;[20] and a couple in their mid-forties whose only child, a daughter, had been ill since infancy before dying at the age of twenty-two. They stressed that they had previously had no religious feelings but had decided to do the pilgrimage as a memorial for her, and in doing so had gained release from their suffering.[21]

I have, on several occasions, come across people "carrying" their deceased kin. For instance, in November 1990 I encountered a man between Temples 4 and 5 dressed in pilgrimage clothing and carrying a small rucksack. He told me he was fifty-three years old and recently retired from the Japanese Self-Defence Force and was doing the *henro* "with" and on behalf of his wife. So saying, he tapped his rucksack to indicate that she was in there, although I was unable to find out (simply because I felt reluctant to intrude further) whether in the form of an *ihai* or as ashes.

In such cases, the *henro* may be undertaken because of the grief of bereavement, with the performance becoming part of the process of healing and overcoming loss. Such sentiments are evident in the comments of the couple mentioned above and in the following account written in 1999 by a male pilgrim who stayed overnight at a temple lodge that kept a book for pilgrims to record their thoughts in.[22] He wrote that the love of his life had died some three years before and how sad he remained as a result. Now he was walking the pilgrimage for her, carrying her photograph at his breast, and as he did so he had felt a deep sense of gratitude because of the warmth and kindness shown him by people he met. As a result, he felt, the pilgrimage was helping to alleviate his pain and loss.

It is not just the sprits of one's own kin who provide the motivation for doing the henro. In 1989 the Japanese newspaper *Yomiuri shinbun* ran two articles about a Japanese electrical company, Eikō, whose head was a devotee of the *henro* and of Kōbō Daishi. Each year, two or three groups of employees from the company were sent on the *henro* as part of the company-training scheme for new managers. The origins of this practice date to 1965, when one of the company trucks struck and killed a young child. The company president went to the funeral and, while there, recalled the death of his own daughter some twelve years earlier. As a result he and the truck driver decided to do the *henro* to atone for the death of the child. Initially, he reported, he was tormented by visions of the dead child and her grieving family, but the more they walked, the less turbulent the visions became, enabling him to attain some peace of mind. Thereafter he and his company continued to remember the dead child and memorialize her each year through their company pilgrimages.[23]

Multiple meanings, multiple purposes

Like many pilgrims, Tomoko had a multiplicity of motives and aims. She was also interested in gaining new experiences through travel and in the self-discovery that this could bring. She had already seen some of the world, having traveled to New Zealand and Europe, and she now wanted to find out more about her own culture. Her interest in the *henro* had been piqued by the NHK broadcasts, which made her think of the pilgrimage as an interesting medium through which to delve into her country's history and cultural heritage, while gaining new experiences through visiting a new part of Japan. Again, such interests are widely felt among pilgrims of Tomoko's age bracket—those who have recently retired after a lifetime of hard work with (as is customary in Japan) relatively little free time for travel and the like.

A comment she made to me as we walked along also hinted at an additional attraction of Shikoku for pilgrims of her generation. Noting how often the local people—especially the children—gave us friendly greetings as we passed, she commented approvingly that people in Shikoku raised their children well in a traditional manner, instilling in them proper respect for others. In an era when it is common to hear older generations complaining about how the young lack respect for their elders and have abandoned traditional modes of politeness, it was striking to hear her speak in this way. I have heard other pilgrims, too, speak similarly, and I sense that this is something that particularly appeals to those of Tomoko's generation and that reinforces, for them, the idea that Shikoku is a bastion of tradition and makes it appealing.

Tomoko also saw, in the pilgrimage, a means of keeping fit and active. Here, again, she displayed characteristics commonly found amongst present-day pilgrims. I have met many people, especially males, who have recently retired and who have been motivated to do the *henro*, amongst other reasons, because it provided a way of keeping fit and gave them a challenge and something to do in their retirement. A number of books have also been published in recent years along these lines by people who, having retired like Tomoko, wish to "find themselves" and learn about their country's culture and religious traditions, while keeping themselves fit in their retirement years.[24]

In the footsteps of others: Asceticism, challenges, miracles

While Tomoko's combination of walking and using public transport, staying in overnight accommodations, breaking the pilgrimage into sections, going at her own pace, and taking advantage of the seasons illustrates a prevalent mode of contemporary pilgrimage, the pilgrimage way of a young man in his early thirties whom I shall call Nakano Kenjirō is one far less widely followed, although deeply rooted in the pilgrimage's ascetic traditions. My wife and I met Nakano-san when our paths crossed in February 1984, when the three of us walked together for several kilometers on two separate days; later, after we had returned home, we had a telephone call from him to tell us he, too, had finished his journey safely. Nakano-san was dressed from head to foot in traditional white pilgrimage clothes, wore a bamboo hat, and carried a staff. His only apparent concession to modern attire was the trainers he wore instead of straw sandals. It was perhaps fortunate that he did so, because it had been a very cold winter, and many of the mountain paths we traversed remained deep in snow. While we, too, had to endure the harsh late-winter snow, we were still traveling relatively comfortably: although walking thirty or more kilometers each day, we were carrying only a light knapsack each, were eating hot food regularly, and were staying overnight in lodges, temples, or wherever we could find accommodation.

By contrast, Nakano-san had a substantial rucksack and was carrying a tent and camping out every night. Each day, too, he begged for alms in traditional style, carrying a begging bowl of the sort used by Buddhist monks, while he observed a strict dietary regimen, eating sparsely and restricting himself largely to uncooked foods such as bread and fruit. He had a history of performing austerities—he told us he had done a number of Zen Buddhist meditation retreats and several long fasts—and considered asceticism to be a way of achieving higher states of consciousness. He viewed his pilgrimage as an austerity designed to purify his body and spirit.

His ascetic journey was also a replication of the journey made some thirty years earlier by a teacher, mentor, and spiritual guide in whose footsteps he sought to follow. This mentor was an acupuncture teacher with whom Nakano-san was about to study as a disciple/trainee, and his pilgrimage was intended to make him worthy of this position. He was following in his mentor's footsteps, for the teacher had, some decades before, done the *henro* in similar fashion. The story Nakano-san told us was framed in the context of miracles, and he stated that, some thirty or so years earlier, the mentor had been terminally ill from cancer and mainstream medicine had been unable to help him. As a result, the mentor had decided, in the manner of sick pilgrims through the ages, to go to Shikoku, walk the pilgrimage, and seek salvation from Kōbō Daishi. According to Nakano-san he had done just that, sleeping out, begging, and maintaining a strict dietary regime. He had returned fit and healthy, cured of his cancer, and with a zealous determination to devote the rest of his life to studying traditional healing practices and to training others in this respect.

Nakano-san's teacher's pilgrimage was in essence a path out of despair and turmoil, but framed by the hope, emphasized in pilgrimage miracle stories, that the saint could provide solace and salvation. Such motivations, in which despair, faith, and hope are intertwined, have been a recurrent feature in Shikoku, found, for example, in the present day among those pilgrims mentioned in chapter 1 who have lost their jobs and are seeking to find new meanings in a life thrown out of kilter by unemployment. The miracle story Nakano-san told is not untypical of the stories that abound among pilgrims, centering on claims of imminent death, the impotence of modern medicine, and miraculous cures acquired via the pilgrimage. It also is based on conjecture, there being no evidence, apart from Nakano-san's narration and his teacher's claim, that this man was in fact dying of incurable cancer—rather than just, for example, feeling unwell and thinking that he *might* be suffering from a life-threatening illness. Such miracle tales, as Imai has noted, are a common theme of conversation among pilgrims.[25] In my experience, too, such oral transmissions, in which miraculous tales may be recycled often at second- or third-hand levels ("I heard this story from someone who was told it at such-and-such temple by..."), often also based on assumptions of severe illness ("I knew I had cancer and the doctors could not help me"), are commonly circulated amongst, and are a staple source of communication between, pilgrims.

Although one does not find many people doing the pilgrimage in quite such an austere way as Nakano-san, his journey is not an isolated one. Asceticism continues to be an element in the wider pilgrimage framework. During my research I have come across various examples of pilgrim asceticism. Perhaps the most extreme was the pilgrim mentioned in the previous chapter, for his self-publicizing tracts posted at the temples and for doing the pilgrimage barefoot. His journey took place in early spring and before the winter snows had melted in some places. People from temple priests to the others he was walking with had implored him to get some footwear when it became clear they would have to go some distance through the snow in the mountains of Ehime Prefecture, but he refused, insisting that he was doing the pilgrimage as an austerity and hence would remain barefoot.[26]

Some pilgrims combine Nakano-san's method of camping or sleeping out with periodic overnight stays in inns and lodges, as was the case with a young man I met in April 2000 who was in his early twenties and had just graduated from college. Because of the economic situation, he was unable to find a job and hence had decided to make use of his enforced free time to find out about himself—and learn about his own cultural traditions, for he was from

Shikoku—by doing the pilgrimage. He was carrying a large rucksack with a tent, sleeping bag, mat, and camping stove and was planning (I met him during his first week) to camp most nights but to stay one night in four at a lodge where he could have a bath, a comfortable night, and good food.

Like Nakano-san, this young man saw the pilgrimage as a personal challenge, something that would test his mettle and strengthen him personally. Unlike Nakano-san, however, who spoke in language relating to spiritual advancement and religious asceticism, he eschewed expressions of piety or devotion. For him the challenge of the *henro* and the desire to "find himself" could be articulated without reference to such terms—or even to the notion of asceticism. This is quite common among contemporary pilgrims, who often, as Hoshino has noted, speak of the "challenge" posed by the *henro* and see this as a means to "find themselves." As Hoshino recognizes, such attitudes and motivations can be readily expressed without any overt mention of faith, asceticism, or devotion to Kōbō Daishi.[27] At the same time, however, they are indicative of the continuing strand of asceticism found in the *henro*, even if the language used to articulate it is framed around notions of challenge and self-discovery, rather than of austerities, devotion, and enlightenment.

Broken hearts and other misfortunes

It has already been seen that misfortune—in the shape, for instance, of illness, unemployment, or bereavement—is a recurrent motivating factor. Those who officiate at pilgrimage temples have frequently commented to me about this, noting that those alone on foot are especially likely to be driven by such feelings. This point was made one day while I was drinking tea with the wife of a temple priest and her son, the deputy head priest. A young woman seemingly in her early twenties and dressed in pilgrim's clothes walked into the temple courtyard, prayed, and made offerings at the temple before taking a pilgrim's book out of her rucksack and going to get it stamped. Observing her, the head priest's wife uttered one word: "*shitsuren*" (loss of love/broken affair). Her son nodded in agreement as she added that it was not all that common to see young female pilgrims on their own on foot. When such people stayed overnight at the temple's lodge, she always tried to talk to them. What almost invariably emerged were stories of unhappy and broken romances. It was for such reasons, she opined, that young women most commonly walked the pilgrimage alone, to get away from their problems, to work their way through their unhappiness, and to rebuild their lives.

Her admittedly impressionistic comments resonated with other accounts I have come across. I was once given a copy of an unpublished pilgrimage journal written by a young woman who recorded how she had turned to the pilgrimage in similar fashion, after a broken affair.[28] Takamure Itsue, who was mentioned in chapter 1, set out on her 1918 pilgrimage after an unhappy relationship, and her pilgrimage account shows that many of those she met assumed that some personal turmoil—either a vow she needed to fulfill, an illness, or some personal loss—was behind her pilgrimage.[29] Takamure later became a well-known writer and a prominent early figure in the feminist movement who wrote widely about her Shikoku experience; as such, she has come to be an inspirational model for similarly unhappy younger women. The aforesaid priest's wife emphasized this, stating that often the lovelorn female pilgrims she talked to said that they were inspired to become pilgrims after having read Takamure's work. The journalist Satō Ken, too, reports meeting a female university student who had been inspired to walk the pilgrimage after reading one of Takamure's pilgrimage books that had been given to her by her father.[30]

Takamure, through her youthful pilgrimage, has thus become a role model for young women of later eras and has created a series of inspirational footsteps for them to follow. Indeed, one of the most interesting pilgrimage accounts of modern times is that of Tsukioka Yukiko, a young woman who studied the *shamisen* and who, at the age of twenty-four, decided to do the *henro* on foot in the style of female ascetic *shamisen* players of premodern times. Tsukioka was also inspired by the example of Takamure and refers, throughout her own account, to Takamure; indeed, her very title (*Heisei musume junreiki*—Pilgrimage journal of a young woman of the Heisei [i.e., present-day] era) reflects the title of Takamure's initial pilgrimage account, *Musume junreiki* (Pilgrimage journal of a young woman).[31]

This is not to suggest that all young female pilgrims are motivated by unhappy affairs, as was, indeed, shown by the example cited in the last chapter of Araki Michio's young female student who did the *henro* as a memorial for her grandfather. Yet personal misfortune appears to be a prevalent motivation for many. Araki reports that another female student of his became a pilgrim because of personal misfortunes and torments that led her to question everything about her life and to drop out of college. She went to Shikoku, taking fifty days to walk the pilgrimage, during which time she felt all her suffering melting away. On her return she visited Araki, who comments that she was positively glowing with life. For her the pilgrimage was clearly a transformational experience—just as it was for Nakano-san's teacher and for many others who have found, in the *henro*, a means of overcoming problems and coming home renewed.[32]

Misfortunes are not, of course, limited only to female pilgrims: the aforementioned priest's wife and her son both considered that, from their encounters with hundreds of young walkers of both sexes over the years, most had become pilgrims after being beset by personal problems. There are also various cases of young males whose broken hearts have led them to Shikoku, including Nakatsuka Mōhei, the pilgrim whose extended pilgrimage between 1865–1922 began when he was prevented from marrying a girl from his village because his family considered she was not a suitable match. He then set off for Shikoku as a means of dealing with this upset—and never returned alive.[33]

Contemporary male pilgrims, too, may also be motivated by matters of the heart. In chapter 1, when I drew attention to the problems of middle-aged males who had become pilgrims after losing their jobs in the Japanese recession, I commented that some had also lost their families and homes as well. One particularly poignant case that has remained in my memory is a man, aged, it would appear, in his early fifties, whom I met near Temple 7 in April 2000. From his clean white pilgrim's clothes, new bamboo hat, and staff, I could tell that he had not been on the pilgrimage long. Indeed, he was wearing shoes more suited to an office than to a fourteen-hundred-kilometer walk, had no guidebook, and was unsure whether he was on the right path. The story he told me was that he had lost his job and thus spent more and more time at home, where he began to get into recurrent arguments with his wife, so that the marriage began to fall apart. He had walked out in the middle of one such argument and gone to stay with his daughter, but she had given him short shrift, telling him that if he wanted to rescue his marriage he needed to sort himself out first. Feeling he was the primary cause of his marital discord, he wanted to do something that would demonstrate his repentance and improve his state of being. Having seen a television program about the *henro* and heard that people did it as a way of improving themselves, he had come on impulse to Shikoku, arriving the day before and going straight to Temple 1, where he stayed overnight and purchased his pilgrim's "uniform." Now he was, as he put it, coming face-to-face with himself and his problems and was trying to work out a new way forward by getting rid of his internal anger and, through this, finding a way to repair his marriage.

His initial departure was, in other words, impulsive rather than planned —an indication that not all pilgrims plan their travels meticulously or at all (indeed, his shoes were so inappropriate for walking any distance that he knew he had to get better footwear as soon as possible) and that spontaneity, especially in reaction to personal circumstance, may also be a factor leading people along the *henro* path. It was brought about because of despair and personal misfortune coupled with the desire for repentance—a recurrent theme among pilgrims, as, indeed, the Emon Saburō story shows[34]—and the wish to reform his life so that he could make a new beginning by returning, renewed, to his wife.

Multiple performances: A lifetime of pilgrimage

The pilgrims I have cited thus far were all first-time pilgrims in Shikoku, but this does not mean that all pilgrims are of a similar ilk: as was noted in chapter 1, there are people who have done the *henro* many, even hundreds of, times. This is the case with my next pilgrim, who illustrates how people may perform the *henro* repeatedly over many years or decades—and by a variety of means—thereby acquiring status and authority.

Tabuchi Yoshio was an elderly man whom I met in Osaka in December 1990.[35] At the time Tabuchi-san was in his eighties and was a well-known and highly respected pilgrim, one of a small number who had been awarded the highest rank of *sendatsu (tokunin daisendatsu)* attainable by lay pilgrims under the system of formal rankings developed by the Shikoku Reijōkai (see chapter 5 for further details). His status accrued from a lifetime as a pilgrim, devotee of Kōbō Daishi, and steadfast leader and supporter of pilgrimage faith associations. He also had close connections with the Shikoku Reijōkai and a number of individual temples, where he would stay during his pilgrimages. He was head of the Kansai Sendatsukai (Kansai Region Association of Pilgrimage Guides), which he had helped form in 1980 and through which he helped promote the pilgrimage, and leader of the Rakushinkai, a pilgrimage faith association whose prime purpose was to organize pilgrimages in Shikoku. He also (as is often the case with such high-ranking *sendatsu* with long histories of pilgrimage behind them) had a number of close associates who regarded him as a special mentor.

Tabuchi-san came from near Tanabe in the Kii Peninsula where the cult of Kōbō Daishi was extremely strong, and he grew up hearing from his parents about how, when they had been ill and the doctor was unable to do anything for them, they had been cured through faith in and prayers to Kōbō Daishi. Then, when Tabuchi-san was twenty-one, his father was diagnosed as suffering from tuberculosis, and rather than seeking medical treatment had set out on the pilgrimage. He was cured and returned home well; the next year, 1929, he went again, this time taking Tabuchi-san with him. This was Tabuchi-san's first pilgrimage, and the impression of it and of the people he met clearly stayed with him.[36] Between then and December 1990, he made 115 pilgrimages around the island by various means.

In his earlier pilgrimages he had always walked, but as he got older he began to use buses. Unsurprisingly, by the time he was in his eighties, he always traveled this way, usually acting as guide to groups of pilgrims, leading them in prayer and instilling faith in them by recounting miracle stories. He is not unusual in having walked and used buses, for many pilgrims do the *henro* numerous times by a variety of means. On my last visit to Shikoku a priest I knew well and who knew of my particular interest in such pilgrims gave me the *fuda* of a man who had done the *henro* 166 times. According to the priest, this man had done the *henro* by foot a number of times, often engaging in arduous ascetic practices and once even doing it barefoot (he was not, however, the person mentioned earlier in this chapter), but he also had done it many times on buses and in organized tours. Kagayama Kōichi also records how, during his pilgrimage in Shikoku, he met a forty-nine-year-old man from Wakayama who had done the *henro* 102 times—60 times by foot, 23 by car, and 19 by bicycle.[37]

It is not, in other words, just that there are a variety of means by which one can do the *henro*, but that people may do it many times by different means. Perhaps more commonly this may be, as in the case of Tabuchi-san, a shift from foot to bus pilgrimages as people get older, but this is not always so. Those who travel by bus may be stimulated to do it again on foot, intrigued by the possibility of seeing the *henro* through a different lens. A sixty-four-year-old female pilgrim from Osaka made this point in a newspaper interview in June 2001, saying that she had done the pilgrimage three times by bus and car and had enjoyed observing the Shikoku scenery through vehicle windows. However, she felt she was missing something and so decided to walk next time, as a result of which her perspective on the pilgrimage landscape had altered and she had acquired a new realm of experiences by noticing all manner of small yet significant things, such as the sounds of insects or the presence of ants as she walked on mountain paths.[38]

Tabuchi-san still expended a great deal of energy on the pilgrimage and maintained an active schedule. In the 1980s and early 1990s he was doing it around five or six times a year by bus, which meant being on the road for close to sixty days per year, a considerable investment of time and energy for a man in his eighties.[39] Much of the time between trips was spent preparing for the next one or taking part in activities related to his position as a *sendatsu* and head of the Rakushinkai and Kansai Sendatsukai. It was, indeed, at one such event (which will be discussed in chapter 5) that I met and interviewed him. He had done several other pilgrimages in Japan, but Shikoku remained the main one for him because of its special nature and the power of Kōbō Daishi. One could, he asserted, attain enlightenment (*satori*) and receive countless benefits (*go-riyaku*) from doing the pilgrimage. Indeed, he told me, if one were sick it would be better to do the pilgrimage than go to the doctor—a sentiment he doubtless imbibed from his parents and their tales of the healing powers of Kōbō Daishi.

Of all the pilgrimages he knew in Japan, the *henro* was the one, in his view, that people were most likely to do again and again, a point I, too, affirm from my studies of Japanese pilgrimage.[40] Certainly his own pilgrimage career showed this, as of course does the case of Nakatsuka Mōhei. I also met several others among Tabuchi-san's colleagues in the Kansai Sendatsukai who had done the *henro* dozens of times, and I have also been given numerous gold *fuda* by pilgrims I have met, indicating that they have done the *henro* fifty times or more. Many of the pilgrims who appear in this book have done the *henro* many times, not simply because I have found the stories and experiences of such multiple pilgrims to be especially resonant, but because such people are numerous and a prominent part of the pilgrim community.

This is evident, too, from the growing numbers of people who have attained the title and rank of *sendatsu* from the Shikoku Reijōkai. To qualify as a *sendatsu* one has to complete the *henro* at least four times; in 2000 there were over seven thousand people registered as *sendatsu,* many of whom had been promoted to higher ranks within the system, thereby indicating that they had done the pilgrimage several more times still.[41] The numbers of such people are growing year by year: through the 1990s the number went up by several hundred per year. Many of those who go by bus also go back again (and again), as was affirmed by officials of bus companies such as Iyo Tetsu, Setouchi, and Kotosan, all of which ferry large numbers of pilgrims around Shikoku. Officials of these firms estimate that around 40–50 percent of the pilgrims who participate in their regular scheduled pilgrimage tours are doing it for the second time or more.[42] This does not mean that each of their multiple performances is a repetition of a previous pilgrimage. Rather, as Tabuchi-san has commented, for him each performance of the *henro* is a new experience; the pilgrimage is not so much repeated as made anew each time he travels.[43]

Multiplicity and motivations

There are numerous reasons why pilgrims do the *henro* time and again. In the pilgrims' eyes, doing it bestows spiritual merit on the performer, which can thereby assist him/her to attain all manner of benefits ranging from good fortune to salvation. By doing it repeatedly, Tabuchi-san emphasized, one piles up merit. This practice of performing rituals and other such acts many times so as to pile up merit has a long history in the Buddhism of East Asia, seen in acts such as performing multiple prostrations or recitations of mantras and sutras, and multiple performances of the *henro* can be seen in the same light.[44] Many of the pilgrims I have talked to think similarly, believing that each pilgrimage they do helps them accrue spiritual merit and eradicate negative karma and that therefore doing it again and again will enable them to build up increased merit. Perhaps this point was made in its most extreme form by a young man my wife and I met in the courtyard of Temple 83 in 1984 as we were nearing the end of our forty-day pilgrimage. He was doing the *henro* by car, and, rather than making any comments about how good it must be to walk (a common refrain from those who travel by car and bus), he chided us for using such a means of travel. If we would only go by car, he said, we could do the *henro* six times in the time it took to walk and thereby accrue six times as much merit!

Devotion to Kōbō Daishi is another important factor in multiple performances of pilgrimage: for pilgrims such as Tabuchi-san, Kōbō Daishi is the guiding light of their lives, and the *henro* is thus an act of devotion through which they can express their faith in him. Repetition is therefore an expression of continuing or increased devotion. Gratitude is also a recurrent motif, with many pilgrims motivated to do it again and again in order to give thanks for benefits received. Tabuchi's father is an example of someone who, believing he was cured by Kōbō Daishi during his first pilgrimage, became eternally grateful thereafter and made his subsequent pilgrimage with his son as a journey of gratitude and thanks.

Multiple performances are also a way of acquiring special status. Being able to acquire the rank of *sendatsu* spurs some to do the *henro* many times, while ardent pilgrims such as Tabuchi-san can acquire exalted status for such reasons. There is also, I consider, an element of competition involved in such multiple performances—a point suggested by Nakatsuka Mōhei's commemoration of his 137th circuit, which, he believed, meant he had done it more times than anyone else—as well as an element of peer pressure. People such as Tabuchi-san and his associates spend much of their time with others who do the *henro* repeatedly, and hence they exist in a milieu in which recurrent pilgrimages are a norm. Thus they are consistently encouraged to keep doing it themselves and in turn are consistently encouraging, by example, others to do so as well.

One of the most compelling reasons for multiple performances, however, may be the simple fact that pilgrims like doing it and hence want to experience it again. One should never underestimate the importance of simple enjoyment when seeking to explain or understand behavior. Certainly many of the pilgrims I have met liked the experience so much that they wanted to do it again—a point that surfaced, for example, in the pilgrimage party I discuss in chapter 7. This enjoyment may lead to what might be termed a form of addiction, in which the *henro* becomes such a captivating and beguiling experience that pilgrims are driven to return again and again. Indeed, I have heard priests and pilgrims alike use the term *"Shikoku byō"* (Shikoku sickness/disease) to refer to this tendency.[45] This "sickness" will recur again in later chapters, notably chapter 8, where I discuss pilgrims who devote their entire lives to the *henro*. Tabuchi-san, with his 115 circuits and constant involvement with the *henro*, clearly was someone deeply affected by the "Shikoku disease," as were those around him for whom repeated performances of the *henro* were the norm rather than the exception. As will be seen also in chapter 7, the disease seems readily transmitted, indeed contagious: by the end of the pilgrimage tour described there, all the pilgrims in the party were talking of coming again to Shikoku.

As a result of his pilgrimage activities, Tabuchi-san has acquired a special status among pilgrims. He commands the respect of temple priests in Shikoku, too, because of his work in promoting the pilgrimage and in inspiring others to do it and because he is the leader of a pilgrimage faith group and has a group of people around him who regard him as a mentor and spiritual leader. (I should note, too, that Tabuchi-san also spoke to me of other pilgrims who, he considered, were more experienced than he and who he regarded as his spiritual mentors). In this way he forms part of a continuing lineage of inspirational figures who, taking their cue from Kōbō Daishi, follow in his footsteps to promote a tradition of faith framed by a narrative of miracles. In such terms Tabuchi-san has himself been transformed into a holy figure to be venerated by other pilgrims.

Tabuchi-san has carried the same pilgrim's book (nōkyōchō) with him since he began his travels. Each time he visits a temple in Shikoku he gets it stamped, with the result that every page of the book, when I was shown it in 1990, was red, due the number of times it has been stamped with the red ink of temple seals. Tabuchi-san considered that the book had acquired a sacred power because of the accumulated merit of the stamps and that it protected him from misfortune and sickness. To those around him, too, the book was a marvelous object and a source of spiritual power, as were the gold fuda he gave to others; they were, one of his disciples informed me, objects of special power, akin to the amulets (o-mamori) one could get at temples that could protect one from misfortunes and even cure illness.

Local traditions, inherited influences

My next example builds on the theme of lifelong pilgrimage by showing how highly motivated pilgrims may create localized pilgrimage traditions that are handed on down the generations and that embed the practice of the henro into the culture of their local communities. My focus here is on a pilgrimage association called the Shiga Shingyōkai (Shiga Faith and Practice Association), based at Nagahama in Shiga Prefecture northeast of Kyoto, and on Naitō Hirozō, its leader when I visited the association in March 1991, and his father, Naitō Kinpō,[46] the association's founder. Naitō Hirozō's position as head of the association—and his connections with the henro itself— stemmed from the activities of his deceased father, and they tell us much about how, in pilgrimage contexts, authority and status may be passed down the generations and how such practices and devotional cults may be inherited from one's parents.

The story of the Shiga Shingyōkai, as it was told to me by members of the association (and as it is recounted in the volume they have published about their organization), starts with Naitō Kinpō's first pilgrimage to Shikoku in 1923.[47] He did this through a mixture of despair and hope: he had tuberculosis, and medical treatment had failed to improve his situation. Hence, aged twenty-eight and seeking a way out of his troubles, he decided to go to Shikoku in search of Kōbō Daishi's grace. Doubtless he was also impelled by the notion, not uncommon among walkers, that the sheer exercise of walking would play a part in making his condition better. During his pilgrimage his illness disappeared, and he returned home believing himself cured by the miraculous grace of Kōbō Daishi. He henceforth became a dedicated pilgrim, walking the pilgrimage again on a number of occasions, including in 1927 with his new wife soon after their marriage, when they slept out and begged for alms. (This, incidentally, is not the only example I have come across of couples doing the *henro* on their honeymoons: in 1984 my wife and I stayed overnight at the *bangai* temple Ikiki Jizō in Ehime Prefecture and spent the evening talking with the priest and his wife there. They also told us that they had walked the pilgrimage on their honeymoon, taking close to three months to do so, and had begged for alms and slept out when no accommodation was available—even though they had done it in winter. Like Naitō Kinpō's wife, the priest's wife from Ikiki Jizō spoke warmly of the experience.)

Naitō later did the *henro* by foot again in 1935 with his son, then aged nine. He also became active in promoting the pilgrimage and the virtues of Kōbō Daishi in the Nagahama area, so that others were encouraged to go to Shikoku. During the 1930s, the Shingyōkai developed as a faith-based association, and members began to walk together on group pilgrimages—a practice that continued, after a hiatus during and after World War II, until the 1970s, when they began to use buses for organized group pilgrimages. Naitō's endeavors were facilitated by a priest from Anrakuji (Temple 6) who gave him a statue of Dainichi Nyorai (the main Buddhist figure of worship in Shingon Buddhism). Naitō carried it back to Nagahama and installed it there in a hall of worship that Shingyōkai members had built on land provided by a devotee. This became the headquarters of the Shingyōkai and is where devotees meet regularly and hold services, especially on the twenty-first of the month (Kōbō Daishi's holy day). The association founded by Naitō has grown into a fairly substantial group, with branches throughout the prefecture and a membership, in the 1990s, of around one thousand people.

Naitō Kinpō built the association up through personal example and spiritual leadership; many elderly members spoke warmly of Naitō's inspirational guidance, even attributing to him miraculous healing experiences they had received. Two men spoke to me of how family members—one a child, the other a wife—had been ill but had been cured through the grace of Kōbō Daishi and the assistance of Naitō. Naitō's importance to members of the association is reflected in a large statue they have had made of him, which stands alongside—and which is similar in size to—a statue of Kōbō Daishi in the courtyard of their hall of worship. Thus while the association was focused on Kōbō Daishi and the *henro,* its now deceased founder has also become a focus of reverence and source of miracles.

When Naitō Kinpō died in 1973, his son Hirozō took over as head of the association. In 1991, when I met him, Hirozō's son was deputy head of the Shingyōkai and destined to be its next leader, while his mother—Naitō Kinpō's wife—continued to be involved in the running of the group. Naitō Hirozō, as has already been mentioned, first did the *henro* in 1935 as a boy accompanying his father. He then did it on foot in 1946 after returning from

Manchuria, where he had been sent on military service at the end of World War II. According to Hirozō, many of his companions were killed, and he made a vow to Kōbō Daishi that if he were to survive he would do the *henro* as a gesture of thanks. Subsequently, he has continued to perform the *henro*, to carry on his father's activities, and to bring his own son up in the family tradition of pilgrimage.

The Naitō family and the Shiga Shingyōkai have developed particularly strong links with Anrakuji (Temple 6), the temple from which Naitō Kinpō received the image of Dainichi enshrined in the Shingyōkai's hall of worship. Naitō formed a close friendship with the temple's former head priest (Hatada Zuihō), who had given him the Dainichi statue; his son Hirozō became close to Hatada Zenpō (the now deceased successor to Zuihō at Anrakuji), and Hirozō's son has become close to Hatada Shuhō, Zenpō's son and successor. There has thus been a continuing relationship between temple and pilgrimage association that has passed on down the generations. This relationship, too, illustrates how the pilgrimage temples and their priests can play a role in building the pilgrimage community, for the friendship and support of the Hatada family and their temple have given great assistance to the Naitō family and their pilgrimage association and have contributed greatly to the embedding of pilgrimage faith among the local community in the Nagahama region.

The Shingyōkai maintains an active schedule through regular worship in Nagahama and through events beyond the immediate region, such as an annual visit to Kōbō Daishi's mausoleum at Kōyasan.[48] It also organizes several pilgrimage trips a year, including a complete circuit of the route that is done in two sections by bus, from Temple 1 to Temple 36 in autumn and from Temple 37 to Temple 88 in spring. This usually attracts a party of around one hundred people. A walking pilgrimage of the Awa temples (1–23) also takes place in March each year, while twice a year, during the school holidays in late March and in July, they organize a children's pilgrimage. The children's pilgrimages (which started in 1958) usually involve around one hundred children and about twenty or so adults, last for around five days at a time, and follow the pilgrimage path in the Awa region. They do this section of the pilgrimage because it is the closest geographically to Shiga and because it is easily walked since the temples are close together and the route well marked. The main emphasis in the children's pilgrimage is on exercise and walking, and they deliberately downplay any religious imagery by getting the children to wear everyday clothing. Members believe that emphasizing the religious connotations of the pilgrimage by asking children to wear *hakui* is more likely to put the children off than encourage them and thus would be counterproductive in the long term.

The children's clothing is the one instance where the association and the priests of Anrakuji appear to have different views, with the priests feeling that the children should be asked to wear *hakui*. The dispute, however, is good-natured and reflects a mild difference of opinion rather than any serious conflict between two institutions with close relations and mutual interests. Even though the Shingyōkai downplays any religious imagery in the children's pilgrimage, stories of miraculous events and cures are never far from members' minds even in this context, and I was told stories of how sick children taking part in the pilgrimage had experienced sudden cures as a result.

Many members of the Shingyōkai are affiliated with the Jōdo Shin (True Pure Land) Buddhist sect, which has traditionally been strong in the Shiga region. For members, however, such "official" sectarian affiliation relates primarily to customary practices of caring for the dead and memorializing their ancestors and is of little relevance in terms of their faith in Kōbō Daishi or their pilgrimages. It indicates, again, that the pilgrimage goes across sectarian barriers: although Jōdo Shin followers are not, according to their sectarian tenets, supposed to engage in worshiping figures such as Kōbō Daishi or in practices such as the *henro*, many do so. According to the Waseda survey, around 13 percent of Shikoku pilgrims are affiliated with the Jōdo Shin sect, the second highest rate of affiliation after Shingon.[49]

The Shingyōkai members I met were, like Naitō Hirozō, mostly in their sixties or above and came from a variety of occupations, including schoolteachers, farmers, railway workers, housewives, and retirees. Most had been doing the pilgrimage many times, over many years, with the group. Some had inherited the *henro* tradition from their parents, were second- or third-generation members of the Shingyōkai, and were actively engaged in passing on the tradition to their own offspring. They saw organized events such as the children's pilgrimage as vitally important for continuing the *henro* custom in the region and building the foundations for the future. As such, the Shiga Shingyōkai is an example of how pilgrimage customs and practices may be part of a local religious culture, passed on from generation to generation, and of how pilgrimage traditions may be carried on outside the immediate geographical region of the pilgrimage sites themselves.

The Shingyōkai is only one of a number of faith associations outside Shikoku that are focused on the *henro* and that have developed the culture of pilgrimage within their local communities. Other examples include the Arita Settaikō, a faith association based in Wakayama Prefecture that specializes in organizing annual collections of goods and food that it then takes to Shikoku to distribute as alms to Shikoku pilgrims. Like the Shingyōkai, the Arita Settaikō was founded by a local man who made a pilgrimage in Shikoku and then returned fired with devotion to his home village, where he established a tradition of alms gathering for the benefit of Shikoku pilgrims. Like the Shingyōkai, too, the Arita association has helped pass on its tradition of pilgrimage support through the generations, as well as established its own Daishi hall of worship at which community-based events and regular worship services occur. The main image in this hall of worship was given to the association in 1910 by Ryōzenji (Temple 1), with which the Arita Settaikō has a particularly strong and continuing bond. It also maintains a hall in the precincts of Ryōzenji, where members stay each year while they distribute alms to pilgrims.[50] The Arita Settaikō and the Shiga Shingyōkai are thus reminders that pilgrimage is not simply related to transitory visits to and around holy places, but may be something with deep roots in local communities that may be inherited through one's community and familial connections. The connections between these associations and particular temples on the route also illustrate how pilgrimage sites and pilgrims need not exist in a context of tension and contest, but can engage in a continuing relationship that is mutually supportive and rewarding.

Through the generations: Family, inheritance, and motivation in the pilgrimage

The case of Naitō Kinpō and the Shingyōkai provides a further example of how ardent pilgrims can acquire spiritual status through their pilgrimage deeds and how they can create their own traditions of pilgrimage and veneration. It also points to the importance of inherited customs within pilgrimage: while pilgrimage may be something spontaneously engaged in by the desperate, the sick, and those seeking temporary escape from society, it may also be something that is deeply rooted in their cultural lives and inherited family traditions. Pilgrims, in short, may well, like Naitō Hirozō, become pilgrims because their parents and relatives were pilgrims.

One can find numerous examples of this pattern in the contributions made by pilgrims to the monthly newsletter *Henro*. Thus in an article in March 1989 titled "Watakushi no nōkyōchō" (My pilgrim's book), Kondō Tō recounts how his grandfather sold one of his rice fields in 1899 so that he could make a pilgrimage in Shikoku, which took him sixty days. On his death in 1916 he gave his pilgrim's book to Kondō's parents, asking them to pass it on down the generations of their family and to carry on the tradition of doing the *henro*. Kondō thus inherited both the practice and book from his parents and in 1964 did the *henro* for the first time (he has done it several times since), carrying his grandfather's book with him. He recounts, too, how this book formed another link with the past in that the official who stamped the book at one temple recognized the calligraphy in it as having been done by the wife of a previous temple priest.[51]

In December 1989 *Henro* reported that an eighteen-year-old female high school student, Asabukawa Satomi, had just become the youngest ever *sendatsu* in Shikoku. She, too, had imbibed the custom from her family, first being taken around the pilgrimage by her family when she was a baby and then as a child. Later, she joined organized pilgrimage groups, and by the time she turned eighteen she had done the *henro* over ten times.[52] In an article in *Henro* in 1988, Matsuura Harutake spoke of how, on the occasion of his one hundredth pilgrimage, he celebrated the event with his family by taking his wife, daughter, son, and grandchildren, as well as various friends and associates, with him on a special commemorative pilgrimage.[53] The tradition of pilgrimage has been passed on through the Matsuura family, as became clear to me when his son sent me a copy of the journal he had kept of this occasion, which emphasized the family's long standing *henro* tradition in which several members had become *sendatsu*.[54]

Priests in Shikoku have frequently commented to me about this practice of passing on the custom of pilgrimage to one's offspring. In April 2000, the head priest at Taisanji (Temple 52) told me that the summer school-holiday period is quite busy for temples because of the numbers of families who come as pilgrims with their children. Asabukawa's experiences of initially being taken on pilgrimage as a baby are not uncommon either; I have frequently come across family groups at the temples carrying babies for whose benefit they are traveling. Such familial and generation-based traditions may be especially strong among the people of Shikoku. When I examined the *osamefuda* left at one of the *henro* temples in Tokushima Prefecture, I repeatedly came across them stapled together in bunches. Each separate *fuda* bore the name and age of one pilgrim, and the fact that every one in the bunch bore the same surname indicated that they had been written by a family group. The ages given showed that normally these were extended family groups spanning a number (often three, but occasionally four) of generations. Almost always, too, these family groups came from Shikoku. Thus one family from Takamatsu in northern Shikoku, evidently a four-generation family group traveling together, had left *osamefuda* all bearing the same surname: a female (aged eighty-three), a male and female aged fifty-six and fifty-one respectively, a male and female aged thirty-four and thirty-three respectively, and two children, a girl of seven and a boy of five. Another set had been left by the Kawasaki family of Marugame, Shikoku, consisting of a male (clearly the grandfather) aged seventy, a couple (husband and wife) both aged thirty-six, and a son aged fourteen. Sometimes the bunches of *osamefuda* stapled together gave names and Shikoku addresses for those of the older generation, but with a Tokyo or Osaka address for the younger ones, suggesting that the offspring had—as is common in an era of regional depopulation—left home and gone to study or work in the main cities but had returned home to do some or all of the pilgrimage with their parents, perhaps as a marker of regional and familial identity. This may possibly also be a residue or continuation of a local initiatory tradition that endured in premodern Shikoku and that will be discussed in chapter 4.

While the influence of previous generations can be exceptionally important in making people into pilgrims, it does not mean that succeeding generations necessarily have the same motivations as their parents or relatives. For
example, at Temple 38 at Cape Ashizuri in March 1991 I met a man in his
mid- to late forties with a party of pilgrims in a minibus. It was, he said, his
twenty-sixth pilgrimage; he had done his first pilgrimage at the age of twenty-
two or twenty-three (he could not remember which) and now did it every
year, always by car or bus since he ran a small business and had no time to
walk. Often, as on this occasion, he acted as the leader of a party of pilgrims.
He had inherited the custom of pilgrimage from his parents, who initially did
the *henro* on foot and then later did it well over one hundred times each by
car or bus. Yet, interestingly, he had a rather different perspective on the
henro than them. His parents, he reported, had done it so often out of a deep-
seated, Kōbō Daishi–centered folk faith, which, he said, was part of the common consciousness of their pre-1945 era generation. By contrast, he felt little
such faith, despite having grown up in a household in which the *henro* was

Family pilgrimages and passing on the pilgrimage tradition: couple with baby on the
pilgrimage.

considered a normal part of family life. He was, however, deeply conscious of what he saw as modern society's lack of spiritual roots, and hence, in seeking to deal with his own sense of unease, felt it natural to turn, in his early twenties, to the pilgrimage tradition that ran in his family. While his pilgrimages were, he said, fueled by the wish to find his own spiritual roots, they were also focused on trying to understand more about his parents, who had done the *henro* so many times.

In such terms, many of those who become pilgrims in Shikoku are influenced by their parents and family backgrounds, as well as by the communities they live in. Where there are strong local or regional pilgrimage associations—as in the area where the Naitō family live, where members of the Arita Settaikō live in rural Wakayama, or in Shikoku itself—the potential to become a pilgrim may be enhanced. Equally, when one's parents or grandparents have done the *henro,* or where there is a strong family tradition of Kōbō Daishi veneration, one may inherit—and pass on—a tradition of pilgrimage. In such cases the pilgrims may not have any clear motivation (in terms of an immediate goal or need) for doing the pilgrimage, but may be engaged in it primarily because it is a part of their way of life and of their cultural and familial inheritance. Inherited tradition can thus be a crucial element in the pilgrimage dynamic, providing a thread of continuity through which participants from different generations can join together in a shared endeavor.

Pilgrims by bus: Temporary communities, escape, and cultural belonging

Going by bus on organized tours is nowadays the most common way of doing the *henro.* The Waseda survey shows that at least 70 percent of all pilgrims in the late 1990s went by bus or car, with virtually half (49 percent in all) doing it in the company of eleven or more people—a clear indication of the dominant position of organized bus pilgrimage tours.[55] Such pilgrimage tour groups may be—like the Shiga Shingyōkai pilgrimage parties that travel around Shikoku each spring and autumn—organized by faith or regional associations, or they may be groups organized by a Buddhist temple, led by its priest and consisting of temple parishioners. Others still may be parties organized by companies such as Iyo Tetsu, which run regular tours to which people may sign up individually.

Sawamura-san, a thirty-three-year-old woman working at a museum in Tokyo, was such a person. I met her while she was traveling as one of thirty-three pilgrims on one of Iyo Tetsu's monthly pilgrimage tours in 1990. It was her first pilgrimage, and she was one of the youngest in the party, most of whom were over sixty. However, she did not find this a problem and had enjoyed traveling with older people—so much, indeed, that she had determined to do it again the next year, a sentiment expressed also by several other pilgrims on this same bus. Although traveling alone, she had found good companions in the bus party and had formed a temporary social bond with them—enough to make them talk of meeting up on pilgrimage again the next year. She had booked with Iyo Tetsu because she had no experience of the pilgrimage but knew of the company's reputation, and hence could leave the details of travel to them while getting on with enjoying her pilgrimage without worry.

Her reasons for doing the pilgrimage were multiple, although her primary concern was with nature and the environment. Living in Tokyo, she felt distant from nature and had been drawn to the pilgrimage because she felt that Shikoku was still predominantly a natural environment where she could enjoy beautiful scenery and fresh air; she was particularly enthusiastic about the Kōchi coastline. She also said that her cat had recently died and that her pilgrimage was thus also a memorial *(kuyō)* for her pet.[56] A further reason for her journey was that she was thirty-three—the unlucky year *(yakudoshi)* for women—and hence she was doing it at this time to ward off danger. Also, she was getting a pilgrimage scroll stamped during her journey and planned to use it as a protective talisman at her home, hung up in an appropriate place to ward off bad luck.[57]

Like Sawamura-san, Koyama-san—a retired insurance broker from Osaka in his late sixties—was also traveling individually but had joined a small pilgrimage party run by a company from Osaka. He, too, had forged a temporary bond with his traveling companions. Koyama-san will feature again in chapter 7, when I describe the pilgrimage tour he (and I) went on in November 1990. He became my closest companion on that tour, although he also got on well and interacted with the other pilgrims too. He was doing the *henro* in sections, by the *ikkoku mairi* method, and this was his third visit to the island; he planned to complete the pilgrimage the next year with the same pilgrimage travel firm. The temporary bonds that developed in the party, all of whom he had traveled with before on his previous *ikkoku mairi* visit, were clearly important to him, and he was keen to establish if there would be a chance of meeting up again with these companions on subsequent outings.

Koyama-san made it clear that his main interest was not in praying, and I can barely recall him speaking about a sense of personal faith in Kōbō Daishi during the three days we traveled together. Of the entire group he was the least focused on devotional activities and often only engaged in cursory prayers at the temples before wandering off to take photographs. He was a keen photographer who carried several cameras and took dozens of rolls of film during the three days we were together. His main focus was the natural scenery of Shikoku and the surroundings of the old temples, which presented him with an ideal opportunity for engaging in his hobby. He was also moved by the natural environment of Shikoku and wanted to spend time experiencing it while having a temporary break from his normal routines and family life. Although retired, he still felt constrained (as do many older Japanese) by social and cultural pressures into feeling that taking holidays is a rather self-ish and indulgent practice. Thus the pilgrimage was ideal for his purposes: he could essentially make a brief escape from home, have a holiday, experience the scenery, engage in his hobby, and yet swathe that escape in a veneer of respectability by emphasizing that he was going on a pilgrimage to pray for his family. He also felt that engaging with his cultural traditions through the *henro* was a means of self-development through which he could learn more about his own society and about himself.

Koyama-san is not untypical of many pilgrims past and present. In pre-modern times, the Japanese feudal authorities that placed severe restrictions on travel in order to keep a tight rein on society largely absolved those who wanted to travel for religious purposes to important temples and shrines. Hence pilgrimage provided one of the few (if not the only) opportunities or excuses for getting away to see the world beyond the confines of one's vill-age or local community.[58] Even in the modern day, when there are no legal restraints on travel, some people—and this appears especially so for older-generation Japanese—still feel the pressure of social constraints and are reluc-tant to simply go traveling. For such people—and Koyama-san clearly was of this ilk—the Shikoku pilgrimage, with its abundance of natural beauty and its resonant images (strongly reinforced and promoted in recent times by pro-grams such as those put out by NHK) of tradition, fills a need and offers the chance of getting away in an acceptable cultural framework.

Koyama-san was also very keen to get a completed pilgrimage scroll, and he talked about how, once he had finished, he would have it embossed, mounted, and hung up at home. It was not, for him, an object of devotion but of artistic beauty, and a representation of his accomplishment in doing the pilgrimage. Getting the scroll, in other words, was an essential part of his pil-grimage and intrinsic to his motives. Koyama-san, in such terms, was a pil-grim more clearly driven by motivations such as the desire to escape, to take photographs, and to bring home a beautiful commemorative scroll than any-thing else. However, he chose the medium of pilgrimage as the most appro-priate and satisfying way to express such feelings; simply to become a tourist and go, for instance, to a famous resort where he could relax and take pho-tographs would not have been adequate or appropriate to his purposes and inclinations.

Something to do together: Couples, worldly benefits, and ancestral offerings

Bus pilgrims such as Sawamura-san and Koyama-san, who travel individu-ally, are in something of a minority compared to those who are accompanied by friends, close relatives, or family members, with the most common of all such companions, according to surveys, being a spouse.[58] The Matsudas, both aged sixty-four, both from Osaka, and traveling in the same party as Koyama-san and myself, were good examples of this. They were on their final leg of a four-stage pilgrimage, having done the other three sections on previous tours with the same company, but they were already talking, as our party ended its journey, about doing the *henro* again in a similar manner, in a small group by minibus.

Sometimes, when one encounters people doing the *henro* together, it is because one of them has particular wishes or needs that they seek through the pilgrimage, while the other is going along primarily as a companion. This was the case with two middle-aged women I briefly walked with on the path between Temples 18 and 19 in April 2000. One of them told me they were both from Shikoku but that it was really she who was doing the pilgrimage—as a series of "day trips" in which she would drive to a set point on the route, walk for the day, then take public transport back to the car and drive home. The next time she would drive to where she had finished on the previous occasion. She was doing it as a memorial for her mother, who had died three years earlier. Her companion had no specific motives, save that she had been asked by her friend to come along to keep her company. While she claimed to have no real purpose other than friendship, she was, however, carrying a scroll, which she was getting stamped at each temple, so that she would have a memento of the journey.

The Matsudas, by contrast, appeared to have a set of shared purposes to their pilgrimage. They were both keen on visiting temples and shrines and regularly went to such places in the Osaka region where they lived, especially those that had great historical or cultural meaning and value. They always got a pilgrim's book or scroll stamped at the temples they visited, and they were looking forward to completing their Shikoku scroll on this journey. They were partially retired and could leave their family business (a shop) in the care of a grown-up daughter. Hence they were beginning to have some free time and saw pilgrimages as a means by which they could enjoy that time together. Making pilgrimages was thus something of an emergent retirement hobby for them.

They combined this hobby with practical prayer and worship, praying for the welfare of their ancestors and hoping that the merit they gained through the pilgrimage could benefit the spirits of their departed kin. They also sought and prayed for practical benefits in three areas: their own continued good health, the prosperity of their family business, and the education success of their grandchildren. To facilitate their prayers they carried with them a large number of copies of the *Hannya Shingyō*, which they, their family, and friends had made prior to their departure and which they offered at the temples they visited. In this way, their family and friends were included with them as they prayed and were surrogate participants in their pilgrimage.

Praying for worldly benefits is a major element in the religious culture of Japan, one of the most common of all activities at Buddhist temples, while figures such as Kōbō Daishi are particularly highly regarded because of their reputed capacity for working miracles and for interceding to assist humans in this world.[60] For pilgrims, too, such prayer requests are highly important elements within their travels, a point that can be seen through an examination of the requests that pilgrims may write, along with their names and other details, on the *osamefuda* they leave at temples. A study I carried out on *osamefuda* left at one pilgrimage temple in 1990 indicates that around one-sixth of all such have written prayer requests on them.[61] The most commonly requested benefits were, in order: good health, the benefit of the ancestors, family safety, healing/recovery from illness, travel safety, education success, and finding a good marriage partner and related matters (e.g., conceiving children and safe childbirth).[62] Other, less widely cited requests included prevention of misfortune and prayers for *mizuko* (the spirits of babies who die in the womb, usually because of abortion). Often such prayers correlate with the ages of those who write them: younger people and children, for instance, are more likely to seek education success than to ask for good health, while the general prevalence of prayers for good health in itself reflects the age profile of the pilgrimage community. My survey correlates to a great degree with an earlier study by Tanaka Hiroshi in 1973 that examined 1,552 *osamefuda* at two temples and found that family safety, business prosperity, health, traffic safety, education success, and the like were the main items sought.[63]

The Matsudas' requests (good health, business prosperity, and education success for their grandchildren) thus reflect a fairly normative array of requests sought by pilgrims. Praying for such benefits is so common among pilgrims that it should be considered one of the standard elements of the *henro*; indeed, one *expects* pilgrims to do this. Mr. Matsuda took a pragmatic view on this point, and, like most pilgrims I have met, he felt that if one is going to do the pilgrimage and be at the temples, one might as well seek such graces and favors from Kōbō Daishi. Few pilgrims I have talked to in Shikoku have excluded the idea of praying for practical benefits from their motives and focuses: members of the Shingyōkai, for example, emphasized that a primary motive behind their Shikoku pilgrimages—and a central element in the prayers they offered at the temples—centered on practical, worldly benefits.

Pilgrims without motive? Learning along the way

Although I have thus far introduced a number of pilgrims and the reasons they had assumed the mantle of Shikoku pilgrims, this does not mean that all pilgrims in Shikoku necessarily have clearly defined motivations or know why they are doing the *henro*. In a sense this issue has been encountered when I introduced the phenomenon of those who have inherited the custom of pilgrimage from their parents and families and who may thus find themselves doing the *henro* without really knowing why they did so. Sometimes, too, pilgrims appear to have, or are unable to, articulate a reason or motive for their journeys.

This appeared to be the case, for instance, with a sixty-eight-year-old man from Takarazuka near Osaka whom I met in October 1990, when we both stayed overnight at one temple. He was traveling on a 50 cc moped and carried a video camera with him with which to record his experiences and to film the temples and the activities going on at them. He also carried a scroll with him that, he said, would be a souvenir and reminder *(kinen)* of his journey. However, when he was asked, in the course of a three-way conversation with myself and another pilgrim in the same room, why he was doing the pilgrimage, he appeared unable to answer, stating several times that he had no idea or motive, nor any clear plan of how long it would take to complete it. He was doing the pilgrimage in stages, a few days at a time, but had no specific plan of how long he would spend on the road each time. Despite his apparent vagueness, however, he did reveal some worries about his health, and especially about his heart, to the extent that, reading between the lines, I concluded that he was probably doing the pilgrimage either to pray for good health or in order to accrue merit that would help him after death—or perhaps both—but that he was either reluctant to say categorically what his motives were or was just unclear about them.

Such reluctance is not uncommon. Indeed, I have even, on occasion, come across people who have initially denied that they were pilgrims. My wife and I, for instance, met a young man on a bicycle while we were walking the *henro* in 1984. We met him a number of times either at places where we stayed overnight, in the courtyard of temples, and, on one occasion, along the highway as he cycled past us, stopping briefly to chat. He was, he told us, a student using the university vacation to cycle around the island, and he just happened to be stopping at the temples because they offered useful reference points on his journey and because they were interesting places to see. He insisted, however, that he was not a pilgrim, and he was not wearing pilgrim's clothing—although he did have a pilgrim's book that was, he said, going to be a souvenir of his trip. Toward the end of our journey—near Temple 85—we found ourselves staying in the same lodge again, but this time he had completed his circuit and was on his way back home. At this point he came over to talk to us and to tell us that yes, indeed, he was doing the *henro* but that he had previously not wanted to talk about it or engage in discussion about his feelings. While he was still doing the pilgrimage he felt unable to speak about it or articulate any clear idea of why he was doing it. Indeed, he had wanted to keep his very engagement in the venture secret, and it was only now, after having completed the circuit, that he felt able to talk about it and start understanding why he had done it.

Sometimes pilgrims are less than clear about why they are doing their pilgrimages whilst they were en route—but are more able to speak about them afterward. One pilgrim I met on the road, for example, did not want to talk about his pilgrimage (apart from telling me that he had no religious faith [mushūkyōshin]) because he did not feel capable of talking about the henro while he was in the middle of it. He did, however, take my phone number and say he would get back to me later. A couple of weeks afterward he did, indeed, call up and invite me to visit him, at which point he readily opened up about his pilgrimage, talking of how he had decided to do it in his retirement, both as "something to do"—as a way of keeping fit and getting in touch with nature and with Japan's cultural heritage—and as a way of learning about himself and storing up karmic merit for when he died. He had also read quite a bit about the henro (including Takamure's writings) and felt that the essence of pilgrimage was in whom one met on the route. As such, our meeting had been, for him, symbolic of the essence of pilgrimage—a reason he had been willing to get in touch with me again and to invite me, my wife, and daughter to his house to talk about the henro.[64] Even the Matsudas—whose multiple motivations I have mentioned above—said that they were still learning, as they were doing the henro, why they were doing it and were still finding more reasons for doing it. As will be mentioned in chapter 7, it was when the party they and I were traveling with had completed its journey after visiting Temple 88 that some members of the party really wanted to talk openly about their motives and intentions.

There is a sense here in which doing the pilgrimage is a learning process through which participants "become" pilgrims and, as they do, come to understand why they are doing it. The man cited earlier who was "carrying" his deceased wife in his rucksack expressed this view by saying that even though he had a clear motive in doing the pilgrimage "with" his wife, he remained unsure as to how to behave as a pilgrim and what his pilgrimage was, deep down, really all about, but that he thought he would find out as he went along. He was, in effect, becoming a pilgrim through the process of doing the pilgrimage: as he did so, his understandings of why he was doing it and what it meant were developing. Pilgrims may have reasons that lead them to take on the mantle of the pilgrim, but they may in effect only learn how to become pilgrims—and why they are pilgrims—while they are in the process of doing the henro. They may, like the young cyclist mentioned above, become more confident of talking about their journeys, motives, and experiences as they grow in experience and when they complete the henro. One should not assume that pilgrims' motivations are necessarily determined only prior to departure, for it is often through the process of doing the *henro* that participants can gain any realization of why they are pilgrims.

A multiplicity of motives and meanings

In this chapter I have introduced a number of pilgrims whose stories illustrate many of the themes found in contemporary Shikoku pilgrimage practice, many of the ways of doing it, and many of the reasons people become pilgrims in Shikoku. The examples I have cited are only an indication rather than a comprehensive account of the vast array of themes and motives found in the pilgrimage community. What is certainly evident is that pilgrims not only do the *henro* in a multiplicity of ways—and often many times—but that they may be impelled by a multiplicity of motives, ranging from personal despair and asceticism to tourism and a wish to get away from home for a while. Pilgrims rarely have just one motive, but often several simultaneously.

Many of these meanings and motives were found among pilgrims in earlier ages as well. As I have also emphasized, the footsteps of those who have trod the way before can impact greatly on pilgrims in the present. This has been seen with Nakano-san's journey in the footsteps of his mentor and in the pilgrimages of those who have followed in the footsteps of earlier generations of their families and communities. Such imprints are part of the historical consciousness of the *henro* that continues to influence and shape the present. I commented on this in chapter 2, when I talked of how the things that pilgrims of former eras left behind play their part in framing and creating pilgrimage consciousness and understandings in the present. It is now time to examine these issues more directly and to examine how these imprints of the past were made. To this end I now turn, in the next two chapters, to the historical development of the pilgrimage from its earliest days until the present.

4 History, Footsteps, and Customs

Making the Premodern Pilgrimage

This chapter discusses the development of the *henro* up to 1945. It draws especially on Japanese academic sources[1] and the work carried out by local historians, historical societies, and regional government offices in Shikoku on the subject, along with the diaries and records of pilgrims from the seventeenth century onward.[2] It also recognizes that the documented history of the *henro* may not be as important to residents and pilgrims as is its legendary landscape: while Kōbō Daishi may not have established the pilgrimage in 815, or Emon Saburō at some later date through his painful wanderings, these stories are central to the belief structure of the pilgrimage and to its popularly understood history.

The *henro* does, however, have a "real" history that needs to be understood, for it, too, has shaped and affected the way the pilgrimage has been made. Like many practices that have emerged out of folk tradition, this history is initially fragmentary, and it takes clearly documented shape only in the seventeenth century. However, there is enough evidence in texts and inscriptions to give a general picture of its development from the latter Heian (794–1185) era onward and to indicate that it emerged out of the ascetic practices of specialist practitioners, gradually becoming transformed into a popular practice in the sixteenth and seventeenth centuries.

Theories, origins, asceticism

The *henro* was one of several pilgrimages that emerged in the latter Heian period linked to the activities of religious mendicants and wandering proselytizers known as *hijiri*, whose seminal role in popularizing folk Buddhist faith in Japan has been widely discussed by Japanese scholars.[3] The *hijiri* promoted the virtues of Buddhist figures of worship and emphasized pilgrimages to important temples and other holy places as a way of deepening faith, attaining salvation in this or the next life, and gaining merit and worldly benefits. Among such pilgrimages was the Kumano *mōde,* or pilgrimage to Kumano, a mountainous region in the Kii Peninsula south of the ancient capital of Nara closely associated with Japanese foundation myths and visualized as a figurative representation on earth of Kannon's Pure Land. Another was the Saikoku sanjūsankasho junrei, the thirty-three-temple Saikoku pilgrimage, which begins in Kumano, circles western Japan around the old capitals of Nara and Kyoto, and takes the pilgrim to thirty-three culturally significant Buddhist temples enshrining Kannon.[4]

These have both influenced later pilgrimage development in Japan. Influences from Kumano are considered to have been central to the development of the Saikoku route and can be seen also in the *henro,* while Saikoku served as a model for later replicated pilgrimages throughout the country.[5] Both were associated with centers of power and culture, their early clientele consisting primarily of aristocrats and members of the Imperial court who followed in the footsteps of the ascetics who developed the routes and served as guides on them. As economic conditions improved in subsequent ages, this clientele expanded to include the growing artisan and merchant classes from cities such as Kyoto and Osaka.[6]

By contrast, the Shikoku pilgrimage was not associated with centers of culture and power. However, like Kumano and Saikoku, it did have ascetic origins. The earliest evidence of a pilgrimage comes in the late twelfth century, when two texts, the *Konjaku monogatari* and the *Ryōjin hishō,* mention a pilgrimage-like ascetic practice in Shikoku. One of the *Konjaku monogatari* stories refers to three Buddhist monks performing the *Shikoku shugyō* (Shikoku austerity) by traveling around the coast of Shikoku along the *heji* (the route around the island). The *Ryōjin hishō,* virtually contemporaneous with the *Konjaku monogatari* and compiled by the ex-emperor Go-shirakawa (1127–1192), also speaks of Buddhist priests doing austerities by following the Shikoku *heji.* While neither text indicates a set route and sites, the austere journey around the island that both refer to is believed to be the precursor of the *henro.*[7]

What inspired the establishment of this trail of footsteps is a matter of dispute. Shinjō Tsunezō thinks that devotion to Kūkai/Kōbō Daishi led Shingon ascetics from Kōyasan to visit places in Shikoku associated with his life, establish an austerity around the island, and turn Shikoku into a "holy land" *(seichi).*[8] Among early Kōya and Shingon pilgrims, Shinjō cites Zenhan from Tōji in Kyoto, who visited Shikoku in the Kōhei (1058–1065) era and renovated a temple (now Temple 72) associated with Kūkai's childhood legends.[9] Other such figures included Saigyō, the poet/monk and devotee of Kōbō Daishi who lived for many years at Kōyasan and who, in 1168, went to Shikoku to perform austerities at sites associated with Kūkai.[10]

Not everyone, however, agrees with Shinjō. Kondō Yoshihiro argues that the austerity was a transplantation into Shikoku of the Kumano pilgrimage, which linked a series of places known as ōji (supposedly ninety-nine, but according to Kondō, less, and possibly eighty-eight in number)[11] where pilgrims worshiped on their way from Kyoto to Kumano. This route, which went down the coast of the Kii Peninsula before cutting inland into the mountains of Kumano and then reaching the southern shore of Kii at Nachi, viewed as the gateway to Fudaraku, Kannon's Pure Land, was also known as a heji. Kondō's thesis is that Kumano ascetics extended the cult's influence to Shikoku and that the presence in Shikoku of numerous pilgrimage sites along the shore (e.g., the promontories of Ashizuri and Muroto, both also gateways to Fudaraku), as well as of other temples with connections to the Kumano cult, indicates this influence. Although Kondō recognizes that faith in Kōbō Daishi is a seminal feature of the pilgrimage, he considers that it became so after the initial impetus came from Kumano.[12]

Gorai Shigeru also recognizes the importance both of Kōbō Daishi and Kumano but suggests that the pilgrimage emanated not so much from these as from an ancient, nature-based religious tradition centered on the sea, which forms a cardinal feature of Japanese geography and nature and which was subsequently overlaid with practices based in mountain worship and asceticism. Gorai's view is that the ascetics who went around Shikoku were following a coastal route because of this sea-venerating tradition that predated Kūkai, who would have followed similar practices in his travels in Shikoku, and that provided the foundations for the henro.[13]

Interesting as Kondō and Gorai's theories are, neither can be readily substantiated. Gorai's reminds us of the importance of the natural landscape in shaping the henro—and it also helps underline the importance of local practices and customs that predated but later became manifest in the henro. Yet the lack of empirical evidence means that Gorai's theory remains largely speculative. Equally, there are problems with Kondō's thesis. As Yoritomi Motohiro and Shiragi Toshiyuki show, Kumano/Fudaraku beliefs and practices are important in Shikoku, with thirty-nine of the eighty-eight temples having founding legends, names, or figures of worship that connect them to Kumano cultic influences and practices.[14] Yet they question whether this amounts to proof that its origins lie in replicating the Kumano cult, since less than half the temples have Kumano connections: if the henro were based on Kumano, they rightly ask, should not the figure be far higher?[15] In their view, the henro was initially an ascetic practice that incorporated a variety of elements ranging from Kumano faith to the Kōbō Daishi cult, with the latter gradually becoming its central organizing principle.[16]

I agree with Shinjō that the travels of ascetic devotees of Kōbō Daishi were the most likely impulse in the formation of the henro, but that, as Yoritomi and Shiragi have argued, their influences incorporated and built on other extant traditions and practices. This again suggests that the henro was an "encompassing" phenomenon that fused the practices and footsteps of followers of the Daishi cult with Kumano-centered beliefs and local customs and practices such as those centered on the sea, the *reizan,* and other features of the island's landscape. Kōbō Daishi served as its central organizing focus due to influences from Kōyasan and because he was a local religious figure, while the myriad *henro* beliefs and practices that developed became closely connected to popular beliefs centered on Kōbō Daishi at Kōyasan. These include concepts of enlightenment, associations with the cult of the Future Buddha Miroku and of future salvation, the promise of after-death salvation in the Pure Land, practical benefits such as healing, the importance of performing ritual services for the dead, and the notion that performing pilgrimages enables the living to accrue merits that will benefit themselves and their ancestors.[17]

Many other holy figures were associated with the pilgrimage, albeit sometimes—as with the popular Buddhist figure Gyōgi mentioned in chapter 2—more in legend than actuality. Generally, though, their influence was subsumed within the Daishi cult, as was noted in chapter 2 with the example of the transformation of the *bangai* Saba Gyōgi into Saba Daishi. In seventeenth-century chronicles the site is called Saba Gyōgi, and only in the eighteenth century—when priests and mendicants linked to Shingon and Kōyasan actively promoted the pilgrimage (see below)—do the story and site become attributed to Kōbō Daishi.[18]

Other prominent figures linked to the emergent pilgrimage include the aforementioned Saigyō; Shinkai Shōnin, one of the senior disciples of Hōnen, founder of the Jōdo (Pure Land) sect in Japan, who did the *Shikoku shugyō* in 1297;[19] and Ippen Shōnin (1239–1288), the founder of Jishū, the itinerant Buddhist movement whose practitioners performed the *nembutsu* (the chant in praise of the Buddha of the Pure Land, Amida). Ippen, who was born in Shikoku, led his group of wandering ascetics to Kōyasan and Kumano before returning to Shikoku, performing austerities at Iwayaji (Temple 45) and visiting sites associated with Kōbō Daishi, including Zentsūji, just before he died,[20] while followers of Jishū later visited Shikoku to follow in the footsteps of their founder.[21] A further connection between Ippen and the *henro* is the notion that circulated among pilgrims in later centuries that Ippen was the reborn Emon Saburō.[22]

Figures such as Ippen and Shinkai, with their associations to the *nembutsu* and Pure Land traditions, strengthened the focus on Pure Land faith and postdeath salvation in the *henro.* They were also part of a wider process in which numerous ascetics and mendicants, ranging from famed figures such as Saigyō to anonymous *hijiri* who invented legends and stories or performed acts of healing and asceticism that were then attributed to Kōbō Daishi, contributed to the formation of a pilgrimage framed around the figure of Kōbō

Daishi, who served as their role model and inspiration. In this cumulative process, the *henro* acquired legends, practices, and beliefs—primarily, though not wholly, centered on Kōbō Daishi—and became a storehouse of spiritual power that proved attractive to future generations of pilgrims.

The impetus for the "austerity" and subsequently the pilgrimage came from outside the island, notably from Kōyasan. There is little in the historical records to suggest that Shikoku residents (except returnees such as Ippen) or temple priests played much part in this initial process, although there is plentiful evidence, as will be noted later, that thereafter, local and regional authorities and people played an important role in its development. Temple priests, however, apart from occasional comments in pilgrims' journals, remain a rather anonymous element in the *henro* until the mid-twentieth century.

Inscriptions, ideograms, numbers

During the Kamakura (1185–1333) and Muromachi (1333–1578) eras, there are further references to monks, mainly of the Shingon sect, performing what is described as a *heji*, a *henro* (albeit with different ideograms than in the present),[23] or a pilgrimage *(junrei)* in Shikoku. This latter term first appears in the *Dainihonkyō sodenjushō* from the Nanboku period (1336–1392), where the Zentsūji priest Yūkai (d. 1416) refers to pilgrims to his temple doing the "Shikoku pilgrimage" *(Shikoku junrei)*.[24]

Further evidence is found in an inscription, dating to 1406, in Kawauchi in Kagoshima Province in Kyushu, that refers to an ascetic who had done the Shikoku *henro*.[25] From this period on the term "*henro*" (albeit not yet with the current ideograms) became the norm for referring to the pilgrimage. Its usage, and that of *junrei* (pilgrimage), instead of *heji*, implies a shift from an ascetic *practice* involving traveling to places to do austerities, toward a *pilgrimage* focused on a route linking specific sites of worship.[26]

While it is fair to surmise that the initial austerity had, by the fifteenth century, become a "pilgrimage," it is unclear why—or when—it acquired eighty-eight designated places of worship. Seemingly the earliest reference to the number eighty-eight is an inscription dated 1471 on a gong in a village temple in Tosa referring to a local *hachijūhakkasho* (eighty-eight-site pilgrimage route).[27] However, this inscription may be problematic. Recently Matsuo Gōji has challenged the acceptance of this date, arguing that the poorly inscribed ideograms in fact indicate a late eighteenth century date.[28] Certainly a later date is more likely for the existence of a local eighty-eighty-stage pilgrimage route, for there is otherwise no evidence of the development of local Shikoku-style pilgrimage replications until the seventeenth century. The earliest verifiably dated such route is one in Mikawa in Honshu, which appears to have developed in 1625 when Hoya Shōnin, a local ascetic, did the *henro* several times, brought back earth from the Shikoku temples, and installed it in eighty-eight temples in Mikawa, thereby establishing a replica route there.[29]

Indeed, there is no evidence (apart from this inscription) of the number eighty-eight being used in Shikoku until 1653, when the Shingon priest Chōzen states, at the end of his pilgrimage journal, that he visited eighty-eight *fudasho* (pilgrimage sites).[30] Equally, there is no indication, either in Chōzen's or any other text, as to why—in an island with considerably more than eighty-eight temples—these eighty-eight were chosen. My view—and I stress it is speculative—is that the *henro* expanded to encompass important geographical locations, regions, and cultic beliefs and practices on the island to the extent that once these were all absorbed into the *henro*, they numbered around eighty-eight places—and that this figure, as a result, became used as a framing device for the *henro* because it had some significance in esoteric Shingon terms (see appendix 2 and also later in this chapter). The sites incorporated in the *henro* included places associated with Kūkai's life and with the legends of Kōbō Daishi and Gyōgi, ascetic retreat centers, holy mountains, and centers associated with the spirits of the dead. They also included local pilgrimage routes such as the Awa *jūkasho* (ten sites of Awa), nowadays Temples 1–10, along the course of the Yoshino river, the Awa *gokasho* (five sites of Awa, Temples 13–17 around the castle town of Tokushima), and similar local routes around other important political centers of premodern Shikoku (e.g., the castle towns of Kōchi, Matsuyama, Imabari, and Takamatsu): over half the eighty-eight sites are on such local pilgrimages.[31]

These sites and routes were assimilated into the island-wide pilgrimage while continuing to exist as local routes in their own right. Maeda found *fuda* left by pilgrims at Temple 52 dating from the 1650s and marked *nanakasho mairi* (seven sites' pilgrimage), indicating that they were doing the local route around Matsuyama.[32] Such localized "pilgrimages within the pilgrimage" continue: Hoshino, researching the records of a pilgrims' lodge in Ehime Prefecture in the 1930s, found that a substantial number were doing the local route rather than the full *henro*.[33] During my fieldwork, too, I have met many people—invariably from Shikoku—doing these shorter local routes, which continue to exist as independent entities that tie locals into the wider *henro* structure.

Other notable institutions that became *fudasho* were the island's four Kokubunji—state Buddhist temples established by the Imperial Court in each province of the country during the eighth century—and its four Ichinomiya (Shinto shrines similarly established in each province for the protection of the realm), which were probably incorporated because of their institutional importance. The Ichinomiya also indicate that the *henro* was not confined to Buddhist institutions: premodern Japanese religious institutions often combined both shrine (Shinto) and temple (Buddhist) elements within one complex, and seven of the *henro* sites, including the four Ichinomiya, were of this ilk.

Graffiti and other inscriptions

Inscriptions found at sites such as Kokubunji (Temple 80) and Jōdoji (Temple 49) indicate that from the sixteenth century, the *henro* was no longer just an ascetic practice, that pilgrims were traveling in groups as well as individually, and that the term *"dōgyō"* had entered pilgrimage vocabulary. Graffiti at Kokubunji from 1528 record the visit of a party of five pilgrims *(dōgyō gonin)*,[34] while at both Kokubunji and Jōdoji they show that the cult of Kōbō Daishi had transcended sectarian boundaries by recording the pilgrimages of Tendai Buddhist priests from Enkyōji, one of the Saikoku pilgrimage temples.[35] Daiei era (1521–1528) graffiti at Jōdoji indicate that laypeople were now appearing among the pilgrims, with a reference to a pilgrim from Echizen—a fair distance from Shikoku—whose name suggests a layperson of comparatively high social status. Late sixteenth-century graffiti show that members of the peasantry and the masses had also become pilgrims.[36]

Thus by the late sixteenth century, the *henro* was a mass activity with a clientele from across the social spectrum—although increasingly, it would appear, from among the poorer classes of society. Strikingly, too, it continued to attract pilgrims at a period when civil war gripped the country. Even the destruction of thirty-one pilgrimage temples during the Tenshō era (1573–1586), when internecine warfare started out amongst the feudal lords of Tosa and engulfed the island, had relatively little effect in slowing down this process, although it probably led to the loss of valuable historical materials that could have provided information on the early pilgrimage.[37]

In 1571 an inscription at the Tosa Ichinomiya records a group of seven pilgrims, including both priests and laymen, from temples in Bitchū on Honshu. They end their inscription with the *nembutsu*—an indication of the importance of Pure Land beliefs in the pilgrimage—and record that since they had not found lodgings, they had been allowed to stay overnight at the shrine. That they recorded their inability to find lodgings suggests, according to Yoritomi and Shiragi, that by this period overnight accommodation was generally available and that ascetic practices such as *nojuku* (sleeping out) were no longer the norm.[38]

The indication that pilgrims could readily find lodgings is not necessarily evidence of an organized lodging infrastructure, but it suggests that alms-giving *(settai)*, which included the provision of free lodgings *(zenkonyado)*, had become established in the island's culture. The first inscription of the Emon Saburō legend (on a plaque at Ishiteji, Temple 51) dates from 1567 and shows that pilgrims by this period were adept at soliciting alms and developing stories to encourage the practice.[39] By the late sixteenth century, the flow of pilgrims was sufficient to persuade regional authorities of the need to provide institutionalized assistance for them. In 1598, the Awa fief constructed eight *ekiroji* (lodging temples) for pilgrims; in his 1653 pilgrimage journal the priest Chōzen mentions six such places and stayed at two.[40] Seventeenth-century records show that wayside halls of worship and local village halls were designated as *henroya* (shelters for pilgrims). Such provision appears to have been made more to control pilgrims and keep them in one place and out of the homes of villagers than from notions of charity. Moreover, Shinjō suggests that such places were dirty and a source of disease, and those pilgrims of any means avoided them.[41]

Pilgrims also began to leave more durable evidence—such as commemorative stones and *osamefuda*—behind. The importance pilgrims vested in commemorating their journeys has provided valuable evidence in the form of stones, inscriptions, diaries, and journals. It also shows that some pilgrims did the *henro* more than once. A 1591 inscription at Kure in Tosa refers to an ascetic probably named Kanshin (the ideograms are unclear) who had done the pilgrimage seven times, while a stone at Suzaki in Tosa appears to have been erected in 1618 to commemorate the donor's pilgrimage.[42] By the mid-seventeenth century pilgrims were also leaving *osamefuda* (usually of wood or metal) at the sites to record their visits; the earliest are a wooden *osamefuda* from 1640 at Temple 52 and a bronze one from 1650 at Temple 53.[43] This latter, from a local man from Iyo who placed *osamefuda* at temples throughout Japan, contains the first use of the modern ideograms 遍路 for *henro*.[44]

In 1638 the first written pilgrimage account appeared, by the monk Ken-myō recording the pilgrimage he made accompanying Kūshō (1573–1650), a high-ranking priest from Daikakuji in Kyoto. It is sparing in detail, starts from near Temple 45, consists primarily of the names of places visited, and gives little description of the pilgrimage or pilgrims. While it emphasizes the importance of Kōbō Daishi, it makes no mention of the number eighty-eight or of any set order.[45]

Chōzen's pilgrimage

In 1653, Chōzen (1613–1680), a senior Shingon priest and scholar from Kyoto with close connections to Kōyasan, did the pilgrimage and left an account, which is the first extended description of the *henro*.[46] It is the first to mention eighty-eight sites *(fudasho hachijūhachi)*,[47] although these were not referred to by numbers. Chōzen started his pilgrimage at Idoji (now Temple 17), proceeding clockwise around the island and finishing by going to the last few temples in what would nowadays be seen as the reverse order, from Kirihataji (Temple 10) to Ryōzenji (Temple 1). His account shows that only twelve of the temples had *daishidō*.[48] It took him ninety-one days—far longer than nowadays because he had to make detours around inlets and rivers where no ferry services existed, at times having to wade across rivers swollen by rain or wait long periods until boatmen turned up. He also had to endure numerous discomforts, including sleepless nights because of high winds and rain.[49]

He records disapprovingly that several of the temples were in a poor state and that some had no priests or were cared for by laypeople—including Idoji, where his pilgrimage started.[50] Chōzen's priestly status helped, for he was put up at several temples—hospitality not normally available to ordinary pilgrims. He also received hospitality from local people, who provided alms such as free lodging because, Chōzen records, they thought that this would bring them spiritual rewards, notably rebirth in the Pure Land.[51] Chōzen thus shows that *settai* and the stories associated with it (he also recounts the Emon Saburō story) were by this time part of pilgrimage consciousness, well known to pilgrims and locals alike.[52]

Chōzen records purchasing a document titled *Henro fudasho no nikki no ita* (Record of the diary to the pilgrimage temples) at a lodge between Temples 23 and 24, noting that "everyone" at the lodge purchased this.[53] This comment and the title of the text (which is no longer extant) have caused Yoritomi and Shiragi to speculate that this might be an early pilgrimage guidebook.[54] Chōzen's comment indicates that some form of nascent commercial infrastructure was in existence, with *henro*-related materials available for purchase and pilgrims with funds to buy them. It also shows that the *henro* had become enough of a mass activity for people to think of producing guides to sell, that some pilgrims wanted guidance, and that some people had become well enough versed in it to take on this role. Thus he records the presence of organized pilgrimage groups, staying overnight at one point with a party of thirteen such pilgrims, and notes meeting parties of pilgrims led by *sendatsu* at Temples 12 and 21.[55] His account also shows that asceticism was still important; he met, for example, a group of ascetics doing the *henro* anticlockwise at one stage.[56] Yet while travel was generally tough, there was also scope for social and leisure activities as well if one had the wherewithal. Thus Chōzen stopped at the Dōgo hot springs to bathe and rest his limbs—a practice followed by pilgrims throughout the centuries—and stayed at a temple in Imabari run by an old friend from Kōyasan with whom he stayed up late sharing stories.[57]

Guidebooks, pilgrimage stones, and "the father of the pilgrimage"

Chōzen's account shows that by the mid-seventeenth century, the pilgrimage had taken shape as an eighty-eight-stage route, with an infrastructure including pilgrims' lodges, almsgiving support, groups of pilgrims being led by guides, and a nascent market of pilgrimage items for sale. From this period, increasing evidence that some pilgrims performed the *henro* repeatedly emerges. Thus Yūben Shinnen (?–1691) writes in his 1687 guidebook, the

Shikoku henro michishirube (Guide to the Shikoku pilgrimage route), about the grave, between Temples 85 and 86, of Dōkyū, a Zen monk who did the *henro* twenty-seven times, twelve of them barefoot, and who died in 1684 at the age of fifty-three. Stating that Dōkyū was a devotee of Kōbō Daishi who had passed to the Pure Land, Shinnen asks pilgrims to honor his memory.[58] Besides being aware of Dōkyū's reputation, Shinnen might also have met him since he, too, devoted much of his life to the pilgrimage in the same period. Indeed, Shinnen is one of the most important figures in the pilgrimage's history, described by Ōishi Mitsuzen as the "father of the Shikoku *henro*"[59] and by Hoshino as the "father of its mass popularization" *(taishūka no so).*[60] It was from Shinnen's era—and in no small way due to him—that the pilgrimage became a mass practice attracting a clientele from much of Japan.

Details of Shinnen's life are sparse; he probably died in Shikoku in 1691, although his date of birth is unknown.[61] His association with Shikoku may have spanned over half a century; Kenmyō's 1638 account refers to Shinnen-an—a hall of worship and pilgrims' lodge between Temples 38 and 39 that was probably established by Shinnen and can still be seen today.[62] Shinnen had connections with Kōyasan, was an ascetic devotee of Kōbō Daishi, and may have been ordained as a Shingon monk. He had a hermitage in the Terashima District of Osaka, where he had various devotees and patrons who helped finance his activities, including producing pilgrimage guidebooks, putting up the first known stone pilgrimage markers, and making about twenty pilgrimage circuits of the island.[63]

Shinnen appears to have instigated the practice of putting up pilgrimage stones *(henro ishi).* These indicated directions and distances, were marked with a stone hand pointing out directions, and usually bore the words *"henro michi"* (pilgrimage route) and the names of the donors who paid for them. The oldest extant *henro ishi* is located near Matsuyama, dates from 1685, and was probably erected by Shinnen.[64] In all, Shinnen claimed to have erected around two hundred such stones, although only twenty-four of these have survived and can still be seen today.[65]

Shinnen also produced the earliest extant guidebook, the *Shikoku henro michishirube,* in 1687. Describing it as *Daishi go henro* (Kōbō Daishi's pilgrimage),[66] the *Michishirube* starts at Ryōzenji, the first temple pilgrims would reach if coming to Shikoku from Osaka, where Shinnen was based. Shinnen describes Ryōzenji as Temple 1 and thereafter numbers the temples in the order pilgrims walking clockwise around the island would visit them. He provides details about each in turn (e.g., its location, name, main image of worship, its *go-eika* [pilgrimage song]) and some rather limited information about how to get from temple to temple.

The *Michishirube* proved useful for the growing numbers of pilgrims in this era, and it long remained the standard guidebook of the Tokugawa period, published in several editions, for much of the period, going through three printings per year.⁶⁷ The sites included in it also became authoritative: since the late seventeenth century the sites included in the *henro* have remained largely fixed, although, as will be seen later in this chapter, there have been some small fluctuations as political disturbances and transport developments have changed the precise location and nature of some sites. Shinnen subsequently visited Jakuhon (1630–1701), a scholar-monk and priest at Kōyasan whom he persuaded to write another, more detailed, guidebook using Shinnen's materials. Jakuhon's *Shikoku henro reijōki* (Record of the holy places of the Shikoku pilgrimage) was published in 1689 in a seven-volume set sponsored by sixty-six donors, many from Osaka and associated with Shinnen. It was sold widely at shops in Osaka, Kōyasan, and the four provinces of Shikoku.⁶⁸

Old *henro ishi* (pilgrimage stones) providing directions for pilgrims. The new white-backed marker to the side was put up by Miyazaki Tateki and the Henro Michi Hozon Kyōryokukai (see chapters 2 and 8).

Jakuhon's guidebook contains more details about the sites and their foundation stories than Shinnen's,[69] and while the *Michishirube* has a few simple prints of Buddhist images, Kōbō Daishi, and pilgrims, Jakuhon's text contains detailed woodblock print pictures of the temples. It differs from Shinnen's text in various ways. While Shinnen's route starts from Ryōzenji, thereby reflecting the convenience and needs of pilgrims from Osaka, Jakuhon's starts at Kūkai's birthplace, Zentsūji, suggests that this Shingon temple with close links to Kōyasan is associated with the origins of the pilgrimage, and ties the *henro* more closely to centers of Shingon authority. Jakuhon does not give the temples numbers and follows a different order (ending at what is now Temple 65) from Shinnen's guide. Jakuhon states that this is an eighty-eight-stage pilgrimage, but mentions ninety-three sites, including several *bangai*. He also states that it is unclear when the pilgrimage was formed, by whom, or why it had eighty-eight sites on it.[70] Jakuhon's guide shows that thirty-five of the eighty-eight temples had *daishidō*—far more than in Chōzen's time, but also indicating that the focus on Kōbō Daishi was not as complete as in the late eighteenth century, when virtually all the temples had *daishidō*.[71]

In 1690 Shinnen produced another important text, the *Shikoku henro kudokuki* (Record of the miraculous virtues of the Shikoku pilgrimage), setting out twenty-seven pilgrimage miracle tales that he had collected from pilgrims, including the Emon Saburō legend. Prevalent themes in the text are that any pilgrim could be Kōbō Daishi, that Kōbō Daishi can be encountered in the pilgrimage, and that people should give alms to pilgrims. Several tales tell of people who, on doing the pilgrimage, are cured of disease (in Tale 13, e.g., a person from Izumi near Osaka suffering from leprosy is miraculously cured through becoming a pilgrim) or, through helping pilgrims, are absolved of sins or reap other rewards. In Tale 4, a woman who had just walked some distance to get water for her child unhesitatingly offers it to a passing thirsty pilgrim. She is rewarded for her good deed when the pilgrim (i.e., Kōbō Daishi) strikes his staff into the ground to produce a spring of abundant pure water, which means that she no longer has to go in search of water each day and that her village and descendants will be blessed similarly. Other tales, though, show the retribution that befalls those who meanly refuse to help. Thus in Tale 16 a pilgrim sees a fisherman collecting large numbers of shellfish and asks him for one. The fisherman refuses, claiming that they are inedible. This mendacity produces immediate retribution as the shellfish turn to stone and become inedible ever after. The *Kudokuki* thus reinforces the practice of *settai*, affirms the sanctity of pilgrims, and promises rewards ranging from healing to absolution for those who do the *henro* and for those who help pilgrims—and retribution for those who do not.[72]

Jakuhon wrote an introduction and afterword for the *Kudokuki* in which he was no longer unclear about who founded it and why there were eighty-eight sites. Now he states that the pilgrimage was established by Shinzei (800–860), a disciple of Kūkai's at Kōyasan and priest of the Shingon temple Takaosanji, and that the number eighty-eight has significant Buddhist connotations linked to the eradication of evil passions *(bonnō)*. There are, Jakuhon says, eighty-eight such passions that act as hindrances to buddhahood, and the eighty-eight pilgrimage sites are a means of eradicating them.[73] He also extols the more worldly virtues of the pilgrimage, which will bring rewards and prosperity to all who do it.[74]

Jakuhon's revisions, which clearly assert links between the *henro*, Shingon Buddhism, and Kōyasan, doubtless reflect the interest of Kōyasan Shingon authorities in developing and stamping their imprint onto the emerging pilgrimage. Certainly his and Shinnen's activities helped intensify links between Kōyasan, Kōbō Daishi faith, and the *henro*. Their lead was followed by others from Kōyasan who contributed to the *henro*'s growing popularity in the eighteenth century by proselytizing among the Shingon faithful.[75] Further publications during the eighteenth century similarly emphasized Shingon orientations, including the earliest map of the *henro*, produced in 1763 by Hosoda Shūei, who had done the pilgrimage in 1747 using Shinnen's *Michishirube* as his guidebook. His map is simple, outlining the island and the approximate locations of the temples; it mentions three routes, one for pilgrims entering at Naruto and starting at Ryōzenji and two for those entering the island on its northern coast, via the ports of Tadotsu or Marugame, and starting at Zentsūji. At the center of the map is a seated Kōbō Daishi along with an inscription from a senior Kōya priest, Kōhan, affirming the esoteric Shingon orientations of the pilgrimage and the significance of the number eighty-eight, which, Kōhan states, represents eighty-eight evil passions and the places through which these can be eradicated.[76]

Miracles and moral landscapes

Shinnen and Jakuhon's texts, with their mixture of practicalities and miracles, provided the basis for subsequent Tokugawa-era guidebooks and for modern guidebooks, which similarly combine practical details (e.g., how to get to the temples, where to stay) with the legendary/miraculous (temple founding stories, legends and miraculous events).[77] The *Kudokuki* provides a moral landscape for the *henro* in which Kōbō Daishi's presence is pervasive and in which wondrous events occur, with sufferers of leprosy being cured through faith and pilgrimage, passing pilgrims being able to bestow benefits on those who help them, and shellfish turning into stone because fishermen behave meanly. It evokes the recurrent importance of miracles in the construction of the pilgrimage and shows how absolution, salvation, and worldly benefits had become central issues of concern to pilgrims.

Such moral structures of reward, retribution, and absolution are replicated in numerous stories that circulated in Shikoku during and since the Tokugawa era to offer pilgrims hopes of salvation and cure and to remind them of the importance of moral actions and repentance. One of the best-known stories of this ilk is that of Okyō at Tatsueji (Temple 19). Tatsueji is regarded, in pilgrimage lore, as a "barrier gate" *(sekisho)*, the spiritual equivalent of the border gates between fiefs where pilgrims had to present their travel permits before being allowed into the next domain (see below). Similarly, in pilgrimage lore, there were four temples, one in each domain, that served as spiritual barriers through which pilgrims could pass only if they were in a morally fit state. These were Tatsueji, Kōnomineji (Temple 27), Yokomineji (Temple 60), and Unpenji (Temple 66). As with so many aspects of pilgrimage lore, it is unclear how they came to be so designated.

According to the story, Okyō, who came from what is now Shimane Prefecture, had been sent to Osaka as a geisha (in reality probably a prostitute) to help resolve her family's financial problems. She became involved first with one lover, then another, and then, with the second, killed the first to be free of him. Okyō and her lover then escaped to Shikoku disguised as pilgrims and aiming to hide there to evade justice. When, however, they reached the first barrier temple, Tatsueji, Okyō's hair became entangled with the temple bell rope, and she could be released only by having all her hair cut off. The incident made the couple realize that they could not escape from their evil deeds, and they confessed to the temple priest. Okyō's tonsured head convinced her that she should become a nun in order to gain absolution, and she did so, living in a hermitage near the temple. Her partner also gave up his previous life to work at the temple. Enough detail exists to suggest that the story (doubtless embellished but commonly dated to 1803) has some historical basis, and, as with the Emon Saburō story, the moral story is illustrated by physical remains. At Tatsueji one can see a bell rope entangled with hair, as a physical reminder of the story, while not far away, on the path to Temple 18, a stone inscription informs passersby that this is the site of Okyō's hermitage, where she tended to pass pilgrims. Okyō's story of wickedness, retribution, repentance, and absolution reinforces the messages of the Emon Saburō legend that for pilgrims to attain sanctity and salvation, they need to follow moral rules, to be free of sin, and, if not, to repent of them.

Okyō's story is interesting also in that it affirms the miraculous powers of the temples themselves. Tatsueji is one of many pilgrimage temples with a corpus of miracle tales that effectively tell pilgrims that the sites and their figures of worship can, like Kōbō Daishi, be sources of the miraculous and provide the benefits (e.g., salvation, absolution) that pilgrims seek. Iyataniji (Temple 71), whose collection of discarded leg braces and the like was mentioned in chapter 2 and whose priests continue to affirm the importance of miraculous events at the site, is another temple with a similar collection of miracle tales.[78] In such contexts the temples are asserting that while Kōbō

Daishi is central to the pilgrimage, he is not its only source of miraculous powers and benefits, and that they are locations of power and miracles in their own right.

Holy footsteps, influential pilgrims

Shinnen was a seminal figure in the development of the *henro*, making the pilgrimage more widely known through his stones, guidebooks, and miracle tales. As such, he is a striking example of how individuals can help make the pilgrimage and create a series of footsteps for others to follow. During the Tokugawa period and beyond, one can find numerous examples of similarly driven pilgrims who helped develop the pilgrimage and thereby added to its landscape. Prominent among them was Bukkai (1710–1769) from Iyo in Shikoku, a prominent *mokujiki* (tree eating) ascetic[79] who did the *henro* twenty-one times and did austerities at Sankakuji (Temple 65), where he spent two years, and other temples. Bukkai also established pilgrims' lodges and *settai-sho* (place for distributing *settai*) at Iriki in Tosa in 1755.[80]

Shinnen's example of erecting pilgrimage stones was followed by others, including Takeda Tokuemon (d. 1814), like Bukkai from Iyo, who appears to have turned to the *henro* to assuage his grief after five of his children died in the late eighteenth century. Thereafter he did the *henro* around three times a year until his death, while putting up around seventy *henro ishi* in the period 1794–1807.[81] Kiyoyoshi considers Takeda to be important because of his understanding (not fully evident in Shinnen's stones) of distances and directions: Takeda's stones contained details of distances and were put up at fixed intervals of a *ri* (just under four kilometers) and also where there were divergences in the path, and hence they helped pilgrims develop a deeper understanding as to where they were on the route.[82] Other such figures include Shōren (mentioned in chapter 2), about whom little is known save that he probably was a monk who put up numerous pilgrimage stones (around eighty can still be seen) during the period 1804–1818 inscribed with figures of Kōbō Daishi and directions,[83] and Tada Emon, who did the *henro* 136 times in the nineteenth century. While little is known about Tada, the number of circuits he did indicates that he spent many years, and possibly a lifetime, on the *henro*, dying on it in 1862. His gravestone can be seen near Temple 88.[84]

In terms of fame and influence, the most prominent pilgrim in Shikoku since Shinnen is Nakatsuka Mōhei, whose life essentially became an incessant pilgrimage around Shikoku. Nakatsuka was born in 1845 in Yamaguchi Prefecture and, as was noted in chapter 2, left home and set out on the pilgrimage in his early twenties because he was frustrated in his wish to marry a local girl. He did not stop, however, spending most of the rest of his life as a pilgrim, doing it 282 times over a fifty-six-year period, making six or seven circuits a year until he got older and reduced his pace. He was initiated into the Buddhist priesthood at Temple 76 on his thirtieth circuit in 1877. He left Shikoku twice—in 1878 to visit mountain religious sites on Honshu and in 1882 to do the Saikoku pilgrimage. Otherwise, he remained a Shikoku pilgrim, resisting calls from his family to return home and stating that he would do so only when he died.

In 1883, to commemorate his sixty-fifth circuit and to encourage others to become pilgrims, he published a guide that incorporated a new edition of Shinnen's *Michishirube*, while in 1891 he gained a license from the Buddhist temple Shogōin as a certified performer of healing rituals. Through his extended pilgrimage he attained an exalted spiritual status, revered by many in Shikoku and part of a living tradition of sacred pilgrims that started with the *hijiri* of earlier times.[85]

Nakatsuka erected 237 pilgrimage stones through donations he solicited. Many of them marked stages in his pilgrimage life, the first being put up in 1886 to commemorate his eighty-eighth circuit. In that year, his forty-second (i.e., his *yakudoshi*), he put up nineteen stones; this suggests that Nakatsuka identified with Kōbō Daishi, who, according to pilgrimage foundation legends, did the *henro* in his *yakudoshi* year.[86] He later erected another batch of stones to commemorate his 100th pilgrimage, and fifteen further stones on his 137th circuit, when he surpassed Tada Emon's 136 circuits. Nakatsuka was concerned about getting others to follow in his footsteps, and his stones generally contained exhortations to this end,[87] while his personal influence and presence on the route for over half a century further served to inspire others. Nakatsuka was thus another powerful individual figure whose historical traces can still be seen in his stones and who remains part of the individual tradition of making and shaping the pilgrimage in Shikoku.

Alms, solicitation, manipulation

The *henro*'s development was enhanced also by local customs and practices ranging from *settai* and local devotion to Kōbō Daishi, to pilgrimage-centered initiation practices. *Settai* was important in attracting pilgrims in the Tokugawa era and in creating bonds between pilgrims and locals. *Settai* has, of course, been part of the pilgrimage landscape from early on, with the Emon Saburō story providing a legitimating foundation that is reinforced through the miraculous tales of Shinnen's *Kudokuki*. The establishment of organized *settai* provisions through the *ekiroji* established in 1598, and the more informal but widespread practice of offering *zenkonyado* (free lodgings)—a practice that was extant, as was seen earlier, in the sixteenth century and widespread by the time of Chōzen's 1653 pilgrimage—show that *settai* was a noted aspect of *henro* culture by the time Shinnen's guidebooks helped usher in the era of mass pilgrimage.

The Tokugawa period was one in which, by and large, the turbulence of sixteenth-century Japan gave way to a more stable and peaceful period, with better economic conditions and growth. Such improvements produced more people with the wherewithal to become pilgrims (see below) and provided people in Shikoku with more resources to give pilgrims. By the mid-eighteenth century, pilgrims were clearly benefiting not only through free lodgings but also from food and other items: the ascetic Kai Mokujiki Shōnin records that pilgrims were being offered items such as straw sandals and rice when he made his pilgrimage in 1763.[88] Rice was especially welcome, as pilgrims could use it in lieu of the fees they normally paid at pilgrims' lodges.

Hence many pilgrims actively—in the manner of Kōbō Daishi standing before Emon Saburō's door—sought alms. Indeed, it became an accepted part of pilgrimage practice to solicit alms on a regular basis—a practice that at times caused regional authorities to rail against pilgrims, many of whom they suspected of being freeloaders more concerned with what they could get out of the populace than with doing the pilgrimage (see below). Some people continue to think that pilgrims should solicit alms as part of their pilgrimage practice. In 1984, when my wife and I arrived early at an old pilgrims' lodge, the lady in charge asked us if we were going to go out and solicit alms and seemed surprised when we said no. She said that many foot pilgrims still did so and that she encouraged this, since, in her view, it was part of the pilgrimage practice to stand before at least three houses or shops per day with a begging bowl seeking alms. The author Hayasaka Akira, who was born and brought up in a village on the *henro* route in Ehime, recalls that during his childhood in the 1930s, there used to be as many as thirty pilgrims every day begging for alms before the village shop and receiving handfuls of rice in return.[89] Nakano-san, discussed in chapter 3, carried a begging bowl for this purpose, while, when we returned to Temple 1 at the end of our 1984 pilgrimage, we met an elderly male pilgrim soliciting alms there. He wrote down the names of those who gave him alms—and who, he said, would spiritually be part, and share in the merit, of his pilgrimage. He planned to beg every day, for otherwise he would not have enough money for lodgings or food. In my visit to Shikoku in April 2000 I also met pilgrims who sought alms regularly in this way.

Why pilgrims sought alms is relatively straightforward. The economic benefits were obvious: free food, lodgings, and the like made the pilgrimage possible for many pilgrims who depended on alms to keep them going. Indeed, some pilgrims in Shikoku in the Tokugawa period became "professional *henro*," eking out an existence on the road through the alms they solicited, either because they found this a conducive way of life or because they suffered from diseases (most commonly leprosy) that rendered them social outcasts and effectively forced them to remain transient and dependent on the charity of others.[90]

The religious connotations of soliciting alms are significant. Carrying a begging bowl and seeking alms is a traditional element in the lifestyles of mendicant Buddhist monks, symbolic of their lack of attachment to the world and important in cultivating the Buddhist virtue of humility. The pilgrim, who is for the duration of his/her pilgrimage following the path of a mendicant, thus signifies this identification by soliciting alms like a Buddhist monk. Begging for alms, too, identifies the pilgrim with, and ties him/her to the image of, the mendicant Kōbō Daishi.

The practice, too, is an affirmation—from the pilgrim's perspective—of the message inherent in pilgrimage stories of reward and retribution: that pilgrims were special, holy, and deserving of special treatment. Being given *settai*, in effect, could be seen as recognition of that special nature. Indeed, pilgrims often *expected* to be given *settai* and saw it as an indicator of their status, while many, according to Kojima Hiromi, were influenced by the wish to "receive things" *(monomorai)*, thereby adding an acquisitive dimension to their motives.[91] Some pilgrims—especially from the nineteenth century, when almsgiving appears to have been particularly widespread—even counted up the times they received *settai:* Arai Raisuke's 1819 pilgrimage account records no less than twenty-eight instances of *settai* in one day,[92] while Nonaka Hikohei, in 1836, recorded over fifty instances of *settai*. By specifying the places where *settai* was given regularly by groups and individuals, Nonaka's account served as a virtual guidebook to *settai* in Shikoku at the time.[93] Modern walkers, too, as will be noted in chapter 6, also often become preoccupied with *settai*, which can become an important element in their pilgrimage experiences.

Giving alms, supporting pilgrims

Settai is, in some senses, a form of sacred manipulation, a means of inducing gifts through the construction of images of sanctity and threatened retribution. Certainly some pilgrims used these images to encourage almsgiving, even sometimes resorting to direct threats, and this caused some Shikoku residents to view pilgrims as dangerous and mercenary and led regional authorities to impose periodic crackdowns on pilgrims when their attempts at solicitation became troublesome. These are points that I will return to later in this chapter.

Despite such problems, a widespread tradition of almsgiving developed in Shikoku both on individual and institutional levels. Maeda suggests four primary reasons why people gave alms to pilgrims.[94] One is a sense of common feeling with pilgrims: since many in Shikoku did the pilgrimage or part of it, they were aware of the hardships and remembered the help they had been given as pilgrims and hence wanted to repay this by helping others. This is a motive I have encountered, too, among local residents in the present day. Maeda's second reason (which I consider to be the most important) is the deep-rooted faith in Kōbō Daishi in Shikoku and the view that one is really giving alms to Kōbō Daishi and will, in return, be rewarded with his grace. The third is that offerings to pilgrims are a means of acquiring merit for the dead; thus people would especially give alms on anniversaries or memorial days associated with the dead, believing that such donations would help their deceased kin in their journeys to other realms. Maeda's fourth reason is that, in giving alms to pilgrims, one is in effect sharing in their pilgrimage and its merits, a motive especially potent for those who have not made the pilgrimage, or are unable to do so. On this point, I consider that *settai* is thus a means of expressing a sense of *dōgyō*, of doing the pilgrimage with someone else.

I would supplement these with other, often related, reasons. The pilgrim is an especially sacred and marginal figure—and hence is like a deity who can provide benefits but who, if improperly treated, can be dangerous and hence needs to be appeased through offerings. The pilgrim's liminal position between the mundane and sacred worlds, and his/her identification with Kōbō Daishi, marks him/her out as a potential healer and source of power. The folk belief encountered by pilgrims such as Tosa Fumio in the modern era and outlined in chapter 2 that pilgrims can aid the sick indicates how this idea of the pilgrim as holy and powerful can spur almsgiving. S/he also may serve, in similar ways, as a specially efficacious conduit to the sacred, a point that came through to me in 1984, when, walking along the road toward one of the pilgrimage temples, I was given two one-hundred yen coins by a young mechanic who hailed me from a garage forecourt. He told me to keep one of the coins as *settai* and to offer the other at the temple on his behalf, saying it was more efficacious channeled through a pilgrim than being offered by him.

While giving *settai* is closely linked to the image of the pilgrim as a representative of Kōbō Daishi, it was also, at times, a manifestation of local protest against regional and feudal authorities. Hoshino's research shows that even when the authorities imposed periodic bans on giving *settai*, local people often continued to give alms and that they did so in part as a gesture of defiance and protest against their feudal rulers.[95] Nor was the practice only individual in nature: Nathalie Kouamé has assembled detailed evidence from local records to show that *settai* was not simply spontaneous and based in piety or fear, but was organized and embedded in the island's social structures and local communities. Kouamé shows that households were assessed by local village authorities and, based on their wealth and land, asked to make particular levels of "donation" to village or community collections (usually of rice), which would then be given out in an organized fashion to pilgrims as *settai*.[96] Often, these alms were distributed on special days, such as village festivals and holy days associated with Kōbō Daishi, or, indicative of the link between *settai* and the ancestors, at important Buddhist ritual occasions for commemorating the ancestors such as the *higan* (spring and autumn equinox) festivals.[97] Such organized almsgiving was not uniform throughout the island, however; as Shinjō demonstrates, it was contingent on local religious orientations: areas where affiliation was primarily to Jōdo Shin or Nichiren Buddhist sects were less likely to give *settai* than those where Tendai or Shingon affiliation was high.[98]

Not all Shikoku residents readily gave *settai* or saw pilgrims as holy figures. Pilgrims in Shikoku were, as will be discussed further shortly, highly ambivalent figures, seen by some as sacred figures and by others as dangerous, troublesome, and disruptive intruders liable to be disease carriers, thieves, or miscreants intent on living off the generosity of locals. Regional authorities, too, also displayed a similar ambivalence: while, as was noted above, they often tried to restrict almsgiving and considered pilgrims to be potential threats and freeloaders, they also recognized that some pilgrims might be sincere and that almsgivers might give not out of fear but through genuine faith. Hence authorities in Tosa issued a decree in 1791 permitting the giving of alms even to illegal pilgrims (i.e., those without appropriate travel permits) if such donations were based in faith in Kōbō Daishi.[99] Equally, regional authorities recognized that while they might attempt to restrict the activities of pilgrims, they also were responsible for the welfare of those within their domains. Hence while attempting to restrict and regulate the flow of pilgrims, they also legislated to establish support structures to look after their welfare. From the *ekiroji* of 1598 onward, regional authorities throughout the island instituted systems and regulations to support sick pilgrims and deal with the corpses of pilgrims who died on the route, an issue that I will discuss more fully below.

Thus *settai* was embedded in the Shikoku landscape and linked to local customs and communities. From the early nineteenth century onward, too, the practice was taken up by groups based outside the island that gathered goods and donations in their home regions and then traveled to Shikoku to distribute them as alms. In 1800, a pilgrim from Awa published a guidebook, the *Shikoku henro meisho zue* (Guidebook to the sights on the Shikoku pilgrimage route), in which he mentions receiving alms between Temples 64 and 65 from an Osaka-based pilgrimage association.[100] Other journals from this era also indicate the existence of almsgiving activities by groups from outside Shikoku.[101] The Arita Settaikō from Wakayama Prefecture, mentioned in chapter 3, is one of the most prominent of these associations, with its members believing that its origins date back to the early nineteenth century.[102]

Local pilgrims, initiation, and play

One reason people in Shikoku gave alms was because many pilgrims were from Shikoku, often doing just part of the *henro* as an initiation rite. Like so many folk customs, it is unclear when this custom first developed, but as Maeda has shown, through much of the Tokugawa period it was customary for age-sets of Shikoku youths of both sexes to set out from their villages to do local pilgrimages or *ikkoku mairi* pilgrimages, whose completion would confer marriageable status on them. Such activities also had a social use, for they enabled these age-sets to meet up with young people of marriageable age from other villages and hence find potential partners—which, naturally, at times gave their pilgrimages an air of frivolity.[103] The custom was not limited to Shikoku: Hoshino states that young women from other areas around the Inland Sea who were preparing to get married would do the *henro* as an initiation rite.[104]

Such pilgrimages were not always leisurely or enjoyable affairs; there are records in the Tokugawa period of young locals who, expected to do the whole *henro* as an initiation rite but lacking adequate funds, would run around the route to reduce the time they needed to be on the road. Among such pilgrims, known as *hashiri hendo* (running pilgrims),[105] was a young man named Kentarō from Tosa who, according to records, did the *henro* in thirty-two days in 1805—remarkably fast for the era, and around half the time it normally took —running most of the route, depending on *settai* and stopping only briefly at the temples.[106]

Such local, initiatory pilgrims, whether running or seeking out potential partners among other pilgrims of their age-set, represent a further strand in the ways in which the *henro* became woven into the island's culture. As I suggested in chapter 3, this tradition may also help to explain why so many of the *osamefuda* I examined indicated family groups of Shikoku residents visiting the temples with younger-generation family members, often in their twenties, who, judging by their addresses, lived outside the island but were returning to visit the pilgrimage temples with their parents.

Growth, development, and economic influences

The patterns of travel followed by the growing numbers of pilgrims in Shikoku also shaped the development of the pilgrimage. Shinnen's guidebook, as was mentioned earlier, placed Ryōzenji as Temple 1, and this numerical order was affirmed through the flow of pilgrims who came to the island from Shinnen's base in Osaka. By 1710 guidebooks and references to the *henro* listed Ryōzenji as Temple 1 and used the numerical order in existence today, while, as was noted earlier, the sites involved in the *henro* and their locations had by and large become fixed.[107] Thus the mass flow of pilgrims produced a normative structure and order to the *henro*. It also indicated the influence of the Osaka region in shaping the pilgrimage. The closest major population center to Shikoku, Osaka developed strong economic links with Shikoku in the Tokugawa period, notably with Awa through the salt and indigo trades. Such economic links fostered greater communications between the regions and thereby encouraged pilgrims from Osaka to go to Shikoku; indeed, it may well be that regional authorities encouraged the flow of pilgrims because this contributed to these growing economic ties.[108]

Osaka came to be seen as an important pilgrimage market by the *henro* temples, some of which, in the early eighteenth century, actively promoted themselves there. In 1713 Shidoji (Temple 86) sent its main image of worship *(honzon)* to Osaka in a *degaichō* (exhibiting the main image of a temple) event. Such events, aimed at attracting visitors to distant temples by exhibiting their images of worship in major population centers, were widely held in Tokugawa Japan. Shidoji was clearly building on the bonds that had developed with Osaka by seeking to further increase the flow of pilgrims from there.[109]

Economic development and social factors also impacted on pilgrimage and travel in the Tokugawa era, with economic growth and the emergence of a moneyed economy providing the means for people to travel, while an improving infrastructure of routes and lodging facilities made pilgrimage more accessible. The growth, too, of urban artisan and merchant classes with incomes and an interest in seeing other places further helped stimulate pilgrimage, while political stability under the Tokugawa regime made travel increasingly safe.[110] Pilgrimage was also encouraged in some instances, as James Foard has argued with regard to the Saikoku pilgrimage, by the Tokugawa government as a means of building a sense of national consciousness and identity.[111]

The Tokugawa regime also in some ways restricted travel by requiring people to get permits to leave their feudal domains. However, such restrictions were not always enforceable as increasing numbers of people sought to broaden their horizons and see other parts of their country.[112] Moreover, even when travel was regulated, exceptions tended to be made for those claiming special (i.e., religious) reasons for their travel; hence travel permits were generally granted for those seeking to visit pilgrimage sites such as Ise, Saikoku, and Shikoku.

The economic conditions of the Tokugawa era helped give rise to a number of peak pilgrimage eras in Shikoku. The Genroku era (1688–1703), when Shinnen was active, was one such, a time of economic growth in which pilgrim numbers grew in Shikoku. Such growth also led to infrastructure improvements that made the pilgrimage less arduous and time consuming. While pilgrims such as Chōzen had had to make detours around inlets or wait until rivers subsided, pilgrims from the Genroku era onward benefited from the improved provision of bridges and ferries. Hence while Chōzen had taken ninety-one days, pilgrims by the eighteenth century could get round in little more than half that time.[113] Transportation improvements in Tokugawa also included better highways and improved boat services across the Inland Sea, which thus made it easier for people to get to Shikoku and helped increase pilgrim numbers.[114]

Later periods of economic growth, too, had similar impacts. The research of Maeda and Kouamé into *osamefuda* at various sites (including, in Kouamé's case, *osamefuda* from a household in Iyo that, through successive generations, lodged pilgrims during the eighteenth and nineteenth centuries) indicates that the Shikoku *henro* experienced peaks that coincided with periods of economic growth, notably in the Genroku, Hōreki (1751–1763), Meiwa (1764–1769), Bunka (1804–1818, but especially, according to Kouamé's study, in the period 1807–1810), and Bunsei (1818–1830) eras.[115] While numbers are difficult to ascertain with any certainty in premodern times, documentary evidence dating from 1764, which records that approximately two hundred to three hundred pilgrims passed through one village on the pilgrimage route each day between the second and seventh months of the year of the lunar calendar, suggests there might have been as many as 36,000–45,000 pilgrims per year in the 1760s.[116] Yet even in periods of economic crisis, numbers appear not to have declined greatly in Shikoku. Kouamé's research indicates that pilgrim numbers may even have grown between 1833–1839—a period of famine—and she suggests that this could have been because of desperation, with people becoming pilgrims and seeking alms because they had no food.[117] It was in this period of famine that Nonaka Hikohei (see above) received such copious amounts of *settai*, indicative, it would appear, that local support toward pilgrims was not necessarily dependent on favorable economic conditions.

Entertainment, tourism, and pilgrimage in Tokugawa Japan

As Constantine Vaporis has demonstrated, during the Tokugawa era pilgrimage became increasingly infused with tourist motifs, and pilgrims spent more and more time on sightseeing both during their pilgrimages and on the way to and from sacred sites. As a travel industry developed, Vaporis argues, pilgrimage increasingly became a secularized tourist activity.[118] Certainly, in an era in which the modern concept of "travel for the sake of enjoyment" was not as yet accepted, pilgrimage had become a medium for the expression of an emergent tourism.

However, this appears to have been less so in Shikoku than on other major pilgrimage routes of the era, probably because of the general poverty of Shikoku pilgrims, the marginalized status of the island, and the arduous nature of the pilgrimage. Moreover, unlike Saikoku and Ise, which were focused around great national and cultural centers (in Saikoku, ancient capitals and major temples replete with cultural treasures; at Ise, national shrines associated with the Imperial household), Shikoku's temples were generally not culturally prominent, and the island was not central to notions of national identity and culture. Compared to Saikoku and Ise, which developed infrastructures of lodges and places of entertainment to cater to the growing tide of pilgrims seeking the chance to let go and indulge themselves away from home, Shikoku had, as Vaporis puts it, a "relative lack of brothels," which, he suggests, enabled the *henro* to retain a more religious flavor than other prominent Tokugawa pilgrimages.[119]

One reason for this was that, as Maeda has indicated, pilgrims were fewer in Shikoku than in Ise or Saikoku, and their economic status generally lower.[120] Maeda—who categorizes Saikoku pilgrims largely as better-off artisans and merchants—and Shinjō think that a sizable number of Shikoku pilgrims were impoverished, Shinjō estimating that around 10 percent of Tokugawa-era Shikoku pilgrims were dependent on begging.[121] Shinjō, too, shows that far more pilgrims died in Shikoku than Saikoku—probably because they were in a worse condition and poorer than those in Saikoku.[122] Maeda also notes that in periods of famine, such as in the 1830s, pilgrim numbers tended to fall dramatically in Saikoku but not in Shikoku—further indication that the *henro* community was less focused on enjoyment and more on austere travel.[123]

This "relative lack of brothels" does not mean, however, that Shikoku pilgrims were *necessarily* more morally upright than those who went to Saikoku and Ise, as, indeed, the word "relative" hints! Rather, Shikoku pilgrims were less able to seek entertainment in paying establishments. They did not necessarily remain chaste; while many pilgrims maintained their ascetic endeavors, there is evidence in the continuing efforts of regional authorities to control what they saw as disruptive pilgrims (see below) that some pilgrims behaved badly. However, much of this behavior, it appears, occurred *within* the pilgrimage community rather than in brothels and the like. The "age-sets" of Shikoku youths on initiatory pilgrimages certainly contributed to this atmosphere, but there is also evidence that sexual liaisons occurred between pilgrims on the route and that some male pilgrims regarded female pilgrims as potential objects of sexual gratification. Takamure's accounts of walking the *henro* in 1918 show that, as a young woman, she was propositioned by lecherous male pilgrims, and they show, too, that some of the female pilgrims she encountered in her travels engaged in sexual liaisons, perhaps to fund their journeys.[124]

One should not assume, however, that all Shikoku pilgrims were poor. Kouamé, while accepting that some pilgrims were dependent on *settai*, argues that Shinjō's assertion that 10 percent of *henro* were beggars is little more than unfounded speculation and that Maeda is making false assumptions when he suggests that because there were comparatively more women doing the *henro* than other Japanese pilgrimages in the Tokugawa period, Shikoku pilgrims were therefore necessarily poor. As Kouamé rightly notes, this implies that being female is indicative of one's economic status—when, of course, this need not be the case.[125]

Indeed, Kouamé demonstrates that, alongside the poor, there were also pilgrims—some female—who had funds for food, lodging, and entertainment. Her studies of local records and of pilgrims' journals in the Tokugawa period show that quite a few pilgrims visited Konpira Shrine as a diversion, that many spent several nights at the Dōgo hot springs, and that while there, they spent money on luxuries such as *sake* and tea. In all, Kouamé considers, the pilgrimage provided local people in Shikoku with an income stream that while not substantial was nevertheless welcome.[126]

Evidence of tourist-oriented pilgrims can be found in the appearance of guidebooks such as the aforementioned *Shikoku henro meisho zue* (1800), which describes good places for pilgrims to visit and indicates that relaxed travel and enjoyment had become a dominant motif of the pilgrimage for at least some pilgrims. The *Meisho zue* also shows that by this time there were plentiful ferries across rivers and that it was quite easy for pilgrims to purchase food and sustenance along the way; thirty-seven of the temples by the beginning of the nineteenth century had teahouses *(chaya)* vending food and tea on their grounds.[127] Arai Raisuke's 1819 journal also illustrates similar themes. Arai made no specific, faith-centered vow before starting, his journey was relatively peaceful, and he indulged himself by smoking, drinking *sake*, and visiting popular sights such as Konpira Shrine and Dōgo, where he tarried for three days.[128]

Pilgrims: Provenance and gender

In effect, there appear to have been all manner of people doing the *henro*, from the poor and the "professional *henro*," to the relatively well-off, to fugitives from justice such as Okyō, to local initiates, to, as will be seen shortly, the sick and dying. However, there are relatively few clear records of accurate pilgrim numbers or of the ages, provenance, or social class of Shikoku pilgrims in Tokugawa times, although one or two suggestions can be made about their overall constituency.

Maeda's analysis of Shikoku death registers over more than two centuries from 1666–1880 provides the best data available to enable some understanding of where pilgrims came from in an era where few pilgrims left written records. Maeda's studies indicate that after those from Shikoku, most pilgrims came from areas proximate to Shikoku, across the Inland Sea, and hence a short boat journey away from it. Provinces such as Bitchū and Setsu, the latter including Osaka, were followed by Harima, Bigō, and the area around Kyoto—again, all fairly heavily populated areas bordering or close to the Inland Sea. Following these were areas in the southern part of Honshu and the relatively heavily populated areas of northern Kyushu (areas with adequate seas links to Shikoku) and the slightly more distant but heavily populated area of Owari (around Nagoya), an area that has traditionally produced many pilgrims. Beyond this, a smaller number came from the more distant but heavily populated area around Edo (now Tokyo) in eastern Japan. None-theless, the proportion of Edo pilgrims was small overall.

More distant and less densely populated areas—notably the Hokuriku region, Tōhoku (northern Japan), and the southernmost parts of Kyushu—were the least well represented areas in the Tokugawa age, primarily because they were distant and hence required a longer and more trying journey just to get to and from Shikoku than from places such as Osaka and even Edo.[129] While practical realities of distance and population density clearly deter-mined the provenance of Shikoku pilgrims in the Tokugawa period, it is per-haps worth emphasizing here that the *henro* tended to draw pilgrims from closer to, rather than farther away from, the island, if only to underline the point made in chapter 1 that one should not assume that pilgrims to major sites necessarily come from afar. As the Shikoku case indicates, it is not just that a large number of its pilgrims come from the island but that its surround-ing regions have been the next most common areas from which its pilgrims have traditionally come.

The pilgrimage population, strikingly, contained a sizable female pres-ence—far more than on other pilgrimages in Japan. Based on archival infor-mation ranging from death registers, to collections of pilgrims' passports (*ōrai-tegata*), to the *fuda* acquired by the Ochi family of Agata in Iyo from pilgrims they lodged between 1799–1862, Kouamé shows that over 30 percent—and perhaps slightly more still—of Shikoku pilgrims were female.[130] Hoshino, too, affirms a high female presence and suggests that one reason for this was because Kōyasan was prohibited territory for women until 1873, when reforms introduced after the Meiji Restoration ended the prohibition on females entering Kōyasan. In Tokugawa times, female devotees wishing to "visit" Kōbō Daishi could not go there and thus might turn to Shikoku instead.[131]

Marginality, death, and disease

Many pilgrims in Shikoku were poor and existed in desperate circumstances. Many, too, were sick and died on the road. Such extreme situations meant that pilgrims were potentially dangerous and disruptive, which affected the perceptions that local people had of pilgrims and affected the ways in which regional and local authorities regarded them. Death was certainly a common factor on the pilgrimage. Even during his largely comfortable pilgrimage in 1819, Arai Raisuke was well aware of the prevalence of death. On one day alone he records seeing the bodies of two dead pilgrims and hearing about the death of a child pilgrim at the lodge where he had spent the night. Unsur-prisingly, Arai records that he was depressed by this close presence of death.[132]

The presence of gravestones along the route and the image of Shikoku as the "country of death" have been mentioned in chapter 2. Maeda's studies and pilgrims' journals such as Arai's indicate that this association with death was a daily reality for Tokugawa pilgrims. Maeda found 1,345 recorded deaths of pilgrims in the pilgrimage temple death registers he examined, while many temples, such as Tatsueji, which has thirty-seven Tokugawa-era pilgrim graves, interred numerous pilgrims in their graveyards.[133] My examination of the death register *(kakochō)* kept by Gokurakuji (Temple 2) indicates that even in the nineteenth century pilgrim deaths were not uncommon in temple precincts. In 1811, for instance, a male pilgrim named Kakubei, from Ishikawa in Kaga Province, died at Gokurakuji and was given a Buddhist posthumous name and funeral there. In 1832 a pilgrim from Harima died at the temple gate and was given a funeral and posthumous name, and another from Mihara on Awaji Island died on the temple grounds.[134] Since Gokurakuji is close to the port of Naruto, where many pilgrims entered the island, it is possible that some of these came to Shikoku already sick and were seeking either a miraculous cure through Kōbō Daishi's grace or the hopes of postdeath salvation through dying in the enhanced state of grace of a pilgrim. Hence some of them were not able to get very far before they expired.[135] Pilgrim deaths decreased in number in the latter part of the nineteenth and earlier twentieth centuries, probably due to improved health services as the country modernized and because better transport meant that it became easier to return the bodies of dead pilgrims to their home regions, thus meaning that they did not appear in Shikoku death registers.[136] However, deaths still occurred from time to time to remind pilgrims of the association of the *henro* and death: Takamure mentions an article in a Shikoku newspaper about the death of a seventy-four-year-old female pilgrim in Kōchi in 1937.[137]

The prevalence of death was in part due to the numbers of pilgrims who went to Shikoku on "kill or cure" pilgrimages. One of the most common illnesses that afflicted Shikoku pilgrims was Hansen's disease (leprosy). While there are no data available to indicate how many pilgrims suffered from this, there is evidence that some did and that a link existed between the *henro* and the disease in the popular imagination.[138] The disease has always, because of its disfiguring effects, coupled, erroneously, with fears of contagion and—especially in premodern times—notions that it was the result of or punishment for some fearful sin, cast fear into populations across the world, and Japan was no exception.[139]

Those who contracted the disease were often driven from their homes because of the fear that they would otherwise spread it, some even being chased away by their own families, who were concerned that if such news got around, all in the family would be ostracized. Sufferers often became outcasts chased from place to place, so that many found a life of permanent travel, becoming a pilgrim in Shikoku and sustaining themselves through begging for alms, was a necessity rather than an option. Shikoku, too, was appealing to sufferers because of its promise or hope of miraculous cures, as evidenced by the *Kudokuki* tale of the pilgrim who is cured of the disease through the *henro*. Both Hoshino and Shinjō consider that many permanent or professional pilgrims in Shikoku in the Tokugawa period suffered from the disease.[140] Many did the pilgrimage until they died, and some, according to Maeda, sought to protect their families from the apparent stigma of leprosy by carrying documents stating that in the event of death they were to be interred where they died and that their families were not to be informed of their condition.[141]

Such, too, was the association between the disease and the pilgrimage that according to Maeda, in certain parts of Japan in the Tokugawa period, if one stated that someone had gone to Shikoku, it was widely surmised that s/he had leprosy.[142] Sufferers did not, however, necessarily meet with sympathetic reactions from other pilgrims and were frequently barred from pilgrimage lodges or made to sleep in separate huts, while in places there were even separate paths for them to use.[143]

Sufferers of the disease were common until the late 1930s, when police roundups forcibly removed leprosy sufferers from the route and placed them in special sanatoriums. Various pilgrims and temple officials who were in Shikoku in the 1920s and 1930s have spoken to me about their memories of pilgrims with the disease. Thus an elderly man who worked in the office of one of the Awa temples recalled pilgrims in the 1930s coming to the temple and holding out their books to be stamped, their hands and faces bearing the ravages of leprosy.[144] Sometimes the memories of suffering pilgrims have led temple priests to engage in charitable actions related to the disease. Thus the priest of Gokurakuji, who recalled childhood memories of seeing pilgrims suffering from leprosy visiting his temple, told me how, when visiting Burma (where his father had died during the World War II), he had been struck by the widespread incidence of the disease, recalled the prewar Shikoku situation, and decided to use some of his temple's wealth to support charitable institutions in Burma that helped sufferers.[145]

"Sacred thieves and contagious saints"

While legends wove an aura of holiness around the pilgrims and placed them in the transcendent company of Kōbō Daishi, they could also be seen as potentially dangerous and fearful. This was doubtless because so many of them were effectively marginal figures, impoverished and dependent on alms and potentially contagious carriers of diseases who might also be fugitives from the law. In this context, it might be that Shikoku attracted people in marginalized situations—a point made also by Dubisch in her study of pilgrims to the Greek island of Tinos. Dubisch notes that many of its pilgrims come from groups and classes that are marginalized in Greek society, and this causes her to wonder whether pilgrimage, rather than being a process in which pilgrims step outside their normal social milieu and become liminal, in effect draws to it those who are already liminal and on the margins of society.[146] Tokugawa Shikoku partially substantiates this idea and suggests that some pilgrimages (and Shikoku, with its generally poor clientele, would fall into this category) might well specifically attract a marginal clientele, thereby helping to create an aura of liminality around themselves.

Certainly the island's authorities were concerned enough about pilgrims to issue various texts and decrees against them. Thus a text issued by the Tosa authorities in 1810 denounced pilgrims in no uncertain terms; some pilgrims, it stated, did not respect local customs, created a nuisance and feigned illness so as to solicit alms from the locals, hawked false medicines and cures, and even turned to thieving to support themselves.[147] Sometimes they were even fugitives from the law who had disguised themselves as pilgrims in order to evade justice and eke out an existence on alms or through criminal deeds. Shikoku pilgrims were thus held in low esteem, as is indicated by Maeda's statement that in the Hokuriku region, saying that someone had gone to Shikoku (to become a pilgrim) was tantamount to saying that s/he had run away because of debts.[148]

The often wild nature of pilgrims is illustrated, even in the early twentieth century, in Takamure's writings (see below), while the dangerous image they possessed among ordinary people is illustrated by the comments made to the journalist Imai Misako when, during her Shikoku pilgrimage in the early 1980s, she visited an old friend who had grown up in Shikoku. The friend said that as a child she had been warned of the dangers of associating with pilgrims and that her parents, using images reminiscent of the tales of bogeymen in Western folklore, would warn her that if she were naughty or careless, the pilgrims might come and take her away.[149] Even in the 1960s, the temples still warned about the dangers of false pilgrims intent on stealing from others: in his 1962 pilgrimage account, Kannuchi Shinzō writes that at Ryōzenji he was given a list of advice emphasizing the common bond that existed between pilgrims but warning that some pilgrims could be thieves or worse and that one should therefore be wary of others on the road.[150]

Pilgrims, in other words, were ambivalent in image: one gave them alms because of their holy nature and association with Kōbō Daishi, yet kept them at a distance because they might spread disease, steal, or be criminals on the run from the law. They were, in effect, "sacred thieves and contagious saints,"[151] imbued with all the sanctity and danger that such marginality and ambivalence implied.

Authorities, regulations, and care

The ambivalent nature of pilgrims as sacred thieves and contagious saints and the admixture of different types of pilgrims, from young initiatory pilgrims on the lookout for partners to ascetics, devout followers of Kōbō Daishi, and pilgrims suffering from leprosy and intent on begging to keep alive, caused problems for regional authorities in Shikoku throughout the Tokugawa period and well into the twentieth century. Despite the possible economic benefits that pilgrims might bring, they were also liable to cause disruption and be a drain on the economy through their begging or when they fell ill or died. This problem was most strongly felt in Tosa, which was the longest section of the route; hence pilgrims spent longer there than in the other three fiefdoms. Also, it had the warmest climate, and it was not uncommon for beggar-pilgrims to try to pass the winters there before heading to the north of the island when the weather improved.[152] Concern, too, over the threat pilgrims might pose to public order led authorities, not without cause—since there were various cases of pilgrims causing public disorder during the Tokugawa era—to issue various edicts (of which the aforementioned 1810 Tosa edict is but one) and implement regulations restricting the movement and activities of pilgrims and punishing them for misdeeds. Yet, at the same time, the authorities recognized that even if pilgrims might be potentially dangerous and disruptive, they could also be genuinely devout and sincere in their practices, and that, as administrators of justice and the law, they had an obligation to help care for those within their midst. This dualistic attitude, reflective of the ambivalent nature of the pilgrims, comes out in the various laws and treatments applied to pilgrims in the Tokugawa period.

In 1663 the Tosa feudal authorities (who seem to have been both the most demanding and draconian in their dealings with pilgrims and also the most active in issuing decrees to ensure that pilgrims in need were cared for) issued various regulations relating to pilgrims, which formed the basis for all subsequent Tosa policies toward pilgrims. They stipulated that pilgrims could enter or exit Tosa only at two points (one at each end of the domain) and would be allowed in only if they carried a valid travel permit (*ōraitegata*) issued by the authorities of their own domain, which they had to present to local authorities wherever they traveled, and they fixed a maximum number of days that pilgrims could stay in Tosa.[153] This latter regulation was probably enacted because of the previously mentioned tendency for pilgrims to linger there in winter. A decree in 1719 limited pilgrims to thirty days in the fief.[154] Other domains also demanded that pilgrims produce travel permits. Pilgrims were often vetted—most strictly, it would appear, by Tosa border guards, although those in other fiefdoms could also be strict and refuse entry to those they suspected of not having adequate funds—to ensure they had adequate funds to support themselves while in the domain.[155] Later decrees also sought to establish that those claiming to be pilgrims were genuine, as evidenced by a decree from Tosa in 1838 stating that anyone trying to enter the domain as a pilgrim but without a *nōkyōchō* (pilgrim's book) would be refused entry.[156]

The Tosa authorities' decision, in 1663, to regulate pilgrims appears to have been founded in the concern that pilgrims were beginning to fall sick and die on the island. Two pilgrims from Edo are known to have died around this time,[157] providing local authorities with the dilemma of how to deal with the corpses of the deceased and with sick pilgrims. Concern about fugitives and miscreants also played a part here. Thus a succession of decrees sought to ensure that pilgrims behaved properly (e.g., by preventing them from begging other than on the direct path between temples) and to impose punishments for bad behavior. Tosa, no doubt in part because of its aforementioned problems with pilgrims trying to linger there had particularly harsh punishments, including branding pilgrims on the forehead or inflicting floggings for major breaches of pilgrimage regulations.[158] At times of famine, too, the Tosa authorities sought to prevent villagers from giving away much needed food to pilgrims.[159] This does not mean that Tosa alone punished pilgrims for infringements or acted harshly toward them, for other fiefs, too, sought to restrict the activities and passage of problematic pilgrims. In 1712, for example, Iyo border guards, fearing the importation of diseases, refused entry to a group of sick pilgrims coming from Tosa.[160]

Yet, while thus serving to control pilgrims, island authorities also recognized that most were not dangerous but were, rather, sincere in their activities and therefore merited support and sustenance when they fell into trouble, became ill, or died. Indeed, Kouamé asserts that the regulations that Shikoku authorities imposed were based on a sense of reciprocity of rights and duties between pilgrims, authorities, and local communities. While pilgrims were obliged to behave in appropriate ways, to carry the correct documents, and to follow the rules laid down by the authorities, they also had rights and could expect proper treatment in times of need.[161]

The 1598 establishment of *ekiroji* was an early recognition of this, as were laws from the latter part of the seventeenth century onward that obliged local and village authorities to care for sick pilgrims if they were unable to continue on their journeys.[162] As Kouamé shows, a well-established system of support developed to assist such pilgrims. Those who died were given funerals and their corpses dealt with in an appropriate manner, complete with Buddhist memorial services and posthumous names (as with the deceased pilgrims cited earlier from Gokurakuji's death register).[163] Indisposed pilgrims were assisted on their way homeward through networks of intervillage cooperation, with pilgrims helped from village to village and eventually to the ports leading out of Shikoku.[164] Yamamoto describes the workings of this system via the repatriation process of a woman from the Izumo region who came to Shikoku as a pilgrim with a female companion in late 1787 but, after becoming separated from her, fell grievously ill in the region of Temple 21. She was first cared for where she became ill, and when she had recovered sufficiently, was aided on her journey back to Izumo—a process that involved her being accompanied by various people who passed her on from village to village across Shikoku and then across the Inland Sea and through Honshu until, in spring 1788, she got back home.[165] The networks that developed around aiding sick pilgrims to return home contributed, according to Kouamé, to a sense of regional identity in Shikoku, forging links between villages and across regions.[166] Through such networks and support mechanisms, the authorities in Shikoku demonstrated that while they could be tough with miscreant pilgrims, they would also support pilgrims when they were devout. In other words, while they recognized that pilgrims could be contagious, deceitful thieves, they understood that they could also be saints worthy of assistance.

The Meiji Restoration: Trauma, destruction, repression

The first half of the nineteenth century has been described by Kouamé as a "golden age" in Shikoku, when pilgrim numbers were high, a relative balance had been established between the need to regulate and support pilgrims, and economic conditions facilitated the growth of pilgrim numbers and infrastructure support.[167] However, this picture was to change as Japan was thrown into turmoil when the country came under external threat, opened to foreign powers, and underwent a traumatic period of change in which the Tokugawa feudal regime collapsed and a new, modernizing nation-state that drew on Western institutional models came into being through the Meiji Restoration of 1868. This turbulent period had a major impact on the *henro* as well.

The new Meiji government was determined to modernize the country—a process that included displacing Buddhism as the main religion of state, elevating Shinto, and eradicating supposedly "superstitious" and "folk" practices. This policy resulted in the *haibutsu kishaku* movement, a government-inspired campaign to drive out Buddhism, close Buddhist temples, and force Buddhist priests to return to lay life, as well as the policy known as *shinbutsu bunri*, separating the Shinto gods *(kami)* and the buddhas, an activity that saw the enforced separation of institutions that had formerly contained both Shinto and Buddhist figures and halls of worship. In the early 1870s thousands of Buddhist temples were razed, and many that had, in Tokugawa times, shared premises with Shinto shrines were closed down, while complexes that had incorporated both Shinto and Buddhist figures of worship and institutions were forcibly separated into distinct entities, usually through the expulsion of their Buddhist elements.[168]

Many of the *henro* temples were affected by these attacks. The seven pilgrimage sites that combined Shinto and Buddhist institutional themes were transformed into Shinto shrines as their Buddhist images of worship were ejected and their temple structures leveled. While these policies and activities were in evidence throughout Shikoku (e.g., the Buddhist elements were expunged from all four regional Ichinomiya sites), it was in Tosa that the most extreme impact was felt. Seven of Tosa's sixteen *henro* sites were destroyed or closed down, and several others were badly damaged and left untended for years. Kōnomineji (Temple 27), for example, was left in ruins for almost two decades and its main image of worship kept at the nearby Temple 26 until Kōnomineji was restored in 1887.[169]

The anti-Buddhism campaign proved to be unpopular and was eventually abandoned in the mid-1870s, after which many of the temples that had been damaged were gradually restored as and when their priests and communities were able to raise funds to that end. The effect of the campaign on the *henro* was quite striking in that after it was over, the sites on the pilgrimage were all Buddhist. Prior to the Meiji era, as has been mentioned earlier, the eighty-eight sites had included shrines and shrine-temple complexes, but after the early Meiji assault on Buddhism, all the sites became Buddhist temples—a situation that remains to the present. Overall, then, the impact of the Meiji Restoration and its policy of separating Shinto from Buddhism was to give the pilgrimage a more explicit "Buddhist" orientation.

The impact of the anti-Buddhist campaign took some time to be cleared up and left one severe problem that lingered for several decades. This involved the thirtieth site, Zenrakuji, which was located within the Tosa Ichinomiya shrine-temple complex and was where pilgrims visiting the complex got their books stamped. In 1870, however, the Shinto shrine priests at the complex banned pilgrims from the premises, complaining that they were disruptive, liable to cause fires and behave inappropriately before the gods.[170] Thereafter, they transformed the complex into Tosa Jinja (Tosa Shrine) and had the Buddhist elements within it destroyed. Zenrakuji's main image of worship was taken away and, in 1876, placed under the protection of another temple, Anrakuji, in Kōchi City. Anrakuji, too, had been destroyed in the *haibutsu kishaku* movement, but as attempts to repair the excesses of the anti-Buddhist movement progressed, it was rebuilt in 1876. Because it contained the main image from the pilgrimage site, it became Temple 30 and was visited as such by pilgrims. Eventually, too, Zenrakuji was also rebuilt, albeit much later in 1929, by which time Anrakuji had long become used to its position as Temple 30. However, those behind the rebuilding of Zenrakuji argued that their temple, as the site of the original *fudasho*, was the rightful Temple 30. This was, unsurprisingly, resisted by those in charge of Anrakuji, and hence a dispute arose over the legitimacy of each temple's claims to be Temple 30, Anrakuji's being based on its possession of the original site's main image of worship and Zenrakuji's on its possession of the original site. For several decades an uneasy compromise existed in which guidebooks listed both sites as Temple 30, both were permitted to stamp pilgrims' books as Temple 30, and pilgrims chose which to visit. This problematic position was resolved in 1994 through mediation by the Shikoku Reijōkai, with Zenrakuji being declared Temple 30 and Anrakuji acquiring special status as its *okunoin* (inner sanctum), which pilgrims are encouraged to visit. Reijōkai officials insisted to me that everyone was content with this solution, and certainly the temple officials I met at Zenrakuji in May 1997 were happy with a solution that meant every pilgrim would visit their temple. By contrast, there were no pilgrims around when I went to Anrakuji, and while the priests there said they accepted the new position, it was evident that they were being more diplomatic than frank.[171]

Ban the pilgrimage and arrest the pilgrims!
Anti-*henro* sentiments in Meiji Japan

The upheavals of Meiji did not affect just the temples. Aggressive anti-pilgrim policies such as the aforementioned Ichinomiya Shrine ban on pilgrims were supplemented by demands that the pilgrimage be banned because it was "superstitious," out of kilter with the modern, rational society that Meiji Japan aspired to become, and liable to foster instability by encouraging people to become wanderers and beggars. Such demands occurred in the context also of a nationwide law that was promulgated in 1872 banning the practice of *takuhatsu* (the act of begging for alms carried out by Buddhist monks) and that not only impacted on and restricted the activities of pilgrims, but also made them appear to be out of step with the law of the land.[172] Such demands occurred, too, at a time when nationwide campaigns were being conducted to improve hygiene and eliminate diseases such as trachoma; in this context, the presence of itinerant pilgrims who had long been seen, in Shikoku, as contagious outsiders and potential carriers of disease could be seen as especially problematic.[173]

The emergent Japanese mass media of the era, notably in Tosa, were quick to pick up on these issues and to demand action against pilgrims. Thus the *Tosa shinbun* of May 9, 1876, demanded that all pilgrims be thrown out of the region, claiming that they were almost all vagrants, few of whom came to pray and most of whom were intent on treachery and theft. Repeating all the prejudices and local demonic folklore that surrounded pilgrims, the paper claimed that they were carriers of diseases who might spread infections among the local populace; they could simply die by the wayside and their corpses spread diseases; their begging was a nuisance and frightened locals; and, if they did not get enough through their begging, they might resort to theft or even kidnap young children. The paper, whose views were reiterated in other newspapers in the region, further called for *settai* to be banned and for the police to strictly control pilgrims.[174]

Such views clearly carried weight with the authorities. In the same month, the newspaper reported that police had forced a number of beggar-pilgrims to leave the province,[175] while further newspaper reports in Iyo and the rest of Shikoku spoke of police roundups of pilgrims *(henrogari)* who were unable to satisfy the authorities that they were genuine, while those with no demonstrable means were expelled or arrested.[176] Such roundups continued well into the twentieth century, contributing to a sense of fear and marginality among pilgrims amply demonstrated by Takamure's 1918 account of how the pilgrims she encountered were worried by rumors of *henrogari*.[177]

Such hostility and unrest caused pilgrim numbers to fall steeply.[178] Yet, despite all, some pilgrims continued to travel, Nakatsuka Mōhei remained on his incessant pilgrimage, and many locals still defiantly gave alms as they had in Tokugawa times even when their feudal lords banned *settai*. In 1881 the ban that had been imposed throughout the country on begging was rescinded,[179] although the authorities in Shikoku continued to maintain restrictions on how and when pilgrims could seek alms there. As stability and economic growth replaced the turbulence of the early Meiji years, however, the attitudes of the authorities appear to have softened, and pilgrim numbers began to grow again: by the 1890s accounts indicate that as many as five hundred pilgrims a day were visiting the temples during the prime (March–May) period.[180]

Takamure Itsue and the wildness of pilgrimage

Despite the less than sympathetic attitude of regional authorities in Shikoku and the continuing threat of pilgrim roundups, this general revival in pilgrim numbers appears to have continued into the early decades of the twentieth century. Certainly, by the time Takamure set out on foot from her home in Kumamoto in Kyushu in 1918 to walk the *henro*, it is evident, as her accounts of her journey indicate, that there were plentiful pilgrims in Shikoku and that despite the activities of the authorities and the demands of newspapers and others in Shikoku, many of them were little more healthy or upright than in earlier times. Takamure's journey took several months, and she wrote extensive accounts of it that provide insights into the experiences and emotional dimensions of pilgrimage and the ways in which it transformed her life (see below, and chapter 8). Her writings also provide some of the most vivid accounts of what the *henro* was like in the earlier part of the twentieth century. Takamure, in fact, wrote a number of accounts of her pilgrimage, the first in a series of articles for a newspaper in her home town of Kumamoto written during her pilgrimage and later collated into a book, and two further volumes written two decades after her pilgrimage, when she was living in Tokyo and returning in her mind—often nostalgically—to the formative event of her life.[181]

Her initial contemporaneous account provides a stark picture of the ups and downs of *henro* life. Hardship was an intrinsic part of the pilgrim's path, and Takamure informs us of the difficulties she had because of the physical strains of walking, having to sleep out when no accommodation was available, the fears of police roundups, and the presence of sick and dying pilgrims. Pilgrims' lodges were often dirty, crowded, uncomfortable, and difficult to rest in, their communal rooms full of the wild, the mad, the sick, and the destitute.[182] She became aware of leprosy for the first time when she saw its presence among pilgrims,[183] and she encountered sexual discrimination not only in the advances made to her but in being made to wait, because she was female, to use the bath at lodges until all male pilgrims had bathed.[184]

Yet she also had good experiences, received *settai,* and felt a sense of bonding with her fellow pilgrims. When she wrote again about her pilgrimage experiences during the 1930s, it is clear that such positive sentiments outweighed any others, and she speaks of the sense of *henro ai* (pilgrim's love) and *dōgyō* (doing the same practice, togetherness) that, she felt, permeated the pilgrimage and bonded all pilgrims together. These sentiments came to the fore when staying at Shinnen-an, where she speaks of how *dōgyō* relates to the pilgrim's relationship with all his/her fellow pilgrims and with the atmosphere of mutual love that is produced in the pilgrimage, commenting that

> no matter how much of an unbeliever anyone is, if they just once visit Shikoku, they will definitely feel this atmosphere of pilgrimage love.
> In Shikoku everyone, whether a wretched pilgrim begging for food, an unfortunate wracked with illness, or the proud daughter of a rich family, will, even if they have no connections with each other, without fail greet each other with a respectful gesture of veneration.[185]

In Shikoku, Takamure states, one meets the blind, the leprous, and all manner of other unfortunates who, in other settings, one might recoil from but who, in Shikoku, become one's spiritual guides *(sendatsu);* in this one corner of Japan, she affirms, one can be joyful that the worlds of freedom and spirituality have been preserved.[186]

Takamure's later accounts of her pilgrimage are clearly tinged by nostalgia—a nostalgia intensified by the fact that she spent the decades after doing the *henro* working as a writer in isolated circumstances in Tokyo. Yet they also resonate with the experiences recounted to me in oral testimonies by pilgrims I have interviewed who did the pilgrimage during the 1920s and 1930s and by Shikoku residents who remembered this era. Their recollections, too, generally substantiate the picture found in Takamure's writings of disease, poverty, hardship, uncomfortable lodgings, and the need to seek alms, along with warm—possibly rather nostalgic—reminiscences of community feelings and togetherness.

The reminiscences of members of the Shiga Shingyōkai—including the widow of Naitō Kinpō as she recalled her 1927 honeymoon pilgrimage with her new husband—are fairly typical of such interviews. Naitō's widow spoke of sleeping out and begging to get enough rice to eat and to hand over as rent at pilgrims' lodges. She and her friends also reminisced about the *senbei futon* (rice cracker futon, so called because Japanese rice crackers are thin and hard), which were thin, hard, matted, and often infested with lice from constant use at *henro* lodges, and of crowded, unclean, and noisy communal rooms. As they spoke of such discomforts, however, they also emphasized the camaraderie and shared sense of purpose that existed at such places, and their discussion took on an air of nostalgia, comparing those difficult times favorably with the more comfortable setup of the present, with its clean and spacious inns, good and plentiful food, and excellent transport facilities and organized tours that enable pilgrims to reach their destination in time for a good bath and meal. All of this, they felt, detracted from the sense of shared purpose and communal belonging that existed among prewar pilgrims; the pilgrims today had it easy compared with them. However, when I asked if they would prefer to go back to the hardship of those days, walking, begging, sleeping out or on *senbei futon* rather than using the bus tours that the Shingyōkai now organizes, they laughed and said no—the hardships were good to *have experienced,* and they wished that everyone could have the chance to do so once. However, now they were content to live in and experience the comfort of modern pilgrimages.

Modernization, transport, and tourism

If the Meiji period gave rise to concerted hostility toward the pilgrimage, the modernizing processes it set in motion also aided the pilgrimage's development. As Japan built up its industrial and technological capacities, it developed an efficient transport infrastructure that, aligned with the country's growing economic wealth, gave pilgrims increasing choice in how they made their pilgrimages and brought increasing numbers of pilgrims with money to Shikoku.

From the nineteenth century onward one finds an increasing use of horse and cart as a means of transportation in Shikoku and of new roads capable of accommodating them, as well as improved ferry and boat services along the coast.[187] Those with money took advantage of such services, as is demonstrated by the journey of the Shingon priest Kobayashi Uhō and a companion in 1907, who walked much of the way but who also used horse and cart services and ferries and boats when they were available.[188]

The advent of train and bus services in the early twentieth century enabled pilgrims to move rapidly along some parts of the route—and even, in one case, led to a change of position for one temple when, in 1921, Hōjūji (Temple 62) was demolished and rebuilt a short distance away because it stood in the way of a planned new railway line.[189] In the 1920s, too, the internal combustion engine began to make its mark, with the advent of local bus services, hire cars, and taxis. This developing transport infrastructure, along with economic growth and increased facilities for transferring money and accessing bank accounts, helped propel what Hoshino has called a "travel boom" in the 1920s and 1930s, which led to growing numbers of pilgrims, often well enough off to utilize taxis and hired cars, visiting Shikoku.[190]

At the same time, too, there was an expansion in lodging facilities as temples began to provide such services for pilgrims. While pilgrims had often been able to sleep in the precincts of some temples, during the 1920s some temples began to build specialized temple lodges *(shukubō)* for pilgrims with funds to pay for it. The first to do so on a regular basis appears to have been Temple 61 (Kōonji), which initially constructed a temple lodge because of its popularity as a place to pray for safe childbirth, which led to large numbers of women coming to visit at festival times. The lodge thus constructed was also used by pilgrims. It became evident that pilgrims liked being able to stay at temples, and Kōonji became especially popular in this respect, expanding its lodge until, now, it is an extensive modern building capable of housing several hundred pilgrims each night.[191] Other temples followed Kōonji's lead, with the result that eventually the majority of temples provided *shukubō*, which, as was noted in chapter 3, have become a favored overnight option for pilgrims.

The increase in pilgrim numbers in the 1920s was aided by a change in the attitude of the mass media toward the *henro*. Whereas in the aftermath of the Meiji Restoration the mass media had generally been hostile, portraying the *henro* as a manifestation of the antiquated and superstitious past that had to be eradicated in the drive toward modernization, by the 1920s attitudes had changed, with some in the media starting to look at it not as a symbol of a degraded past, but as a sign of tradition that stood against the march of modernity that threatened Japan's cultural heritage. In March 1927, for example, Aibara Kumatarō, a Tokyo newspaper editor originally from Shikoku, made a series of radio broadcasts about the pilgrimage and his experiences growing up on the route, contrasting what he called "the different world" *(betsu no sekai)* of the pilgrimage, in which traditions were preserved and people had pure hearts and helped each other by providing alms and lodging to pilgrims, with critical comments about the modern, urban lifestyle that was developing in Japan.[192] Aibara, who subsequently published a book about his experiences of growing up in Shikoku,[193] thus promoted an idealized image of the pilgrimage not dissimilar to that highlighted in modern media portrayals and recent television documentaries. His broadcasts were a forerunner of the imagery that has framed the *henro* in the postwar era and has proved intrinsic to its appeal in the present day.

Other journalists who drew attention to the pilgrimage in this era included Shimomura Kainan and Iijima Hiroshi from *Asahi shinbun,* who did the *henro* using a variety of modes of transport in order to write a series of newspaper articles about it; they later published these articles as a book.[194] From the

1920s onward, too, the improvement in transport facilities was mirrored by a growth in the number of guidebooks about the *henro,* often with a tourist orientation.[195] Shima Namio, for example, wrote a series of articles (later published as a book) for the travel magazine *Tabi* about his pilgrimage done during four visits to Shikoku between 1926 and 1928. Shima drew attention to the island's historical and scenic attractions that could be visited en route and provided information about transport facilities that could make the pilgrimage more convenient and comfortable. Thus, for example, he advised pilgrims going from Temple 11 to Temple 12 (which are connected by a steep path through the mountains) to take an easier, roundabout route by bus to a village from which they could readily walk up to Temple 12.[196] Interestingly, while Shima begins his account by declaring he has no faith or belief,[197] his views appear to have changed as he traveled, for he later extols the "pure spirit" of the pilgrimage, which is, he says, founded in feelings of gratitude, repentance, and austerity.[198]

Other guidebooks of the era similarly emphasized convenience and tourism. Adachi Chūichi's 1934 guidebook *Dōgyō ninin Shikoku henro tayori,* for example, provided information on the sites, convenient modes of travel, and other sights of interest around them. The book proved popular, going through eight editions between 1934 and 1937.[199] Pilgrims were clearly keen to use the island's transport facilities; thus in 1931 Miyao Shigeo did the *henro* in just twenty days, walking when the sites were close together but taking buses, cars, and trains as available and when the temples were far apart. He also emphasized that his main motive was sightseeing *(kengaku)* rather than faith and devotion.[200]

Even Buddhist priests such as the Rinzai Zen monk Ōzeki Gyōō, whose devotion to Kōbō Daishi was noted in chapter 1, warmly embraced modern transportation. Ōzeki's 1936 pilgrimage account combines discussions of devotion, legends, and miraculous events with descriptions of how he took time out to enjoy the island's amenities and to make his journey easier. He, for instance, rested for two days at Hiwasa, near Temple 23, where he went swimming, and then used a hired car to get to Temple 24—a journey that would have taken two days by foot.[201] Elsewhere he used rickshaws, trains, and cars, especially when the temples were far apart.[202] Ogihara Seisensui's account of his 1938 pilgrimage also indicates a similarly relaxed attitude, in which he states that he felt no obligation to walk and that while the slow pace of foot travel was rewarding, he also found bus and train services to be useful. Ogihara's account gives a sense of the commercial infrastructure of the time, referring to shops that sold pilgrimage equipment and to advertisements he saw by the roadside for pilgrims' lodges. Ogihara also mentions visits to coffee shops, which were then clearly a rarity in Shikoku, as is clear when he comes across one in the town of Uwajima and remarks that this was his first chance to drink coffee in ten days.[203]

Not everyone approved of such developments, however. Complaints that such modern developments went against the spirit of the *henro* were voiced by some, including the Tokyo-based Shingon priest Tomita Gakujun. Tomita —who deeply influenced Takamure during the 1930s—established an association, the Henro Dōkōkai, in 1928 to promote the pilgrimage and subsequently, between 1931 and 1942, also published a monthly magazine titled *Henro*. Through its pages Tomita waged a campaign in which he published various editorials and articles insisting that modern (e.g., trains and cars) modes of transport were contrary to the true spirit of the *henro* and that people who traveled by them were not genuine pilgrims.[204] Tomita's criticisms articulate a recurrent issue raised over the centuries in Shikoku, as in studies of pilgrimage in general, about whether the means by which people travel or the ways in which they behave have a bearing on their status as pilgrims. Tomita, in speaking of "genuine" pilgrims, is using the same notions as those of Shikoku authorities in the Tokugawa period when they sought to differentiate between those they saw as genuine and those they saw as false pilgrims—and they can be found also in the criticisms cited in chapter 1 by those who view present-day bus pilgrims similarly, as well as by the pilgrims to Santiago discussed by Frey, who dismiss those who go by bus and car as tourists.

Early twentieth-century pilgrimage patterns

Mass transportation in the first half of the twentieth century did not initially broaden the areas from which pilgrims came to any great extent. The most comprehensive study of pilgrimage patterns in this period is by Hoshino, based on an extended study of the records of pilgrim lodges in Kuma in Ehime Prefecture, close to Temple 44, during the 1930s and early 1940s.[205] The pilgrimage temples in this area also form a local pilgrimage done as an initiation ritual, and Hoshino is aware that many pilgrims staying at the lodges were probably engaged in this activity, rather than doing the *henro* as a whole. This suggests that the practice of doing initiatory pilgrimages remained strong during the 1930s, a point confirmed by Hayasaka Akira, whose childhood memories of the *henro* from the 1930s include not only mendicant pilgrims (see above), but also large numbers of young women from his local region doing the *henro* as a prenuptial initiation rite.[206]

Hoshino's study shows that the majority of those staying at the pilgrims' lodges (56 percent in all) were from Shikoku, a figure that is perhaps disproportionate because of the local pilgrimage route. Nonetheless, it provides ample evidence that in the 1930s, as in the Tokugawa era and the modern day, local people featured prominently among the pilgrims. The next most prominent regions for pilgrims were the Kinki region around Osaka, followed by Kyushu, then Chūgoku (the region north of Shikoku across the Inland Sea), and then Chūbu (the region around Nagoya). With the exception of

Kyushu, which seems to have become more prominent as a place of pilgrim origin by this era, these are the areas from which the bulk of Tokugawa pilgrims came. Even in this era, the *henro* did not attract many people from farther afield: less than 2 percent came from the densely populated Kantō region around Tokyo. Generally, it would appear that those from within Shikoku were more likely to travel in groups, while those from farther afield traveled individually, or if in groups, because of having met up with other pilgrims on the island. The majority—reflecting the saying about Shikoku coming alive in spring with the sound of pilgrims' bells—came in March (17.7 percent), April (37.6 percent), and May (13.1 percent). More (65 percent in all) were male, compared to 35 percent for females—a figure that suggests a shift was going on in the gender balance that has continued thereafter. As was noted earlier, around 30 percent of the pilgrims in the eighteenth and nineteenth centuries were female, and as I commented in chapter 3, nowadays females are in a clear majority. Hoshino also shows that the main age groups represented in the *henro* in this period were those aged between twenty and twenty-nine (18 percent) and those aged between sixty and sixty-nine (19 percent).[207]

Temples, Shingon Buddhism, and organized publicity

While critics such as Tomita were unhappy about the impact of modernity, it is clear that many in authority at the temples were happy at the potential it offered for increasing pilgrim numbers and—for Shingon authorities on the island—utilizing the pilgrimage as a means of enhancing sectarian agendas. These two themes were among the most important developments in the *henro* in the period up to World War II, along with increased cooperation between the temples, and they have remained prominent features in its postwar history too.

Until the twentieth century there is little evidence of any serious coordinated activity between the temples—a point that may go some way toward answering why the temples appear to have been rather anonymous in the pilgrimage formation process. This lack was most likely due to the fact that communications were difficult until the modern age, while the geographical spread of the temples meant that their main source of news about each other came from pilgrims. However, as the age of modern communications and swifter transport progressed, it became easier for the temples to maintain close contact with each other and develop lines of cooperative action. In 1912, for example, the twenty-three Awa temples formed an association and began to hold regular meetings aimed at coordinating the pilgrimage route in its region. No further attempt at developing a formal organizational structure occurred, however, until after World War II.[208]

However, in the 1930s there were attempts at getting closer cooperation in which the Kōyasan Shingon sect was deeply involved. In 1934 it commemorated the 1,100th anniversary of Kūkai's death/entry into nirvana by encouraging people to visit places associated with Kōbō Daishi and Shingon and promoting both Kōyasan and the *henro* in this respect—as it was to do again half a century later in 1984, on the 1,150th anniversary. It also commissioned the artist Yoshida Shōsaburō to paint pictures of the *henro* temples as part of this publicity campaign.[209] In this period, too, the sect further emphasized the links between the *henro* and Shingon by affirming the image of the *henro* as a four-stage journey to enlightenment and as representing a sacred mandala. Tomita played a prominent role here, using the medium of his pilgrimage association and magazine to emphasize Shingon sectarian dimensions to the *henro* and to argue that it was a setting for esoteric Shingon Buddhist training.[210]

Further cooperation aimed at promoting the pilgrimage occurred in 1937, when the eighty-eight temples were persuaded to organize a *degaichō* in Osaka. This was the first time all eighty-eight were involved in such a joint venture, which was organized at the instigation of the Osaka-based Nankai Railway Company, which serves Kōyasan and has close connections with the Shingon sect. In the *degaichō,* copies of the main images of all eighty-eight temples were exhibited in a park in Osaka, along with information about the pilgrimage and its customs. The event was widely publicized through newspaper advertisements and events, including parades and the use of well-known stars of the era. It ran for forty-three days between May and June 1937, drawing around two hundred thousand visitors and providing the pilgrimage with immense publicity.[211]

However, the event happened at an inopportune time, when Japan had become embroiled in overseas military activities in China and elsewhere and when the specter of war was looming over the country. Not long afterward, Japan went to war—and eventual defeat—against the Allies. Such turmoil, and its economic effects, naturally affected pilgrim numbers; even at the time of the *degaichō* pilgrim numbers had started to be affected, while during the war period the pilgrimage and its temples were neglected for obvious reasons. The publicity generated by the *degaichō* thus had little impact. However, the event is significant in that it showed the temples that they could work with commercial organizations to promote the pilgrimage and showed how, through skilful marketing and publicity, they could bring the pilgrimage to the attention of a wider audience—themes that have come to characterize much of postwar *henro* history.

Ambivalence, marginality, asceticism, and leisure

The history of the *henro,* as this chapter has indicated, is one in which, from ascetic beginnings, the pilgrimage developed into a mass practice, attracting a wide variety of participants from ascetics, the sick and dying, and seekers after miraculous cures, to local youths in search of partners and those who were happy to use trains and enjoy relaxing diversions. The multiplicity of themes within the *henro*'s development also indicates a variety of often contradictory and ambivalent strands in which pilgrims could be seen as sacred figures and contagious thieves, as dangerous and disturbing threats to peace and the public purse and genuine devotees who merited support and care. The ambivalence of earlier eras carried over into the twentieth century, when, as pilgrims became better off and more able to make use of modern transport infrastructures and as the pilgrimage itself became safer for travelers, voices came to be raised about whether such pilgrims could be "genuine."

By the 1930s the *henro*, while retaining an ascetic, arduous, and liminal dimension, was beginning to be increasingly subsumed with images of modern travel, comfort, and tourism. These were to become dominant images in postwar Shikoku, an era in which impoverished and sick pilgrims virtually disappeared, while those who could travel in some style increased in number and the sorts of facilities that could support them in this grew rapidly. At the same time, the levels of organization within the pilgrimage increased as the temples mobilized and developed a coherent organizational structure and as interactions between external interests and pilgrimage organizations began to form. These are themes that have their origins in the prewar period but that came to the fore and have characterized the pilgrimage in the postwar era. It is to this era and these issues that I turn next.

5 Shaping the Pilgrimage

From Poverty to the Package Tour in Postwar Japan

Nowadays Gokurakuji (Temple 2) looks well off. Its buildings, from the priest's house to its *shukubō*, are in excellent condition, either new or renovated to the highest standards, its gardens are well maintained, and its Buddhist statues resplendent. Its opulence stems from its status as a pilgrimage temple and from the pilgrims who are a prime source of income, paying fees when getting their scrolls and books stamped, making monetary offerings when they pray, and perhaps also purchasing amulets and the like and paying for other religious services.

Income is boosted when a temple runs a successful *shukubō*, as does Gokurakuji, whose well-equipped, clean, and friendly lodge run by the priest's wife and local helpers accommodates large parties of pilgrims, especially during the peak spring pilgrimage season. When I visited it in April 2000, for instance, there were ninety-seven pilgrims, in three separate parties, staying overnight—typical, I was told, for the time of year. Gokurakuji, like many temples, also runs a shop where pilgrims can buy pilgrimage items and souvenirs—and which also does a good trade, especially from overnight visitors.

Such prosperity contrasts with the picture of marginality and poverty painted in the previous chapter and with the situation immediately after World War II. According to pilgrims and priests who remember the era, many of the temples were run-down and some were without priests. Gokurakuji was a case in point: its head priest had been ordered to serve as an army chaplain in Burma and had died there, leaving the temple officially in the hands of his six-year-old son, who was looked after by other family members.[1] Economic conditions meant that locals were unable to support pilgrims; one Shikoku resident recalled that *settai* disappeared in her village in this era.[2] (As will be seen in chapter 6, the custom has not, however, died, for as the economic situation in Shikoku improved, people began giving alms again, primarily to those on foot).

Naitō Hirozō recalled that when he made his 1946 pilgrimage mentioned in chapter 3, the temples were in disrepair and little food or *settai* was available. There were few pilgrims, mostly grateful returnee soldiers like him, giving thanks to Kōbō Daishi for helping them survive the war.[3] Some were escaping personal tragedies of the war, such as the elderly pilgrim who told the nun Tezuka Myōken, when they met on the pilgrimage some decades later, that he had returned from Manchuria at the end of the war to find his home in Osaka destroyed by bombing and his wife and children dead. In grief he set off for Shikoku to become a pilgrim and had lived as such for the next thirty years, making, he said, his home under the Shikoku sky.[4] Even in the early 1950s pilgrims such as these would not have had many companions: Shimizutani Kōshō, a priest from Asakusa Kannon Temple in Tokyo and a prominent writer on pilgrimage who visited Shikoku in the mid-1950s, spoke to me of poor, run-down temples, few pilgrims, and temple priests very unsure of the future.[5]

Yet from the mid-1950s onward, immense changes have appeared in the *henro*, affecting its infrastructure and the style of travel of pilgrims, to say nothing of their status. The transformation of Gokurakuji from its impoverished, priestless state of 1945 to its current condition is indicative of this process, which is in many respects the most striking feature of the *henro*'s post-

Gokurakuji's courtyard, temple office, garden, and new buildings.

war history. This process, in which poverty has been replaced by financial well-being, has been accompanied by a change in the general image of the pilgrim, from a potentially dangerous outsider leeching off Shikoku society to a source of income for the local community and symbol of cultural heritage. This process is linked to the emergence of postwar Japan as an economic power and to questions about cultural identity and heritage that have accompanied Japan's rapid transformation into a technologically advanced society. In this process pilgrimage has changed from being frowned on by civic authorities into a practice feted by television documentaries as a manifestation of Japanese cultural heritage and proclaimed by regional authorities as a central feature of the island's heritage and economy.

Nor can this process be separated from the development of formalized structures, interest groups, and organizations that have promoted the pilgrimage in the modern period. Prominent amongst these are the Shikoku Reijōkai, which was formed in the postwar era to provide greater coordination between the temples and which has assiduously promoted the pilgrimage and established a formal system of granting recognition and status to those who do the pilgrimage regularly, and various commercial organizations, particularly Shikoku-based bus companies, that have developed package-tour pilgrimages on the island. This transformation will be a prime focus of this chapter, as will the development of the modern pilgrimage infrastructure and the activities of the temples and their priests.

And then came the buses: Iyo Tetsu and the development of package tours

It was the world of commerce that provided the initial impetus for this postwar transformation. In effect, the "modern" era of pilgrimage in Shikoku began on April 28, 1953, when the first commercial package-tour bus pilgrimage set out from the offices of the Iyo Tetsu Company in Matsuyama. This was not the first ever Shikoku pilgrimage bus tour: in 1933, the Anan Jidōsha Company of Osaka had taken fifteen people on an all-in *henro* bus tour, but this appears to have been a one-off event.[6] The Iyo Tetsu tour, however, was followed by others organized by the company, while other firms quickly followed suit, so that within a few years commercially organized pilgrimage tours had become the dominant mode of pilgrimage in Shikoku.

This development resulted from changes to the laws regulating bus companies and the business acumen and long-term thinking of Iyo Tetsu officials. In 1951, Japanese commercial transport law was amended to permit hiring out buses for organized tours, whereas previously companies had been able to run buses only along timetabled passenger routes. This change, at a time when the war-stricken economy was improving and people were beginning to seek new leisure outlets but prior to the age of mass international tourism, facilitated the growth of package tours to tourist destinations inside Japan. Iyo Tetsu officials, thinking about the long-term future of the firm, recognized that economic development would lead to increases in car ownership and a resultant fall in the use of local and regional bus and tram services, which were the company's mainstay, and hence established a bus hire and package tour section as part of a strategy of diversification. Company officials also realized that the *henro* provided an ideal focus for such tours—especially because there were few other sites to attract people to the island. Their strategy—of arranging "all in" tours appealing to people who had the money to do the pilgrimage but not the time or inclination to do so by existing means on their own—has been highly beneficial to Iyo Tetsu, which remains the single largest provider of pilgrimage transportation in Shikoku.[7]

In essence, the Iyo Tetsu Company was building on the tradition, established before the war, of pilgrims using modern forms of transport. Indeed, an influential guidebook first published in 1953 estimated that around 80 percent of pilgrims used some form of transport during their pilgrimages. This guidebook, *Namu Daishi* (Hail to Kōbō Daishi), was published under the auspices of the Shingon sect and asserted a distinctly Shingon doctrinal orientation to the *henro* by stating that it represented the Taizō mandala and that the number eighty-eight represented the eighty-eight evil passions to be eradicated. It also noted that the historical way of doing the *henro* was by foot, but because of modern time pressures, it affirmed the value of new modes of transport such as buses. The guidebook, published under the auspices of and bearing the imprimatur of Shingon Buddhism, thus effectively legitimated traveling by bus, while several advertisements in it for regional bus services that pilgrims could use to get between the temples further appeared to emphasize this point.[8]

On April 28, 1953, Iyo Tetsu's first tour party of twelve individuals, aged between sixteen and seventy-five and each paying 13,600 yen for a tour scheduled to last fifteen days, set out from Matsuyama on what was called the *Kōbō Daishi junshaku Shikoku hachijūhakkasho meguri* (Kōbō Daishi Buddhist teaching pilgrimage to the eighty-eight sites of Shikoku).[9] This tour —at a time when the road infrastructure was poor—was far from comfortable. The pilgrims had to provide their own rice, miso, and other foodstuffs, make do with sparse accommodations, and endure bumpy, narrow roads, often having to disembark and walk quite long distances to reach temples without adequate access roads. Nor did the tour go to schedule due to frequent breakdowns, which necessitated an extra day being added to the schedule—for which the pilgrims were asked to pay an additional one hundred yen to cover costs![10]

Despite such inconveniences, feedback was positive, and Iyo Tetsu planned further ventures. Their experiment caught the attention of two other Shikoku companies, the Setouchi Bus Company of Imabari and the Kotosan

Company in Takamatsu, which shortly followed suit. Within a year or so new editions of *Namu Daishi,* the guidebook mentioned above, were carrying advertisements from these companies for all-in tours.[11] They are now the second- and third-largest carriers of pilgrims in Shikoku after Iyo Tetsu.

The market was clearly ready for such ventures. Iyo Tetsu increased its tours until, by 1965, it was sending out over one hundred buses full of pilgrims a year,[12] and bus tours had become the dominant mode of pilgrimage in Shikoku, used by over 70 percent of pilgrims.[13] Numbers have largely continued to grow since then. Between 1965 and 1975 Iyo Tetsu alone saw an annual increase of over fifty buses per year; by 1975 it was running 600 bus tours a year, by 1985 over 950, and by 2000 well over one thousand.[14] Since each bus carries an average of thirty to forty pilgrims, this means Iyo Tetsu alone is nowadays carrying between 30,000–40,000 pilgrims per year in Shikoku. Setouchi and Kotosan also experienced rapid growth—Setouchi, according to its officials, by the 1990s carrying around 27,000 per year and Kotosan around 8,000.[15] This rise has been accompanied by improvements in the quality of services (see below), with efficient and comfortable coaches that, unlike the first Iyo Tetsu tour, are not liable to break down and can transport pilgrims in some comfort.

It is not just Shikoku-based companies that are active in the bus pilgrimage trade, for nowadays companies outside the island have also built up businesses organizing pilgrimage, one of which I will discuss in chapter 7. According to temple priests and bus company officials, in recent years northern Japan, notably Iwate Prefecture, has become a growth area, due to the involvement of a tour company from there.[16]

Pilgrimage growth has not come about just through package tour buses alone, however. Modern developments have facilitated the use of a variety of other means of travel, from minibuses with small pilgrimage groups to pilgrimages by car. This latter category has grown substantially as car ownership has risen and appears especially popular with family groups. Another mode of organized pilgrimage widely used is by taxi, which is quick and relatively cheap. Local Shikoku taxi firms have become expert in organizing tours for groups of four or so pilgrims; a representative of one such firm—whose offices are conveniently located near to Temple 1—told me that groups of four or five pilgrims regularly hired his companies' taxis with a driver to take them round the whole route. His drivers had become versed in the route as a result and were able to do it in just under a week for a price per individual (including the cost of lodging the driver each night) that was little different from the charges made by companies for bus tours.[17] In addition, of course, there are walkers (a category that has grown in recent years, as was noted in chapter 1), those who walk partway and also use public transport, and the rare few who take helicopter tours.

Numbers and growth

In numerical terms, bus pilgrimages constitute the largest segment of the contemporary pilgrimage population, and their rising numbers are indicative of the general pilgrimage growth in Shikoku in the postwar period. Pilgrim numbers have fluctuated somewhat over the past five decades; by the late 1960s, studies suggest there were around 15,000 pilgrims per year doing the *henro*, mostly by bus,[18] with the numbers rising steadily through the 1970s, reaching a peak at the end of that decade when Kōonji, the temple with the largest *shukubō*, lodged 35,000 pilgrims alone.[19] Throughout the 1980s the temples regularly estimated that "around 100,000 pilgrims" did the *henro* each year, although studies by Satō Hisamitsu based on the numbers who got scrolls and books stamped at pilgrimage sites indicate the number was lower, at around 40,000–50,000 per year.[20] In 1991, data gathered by the office at Temple 41 showed that 79,000 pilgrims visited the temple in that year.[21] In the late 1990s numbers continued to rise, with Iyo Tetsu running over one thousand bus tours per year and with the numbers of walkers well into four figures, and estimates by bus officials, temple priests, and local journalists alike are that in excess of one hundred thousand pilgrims per year are now doing the *henro*. While such figures may be vague, it is certainly clear, both from Iyo Tetsu's figures of the numbers of people annually taking its tours and from the observations of those at the sites, that numbers have been, in the past few years, higher than at any time in the postwar era and probably in history.

In chapter 3 I indicated that the majority of pilgrims nowadays are female and that overall those aged sixty and over are the most numerous—clearly a result of the increasing accessibility of the pilgrimage due to bus tours. This has made the *henro* a truly national pilgrimage in that its clientele now comes from just about every region of Japan. In the Tokugawa era, as was noted in chapter 4, the pilgrims were overwhelmingly from regions in and around the island, with more distant regions such as Tōhoku barely, if at all, represented. Now, Shikoku can be quickly reached from all of Japan, and this has widened the levels of participation of people from places such as Japan's northern island of Hokkaido as well as Tōhoku; now, according to the Waseda researchers, people from these areas constitute 2.5 percent of the pilgrimage population[22]—still a small minority but far more than in the Tokugawa period and the early twentieth century. Pilgrims from Kantō (the region around Tokyo), too, have increased in number and now constitute 14.6 percent of all pilgrims, compared with less than 2 percent in the 1930s, according to Hoshino's survey.[23] On this score alone it would be fair to describe Shikoku as a national pilgrimage—even more so than Saikoku, 95 percent of whose pilgrims, according to surveys by Satō Hisamitsu, come from the region (the Kansai-Kinki area) in which it is situated.[24]

As my account in chapter 3 suggested, there are multiple personal reasons drawing people to the *henro*. There are also various other general factors that have created the environment for this growth in pilgrim numbers, of which the impact of modern transportation, coupled with Japan's postwar economic wealth, are obviously important. Improving health care and life expectancy, too, have played their part: as the priest of one temple commented to me recently, people now generally retire at sixty-five but still have many years of life to look forward to and are often still fit enough to do the pilgrimage. Both Satō Hisamitsu, in surveys of pilgrim attitudes in the late 1980s, and Hoshino, through fieldwork interviews with pilgrims, have found that a major impetus for many was the wish to seek antidotes to the materialism of modern Japan and to engage in a spiritual search, along with a desire to escape, albeit temporarily, from the pressures of modern society—a desire linked to a general nostalgia and interest in "tradition" in the face of the seemingly inexorable rise of modernity.[25] Such themes, which were touched on in chapter 1, were part of a more general growth in interest in visiting places in Japan associated with Japan's cultural and spiritual heritage—a theme that was widely encouraged by organizations such as JR (Japan's national rail

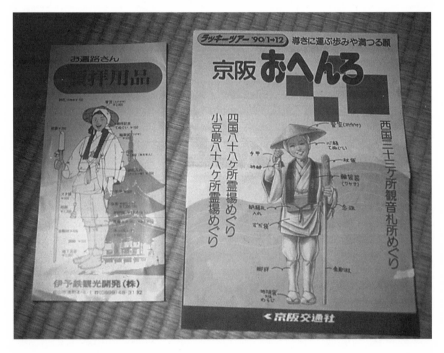

Publicity leaflets advertising pilgrimage tours run by Iyo Tetsu and other transport companies.

company), which has run various promotional campaigns to encourage people to "discover Japan" and has been influential in stimulating a massive increase in domestic travel, especially from the 1970s onward.[26] In this context the majestic scenery of Shikoku, conjuring up images of rural tranquility unspoiled by modernization, and the endurance of pilgrimage customs such as the pilgrim's attire have helped make the *henro* stand out as a symbol of cultural tradition—a factor that has not only heightened its appeal to contemporary pilgrims but that has, as will be discussed later in this chapter, been central to pilgrimage publicity produced by the temples and the bus companies.[27]

Regional governments, roads, and cable cars

This growth has been facilitated, too, by the support of Shikoku's regional governments, which, in the postwar era, have recognized that modern pilgrims are liable to bring money to the island. As officials of the Reijōkai have informed me, Shikoku regional government agencies, from highways agencies that have facilitated the development of better roads as well as road signs making it easier to get to the temples, to tourist boards that have helped publicize the pilgrimage, have played a positive role in encouraging pilgrimage development.[28]

The development of new roads has speeded up the journey around the island and made previously remote temples accessible. In 1984 a forest road was built up to Yokomineji (Temple 60), until then the last temple without road access. Now pilgrims can get to it by transferring to a minibus shuttle service along the forest road. Such developments have impacted on the order that pilgrims may follow. Before the forest road was built, buses would visit Temple 59, then drop the pilgrims off at the mountain path up to Yokomineji and drive round to pick them up where they descended on the path leading down to Temple 61. The forest road, however, leads off a road closer to Temple 64; as a result, bus tours usually now go from Temple 59 to Temple 61, then in order to Temple 64 and after that to Temple 60 and then on to Temple 65. A repercussion of this change is that the *bangai* temple Ikiki Jizō, situated along the old route between Temples 59 and 60 and formerly a popular calling place for pilgrims, is less visited nowadays save by foot pilgrims, for whom it remains on the most direct route between Temples 59 and 60.[29] Other *bangai,* too, have had a loss of visitors due to such route changes, while others directly on main roads—notably Saba Daishi (see chapter 1)—have seen their visitors increase due to bus tours.

Other major developments include the building of three bridges linking Shikoku to the mainland: the first was opened in 1988, the others at the turn of the twenty-first century. These have made it quicker still for bus tours to get to Shikoku and have given rise also to *higaeri* (day trip) pilgrimage tours

from the mainland; the Nihon Kōtsū Company, based in Osaka, began to promote such tours during the 1990s, and in 2000 alone, according to the priest
of one temple, it had already, by April, brought around nine thousand to ten
thousand people on *higaeri* tours from Osaka.[30] Other companies, including
the Kotosan Company, also run *higaeri* trips that enable pilgrims to complete
the whole tour gradually in this way. This service is largely used by people
either from Shikoku itself or, with the opening of the bridges, from adjacent
areas in Honshu. Pilgrims who come from farther afield remain more likely to
do the pilgrimage in one go than in a series of shorter trips, although increasingly fast transport to and from Shikoku is making even this distinction less
clear, as the example of Tomoko in chapter 3 shows.[31]

Another development has been the building of ropeways and cable-car
services up to some of the mountain temples. Unpenji (Temple 66), the highest site on the route, can now be reached by such means, offering the pilgrim
a new way of approaching the temple and seeing the landscape: when I visited Unpenji with a pilgrimage party in 1990, before the completion of its
ropeway, we, like every other tour group, went up the narrow, winding roads
and then walked some distance to the temple. When I visited the temple in
April 2000, it was clear that few buses came up there anymore. Now they went
instead to the ropeway station, and the pilgrims then made their way up to
the temple by the ropeway. Such developments are evidence, too, of continuing interactions between commercial companies and the temples. In July
1992 a new cable-car service was completed leading to Temple 21; the head
of the company who built it then donated a new statue of Kōbō Daishi to the
temple, and this donation was marked in April 1993 by a commemoration
service for the statue and the cable-car service.[32] Unpenji has recently built
a new *daishidō*, and a sign there indicating that the head of the ropeway company was the single donor also illustrates this point. Such commercial interactions between transport firms and temples are not special to the Shikoku
temples but are found widely in Japan, as evidenced, for example, by the
links between the Nankai Railway Company and Kōyasan mentioned in the
previous chapter.[33]

Pilgrims' lodges and changing patterns

The development of a modernized transport infrastructure, expanding numbers, and the growing economic power of pilgrims in the modern era have
been accompanied by improved facilities to make the pilgrimage more comfortable and to provide services considered better suited to the needs of pilgrims accustomed, in their tour buses, to convenience and comfort. Everyone, from temple priests and lodge owners to bus guides and the people
operating other services such as restaurants and souvenir shops catering for
the pilgrimage trade, has commented to me that modern pilgrims have

increasing expectations about what they want in terms of support and material comforts from their pilgrimages—a list of expectations that may involve not just efficient buses that do not break down but clean lodgings, decent food (rather than having to bring their own rice, as with pilgrims on Iyo Tetsu's first package tour), and good facilities at the temples.

This has greatly affected pilgrims' lodges and *shukubō*. Bus tour pilgrimages did not immediately give rise to improvements in such facilities, as is evident from a book of photographs of the *henro* published in 1956 that shows crowded lodges with pilgrims crammed together and sleeping in long rows.[34] In 1961, when Kagita Chūsaburō walked the *henro*, things had not changed much: the lodges he stayed in were barely comfortable, with hard futon that made it hard to sleep—and even lice, which bit him on one occasion.[35] Lodges could still, in the 1960s, be places frequented by miscreants, as the warning given to Kannuchi Shinzō (see chapter 4) that his fellow pilgrims might include possible thieves, indicates. Pilgrims, too, could still be regarded as marginal figures—as Kagita found one night when he was refused accommodation at an inn simply because he was a pilgrim.[36]

Yet as bus pilgrimages became prevalent, road infrastructures improved, and people became better off due to Japan's rapid economic growth from the 1960s on, such fears subsided, especially as pilgrims began to expect the better accommodation and food that their new economic wealth allowed. Lodge owners informed me that from the 1960s on pilgrims began to expect individual rather than large communal rooms and to ask for delicacies rather than basic foodstuffs. They also got not just better but more equal facilities: whereas prewar pilgrims' lodges usually had but one bath, leading to the discrimination faced by Takamure and other female pilgrims, modern lodges have separate baths for both sexes, normally, too, with a steady supply of hot water so that pilgrims can bathe at any time they wish.

In the post-war era, too, and with the development of bus tour pilgrimages, *shukubō* have become prevalent. Kōonji's successful prewar *shukubō* venture pointed the way, while the close connections between the temples and bus companies (see below) have facilitated this development by ensuring that many commercial firms use *shukubō* during their tours. Priests from the Reijōkai have been active, too, in encouraging pilgrims and bus parties to stop at the temples wherever possible and instilling the view that staying at the temples is the most authentic mode of pilgrimage.

Bus pilgrimages have had a major impact on the patterns of lodging available. Old-style pilgrims' lodges, which tended to be small and catered to individual foot pilgrims, have rarely survived the changes. The example of a lodge we stayed at in 1984 near Temple 43 is typical. Its owner told us that she was almost wholly dependent on foot pilgrims, whose numbers were in decline ever since the rise of bus pilgrimages. Her lodge, with simple food and one bath, capable of taking only one or two people at a time, did not meet with the standards expected by tour companies and could not handle parties of a dozen or more. Thus she only got small groups staying when they had nowhere else to go, and since walkers were fewer than in earlier eras, the income from the lodge was barely enough to support her. When she died or became incapable of continuing, the lodge would close because her offspring were not interested in a venture whose income was insufficient for someone with a growing family. When I was back in the area in 2000, the lodge had closed; I had seen similar things happen to at least two other pilgrims' lodges —each also run by single, elderly ladies—we had stayed at in 1984 and that had closed by the 1990s.

This decline is manifest in Hoshino's study of Hatakenogawa, a village near Temple 44 that had had ten pilgrims' lodges in the prewar period. The rise of bus pilgrimages, coupled with the opening of a new road bypassing the village, led to all but one lodge closing by the 1970s.[37] Similarly, the owner of Chōchinya, a large pilgrims' lodge just outside Matsuyama, told me that even in the 1950s there had been around fifteen small lodges in the area, which was a convenient place for pilgrims to stay since it was a good day's walk from Temple 45 and at the place where pilgrims came down from the mountains of Ehime to the temples around Matsuyama. Her family were farmers who for generations put up pilgrims during the peak spring months, and a century ago their lodge took in around three hundred pilgrims per year, with pilgrims staying in communal rooms and providing their own rice. As the numbers of walkers declined, however, the lodges in the area began to close, and as bus tours became the predominant mode of travel, her lodge— because, she said, it was located directly outside one temple and had space for buses to park—became the one where they stopped. As this happened, it cornered the market and grew in size and facilities, while others closed. Now it is the only one in the area, lodging one thousand or more pilgrims per month.[38]

Chōchinya is now a preferred overnight stop for many tour groups because it is able to house several large parties in comfort. It is an example of a growing pattern through the 1970s and 1980s—of the numbers of lodges declining, and the rise of large lodges and *shukubō* capable of taking large parties and by and large located at a day's bus pilgrimage travel apart. Such lodges generally have long histories; Chōchinya is a good example here of a family with several generations' experience of accommodating pilgrims that has been able to flourish as others fell by the wayside. The lady in charge at Chōchinya had a good explanation for why her lodge had succeeded: it was not just because of the lucky position and space for buses, but because Kōbō Daishi (to whom they were devoted) had been good to the family and repaid their faith, enabling them to continue their tradition of supporting the pilgrimage and passing on pilgrimage customs.

Her rhetoric covered sharp business acumen. It was evident that her family had managed to adapt to the changing circumstances, note the emergence of the bus trade, and link up with appropriate companies in ways the neighboring lodges had not.[39] Yet at the same time, the owner—like the lodge owner mentioned in chapter 3 who washed the "feet" of Kōbō Daishi—actively maintains pilgrimage customs and emphasizes the link between pilgrimage and faith. In 1984 we stayed overnight there, and when we paid the next morning, the owner (the same person I had interviewed in 1990, although she did not recognize me from the earlier visit) handed back part of the money as *settai*. She also explained that this was not a special favor to foreign pilgrims but one often made to help those on foot. While running a lodge was her business, it was also rooted in her family traditions, her personal faith, and the culture of her island, so that business, identity, and faith were tied together.

The rise of large-scale lodges and the decline of smaller ones, especially during the 1970s and 1980s, have inconvenienced walkers, for whom finding accommodations can be problematic. This is a point I will return to in chapter 6, but suffice it here to say that it was one of the constant problems we faced in our 1984 pilgrimage. Often there were no lodges available within a day's walk of where we had spent the previous night, and many lodges were geared to the bus trade and either had no rooms for just one or two people or were reluctant to let them out because they preferred to use them for larger parties. This complaint recurs in the comments of foot pilgrims in the modern times, is a central part of their Shikoku experiences (see chapter 6), and has also been a factor in discouraging walkers.

One should also note that even temple lodges might disappear from time to time, a point brought home to me in an interview with one temple priest and his wife in 2000, when they told me that their temple closed its *shukubō* in 1989 and that others also might well be closing in the near future. The reason was that *shukubō* have normally, as with Gokurakuji's cited earlier, been run by the wives of temple priests with assistance from local people, usually women. In the case in question, the priest's wife lost her main help when her daughters married and left home (both marrying into other temple families on the island) and she was unable to find anyone local to work there since it was in a sparsely populated area. The wife felt, as she got older, that she was unable to cater on her own to pilgrims who, she said, were increasingly demanding in what they expected. Hence they had taken the decision to close down their lodge.[40]

Commerce and innovation

Regional governments have supported the *henro* in the modern day not just because it is a manifestation of the island's cultural heritage, but because it has brought money to the island and helped maintain businesses and economic life in an area that has struggled as its traditional economic support structures—such as agriculture and, in the earlier twentieth century, ship building—have declined. Pilgrims have compensated for some of this economic shortfall: as will be described in chapter 7, nowadays they spend substantial amounts of money in Shikoku not just on lodgings and at the temples, but on souvenirs, food, scrolls, and much else. As a result, the *henro* is an important factor in Shikoku's economy, supporting various businesses from bus companies and lodges to restaurants, souvenir shops that are found around many of the temples, most notably Temple 88, photographers who specialize in commemorative photographs of pilgrims (see chapter 7), stone masons who carve the stones and commemorative plaques found along the route, and scroll manufacturers who, as one such person whom I interviewed in November 1990 stated, have benefited from the interest of modern pilgrims in acquiring these striking artifacts.

The pilgrimage market is constantly in a state of innovative development as vendors and temples alike seek to produce new goods to interest pilgrims. Given that pilgrims tend to do the pilgrimage a number of times and that repeaters form a sizable section of the market, such continuing innovation is important in order to ensure that they always can find something new to purchase as a reminder of their journeys. This consistent focus on new goods is evident in the newsletter *Henro*, which regularly runs features about new pilgrimage items. The January 1999 issue, for example, highlighted a new *hakui* with a map of the island and its eighty-eight sites on the back that was now on sale at the temples. The importance of new items was emphasized to me by the owner of a shop catering to pilgrims near Temple 19. His family had run it for four generations and over one hundred years, during which time they had always sought—and needed—to find new goods that would appeal to pilgrims. Without such new products on a fairly regular basis his shop would not, he said, be able to continue. When I visited in April 2000, the shop had recently started selling Kōbō Daishi/Shikoku pilgrimage key chains, which he thought were likely to be a good sales item.[41]

Along with such goods, mention should also be made of the growing number of books about the pilgrimage that have appeared in recent years. In the 1930s, as was noted in chapter 4, publications about the *henro* began to grow, and this trend has continued in the postwar period, and especially since the 1970s. Among such publications have been numerous colorful guidebooks—including a number produced by the Reijōkai and other organizations such as NHK—as well as photo essays that draw attention to Shikoku's scenery and the age of its temples, various accounts by journalists who, like their counterparts in the 1930s, have visited the island and walked sections of the route in order to produce reports about the *henro* and write about its cultural heritage, and numerous journals by pilgrims who have done the pilgrimage, usually by foot. I will briefly mention some of the images used in such publications, especially guidebooks, later in this chapter and will discuss the contents of some of these pilgrims' journals in chapter 6. The point to note is that a small publishing industry has developed around the *henro* in recent years: every time I return to Japan (and I usually go back annually) I find several more such have been published, all of which help further fuel interest in the pilgrimage.

Service and piety in the pilgrimage business

People working in the pilgrimage service industry[42] are aware that theirs is not a business founded purely on business imperatives. Companies such as Iyo Tetsu, Setouchi, and Kotosan are certainly built on commercial foundations, and their business revolves around commercial transactions with pilgrims who pay them for their services. The companies fully recognize that their success is founded on providing people with an efficient and convenient means of doing the pilgrimage, and their advertisements assure potential pilgrims that their services enable them to travel with peace of mind and in comfort.[43] As a company official emphasized to me, pilgrims on Iyo Tetsu buses know that someone will make sure their scroll is stamped, that they will get to each temple, that their accommodations and food will be taken care of, and that therefore they can focus all their energies on their devotions, the temples, and their companions.

Yet the companies are well aware that their success is built on more than just getting pilgrims efficiently from point A to point B and ensuring that they reach their lodgings and are fed each evening. They know, for instance, that the clientele they cater to might have wishes and orientations different from those on tourist excursions and that issues of faith and devotion need to be catered to. Moreover, their business involves engaging with, and hence addressing the attitudes and concerns of, the temples. Such relations depend not on simple commercial transactions, but on ensuring that the services they provide are sensitive to, and the ambience they create is in accord with, the sentiments of pilgrims and temples alike.

As an Iyo Tetsu official said to me, the company's reputation depends on meeting such expectations and on being known as a company in whom pilgrims and temples can place their trust. The reason so many people sign up for its tours and so many pilgrimage groups want to hire its buses, drivers, and guides, he said, is because of the effort it puts into maintaining its reputation in this context. Iyo Tetsu thus expends much effort on ensuring that its services are sensitive to the orientations of its pilgrims and seeks to create an appropriate ambience by ensuring that the pilgrims it carries follow the correct behavior expected of pilgrims by wearing appropriate pilgrimage clothing, participating in worship, and following the guidance of tour leaders.

The company's officials, and the drivers and guides who actually look after the pilgrims, are expected to show respect for the religious sensitivities and needs of pilgrims, and many do more than that. The employees of Iyo

Tetsu (and of other Shikoku-based companies) I have talked to appear to be deeply devoted to the *henro* in terms of personal faith and/or because of its importance in the culture of their home region—as was illustrated by the Iyo Tetsu official who affirmed, at Ishiteji, that the Emon Saburō story was true (see chapter 2). This particular official (who was a bus guide when I first met him but who, when I interviewed him again a decade later, had become a senior manager in the company) told me that through his work and constant interactions with pilgrims he had developed a deep faith in Kōbō Daishi and in the efficacy of the pilgrimage. Being able to link this faith to his work was very important, and he felt that his life had been transformed as such.

The importance of maintaining appropriate decorum on the pilgrimage means, according to company officials, that sometimes its guides may remonstrate with pilgrims who, they feel, are not behaving appropriately or are disturbing the equilibrium of others. Perhaps the most amusing story I have heard during my research in Shikoku relates to this and was initially told to me by an Iyo Tetsu official but subsequently corroborated by a temple priest. It concerned a group of young priests from Kōyasan University, run by the Shingon sect and an academic training ground for its priesthood, who were on a graduation bus pilgrimage tour of Shikoku. Although the pilgrimage was intended to engage them in a practice related to the founder of their faith, it became clear that the recently graduated young priests were more intent on celebration than anything else. As a result, the bus guide became annoyed, reprimanding and lecturing them about the importance of Kōbō Daishi and about correct pilgrimage behavior!

My interviews with employees from Kotosan and Setouchi indicate attitudes very similar to that of Iyo Tetsu. A senior representative of Kotosan emphasized to me how important it was to ensure that Kotosan pilgrims maintained a pious attitude and that the atmosphere on Kotosan buses was reverent. That was critical in order to put the pilgrims at ease and meet their needs. Equally, he stressed that the company had to maintain close relations with the temples and be sensitive to their views not merely out of commercial considerations, but because they were engaged in a shared enterprise vital to the culture and life of Shikoku.[44] For companies based in Shikoku, too, as this comment indicates, consciousness of the importance of the *henro* and Kōbō Daishi in the island's folk religious culture and cultural heritage is also critical.

I gained some insight into how companies such as Iyo Tetsu go about their business and how they seek to create an appropriate atmosphere for the pilgrims they serve when I joined an Iyo Tetsu tour group in October 1990 as they were on the way to their last temple (Ishiteji, which is only a short drive from the Iyo Tetsu offices in Matsuyama). The group of thirty-three pilgrims was looked after by two guides and a driver who had traveled all the way with them, ministering to their needs and taking care of their scrolls and books. For their visit to the last temple (Iyo Tetsu tours generally finish at Ishiteji), they were augmented by an official from the company's head office and an assistant who came to congratulate them on behalf of the company for completing the pilgrimage.

The company had arranged for a service of thanks for completing the pilgrimage to be conducted by priests at Ishiteji, after which the pilgrims and Iyo Tetsu officials went to a tatami room in the temple for a celebratory meal and a "closing ceremony." The officials told me that this was regular for all Iyo Tetsu tours, as was an opening ceremony. In this closing ceremony, the five Iyo Tetsu workers knelt before the pilgrims, bowed their heads to the floor, and thanked them for traveling with the company. The official from the head office then handed out to each pilgrim their stamped scrolls and books, along with a number of souvenirs and commemorative gifts from the company to each pilgrim. He then asked if anyone was on his or her first pilgrimage; when a number raised their hands, he congratulated them on their first full pilgrimage, hoped they had enjoyed it, and said he expected that at the start they had felt uneasy and unsure of what they were doing. However, he hoped—and expected—that this feeling had soon worn off and that they had come to feel at ease and have a valuable pilgrimage. Their nods of satisfaction suggested that this had, indeed, been so. In return, one pilgrim, representing the party, made a reply speech of thanks, and everyone bowed deeply and thanked the guides before the ceremony ended. Afterward, the officials told me, they would take the party to the Dōgo hot springs, just down the road, for a relaxing bath before going back to the Iyo Tetsu offices, where the tour would end.

The satisfied responses of the pilgrims indicated that the service and the balance of organization, piety, and care fitted their needs well, a view summed up by a sixty-seven-year-old male pilgrim who told me that this was his third pilgrimage with Iyo Tetsu. He had done it each year since retirement and planned to repeat it annually until he died. His three main reasons for doing it, he said, were, in order, faith, tourism, and health (shinjin, kankō, kenkō). He would always travel with Iyo Tetsu and had already booked a place on a tour for the following year because he liked the consideration the company showed for pilgrims and the warm feeling of community that its tours engendered. A female pilgrim in her sixties echoed his sentiments, saying that Iyo Tetsu's tours offered the possibility of making friends and enjoying the pilgrimage in a convivial setting. She also felt the henro had improved since she first did it five years earlier because the roads and facilities were better and everything was cleaner. Such sentiments are not exceptional; Iyo Tetsu officials have informed me that around 50 percent of their clients are repeat pilgrims. The culture of repeat pilgrimages in Shikoku (mentioned in chapter 3 but to be further discussed in later chapters) is an added stimulus to the company to ensure that its services are good.

While this emphasis on care and devotion has roots in the commercial orientations of the companies, it is not, as the above indicates, just a manipulative facade intended to attract customers and put a pleasant spiritual gloss on a purely commercial activity. The success of Iyo Tetsu is directly linked to the concerns of the company and its officials for the type of service and business they have become engaged in. They are successful as a business because they provide efficient services supported by attitudes and modes of conduct that meet with the approval of pilgrims and the temples alike; the service they provide is their best means of advertising their tours and encouraging pilgrims to travel with them again.

I have also heard one Iyo Tetsu official, like the lady at Chōchinya, link commercial success and devotion: Kōbō Daishi had, he suggested, favored the company because of its good attitude. While one might note that such invocations of piety are not uncommon in those who engage in commercial activities and that in many respects they serve to legitimate business practices, one should also remember that part of the success of businesses associated with the pilgrimage is their capacity to make pilgrims feel that those providing the services are doing so in a spirit of dedication to the pilgrimage and Kōbō Daishi. In such contexts, the long history of the family running Chōchinya and caring for pilgrims is as much an advertisement for their success as is the service those companies such as Iyo Tetsu provide to their pilgrim customers.

In such contexts bus and pilgrimage tours contribute to the pilgrimage environment through their services, their treatment of pilgrims, their reinforcement of correct modes of deportment for pilgrims, and their reiteration of other aspects (e.g., the miracle tales and legends surrounding the temples) of the pilgrimage landscape. I would suggest, too, that these companies, through their insistence that pilgrims wear appropriate pilgrimage clothing, have been an important factor in the maintenance of the image of tradition in Shikoku, just as have lodge owners who ensure the maintenance of pilgrimage customs over the generations. It has been widely noted by observers that one is far more likely to see pilgrims dressed in traditional pilgrimage clothing in Shikoku than on other major pilgrimage routes in Japan; in Saikoku, for example, it is relatively uncommon to see pilgrims wearing white pilgrimage shirts or other traditional pilgrimage accoutrements.[45] This maintenance of tradition is characteristic of Shikoku and, according to several Shikoku priests I have spoken to, owes much to companies such as Iyo Tetsu and Kotosan. A female official at Temple 5 similarly commented to me that people who went on organized tours were far more likely to wear traditional pilgrims' clothing than those who went by car or individually and were also far more likely to recite sutras and engage in extended devotions at the temples. I have already made this latter point in chapter 1, and her words were reinforced in my mind the next day when I sat watching pilgrims at Temple 10. As I did so, a Setouchi Company tour arrived, and its participants—all dressed in white—disembarked to engage in a long series of chants and prayers while kneeling on the ground (an act that caused some of the older tour members some discomfort) before the temple's main hall of worship. Their extended prayer rituals lasted over twenty minutes; during that time, a number of individual pilgrims came, prayed, and moved on.[46]

Shikoku temple priests value the contribution of commercial companies in such contexts. My first encounter with the Kotosan Company occurred while I was visiting one temple to interview its priest, who, when I arrived, was engaged in earnest conversation with a representative of Kotosan, who was arranging for a number of company tour parties to stay overnight at the temple and receive special sermons from temple priests. (One of the facets of tours arranged by these companies is that they can provide pilgrims with extended access to temple priests). After the representative left, the priest spoke positively about the official and the company, stating that they were genuine in their pronouncements of piety and that they provided a good service for their pilgrims. This did not appear to be mere politeness on his part or an attempt to sanitize the commercial elements of pilgrimage, for, in the same conversation, he made negative comments to me about another travel firm (not from Shikoku) that ran pilgrimage tours but that was, he felt, rather mercenary in nature.

The Reijōkai has recognized the significant contribution made by Iyo Tetsu by awarding it the rank of *sendatsu* (pilgrimage guide), a status granted as a rule only to those who have done the *henro* at least four times and who have demonstrated their commitment to supporting and promoting the pilgrimage (see below for a full discussion of the *sendatsu* system in Shikoku). In Iyo Tetsu's head office in Matsuyama there is glass case containing a red pilgrim's staff *(akazue)*, presented to it by the Reijōkai in recognition of its endeavors in developing and promoting the pilgrimage. Indeed, Iyo Tetsu was the first entity or person to be awarded the status of *sendatsu* when the system was inaugurated in the 1960s; each *sendatsu* is given a number upon registration, and Iyo Tetsu's is number one.[47]

The Shikoku Reijōkai: Origins, organization, and activities

The development of the Shikoku Reijōkai has been another important feature of the postwar pilgrimage, and it has, along with the expansion of pilgrim numbers and the emergence of package tours and the pilgrimage service industry, been a critical factor in shaping the modern *henro*. While there had been some attempts (notably the *degaichō* of 1937) to get the temples to work together beforehand, it was not until the postwar era and an age of more rapid transport and communications—including, first, telephones and later computers, faxes, and the Internet—that the temples were really able to maintain close contact with each other throughout the island. The rise of bus tours clearly had an effect as well, making it all the more necessary for the temples to speak with a coordinated voice when trying to arrange schedules and the like.

It seems hardly coincidental that the Reijōkai began to develop as an organization in 1955, a time when organized bus tours were beginning to take off, and that a formal organization was set up in 1956, with the then priest of Anrakuji (Temple 6) installed as its first head.[48] The Reijōkai's structure was based on the fourfold administrative structure of the island, with the temples of each domain/prefecture being grouped in regional sections, which elected (and continue to do so on a periodic basis) a regional head and administrative officers from amongst the temple priests of their region. The headship and other senior positions (such as the chief administrative officer) rotate among the four sections on a four-year cycle. This rotation at the regional and overall level means that most priests at some stage occupy senior positions in the Reijōkai. The representatives of all eighty-eight temples meet by regulation at least once, but usually, depending on need, three or four times per year. Zentsūji has a special status because of its position as the birthplace of Kūkai, and its head priest is designated president *(sōsai)* in perpetuity of the organization.[49]

The Reijōkai gave the temples a coordinated voice at a time when the pilgrimage began to grow in popularity, and it enabled them to play a coherent role in producing publicity for the pilgrimage and in dealing with interest groups such as NHK when it has sought to produce programs about the *henro*. The Reijōkai also deals with the overall financial affairs of the temples as an organization.[50] Other activities and responsibilities include running and regulating the *sendatsu* system, which will be discussed shortly. The Reijōkai cooperates with external organizations—from travel firms to television companies—that are interested in the *henro* and represents the interests of the temples to them. It works, too, with regional and government authorities in consultations on road building and improving transport infrastructures, representing the interests of the temples and encouraging regional support for the pilgrimage.

The Reijōkai ensures that all the temples operate in the same way, determining a standard fee that will be charged for stamping pilgrims' books and scrolls and for staying overnight at *shukubō* and stipulating the hours that each temple must remain open for pilgrims to get their books and scrolls stamped. This latter regulation was instituted to ensure that disputes did not occur when pilgrims turned up late (as they had the habit of doing) and found that while some temples were willing to stamp their books, others were not. Now Reijōkai rules state that temples are expected to keep their offices open from 7:00 A.M. to 5:00 P.M. for this purpose.

The organization sets out appropriate modes of behavior for pilgrims (such as the ten rules or prohibitions mentioned in chapter 1). It organizes and oversees all aspects of publicity, including the production of pamphlets, guidebooks, and other publications designed to provide information on, and attract people to, the pilgrimage, and organizes various public events, including lectures and other such meetings to disseminate knowledge about the pilgrimage. It also oversees the editing of the monthly pilgrimage newsletter *Henro* (see below) and mediates in disputes between the temples (as was evidenced by its resolution of the Temple 30 conflict mentioned in the previous chapter).

The Reijōkai also seeks to provide improved facilities at the temples suitable for pilgrims in the modern age. One of its main activities here has been the provision of good toilet facilities at the temples; until recently, many temples had rather primitive toilets, and this had been a source of complaint and dissatisfaction among pilgrims for some time, voiced frequently in surveys. As a result, in 1987 the Reijōkai instituted a campaign to improve such facilities; in 1984, when I first went to Shikoku, most temples had only insalubrious toilets without flush facilities, whereas nowadays they tend to have ultra-modern, clean lavatories.[51]

The activities of the Reijōkai—especially due, I think, to the prominent role played in the organization by priests from Shingon temples such as Zentsūji and Anrakuji (Temple 6)—have clearly intensified the emphasis on Shingon Buddhist images and teachings in the pilgrimage. I have already mentioned this in chapter 2, where I stated that the Shingon-derived image of the pilgrimage as a fourfold journey to enlightenment is relatively modern, one that appears to have come to the fore through Reijōkai publications.[52] This emphasis on Shingon teachings is something that has the potential to also create tensions, not least because not all the temples are of the Shingon sect.[53] It also tends to show that the temples and pilgrims do not necessarily have the same views—a point also rooted in the ambivalence of Kōbō Daishi as sectarian founder and figure of worship within one established Buddhist tradition and as a sacred figure within the broader folk tradition.

A pilgrimage temple and its networks

While the Reijōkai serves as a coordinating body, each temple engages in its own way with the pilgrims. Some temples (I speak here from general observations over the years) appear to have relatively little contact with pilgrims, not running *shukubō* or interacting at any great level with those who visit, apart from stamping their books and providing space for them to pray. Others maintain close connections with individual pilgrims and pilgrimage associations alike—as with, for example, Ryōzenji and its connections with the Arita Settaikō—and are heavily engaged in supporting pilgrimage activities through these connections and through the Reijōkai.

Anrakuji (Temple 6) is one such example. The Hatada family, which has run the temple for several generations, has been encountered before, in chapter 3, in terms of its ongoing connection with, and support for, the Naitō family and the Shiga Shingyōkai. The family maintains connections with other pilgrimage associations, such as the Toho no Kai, whose commemorative marker outside Anrakuji was mentioned in chapter 2. On the occasions I have visited the temple, I have noted, too, how well the Hatada family and local people who work at the temple appeared to know the pilgrims who visited the temple—evidence of a familiarity based on the practice I have commented on earlier, of pilgrims doing the *henro* again and again. Anrakuji has a good reputation among pilgrims, its large *shukubō* being a popular stopping place for tour groups and individuals alike, and many pilgrims I have interviewed have spoken of how they like to go back there regularly. It is not just the priests themselves who are important in this context, but also their family members, especially wives, who are involved in running the *shukubō*, catering to the pilgrims and helping maintain good relations with them. Equally, pilgrims have commented on how such temples and temple families provide them with a sense of both continuity and change in the pilgrimage. Matsuura Harutake, a pilgrim from Aichi Prefecture whose pilgrimage experience spreads over several decades and over one hundred circuits, wrote, in 1988, about how, when he first did the *henro*, Hatada Shuhō was a small child at the local school but was now a grown priest at Anrakuji with a family.[54]

Anrakuji has also been actively engaged in the Shikoku Reijōkai from the outset, providing its first head in 1956. Its priests have, through the generations, held senior positions in the organization since then and have been actively engaged in writing about the pilgrimage in a variety of ways: its former head priest, Hatada Zenpō, wrote a number of articles and pamphlets on the *henro*, while his son and successor, Hatada Shuhō, has been involved in historical research on the pilgrimage.[55] Hatada Zenpō was especially closely connected to Kōyasan, having studied there and been a Kōyasan Shingon teacher whose job was to travel around Japan preaching about Shingon Buddhism in the 1950s before becoming head of Anrakuji.[56] His commitment to Shingon teachings and his emphasis on the pilgrimage as a mandala (see chapter 2) have been important, too, in influencing the Reijōkai's advancement of Shingon teachings through the pilgrimage. Like other Shikoku priests I know, the priests at Anrakuji have been firm devotees of Kōbō Daishi, in their case emphasizing that this faith is linked to Kōbō Daishi's position as the founder of Shingon Buddhism.

Anrakuji is but one of eighty-eight temples on the route, but it is fair to say that it has been one of the most influential and active in its engagement with pilgrims and in shaping understandings of the *henro*. It is one more in the cacophonous array of voices that are found in the pilgrimage, a voice that strongly supports the pilgrimage yet has its own distinctive agenda and views, which are influenced by the temple's sectarian orientations and which at times—even while helping and providing support for pilgrims—may, as the difference of opinion with the Shiga Shingyōkai over whether those doing that association's children's pilgrimage should wear traditional pilgrimage clothing (see chapter 3) indicates, speak in a different register from, and present alternative perspectives to, those of pilgrims.

The *sendatsu* system: Roots, roles, and responsibilities

One of the Reijōkai's most important initiatives was the establishment of a *sendatsu* system *(sendatsu seido)* in February 1965.[57] The word *"sendatsu"* consists of two ideograms, "before/at the front" and "stand," suggesting someone who has "gone before/ahead" or who stands in front (of a group of pilgrims). It has a long history relating to people with enhanced knowledge of pilgrimage routes who are therefore able to "go in front" of and guide others on pilgrimage. Historically, *sendatsu* are associated both with the ascetic and commercial dimensions of pilgrimage, since the people who guided others on pilgrimages generally did so in a professional capacity. The *sendatsu* who, from the late Heian era onward, acted as guides on the pilgrimages to Yoshino and Kumano were also proselytizing agents who, during the Muromachi era (1338–1573), widened the pilgrimage's clientele beyond the aristocracy and court to warriors, farmers, and other sections of the populace.[58] The term *"sendatsu"* also had hierarchic connotations within the world of asceticism, and a ranking system of *sendatsu* based on spiritual achievements and the numbers of pilgrimages one had performed developed within the mountain ascetic tradition of Shugendō.[59] *Sendatsu* were thus, in general terms, figures associated with multiple performances of pilgrimages, guiding others, proselytizing, and the commercial structures of pilgrimage. While the position is an individual one associated with the holder's personal history of pilgrimage practice, it is also inherently linked to group pilgrimages in that the word *"sendatsu"* refers to someone who stands in front of (a group).

Sendatsu appear to have been relatively rare in Shikoku in earlier times. The first mention of the term in Shikoku is by Chōzen in 1653, who records meeting a group of pilgrims led by a *sendatsu*.[60] Otherwise, there is scant evidence of the term, possibly because the individualized pattern of Shikoku pilgrimage, coupled with an emphasis on asceticism that went hand in hand with an undeveloped pilgrimage infrastructure, and with the general poverty of Shikoku pilgrims, provided little opportunity for the development of a professional class of *sendatsu*.

In 1965, however, the Reijōkai decided to establish the rank of *sendatsu* for pilgrims in order to facilitate development of the pilgrimage, build stronger links between the pilgrimage community and the temples, and, it would appear, to promote Shingon ideas in the pilgrimage. The system was established with seven ranks (see below), and a number of well-known pilgrims were immediately granted the rank, as was Iyo Tetsu. In 1967, the Reijōkai produced a handbook, *Sendatsu hikkei* (The *sendatsu* manual), outlining the attributes and activities considered important for *sendatsu*. These included leading other pilgrims in acts of worship, narrating miracle tales so as to fire pilgrims with enthusiasm, and encouraging people to become pilgrims. The handbook also contained a brief (if not always historically grounded) account of the pilgrimage and of the life and legends of Kōbō Daishi, along with chronicles of miraculous events associated with the sites and a summary of the teachings of Shingon Buddhism.[61]

The Reijōkai has sought to strengthen links between pilgrims and temples by asking *sendatsu* to get parties they travel with to stay overnight where possible at *shukubō*.[62] It also suggests that pilgrims should travel with experienced *sendatsu* wherever possible, especially on their first pilgrimage, for this will help them avoid making mistakes or getting lost and will make sure they perform the correct prayers and actions at the temples.[63] Shimada Taiichirō, who led the pilgrimage tour I discuss in chapter 7, told me that a major reason first-time pilgrims sought out his services was because they wanted to be sure to follow the correct patterns of behavior and not make mistakes and because they knew that going with a *sendatsu* in an organized party would enable them to do this. The presence of *sendatsu* and the structure of organized parties, in other words, provides a comforting mode of reassurance for pilgrims that they will do the pilgrimage in the right way.

In 1967 the Reijōkai instigated regular meetings for *sendatsu*: the *kenshūkai* (study/training meeting) each September and *sendatsu taikai* (an annual general meeting) each December, both normally at Zentsūji. The *kenshūkai* involves lectures and training sessions led by priests from the Reijōkai or Shingon institutions such as Kōyasan and includes studies of Shingon teaching. The *sendatsu taikai* centers on ceremonies celebrating the induction of new *sendatsu*, the promotion of existing ones, and the commemoration of *sendatsu* who have died during the year. Each year the attendance at this meeting is around nine hundred or so people, according to Reijōkai officials. Iyo Tetsu and other bus companies send representatives to the meetings, while the Kotosan Bus Company provides support staff to help organize and run these meetings.[64]

The *sendatsu* system: Structure, promotions, and numbers

There are seven ranks of *sendatsu* in Shikoku as follows.

1. *Sendatsu*—people who have done the pilgrimage four times; there is no regulation about how this is done.
2. *Gonchū sendatsu*—*sendatsu* who have subsequently done the *henro*

at least twice more; one needs also to wait two years after attaining the previous rank.

3. *Chū sendatsu*—those who have done the pilgrimage at least twice after attaining the previous rank and waited two more years.

4. *Gondai sendatsu*—those who have done the pilgrimage three more times and waited three years after attaining the previous rank.

5. *Daisendatsu*—those who have done the pilgrimage three more times and waited three years after attaining the previous rank.

6. *Tokunin daisendatsu*—only ten people hold this rank at any one time; they are selected by the Reijōkai from the ranks of the *daisendatsu* because of their work in promoting the pilgrimage, the status and respect they have acquired among fellow pilgrims, and their relationship with the Reijōkai.

7. *Genrō daisendatsu*—this is limited to five people only, who must be Buddhist priests and who are chosen because of their dedication to the pilgrimage, evidenced, for example, by their work in organizing pilgrimage parties and bringing substantial numbers of pilgrims to Shikoku.[65]

Those who do the *henro* in a professional capacity, for example as drivers and guides for commercial firms, can usually hold only the basic rank. Many who work for Iyo Tetsu, Kotosan, and Setouchi are *sendatsu*—a point mentioned proudly to me by officials from these companies as indicative of their commitment to the pilgrimage. The leader of the pilgrimage tour discussed in chapter 7 was similarly proud of his rank of *sendatsu* and saw in it affirmation of his devotion and a status that made him more than just a "mere" travel guide.

Attaining each rank involves a fee—30,000 yen for the initial rank and a further 30,000 yen for each subsequent stage, with 50,000 yen for *gondai sendatsu* and above.[66] In return, *sendatsu* receive from the Reijōkai a number of items including a *wagesa* (a Buddhist stole that is a symbol of lay Buddhist ordination), a cassette tape of pilgrimage songs, a special *sendatsu*'s pilgrimage staff, and a copy of the *sendatsu* guidebook and rules. *Sendatsu* also receive copies of the monthly newsletter *Henro*. Each year, too, the Reijōkai holds special memorial services in Shikoku, and at the *sendatsu* memorial it has built in the graveyard at Kōyasan, for deceased *sendatsu*.

To ascend the ranks requires support from, and approval of, one or more temple priests. Technically, at least, one needs to be known to one or more priests as a pilgrim who actively helps promote the pilgrimage, although usually an informal statement of support from a well-known *sendatsu* can suffice. Attending training sessions for *sendatsu* is also important. Hence acquisition of status and advancement depend on a combination of doing the *henro* a number of times over an extended period, developing connections with the temples and priests, and participating in the meetings organized by the Reijōkai.

The following two cases illustrate how the system works. The first, from 1990, concerns a female *sendatsu* applying for promotion from *gondai* to *daisendatsu* status. Her application stated that she first did the pilgrimage on foot in 1955, had done it eight times since, each time on an Iyo Tetsu bus, had attended the annual study/training meeting fifteen times, and was a member of an almsgiving association. Her application was supported by several priests who certified she was a devout pilgrim. The second example, from 2000, was of a male who, between 1987 and 1997, had risen to the level of *daisendatsu*. He became a *sendatsu* in December 1987 and, according to his application, had successfully attained the rank of *gonchū sendatsu* in December 1989 and then, in December 1991, of *chū sendatsu*. Each time he had fulfilled the basic obligations and applied immediately after the statutory waiting period of two years had elapsed. He maintained the same dedicated regularity in his two subsequent advances, waiting just three years and doing the *henro* three more times to apply, in December 1994, as a *gondai sendatsu* and again, in December 1997, as *daisendatsu*. His application, too, indicated attendance at *sendatsu* training meetings and support from temple priests. Both applicants were in their sixties, and this is not unusual: as was noted in chapter 3, the sixty to sixty-nine age group is the largest among pilgrims, and it is so also among *sendatsu*, largely because people of this age have more time, due to retirement, for making pilgrimages regularly. However, as the example of Asabukawa Satomi, the eighteen-year-old girl mentioned in chapter 3 who attained the rank in December 1989, indicates, some are far younger.

Sendatsu numbers and growth

Sendatsu numbers have, like pilgrim numbers in general, risen steadily over the years. In 1980 there were 2,590 registered *sendatsu;* by 1991 there were over 5,200, and by 2000 over 7,000. At the turn of the 1990s there tended to be around 400 new *sendatsu* each year along with around 300 promotions— as well as around 100 or so deaths on average—and this pattern has continued since.[67] Their regional distribution is similar to that of pilgrims in general: in 1991, 1,658 of the 5,233 *sendatsu* (31 percent) were from the four prefectures of Shikoku, 696 (13 percent) from Osaka, and 881 (16.8 percent) from Aichi Prefecture. These latter areas also have strong, locally organized *sendatsu* associations. Reijōkai officials have commented to me that there is a correlation between the strength of regional *sendatsu* associations and the numbers of pilgrims that come from a region; generally, too, they cite the Kansai Sendatsukai, headed by Tabuchi Yoshio (see chapter 3) and based in Osaka, and the Aichi regional *sendatsu* association as examples of this point and speak warmly of the work being done by these groups.[68] In recent years, too, there has been an increasing number of *sendatsu* from Kantō and northern Japan, areas that have also seen recent growth in pilgrim numbers.

The Reijōkai is well aware of the influence of *sendatsu* in ensuring that pilgrims keep coming to Shikoku; indeed, one of the reasons the system was set up was for such reasons, and it has largely been a success—one that has led priests on other pilgrimages in Japan to follow suit and establish their own *sendatsu* systems in recent years.[69] I will give one example here of how *sendatsu* can help publicize the pilgrimage, and it concerns my meeting in December 1990 with Tabuchi Yoshio. The meeting occurred at the Tsūtenkaku, Osaka Tower, in southern Osaka, where Tabuchi and his colleagues in the Kansai Sendatsukai were organizing a five-day event designed to promote the pilgrimage. The event centered on a *sunafumi* (miniaturized version of the Shikoku pilgrimage). The term *"sunafumi"* means "stepping on the soil," and the miniaturized pilgrimage was just that: inside the Tsūtenkaku an eighty-eight-stage circuit had been set up, with each of the temples represented by a hanging scroll, miniature altar, and small Buddhist image. On the ground before each was a bag of soil from the temple so that as people walked around the tower they trod on soil from each of the temples, thus symbolically "walking" the pilgrimage. Priests from the Reijōkai attended on different days to bless the "pilgrims" as they went round.

The event had been widely publicized by the Kansai Sendatsukai through posters, leaflets, and newspaper advertisements. Numerous *sendatsu* were on hand—dressed in their pilgrimage clothes—to greet visitors, answer questions, and encourage them to do the pilgrimage. As Tabuchi and his colleagues explained to me, their aim was to introduce the pilgrimage to people who had not previously done it and to reawaken the memories of those who had, thus getting them to think about doing it again. The event was a success, with over two thousand people taking part and temporarily becoming Shikoku pilgrims. Many told the organizers that they were keen to become pilgrims, while those with previous pilgrimage experience stated that they wanted to do it again.

Sendatsu and the trail of miracles

One role the *sendatsu* is expected to perform is that of narrating miracles as pilgrims travel around the route, and in chapter 7 I will give an example of how such miracle narratives can be woven into pilgrimage experience. Yet *sendatsu* are not just reporters of tales and trails of miracle; they may also be active agents in the creation of miracle stories. The collection of miracle stories from which the story of Ogasawara Shōichi and his motorbike (see chapter 2) was taken largely centers around the miracles claimed and reported by contemporary Shikoku *sendatsu* who thus become parts of the miracle narrative in their own right. Sometimes, too, through such miracle stories, *sendatsu* can acquire enhanced status, as is the case with Mizutani Shigeji, a *tokunin daisendatsu* from Aichi Prefecture who, with his wife Shizu, is the focus of one of the best-known modern miracle narratives. Shizu had become so ill with spinal tuberculosis that they felt they would not be able to do the *henro* for much longer, setting out, in 1962, on what they assumed was a final pilgrimage. At Kōnomineji (Temple 27), situated on a steep hillside overlooking the sea, they laboriously made their way to the temple and prayed to Yakushi, the Buddha of healing enshrined at the temple. As they left, Shizu experienced a dramatic sensation in her body; Yakushi had intervened to cure her, her pain disappeared, and she was thereafter able to travel without difficulty.[70] Her miraculous healing experience has entered the annals of contemporary pilgrimage lore, reproduced many times in pilgrimage literature and passed on among pilgrims by other *sendatsu*—often with added embellishments to further dramatize it: I have been told it by Tabuchi Yoshio and several others on different occasions.[71]

Mizutani has also been linked with other miracles, as the following story —one I have heard a number of times in Shikoku—indicates. It states that he had given one of his gold *fuda* to a man he met, who kept it in his pocket as a lucky amulet. The man's workmates, however, were skeptical, regarding his carrying of the *fuda* as little more than superstition. One day, as they were digging a trench, he cut through a power cable. There was a sudden flash, and he was flung backward down a bank by the shock. His workmates, horrified, assumed immediately that no one could have survived such a thing, but they were amazed when he—somewhat reminiscent of Ogasawara-san in chapter 2—clambered back unharmed. The only real damage was to Mizutani's *fuda*, which was still in his pocket but now charred. According to the story, the *fuda* had absorbed the electric shock and saved him; in versions I have heard, too, his workmates instantly ceased their skepticism and became convinced of the wondrous benefits of the pilgrimage.[72]

Thus Mizutani has acquired a special status among pilgrims, and his *fuda* have come to be seen as specially charged protective amulets, just, as I noted in chapter 3, as has that of Tabuchi Yoshio. The association between *sendatsu*, their *fuda*, and the promise of spiritual power is found widely in the *henro*; Mori Harumi, for example, relates how a fellow pilgrim's son was healed after the pilgrim was given the brocade *fuda* of someone who had done the *henro* over one hundred times.[73]

Status and criticism

Not all *sendatsu* are, however, inspirational figures, and there has been criticism that the *sendatsu* system is effectively a means through which the Reijōkai can gain loyal support by granting pilgrims rewards and status just for doing the *henro* several times and supporting the temples. This point was made clear during a conversation with two Buddhist priests at a *bangai* temple when a party of pilgrims, consisting of around thirty people and led by a male *sendatsu* in his sixties who directed everyone in their chanting and prayers, visited the temple. Both priests commented afterward that several people in the party carried the special staff of a *sendatsu* but took no role in leading others and appeared to just passively follow their leader; they were, the priests said, "paper *sendatsu*" who had acquired the status just by sitting on a bus. I have heard similar critical comments about "paper" and "sedentary" *sendatsu* from others in Shikoku—notably, for example, from Miyazaki Tateki of the Henro Michi Hozon Kyōryokukai, whose emphasis on the importance of walking has led him to suggest that the only true *sendatsu* are those who go by foot and that those who get the accreditation by riding on buses are not real *sendatsu*.[74]

Some of these criticisms are valid. Many people are interested in the position primarily for reasons of status, for it allows them to wear a badge of devotion through their special *sendatsu* accoutrements and hence to stand out from their fellow pilgrims. This was what had attracted a female *sendatsu* I interviewed in November 1990. She said she had become a *sendatsu* (and subsequently received promotion up to *chū sendatsu*) because she did the pilgrimage regularly with a pilgrimage association whose leader encouraged others to acquire this rank. She was keen to do so and to wear the accoutrements (her *chū sendatsu wagesa* and staff) because she saw them as signs of her devotion and the time she put into the *henro*. She was, however, neither interested nor willing to take on any more active role by, for example, providing a commentary about the temples to others or standing at the front of the group leading them in prayers. For her, holding the *sendatsu* rank was a mark of status and recognition rather than of obligation to be more proactive in the pilgrimage.

Hierarchy and gender

The formalized, hierarchic structure of the *sendatsu* system essentially implies that those who do it more times than others and who maintain close links with the temples are of higher status than others. This appears to go against the egalitarian and leveling symbolism in which all pilgrims are equal through being with Kōbō Daishi. Yet while contributing on the one hand toward hierarchic tendencies, the *sendatsu* system has, on the other, helped to reduce inequalities, specifically by enhancing the status of female pilgrims who can acquire recognition and status through multiple performances of the *henro* and thus achieve equality with, and even status enhancement over, male pilgrims. In earlier times, when everyone walked and female pilgrims had to endure the additional hardship of discrimination, it was rare to find females who did the *henro* more than once or acquired enhanced status through multiple performances. Nowadays, however, especially thanks to modern transport development, this has changed: since the majority of pilgrims now are female, it is unsurprising that many *sendatsu* are likewise, including several of the *tokunin daisendatsu*.[75] The *sendatsu* system may thus emphasize status and hierarchy, but it also offers a means of amending earlier imbalances and providing female pilgrims with the opportunity to acquire similar, or higher, status to men.

Modernity and ambivalence

The *sendatsu* system clearly encourages multiple performances, and it and the figure of the *sendatsu* are very much products of modern Shikoku pilgrimage culture and its group-oriented nature and of the organizing dynamic of the contemporary *henro,* through which the Reijōkai seeks to influence pilgrims in ways that concur with the temples' interests. Yet the system also reflects tensions between the Shingon orthodoxy exemplified by the Reijōkai and many of the temples, and the Japanese folk tradition manifest in the attitudes of pilgrims. Shinno Toshikazu has commented that the *henro* manifests two faces, one connected to Shingon orthodoxy and the other to Japanese folk traditions,[76] and one can see aspects of these two faces in the context of the *sendatsu* and what they stand for. While *sendatsu* can be closely associated with the temples, the Reijōkai, and tendencies toward orthodoxy in the pilgrimage, they also can function as agents for the continued assertion of the individualizing orientations of the *henro*. Their interest in asserting the primacy of miracle stories reinforces some of the basic starting points of pilgrimage—the rumors of miracles and the affirmation that the holy can be directly and personally encountered—which offer pilgrims the hope and possibility of being able to experience or come into contact with the sacred without needing the mediation of priests and other authority figures.[77] In disseminating tales of wonder, *sendatsu* are effectively sowing the potential seeds of individual interpretation, thereby encouraging other pilgrims to think that they, too, may experience miracles and be able to tell their own legends and stories—and hence be independent agents unbounded by the authority, parameters, and doctrinal orientations propounded by the temples.

Moreover, *sendatsu* can themselves become authority figures and sources of spiritual power and inspiration—as can be clearly seen with Tabuchi Yoshio or Mizutani Shigeji. Hence while the Reijōkai has created, through the *sendatsu* system, a structure through which it can advance a Shingon/temple orientation to the pilgrimage, it has also helped enhance the status of figures who can stand as alternative sources of authority. When the *fuda* of experienced *sendatsu* such as Tabuchi or Mizutani become sacred objects in the eyes of other pilgrims, and when miracles are attributed to them, they become alternative focuses of faith and authority to the priests, the temples, and the Reijōkai—and may well, indeed, be more widely listened to than them.

In such terms, then, the *sendatsu* may be ambivalent, associated with the structures and group travel of modern pilgrimage yet also imbued with its individualizing folk orientations. The *sendatsu* is a figure honored by marks of status from the Reijōkai because of devotion to Kōbō Daishi and the pilgrimage, and s/he symbolizes the structure of the pilgrimage as a journey in the footsteps of a sacred person. S/he is a figure associated with the miracle narratives that are so crucial to the folk and populist dimensions of the pilgrimage and that offer unmediated access to the sacred. Yet s/he is also and equally a figure associated with the group, organizational, commercial, and promotional dimensions of modern pilgrimage. While the *sendatsu* may, in the modern day, be generally a figure seated on a bus, s/he nevertheless symbolizes many themes and meanings of the pilgrimage that relate to both its social and ascetic/individual orientations. S/he is implicitly always alone, out front, going in front and therefore standing in the footsteps of Kōbō Daishi, the original one who "went before," creating the footsteps and path for others to follow while simultaneously being part of the socializing and promotional dynamic of modern pilgrimage, a symbol of the bus age.

Bus companies, *sendatsu*, and the Reijōkai

The criticisms that are directed at "passive" *sendatsu* may also be a sign of unease at the influence of commercial companies and the close associations they have with the Reijōkai. Such links have been touched on earlier, for example, in my comments about how Ishiteji provides facilities for Iyo Tetsu during their tours and about the assistance of Kotosan in helping the Reijōkai organize meetings for the *sendatsu*. Another example of such cooperation, which has provided members of the pilgrim community with a viable medium of communication that links temples, companies, and *sendatsu*, is the pilgrimage newsletter *Henro*, which has been published each month since April 1984. Normally eight pages long, it contains articles and information about the pilgrimage ranging from descriptions of the temples and their history, to articles by temple priests, to short accounts by pilgrims about their experiences, to news about the pilgrimage. The newsletter is published and funded by the Iyo Tetsu Company but is edited in close cooperation with the Reijōkai and sent out free to all *sendatsu*. The Reijōkai can communicate regularly with its *sendatsu* through *Henro*, passing on announcements and reports of *sendatsu* meetings, training sessions, and other such news while encouraging *sendatsu* to act in the service of the temples. *Henro* also serves as a valuable publicity medium for Iyo Tetsu, which can constantly remind *sendatsu* of its organized tours, bus charter services, and support for the *henro*.

Imag(in)ing and making (pilgr)images

The emergence of the Reijōkai, along with the rise of commercial companies engaged in the pilgrimage business, has produced a coordinated framework through which the pilgrimage can be represented as a "product" of vital importance to Shikoku and through which the image of pilgrim as a symbol of national identity and culture can be advanced. This image has been created at least in part through skillful publicity produced by the Reijōkai, often in conjunction with other interest groups or media organizations—the recent NHK television series cited earlier is one such example. This was not, I should stress, the first time that NHK or other broadcasting companies had focused on the *henro*: in 1990, NHK broadcast a documentary about the pilgrimage, and other regional television companies have followed suit. Such publicity invariably focuses (as my comments on the NHK programs in chapter 1 indicated) on images of white-clothed pilgrims walking amidst trees along mountain paths flanked by moss-covered Buddha statues, as if to emphasize that through the *henro* one can escape modern society and get back in touch with nature and the rhythms of traditional Japan. Often the pilgrim(s) depicted walking along the *henro* path in such photographs or publicity materials are pretty, young females, as if to further heighten these images of beauty. That such people may not really be pilgrims but models chosen to enhance the idealized settings of pilgrimages is apparent from their spotlessly white new clothes and footwear—never a likely eventuality for anyone actually walking the *henro!* Often, too, such images of nature and separation from the modern world are intensified by the absence of any signs of modern times, such as paved roads or telegraph wires.

Two examples of how the Reijōkai presents the pilgrimage can be found in guidebooks it was involved in producing in 1989 and 1990. The first, published by the leading Japanese publishers Kōdansha and edited by the Reijōkai, contains numerous glossy and scenically striking photographs of temples surrounded by trees and swathed romantically in early morning mist, of Buddha statues and white-clad pilgrims on forested paths, along with various articles by temple priests and others extolling the virtues of the pilgrimage and its cultural significance. Despite the fact that the majority of pilgrims travel by bus, not one photograph shows any pilgrim other than on foot or wearing sun hats (the norm these days), rather than traditional bamboo hats. The only photograph in which a vehicle appears depicts pilgrims greeting some elderly women in a minibus who are waving at them. The minibus appears to have slowed down for this purpose, and the photograph seems to convey an image of cheerful interaction between walkers and those in motor vehicles—not, as frequent complaints by foot pilgrims about having to endure the noise and fumes of passing traffic (see chapter 6) indicate, a very normal scenario. In fact, the picture was stage-managed, as one of the pilgrims in the photograph (whom I interviewed during my research) told me: he and some fellow pilgrims were asked by the photographer to pose next to a stationary minibus, whose occupants were asked to wave to them.[78]

The second example is of a book published in 1990 to accompany the aforementioned NHK documentary of that year and edited by NHK with editorial supervision from the Reijōkai. It also focused on the above images, with a strong focus on temples, ancient buildings, and statues. The book contained a number of short testimonials or comments about the *henro* from well-known figures in Japanese life, including writers and actors as well as public figures such as Umehara Takashi, the influential writer and then director of the Nichibunken (International Research Center for Japanese Studies), established by the Japanese Ministry of Education. These articles informed readers why the writers were interested in particular temples or aspects of the *henro* and asserted that it was a central and significant facet of Japanese culture and tradition.[79] Such publicity materials and the images they conjure up tap into the oft-noted vein of nostalgia and cultural longing prevalent in modern Japanese cultural discourse (see chapter 1) that has created an imaginative vision of the pilgrimage as a journey to and through Japan's "spiritual homeland" *(kokoro no furusato)*—an image widely used in popular literature about the pilgrimage and widely emphasized, for example, in Iyo Tetsu pilgrimage advertisements.[80]

As was stated in earlier chapters, such images have raised awareness about, and increased the popularity of, the pilgrimage in recent years. Many people, like Tomoko and Sawamura-san in chapter 3, have been drawn to Shikoku because of its natural scenery and contemporary associations with heritage, tradition, and identity. Especially for urban dwellers in Japan's major cities, Shikoku still retains a sense of rural and (relatively) unspoiled beauty. There is an irony here, of course, in that while such publicity has focused on tranquil mountain paths, most of the pilgrims who have been stimulated by it travel by bus along highways. Moreover, as bus pilgrimages became more prevalent, the numbers going by foot declined until by the mid-1980s, according to temple priests, there were little more than two hundred people a year actually walking it all.[81] As a result, in many places the old footpaths disappeared, either because they had been paved over and turned into roads or because they were so little used that they became overgrown. Thus the image of pilgrims walking on forested mountain paths was, ironically, accompanied by the disappearance of the very paths that made the *henro,* in publicity materials and posters, so attractive.

This is not, however, to suggest that the images conjured up by poster girls in pilgrims' uniforms are intended to mislead pilgrims. The messages they send out are important in the ways in which pilgrimage is understood and experienced by pilgrims today. Pilgrims such as Sawamura-san are attracted by these images of tradition and nature yet labor under no illusion that in

Shikoku they will step outside the parameters of the modern world entirely and spend all their time on mountain paths. They have, after all, signed up for bus tours that are advertised as comfortable and convenient, but through their medium they can simultaneously, perhaps at times for a few moments when climbing the steps up from a temple car park to its main hall, find themselves in the midst of traditional settings. In this context the bus tour framework offers modern pilgrims an avenue, via the modern and convenient, through which they can emotionally touch upon and feel themselves suffused with the traditional.

Of tradition and the modern: A walk across the bridge

This juxtaposition of images was evident in 1988 when the Seto Ōhashi, the first of the three bridges built across the Inland Sea to connect Shikoku to the Japanese mainland, was opened. The Seto Ōhashi was a great feat of engineering, one of the longest suspension bridges in the world, and its completion was greeted in Japan with great pride, as a triumph of Japanese skill, technology, and modern achievement. The bridge's opening was a major affair, celebrated by various events and exhibitions designed to highlight the technological achievements involved and to draw attention to the culture and traditions of Shikoku as it became linked to the mainland. Naturally, the *henro* featured prominently, being represented, for example, in an exhibition about travel and communications in Shikoku that included a miniature *sunafumi* version of the pilgrimage.[82]

Before the bridge was opened to traffic, a day was set aside for an event in which pedestrians were permitted to walk across it. This event was used by the Reijōkai, in conjunction with regional bus companies and *sendatsu* associations, to publicize the *henro,* and they ensured that large numbers of white-clad pilgrims participated in the event. As a result, amidst the crowd—estimated at around ten thousand—that crossed the bridge were numerous pilgrims: in photographs of the event the white of the pilgrims' clothing stood out to suggest that this was, in effect, a pilgrimage event.[83]

Since the event featured widely in subsequent media and news reports, it provided widespread publicity for the *henro*. Photographs of the walk were used in a poster advertising the *henro* and juxtaposing two contrasting yet complementary images of the pilgrims representing tradition and the bridge representing the modernity and technological advances important in the self-image of Japan in the late 1980s, when its economy was booming and it had become one of the leading technological forces in the world. The image is striking in that the pilgrims and the tradition they represented were not set apart from modernity; rather, they combined with it, the modern serving as a means of accessing the traditional, just, indeed, as bus tours have served to allow urban Japanese to readily access the tradition of pilgrimage. In such images, tradition and modernization are fused, with the modernity of the bridge serving as the framing device for the prominence of tradition.[84]

The above are but some of the activities the Reijōkai has been involved in while seeking to heighten awareness of the *henro* and encourage more people to become pilgrims in Shikoku. Other activities include its involvement in the 1,150th anniversary celebrations of Kūkai's death/entry into nirvana, celebrations that included campaigns to encourage people to visit Kōyasan and Shikoku and a *degaichō* event it organized in 2003 in Tokyo. Furthermore, the Reijōkai remains actively involved in the continuing production of publicity materials, most recently including CD-ROMs and videos of the pilgrimage as well as a web site to provide information on, and promote, the pilgrimage.[85]

One should note that it is not just the Reijōkai that has publicized the *henro* in such ways. As I mentioned earlier, there have been numerous books on the *henro* in recent times, many of which similarly focus on and use the photogenic beauties of Shikoku and the images conjured up by the *henro*. Thus a pilgrimage guidebook by Fujita Shōichi from 1996 contains numerous photographs of the natural sights of Shikoku, its temples, and white-clad pilgrims—but not of cars or buses—and portrays the *henro* as a journey through nature in the company of the buddhas.[86] Other examples one could cite here include a guidebook by Miyazaki Tateki, which is full of similarly beautiful photographs of the Shikoku landscape and temples, rocky coastlines, azure sea, hills bathed in subtle evening shades, and mountain temples and pilgrims—again with no signs of any of the manifestations of modern life in the form of buses, telegraph wires, and the like to be seen.[87]

Complaints and the decline of foot pilgrims

The 1990s, as has been noted, saw a renewed growth in pilgrim numbers, leading to continued improvements in the infrastructure and in the prosperity of the temples. The visual impact on the *henro* has been striking—from the new buildings at temples such as Gokurakuji, to new buddha images and signposts along the route, to new roads and cable cars. This continually developing, moving landscape and the increased wealth that has come along with it has not, however, been to everyone's liking. The critical comments about modern pilgrims I cited in chapter 1 from the lady who ran a teashop have been reiterated by many others. As early as 1961 Kagita was complaining about bus-tour pilgrims whom he felt failed to show appropriate levels of faith as they rushed around the island.[88] When Kesaya Noda, a Japanese-American woman, walked the pilgrimage in 1981, she commented on the haste of bus pilgrims and reported how local people felt that the spirit of the pilgrimage had been lost because of the change from foot to buses.[89] Local media have also added their voices to such feelings: an article in the *Shikoku shinbun* in July 1987, for instance, complains that the pilgrimage has turned into a tourist activity *(kankōka)* because of package bus tours that have eradicated old-style traditional lodgings and given rise to modern hotels and *shukubō* akin to hotels.[90]

Such sentiments—notably about the "loss" of pilgrimage spirit—have been frequently reiterated to me by pilgrims and locals alike. A priest from Shikoku whom I interviewed in 1991 and who had done the pilgrimage in the late 1950s bemoaned what he felt was the loss of a communal spirit among pilgrims. When he had walked, everyone stayed in communal rooms *(aibeya)* and shared stories and miraculous experiences. Now, he said, everyone went by bus and had far less communication with others, and the sense of miracle inherent in the *henro* had disappeared.[91] Such sentiments are perhaps, however, given the nature of communal pilgrims' lodges of earlier times, as much the products of nostalgia as anything; the priest's comments reminded me of the members of the Shiga Shingyōkai cited in the previous chapter for whom the harshness of prewar pilgrimage was a cause for nostalgic reflection. I would also note that my account, in chapter 7, of bus-tour pilgrimages will show that such pilgrims often interact with those outside their group and that shared stories of miracles are prevalent in their communications with other pilgrims.

Certainly as bus tours became the norm, walkers faced increasing difficulties. The high-speed culture of Japan, coupled with the very convenience of buses and organized tours, made walking an increasingly marginal activity from the 1960s on, and it became even more so because of the disappearance of old paths. The aforementioned lack of convenient lodgings for walkers also made it an increasingly difficult option. In the rapidly modernizing society of the era, too, there was a general sense that going on foot was a rather low-status means of doing the pilgrimage. A male pilgrim whom my wife and I met in 1984 summed this feeling up by telling us that nowadays anyone with means went by bus or car and that only "students and foreigners" *(gakusei to gaijin dake)*—two clearly low-status groups—went on foot. At the turn of the 1990s few people seemed to walk, and one temple priest I knew even thought, rather gloomily, that walkers would die out altogether and that the future of the *henro* would be wholly motorized.

Revival and new webs of meaning

By the latter part of the 1990s, however, the number of foot pilgrims had risen sharply, stimulated in part by the general rise in interest in the pilgrimage. Some were captivated enough by its images of tradition, for instance, to want to experience it in traditional fashion on foot. Other reasons also began to play a part, notably the growing concern with personal health and physical exercise in an age where sedentary occupations have become the norm. This has led to an increased interest in walking. In 1997 a survey by the prime minister's office on sports and physical activities showed that walking was the most popular such activity in Japan, cited by 31.8 percent of respondents.[92] Pilgrims such as Tomoko and others cited in chapter 3 who see walking as a means of keeping active in their retirement years have found, in the *henro*, a useful means of combining this desire to keep healthy with the wish to delve into their cultural roots, with the result that the numbers of such pilgrims—often doing the *henro* in stages, as was Tomoko—have steadily risen. The recent surge in walkers' numbers, too, has been fueled, as was noted in chapter 1, by growing numbers of unemployed people hit by Japan's economic woes of the 1990s and who see, in the *henro*, a means of challenging themselves and searching for new meanings in the midst of their personal troubles.

The revived interest in walking has been accompanied and stimulated by improvement in the support structures for walkers. This has especially been so since Miyazaki Tateki founded the Henro Michi Hozon Kyōryokukai after he had walked the pilgrimage and become frustrated at the lack of signs and good paths for walkers. I will discuss Miyazaki more fully in chapter 8, but suffice it to note here that from the late 1980s onward Miyazaki has devoted much of his time to making and putting up signposts to assist walkers and to clearing overgrown sections of the path. In 1990 he compiled a detailed walkers' guidebook, complete with precise information on distances by foot along every section of the route and maps to scale showing minute details ranging from contours and wayside markers to places where one can acquire food, drinks, and lodgings. The guidebook has been very successful and by April 2000 was in its sixth edition and had sold twenty-three thousand copies, becoming an almost essential item of pilgrimage equipment for walkers, carried by many of those I have met on foot in the 1990s and beyond. It and the signs that Miyazaki and others have put up have made walking a much more practical option than it was in 1984, when we walked the route and had to find our way using a guidebook designed primarily for pilgrims going by bus or car and with few signposts to assist us.

In the 1990s, too, Shikoku regional governments, conscious of the position of the *henro* in local culture, also put efforts into improving footpaths and putting up signs to help pilgrims.[93] This has also led to something of a renewed focus on the needs of walkers along the route. In a number of places, new lodges have been established in locations convenient for, and catering primarily to, foot pilgrims, who now constitute a growing part of the pilgrimage community and whose particular needs are, in turn, creating a market for such new facilities.[94] This has also—with the successful activities of the Henro Michi Hozon Kyōryokukai in particular—produced new voices and interpretations of the pilgrimage that are alternatives to the temple—and sectarian—orientations of the Reijōkai. In the past few years—and assisted by the growth of the Internet and its emerging capacity to produce communities forged in cyberspace—a variety of new forums for discussing the pilgrimage and sharing experiences have developed, largely created by people who have walked the *henro* and want to share and converse about their experiences with others and maintain the sense of community they experienced as pilgrims.[95] Such phenomena are still in their early stages, and it is as yet difficult to assess their impact or influence, yet they suggest that a growing interest in the *henro* is being accompanied by an interest in sharing experiences and forming new voices within the pilgrimage community—an issue that will be central to future research on the pilgrimage.

Shifting landscapes in the new century

This account of the developments of the *henro* in the post-1945 era has shown the immense effects on the pilgrimage landscape of organized bus tours and modernization processes. The rise of the Reijōkai and the structural developments (e.g., the *sendatsu* system) it has instituted, coupled with the influence of commercial interest groups from bus companies to large scale pilgrims' lodges and media concerns, have turned the pilgrimage into a mass activity suffused with images of comfort, group travel, tradition, and cultural heritage. In that process the *henro* has certainly become transformed from its earlier marginalized status to its current position as national pilgrimage and symbol of cultural heritage—even if there are still some in Shikoku who regard pilgrims in a negative light, not so much now because they are poor and dangerous but because they are well-off, traveling by bus, and not behaving as pilgrims of yore.

As the *henro* in postwar Japan shows, pilgrimages can change not just in nature but also in public perception over the ages, dependent on conditions such as changing economic situations and the politics of memory, tradition, and cultural heritage. In the postwar era the Shikoku landscape has been reshaped and remade constantly through new developments and the changing dynamics of pilgrimage practice. The visual landscape is in a state of constant flux as new markers and visual phenomena appear, while the emotional landscape similarly—through the images produced by the Reijōkai and media concerns and now, it would appear, through the new communities in formation through the Internet—takes on new and renewed meanings. This continually shifting landscape, influenced by the processes of modernization that have fused with the images of tradition in which the *henro* is bathed, has, in the 1990s and the beginning of the twenty-first century, attracted increasing numbers of pilgrims whose experiences and understandings have been shaped by and have drawn meanings from it. It is to such issues that I turn in the next two chapters, where I look, respectively, at how pilgrims on foot and by package tour experience their pilgrimages.

6 Walking Pilgrimages

Meaning and Experience on the Pilgrim's Way

In the preceding chapters I have examined various aspects of the *henro*—notably its landscape and historical development—that frame and help shape the experiences of the pilgrims who themselves are constantly in a process of making and (re)shaping the pilgrimage at any given juncture. In the following three chapters I focus more directly on the pilgrims and on their experiences and performances. In chapters 6 and 7 I examine pilgrims as they engage in the pilgrimage, and in chapter 8 I look more closely at an issue I have raised earlier in this book: that pilgrims often do not just make one pilgrimage in Shikoku, but may return again and again. Many of the pilgrims introduced thus far in this book, such as Tabuchi Yoshio and Shinnen, have done the pilgrimage many times and have had an extensive and often lifelong engagement with it. Yet as I have noted before and as I will discuss in more detail at the start of chapter 8, such matters have rarely been discussed in studies of pilgrimage, which have tended to focus on goals and sites and at pilgrims in the moment of their practice of pilgrimage. This focus is unsurprising, given that the most visible aspects of pilgrimage naturally relate to sites and the pilgrims at them, and also because—as chapters 6 and 7 indicate—pilgrims, while in the midst of their pilgrimages, are very much focused on goals and (in the case of Shikoku) the next site or place they will visit, while their accounts and diaries of their experiences also frequently center on such matters.

However, at the same time this focus is problematic in that it omits adequate discussion of the ways in which pilgrimage might itself be, in the eyes and practices of its participants, something more than a transitory and (to use Turner's term) liminal process. Hence while chapters 6 and 7, as accounts of pilgrims in motion and their experiences of performing pilgrimages, show how pilgrims in motion are goal-centered, chapter 8 will discuss how pilgrimage can become what I describe as a way of life for some participants and a central organizing dynamic in their lives, to the extent that perceptions of pilgrimage as primarily a liminal, transient, or one-time only event can be seen to be rather problematic.

Walkers and pilgrims on buses

My examination of the feelings and experiences of pilgrims as they perform their pilgrimages in Shikoku in this and the next chapter will center on two categories of pilgrim, those who walk and those who travel by organized bus tours. These are the two dominant modes of pilgrimage practice historically and in contemporary terms—foot pilgrimage holding sway until the advent of mass tours in the 1950s and now showing signs of revival, and buses nowadays the most dominant form of pilgrimage, one that, as chapter 5 has shown, has greatly shaped the *henro* in the present day.

I focus on these two modes of travel also for practical reasons, since they are the ones with which I am most familiar. Besides walking the whole pilgrimage once, I have, in numerous visits to Shikoku, spent many days walking between the temples and meeting pilgrims. There are also far more published materials, in terms of pilgrims' journals and accounts, by walkers than by pilgrims who have used any other mode of travel. From Kenmyō and Chōzen in the seventeenth century to the present day, walkers have often recorded their experiences and published accounts of their pilgrimages. By contrast, there are few published accounts of other forms of pilgrimage, whether by organized tour, taxi, or bicycle.[1] Apart from walking, my most extensive fieldwork research has been with bus pilgrims. Over the years I have traveled with bus pilgrimage parties, normally for short periods, but once—an account of which forms the main focus of the next chapter—doing an *ikkoku mairi* tour with a party of pilgrims. When I have stayed at temples and pilgrim lodges overnight, too, I have often encountered bus parties there as well, enabling scope for further interviews and communication.

By contrast, my access to and interactions with other pilgrims (e.g., those by car, taxi, or bicycle) has been limited usually to fleeting encounters at sites. Since I have not been on a helicopter tour, and since I have as yet not come across any accounts of people who have, I am unable to make any comments on that mode of travel in experiential terms. Thus this and the next chapter will look at walkers and bus pilgrims as examples of the most normative types of pilgrim in Shikoku and as the primary foci of my fieldwork research. This chapter will focus on those who go by foot, and the next will turn to bus pilgrimages.

Seeing the pilgrimage: Through the walker's eyes

Pilgrims see and experience the pilgrimage in different ways depending on their modes of transport; the view from a bus is obviously different from that out of a helicopter window or from the perspective of a pilgrim on foot. Differences of style—for example, in terms of speed, lengths of time taken, and energy spent getting to and from temples—indicate that those on buses and those on foot are likely to travel different paths and pass through different modes of experience even though they are all *dōgyō*, engaged in the same practice together with Kōbō Daishi. Such differences also affect pilgrim behavior at the sites and between them, as I have noted before in my comments that those on foot tend to spend less time and to perform fewer rituals of worship at the sites than do those on organized tours. The comments of a *bangai* temple priest to me are worth citing here. Walkers, he said, often came to his temple, but they rarely worshiped much. They just, he complained, got their books stamped, had a quick look around, and then moved on. They were, he felt, "just walking" rather than engaging in the faith-centered endeavor that, in his view, the *henro* ought to be. They were just using the temples as points of reference on a long walk rather than as places for expressions of devotion and prayer. In his view bus pilgrims were closer to the heart of the pilgrimage because they actually engaged in extended prayers and acts of devotion at the sites.

I have heard similar opinions from other priests in Shikoku. However, one should also note that temples do not consider it appropriate for those who are "just walking" or who fail to overtly demonstrate faith by engaging in worship to be denied having their scrolls and books stamped. While the Catholic authorities at Santiago ask those who arrive at Santiago to give their motives for their pilgrimages before handing out the Compostela, or certificate of completion of pilgrimage, and refuse to do this for those who do not provide a religious motive for their journeys,[2] the Shikoku temples make no differentiation between pilgrims, treating them all the same by stamping their scrolls and books without question.

The behavior of foot pilgrims at the sites—and their perceptions of those sites—is shaped by the physical conditions of their journeys. Unlike bus pilgrims, who exist in a communal atmosphere that, especially when they are led by *sendatsu,* stimulates participation in prayers and devotional acts and who travel in a way that enables them to focus their energies on the temples, walkers expend much of their energy just getting to and between the temples. They thus tend to be impelled by the process of walking and the physical challenges this imposes. In such circumstances it is unsurprising that they do not engage in quite the levels of devotion at the sites as are seen among bus pilgrims or that their journals tend to focus more on the periods spent walking between temples than they do on the temples themselves. The account of Harada Nobuo, a man who walked the *henro* in 1998 just after retiring in his early sixties, is typical in this respect in that it provides plentiful descriptions of the paths, roads, vegetation, and flowers seen as he walks but tends to make only perfunctory comments about the temples themselves.[3]

In effect, those on foot tend to see the route as their focus, with temples as reference points on it, special signposts or sacred nodes in what is itself an extended sacred space that is simultaneously linear (the route, the legendary path trodden by Kōbō Daishi) and encompassing (the landscape and sacred arena of Shikoku). By contrast, as my account in the next chapter will indicate, those on buses find their main focus to be on the temples themselves, and while the journey and the space between them provides a setting for prayer and miracle narratives, it is largely a means of getting to the next temple rather than the central focus of their endeavors.

My experiences of foot and bus pilgrimage are probably a fair representation of this point. Thinking about my 1984 foot pilgrimage, the memories that abide are primarily of paths, roads, and the places in between (as, indeed, are my recollections of the day I spent in April 2000 walking with Tomoko, where I recall and delighted in the quiet mountain paths while quickly getting away from the noisy temples). Conversely, memories of my 1990 bus pilgrimage center far more on the sites than the route between them, and my primary recollection of the spaces in between is of the interior of the microbus, the narratives of the tour leader, and the faces and comments of the pilgrims in the party.

Attitudes to the temples may vary accordingly, as well. For those traveling by bus there is a growing sense of expectancy as they travel between or approach sites; this is what they have come to visit, and hence when they arrive at the sites, there is generally an excited readiness to pray, chant sutras, and engage with the location. Those on foot, however, often find that the noise and chaos of temple courtyards contrast disturbingly with the quiet they have experienced between sites, and hence they may be keen to hurry on rather than tarry at the sites—as my comments in the introduction about making a hasty escape from Temple 41 indicated.

Harada comments that there were many days when he barely spoke to anyone while walking, apart from perhaps a brief word or two with the people who stamped his book at the temples. On days when he did not visit a temple at all he might not speak to anyone.[4] In such contexts, the noise and bustle of temple courtyards can be unsettling, a harsh rupture in the experiences of pilgrims accustomed to being immersed in their own thoughts. Certainly Harada's journal indicates that at various points the shock experienced on reaching temples thronged with pilgrims became an intrusion on his inner thoughts, the quiet he had been used to, and the simple process of walking.[5] Those spaces in between, too, are where foot pilgrims are likely to have encounters with local people and to receive *settai*—a prominent theme (see below) in the experience of walkers, one that raises their spirits and elevates their sense of self-worth. Between temples, then, foot pilgrims may thus feel special and distinctive. When they reach temple courtyards and find themselves in a crowd of pilgrims (mostly those who have arrived in buses and cars), their distinctiveness is submerged or lost in the throng.

Henro boke and self-absorption

Harada comments that he gradually became used to the process of walking, entering into a state he calls *henro boke* (literally, "pilgrimage senility" or blankness of mind, but which is perhaps best rendered as "pilgrimage immersion"), in which he lost sight of the world around him and became immersed in just walking. This feeling developed after about twenty-five days on the road, after the initial excitement of becoming a pilgrim had worn off and after he had become used to all the pains and difficulties of walking every day.[6] As he entered into this state of *henro boke*, Harada became absorbed in a world of simplicity in which everything centered around just walking, eating, and sleeping—a state of mind that he relates to the Buddhist notion of selflessness *(muga)*.[7] As he walks, Harada records, life becomes increasingly simple and straightforward, with few needs for sensual delight; each evening all he seeks is somewhere to stay, a bath, food, one bottle of beer (he does not give up alcohol entirely but limits himself to one beer per night), and a good sleep.[8] He watches no television and hears no news—and when, at one point, he does come across a newspaper, he finds the contents to be trite, concerned with scandal, and of little enduring value and meaning.[9]

This feeling of simplicity—walk, eat, sleep, get up, walk again—is widely felt by foot pilgrims. It was certainly one of the most striking experiences that Dorothy and I felt as we walked—often a few meters apart, absorbed in our own thoughts for much of each day—in 1984. Having but one simple routine to do each day—effectively, get up, eat, leave, put one foot in front of the other, visit the next temple, get to the next lodge, eat, and sleep—liberated us from the normal issues of daily life and the trials and stresses of work and provided a clear focus to everything we did. Life became simple and the world beyond the pilgrimage, beyond the simple process of walking, ephemeral. News, politics, sport, and much else that normally interested one or the other of us just lost its importance; even when we stayed in places that had a television we hardly felt interested in watching the news or other programs. In the evenings we did not need to think about what we might do or what we might eat; exhausted after the long walk each day, we just got in the bath, ate what the pilgrims' lodge provided, tried to summon up enough energy to write our daily diaries and talk a little—and then slept.

This can make walkers become remarkably self-absorbed—and often, too, so focused on and convinced of their own value that they expect special treatment and favors not accorded to (for example) those on buses. This self-absorption does not mean that such pilgrims have no cares or interest in their fellow pilgrims; indeed, the journals of walkers such as Satō Takako, Harada, Kagayama Kōichi, and others that will be referred to in this chapter contain vignettes recording encounters with other pilgrims as well as local people who assist them.[10] Yet although they walk at times with other pilgrims met on the route, there is also a sense in which they are glad to get back on their own again. Harada, whose account shows that often when he meets other pilgrims on foot they do little more than make a cursory greeting and move on,[11] comments that "there are also times when it is good to walk and talk with other pilgrims," recording, for example, how he walked for two days with a businessman from Tokyo who was doing the *henro* and whose life of international business and travel fascinated him, and from whom, Harada records, he learned a lot. However, they, too, were conscious that this was a transitory relationship and parted company ostensibly because Harada was a faster walker, but clearly also because each wanted to be with his own thoughts.[12] I am conscious that when we walked with Nakano-san, the ascetic pilgrim described in chapter 3, we and he were all pleased to have new company for a while—but that there came a point when he definitely wanted to be left to his thoughts and company, and we to ours. In such contexts, Harada comments that at least one of the ten recommended rules and prohibitions for pilgrims—that of not using bad language to others—was relatively easy to maintain because he spoke so little with them.[13]

A striking example of self-absorption occurs in the account written by Kagita Chūsaburō of his 1961 pilgrimage. Kagita was a businessman with good connections in the legal and political worlds, and the foreword to his book was written by Ikeda Hayato, the former Japanese prime minister who also had done a Kōbō Daishi pilgrimage and who wrote that he had been cured of illness as a result.[14] Kagita had been ill with pancreatic problems (and also hemorrhoids) and had been told by doctors that he would require two months' hospitalization to get better. Rather than doing this, he decided to take two months off work and do the *henro* instead, viewing this as a way to cure his ills. A friend—a court judge—decided to accompany him, and they took temporary Buddhist ordinations for the duration of their travels—a point that Kagita clearly thinks accorded him special status enabling him to criticize others he met who failed, in his view, to attain the same standards as himself. At various times temple priests are criticized for not maintaining their temples properly, inn keepers are castigated for their venal attitudes, and bus pilgrims for their haste and tourist behavior, while even his own companions (the judge and a young man who joined them during their pilgrimage) are seen as failing to meet the standards Kagita demands.[15]

Yet while at times criticizing those he meets or travels with, Kagita's account is more striking for the relative lack of mention of others, notably his traveling companions, one of whom walked for forty-three days with him, the other for thirty, in comparison to the amount of time he spends talking about his health and thoughts. On page 166 of his book, for example, Kagita comments that Kawano-san was parting company with them after thirty days. At this point I had forgotten completely who Kawano-san was, so rarely had he been mentioned, and it was only after searching back through the book that I found two references to him. The first, on page 57, noted that a young man called Kawano had joined up with them—an event Kagita sanctioned because he saw himself as assuming the role of guide and mentor to what appeared to be a troubled young man—and the second a few pages later, when Kagita records some critical comments about Kawano's poor attitude and spirit. Other than that, Kawano-san had not featured at all, being mentioned less often than Kagita's hemorrhoids. While these were obviously of immediate concern to Kagita, and while his critical remarks about Kawano-san's poor spirit suggest that Kagita regarded him as a pain in a similar location, it is nevertheless striking and indicative that so little can be said about companions with whom one has walked so far and for so long.

Sleeping, eating, going to the toilet

Even while becoming increasingly absorbed in the simplicity of "just walking," foot pilgrims still need to deal with the basic practicalities of the pilgrimage, and these usually leave abiding memories. Kagayama, commenting on his 1999 pilgrimage, states that pilgrims who walk might forget the pilgrimage temples and their surroundings, but their memories would always be deeply engraved with impressions of where and how they slept.[16] Such locations, Kagayama considers, were more memorable points on the *henro* than the temples—a point evident also in Harada's account, which says far more about the places he stayed than the temples he visited. It resonates, too, with my

Pilgrims led by a *sendatsu* praying at Temple 84.

memories of walking, in which places we stayed—notably the old-style pilgrims' lodges—have stayed more vividly in my memory than most of the temples. Miyazaki Tateki of the Henro Michi Hozonkyōryoku Kai also emphasizes the importance of basic practicalities when he states that foot pilgrims have three main concerns: places to sleep, eat, and go to the toilet.[17]

This emphasis on pragmatic concerns indicates a rather different realm of perception and experience from those bus pilgrims who travel with a fixed schedule through which they are assured of from the outset food, a good bath, and comfortable accommodations each night. Walkers, by contrast, face a daily struggle due not just to the physical effort required to walk thirty or more kilometers, often in mountainous terrain and in all weathers, but because of the incessant state of insecurity and uncertainty related to simple, everyday necessities that even those immersed in a state of *henro boke* have to deal with. Such recurrent needs can create an almost constant sense of unease and tension that is central to the foot pilgrimage experience. Pilgrims' journals reverberate with such questions: where will I get to today? Will I be able to get to a lodge that can accommodate me (a question of much uncertainty in that lodges may be spread far apart, are usually more geared toward the bus trade, and do not always have room for solitary travelers)? Will there be places to eat when I am hungry?

Harada, for example, writes of how each evening he would pore over maps to work out where he would be the next evening and whether there would be somewhere to stay—and of working out alternatives, such as shortened or lengthened days of walking if there was nothing available at a reasonable distance by foot from his current overnight accommodations.[18] As Harada notes, there were days when available lodgings were far apart, meaning that sometimes he needed to walk forty kilometers or more in order to get to lodgings and how, as a result, he ended up walking the *henro* more quickly than he had planned.[19] Although Harada thought that doing the pilgrimage on foot and just concentrating on walking would be stress free, there always remained, despite his sense of selflessness and "pilgrimage immersion," an underlying unease in his journey.[20] Transience made everything simple and straightforward—and simultaneously created a new set of tensions.

Time and speed

Along with—and closely linked to—this emphasis on practicalities and basic necessities, walkers often display a concern, and at times an obsession, with speed and distances. Even though they travel at a far slower pace than, and may complain about the haste of, bus pilgrims, speed remains a matter of concern and even pride for many of those on foot, while their accounts frequently emphasize the distances they cover each day. Sometimes, as with the *hashiri hendo* of the Tokugawa period, such speed may be spurred by the financial need not to incur too many nights' lodging fees, but a more potent factor is that lodgings are often far apart, meaning that pilgrims may have to walk fast in order to get to their next night's lodging. This helps them build up a momentum, which reverberates through their pilgrimages—a point that was central to our pilgrimage experience in 1984. We started from Temple 1 in the first week of February because this was the only time we could absent ourselves from work, and from the outset we experienced cold, often snowy, weather, which meant we never wanted to linger long but—in order to keep warm— kept walking. Moreover, as this was outside the main pilgrimage season, many of the lodges in Awa were not open for business, making it harder than normal to find places to stay. For our first few days in particular, we had to walk fast in order to get to the next available place that could accommodate us. In such conditions, we quickly got used to a fast pace. We were also— like many pilgrims—constrained by time: we knew we had a maximum number of days (around forty-five) in which to complete the *henro* before we had to get back to our jobs at Japanese universities and hence could not afford to tarry long anywhere. As a result, even when it became clear that we would easily get back in time, and as the weather warmed up, we found it hard to slow down, while our strength built up so that we became increasingly able to cover long distances. On one day, well over halfway through the pilgrimage, we had to cover just over thirty kilometers to reach the lodge where we had arranged our next night's accommodation—yet we found ourselves easily getting there in the early afternoon, leaving us somewhat disoriented because we had nothing else to do for the rest of the day. Like Harada, we finished the *henro* a few days earlier than expected.

Pilgrims often, in such contexts, become obsessed with the distances they can cover and the time it takes them. Thus Watanabe Yasuhiro, who took a rapid thirty days to walk in the late 1990s, carefully records how far he walked each day in his journal.[21] In published pilgrimage accounts, the number of days taken to walk the pilgrimage is frequently flagged up in the book's title or subtitle, as if this were one of the most important aspects of the journey. Thus Shiraga Tadashi's book, *O-henro,* has a subtitle telling us this is an account of his forty-two-day walk around the Shikoku pilgrimage,[22] while Harada's subtitle informs us that his was a "35 day, 1200 kilometer" pilgrimage. Other accounts, too, emphasize how many (or rather, how few) days the author/pilgrim has taken to complete his pilgrimage. Thus Nishikawa Arao, who decided to do the *henro* when he retired, more as a challenge than because of any sense of faith, took just thirty-one days to walk the entire route, and his journal reads accordingly, as an account of something akin to a route march.[23] Watanabe Yasuhiro's thirty-day pilgrimage—and his resultant diary, with its emphasis on distances covered—has already been mentioned above, but others may have completed the whole circuit even more quickly. Harada, for example, records meeting a young man aged twenty-three from Osaka who completed the *henro* in just twenty-nine days, largely by running, sleeping out, and eating snacks bought at shops. This young man appeared to have had little or no motivation related to faith, telling Harada merely that he was at a loss to know what to do in his life, so he came to Shikoku to become a pilgrim. He did, however, feel that through the pilgrimage he had acquired a sense of confidence.[24]

Harada, too, proudly records his own capacity to cover long distances, noting that he walks farther in a day than Bashō, the celebrated Tokugawa-period poet and pilgrim, managed.[25] Tsukioka Yukiko, too, touches on the issue of pilgrims who talk about their speedy prowess, mentioning an elderly male pilgrim who briefly walked with her but who normally, he let her know, did sixty kilometers a day.[26] Pilgrims I have interviewed, especially those met while on the road in Shikoku, often broach the subject of distances covered and speed without any prompting. Thus, for example, a male pilgrim I met near Temple 3 in April 2000 (he was heading back toward Temple 1 before returning home) immediately began to regale me with facts and figures about his pilgrimage: it had taken him just thirty-two days, and he had averaged forty-five kilometers per day. He also emphasized that he had no faith *(mushinkō)* as such and that his journey was primarily motivated by a wish to improve his health.[27]

There is a latent irony in this emphasis on speed, given that many walkers do the pilgrimage as a means of escape or release from the pressures of modern, speed-focused society—and since a major criticism they make of bus pilgrimages is that *they* travel too fast! Yet at the same time it is perhaps only natural that people who spend long periods walking, need to cover long distances and reach overnight accommodation, and are concerned about matters of fitness become fixated on time and speed. There may also be a competitive element to this as well, often underpinned by machismo, for it should not escape the reader's eye that all the examples I have cited here are of male pilgrims. A similar observation has been made by Frey with regard to male pilgrims on the Santiago Camino, many of whom "boast about the number of kilometers they are able to travel every day" and who may do far more than the normal walkers' daily average.[28] My sense is that male pilgrims in Shikoku (many of whom are retired and who like to emphasize this while talking of speed in a "I am sixty-eight years old, retired, and I can do forty kilometers a day!" manner) are much the same.

This emphasis on speed is one means by which pilgrims seek to distinguish and mark themselves out as special. In such contexts, while female pilgrims appear to be less focused on speed and the wish to inform everyone of how quickly they walked, they are often equally keen to emphasize, in their written accounts, their own special characteristics, usually by drawing attention to their gender and, sometimes, age, as if these were striking and defining characteristics that mark out and give their pilgrimages special status and significance. Satō Takako's account of her foot pilgrimage, for example, informs us in its subtitle that this is the account of a "healthy old lady" *(genki na obāsan)*, Mori Harumi emphasizes her gender in the title of her account, and both Takamure in 1918 and Tsukioka in 2000 emphasize in the titles of their accounts their status as young women *(musume)* on pilgrimage.[29]

Scenery, nature, tranquility, beauty . . .

While impelled by practical needs, speed, distances, and achievements, this does not mean that walkers race on, unmindful of the environment in which they travel. The scenery and landscape of Shikoku, discussed in chapter 2, is a prominent attraction of the *henro*, featuring widely in pilgrims' accounts. While pilgrims emphasize the effort, pain, and sweat involved in some of the more demanding and mountainous parts of the route—notably the steep slopes known as *henro korogashi* (literally, "pilgrimage tumbling/falling place") leading to and from temples such as Shōsanji (Temple 12) and Yoko-mineji (Temple 60)[30]—such references are mingled with wonder at the natural beauties and scenery involved. Thus Kagayama, even as he records being out of breath, sweating profusely, and struggling to climb up Hatchōzaka, a steep ascent between Temples 44 and 45 that has tested the mettle of many pilgrims, is able to record his wonder at the dramatic scenery that is manifest as he climbs and sweats and at the awesome aspect of the precipices and overhanging rocks through which he walks.[31] Harada, too, constantly records the natural beauties and features of the island and the *henro*—the joys and beauties of Shikoku in a spring breeze, the splendid scenery of the Kōchi coast, and the tranquility of places when there is not other human presence, where the only sounds are the voices of birds and where he is surrounded by wild flowers and greenery.[32]

And highways, traffic, and tunnels . . .

Whilst walkers enthuse about the Shikoku scenery and the quiet mountain paths, they also complain frequently about the relative lack of places where they can get away from the modern world. Harada comments that only around 150 kilometers of the *henro*—not much more than 10 percent—runs along such paths, while Hirota Mio complains that most of the time is spent walking along roads.[33] Takada Shinkai comments that there are few places where the pilgrim can walk in peace and especially complains about how painful and unpleasant it is to have to walk so much on asphalt and concrete—again, a concern that surfaces in many pilgrims' accounts.[34] Hirota and Imai Misako both also voice a common complaint, saying that not only do walkers have to spend a lot of time following roads, but that these are often narrow and with little space for walkers, who are frequently troubled by the proximity of cars and trucks hurtling by.[35]

Pilgrims find this especially problematic when they have to follow major highways. Perhaps the place that causes the most common gripes and least pleasant memories is the long stretch of road between Temples 23 and 24, where the walker has little choice but to follow the often narrow highway that is hemmed in between the hills and the coastline and that follows the course of the old *henro* path, which it has covered over. The only space for anyone on foot (or bicycle) for much of the way is a narrow lane marked off from the main carriageway with a painted line, less than a meter wide and too narrow for pilgrims to walk together side by side even if they wanted to. The road bears heavy traffic, and it is very hard not to feel intimidated by the speed, noise, and closeness of the vehicles along it—a feeling that is especially wearing given that it takes close to two full days to cover this part of the route. It was one of our least favored places on the whole pilgrimage, and many others, such as Harada (who also found visibility poor in this area and felt especially worried along a stretch where there were no houses or signs of life for several kilometers), have voiced their negative feelings about it as well.[36] Indeed, many pilgrims have been so put off by this part of the route that they give up walking here and take buses and trains instead as far as Temple 24.[37]

Tunnels also cause pilgrims a great deal of distress and turmoil. There are many places in Shikoku's mountainous terrain where the roads pass through long tunnels, and often, due to the disappearance of old paths, the pilgrim has little choice but to use them too. Some are a kilometer or more in length and are not well lit—or, indeed, especially wide. Again, our 1984 pilgrimage diaries record several places where we felt ill at ease in such places, while Hirota comments about the unease of having to go through long road tunnels.[38] Tsukioka is more direct still, describing one tunnel (some seventeen hundred meters long) that she went through as an "exhaust gas hell."[39]

And other complaints . . .

It is not just the noise of the temples or the turmoil of highways and tunnels that cause foot pilgrims to complain or feel unhappy at their lot. The problems of finding overnight accommodation, which I have already mentioned in chapter 5 and earlier in this chapter, are at times exacerbated for walkers because many large lodges and *shukubō* get fully booked out by large-scale pilgrimage tour groups, especially in the peak (i.e., spring) season. Even in 1961, Kagita found that there were times when he was unable to get lodgings at *shukubō*,[40] while Takada Shinkai—reiterating a common problem that I have heard frequently from those walkers I have met over the years—complains that it is sometimes hard for solitary walkers to find space at pilgrims' lodges and *shukubō*.[41] Kobayashi Atsuhiro, too, complains about a lack of lodgings for walkers and of having to sleep out on occasion when he could not find somewhere to stay.[42]

Besides accommodation problems, foot pilgrims often feel frustrated when they arrive at the *nōkyōjo* (the temple office where pilgrims' books and scrolls are stamped) and find that they have to wait in a queue while large numbers of books and stamps belonging to bus pilgrims are stamped. Harada expresses annoyance at such a situation, complaining that his schedule was delayed by having to wait for thirty minutes in one case.[43] A common feeling among walkers is that they should be given precedence over people in groups in such contexts.[44] Interestingly, such complaints seem to be directed against the temples and those working at its offices rather than at the bus pilgrims themselves; while walkers overall tend to see their way of traveling as being closest to the spirit of the pilgrimage, there is a general sense within the pilgrim community as a whole that bus pilgrimages are a practical means of accomplishing the *henro* in the context of modern society and the demands it makes on people.[45] Moreover, as my comments on *settai* (below) will indicate and as my description of bus package tours in the next chapter also notes, when those on bus pilgrimages do encounter walkers, they often treat them well and in a friendly manner—for example, by giving them *settai* or praising them for their ardor in walking the route (a compliment we received countless times). In such contexts, potential tensions may be diffused through personal contact.

Another related complaint that appears especially keenly felt among walkers (whose schedules are less predictable than those on buses and who may at times thus arrive at temples quite late in the day) is that *nōkyōjo* are as a rule open only until 5:00 P.M. Many feel that this is too short a period— one that, in effect, makes temples into something akin to offices or businesses (and priests into "salarymen"). Such complaints have been voiced most frequently to me by pilgrims on foot, but I have heard such complaints also from those who travel by other means as well. The comments of a lady who was in her mid-sixties, who had been born and brought up in Shikoku (she lived in Matsuyama), who had done the pilgrimage by bus, and who knew a lot about the temples because her son worked in the pilgrimage service industry, are perhaps typical of those I have heard over the years. The temples, she said, are just like offices, keeping office hours and doing little more than stamp scrolls and books and take money as fees, while the priests that run them are just like salarymen, working for and running a company business.[46] Tsukioka comments on the atmosphere that can occur at *nōkyōjo* especially when large groups of pilgrims descend on them to get their books and scrolls stamped, at which times she says they become like factories.[47]

Harada states that, like many pilgrims, his main impressions of the temples are of the offices where he got his book stamped rather than of the temples themselves. These were the places where pilgrims were most likely to have any interactions and encounters with people working at or looking after the temples—and that such impressions tended to be negative, of unfriendly priests or assistants who take their books, inscribe and stamp them, and take the fee with barely a word or friendly gesture.[48] Again, this is a refrain I have heard on numerous occasions.

I can identify with all the above frustrations and complaints. The sense of being aggrieved to see a line of people clutching piles of books and scrolls when one enters a temple office, the feeling that they have got there the easy way by bus or car when you have just walked and struggled for several hours, and that you may have to wait a long time to get your one book stamped while someone (probably not the priest and probably not smiling or appearing friendly) works their way through hundreds of books and scrolls, can be galling. Yet there are caveats to such perceptions. The first is that the demand that walkers should be given preference undermines the implicit egalitarianism of the pilgrimage expressed by the concept of dōgyō. Walkers who demand precedence are, in effect, saying that they are "more equal than others"—a view that is not borne out or validated by any pilgrimage rules, for, as I have pointed out in an earlier chapter, there is no set regulation that says how the pilgrimage "ought" to be done.

Moreover, despite such complaints, in my experience individual pilgrims and those clearly traveling on foot are very often privileged in this respect. When we walked, we repeatedly noted that when we entered temple offices to find a queue of people, someone working there would beckon us forward, ask if we were walking (for most, though, our weathered faces and grubby clothes were such a clear indication that they did not need to ask), and stamp our book out of turn—and not infrequently waive all or some of the fee as settai. Priests, their wives, and other temple workers whom I have discussed this matter with inform me that they almost invariably do this for walkers. They also tend, at the same time, to have negative impressions of pilgrims who overtly display or manifest a sense of self-importance or who expect to be able to jump queues and may well make such pilgrims wait their turn as a result (see chapter 7 for an example of such an event).

The apparent surliness of those stamping books, too, is also something I can understand. When one has spent all day dealing with thousands of books and scrolls, it is probably hard to manifest new enthusiasm when a pilgrim arrives late in the day. While each pilgrim naturally regards him/herself as individual and special, for someone who has spent all day working at a nōkyōjo, s/he can appear to just one more person in a stream of many thousands. Pilgrims can, in such circumstances, misjudge the apparently unsmiling faces and attitudes of those at nōkyōjo. My most hostile memory of a priest during our 1984 pilgrimage occurred when we arrived late at a temple, needing to get our book stamped and hoping to stay at its lodge. The priest appeared to be unimpressed at two foreign pilgrims turning up late, expecting their book to be stamped (we felt he did this with little apparent grace) and to be put up overnight. In fact, there had been a misunderstanding, for the priest at the previous temple had assured us that this temple had a functioning *shukubō* and that there was no need to call in advance for places. He was unaware that the lodge had been closed for repairs. The priest at the temple we had reached somewhat abruptly told us this, seemingly showed no interest in helping us find somewhere else, even though it was rapidly becoming dark, and somewhat rudely, we felt, suggested we walk a few kilometers to the next town where there might be a business hotel open. We left the temple in ill humor, me muttering imprecations that questioned his parentage, suitability for the priesthood, and much else. In 1997, I was back in the region and learned, through other sources, that the information I was seeking on one point of my research was available at this temple. I went there in some trepidation, hoping either that the priest would not be there and that I could ask someone else or that he would not recognize me from over a decade earlier. He was there, and he did not recognize me. He was, however, extremely friendly and could not have been more helpful. I left feeling guilty at my earlier hostile thoughts, aware that we had doubtless caught him at a bad time before and had probably made things worse by our attitude. Priests and other *nōkyōjo* officials I have talked to also tell me that it is not always easy to maintain a friendly visage when dealing with pilgrims, especially when they come across in a self-righteous manner.

Moreover, as I have noted above, those working at the temples may well display special kindness—by, for example, reducing the fee as *settai*—to individual pilgrims. On many occasions it was through the good offices of priests or others working in *nōkyōjo* that we were able to arrange accommodation. Harada, even as he complains about people at the *nōkyōjo*, recognizes that there were many who took great care to inscribe his book and who—recognizing from his sunburned face that he was walking—would offer him tea and other forms of *settai* and provide detailed directions on how to get to the next temple.[49]

Similarly, complaints about "office hours" can be unfair. The reason the temples decided to regulate the hours they remained open to stamp books and scrolls was that pilgrims would turn up at all hours expecting to be dealt with—again, indicative of the ways in which (some) pilgrims consider themselves to merit special treatment. Yet it is not unknown for priests or assistants to accommodate the needs of pilgrims who appear after hours; as Tsukioka notes, while there are those who shut up shop on the dot, others will, depending on their feelings and circumstances, stamp scrolls and books out of hours.[50] Priests I know say much the same; much, in effect, depends on the attitudes they encounter among pilgrims. Pilgrims who brashly expect to be given precedence or to be dealt with out of hours just because they are walking may well find themselves rebuffed and frustrated, while those who take their turn in the queue or politely apologize for turning up late and ask-ing if their book can be stamped are more likely to receive kind treatment.

Hardships, smiles, and *settai*

During our pilgrimage in 1984, our frustrations (over problems of accommo-dation, in particular) surfaced on one occasion when we were asked by a tem-ple priest how our pilgrimage was going. We both gave vent to our feelings, and I unleashed what I now realize was a typical foot pilgrim's self-righteous diatribe about the lack of accessible lodgings at convenient places for walk-ers, as well as about the traffic, lack of decent signposts, the weather, and much else. The priest smiled and gently reminded us that we did not *have* to do the *henro;* we had chosen to do it and hence should accept the way it was. It was a *shugyō* (austerity) and hence one should not expect it to be easy, comfortable, or convenient. If one chooses to walk a fourteen-hundred-kilo-meter pilgrimage known for its ascetic orientations, one should expect to meet some difficulties and setbacks. In a modern society such as Japan, one should expect such a long journey to involve some periods on roads and that there would be some traffic on the island. If one is going to spend thirty to forty days walking around an island, one should expect it to rain sometimes, while one is bound to have some accommodation problems if one wants to spend forty or so successive nights in different places. If we really wanted ease, comfort, and an assured place to stay each night, we should take an organized tour that would deal with such issues and keep us out of the rain and cold. And, he also commented, we doubtless received *settai* and other forms of help from people in Shikoku, had periods when we were in beauti-fully scenic places, when the weather was sunny and warm, found many good lodges at which to stay overnight where the food was nourishing and the welcome warm, and had many other good experiences along the way. The journey, he commented, using an image similar to that used in the Shi-koku Reijōkai's 1984 collection of miracle tales, which portrays the *henro* as a metaphorical journey through the valleys of death and the mountains of life, was one through highs and lows, valleys and mountains in which the lows and difficulties were what should teach us to appreciate the highs. Hard-ship, in other words, was intrinsic to pilgrimage experience; without being tested by it, one could not appreciate the benefits and positive aspects of the pilgrimage.

He was, of course, right on both counts. I will look more closely at his point about pilgrimage being *shugyō* and about how foot pilgrims express and write about their physical suffering shortly, but first I will affirm that the bad days and problems we had were more than outweighed by positive experi-ences of the sort he mentioned: sunny days, beautiful scenery and paths, the kindness of local people and of numerous priests. *Settai* in particular is an abiding positive memory of ours—as it is in walkers' accounts in general. While complaints about all manner of annoying inconveniences permeate pilgrims' accounts, so, too, do the positive feelings engendered by *settai*—feelings that recur in every account written by a foot pilgrim I have come across and in just about every conversation I have had with pilgrims on foot over the years.

Although, as was noted in chapter 5, *settai* had virtually died out by the late 1940s, it began to reappear in later decades as Japan's economy was rebuilt, supported not just by island inhabitants, but also by externally based organizations such as the Arita Settaikō (see chapter 3), which resumed its activities in Shikoku as the economy improved. While in the economically more prosperous era of today fewer pilgrims, compared with Tokugawa times, actually need alms, the practice remains widely supported in Shikoku, seen by locals as a continuing element in local identity and culture and regarded by pilgrims and locals alike as a defining characteristic of the Shikoku *henro*.

Settai is nowadays most commonly experienced by walkers, although this does not mean that people do not give also to those on buses. The Arita Settaikō, which hands out alms from its stall at Temple 1 for one week per year, does so to all—whether traveling in organized tours, in private cars, or on foot—who enter the temple. Other fixed *settai* stalls do the same. However, for the most part *settai* is more often given out to those on foot than those on buses, both because the pilgrims that potential donors are most likely to encounter, unless they are in the courtyards of temples, are those on foot and because—as various conversations with people in Shikoku indicated—there is a general feeling among potential donors that foot pilgrims are deserving of support in a way that bus pilgrims are not. This latter point was evident to me when we walked the pilgrimage: on several occasions we were given *settai* in direct view of bus and car pilgrims who were not similarly privileged. On one occasion (and certainly not the only one), for example, a priest's wife, busily stamping scrolls and pilgrims' books and collecting fees at the temple office, called us forward, stamped our books, stated that we need not pay the standard fee as we were walking, and handed us some *okashi* (Japanese cakes) to us as *settai*. She then resumed stamping the books of the bus pilgrims and charging them for this service. No one complained or commented that this was unreasonable; my general feeling is that pilgrims who travel by bus feel that walkers who are treated in this way merit it and regard such support in a positive light.

Settai is a common and recurrent experience of foot pilgrims in Shikoku. While it is rare to come across cases such as the pilgrim from 1819, mentioned in chapter 4, who received *settai* twenty-eight times in one day, receiving large amounts of *settai* is not uncommon. When Satō Ken, a journalist for the *Mainichi shinbun*, was walking the pilgrimage in 1988, he met a young Japanese Buddhist priest with a Thai wife. The couple were walking and doing *takuhatsu* (the traditional Buddhist monk's begging round) as they went. Satō met them again five days later, at which point they had more money than previously because of various monetary donations they had received as *settai* in the meantime.[51]

Even pilgrims who do not solicit alms receive it frequently: a couple interviewed by Hoshino who took sixty-one days on their *henro* in 1996 recorded receiving fifty-six cases of *settai* ranging from money and drinks to tea, fruit, and cakes.[52] On one of our first days of pilgrimage in February 1984, a priest we met who was traveling as a pilgrim and who knew Shikoku well from earlier pilgrimage visits told us as we talked about how cold the weather was, that the warmth of the people of Shikoku would drive the cold away, and that as we traveled we would encounter this warmth through the help they gave us. His predictions were accurate, for during the forty days of walking we received all manner of alms from people throughout the island—including fellow pilgrims. On one occasion, as we were walking along a road just outside Matsuyama, a bus full of pilgrims stopped, and someone thrust three thousand yen in notes in our hands. The person who gave us the alms told us that they had heard, from the priest at the previous temple, that two foreign pilgrims were walking the route and that the party of pilgrims she was leading had had a collection among themselves so that they could give us a gesture of support. On another occasion, too, when we encountered a large party of pilgrims led by a Buddhist priest at Temple 58, he instructed one of the party to go to their bus and bring us some *settai*; apparently they carried various snacks and sweets that could be given to other pilgrims met along the way. While we—like most walkers—at times expressed negative views about bus pilgrims, we were also frequently touched by the kindness and supportive comments that we received from them in this way.

During our pilgrimage we received all manner of *settai*, from money to foodstuffs, to canned drinks, to useful objects such as tissues and small hand towels. Shopkeepers often would throw in an extra item or two when we went into a shop to buy something, and occasionally people would haul us in off the street to partake of some food or drinks with them. Usually the gifts would be useful, encouraging, and fitting to the moment: on one bitterly cold and windy day, a car stopped by us and a man popped two hot drinks into our hands and sped off before we could stammer our thanks, and on another, as we trudged along in pouring rain, a truck driver screeched to a halt and thrust an umbrella into Dorothy's hands.

Sometimes, though, the gifts would be less practical, especially given that pilgrims traveling light, as we were, with small backpacks, have limited space (and limited inclination) to carry bulky or weighty offerings. On one occasion, the retired priest of one temple gave us a hanging scroll of the *Hannya Shingyō* that he had done by hand. It was too long to fit inside our small backpacks, but we felt we had to carry it for some distance with us, and thus for the next week I walked with it sticking out the top of my pack, wrapped in plastic to keep it dry when it rained, before we felt we had taken it far enough and stopped at a post office to mail it home. On another occasion, as we sat eating our lunch in a temple courtyard, the priest's wife (who had earlier stamped our book for nothing) came out carrying a bag of *settai* for us. It contained fourteen huge apples, four large oranges, and four cans of fizzy drinks. Pilgrims are supposed to honor the gift of *settai*, since this represents an offering, via the pilgrim, to Kōbō Daishi; to refuse *settai* is to deny the donor the opportunity of gaining merit and sharing in the pilgrimage, and hence one is supposed to accept offerings with good grace. Smiling somewhat weakly, we thus accepted the kind donation, thereby consigning ourselves to a ferocious fruit-eating campaign and bulging rucksacks for a couple of days. The fizzy drinks, however, were just carried a short way and then donated to a small, wayside Buddhist statue.

At temple lodges and other inns we often had our overnight fees reduced —or money given back to us when we paid—while on a couple of occasions people put us up in their homes as *settai*. Once we were walking through Kōchi Prefecture when a man driving a grocery truck stopped, gave us his address, and told us that we would be passing through his village the next day. We were, he said, to stay with him and his family as *settai*. They lived in the area between Temples 38 and 39, a part of the route that took close to two days to walk and where there were no lodges in the region (it was the area in which Shinnen established his lodge in the seventeenth century for similar reasons). Hence his family offered lodgings to those on foot, though not, as he made clear, to those traveling by other means. We accordingly stayed with his family the next evening. Later, after we had completed our pilgrimage, we received a phone call from Nakano-san, the ascetic pilgrim mentioned in chapter 3, informing us that he had finished his pilgrimage and that he had been invited to stay at the same place. Although, since he was sleeping out as part of his ascetic vow, he had had to refuse the invitation, he had stopped there to talk to them and accept some food. While there, he had seen our names in the visitors book the family kept and had been able to hear from the family of our progress around the route. Sometimes, one encounters cases of local people who actively advertise free accommodation. Shiraga, for instance, reproduces a photograph he had taken of a sign attached to a house near Kōchi that offered free lodging as *settai*. Since Shiraga was passing by in the middle of the day and wanted to press on, he had no need of this generosity, but he records that he was invited in and given lunch as *settai*.[53]

Our experiences appear to be little different from those of other pilgrims who have written about their own. Tsukioka records getting frequent donations of *settai*, including twice being given ten thousand yen (over £50) in cash, the second of which came shortly after she had already received three separate gifts of *settai* in quick succession.[54] Takada Kyōko speaks of becoming accustomed to *settai*, so often was she given it as she walked,[55] while Satō Takako comments that frequently, as feelings of exhaustion were weighing upon her as she walked, someone would call her over and give her a can of juice or the like as *settai* and how this would revive her and give her renewed strength to walk on.[56]

It is not just material gifts, however, that energize pilgrims and make them feel that their efforts are being supported, but also the general levels of kindness and support that they receive from local people. Harada, while reflecting on the various things he had received as *settai*, states that more striking than any amount of material objects and gifts was the warmth and kindness he received from local people, who went out of their way to help him and to provide directions and assist him when he got lost, and whose moral support through smiles and general encouragement lifted his spirits frequently. The smiles and warm greetings of strangers as we walked around Shikoku in 1984 remain an abiding memory of that journey. Pilgrims I have talked to have told me that they felt such support—the smiles, bows, and encouraging comments received from people along the way—manifested, for them, the real essence of *settai* and helped them on their way with moral encouragement. For Harada, this spirit of kindness was summed up by the little table set out by the roadside not far from Temple 44. On it were a pile of sweets, a drawing of pilgrims, and a note explaining that the table had been put there by a primary-school girl to offer *settai* to foot pilgrims—and saying *"ganbatte kudasai"* (please keep going) because the next temple was not far off.[57]

Lifts, gifts, dilemmas, regrets

While *settai* provides foot pilgrims with warm and positive feelings that give valence to their pilgrimages and make them feel valued and respected, it can also in some contexts provide them with serious dilemmas, tensions, and, sometimes, regrets. This is especially so when someone stops in a vehicle to offer a lift—something that probably occurs more often (at least in our experience) when the weather is bad and when the driver feels that a pilgrim tramping through the pouring rain might really need some help. Since *settai*, as has been noted, should not be refused and since the offer is intended as a gesture of help (motorists are not certain that the pilgrims they offer lifts to are necessarily committed to walking every step of the way), walkers who have vowed to, or want to, walk every step of the way are placed in a dilemma of whether to refuse and possibly cause offense or to accept and hence not walk the whole way. Satō Takako muses on this when she is offered a lift by people she meets at one of the temples—and of how, when she politely refuses because she feels able to walk, she realizes that her refusal and the request, which had put her in this position, had embarrassed the people who asked her.[58] Kagayama writes about the same dilemma, worrying that to decline would be to deny the potential donor the opportunity to do a good deed, and he also is concerned lest, for donors, giving *settai* might be linked to previous experiences of so doing; in other words, if someone offers *settai* and is refused, they might not do so again.[59]

Such ambivalent feelings were also felt by Harada when he was offered a lift as he was walking along a road where lorries were roaring past and annoying him and just as it had started to rain hard. The circumstances made Harada think seriously about accepting before he politely declined.[60] However, later in his journey he was willing to accept a lift in order to get him out of difficulties, for, walking in the pouring rain, he had missed a signpost and gone several kilometers in the wrong direction. This unexpected diversion meant that he would not reach his arranged lodgings until very late at night—which would inconvenience him and the people at the inn. Thus he decided, on this occasion, to accept the kind offer of a woman at a wayside eating place who knew the owners of the inn he was staying at and who arranged for them to send a car to collect him and to bring him back the next day so he could carry on walking from the same place.[61]

On our first day of walking in 1984, we faced this situation in the late afternoon when the priest of the temple we were visiting (but that did not have a *shukubō*) offered to arrange accommodation for us at the nearest pilgrims' lodge, about two kilometers distant and on the way to the next temple. He duly made a phone call on our behalf and then told us he would take us there in his van. We said no, we were walking the whole way—at which point he talked to us about *settai* and about how, as pilgrims, we should be ready to accept whatever the fates presented us with on our pilgrimage—a perspective similar, of course, to that of the priest discussed earlier who reminded us that we should not complain about what happened on our pilgrimage but regard it all through the lens of *shugyō*. If one were offered a lift, he said, it was better to accept it with grace, even if one only rode for a short distance with the driver, than to refuse. He also commented on the arrogance of some walkers who, he said, were so transfixed by the egotistical desire to walk every step of the way that they rejected—not always politely—sincere and genuine offers of help from those who offered them lifts. In subsequent conversations with people in Shikoku, this criticism has been reiterated several times: from the local perspective and in the eyes of prospective donors, offers of lifts that are turned down in such ways can be seen as a contravention of the normative understandings of the *henro* and the interrelationship between pilgrims and locals. As one person commented to me, pilgrims should not discriminate between forms of *settai*; if they accept gifts of money, lodging, and food, why should they refuse offers of lifts?

Chastened, we climbed in the van for the short drive to the lodge. The next day, when we went to pay for our accommodations, we were told he had picked up the bill already—and that he often did this for walkers, to help them on their way on their first day. He had given us an important lesson about understanding *settai* from the perspective of donors and about the importance of accepting what transpired on the *henro*—yet his generosity also engendered a sense of unease in that we have always remained aware that when we say we walked the Shikoku *henro,* in reality we did not walk it all and that a two-kilometer stretch was done in a priest's van.

While some pilgrims steadfastly refuse all offers of lifts, there are others who will gratefully accept them in the spirit offered or because they are not necessarily committed to walking every step of the way. Takada Kyōko, who speaks of wanting to experience the pilgrimage at her own pace, without using buses, cars, and the like, nonetheless mentions receiving *settai* lifts at times during her pilgrimage.[62] I have met several pilgrims who have accepted lifts when offered—sometimes riding just for a few meters to acknowledge the offer, but occasionally gratefully taking lifts to the next temple or, as with Harada, to save themselves from difficult circumstances. At times, though, accepting lifts can induce a sense of regret (as with our lingering sense that we did not walk the whole way)—as was perhaps best exemplified by a pilgrim I met in 1990 during the package tour described in the next chapter. As our party arrived at Temple 87, we met a pilgrim on foot who was just leaving the temple. He had, he told us, taken thirty-five days and had walked much of the way, although he was not fixated on walking every step and had on occasion taken a bus—notably between Temples 23 and 24—because the walking conditions were not so pleasant. He had also accepted lifts when offered, as *settai,* since this, he felt, was part of the correct spirit of the pilgrimage. After our party had visited the temple, we set off for Temple 88, some twenty or so kilometers distant. As we reached it, we were surprised to encounter this pilgrim again; barely ninety minutes had elapsed since we had seen him at Temple 87, several hours' walk distant. He told us that soon after leaving the temple a pilgrimage bus had stopped and offered him a lift as *settai* and that he had accepted it. He recognized that his acceptance was probably not just due to his customary practice of accepting such *settai,* but because the imminence of finishing his pilgrimage—and the excitement he felt at the prospect of getting to Ōkuboji in quick time—suddenly appealed more than delaying reaching his goal for several hours by walking. Yet this was a decision he had begun to regret. As he commented to me, it would have been more appropriate, in the wider context of his pilgrimage, to have walked the last section and to have approached Ōkuboji more slowly on foot. I suspect that his regret—like ours on that two-kilometer section—is one that pilgrims who accept lifts often face—just as those who turn down such *settai* may also regret breaching pilgrimage customs.

Pain, suffering, memory, and death

The comments of the priest cited earlier—who reminded us that we had chosen to walk the pilgrimage—that this was not meant to be easy but was, rather, a *shugyō* in which one should expect to endure hardships are worth reiterating in the context of the complaints foot pilgrims often make as they travel. Certainly experiences of pain and hardship—not just in the context of the problems pilgrims may endure when they have to walk along a highway or when they are unable to find somewhere to stay—are central features in the experiences of foot pilgrims, few of whom have written accounts that do not feature some descriptions of torment, unease, discomfort, and suffering. Hosoya Masako's account of walking the *henro* in seventy-three days between March and May 1995—a rather slow pace by modern standards—frequently discusses the pains, stresses, and physical tribulations of being a pilgrim, while Watanabe Yasuhiro had days when he suffered from agonizing pains around his hips.[63] Feet are, naturally, the most common source of pain, with Satō Takako, for example, speaking of how her feet hurt and how she was wracked by pain and fear and often burst into tears as a result.[64] Satō Ken, quite early in his pilgrimage, complains of sore feet, while Harada recounts difficult hikes up hillsides, the struggles of battling against the elements, and, in physical terms, the problem of blisters and sore feet.[65] Pilgrims interviewed by Hoshino, too, speak of their trials and tribulations on the *henro* and especially of painful, blistered feet,[66] while my experience of walking involved not just blisters but also chilblains on my hands. This came about because we started walking in early February, when the weather was still bitterly cold, windy, and snowy and I was not wearing gloves. As a result, my hands—facing the wind and the supply of blood to them partially cut because I was gripping my staff—were constantly battered by the wind and snow until, before I was aware of it, chilblains had begun to form. It took several weeks and the purchase of gloves to alleviate the unpleasant pain that resulted. At one point, too, we met a male pilgrim who had been sleeping out and whose face and lips were dry and cracked and whose gums were bleeding from exposure to the elements—indications of the raw suffering and hardship that can accompany those who choose to make their pilgrimages in this way.

Besides such immediate physical pains, pilgrims write of having to endure the torment of getting lost (often as night is closing in and they feel lost in the dark) while looking for places to stay,[67] being wracked by worries about losing one's way,[68] and being drenched to the skin in terrible downpours.[69] Sometimes, too, pilgrims become tormented by a sense of their own failings and self-doubt as they walk—a theme that surfaces on a number of occasions in Harada's journal as he questions his resolve and ability to live up to his personal aspirations. On two occasions Harada records his shame and sense of failure after breaking his resolve to be abstemious during his pilgrimage. On one evening, after a long day walking in isolation, he stayed overnight at a lodge, which housed a number of other guests. At dinner the conversation that ensued—and the presence of company—so aroused him that he broke his normal limit of one bottle of beer, then turned to ordering sake and becoming drunk, with the result that he slept badly and felt guilty at breaking his avowed intent to avoid the pitfalls of intoxication.[70] Later, staying in a hotel on the nineteenth day of his pilgrimage, he fell by the wayside again during an animated conversation with a fellow pilgrim staying at the same hotel, drinking more beer than he planned and feeling, as a result, that he had failed miserably again in his resolve. His sense of suffering at this failure was intensified the next morning when, feeling none too good with himself, he first left his pilgrim's hat behind at the hotel and had to backtrack to get it and then later lost his way entirely. He attributes this catalogue of disasters to his abandon of the night before and is suitably tormented and anguished as a result.[71]

Walking, in such terms, can intensify feelings and leave the pilgrim especially open to raw emotions and feelings. Many pilgrims record how, as they walk and are subsumed by the physical and mental demands of the pilgrimage, they find themselves being brought face-to-face with painful memories of the past. Often such memories center on issues of death, whose presence is so evident in the symbolic structures of the *henro* and the physical remains in its landscape. Harada, for example, in a state of heightened vulnerability on the day after his second overzealous engagement with alcohol, encountered an elderly couple. The man appeared well, but the woman (presumably his wife) was bent and had a glazed expression, reminding Harada of his deceased mother, who had lost her memory before she died. The poignant sight of the man caring for his stricken wife and the memories of his mother (coupled, Harada is aware, by various other pent-up feelings created through the pilgrimage) caused a surge of emotion to pass through him, making him break down in tears.[72] Satō Takako, too, confronted similar feelings early in her pilgrimage. An old lady at Temple 3 gave her an offering of *settai,* and thereafter Satō was beset by memories of her deceased grandmother, of whom the old lady reminded her. Feelings and reminders of death—ranging from the graves of deceased pilgrims to the bodies of dead birds she found on the pilgrimage path[73]—thereafter permeated her pilgrimage as Satō found herself accompanied by the memory and presence of her grandmother. This caused her torment, arousing the ambivalent feelings she had for her grandmother, who, she knew, had loved her but who had also fought with her and left her with abiding memories of estrangement. Yet as her memories flooded back, Satō comments, she felt her grandmother's presence again and rejoiced as a result.[74]

Ambivalence, peaks, and valleys

Yet even while being reduced to tears by pain, emotion, and memory or getting lost in the rain, pilgrims rarely if ever express the wish that they were doing something else or traveling by bus. When pilgrims do, for example, stop walking and use buses, it is usually, as with the pilgrims who hop on trains and buses between Temples 23 and 24, because of the unpleasantly dangerous road conditions, not because of their physical pains. Indeed, the pains and challenges posed by the *henro* are widely seen as cathartic processes that need to be endured and experienced in order that the pilgrim can understand his or her travels. As Harada struggles up steep *henro korogashi*, he speaks of how the sweat that pours from him is cleansing his body of impurities, while Kagita expresses similar feelings, speaking of how the evil passions *(bonnō)* fall away from him with his sweat and effort.[75] Satō Takako, too, recognizes that the value she derives from her pilgrimage is directly connected to the pains and tribulations she undergoes in it and that the tears she sheds through pain and struggle are cathartic, freeing her and enabling her to gain energy and feel better as her pilgrimage continues.[76]

Satō, in other words, effectively affirms the views of the priest who admonished us that setbacks and hardship were integral to positive experiences of pilgrimage and that its highs could be attained only through experiencing its lows. At the same time, however, pilgrims are constantly made aware that this is not a one-way process: the positive can change all too rapidly to the negative. I made this point earlier when I commented about how the joyous contentment of walking along beautiful and tranquil mountain paths in warm sunshine and of feelings of gratitude and warmth through receiving *settai* can rapidly change when, for instance, a pilgrim reaches a noisy temple, is engulfed by hordes of other pilgrims and has to wait for ages at a *nōkyōjo* or s/he struggles to a pilgrims' lodge to find there is no accommodation available, or the weather suddenly turns unpleasant.

Harada's pilgrimage account is typical here. Early in his pilgrimage he enjoyed good weather and enthusiastically walked amidst pleasant scenery, received *settai* and kindness from those he met, and generally appeared to be having a good journey. Then, he notes, it began to rain—just at a point where the *henro* path came to and followed a major highway for some distance. His previously tranquil walk became unsettled by the noise of lorries roaring by, and his mood accordingly became dark and angry—a shift in feeling that repeats itself through much of his journey.[77] Watanabe Yasuhiro's account, too, displays similar changes: from being overjoyed by the "wonderful emotions" *(fushigi no kandō)* and beautiful scenery he experienced in his first few days after setting out from Temple 1, his mood took an abrupt turn for the worse as he ran into heavy rain and winds.[78]

In our pilgrimage, too, we experienced many similarly ambivalent experiences and fluctuations of mood, in both directions. There were numerous occasions when a dispiriting and difficult period—perhaps walking along a noisy road, lashed by biting winds and rain, finding nowhere convenient to get a warm bowl of noodles to resuscitate us at lunchtime, and arriving cold, wet, and hungry at a temple late in the afternoon where a seemingly grumpy temple official took our book and stamped it with barely a glance at us—would be transformed as the official, having stamped our book, would ask us to wait a minute, disappear briefly, and then return with a smiling face and a bag of fruit or a hot drink as *settai*. Similarly, the reverse happened with regularity. I especially recall walking through sunshine and pleasant scenery on the way to the town of Hiwasa, where Temple 23 is located, and arriving there during a festival. The noise at the temple and the crowded streets full of temporary market stalls were a bad enough contrast to the quiet we had become used to, but worse was to come because we had arranged to stay in the youth hostel in town—the only place with any accommodation to spare. It was, unfortunately, where the market traders, too, were staying. We were tired from a hard day's walk and wanting nothing more than the normal quiet, sober evening we had become used to, while they, exuberant after a day's hard work and profit, were in a mood for celebration and were quaffing beer and *sake* liberally. The contrast between our mood and their drunken joviality was stark. It was the point at which our experiences and self-identification as pilgrims made us feel the most estranged from the everyday society around us, and it showed us how positive feelings can quickly turn to anger and annoyance.

One of our darkest and one of our brightest moments on the *henro* illustrate this point too—especially since they occurred within moments of each other. They happened after the incident I mentioned earlier, when we arrived at a temple expecting to be able to stay at its *shukubō* only to be told somewhat abruptly that this was not possible and that we should walk—in the rapidly spreading darkness—some distance to a town where we might find accommodation. This incident happened after a couple of days along highways and some poor weather, and the problem at the temple was that classic last straw that made us question our entire resolve about the pilgrimage. As we sat, depressed, on a low wall outside the temple in the encroaching dark wondering what to do and where we might stay, a woman passing by asked us if we were all right and whether we had anywhere to stay. When we said no, she asked us to stay at her house, which just a few meters away. We spent a lovely evening with her, her young daughter, and her elderly father. Word got around that she had two foreign pilgrims in her house, and various friends dropped by to chat, usually bringing snacks and delicacies for us to eat. Her father went out for a while to an old people's club but returned with several of his friends, who spent the rest of the evening talking to us about their memories of earlier times, the pilgrimage, and pilgrims they had met. For once we did not feel like collapsing into sleep early and were happy to stay up late talking and socializing. A truly low point had been transformed into one of the highs of the whole journey.

Kōbō Daishi, miracles, transformation, and wonder

Sometimes pilgrims regard the tribulations of pilgrimage as trials set for them by Kōbō Daishi in order to test their mettle, a view expressed by Kagita when he wrote of how problems arising during his pilgrimage—such as getting soaked in the rain or getting lost—were created for him and his companions by Kōbō Daishi to this end.[79] On the last day of his pilgrimage, as he headed for Temple 88, Harada lost his way—not for the first time. Earlier in his pilgrimage Harada had been liable to react with anger to such setbacks and disruptions to his schedule (as with his annoyance, mentioned earlier, at having to wait for thirty minutes in a queue at one *nōkyōjo*). Now, however, near the end of his pilgrimage, he had become more able to deal with such events and, rather than getting annoyed, was able to regard getting lost as a final test given to him by Kōbō Daishi.[80]

Through such tests, too, pilgrims such as Harada and Kagita consider that they have traveled along a path of transformation during their pilgrimage. Harada's transformation is evident in his ability to accept, on the last day, what earlier would have made him angry, while Kagita's is related to a sense of dying to his previous existence and gaining a sense of rebirth. As mentioned earlier, Kagita was suffering from health problems when he began his pilgrimage. Early on, too, the demands of walking increased his unease, leading him to think that he might die on the pilgrimage.[81] As he was making the ascent up to Temple 27, however, he experienced a major turning point: as he sweated, he felt all his ills falling away. From then on, Kagita reports, his old pilgrimage (in which he had been expecting to die and was preparing for death) ended and he embarked on a new one, a pilgrimage of life in which he felt reborn and through which he vowed to change his life, give up his business career, and do something with more social value and to work thereafter for the benefit of society.[82] He also, softening his earlier critical comments about the problems he had had with finding accommodation, reflects that simply having to move every day and to experience the necessity of looking for new places every night for forty days or more led him to experience and gain an understanding of the notion of transience, which is of course an important aspect of Buddhist thought.[83] Kagita thus felt healed by the pilgrimage—again, a common experience of walkers, expressed also by Harada, who writes of how, through walking, exercise, and the good water, food, air, and natural scenery of Shikoku, pilgrims can become healthy—not just in physical terms but in terms of self-transformation, self-discovery, and rebirth

—and of how the *henro* thus offers anyone feeling uneasy in the modern world a cure for their ills.[84]

Such themes—the hand of Kōbō Daishi, the sense of healing, and the notion of transformation—are common refrains in pilgrims' accounts. Reflecting at the end of his hard-walking, thirty-day pilgrimage, Watanabe Yasuhiro feels that he did not complete the pilgrimage through his own power alone, but thanks to Kōbō Daishi, who guided him and with whom he walked.[85] Satō Takako, like Kagita, had a sudden, transformative experience in which she "met" Kōbō Daishi and realized that he had been with her through her whole journey—a realization, she states, that bathed her in a sense of happiness and warmth, dissolved her pain, and brought about a sense of awakening.[86]

Even those who reject any notion of faith or assert that their pilgrimage motives relate to the idea of challenge rather than faith find themselves articulating their experiences in terms that, as Hoshino has commented, have religious undertones. Many of those Hoshino interviewed spoke of experiencing a sense of purification through walking, of being given strength from somewhere beyond themselves and gaining a sense of personal fulfillment.[87] Nishikawa, who emphasizes that he has no religious faith at all and that his motives in the *henro* relate solely to the concept of personal challenge, similarly comments that as he walked he had extraordinary experiences through which he felt a sense of transformation.[88]

Full circle: Ending the pilgrimage, tasting the beer

Unsurprisingly, given that they have spent such a long time and such effort on doing pilgrimage, pilgrims, as they come to the last temple on their journeys, are often gripped by emotion as well as by reflections on what they have done. Harada finds himself thinking back to all those he has met along the way—and as he does so, his memories are overwhelmingly positive, as if the bad memories and experiences he had had while walking had been washed away with his sweat and effort.[89] As he comes to Temple 88, Harada records a series of powerful emotions; people congratulate him on completing the *henro*, and as he begins to give thanks to all those who have helped him—Kōbō Daishi, his family, everyone who helped him along the way—he becomes choked by tears and cannot stop sobbing.[90] Kobayashi, too, records that he cannot stop sobbing with emotion as he prays at Ōkuboji.[91]

For Harada this was the end of his actual pilgrimage, and he had no intention of doing *orei mairi*. Nevertheless, having met another pilgrim at the temple and having shared a lunch and a celebratory beer with him, Harada was persuaded to change his plans and go back to Temple 1 with him for this purpose. However, neither felt the need or impulse to walk to Ryōzenji; it is clear that they consider their pilgrimages ended when they visited the last of the eighty-eight temples, a point that is also evident in the behavior of bus pilgrims (see below, chapter 7). Instead, they called a taxi to get them to a station from which they can take a train to Ryōzenji.[92] Harada's main impulse for making the return trip was, he asserts, not so much to do *orei mairi* at Ryōzenji, but to call in at a nearby lodge where he had spent his first night as a pilgrim and whose owner had given him a purse as *settai* (Harada had kept any monetary *settai* in it thereafter). Recalling how much this gift had lifted his spirits, he wanted to go back to tell her he had successfully completed the *henro* and to thank her for her help. However, in a reflection of the emotional ups and downs of the pilgrimage, Harada records how his positive feelings were shaken when he reached the lodge to be told that the lady in question was seriously ill in hospital. It was another lesson for him in how quickly fortunes and fates may change: the lady who barely a month before had appeared healthy and had encouraged him in his endeavors now lay ill in hospital. A day that had had such emotionally positive feelings—and a pilgrimage that had started so positively with this gift—had ended sadly.[93]

While pilgrims may be transfixed by a sense of emotion and achievement and feel that they have been transformed and found a new life through having walked the pilgrimage, they may at the same time also be conscious that they are about to return to the world they had left behind for the duration of their journeys. In contemplating their reintegration into that world, they may also think of the things they have given up while pursuing the simple "walk, eat, sleep" routines of their pilgrimages. Kobayashi, like many pilgrims, had vowed to abstain from alcohol and tobacco for its duration. On the evening before he started his pilgrimage Kobayashi had a final smoke and drink of beer, as well as a liberal amount of *sake*.[94] During his pilgrimage he drew strength from his abstinence. Yet as his pilgrimage neared its end, the zealous and abstemious walker observing the precepts of the way began to think again about worldly desires and cravings, not just looking forward to drinking beer and *sake* and smoking cigarettes again, but starting to anticipate how that first beer and cigarette would taste.[95] Before he finished, in other words, he was anticipating breaking away from the restrictions of the pilgrimage and ending his separation from the everyday world. Nishikawa similarly waxed lyrical about his return to the mundane world at the end of his pilgrimage by drinking *sake*—which he found exceptionally tasty—for the first time in more than thirty days.[96] Although he felt reborn and ready to start a new life, Kagita, too, found his return to the everyday world to be exceedingly pleasurable as he quaffed some celebratory *sake*—his first in over forty days—with friends who came to meet him at Temple 88.[97]

Endings, new beginnings, returns . . .

Physical endings and reintegration into ordinary life do not mean that the pilgrim returns to his/her life as it existed beforehand or that they leave the pilgrimage behind. Kagita's comments, as he walks, about changing his life and doing something that is useful to society (at times he even talks of returning to Shikoku to help run a temple there)[98] are typical of the feelings pilgrims have that their pilgrimages have opened new paths for them and that the end of the physical pilgrimage is the departure point for a new life. Even as pilgrims complete their physical journeys, too, many seek to keep alive the memories and experiences they have developed through their journeys, and, through these memories, to remain part of the pilgrimage community.

I have alluded to this point in earlier chapters by speaking of *Shikoku byō* (Shikoku sickness) and of how pilgrims may do the *henro* repeatedly, may pass on the practice to others in their families, may establish faith associations that affirm and promote a pilgrimage tradition in their home regions, or may become *sendatsu* contributing to regional *sendatsu* associations and the like. Through such means, pilgrims can keep their pilgrimages alive and, indeed, relive them, thereby remaining part of the community of pilgrims— as they can, also, through publishing and sharing their accounts of pilgrimage with others. The number of accounts published by those who have done the *henro* on foot is indicative of this desire, as is the emergence of internet sites (mentioned in chapter 5) through which such pilgrims can share and discuss their experiences and develop links with other walkers.[99] It is, perhaps, ironic that pilgrims who—as the accounts of people such as Harada, Kagita, and others cited in this chapter indicate—often appear so internally focused that they say little about their travel companions or spend days on end barely communicating with others can be so keen to speak of their experiences to, and develop links with, other pilgrims after they have returned home. However, this is also the reflection of an awareness that many such pilgrims come to as they walk and that remains an enduring and central feature of their experiences: that while the journey they are undertaking may have a physical end point, it continues thereafter, shapes the rest of their lives, and gives them a renewed and continuing sense of belonging as members of the pilgrimage community.

I will return to these issues in chapter 8, where I examine how, for many pilgrims, pilgrimage transforms their lives and how their experiences make them return again and again to the *henro*, so that pilgrimage becomes a central defining feature and permanent fixture in their lives. First, however, I will turn, in the next chapter, to the experiences of those who travel by the other dominant mode of pilgrimage in Shikoku in the modern day—that by bus in organized tours.

7 Making Bus Pilgrimages

Practice and Experience on the Package Tour

This chapter examines the dynamics of bus tours by focusing on a tour I did in November 1990, organized by a small travel company from Osaka. It would be difficult to claim that this (or, indeed, any) tour was "typical" of Shikoku pilgrimage bus tours. There is probably no such thing as a "typical" tour; the sheer numbers of them (Iyo Tetsu alone organizes over a thousand tours a year) work against this possibility. As officials and bus guides have commented to me, while many such tours operate on the same schedules and patterns, their individual dynamics vary depending on such factors as the personnel, whether some or all of the pilgrims have done the *henro* before, whether pilgrims in the party know each other from earlier journeys, who the guides are and how they interact with the pilgrims, and even what the weather is like.

The constituency of tour parties varies widely, too. Many are brought together by special interest groups (e.g., a local pilgrimage association such as the Shiga Shingyōkai, a Buddhist temple and its parishioners led by its priest, or a nationally known pilgrimage association such as the Junrei no Kai) that then seek the assistance of bus companies that will provide the buses, drivers, and guides and arrange accommodations and so on. Other parties may be recruited on a more individual basis, run by companies who advertise tours to which individual pilgrims may sign up. The Iyo Tetsu tour group, whose "closing ceremony" at Ishiteji was described in chapter 5, was of this sort, as was the group discussed in this chapter, which was similarly recruited through advertisements combined with the participants' knowledge of the firm concerned. All had, it transpired, traveled with this firm before.

Shikoku pilgrimage parties are by and large temporary, transitory communities that come together for the period of the pilgrimage. Sometimes they are quite coordinated in their activities and intentions, especially if led by a *sendatsu* or priest or traveling under the auspices of an organization such as the Shiga Shingyōkai. In such cases they may travel under a banner indicating the name of their group and shared prayers and requests (see above, chapter 2) and—especially so for temple groups—wear *wagesa* (the traditional stole of Buddhist laypeople) that bear the name of their temple and that stand as a sign of shared identity.

Such shared intent is often reinforced by a common set of understandings about how one should behave as members of a pilgrimage party, a point emphasized in chapter 5, where I commented on how organizations such as Iyo Tetsu asked their tour participants to maintain an appropriate attitude and wear traditional pilgrimage clothing. Normally, too, people on organized tours engage in collective acts of worship and prayer at the temples and between them, as well as in the mornings and evenings before and after the day's pilgrimage activities. Whenever I have traveled with organized groups, it has been common for them to spend some of their time between temples chanting prayers (a factor that does not always make it easy to conduct interviews!) or for the tour leader to narrate miracle stories to keep the pilgrims enthused.

These temporary communities are not necessarily egalitarian, sometimes developing internal hierarchies dependent, for example, on the pilgrimage experiences of participants. Parties usually have a leader who oversees and leads their prayers and other acts of worship during the pilgrimage and at the

Tour guides carrying bundles of scrolls to the *nōkyōjo* to get them stamped for a party of pilgrims (in background).

temples. A Buddhist priest leading a group of parishioners on a tour would be likely to fill this role, as would the head of a pilgrimage association, such as Naitō Hirozō with the Shiga Shingyōkai. Even when pilgrims are recruited on an individual basis (as with Iyo Tetsu's regular monthly tours), the parties thus constituted often, according to company officials, develop their own structures and hierarchies, with someone from within their ranks either assuming the role of leader or being chosen by the rest of the party for this purpose because of his or her previous pilgrimage experience. Thus the pilgrim who spoke at Ishiteji on behalf of the other pilgrims in the Iyo Tetsu tour mentioned in chapter 5 had emerged as their leader because he had done the *henro* more times than others on the tour. Pilgrims often sort themselves out into an implicit hierarchy based on pilgrimage experiences, something that also tends to happen when a number of registered *sendatsu* travel in the same party.

Shared signs of identity and the recognition of a shared social structure do not, however, mean that parties necessarily share common purposes in their pilgrimages. While traveling under banners indicating common aims, individual pilgrims in a party may have wishes, requests, and motives specific to themselves. This will become evident shortly in my description of the pilgrimage party at the center of this chapter, but it is something I have noticed about every group I have had contact with. The Iyo Tetsu party mentioned in chapter 5 is a good example. Though they were traveling together with a common leader and group banner, each pilgrim I spoke to (such as Sawamura-san, described in chapter 3) had a personalized set of motives and expressed the view that their pilgrimages were individual and personal affairs.

Such views may be more overt in groups that have been recruited individually. Those who have signed up individually and who thus have lesser (or no) degrees of social contact with their fellow pilgrims are less likely to be constrained by peer pressure to conform to a set range of actions than are those who travel under a common banner and with common social bonds. This, indeed, is an attraction of individually recruited groups for those who find the regulated, prayer-oriented activity of the tours run by temple associations and the like and the presence of people they know from other social contexts to be too constraining. Thus they may prefer to seek out less regulated groups that will allow them greater scope to determine their own actions at the temples.

This was the case with the people I traveled with in November 1990. They made few attempts to chant together and did not (despite ostensibly being members of a pilgrimage association for the duration of their travels) act as an organized group so much as a collection of people traveling together with diverse purposes. Nonetheless, they clearly felt some kind of shared identity, for in talking to other pilgrim groups, they manifested a sense of togetherness, as they did also when one pilgrim in the group ran into difficulties and needed help. They also demonstrated a sense of commonality with pilgrims outside the group, referring to them as *dōgyō*. As with Tomoko in chapter 3, they appeared to feel a sense of community with others who were doing the same practice—a sense that was strongest within their party but extended to those outside it as well.

Company head, pilgrimage leader

The tour I focus on here was arranged commercially by the Tōyō Kankō (Tōyō Tourist) Company—which specialized in pilgrimage tours—although it went under the banner of the Iwaki-kai, a pilgrimage association. The pilgrims who had signed up to travel with the Tōyō Tourist Company were, for the duration of the pilgrimage, also members of the Iwaki-kai; this sort of temporary relationship appears to be quite common and is similarly found in, for example, Junrei no Kai pilgrimage tours. I traveled with this group due to a mixture of serendipity and practicality. I wanted to undertake a pilgrimage tour as part of my research when Shimada Taiichirō, the head of the Tōyō Tourist Company, mentioned during an interview about the business of pilgrimage that in a couple days' time he would be taking a small group of pilgrims in a minibus to Shikoku and suggested that I should come along.[1] The size of the party (in all we were nine people) was appealing because it would enable me to talk in some depth to, and observe in detail the behavior of, everyone involved. I had found it problematic to get many insights into the feelings of pilgrims in larger parties because of the difficulties of developing in-depth relationships within a large group in a short period of time and because, on large buses, seating patterns are often fixed, so that one ends up next to one person all the time and has few chances to talk much to others. By contrast, in a minibus with a small number of people, I could be within earshot of everyone, develop close links with them, and record what each of them did with greater facility than would have been possible with a larger group.

Shimada-san, who was in his early fifties, combined a number of roles, running the company with his wife, who looked after the office while he was away leading tours, and serving as the company's driver and pilgrimage guide. In this guise he ensured we were fed regularly, got to our lodgings each evening, and had our scrolls and books—which he carried—stamped at each temple. He had thus a schedule to keep to, one that allowed around thirty to forty minutes at each temple. Usually his first act when we reached the sites was to go to the temple office to get the scrolls, books, and shirts stamped while the rest of us would head for the halls of worship. Keeping everyone on schedule and not losing anyone at the sites, however, was not an easy task, for even though the party was small, some managed to frequently wander off or forget the time, requiring Shimada-san on several occasions to chase around temples looking for stray pilgrims. One man, who was keen on photography, tended to wander off seeking interesting things to take pictures of, thereby forgetting to return to the minibus at the designated time, while one of the women had a seeming knack for so immersing herself in prayer at the innermost recesses of the temples that she lost track of the time and had to be collected by someone.

Shimada-san was not just concerned with practicalities. He was a devotee of Kōbō Daishi, took seriously his position as head of a pilgrimage association, and had given various public talks on the subject. In effect he combined business and faith together, spending time on his own devotions at the sites and carrying a pilgrimage book, which he proudly showed me to indicate that he had done close to thirty pilgrimage circuits in Shikoku. He maintained a constant narrative both in the minibus as we traveled between temples and at the sites themselves, as well as in the evening, regaling us with miracle tales, legends, and other stories about the *henro*, the temples, their priests, pilgrimage customs, and so on. As we were going through the narrow lanes leading to Iyataniji, he was especially effusive, telling us that anyone who died on its steps would have all their sins eradicated and go straight to the Pure Land. Such narratives drew a series of exclamations (*"fushigi"*—amazing!) from the party, who clearly enjoyed the images of miracle and wonder he evoked and that drew them into heightened states of expectancy. Shimada-san also spoke of the immense piety of pilgrims in earlier times, the difficulties they faced, and the arduous austerities they performed, all of which intensified the emotions and sense of awe of the group and heightened their involvement in something with deep spiritual and historical roots.

At the sites, too, he would point out interesting features, including things donated by the Iwaki-kai—such as a metal collecting box for *osamefuda* at Temple 70 and a piece of calligraphy done by the previous head of the society at another site. He appeared genuinely interested in the pilgrims in his party, asking everyone about their background, feelings, and so on—which helped me a lot because he effectively drew from my traveling companions information that I had wanted to seek out. He also, as one might expect from someone who made his living from the pilgrimage business, at times introduced other pilgrimages into the conversation, praising their wonders and suggesting to his clients that they might want to try them out.

Because of the practical things he had to do at the temples, he was unable to coordinate our activity there. This left everyone in the party to follow their own inclinations and devices, which all of us much appreciated. Shimada-san did occasionally suggest that we all should chant various prayers together on the bus or at the sites, and each morning, as the minibus set off, he led us in a half-hearted recitation of the *Hannya Shingyō*. The party, however, was generally reluctant on this score and, perhaps mindful of his commercial status, paid scant regard to him as a leader, seeming at times almost willfully determined not to follow his directives. It was an indication of a point I had observed often in Shikoku and made to me on several occasions also by temple priests: that one could try to get pilgrims to follow particular rules or act in a particular way (as the Reijōkai attempts to do), but they will not necessarily listen to or do what others tell them. The pilgrimage is voluntary, pilgrims are free to follow their own inclinations, and many of them like to do just that.

If the lack of cohesion in the party was voluntary, this did not stop some of the members from comparing us unfavorably to other groups. On one occasion, for example, one of the party pointed at a group of some thirty or so pilgrims, led by a priest as they went through a long ritual of prayers, and remarked that they were real pilgrims, led by a real leader and doing it together, unlike our ragged and individualized party. However, although his remarks implicitly criticized Shimada-san and the group, he was also highly resistant whenever Shimada-san made any attempt to get us to chant together. In reality, he, like other members of the group, liked the lack of organization and group coordination, since this gave them all more time to do what they wanted at each site. This, indeed, was one of the attractions of this particular company/pilgrimage association and a reason the pilgrims had traveled with Shimada-san before and probably would again. This does not mean, however, that they neglected acts of worship, for some of them spent a lot of time in prayer and devotions. It was just that they did not want to be pressured into doing so, but wanted to choose individually how they would act at the temples.

The tour: Mechanics and speed

The Iwaki-kai/Tōyō tour began at a ferry terminal in Osaka, where we had been instructed to meet at a particular time in the late evening and whence we took an overnight ferry to northern Shikoku and then drove to Temple 65 and on to the Sanuki temples (66–88). Temple 65 is in fact part of the Iyo section of the pilgrimage, but for reasons of transport convenience the tour included it with the Sanuki temples. We spent two further nights together, one at a pilgrims' lodge, the other at a temple, before returning to Osaka on the final evening. Although the amount of time I spent with the party was short, just under seventy-two hours, it was a hectic period in which we visited twenty-five temples (including an *orei mairi* visit to Temple 1) and one major Shinto shrine, were up from very early in the morning till late at night, and spent all our time together. On the first full day, for example, we disembarked from the ferry at about 6:00 A.M., had breakfast, and then visited Temples 65 to 73 before stopping at a lodge next to Temple 72 at around 5:00 P.M., having an evening meal and bath, and then talking until late before getting out the futon and trying to sleep. By 5:00 A.M. everyone was up again, talking and making themselves ready for the next day's travel. Each day was similarly frenetic. Indeed, such was the pace that afterward I remarked that going by foot was less taxing and that given the choice, I would rather walk the whole fourteen hundred kilometers than do it by bus tour. My companions, however, despite the seemingly hectic schedule (about which they complained), seemed reinvigorated by the experience.

While the pilgrimage might not have been as arduous as the bus pilgrimages Anne Gold describes in her study of Rajasthani pilgrims, which involved not only long journeys and tiring days, but also breakdowns and other problems,[2] it was nonetheless hard going and showed me how problematic it is to dismiss bus pilgrimages as an easy option. They are not: traveling on organized tours can be arduous and involve much haste, hard work, long hours, and very early mornings and late evenings. Each day we visited eight or nine temples and covered around one hundred or more kilometers—not a great distance, but time consuming since many of the roads are narrow and winding, especially when leading to mountain temples. Moreover, at some mountain temples, cars and buses are unable to drive up to the sites, and pilgrims have to walk some distance or climb endless steps, which meant that visiting them took extra time. As a result, the schedule was unrelenting, causing Shimada-san to perhaps drive faster than he should have, in the view of the pilgrims who at times muttered about his speed.

Yet the tour was not exceptional in this respect. Evidence that many tours follow similar schedules came a couple of times on our travels. On our first day we found ourselves traveling together with another tour group, whom we encountered in the courtyard of one temple, then in the car park of the next one, at the temple, and then again as we left. We met them again at the following temple, at which point Shimada-san decided to change our route so we would not continue in convoy with them. We did so—and promptly found ourselves meeting up with another tour group at successive temples! The experience indicated that even if we felt that our tour was going fast, it was effectively following a fairly normal pace for Shikoku pilgrimage tours.

The pilgrimage party and the outsider in their midst

The party consisted of nine people: I, Shimada-san, and seven others. The information about the pilgrims that is given in this chapter emerged over the three days we traveled together, during conversations in the bus, at the temples, over meals, in the evenings after dinner, and even, with the males in the party, in the bath each night. The seven consisted of two couples and three individual pilgrims, as follows (all these names are pseudonyms, though all other details are factual).

Mr. Matsuda, age sixty-four
Mrs. Matsuda, age sixty-four
Mr. Higuchi, age sixty-four

Mrs. Higuchi, age sixty-three
Mrs. Kachi, age sixty-two
Mrs. Kuwata, age sixty-three
Mr. Koyama, age sixty-seven

(I use the titles Mr. and Mrs. here so as to differentiate between the couples, since the Japanese term "-san" is not gender specific.)

All were all either retired or semi-retired. Most had had their own small businesses or shops, while Mr. Koyama had been a health insurance broker. Mrs. Kachi was a widow and was doing the pilgrimage as a memorial for her recently deceased husband, although she did not tell us this until the end of the pilgrimage. Mr. Koyama was married but traveling alone because his wife was not interested in pilgrimages. Mrs. Kuwata, too, was married, and her husband was also a pilgrim who traveled at different times from her so that one of them could always be at home to look after the house and help with the grandchildren. All seven had met before on an earlier Tōyō *ikkoku mairi* pilgrimage, with six of them having done the previous three sections of the pilgrimage in order together, hence they were completing their pilgrimage on this occasion. The seventh, Mr. Koyama, had done two of the four sections and was planning to complete the pilgrimage the following year. On earlier tours, it appeared, another couple had also taken part, but this time they were unable to come, a fact that caused some discussion and regret, since everyone had expected to meet up with them again.

Their acquaintance over earlier stages of the pilgrimage had allowed a degree of group spirit to develop among them. This mood of companionship was tinged with respect for each person's desire for autonomy. Since each had joined individually or as a couple, each was aware that the others wanted to have time alone and not be pushed into communal activities such as group prayer.

Such camaraderie also led them to continue using Shimada-san's company to organize their pilgrimages. This is a pattern often reported by companies involved with running pilgrimage tours in Shikoku: as was noted in chapters 3 and 5, many of those making pilgrimages with Iyo Tetsu and other companies come back to them again. It is common for pilgrims to form bonds with those they have met on previous tours. Officials from Iyo Tetsu have told me that many people return repeatedly to Shikoku using the same bus company and, through striking up a degree of companionship with others met on the buses, often agree to "meet again next year in Shikoku."[3] Several of those on the Iyo Tetsu pilgrimage group I met at Ishiteji (see chapter 5) were talking about doing the pilgrimage again together and were swapping addresses with this end in mind. The tour group I joined had a similar feel, of people who knew each other and were keen to meet up again on pilgrimages—but who appeared not to have socialized in between. This latter point suggested that they wanted to maintain a distance between their home lives and their pilgrimages while maintaining special friendships on the road, which made Shikoku itself more familiar. Thus while doing the Shikoku pilgrimage might mean stepping outside of normative parameters, it can also involve an adherence to the patterns of the known. In entering into "another society," pilgrims may be happiest to retain as much of the known and familiar as possible and to recreate a shared belonging and sense of community that is formed around the patterns of pilgrimage—yet is also distinct from home.

Initially, I was an outsider in this informal community. One reason, of course, was that I was not Japanese—an obvious difference, yet one that appeared less overt than the fact that I had not been a member of earlier parties. I think I was hardly more of an outsider than someone from, say, Tokyo who had not been on previous trips might have been. The party had a somewhat parochial outlook that was underlined at one stage when Shimada-san said the pilgrims who traveled with Iwaki-kai/Tōyō were invariably from the Osaka region because he advertised only locally, whereas tours run by groups such as the Junrei no Kai or companies such as Iyo Tetsu drew people from all over the country because they advertised nationally. At that point Mrs. Kachi said that she was glad to travel with Iwaki-kai/Tōyō because this meant she could travel with people from her own region rather than from distant places such as Tokyo—and all the others nodded in agreement.

The pilgrims were, however, initially uneasy about my status as a researcher and the extent to which I would be intruding on, and analyzing, their pilgrimages. Yet everyone appeared reassured when I told them that I would not be identifying them by name and that my purpose was to use their tour to describe what bus pilgrimage in general was like. This, in effect, meant that they were not being examined in a personal capacity but were being observed as representatives of the pilgrim community. They found this acceptable and, indeed, seemed rather proud to have been chosen in this way. As a result, it did not take long before the ice began to melt and they accepted and talked more freely to me. It helped that Mr. Koyama was extremely convivial and liked to talk about his family and interests and found in me a ready audience for this. Mrs. Kuwata, too, was quick to strike up a friendship and appeared to find me easy to talk to. The group as a whole also found that my knowledge of the *henro*—admittedly from an academic perspective rather than the faith-based narrative they were used to—was interesting and liked to ask occasional questions of me.

They also quickly came to realize that my presence made them distinctive as a group and enhanced their status, making them an "international" (*kokusaiteki*) group, as Mrs. Kuwata told one party of pilgrims we fell into conversation with. I was not just a foreign researcher; I was *their* foreign researcher, and my presence gave their party a distinctive quality and identity not found in other groups. As we traveled together and shared experiences—

including one incident, described below, when Mrs. Kuwata ran into difficulties on the steps of Iyataniji—we grew closer and I became still more integrated into the group.

Affiliations, motives, orientations

Everyone in the group apart from me was affiliated with a Buddhist sect. This is quite normal in Japan, where the vast majority have a formal Buddhist affiliation. Shimada-san was a member of the Shingon sect, as was Mrs. Kachi, the Matusdas were Tendai Buddhist, the Higuchis were members of the Nishi Honganji branch of Jōdo Shin (True Pure Land) Buddhism, Mrs. Kuwata was of the Otani branch of Jōdo Shin, and Mr. Koyama belonged to the Myōshinji branch of Rinzai Zen.

As is common in Japan, none felt exclusively affiliated to their sect. All indicated that they liked visiting shrines and temples and that engaging in acts of worship and praying for worldly benefits was normative for them. All were familiar with most of the famed temples and shrines of the Kansai region around Osaka, such as Kōyasan and Sefukuji, where Kūkai became a monk. The Higuchis liked these places, they said, because they were part of their cultural and spiritual heritage as residents of Osaka. Mrs. Kachi and Mr. Koyama had both done the Saikoku pilgrimage, and the others had visited several of the Saikoku temples, which are all well-known landmarks in their home region. Mrs. Kuwata's husband had also done the Shikoku pilgrimage with Shimada-san's company, and he was currently, she said, doing two other regional pilgrimage routes as well. During our days together they all expressed interest in other pilgrimages, Mr. Higuchi, for example, announcing one evening that he wanted to do the Chichibu pilgrimage as well as Shikoku again. The others, too, all questioned Shimada-san about other pilgrimage tours his company was planning, and he, ever the businessman, encouraged such interest with occasional plugs for future tours.

Their interest in making pilgrimages was stimulated by the fact that they were retired or semi-retired. Mr. Higuchi spoke for them all when he said that, like most Japanese, he had spent most of his life devoted to work and business, had taken few holidays, and had little time for pilgrimages. Now that he and his wife had handed over day-to-day running of their shop to their son, however, they had the time and were determined to do various pilgrimages. However, as is often the case even with retired people, the thought of being away for even the twelve days it took for the full *henro* seemed too much and an evasion of their continuing responsibilities as householders and grandparents. Hence doing the *henro* in four shorter tours was a convenient and preferable alternative.

During our travels, everyone told either me individually or the group as a whole the main reasons they were doing the *henro*. I was interested to note that despite having traveled together before, they had clearly not confided to any great degree in each other about such things. Barbara Aziz, whose critique of group-centered pilgrimage theories was cited in chapter 1, has argued that pilgrims, even within groups, are traveling very much on their own personal pilgrimages, and may, as such, have little interest in the views or motives of others. She cites a Hindu pilgrim who expressed no interest in the motives or experiences of the relatives traveling with her, saying, "[W]hat they feel about Siva is their own: I do not care about them."[4]

The views of the Iwaki-kai party appear to partially substantiate Aziz's views. They certainly did not overtly seek out the motives of their companions. Yet they appear to have refrained from asking such questions more because they respected the autonomy of their fellow pilgrims than because of a lack of *care* about them. Indeed, it was clear that they were interested in such things: whenever I asked such questions, everyone paid attention to the responses and wanted to learn more about the feelings and attitudes of their companions. In that sense I served as a means of enabling them to learn more about their companions, and this, too, helped me become more accepted by the group.

The most interesting revelation came from Mrs. Kachi—not while we were traveling, but after we had visited Temple 88 and she had completed her circuit. Until then all she had said was that she was a widow, and clearly her pilgrimage involved memorializing her husband, especially as she lit numerous candles and offered incense at every site. However, she had not said anything directly on the subject, even though she was normally rather chatty, kept up a constant stream of questions to Shimada-san, and talked especially to Mrs. Kuwata, with whom she seemed close. Since she spoke a lot about her interest in visiting temples and doing pilgrimages now her family had grown up and she had time to spare, we gradually came to assume that this was her main motivation. However, after completing the circuit at Ōkuboji, Mrs. Kachi told us that her husband had only recently died and that her pilgrimage— spread out over four trips but designed to be completed as close as possible to the first anniversary of his death—was a memorial (*kuyō*) for him. This caused the rest of the group to commend her not just because she had done such a superb memorial (*rippa na kuyō*), but because she had not gone on about her loss but had endured it with silent fortitude—a point that, they felt, enhanced the merit of her pilgrimage. Mrs. Kachi, like some of the pilgrims mentioned in chapter 3, was clearly not ready to articulate her motives until she had finished the pilgrimage.

The pilgrims' motives were similar to many already encountered in earlier chapters. Mr. and Mrs. Matsuda, as was stated in chapter 3, were interested in visiting shrines and temples, especially those associated with Kōbō Daishi. They liked getting the stamps of the temples and collecting pilgrimage scrolls and saw such travels as a release valve enabling them to gain some space from the pressures of Japanese society. Mr. Matsuda spoke at length to me of these pressures, of how little time he and his wife had had with their family due to work until they had retired, and how it saddened them to see the stress their grandchildren were placed under by the Japanese education system and the high work levels expected of them. Hence they kept their grandchildren in mind during their pilgrimage, praying for their happiness and education success. They prayed for worldly benefits for themselves—especially for their good health—and included their ancestors in their prayers, having special prayers said for them and hoping that their pilgrimage would help the spirits of departed family members in the other world.

Mr. and Mrs. Higuchi expressed similar interest in traveling to temples and new places, especially those associated with what they saw as their cultural heritage. They were concerned about worldly benefits, particularly relating to their health and the continued success of their shop, now looked after by their son. They also offered prayers on behalf of their ancestors and, like the Matsudas, had special prayers recited for them.

Mrs. Kachi, as I have already mentioned, was doing it for her deceased husband, although her enjoyment of making pilgrimages and praying to the buddhas was clearly also important to her. Mrs. Kuwata, too, emphasized that she liked visiting temples and that, since her husband's retirement and since her children had grown up and left home, making pilgrimages had become her main hobby. She prayed for her ancestors and for good health for herself and her husband, while this pilgrimage was especially devoted to the spirit of her husband's brother, to mark the fiftieth anniversary of his death.

I have already introduced Mr. Koyama in chapter 3 as an example of someone who liked to travel and see new places while using pilgrimage as a legitimation for such things. He was doing the pilgrimage mainly, he said, because he liked travel and photographing temples and natural scenery. He claimed not to have any specific religious motivation, rather stating that the pilgrimage offered a good framework in which to indulge in these hobbies while providing, for his family, a good reason that he needed to keep going off with his cameras. He was also, as was noted in chapter 3, keen to get a completed scroll for his home. Yet while he emphasized the hobby and enjoyment aspects of pilgrimage and steadfastly refused to engage in some of the activities that the others participated in (notably, he declined to have a memorial service done for his ancestors when everyone else did), he also had an interest in Buddhism and its potential to provide guidance in his life. He was at times unhappy at the pace of the tour, complaining that it gave us no time to seek out priests at the temples and learn from them, telling me that when he did the Saikoku pilgrimage, he had made individual visits to each temple, seeking out the priest(s) there and asking them for explanations of Buddhist teaching.

Major concerns that came through related to afterlife issues—most notably in the context of memorializing the ancestors but also acquiring merit for when they died, with six of the seven (Mr. Koyama was a noted skeptic in this context) thinking that doing the pilgrimage would help them in this respect —and concern for their health in the present. Both concerns were linked to the age of the pilgrims, who were entering the latter stages of their lives, with grown-up children, as well as grandchildren, and they were hence focusing their attention on the expectations (which included death) and worries of later life. Thus praying on behalf of their departed kin (which implicitly also relates to preparing for the time when they, in turn, would become ancestors) and for their own good health were especially pertinent. Such emphases are indicated also in the Waseda survey, which showed that praying for the ancestors was the most widely cited motivation for pilgrims, with good health also scoring highly, as well as by the study I did on pilgrims' prayer requests, cited in chapter 3, in which good health was the most commonly cited prayer request, followed by those on behalf of the ancestors.[5]

The Iwaki-kai pilgrims were concerned about their health, and there was plentiful discussion about maladies, especially since both Mr. Higuchi and Mrs. Kuwata had had heart troubles in the recent past. From our discussions it was clear they thought that Kōbō Daishi could help them overcome illnesses, and there was general interest in the possibility of miracles: whenever Shimada-san narrated pilgrimage stories about miraculous cures, everyone became animated and plied him with questions on the subject. Whenever we met other pilgrims, too, they readily engaged in conversations about miracles and joined in the widespread pilgrim habit of passing on and sharing miracle stories that they had heard.

Their interest in good health had highly practical dimensions too, for all of them recognized that keeping in good health was dependent on being active and remaining fit and alert. Visiting temples and making pilgrimages was one way of doing this, Mr. Higuchi commented, for pilgrimages involved physical exertion and kept everyone animated. Even by bus the pilgrimage involves a lot of climbing up steps and walking, and a lot of time is spent in the fresh air and in rural settings that were soothing and mentally calming compared to the city life they were used to. Being interested in pilgrimages and temples encouraged them to keep alert mentally and physically, reading books about temples, culture, and history and getting out of their homes rather than, as Mr. Higuchi opined, just sitting at home vegetating in front of the television, as so many people did. The pilgrims were worried that unless they did such things they could run the risk of becoming senile—an increasing problem in a society with a growing number of elderly people and high life expectancy. Indeed, many pilgrims these days pray for protection against senility during their pilgrimage—or even go on special "prevention of senility" pilgrimages that have become popular in Japan.[6]

While keen to see new places, they were concerned about legitimizing what might otherwise be seen as tourist behavior by pursuing it through the medium of pilgrimage. Having such a framework for their travels was probably important because they came from a generation accustomed to the ethic of austerity and hard work central to Japan's postwar reconstruction. As Mr. Matsuda said, they had grown up in a period when the emphasis was on hard work in order to rebuild the country and extended holidays were not encouraged. They thus felt somewhat guilty, even though now retired, about going off to enjoy themselves. Pilgrimage was valuable in providing a legitimation through which they could get away and in combining enjoyment with spiritual needs. They could travel, see beautiful places associated with tradition and heritage, and engage in actions on behalf of others and pray for their families, kin, and ancestors. Enjoyment and escape could thus be suffused with selfless actions for others and seen as a means of preparing for one's own demise. Such a framework clearly worked for Mr. Koyama's family, who no doubt felt that he had the right, in his old age, to acquire some merit that might be helpful when he died, while for him it provided scope to indulge in his hobby without contravening the work ethic in which he had been acculturated.

Clothes, scrolls, incense, rituals, prayers

As is common for people participating in organized pilgrimage tours, everyone wore items of traditional pilgrims' clothing. Shimada-san insisted on this, and so when I met up with the group, he gave me a *hakui* and asked me to put it on. Everyone else wore *hakui,* and all had pilgrims' hats—Mr. Koyama a bamboo one, the rest white sun hats—and carried staffs. They all had bells attached either to their staff or clothing and hence—like other pilgrimage groups—made a characteristic ringing sound as they disembarked from the minibus and wandered around the temples. They all had at least one item to be stamped at the temples. Between them the seven pilgrims had four scrolls, six pilgrims' books, and three additional *hakui* to be stamped. The Matsudas, with one scroll, two books, and two *hakui,* were the most prolific collectors; the *hakui* were being stamped so that they could wear them in their caskets at death.

All of them had a variety of small items and prayer aids, such as rosaries and *fuda.* All save Mr. Koyama also carried incense holders, incense, and candles, and they all had bags of small coins to offer at the temples and before the various statues in their precincts. They all carried other items appropriate to their own pilgrimage needs: Mr. and Mrs. Matsuda, for example, carried a stack of *shakyō*—copies of the *Hannya Shingyō* that had been done by themselves, their family, and friends—which they offered at the sites when praying for success and good health and for their family and friends, who were in effect accompanying them on the pilgrimage through this medium. In all on this trip the Matsudas had fifty copies—two for each of the twenty-five temples we visited. Mrs. Kuwata, too, carried copies of the *Hannya Shingyō* done by her husband, one of which she offered for him at each temple. Only Mr. Koyama appeared to carry few objects connected with devotion and prayer; apart from a rosary, *fuda,* and coins, his hand luggage consisted mostly of cameras and lenses.

Each person had his/her own routine at the sites. Mr. Koyama would go to the main hall and the *daishidō,* offer coins, and do a peremptory prayer before getting his cameras out and taking photographs. Mr. and Mrs. Matsuda would go to each hall of worship, make an offering of coins and copied sutras, light incense and candles, and then pray together, standing just to the side of the halls of worship and reading from a sutra book. Mr. and Mrs. Higuchi would perform a similar routine to the Matsudas, except that Mr. Higuchi also had a video camera that he used to record almost everything that went on, from views of the temples to the activities of his companions. At times—if, for example, there was a particularly large or interesting looking pilgrimage group at the site—he would leave his wife to do the prayers while he concentrated on his video recording, which was intended, he said, to be both a record and a commemoration of their pilgrimage. Such commemorative recording is quite common, and video cameras as well as cameras and digital cameras are a common item in the luggage of many pilgrims, who probably afterward will bore their friends ("here we are at Zentsūji!") with home pilgrimage videos.

Mrs. Kachi and Mrs. Kuwata tended to spend the longest in worship and prayer, each paying homage to all the statues and shrines, as well as the main hall and *daishidō,* at every site. Both had a seemingly endless supply of small coins and sticks of incense for this purpose, and each went through a litany of prayers as they did so. Usually, Mrs. Kachi managed to outlast Mrs. Kuwata in this activity and often spent the whole time we were at each temple in prayer. Mrs. Kuwata usually took a little time out to have a look around, check out any shops selling trinkets and souvenirs, and have a chat with me or one of the others.

Haste, tranquillity, interaction

On our first day we traveled from Temple 65 to Temples 72 and 73, which are located within a few hundred meters of each other. The hectic schedule had already made the pilgrims complain by the time we arrived, at around 5:00 P.M., at the large pilgrims' lodge where we were to stay. However, it had become evident to me that this sense of rush was relative to the nature of the temples themselves, as I suspect it is for all who go on package tours. When the pilgrims found themselves in beautiful and atmospheric settings in the mountains—such as the paths through the deep forests surrounding Unpenji, for instance—they wanted to linger, breathe in the atmosphere, and imbibe the tranquil surroundings. It was on such occasions that they fretted at the schedule and muttered complaints when Shimada-san tried to chivvy them back to the van. When we visited temples that were less atmospheric or in less dramatic situations, no one seemed to mind the haste and sometimes were ready to move on earlier than Shimada-san had expected. When we reached the lodge at 5:00 P.M.—which meant we had a little time to spare before the bath and meal were ready—some of the party began complaining amongst themselves that we could have stayed longer at Unpenji or Iyataniji (the two mountain sites that had most impressed them that day). However, although we were staying next door to Temple 72 and a five-minute walk from Temple 73, two rather small and not very spectacular temples, no one seemed interested in having another look at them.

The nature and settings of the sites affected the mood of the party and how they interacted with other pilgrims. At easily accessible sites, everyone seemed infused with a spirit of hustle and bustle and rarely seemed to communicate with others outside their group. At Temple 70, for example, we had only a few meters to walk from the car park to the front of the main hall, and little attempt was made at talking to other pilgrims. On such occasions, too, one sensed the potential for tensions to develop as different groups of pilgrims jostled for spaces to pray before the temples or to get their scrolls stamped and move on.

Yet things appeared rather different when we had to make efforts to get to the temples and where the natural settings were most striking. At Unpenji, for instance, the minibus followed a winding road that snaked up through deep pine forests before depositing us at a small car park several hundred meters from the temple. From there we had to walk along a narrow road flanked by high and majestic cedars; the air was crisp and fresh and seemed to uplift everyone's spirits. There were a number of groups either walking from the car park or coming back to it, and everyone seemed to feel drawn together in a sense of mutual purpose. The pilgrims mingled rather than maintaining boundaries between groups, smiled, and nodded in greeting (*yoku o-mairi de* —please have a good pilgrimage visit) to everyone they met. Iyataniji, with its steep steps, caves, and general aura of miraculous expectation, was another place where the pilgrims seemed most open to engaging with and greeting others and feeling, as they were struggling up the steps together, that they were *dōgyō* doing the same practice.

Settai and group consciousness

It was at Iyataniji that a sense of group consciousness really developed. The catalyst for this was that Mrs. Kuwata rapidly got out of breath while climbing the steps. It was then that she told us she had had heart problems and, worried that if she tried to climb farther things might get worse, suggested that we go on while she waited until we came back down. Everyone disagreed and insisted we should all go up slowly together. We rallied round to help her up the steps, taking turns to hold her arm and support her. As we came down, too, we did the same, as everyone consciously strove to keep together as a group rather than, as at previous temples, going at their individual speeds. Mrs. Kuwata's difficulties were a vivid reminder about the demands of the pilgrimage even for those who use buses and the like—and showed how pilgrims such as her would not have been able to manage the *henro* without the aid of modern transport and its conveniences. In previous centuries, if Mrs. Kuwata had been able to attempt the *henro* at all, she might well have ended up as one of the pilgrims whose names are recorded in the death registers of temples such as Gokurakuji.

Her distress led to a further show of togetherness and interaction. There is an old tea shop located on Iyataniji's steps, and when we reached it, two of the party[7] ordered (and paid for) tea and cakes for everyone, saying that this was *settai* from them to their fellow pilgrims. This was the first time that someone in the party had made such a gesture, but thereafter it became common to do so, with each of us buying refreshments for the others whenever the occasion demanded it and offering them as *settai*.

Giving *settai* to other pilgrims or within pilgrimage groups is not uncommon: I have noted in the last chapter how sometimes parties of pilgrims will give alms to those on foot, but sometimes *settai* may also be given within groups, thereby creating a sense of togetherness. It can also help circumvent the nominal prohibition on alcohol set out in the ten rules of behavior advocated by the temples. One evening, for example, I shared the dining hall at a pilgrims' lodge in Ehime Prefecture with a large pilgrimage party from Nagoya led by a Buddhist priest. After leading his group in prayer, the priest announced that various individuals (including some temple parishioners unable to be with the party but whose donations made them part of it in spirit) had donated *settai* to the party to accompany the evening meal. This seemed to consist largely of bottles of beer or *sake*—the latter announced as *hannyatō* (wisdom water), the term traditionally used in Buddhist temples in Japan and through which *sake*, theoretically prohibited as an intoxicant, is transformed into something spiritually uplifting. Sometimes, too, food delicacies are donated in this way; the priest also announced that someone had provided a large plate of sashimi as *settai* to the group.

Meals, bath . . . beer

In the evening we split into two groups, male and female, headed for our respective baths, and spent some time lounging in the hot and refreshing water of the Japanese *furo*. As we wallowed in the hot water, my companions continued to talk about their feelings and motives. Afterward, we were served our evening meal in a large tatami mat room, which had had its sliding doors removed so as to accommodate our group and another larger pilgrimage party. Later, after the meal, the sliding doors were put back in place, thereby dividing the space into four rooms, one each for the males and females of each party.

It is common for pilgrimage parties to engage in religious devotions not only while traveling or at the temples, but also in the mornings and evenings and prior to eating their meals. At times, such communal devotions can become infectious, as happened on this occasion. As we were about to eat, the pilgrimage party at the next table began to chant the *Hannya Shingyō* and other invocations. Mr. Higuchi, embarrassed by the fact that we had made no attempt to pray prior to eating, quickly put down his chopsticks and began to chant, and shortly everyone else joined in.

When the food came, Mr. Higuchi ordered some *sake,* and Mr. Koyama and I ordered beer. Consuming alcohol—at least in the evening—is quite common among pilgrims. While some pilgrims may take a vow of abstinence for the duration of their pilgrimages (as did Kobayashi Atsuhiro, whose dreams of the beer he would drink after finishing his pilgrimage were mentioned in the previous chapter), many do not. The relaxed attitude toward alcohol that is widespread in Japan extends to pilgrim and temple lodges, some of which also provide other forms of entertainment, including karaoke machines, for pilgrims to use. Thankfully the group I was in was not interested in karaoke, but several, including Shimada-san, were happy to have a glass of beer or cup of *sake* with their meal and gratefully accepted the offer from Mr. Koyama and Mr. Higuchi to fill their glasses.

Such activities can thus help to promote a sense of conviviality in the evenings, as was clearly the case here. As we ate and drank, we began to talk together about pilgrimages. Mrs. Kachi spoke of her experiences of visiting the Saikoku temples and famous temples such as Zenkōji in Nagano, which she had been to several times, while Shimada-san outlined his plans for Iwaki-kai pilgrimages in the next year. Conversations carried on late into the evening, even after we had ostensibly stopped at around 11:00 P.M., divided into two groups, closed the sliding doors, and got into our futon, with both groups keeping up a constant chatter. In the adjoining rooms—separated only by traditional Japanese paper sliding doors that are no barrier to sound—the other pilgrimage group also kept up a babble of talk, accompanied by occasional prayers, all of which kept me awake for longer than I wanted. It was not until past midnight that, exhausted, I finally drifted off to sleep.

Distinct impressions: Wonderful temples and insignificant sites . . .

The next morning, the noises began early. By 5:00 A.M., as far as I could make out through my sleepy haze, the group next door had begun to stir, shuffle about, and start talking and then chanting sutras. Our group were soon up and waiting expectantly for breakfast. We set off early to visit Temple 74, which, as I noted in chapter 1, everyone found to be rather unimpressive, before going on to Zentsūji, whose size and grandeur were commented upon by all. Mrs. Kuwata thought everyone should be really thankful that such places existed, and everyone decided they should make a particular effort to pray well there. Everyone seemed rather shocked, however, to see posters of Zentsūji that described it as a *tourist (kankō)* spot; Mrs. Kachi was particularly upset, saying that such places were religious centers and should not be described in any other way. She was also taken aback when Shimada-san said that some pilgrimage tours stopped at tourist sites (including two well-known gorges in central Shikoku) as well the temples.

Later, after everyone had been around the temple and returned to the bus, there was much laughter because it transpired that Mrs. Kachi had somehow managed to pray at the wrong place. Zentsūji covers a wide area, and somehow she had thought the *daishidō* (which is the most prominent building in the complex) was the main hall of worship, and after worshiping at it had then prayed at the building near it (which she thought was the *daishidō*). She had managed to miss the main hall of worship completely.

Beer at the wrong time

Although drinking alcohol in the evenings is regarded with equanimity, this does not mean that it is encouraged at other times—a point that became clear at lunch on the second day. Mr. Koyama ordered a bottle of beer and was pouring a glass when Shimada-san saw him and got cross, reprimanding him for a breach of pilgrimage etiquette. While, he said, it was reasonable to have a drink after completing the day's travels as a refreshing reward for one's efforts and a way of relaxing, it was not right to imbibe while in the process of being a pilgrim and visiting the sites. It was an interesting comment, indicating that for Shimada-san, the evenings after one had stopped visiting temples were in effect a break from the process of pilgrimage. Lunch was clearly not so.

Interestingly, too, and evidence of the extent to which pilgrims do not feel constrained by the rules others try to impose on them, Mr. Koyama took little note. Downing a mouthful of beer and then topping his glass up, he commented that it was his pilgrimage and it was up to him whether or not he had a lunchtime beer. The other pilgrims, although they did not speak up openly, appeared to support him. Mrs. Kachi, who was probably the most distant from Mr. Koyama in that she appeared the most, and he the least, devout in the party, said later that she felt it was up to him whether he had a beer and that she did not think he should be obliged to follow a set of rules if he did not want to.

Mrs. Kachi's support for Mr. Koyama was an indication that although the group consisted of individuals keen not to intrude on each other's pilgrimages, members also felt a sense of common belonging and support. On other occasions, too, Mr. Koyama expressed views that went very much against Mrs. Kachi's reasons for doing the pilgrimage, such as when the pilgrims had decided to have special prayers said for the benefit of their ancestors at one temple and Mr. Koyama was the only person to decline, saying that in his view the whole business of having memorial services done after people had died was ridiculous. Yet even though the comment was made as the others were writing out the names of ancestors for whom they wanted the service done, no one seemed to take offense, while Mrs. Kachi just wagged her finger at him in a jocular manner. Yet she was doing the pilgrimage for her dead husband and asking for a memorial service that she felt would help his spirit. Even though she and Mr. Koyama thus appeared to have very different views, they appeared to be able to get on together, see themselves as parts of the same group, and live with each other's views.

Interactions

The diverse group thus developed a sense of common belonging within which they could accommodate highly divergent views and differing individual motivations. This sense of togetherness was evident when we talked with other pilgrimage groups. The Iwaki-kai pilgrims were conscious, in particular, that my presence, as a Western academic journeying with a small party of Japanese pilgrims, was something that made our party different. This clearly encouraged them to draw attention to my presence and identify themselves with the group, even as they eschewed the sorts of communal activity performed by many of the other groups we saw.

Pilgrimage package tours have the potential to create barriers between groups, with each group traveling in their own bus and staying in their own rooms overnight. A refrain of older pilgrims who remember the prewar period is that the traditional communal rooms (aibeya) in pilgrims' lodges have disappeared, so that now pilgrims have less chance to mingle together overnight. This may be a somewhat nostalgic view, since, as Takamure's account of pilgrims' lodges shows, communal rooms could be places of bedlam and unease, yet there may be some validity to such worries. Often the only times pilgrims do meet up is in contexts when they are effectively competing with others. When several groups arrive at a temple together, there may not be space for all of them to stand directly in front of the halls of worship to do their prayers, and hence some jostling for position occurs. Queues develop at the offices where scrolls and books are stamped, and hence pilgrims—and their guides, who, like Shimada-san, may be taking care of this business—strive to get ahead of others seeking the same service—and become frustrated if they have to wait. At restaurants and in lodges, too, tensions and frustrations may occur when groups have to wait to be served because another party has arrived just before them.

And yet it would be wrong to overemphasize this tension or to suggest that the *henro* creates the sort of rigid boundaries between groups that Michael Sallnow perceived between pilgrimage groups in the Andes and that gave rise to his initial critique of Turner's notion of *communitas* and to the development of a theory of contest.[8] There were times when our group, caught up in the haste of temple visits, saw other groups as rivals who often did things (e.g., chanting) better than us or who got better positions before the temples. However, there were also many occasions—the walk to and from Unpenji, for example—when a harmonious atmosphere existed between groups, while the general readiness of our group to engage in conversations with others indicated that they were not intent on maintaining rigid boundaries.

The concept of *dōgyō* certainly helps in this context, as does the very structure of the *henro*. Because there are eighty-eight sites to visit, pilgrims may well encounter each other again and again. I noticed that the Iwaki-kai party reacted positively when they met again pilgrims whom they had seen at earlier sites; it was as if something familiar had entered their landscapes. Pilgrims can bump into each other frequently, especially when the temples are close together. Temples 13–17, for example, are so close together, and the streets around them so narrow, that walkers often get to the next temple as quickly as buses. Indeed, often buses drop their passengers at one end of the path between these temples and pick them up at the other end. I have walked this section several times and have found myself keeping pace with bus and car groups. Meeting several times in a day encourages familiarity and can thus reduce any potential tension that might otherwise occur. This appears somewhat different from, for example, the Santiago Camino, where it may be possible for different types of pilgrim (e.g., walkers and those coming by plane) to meet up only at the sacred goal—a point that might explain why the foot pilgrims Frey interviewed seem so critical of other pilgrims (see chapter 1). When one has walked several hundred kilometers and arrives tired and dusty at Santiago, it is doubtless galling to see others looking fresh because they have just flown in.

The Iwaki-kai pilgrims were certainly open to interactions with others, especially when they became familiar through repeated meetings. This came through on our first day, when we ate lunch in a noodle shop in one temple courtyard. A group whose schedules we had found ourselves dovetailing with came in soon after. Having seen them three times already, it was as if we knew them, and everyone acted as if their friends had just turned up. They sat at the next table, and everyone began conversing, asking questions about where everyone came from, our pilgrimages, and so on. Much of the discussion (after the Iwaki-kai pilgrims had explained my presence, that is) centered on tales and rumors of miracles. I have commented earlier about how pilgrims pass on and repeat miracle stories to fellow pilgrims. This point came out as we talked to the other group, for Mrs. Kuwata and Mrs. Kachi, in particular, were adept at recounting stories they had heard from Shimada-san and were excited as the pilgrims in the other party told us of stories that someone had told them. Needless to say, when we later got into conversation with other pilgrim groups, Mrs. Kuwata and Mrs. Kachi lost little time in recounting these stories as well. It was evident, too, that telling and recycling miracle tales in this way is part of the enjoyment of such pilgrimages, which everyone seemed to engage in readily and which served as a means by which pilgrims could interact with and talk to each other.

Becoming tourists, visiting Konpira

In the afternoon of our second day we briefly became tourists when Shimada-san announced that since we had made good time, we could make a diversion to the town of Kotohira to have lunch (it was during this lunch that he criticized Mr. Koyama for drinking beer) and visit Konpira Shrine, the best known Shinto shrine in Shikoku. This, Shimada-san said, was a bonus extra to the tour, which caused the party to thank him gratefully. Konpira Shrine has been a frequent port of call for Shikoku pilgrims since the Tokugawa era, and it continues to receive a steady flow of white-clad pilgrims among its clientele. Hence when we visited, we were not doing something out of the ordinary for Shikoku pilgrims. However, since the visit was not in the pilgrimage itinerary that the group had signed up for, they treated it as something extra.

Shimada-san parked the bus at the restaurant-cum-tourist shop in town where we had lunch and waited for us there. I later asked him whether he always took pilgrims there and he said yes; calling it an extra was just a way of making everyone feel they were getting special treatment. In reality, he (like most pilgrimage tour operators) had special contractual links with particular places where he would stop overnight or for lunch. By guaranteeing that he would bring so many pilgrims or groups per year, he could get special rates for food, as well as a commission on any sales of goods and souvenirs that might be made to the pilgrims. The shop (like many places in Shikoku) offered a special service whereby goods could be shipped direct to the pilgrim's home, to arrive there the day after their pilgrimage ended. After lunch, encouraged by Shimada-san, several of the group indulged in a souvenir-buying spree, giving the shop their addresses and the date when their pilgrimage was to end so that the souvenirs (mostly local foodstuffs, such as local Sanuki noodles) could be sent directly to their homes.

After lunch, we prepared for the ascent to the shrine—a climb of over one thousand steps. As we did so, Shimada-san advised everyone to retain items such as the staff and *hakui* that marked them out as pilgrims. However, after some discussion on this score, everyone apart from Mrs. Kachi took off their pilgrims' shrouds, and only Mrs. Kuwata held on to her staff, as if, it would appear, they wished to detach themselves temporarily from their guise as pilgrims. The eight of us then climbed, slowly so as to ensure that Mrs. Kuwata and Mr. Higuchi, with their heart problems, would not be placed under duress, up to the shrine buildings. While there everyone acted in much the way they had at the pilgrimage temples: Mr. Koyama (who told me he had been to the shrine four times before) clicked away with his cameras, Mrs. Kuwata and Mrs. Kachi prayed and threw coins into offertory boxes, Mr. Higuchi recorded the proceedings with his video camera, and the couples prayed and admired the scenery. Afterward, we descended, stopping to check out various booths and souvenir shops before getting back to the bus, where everyone donned their white shirts again and entered back into pilgrimage mode.

The excursion was an interesting and, it seemed to me, invigorating break in the process of being pilgrims. I was interested that most of the group actually wanted to take off their white shrouds and that they welcomed the chance to slip briefly out of their roles as pilgrims. I was reminded of an occasion when my wife and I had stayed overnight on the outskirts of Takamatsu, over five weeks into our pilgrimage. We felt like a stroll after our evening meal, and, since there was a coffee shop not far away, we went there. Consciously, though, we did not take any pilgrimage accoutrements with us, going in effect as "ordinary" citizens as for an hour or so we escaped our guise as pilgrims. It felt quite therapeutic, a release from our normative reality of the past few weeks. Briefly, our sense of release and difference came about not because we were pilgrims, but because we had stepped out of that role.

I think that such excursions and diversions can have a positive function in the highly charged, nonstop atmosphere of the *henro*. By visiting tourist places and stepping aside, for a short time, from their "pilgrimage mode" and guise, pilgrims can gain a brief respite from the pressures of being on display. Although in one sense each pilgrim merges into the wider mass of pilgrims, at the same time each one is conscious of living in a (temporary) role different from their everyday life. Setting aside that persona temporarily to visit tourist sites can help diffuse the tensions that may build up in the pilgrim's mind and in the internal dynamics of the bus party. This is a shade ironic, since many become pilgrims in order to step aside from their everyday existence and to get away from the pressures and rush of modern life. However, bus pilgrimages, even as they seem to offer a temporary way out of contemporary society, can also *produce* an environment of tension and rush of the sort that pilgrims are seeking to escape, thereby creating, for some pilgrims, the desire to escape from the pilgrimage for a while, a point that was evident when we visited Konpira and briefly shed our guise as pilgrims before returning again, renewed, to the world of pilgrimage.

Money and souvenirs

Later that afternoon, we stopped at a coffee shop where, Shimada-san assured us, they sold extremely tasty cakes. It was another place where he always took pilgrims and where he got a commission. We all were given a "free" cake with our coffee, and afterward (as is the custom) most of the party, except Mr. Koyama, whose stubborn nonconformity I admired, duly bought boxes of them to send home. Their behavior at the shop was not at all exceptional: throughout the journey the pilgrims spent money readily, buying numerous souvenirs and items of local foodstuffs to send or take home. At the shop in Kotohira Mrs. Kuwata alone had spent 7,900 yen, and at the cake shop, too, her purchases ran to several thousand yen's worth of souvenirs and foodstuffs for her family and friends. Mr. Koyama also purchased large amounts of souvenirs, but elsewhere. He just seemed to refrain from so doing when he felt that Shimada-san was cajoling him into purchases and when he suspected that Shimada-san was getting a commission.

The Iwaki-kai pilgrims were not alone in this readiness to spend money on pilgrimage; my observations are that it is a common tendency among Shikoku pilgrims. I have already alluded to the economic benefits that the pilgrimage brings to Shikoku in terms of service industries such as pilgrims lodges, souvenir shops, and the like, and such benefits can be sustained only because pilgrims such as Mrs. Kuwata and her companions want to spend money freely as part of their pilgrimages. In this they seemed similar to the pilgrims Gold discusses, who pursue the Hindu pilgrimage ideal of returning "thinner and poorer" by divesting themselves of money through giving to beggars at sacred sites and spending it wherever possible. Gold shows that Rajasthani pilgrims not only like to spend liberally while on pilgrimage, but that they see merit in doing so; being away from home, too, released any constraints in this context.[9] While the Iwaki-kai pilgrims had little opportunity to give alms to beggars, they certainly had plentiful opportunities to spend money and took them whenever possible. At the temples they purchased amulets and lucky charms and paid for special prayers to be read for their ancestors. At the booths and stalls outside the temples they bought trinkets and souvenirs, and when the opportunity presented itself, as at Kotohira, they bought large amounts of local products and foodstuffs to send home. By the time we left Temple 88 (where the purchasing of souvenirs and commemorative items hit its peak) it was fair to say that everyone had got through enough money to ensure that at the very least they would return home poorer.

Enigmatic encounters: False pilgrim or implicit challenge?

Later in the afternoon a rather odd incident occurred when we encountered a man in full pilgrimage regalia and a long black priest's robe at Temple 79. He told me he had been doing pilgrimages in Shikoku for twenty-six years, since 1964, sometimes by foot, sometimes by bicycle, and sometimes by bus leading other pilgrims. In all, he had done the pilgrimage 109 times. He gave me a brocade *fuda* that stated he was a *sendatsu* who ran a pilgrimage association *(kō)*. As we talked, the other members of the group gathered around and, impressed by his regalia, which bore the number of times he had done the pilgrimage, asked him for *fuda*—a request he declined, as they were expensive and he could not dole them out to everyone he met. On being pressed further, however, he said he would do so for donations of four hundred yen. As everyone handed over this amount and got a *fuda,* he spoke again about how many times he had done the pilgrimage and complained about how easy it now was to become a *sendatsu* and about how so many of them got their rank merely through sitting on a bus and doing it the easy way. Mr. Koyama then took some photographs of him with the group before we returned to the bus.

Several of the party were in a state of excitement at having met so splendid a pilgrim, and Mrs. Kuwata told Shimada-san (who had been at the temple office getting the scrolls stamped) about the encounter and showed him the brocade *fuda* she had received. Shimada-san's reaction surprised everyone: how did we know he had done the pilgrimage 109 times? How did we know he was genuine? He looked at the *fuda* and declared he had never heard of him or his pilgrimage association—since he knew the pilgrimage so well, he would certainly have done so if this man had been a genuine *sendatsu* and had really had such a long pilgrimage experience. Anyway, he opined, real *sendatsu* would not sell their *fuda,* and anyone who did so must be a scoundrel preying on gullible pilgrims! He proceeded to scold everyone for having been taken in and for having parted with their money. Nor did he let the matter rest. At the next temple he showed the priests the man's *fuda* and asked whether they knew him or his association. When they answered in the negative, Shimada-san stated that any true pilgrim who did the *henro* so many times would be known to all the priests at temple offices. There is some truth in this. In my experience, temple priests and officials tend to have very good knowledge of those who do the *henro* repeatedly. I have on many occasions sat in temple offices with priests and noted how they appeared to know many of the pilgrims and about pilgrimage associations throughout the country. Shimada-san was clearly well known to many of the temple priests, who greeted him with familiarity when he entered the temples or their *nōkyōjo;* this was the case with the two he had shown the pilgrim's *fuda* to. Yet this does not mean that all who do the *henro* necessarily visit the temple offices or get books stamped every time they do it; I have—admittedly only very occasionally—met pilgrims who do not carry books or scrolls. Hence the fact that priests did not know this man is not absolute evidence that he was, as Shimada-san suggested, false.

However, the others in the party did not seem convinced by Shimada-san's comments and continued to assert that they had been impressed and were pleased to get his *fuda*. Mrs. Kuwata remarked several times that one had to be grateful for being able to receive such a superb *fuda*, while Mr. Higuchi remarked that there was, as he put it, a little bit of Kōbō Daishi about the man. Hence it was perfectly acceptable to make an offering to him; it was no different to offering money before a statue of a buddha. Privately, too, everyone was critical of Shimada-san's comments and asked how he could be so sure the man was a fraud.

I never quite managed to ascertain whether he was a fraud or not, although I felt somewhat suspicious. I was surprised when he offered his *fuda* in return for money and even wondered if he gave me one in order to spur the others on so that he could solicit donations. His striking apparel (besides his priestly robe he had a large bamboo hat of the type usually worn by mendicant priests and a very long and ornate staff) and demeanor seemed designed to draw attention to himself. Sometimes one comes across pilgrims who make overt shows of piety and appear full of their importance in this way; I should also note that they do not always impress their fellows. On more than one occasion I have been at temples when pilgrims have come in dressed in grand robes, gone through long and demonstrative prayer routines, and spoken loudly about how many circuits they had done and so on, in ways designed to make an impression. Often the response of officials and others there has been respectful and polite, only for them to dissolve into amused and mocking laughter after the pilgrim has gone.

I was certainly interested in Shimada-san's reaction. Perhaps he felt that the man was a fraud and wanted to protect his pilgrims. He may, indeed, have come across cases of deception before; thieves and other miscreants, as was noted in chapter 4, were part of the *henro* fabric in earlier eras, and there is no guarantee that they are absent in the present. Yet I felt that it was as likely that his hostile response was because he somehow felt threatened and challenged by someone with apparently more pilgrimage experience than himself. Certainly, the reverential way in which the pilgrims talked about this pilgrim contrasted with their much more businesslike interactions with Shimada-san, to whom no one had shown any real deference. Moreover, Shimada-san had, on the previous day, criticized a woman who was leading a group of pilgrims who had called her *sensei* (teacher) because, he said, she was not really leading them in the right way and hence could hardly be a "teacher." Thus I sensed that he was generally suspicious and critical of anyone who appeared to be an alternative figure of authority or respect and whom the pilgrims he was guiding might compare with himself.

I should note here that it is not uncommon for pilgrims to feel challenged by others or to become defensive in such contexts. When we were walking the pilgrimage in 1984, my first reaction when we met Nakano-san was defensive, as if I felt I needed to justify to myself (and him) why we were not sleeping out and doing the *henro* in the same austere way as he was. I noted, too, that when we met up with pilgrims on buses, they would often start explaining why they were going by bus ("You are young and strong . . . my legs are weak . . . I have family responsibilities and cannot get away for long"), as if they felt that by walking we posed a challenge to their credibility. It is possible, in other words, that Shimada-san's reaction was of a similar ilk—an uneasy, instinctive response to the challenge he felt was posed by someone who had done more pilgrimages than himself. It was an indication that despite the notion that everyone is equal in the *henro*, despite there being no preordained way to do it, and despite it being an individual and personal journey, pilgrims can readily compare themselves to others and can find themselves challenged and threatened by their actions.

Office workers stamping books

Shortly after this encounter we traveled on to Temples 81 and 82, located amidst cool pine forests in the hills overlooking Takamatsu and the Inland Sea. At both we ran into a logjam at the *nōkyōjo* not just of pilgrims, but of representatives of pilgrimage groups who were traveling separately from the main party in order to facilitate the stamping of the scrolls and books. At Temple 81 we met two men who were doing what Shimada-san called *atodōri*, following around behind a large tour bus of pilgrims for whom they were carrying the scrolls. By having the scrolls and books carried separately (they would be forwarded to the pilgrims' homes the day after their pilgrimage ended), the company organizing the tour could keep to a strict schedule and save the pilgrims from having to wait at any site while their scrolls were being stamped.

The men looked slightly incongruous in the pilgrimage environment, for they were dressed like ordinary Japanese office workers in neat blue suits with small company lapel badges. They traveled in a small car, carrying with them some thirty scrolls, sixty-one pilgrims' books, and thirty *hakui*. We met them again at the next temple, where we and they had to wait while a couple of men working for another company had their huge pile of scrolls and books stamped. This pair was going around in front *(sakidōri)* of a very large pilgrimage group so that their pilgrims could avoid delays but get their scrolls as soon as they finished. They were still being dealt with when the two earlier employees turned up with their scrolls and books; the temple officials, rather than cause a major queue to develop, asked the company employees to stamp the books themselves. As Shimada-san fretted at the delay, a couple in their fifties marched into the temple and went straight to the office to get their scroll stamped, evidently hoping that they would get preferential treatment and be able to jump the queue. The priest, however, told them he was very busy, asked them if they had worshiped at the temple, and, when they said no, asked them to go and do so first. They went off—but were back in a very few minutes; before we left another couple came in, and virtually the same performance was repeated.

Temples generally try to ensure that individual pilgrims do not have to wait and will often interrupt stamping the scrolls of tour groups in order to attend to pilgrims on their own or in couples. However, on this occasion the priests did not. The pilgrims' haste and impatience in going straight to the temple office, spending so little time praying before coming back, and trying to push them forward so that the priests would interrupt stamping the scrolls of the parties ensured that they were made to wait. Shimada-san gleefully commented on this when we got back on the bus, complaining about the lack of manners of some pilgrims and about how one should observe the correct etiquette and not try to jump queues. It was another indication of his feisty character and willingness to speak his mind—traits that endeared him to me in many respects. I noted, too, that Shimada-san was always friendly and polite when he entered temple offices, that he never attempted to seek pref-

Bus company officials helping out at one of the temples by stamping pilgrims' books.

erential treatment—and that officials would often respond by stamping his small pile of scrolls and books before they stamped those of larger groups ahead of him.

Vegetarian ham and a bargain for the ancestors

On the second evening, after visiting Temple 83, we stayed in Takamatsu at the local branch temple of Kōyasan (Kōya Betsuin). Kōyasan temples are well known for their vegetarian fare, and the temple leaflet that we were given emphasized that this branch temple continued in this well-known tradition. It came as a surprise, then, to find in the generally excellent vegetarian food served for our evening meal a slice of ham. Later, as I read through further temple literature I had picked up, I discovered that the founder of the Marudai Ham Company had been a generous patron of the temple—a fact that no doubt explained why ham was part of its "vegetarian" meals.

The routine was the same—baths, a couple of beers, and endless talk into the night—as the previous evening. The one difference was that since we were staying at a temple, a priest asked us if we wanted any special memorial prayers read at the early morning Buddhist service, at which point all save Mr. Koyama and I requested prayers for their ancestors. It was as they were filling in the forms the temple provided (which give details such as the name of the supplicant and the posthumous name of the ancestor being prayed for) and placing bank notes to pay the fee for this service into the envelope provided that Mr. Koyama made his critical comment about praying for the ancestors.

Noticing that the Matsudas, when they filled in their forms, asked for memorial services for both sides of their family, I asked if memorializing their ancestors was their main reason for doing the pilgrimage. Mr. Matsuda, laughing, said that it would be good for me to think that, since it was the socially acceptable thing to state one was doing it for the ancestors rather than, say, primarily for personal requests. It was also the done thing, he commented, to have prayers said at the morning service for one's ancestors when staying overnight at temples. He added, in a pragmatic comment that perhaps indicated the commonly ascribed characteristics of Osakans, who are famed in Japan for their interest in money and commerce, that the fee for such services in Shikoku was cheap compared to temples in Osaka. Hence they were getting a bargain—which encouraged them to have the prayers done.

Completion and celebration

We left early the next morning, after the morning service and breakfast, for the final few temples. There were few striking events to note—apart from the encounter at Temple 87 with the pilgrim on foot whose spontaneous decision to take a lift to Temple 88 was mentioned in the previous chapter. The Iwaki-kai pilgrims, showing—as they had all along—a readiness to engage with pilgrims of all sorts, were keen to talk to him at both sites and were graciously complimentary about him for having walked, even as he bemoaned having taken a lift to the last temple.

The last two or three temples appeared not to register greatly with the pilgrims, as the mounting excitement and expectation about getting to Temple 88 and completing the pilgrimage appeared to color their feelings, making them want to hurry past the temples preceding it. At Temple 88 Mr. Matsuda announced that since this was the last temple, we should all worship here seriously *(daiji ni ogamō)*. Everyone appeared to spend longer in prayer than at the other temples. Mr. Koyama seemed to take more photographs, too, and Mr. Higuchi videotaped everything at great length. Everyone made a point of congratulating their fellows on the completion—an interesting point, since Mr. Koyama had not yet been to all the temples and still had one *ikkoku mairi* to go.

At the row of gift shops before the temple, shop workers greeted us warmly, congratulating us on completing our pilgrimage and offering us *set-*

Pilgrim posing for a commemorative photograph at the steps of Temple 88. The stone to her right reads "Hachijūhachibun kechiganjo" (Number 88: the place where one's vow [to do the pilgrimage] is complete).

tai. In reality, this *settai* involved samples of the local foodstuffs sold as souvenirs at the shops. Of course, most of the party eventually bought some to take home as they indulged in a final burst of souvenir buying. At Ōkuboji, too, one could get commemorative photographs *(kinen shashin)* taken, and most tour groups appeared to make use of their services. One could even have such photographs transposed onto personalized telephone cards, which Mrs. Kuwata did, asking me to be in the photograph with her so she could have a souvenir of our travel together. She then ordered two copies of the card, giving the extra one to me.

Reaching Ōkuboji and completing the pilgrimage clearly affected everyone in the party, even Mr. Koyama. It made them more voluble and ready to express themselves, as if, having finished, they now felt that a barrier to self-expression had been taken away. It was at this point that the Matsudas showed me the sutra copies they had been offering at the temples (I had been aware of them but had not yet extracted any information on this subject) and told me that they had been praying particularly for their grandchildren's examination success. Mr. Matsuda then told me what they planned to do with their scroll when they got it mounted: keep it stored at home to be brought out as a focus of prayers at special occasions connected with the ancestors, such as memorial services, death anniversaries, and related festivals. It was at this juncture, too, that Mrs. Kachi revealed that her pilgrimage was a memorial for her recently departed husband. Everyone talked, too, of future pilgrimages they might make and discussed whether it might be feasible for them to meet up on another tour somewhere.

After visiting Ōkuboji we had a lunch of *sekihan* (red beans and rice, a traditional celebratory dish in Japan) at one of the restaurants nearby. Everyone talked of their good feelings at having finished, and Shimada-san—who the previous day had been so critical of pilgrims drinking at midday—ordered some bottles of beer and poured each of us a congratulatory glass or two, of which everyone partook happily. Clearly he regarded the pilgrimage as having effectively ended at this point and felt that in such contexts it was acceptable to drink alcohol, even though we still were scheduled to go back to Temple 1—around an hour's drive away from Temple 88—to perform *orei mairi*. Yet once we had visited Ōkuboji, the general atmosphere and the attitudes of the pilgrims and of Shimada-san suggested that we had finished. No one appeared to consider the *orei mairi* visit as integral to the pilgrimage. It seemed an afterthought, a formality to be carried out, rather than an intrinsic part of the *henro*. As we drove on to Ryōzenji, our normal mood of lively conversation and anticipation gave way to soporific contentment.

We visited Temple 1, prayed cursorily, and left, heading across the bridge to the neighboring island of Awaji and then by car ferry to Kobe. As we waited to embark on the ferry taking us back to the mainland, everyone spontaneously took off their pilgrims' shirts, thereby shedding their pilgrims' guise and reverting to being "ordinary people" again. Once our ferry had arrived at the mainland, Mr. Koyama left us, as it was easier for him to get home by taking a local train from there than coming in to central Osaka with us.

Ending, dissolution, farewell

Even before Mr. Koyama left, the sense of being a group had begun to dissolve, as everyone appeared to sink into individual reveries and thoughts. It was a reminder to me that traveling in a group is convenient and enables pilgrims to develop common bonds and a shared group identity—but that such bonds and identity may also be transient and can quickly fade as individual thoughts take over. While groups may travel as a unit, they consist of individuals each centered in his or her own personal journey and intentions, in which each person has his or her individual experiences within the framework of group travel, but always relevant to them as individuals.

Yet if I was thus reminded about how problematic it was to build theories solely around group dynamics, the tour also showed me that individualized theories of pilgrimage are also problematic. While each pilgrimage is an individual affair, even such individual journeys and behavior occur and are framed within social and group contexts. The Iwaki-kai pilgrims operated within a social framework and set of dynamics that allowed them to be individual and yet operate as an entity that gave them the scope for a highly personalized journey and experience within the comforting setting of an organized tour, in which each participant brought something special and individual to the group. The group was thus a combination of individuals with different views and aims and ideas existing in a temporary community that gave them a sense of identity and purpose and added to their pilgrimages, whose meanings were made within the framework of the social and group contexts in which they were carried out.

We dropped the Higuchis and Matsudas at convenient places and then, at around 5:30 P.M., reached our last stop at Nanba in central Osaka. By then there were just three of us left along with Shimada-san. We disembarked clutching our belongings and, in the case of the others, their staffs and scrolls. We bowed, said good-bye to each other and to Shimada-san, and headed off in our separate directions. Mrs. Kuwata bowed one last time to me as I headed down the steps into the Osaka subway system. Suddenly, I was alone, no longer part of a group, no longer a pilgrim, just another foreigner on the Osaka underground.

8 A Way of Life

Pilgrimage, Transformation, and Permanence

In this final chapter I focus on a striking aspect of the *henro* that raises questions about how pilgrimage has thus far been discussed and studied in academic terms, namely how people may dedicate their lives to it, becoming permanent fixtures on the route or turning pilgrimage into a way of life. This opens up a different angle to the study and analysis of pilgrimage than is normally found in the academic literature, which, as I have previously noted, tends to concentrate on goals, pilgrimage sites, and pilgrims in the process of visiting them. This emphasis on destinations and goals is often reflected, too, in pilgrims' accounts, which, as Frey remarks in the context of the pilgrimage to Santiago, commonly "end when the goal is reached"[1]—a characteristic also evident in Shikoku pilgrims' diaries, which often end at Temple 88. Indeed, my descriptions of walkers' accounts and of bus pilgrimage tours in the previous two chapters have indicated how reaching Ōkuboji is frequently a cognitive end point for pilgrims, and how any subsequent activity, such as an *orei mairi* visit, may be seen as an appendage rather than an integral part of the pilgrimage.

Yet even if pilgrims have contributed, through their writings, to this focus on goals, destinations, endings, and sites, this has in many respects created a distorted picture of pilgrimage, one that is goal centered and interpreted through the mode of transience, a disruption in the normal routines of life, and a temporary "going out" into the sacred world performed by those normally living in the mundane world. This focus has, I think, been strongly influenced by Turner's analysis of pilgrimage as a liminal process involving the formation of temporary antistructures and a visit to a center "out there," but other theories, such as the notion of pilgrimage as an arena for contest, have also produced heavily goal-, place-, and transience-centered analyses of pilgrimage that neglect what happens before pilgrims reach sacred sites and what happens afterward. This has caused pilgrimages to be presented in the literature predominantly as "one off," transient and extraordinary events that contrast with the seemingly normative patterns of stasis, rather than as central or formative themes within religious culture or within the lives of those who perform them, and also largely as appendages on the margins of broader religious traditions. The pilgrimage process in this context, too, is therefore associated with liminality and the margins of religious culture.[2]

There is much that is valid in this. As has been noted in earlier chapters, for example, the *henro* can provide participants with a means of temporary escape or release from their everyday lives. Moreover, as the previous two chapters have indicated, there is a distinct sense in which pilgrims, whilst on their pilgrimages, are very much goal centered and focused on their next port of call. However, at the same time, there is much that is problematic about goal-centered understandings and perceptions of pilgrimage and from viewing pilgrimage primarily through the lens of transience and liminality. Such perspectives fail to recognize that the goal-centered focus of the journey may turn into something more enduring in its aftermath, and they neglect to a great degree what happens after the physical journey of pilgrimage ends. Yet as Gold's study of Rajasthani pilgrims and Frey's work on Santiago both indicate, what happens when the pilgrim is returning or has returned to his/her home, how pilgrimage may impact on their lives afterward, and how completing a pilgrimage may in effect be a starting rather than an end point for participants are also vital elements in the study of pilgrimage.[3]

In my view, too, studies of pilgrimage have paid too little attention to the ways in which pilgrimages, rather than being marginal and transient, can be central organizing themes in the lives of participants. Both Gold and Frey provide some evidence of this, Gold showing how pilgrimages are embedded in the social and religious lives of Rajasthani villagers[4] and Frey demonstrating how pilgrims may return in one way or another to their pilgrimages after reaching the (physical) end or goal. They may, for example, maintain a continuing association with the pilgrimage, whether on an emotional level, through constant mental return to the Camino or continuing engagement in the pilgrimage, through joining Camino-related associations, or returning to work as a volunteer at pilgrimage hospitals. Thus, Frey demonstrates, reaching the sacred goal may be less an act of completion than a point of departure for what comes next in pilgrims' lives.[5]

My study of Shikoku pilgrims not only affirms these points, but also suggests that there may be even greater levels of engagement, return, and repetition than are found in Gold's and Frey's studies. As such, there is a need to reconsider normative anthropological perceptions of pilgrimage and to emphasize the extent to which pilgrimage is entrenched in the cultures that produce pilgrims and how it impacts on and influences the lives of those who become pilgrims. These are the issues taken up in this chapter, where I look at how the *henro* may become a dominant motif in pilgrims' lives and a way of life for some, who effectively become "permanent pilgrims" in Shikoku.

Transformation and renewal

In earlier chapters I have emphasized some of the issues outlined above, showing that the pilgrimage is part of, and central to, the folk religious traditions of Shikoku and is thus embedded in the social lives and religious culture of people in the region. My discussions, in chapter 3, of the Shiga Shingyōkai and the Arita Settaikō, too, show also how pilgrimage practices, customs, and beliefs can be taken home and become central to the belief and practice structures of communities and people in places outside Shikoku, and how a pilgrimage tradition can be passed on to later generations and become an integral part of their lives and cultural inheritance.

Pilgrimages in Shikoku do not end when pilgrims reach the final temple or perform *orei mairi*. Throughout this book numerous examples of pilgrims for whom completing the pilgrimage is evidently not a terminal point and for whom a continuing link with the *henro* is maintained afterward have been given. The Iwaki-kai pilgrims cited in the previous chapter, whose completed pilgrimages served as a stimulus to go on to further pilgrimages, are one such example. The pilgrims who leave objects behind at the temples are another, for they are, in a sense, maintaining a bond with the *henro* that continues after they have ended their journeys, as are those who bring things back (a scroll, a stamped shirt) to use in later memorial and other services. The large numbers of people who attain the status of *sendatsu* and who maintain a continuing relationship with the *henro* through attending regular *sendatsu* meetings are another. There are many for whom the experience of pilgrimage has been so striking that they have remained ardent and continuing pilgrims, not just returning again and again to Shikoku but also establishing and running regional pilgrimage associations designed to inspire others to follow in their footsteps, as has been shown by the examples of people such as Tabuchi Yoshio and Naitō Kinpō.

In all these cases one can see how the transformative effects of pilgrimage can resonate through the rest of a person's life—themes evident also in the cases of Takamure and Kagita, both of whose pilgrimages have featured in this book. Takamure's pilgrimage took place in 1918, when she was twenty-four. She had turned to the pilgrimage after an unhappy affair with the writer Hashimoto Kenzō, but after completing it and having started to develop a reputation as a writer, she then married Hashimoto and moved to Tokyo. The self-confidence she gained through her pilgrimage and her first steps as a writer enabled her to transcend the sense of self-doubt that afflicted her and to establish herself as a feminist writer and historian.

Yet the confident transformation did not last, and Takamure became beset by doubts and illness, turned inward, and became reclusive. As she did so, she returned, mentally, to her formative pilgrimage experiences, which came to signify a means and a path for solving her problems. During the

1930s she wrote of her desire to leave her literary life in Tokyo and head off with begging bowl and white robe again to seek the mental strength and sense of renewal she had got in Shikoku—feelings expressed in her diary in autumn 1933, when she was ill, and again in April 1934.[6]

Takamure never returned to Shikoku, however, remaining with Hashimoto in Tokyo. She did, however, return to the pilgrimage in her writings, producing two further accounts of her 1918 pilgrimage: *Ohenro*, initially published in 1936, and *Henro to jinsei* (1939), as well as a later journal, which further discussed her pilgrimage and her decision to rewrite her experiences. The two volumes were, she insisted, attempts to put her actual pilgrimage—and the things she wrote in it, which she saw as the work of a naive and unhappy young woman—into proper perspective and make sense of them; they were not just repetitions of her earlier newspaper articles.[7] She also advised others who were unhappy to become pilgrims and asserted that the pilgrimage represented her spiritual homeland *(kokoro no furusato)*.[8] As has been seen in earlier chapters, her example has had an impact, and she has passed on her legacy as a pilgrim to others, notably young women for whom she has been a role model inspiring them to become pilgrims.

In essence, Takamure remade the pilgrimage in her mind, indicating as she did how deeply the experience had affected and influenced her and how nostalgically she yearned to experience again the freedom of her youthful pilgrimage. In this context, her experiences appear in a brighter light than before; as Hoshino comments, the sometimes raw depictions of pilgrimage in the young Takamure's newspaper articles have been replaced by a more peaceful, idealized picture in later works.[9] It is from these later writings that Takamure's talk of harmony and "pilgrims' love" comes. Despite her failure to return to Shikoku, Takamure thus constantly remade and reshaped that pilgrimage in her mind, living her life constantly in the light of her pilgrimage experience.

Takamure's example is evidence, too, of how pilgrims, after returning from their pilgrimages, may turn again to them in their minds and reflect on and reassess them in the light of subsequent experience. The pilgrim I cited in chapter 3, who was not willing to talk about his pilgrimage while still on the road but who felt able to do so after he had finished, is another example of this, as are the many pilgrims who, after returning home, return to their experiences by writing up their pilgrimage journals for publication, thereby adding their memories to the accumulated history of the pilgrimage.

Another pilgrim who wrote about his journey and for whom the experience was so powerful that it reverberated through the rest of his life and served as a life-transforming event was Kagita Chūsaburō, who walked the *henro* in 1961, four decades after Takamure. Prior to his pilgrimage, Kagita had been a successful businessman. Becoming ill through overwork and stress, his aim through the pilgrimage was to become well again and take stock of his life. During it, as the account in chapter 6 indicates, he began to think about changing his life's course and turning to new ventures that would be of benefit to the public at large. In an interview published in the *Yomiuri shinbun* in 1990, almost three decades later, Kagita spoke of how the pilgrimage remained the most central, most formative experience in his life, one that had led to a life change and continued to provide him with a sense of vitality. He had moved from business into local politics, devoting his energies to trying to improve the public lot and working for the Liberal Democratic Party (LDP), the main political force in Japan in the postwar era, eventually becoming the mayor of a town in western Japan, a position he held at the time of the *Yomiuri* interview. While those who are aware of the close connections between politics, money, business, and corruption in Japan might wonder whether going into politics and representing the LDP was necessarily the noblest path someone determined to work for the public good in Japan could take, it is clear at least that Kagita's change of career direction was a direct result of his pilgrimage experiences, which effectively transformed his life and continued to resonate through it.[10]

Takamure's and Kagita's pilgrimages were thus starting points for new lives in which the past was transformed and they found themselves drawn to new paths of action. The Shingon Buddhist priest Tattebe Zuiyū has also written in similar terms about his pilgrimage experiences in Shikoku. Tattebe was born into a temple family in the early twentieth century but never knew his father, who died while he was still in the womb. He was raised as a Shingon priest and heir to his father's temple but became troubled by illness and doubts about whether he was committed to this inherited role and quit in 1931 to set out on a pilgrimage of self-discovery in Shikoku, begging for alms, staying in cheap pilgrims' lodgings, and enduring all manner of hardships. The *henro*, however, awakened a new resolve, and when he reached Kōonji (Temple 61), he was so struck by its lively atmosphere and the presence of enthusiastic priests that he decided to stop a while there and take up priestly duties again. The entire sojourn lasted seventeen years. According to Tattebe, the pilgrimage that led him to Kōonji transformed his life, helped resolve his doubts, and made him realize a true commitment to the priesthood. Indeed, he became so devoted to this path that he eventually became the head priest of the Omuro sect of Shingon Buddhism and of Ninnaji, its head temple in Kyoto. For Tattebe the pilgrimage was a transformative experience and a new beginning, as indicated by the appropriate section of his autobiography, titled "My life started with the Shikoku pilgrimage" *(Shikoku henro kara jinsei ga hajimatta)*.[11]

A lifetime of miracles

Sometimes this life-changing transformation through pilgrimage begins prior to actually setting foot on the *henro* path and involves a continuing relationship with the *henro* centered on its trail of miracles. This was the case with

Tsujita Shōyū, a man in his eighties who told me his life story in December 1990. The following is a very much shortened account of his story (supplemented by short written accounts he also has published)[12] that centers on the miraculous events that he believes he has experienced due to the grace of Kōbō Daishi, through which his life has been shaped and guided for over half a century, since illness and a miraculous encounter first made him into a pilgrim. Tsujita was brought up in Osaka Prefecture in a family devoted to Kōbō Daishi; family lore insisted that his great-grandfather had been cured of blindness after fasting and praying to Kōbō Daishi for twenty-one days. Tsujita was to receive a similarly beneficial intercession from Kōbō Daishi in 1937, when, according to his testimony, he fell seriously ill and was at death's door with beriberi, kidney disease, and tuberculosis, and with doctors saying that nothing more could be done for him. According to his account, he was lying in his room, his life ebbing away, when a wandering monk came to the house to pray for him. The monk, who told Tsujita that he came from a temple in Shikoku, said he could help cure him. He performed a series of rituals and invocations in the name of Kōbō Daishi and asked Tsujita to recite certain prayers, which would help him get better. When his strength returned, the monk said, Tsujita should go to Shikoku to do the pilgrimage, after which he would be cured of all his ills. While in Shikoku he should also visit the monk's temple.

Heartened by this message, Tsujita followed the advice, and within days his strength began to return. Feeling he had been saved from death by the monk's intercession, he set off the next spring on a pilgrimage of gratitude to Shikoku. He had positive memories of the pilgrimage, receiving frequent gifts of *settai*, enjoying hearing of miraculous cures that pilgrims had received, and feeling the presence of Kōbō Daishi everywhere he went. He was also inspired by the devotion to Daishi that he encountered among the pilgrimage community. Eventually, he came to the wandering monk's temple and asked after him. The temple priest was mystified when Tsujita gave a description of the wandering monk and said that no such monk lived there. It was then, Tsujita states, that he realized the wandering monk who had come to his door was in fact Kōbō Daishi.[13]

Tsujita returned fully cured and reborn through the *henro*. He was also fired anew by devotion to Kōbō Daishi, especially after his realization that Kōbō Daishi had personally intervened to save him. As a result, he decided to dedicate his life to Kōbō Daishi and to the practice that Kōbō Daishi had established for the benefit of humanity—the *henro*. Since then, he fervently believed, Kōbō Daishi had guided every aspect of his life, every moment of which has been lived in a special relationship with him and the *henro*. Due to family and work circumstances, he was unable to go to Shikoku regularly and had done the pilgrimage relatively few times. However, he had developed close links with local temples near his home that had miniature versions of the Shikoku pilgrimage and did them regularly, and he had on occasion helped organize parties of pilgrims from local temples and had led them in Shikoku, inspiring them with his tales of miracles and the benefits bestowed by Kōbō Daishi. Especially since he retired from his job as a policeman, and since his wife's death, he spent all his time focused on the *henro* and his dedication to Kōbō Daishi, increased his pilgrimage-related activities, and became a registered *sendatsu*. It was because of his desire to draw attention to the merits of the pilgrimage that I was able to interview him; he had seen an article about my research in the Shikoku pilgrimage newsletter *Henro* and through it had managed to get in contact with me, telling me that he wanted to tell his story so that I would in turn pass it on, in my writings, to others outside Japan. In this, he told me, he saw the hand of Kōbō Daishi at work; it was Daishi who had brought us together through the *henro* so that I could tell his story and thereby inform people outside Japan of the virtues and merits of the pilgrimage so that they, too, would visit Shikoku and become pilgrims and devotees.

"Shikoku sickness," return, repetition, attachment

Many years ago, while conversing with the late Oliver Statler, the American writer and pilgrimage enthusiast, we were both trying to articulate why we were so interested in the *henro* when he sighed and remarked simply, "It's addictive."[14] It was a remark I could identify with. (One reason this book has taken so long to finish is that I always wanted to go one more time to Shikoku to do more research. . . .) It also resonates with the remarks referred to in chapter 3 about the "Shikoku sickness" *(Shikoku byō)* that captivates pilgrims and brings them back there again and again. This "sickness" or addiction is something that has resonated through the history of the *henro*, making it for countless people not a transient activity that takes place just "out there" at pilgrimage sites, but a continuing, often obsessive, engagement and unending process.

The very structure of the *henro* facilitates and opens up the possibility of recurrent pilgrimage. Since the route circles the island, it effectively has no fixed or defined finishing point, unlike a linear pilgrimage. Hence it is quite feasible for those who have completed their circuits to simply carry on and still be on the pilgrimage. This can, indeed, be a tempting option that enables pilgrims to evade the troubling question of what to do next—or, indeed, the troubling feeling that may be engendered, especially for walkers, by a rapid return home by train, bus, or plane. Such dilemmas may be more acute in linear pilgrimages such as the Santiago Camino, where pilgrims effectively end at a goal. As Frey shows, pilgrims who walk to Santiago come to a finite end point and tend then to face the dilemma of returning home, normally by the rapid means of modern transport such as trains or planes. Such a sudden return back to the pace of the modern world can be disjunctive and disturbing to the extent that for one pilgrim from Lyon, France, cited by Frey, the possibility proved so disturbing that he turned round and walked home, doing the Camino in reverse and maintaining his association with it for a longer period.[15]

In Shikoku, pilgrims faced with this worry can keep on going and remain on the pilgrimage. While they have reached the end of their pilgrimages by reaching their last temple, they are still on a route and circuit that is in effect continuous, and hence they are as much at a starting as an end point—and hence have the choice, should they so wish, to just keep going onward. This is what Nakatsuka Mōhei did; he had clearly not resolved his troubles and was not ready to return home after he had walked the *henro* for the first time in 1865. At some point, too, the practice clearly became so addictive that he became permanently attached to the route and, like the bereaved returnee solider mentioned in chapter 5 who made his home under the Shikoku sky for thirty years, became a fixture of the *henro*, part of its moving landscape, until he died there in 1922. Nakatsuka and the returnee soldier are by no means isolated cases, for numerous other such examples can be found in Shikoku pilgrimage history—and in legend, both with the figure of Kōbō Daishi permanently wandering as a pilgrim and with the image of Emon Saburō, another archetypal permanent pilgrim who gave up his home to become a wanderer in search of Kōbō Daishi and who died, is buried on, and is part of the route. Figures such as Shinnen are also examples and role models for those who wish to devote their lives to the *henro*. The pilgrimage stones he and other similar pilgrims erected are also physical reminders of this tradition of permanent transience and engaged asceticism, exemplified by figures cited in chapter 4 such as Tada Emon, who did 136 pilgrimage circuits in the nineteenth century and died and was buried on the route in 1862. The "professional *henro*" cited in chapter 4 who lived on the road soliciting alms during the Tokugawa period also fall into this category.

The tradition of permanency and of attaching oneself to the route has continued throughout the modern era and is often linked to taking the Buddhist tonsure as a result of pilgrimage experiences in Shikoku. Here I will cite just a few examples of those who have done this. One example is the Rinzai Zen priest Yamamoto Genpō (1865–1961), who first went on the pilgrimage in 1888. Yamamoto had experienced severe personal loss and bereavement, and his early life was already full of suffering when, at the age of nineteen, he lost his eyesight. This catalog of suffering caused him to start visiting shrines and temples, seeking divine grace and assistance in his search for a way out of this pain. In 1888, at the age of twenty-three, his quest led him to the *henro*. It proved to be a dramatic experience, one he was drawn into repeating again and again, in all completing seven circuits of the route in the next three years until, at the age of twenty-six, an encounter with the head priest of Sekkeiji

(Temple 33) led him to take the Buddhist tonsure in the Rinzai Buddhist sect to which Sekkeiji belongs. Yamamoto thereafter devoted much of his life to the temple and pilgrimage, encouraging and helping the pilgrims who passed by. He became famous as a Buddhist teacher and in his teachings consistently emphasized the virtues of the *henro*, which he proclaimed as the best possible form of austerity and spiritual practice. He also continued to do the *henro* regularly, in all walking it seventeen times, the last when he was ninety-five, the year before he died.[16]

Others, too, have come to Shikoku as pilgrims and stayed there as priests, ranging from the pilgrim who transformed Saba Daishi from a wayside hall of worship into a prominent *bangai* in the post-1945 era and then passed the temple on to his son, who maintains the family tradition of pilgrimage, to the scholar-priest Kiyoyoshi Eitoku, who came to Shikoku as a pilgrim in his twenties in 1974. Kiyoyoshi developed a fascination with the pilgrimage, took the tonsure as a Shingon priest, and stayed thereafter in Shikoku, running a small Kōbō Daishi temple in Niihama in Ehime Prefecture. Kiyoyoshi has dedicated his life to historical studies of the pilgrimage, is an acknowledged expert on pilgrimage stones, and has published journals and books on the *henro*, as well as providing valuable advice and help to researchers such as myself.

Home on the road

The above cases are of pilgrims who, through their encounter with the *henro*, have remained focused on it in ways that make it the center of their lives. At times this focus and dedication leads pilgrims to become like Nakatsuka, whose extended pilgrimage turned him into a permanent fixture on the route. I have encountered others who follow in this tradition of permanent mendicancy. On my first visit to Shikoku in February 1984, for instance, my wife and I met a pilgrim dressed in priestly robes who was pushing a handcart, which, he told us, contained all his worldly belongings. He was in his nineteenth year of pilgrimage and on his fifty-sixth circuit. He was affiliated with a Shingon temple at Kōyasan, where he had taken a Buddhist ordination with the Buddhist name of Unkai (Clouds and Sea). However, although he very occasionally visited Kōyasan, his real home was on the *henro*, and he spent most of his time there on an endless circuit of the island. Through his travels he had developed a regular circle of friends, both among temple priests and local people who lodged him when he passed by and provided him with food and other support. He had, he told us, initially done the *henro* once, liked it, and decided to go round again, until repetition and familiarity took over, with the *henro* becoming his home and *settai* his means of support. On this particular circuit he was traveling anticlockwise (*gyaku uchi*) "just to make a change," as he put it. His decision to change his mode of direction appeared to be an attempt to break away from a growing sense of familiarity with the pilgrimage and to give his pilgrimage-centered life a new impetus. Like the Tokugawa-era pilgrims who annoyed the Tosa authorities, he timed his travels so that he spent the winter period in the warmer climes of Kōchi Prefecture. Unkai not only lived on the *henro*, but as he told us, he expected to die on it too. He would thus forever remain part of the route, with his grave a marker and sign for other pilgrims.

Some years later, in spring 1991, I came across a handcart parked outside a house near Temple 1 on which was a sign indicating that the person who owned it was on his or her 126th pilgrimage circuit of Shikoku. I was unable to find the owner, who was doubtless resting at the home of a regular host, but I doubt if this was Unkai, since he would not have had time to complete seventy circuits in the seven years since I had met him. The cart and its sign, though, were further evidence of permanent itinerancy. Temple priests and others I have spoken to over the years have informed me of a number of such pilgrims who live as permanent residents on the route, often, like Unkai and the unseen pilgrim on his/her 126th circuit, with all their worldly possessions in a handcart.

Not all such permanent pilgrims travel alone. In October 1990 I met a husband and wife living in a small hut in the precincts of one of the pilgrimage temples near Matsuyama. They had given up their home in Fukuoka in Kyushu over three years earlier in order to come to Shikoku because the man, a designer and artist originally from Shikoku, was fed up with his work and the constraints of society and wanted to drop out by returning to his home island to do the pilgrimage while sketching and painting scenes along the way. His wife, who read palms and believed she had powers of divination, was equally keen to break away from everyday society so as to focus on her spiritual interests, so they put all their belongings in a handcart and set out, spending eighteen months walking around the pilgrimage, living in a tent, and begging for alms when necessary. It had taken them so long because whenever they came across a place that they liked, they would stop for a while for him to draw. By the time they completed the route they realized that they had no desire to go back to Fukuoka, as they were effectively at home in Shikoku. Since they had developed a rapport with the priest of one temple, they decided to stay there a while and, with his permission, had built a hut on the temple grounds, where they had (at the time I met them) been living for eighteen months. They supported themselves by helping around the temple, while he also sold his drawings to pilgrims and she performed divinations for a small fee. They planned to walk the pilgrimage again at some point (again sleeping in their tent) and, to all intents and purposes, were likely to remain on the pilgrimage for a long time to come. I have since come across other examples of couples doing something similar, either through reports from temple priests or, occasionally, through the mass media: in 2001, for example, I came across a newspaper article in Shikoku about another couple who were traveling around the *henro* with all their worldly goods in a handcart.

Inscribing your life on the pilgrimage

In this book I have at various points drawn attention to the role of Shikoku residents in making and supporting the *henro*. There are, of course, many people in Shikoku whose lifelong association is linked to their professional interest, as with those who have for generations run pilgrims' lodges, or temple priests whose families have for generations supported the *henro*. Yet often such people are driven not just by commercial or professional interest, but also by a deeply ingrained sense of historical consciousness into dedicating themselves to the *henro*. The pilgrims' lodge owner who ensures that all pilgrims become aware of the custom of washing Kōbō Daishi's feet (chapter 2) and the various family lineages (such as the Hatada family, who have for generations run Anrakuji [Temple 6]) who have cared for the temples and run temple lodges are just a few examples of people I have met in my research who clearly are deeply influenced by a sense of continuing a tradition that is part of their very being and heritage.

There are those, too, who develop a lifelong engagement with the *henro* because of its place in local culture and because of their sense of responsibility as local citizens. This is the case with Miyazaki Tateki, the founder of the Henro Michi Hozon Kyōryokukai, whose activities have been mentioned earlier in this book. Miyazaki is a native of Shikoku who lives just outside Matsuyama, where he made his living as a futon maker. Although from Shikoku, he had not been particularly involved in the *henro* until personal circumstances led him to walk the route, after which he underwent a major transformation, finding a new purpose in life centered on the *henro*.

I first interviewed him in February 1991, not long after he had formed the Henro Michi Hozon Kyōryokukai, which at the time was largely centered on his individual efforts. When I met him again in April 2000, the society was well established, with a regular membership and numerous organized activities. On the first occasion he was still running his futon business but spending most of his money and spare time on the pilgrimage; by 2000, he was in his mid-sixties, had retired, and spent all his time on the society and *henro*-related activities.

Miyazaki's initial engagement with the *henro* was pragmatic, due to sickness. In 1977 (which was his *yakudoshi*) he was forced to spend ten days in hospital, and while there, he determined to change his rather sedentary life, which he realized had weakened his health, and get more exercise. He decided to walk every day to build up his strength, and since there was a pilgrimage temple three or so kilometers from his home, he decided to use it as a goal to walk to and from every day. Subsequently he began to walk farther when time allowed, visiting the other local *henro* temples around Matsuyama and developing a regular circuit. As his health improved he began to think about walking the whole *henro*.

He did this in 1979, mainly for reasons of health. It was not easy, however, because at the time almost everyone went by bus, and the old pilgrimage paths were overgrown and hard to find. There were few wayside markers for walkers to follow, and the available guidebooks were primarily geared toward cars and buses and were unsuitable for walkers.[17] There were numerous places where he got lost or wished that there were signposts available. This annoyed him, and as he walked, he began to think about doing something about it. Initially, he told me, this was just a dream, but when he got home, he realized how renewed he had become through the pilgrimage, and this gave him the impetus to turn his dream into reality. He also felt that as a native of Shikoku he had a responsibility to help with the upkeep of the pilgrimage route, which was an intrinsic part of his island's culture. He felt annoyed that people in Shikoku had allowed the *henro* path to get to such a state and resolved to do something about it.

Thus he started to make signposts in his spare time and go around the route putting them up in relevant places. His first sign was put up in January 1987, not far from his home, indicating the path to Temple 52. He began channeling the money he earned into such activities and reoriented his business activities to this end; on one occasion, for example, he made fifty futon inscribed with the *Hannya Shingyō*, which he then sold to pilgrims' lodges and the like, using the money raised thereby to fund more signposts. By 1991 he had been around the route five times and put up, he estimated, some two thousand markers, usually small wooden boards with an arrow and red pilgrimage figure indicating the way. Both his house and van, at the time, were full of signs and the equipment needed to make and put them up. He spent most weekends driving around Shikoku to appropriate places, often then walking some way along footpaths with his signs, hammers, and other equipment to put the signs up in places useful for walkers. He usually slept overnight in the van during such weekend sorties. By March 2000 he had moved on from wooden to stone markers, putting up his first *henro ishi* next to one of Shinnen's remaining stones. His turn to stone markers is mainly because they last far longer than wooden ones. Reflecting on the fact that many of Shinnen's stones from the seventeenth century can still be seen, he feels that if he does the same, his influence and activities will last down the generations and be indelibly carved into the Shikoku landscape for centuries to come.

Although Miyazaki's initial motivation for doing the *henro* was pragmatic, he now feels a deep sense of gratitude (to Kōbō Daishi, to the gods and buddhas, and to his ancestors) for being able to devote himself to the *henro*. He has spent much time studying maps and texts to ascertain where the old *henro* path might run, especially in areas where it has been lost as new roads have been built. In his van he also carries a variety of tools and equipment for clearing paths, and he often spends weekends clearing and opening up new paths, as well as putting up markers. He founded the Henro Michi Hozon Kyōryokukai in order to support and publicize his activities, and it has grown steadily in membership. In 1991 it was virtually a one-man show, but by 2000 he had thirty dedicated activists working with him on his projects, such as weekend path-clearing activities, which are carried out by groups of volunteers, while numerous others participate occasionally in the group's activities.

In 1990 Miyazaki produced the walkers' guidebook mentioned in chapter 5, which has proved so successful. Its sales have provided him with a steady income stream that has, in turn, enabled him to give up his futon business and concentrate solely on the Henro Michi Hozon Kyōryokukai, which has prospered as a result. When I met him in 1991 he had one van, which he used for his futon business and, on weekends, for his pilgrimage signpost erecting activities. By April 2000 he had several vans.

The success of Miyazaki's guidebook has led to other publications as well, including a special guidebook for people intent on organizing and running pilgrimage groups, which contains detailed information on routes, buses, trains, local transport, and the like. Other publications of his include a colorful guidebook for walkers edited under the auspices of the Henro Michi Hozon Kyōryokukai and an account of the *henro* published under his own name.[18] During the 1990s, too, he began to organize and lead *henro* walking tours, and by spring 2000 he had led 1,348 people on such tours, each of which was a nine-day, eight-night trip along part of the route. Until 1999 he led six such tours per year, but at the time I met him again in April 2000, he had just stopped doing so because of knee problems.

He remains very active, however. The success of his work and guidebooks has made him a well-known figure, and he is often interviewed or featured in the media as a result, which further enables him to publicize his activities and attract more supporters and helpers. He continues to develop plans, ranging from a *henro* guidebook for people of retirement age, to putting up more stone markers, to building a memorial tower for the spirits of all who have died on the *henro*. He is also engaged in further fund-raising campaigns to finance more path clearances.

Miyazaki has, through his activities, made himself a prominent public authority on the *henro*, and he uses this position to express his opinions widely. For Miyazaki the essence of the *henro* is found in the path itself and in the spaces between, rather than primarily at, the sites. This essence is encountered through walking, and hence his mission is to get more people to walk the pilgrimage. He considers the pilgrimage primarily an ascetic exercise related to traditional Japanese folk culture. Indeed, he affirms the image of the *henro* as a manifestation of Japanese tradition with an almost nationalist fervor: he was strongly critical, in our most recent interview, of "Western materialism," which he believes has permeated Japan, undermined its culture, and led to the decline of traditional activities such as walking the *henro*.

His criticisms also extend to bus pilgrims, to *sendatsu* who do not walk (and who are thus not, in his view, really authentic pilgrims), and to the Shikoku Reijōkai, which he thinks places too much emphasis on the temples and not enough on the route and which he thinks has failed to encourage walkers. Despite such criticisms, however, he maintains good relations with the temples and, in 1999, received an award of thanks from the Reijōkai in honor of his achievements; the plaque is proudly framed in his home. Moreover, although he has criticized the Reijōkai, its officials whom I have spoken to pay warm tribute to his endeavors and regard him as an important influence in increasing public interest in the *henro* and in assisting in the recent rise in pilgrim numbers, especially of those going by foot.

Pilgrimage has clearly framed Miyazaki's identity and become the focus of his life in recent years. He is also deeply conscious of the historical legacy of the *henro* and keeps meticulous records of the Henro Michi Hozon Kyōryokukai, which he intends to place in a local museum so that its records will be preserved for later generations. This sense of historical consciousness leads him to identify strongly with the traditions established by seminal figures of the past such as Shinnen. He thus sees himself in a similar context, as someone who has dedicated his life to the *henro* and has made it his raison d'être and who is creating, like Shinnen three centuries earlier, a new series of footsteps for pilgrims of future generations to follow.

Hierarchy, status, empowerment

The reasons pilgrims devote their lives to the pilgrimage may be as varied as the pilgrims themselves, although several points touched on in this chapter may be suggested as relevant. One theme that comes through in just about every story related here is the "addictive" nature of the pilgrimage, which causes people to go back again and again physically and/or emotionally and makes them not want to let go but—as in the cases of Nakatsuka, Unkai, and the couple mentioned earlier—make their homes on the pilgrimage path. Another theme is that doing the pilgrimage again and again is seen as a means of continually improving oneself spiritually, a point made by Tabuchi Yoshio when explaining to me why he did it so many times (see chapter 3), and is linked also to Buddhist notions of repeating practices over and over again as a means of spiritual advancement. Yet another is faith in Kōbō Daishi, which is evident in the stories and narratives of Tsujita and Tabuchi, although less so in those of Miyazaki and others.

Another factor that plays a part with some pilgrims is that repeated performances provide them with a sense of status and empowerment; Tabuchi's special position as an exalted *sendatsu* and mentor comes from his commitment to and multiple performances of the *henro*. Nakatsuka in earlier times similarly became revered as a permanent pilgrim, and people would offer homage to him as he passed by, while permanent pilgrims such as Unkai have become sufficiently well known to provide them with a network of support for their travels. Miyazaki, too, has acquired public status and recognition and remains confident of a place in pilgrimage history because of his dedicated pilgrimage activities.

When status is related to performance, it can generate a sense of competition, which in turn is a factor in encouraging pilgrims to keep going; I have mentioned in chapter 2 how keen Nakatsuka was on commemorating particular numbers of circuits he had completed, especially when surpassing Tada's 136th circuit. I have heard of pilgrims who, in the modern day and assisted by the rapid nature of modern transport, have done the *henro* over two hundred times and who are clearly driven also by a sense of competition to increase these totals and challenge Nakatsuka's "record."

Such multiple performances have created a set of hierarchic values and relations that are also evident and formally stated in the different colors of *fuda* that pilgrim's carry and in the rankings of at the *sendatsu* system. I do not suggest that pilgrims travel numerous times only because of a desire to acquire status, for, as has been seen, a variety of factors play their role in making pilgrims—from Tsujita, with his sense of spiritual devotion and guidance from Kōbō Daishi, to the couple who found their true home on the Shikoku road—recurrent or permanent pilgrims. Nonetheless, I think it is important to draw attention to these hierarchic issues since they can be a relevant factor when considering figures such as Tabuchi, Miyazaki, and Nakatsuka, all of whom have acquired enhanced status through the *henro*. The interest in status and hierarchy is also evident (as is the continuing tendency for people to repeat the *henro* many times) in the growing numbers of *sendatsu* and in the keenness of those who acquire this rank to gain promotions, issues touched on in chapter 5.

While such notions of hierarchy are deeply entrenched in the *henro*, they do not sit easily alongside the idealized notions in which all pilgrims are equal and one with Kōbō Daishi, or with the idealized images of pilgrimage as envisaged by Turner in his concept of *communitas*. This does not mean that equality and *communitas*, in which all pilgrims are equal, are nonexistent in Shikoku; indeed, as has been seen in the context of the pilgrims' clothing, such concepts are well represented in the symbolic constructions of the pilgrimage, while numerous people from Tomoko to Takamure have emphasized the importance of equality among pilgrims. The point is, feelings of commonality exist side by side with hierarchic, status-oriented impulses, in a further indication that one cannot see, in pilgrimage, just a dynamic toward equality and the dissolving of structures amongst pilgrims, or just a tendency toward contest and the creation of status differences. Rather, the often tense juxtaposition of the dynamics of status and equality, and of structure and its dissolution, are illustrative of how the *henro* can encompass and manifest ambivalent and multiple meanings simultaneously.

Repetition in comparative contexts

The numbers of pilgrims who repeat their journeys, who do the *henro* over and over again, and who stay permanently affixed to the route are a striking feature of the *henro*. This does not necessarily mean that Shikoku should be seen as exceptional in the study of pilgrimage. There is evidence, for example, that repeated visits are common on some other pilgrimage routes in Japan, in which pilgrims weave the practice of pilgrimage into their everyday lives. Priests I have talked to who run temples on other Kōbō Daishi–centred pilgrimages, notably the Sasaguri pilgrimage in Kyushu and the one around the island of Shōdoshima in the Inland Sea, tell me that many of those who visit the sites do so repeatedly, and I have met several pilgrims on Shōdoshima who have done this admittedly shorter route (both it and Sasaguri can be done in under a week by foot or two or three days by transport) over a hundred times.[19] Osada Kōichi, one of the Waseda University researchers whose work I have cited several times, told me recently that while doing research on the Chichibu pilgrimage not far from Tokyo, he met a man who visited temples on this route every Monday. I have not, however, come across cases in any of these routes (or others in Japan) where pilgrims become so attached that they become permanent fixtures on the route, and this may be a particular facet of Shikoku not found elsewhere in Japan.

One can, of course, find examples in other cultures of people who become engaged in eternal pilgrimages as wandering ascetics (the tradition of holy mendicancy and renunciation in India comes most readily to mind) and of pilgrimage sites that are seen not simply as sacred places to visit in a transient manner, but as locations in which to dwell. Diana Eck, for example, has drawn attention to the phenomenon of Kashivasi, pilgrims who come to the Indian pilgrimage center of Varanasi (Kashi) and then settle there so as to remain permanently within the sacred center.[20] Frey, too, has drawn attention to the idea of pilgrimage as a lifelong activity through examples of people who dedicate their lives to the Santiago Camino by, for instance, coming to live along the route, working in pilgrimage hostels, and joining pilgrimage confraternities.[21] Indeed, in rather similar terms to my comments about "Shikoku sickness" and the "addiction" of Shikoku, Frey writes of pilgrims who talk about the "pilgrimage bug" and of "serial" pilgrims who have become "hooked" on the Camino. Indeed, she even cites a pilgrim who described the Camino in terms reminiscent of Statler's comment about Shikoku: "*It's addictive.*"[22]

Rather than pursuing the issue, however, Frey appears disturbed by its implications, worrying about the "danger" of repetition and fearing that the pilgrimage might become a habit, something well known and safe, "rather than a stimulant for self-exploration."[23] I do not find this a real "fear," however, based on my experiences of meeting "permanent pilgrims" who have grounded their lives in the *henro* and made Shikoku a second home. This does not mean that the *henro* has necessarily, for them, become safe and lacking in scope for self-exploration. Certainly there is the potential for those who become permanent pilgrims or center their lives on the *henro* to enter what could be seen as rather familiar and comfortable territory. Multiple pilgrims such as Tabuchi, when they visit Shikoku, are not entering a world that stands apart or at an opposite end of a spectrum from their homes so much as going into very familiar territory where they know many people and have many friends and familiar points of reference. Nakatsuka and Unkai, in permanently circling the island, equally passed through landscapes that became familiar through repetition—so much so that Unkai felt tempted to go round the other way for a change. Indeed, the example of Unkai shows that if "permanent pilgrims" do find themselves getting overly familiar with the landscape of their pilgrimage, they can readily change it and make the pilgrimage anew by going round anticlockwise, a possibility not open to those following linear pilgrimages such as Santiago.

There is clearly a sense in which the ostensible gap or opposition between "home" and the pilgrimage arena has been reduced or eliminated through recurrent practice and in which the seeming "other" of pilgrimage has become the deeply familiar. Yet to consider that this necessarily limits the scope for self-exploration or development is highly problematic. For a start, it implies that self-exploration and development cannot be pursued in the realms of the familiar. It also overlooks the point made by Tabuchi in his comment (see chapter 3) that each journey was a new one that offered a sense of renewal and showed the *henro* in a new light. This is something that has come through to me in my dealings with pilgrims who have done the *henro* many times or who have devoted their lives to it. When I interviewed Tsujita and Miyazaki, for example, I found myself dealing with people who were energized by the *henro* and who were constantly finding new meanings and stimuli in it. Miyazaki was constantly, as his various plans and ideas for further developing the activities of his pilgrimage society indicate, looking for and finding new challenges and ways to develop his engagement with the *henro*, while Tsujita, even in his eighties, was still so enthused and fired by notions of miraculous intercession that he wanted to engage with a foreign researcher in order to enhance awareness of the pilgrimage. The *henro* was, indeed, familiar to them, but it was also exciting and provided a continuing stimulus spurring them on to new meanings and feelings. As the example of Unkai shows, too, the potential for change within the realms of the familiar is also ever present, enabling recurrent pilgrims to gain new perspectives on their journeys.

Binary divides and problematic assumptions

There is an irony in the idea of a pilgrim—often considered a transient, in a liminal state away from home—being or becoming permanently "at home" as a pilgrim. The problem, however, lies in the assumption that pilgrimage is a transient event framed around a binary divide between "home" and "pilgrimage site" and between movement and stasis.[24] This is a problem that has developed in the study of pilgrimage especially, I would argue, because of the ways in which fieldwork studies of pilgrimage have been carried out.

While notions of a binary divide may appear to be paramount when one locates oneself at pilgrimage centers and observes pilgrims in the midst of their travels, they are not always sustained when one examines the ways in which pilgrimage fits into the wider contexts of their lives. Rather, as this chapter has indicated, there are many people for whom the *henro* has become the central element in their lives, for whom "home" and the pilgrimage site have become one and for whom the "stasis" of home is effectively transformed into the "movement" of pilgrimage. For such pilgrims—and for those also who have had such transformational experiences that they have returned either physically or emotionally again and again to Shikoku—the *henro* has become their central focus, a way of life and a path of permanency. For some this permanency is manifested in their continuing, incessant circumambulation of the island; for others it means repeated visits interspersed with constant thoughts about and preparations for the pilgrimage or the establishment of organized structures and institutions to maintain the tradition of pilgrimage and its related customs within local communities, as has been seen with the examples of the Arita Settaikō and the Shiga Shingyōkai. In all such cases, pilgrimage has become an unending process, one that is neither a marginal offshoot from a broader religious tradition nor a one-off event or rupture in the normal lives of its participants. As the evidence of Shikoku's permanent pilgrims and its pilgrimage-centered faith associations indicates, pilgrimage cannot be viewed solely through the lenses of marginality and liminality or as a one-off activity. Rather than being a practice existing as an appendage on the margins of mainstream Japanese religious life, the Shikoku pilgrimage is something far more central, a core motif in the social and religious lives of the pilgrims. As such, pilgrimage may be as much about continuities and providing a centralizing theme to its participants' lives and religious orientations as it is about departures, disjunctions, and transience.

Conclusion

This book has discussed how a major pilgrimage has been shaped and made historically and, in the present, how pilgrims have helped make it through their travels and practices and how the pilgrimage has impacted on and become part of the lives of its participants. The pilgrimage culture I have described, with its history, narratives, processes of development from ascetic traces to contemporary commercial pilgrimages, and participants ranging from local people to pilgrims from afar, is particular to Shikoku, which, like any pilgrimage, is in such respects unique. It is always, of course, inexact science to build or posit universal models from single cases and from cases that are by nature specific to particular cultural settings. Yet studies of the *henro* do have something to add to general understandings of pilgrimage, and they also indicate where studies of pilgrimage require further development. The importance of landscape (which, as I have argued, should not be seen as consisting just of the physical terrain) in the construction of pilgrimage is a topic that, as was noted in chapter 2, has been somewhat overlooked until recently and is something that requires further consideration and development in the future. As my references throughout this book (e.g., in chapter 6, when I note how walkers perceive the landscape as they travel) to the influence of the ever-changing pilgrimage landscape indicate, this is a central element within pilgrimage, one that is in a continuing state of change—change that is brought about by pilgrims and by changing conditions and influences and that influences how subsequent pilgrims view and experience the pilgrimage.

The role of local populations (including legislative authorities) in the construction and processes of pilgrimage is another such area where the Shikoku case has vital things to say, reminding us that pilgrimage may not necessarily be just, or even primarily, about traveling to far places. As this volume has shown, the *henro* may be a major national pilgrimage, but it is also very much part of local culture, with a significant number of its pilgrims drawn from its own region and with important traditions (e.g., *settai*) that have been supported by local people and that have played an important part in the development and construction of the pilgrimage. Too often the influences of the "local" have been either neglected or somewhat sidelined in the study of pilgrimage, but, as my study of Shikoku shows, to do this is to potentially neglect some of the most important formative and creative influences in the shaping of pilgrimage. This does not mean that there is necessarily a binary contrast between the pilgrimage as local and as national; it is both at once, with Shikoku residents being able to support and help make their local pilgrimage while also recognizing its national significance, and people from beyond the island able to experience the influences of local tradition within the context of a pilgrimage that is important for them in terms of national cultural identity. Equally, as I emphasized in the previous chapter, the widely assumed notion that pilgrimage is a transitory, often marginal, event centered on pilgrims and goals that are "out there," away from the normative parameters of life, is challenged by the tradition of repeated pilgrimages and permanent pilgrims in Shikoku and by the extent to which the pilgrimage has become a way of life and central organizing principle in the lives of so many of its participants.

The Shikoku case certainly adds further evidence to the growing understanding that grand narratives and overarching theories of pilgrimage (many of which, in my view, have displayed too much of a Western-centric bias and have been based predominantly around Christian pilgrimage)[1] may themselves be problematic and incapable of widespread application.[2] As I indicated in chapter 1 and elsewhere, while Shikoku provides some evidence to partially substantiate some prominent, overarching theories of pilgrimage—for instance, the theories of *communitas* and contest—it also indicates various problems with such theories and demonstrates how, on their own, they may be insufficient as modes of analysis. This does not mean that I find such theories (or, indeed, theories that focus specifically on the individual and on pilgrimage as an individual journey) to be wrong. Indeed, as my frequent dwelling on them indicates, they have been helpful as I have developed my thinking about pilgrimage. The problem is that, viewed from the perspective of my research on Shikoku, they are not enough on their own to encompass the complexities of the *henro*.

My account shows that not only does the *henro* not fit neatly into any of the general theoretical structures that have been posited for pilgrimage, but that it tends—to make use of the terms used by Naquin and Yü, cited in the introduction—toward the chaotic and cacophonous. It is (to return to Dubisch's term) "unbounded" in that it cannot fit into particular disciplinary frameworks or geographical locations; a pilgrimage to a shrine or to a sacred location or region such as Shikoku is not, in other words, just about that shrine or place, but involves much that relates to local identity, home, and (as my discussions of how pilgrimage as a practice may be passed on through the generations shows) family and inherited circumstances. Nor does the notion of a binary divide between home and pilgrimage site work in the context of the *henro*, in which pilgrims may continually circle the island as transients and outsiders yet create a set of familiar footsteps and exist within an "other" world that is simultaneously home.

Such themes point to an ambivalence in the *henro*—an ambivalence that has been a recurrent feature of this book, seen, for example, in my discussions of how the pilgrimage may be both "familiar" (to locals, in terms of the images of cultural heritage or of repeated visits to a location that becomes, in effect, "home") and "exotic" (the pilgrim as outsider, as dressed for death and apart from this realm), and in images such as those of the pilgrim as sacred thief and contagious saint and, in modern times, as symbol of cultural tradition and bringer of economic benefits. The tensions between the egalitarian structures in which pilgrims are equal and one with Kōbō Daishi and the hierarchic implications of the *sendatsu* system and of those who acquire special status through performing the pilgrimage many times are further signs of this ambivalence. So, too, is the question, evident in the differing behavior, perceptions, and experiences of bus and foot pilgrims as well as of temple priests, about where the focus of the pilgrimage lies, in the sites or the route—a dilemma and ambivalence that have different answers depending on factors such as one's mode of travel and locus of perception.[3] The centrality of the *henro* to Shikoku, both culturally and as a linking route through the island, and yet as marginal, skirting its power centers and clinging to its edges, is another such point of ambivalence, which, in the new millennium, may be seen also in the expense and speed of helicopter pilgrimage tours when, down below, a new wave of pilgrims who have lost their jobs, have no money, and are dependent on begging may be walking the *henro* path.

These ambivalent images and tendencies do not constitute binary oppositions. While the pilgrimage can be local, it is simultaneously national, and while pilgrims could be treated as sacred, they could simultaneously be seen as (potential) thieves and carriers of disease. The seeming oppositions and divergent themes within the *henro* exist within one framework in which the well-off traveling by bus or even helicopter, the poor begging for sustenance, the pilgrim doing his or her once-in-a-lifetime pilgrimage by bus with companions from their hometown, and the permanent pilgrim pushing his or her handcart around the route can each participate in the way that suits their purposes, needs, and, of course, wallets. In such terms, each person and group can organize, experience, and interpret the pilgrimage in the context of their own lives and draw from it meanings appropriate for their purposes. The locus of Kagita Chūsaburō's life-transforming experiences and Tsujita Shōyū's realm of miracles is also the scenic place where Mr. Koyama can get away from his family and enjoy his hobby of photography, where NHK broadcasters and others can weave images of cultural tradition and heritage, and where out-of-work and retired Japanese people can engage in a personal challenge that has, they claim, little or nothing to do with matters of faith.

I have argued in this book that all these can exist together because of the encompassing nature of the *henro*, which, for all its manifestations of divergent themes, has the capacity to incorporate and allow all such diverse themes to coexist without contradiction within one framework and to provide each participant with personal meanings relevant to his/her situation. The *henro* as a linking route tying together all aspects of the island and landscape, bringing together all participants within its framework, is underpinned and held together by some potent unifying symbols, most notably the figure of Kōbō Daishi and the belief that all in the pilgrimage are "with" him and are "pilgrims together." Such symbols and concepts provide a sense of shared consciousness that, in my view, largely overrides the numerous points of conflict within the pilgrimage. This point especially came to me when I stood in the hallway of Miyazaki Tateki's house in Matsuyama in April 2000 and saw proudly displayed on his wall a framed certificate of thanks and recognition for his devotion to the pilgrimage, which had been given to him by the Shikoku Reijōkai. Next to it was a photograph of him receiving the award from Reijōkai officials at the annual *sendatsu* general meeting. Miyazaki, as I have noted, has been very critical of the temples and the *sendatsu* system and has spoken vociferously about how, in his view, the *henro* is centered on the route and on walking between them rather than on the temples. Reijōkai officials with whom I raised the question of honoring a vocal critic replied that while they did not agree with his views, they respected him and valued the work he had done for the *henro* and on behalf of all pilgrims. The award was recognition of this. Miyazaki, too, when I asked him about his relations with temples, stated that he had good relations with individual priests, and while he criticized the Reijōkai, he valued the award it had given him and was proud to have been so honored, and he recognized that the Reijōkai, in its own way and from the context of its interests and perceptions, worked hard on behalf of the pilgrimage. Both officials of the Reijōkai and Miyazaki recognized that they shared common ground in and through the *henro*. They were all together, *dōgyō*, in the pilgrimage even as they disagreed on most matters to do with it.

It is through an understanding of these encompassing dimensions and a recognition of how the pilgrimage thereby offers pilgrims and participants scope to engage in their pilgrimages in the ways they seek to so do and to find and impart their meanings within the often chaotic and cacophonous landscape of the *henro* that the study of pilgrimages such as Shikoku might be best approached. In order to understand these encompassing dimensions, it has been important to approach the *henro* from a variety of perspectives and in a multidisciplinary way that incorporates and brings together diachronic and synchronic approaches and that recognizes that pilgrimage is not just about one set of participants or just about the process and the social, group, and individual dynamics of going to particular places. Rather, as I have indicated, the *henro* has multiple dimensions in which a variety of complex factors, including landscape, emotion, the traces of history and legend, as well as the acts and attitudes of participants, from pilgrims to locals, to priests and commercial interest groups and much else besides, interweave to make the pilgrimage what it is at any given point.

All of these elements play their parts in a continuing process in and through which the pilgrimage is constantly developing and creating meanings for its participants. All who are involved in the pilgrimage—whether an individual pilgrim in a tour party whose presence may be fleeting and whose impact, on the surface, may be slight but whose footsteps and cumulative presence over the ages have made their mark on the pilgrimage landscape, an innkeeper passing on pilgrimage customs, a tour operator insisting that his pilgrim-customers maintain traditional clothing customs, or *sendatsu* repeating miracle stories to busloads of pilgrims—are engaged in this process, adding and helping to make the pilgrimage and thereby create meanings both for themselves and those who follow in their wake.

The process of making pilgrimages and of creating meanings is not static. As pilgrims travel and interact with each other and with the sites and route; as priests run their temples, preach sermons to, and engage with the pilgrims; as bus companies run package tours and think of new innovations; as route changes, new bridges, highways, and cable cars give pilgrims new and different views of the landscape around them; as legends develop and miracle stories are retold; as temples, regional authorities, and commercial concerns develop new modes of publicity, customs (e.g., the idea of the pilgrimage as a fourfold journey to enlightenment, which has become a prevalent theme in modern pilgrimage experience), and goods for pilgrims to acquire, they all add to the *henro* and help (re)make its landscape. It is through the multiplicity of meanings thereby created that the pilgrimage is understood by participants, and it is through the seeming chaos and cacophony of sounds, practices, beliefs, legends, miraculous tales, tourism, and the like that the complexity of pilgrimage—a complexity that cannot be reduced to simple theoretical narratives—may be viewed and understood as a continuing process of meanings that are made and remade with every act of every one of its participants.

Appendix 1

The Eighty-Eight Temples on the Shikoku Pilgrimage (in Numerical Order)

The following table gives the numbers, names, ideograms, main images of worship, and sectarian affiliations of the eighty-eight pilgrimage sites. It should be noted that some sites have more than one main image of worship (e.g., Temple 37 [Iwamotoji] has five, while Temple 13 [Dainichiji] has two). Several temples have the same name, notably Temples 4, 13, and 28—all called Dainichiji and all enshrining Dainichi, the main image of worship in Shingon—and Temples 15, 29, 59, and 80, which were the four regional Kokubunji temples and all four of which bear that name. Some temples have both an official and a popular name (e.g., Temples 24, 25, and 26 have both, the former of which is rarely used compared to the latter). In such cases I give the official title with the popular name in parentheses (and similarly with their ideograms).

One point of some interest is that several temples enshrine Shakuson (i.e., Shakyamuni, the historical Buddha), a figure rarely found as a main image in Japan but found as a main image in five of the Shikoku temples. Otherwise, the main images are of popular figures in the Buddhist pantheon such as Dainichi, Jizō, Miroku, Amida, Fudō, Kannon, and Yakushi, as well as Daitsūchishō, a rather rare figure of worship enshrined as the main image of Temple 55.

Temples in Tokushima (formerly Awa, the *hosshin* temples, 1–23)

Number	Name	Ideograms	Main image	Sect
1	Ryōzenji	霊山寺	Shakuson	Shingon
2	Gokurakuji	極楽寺	Amida	Shingon
3	Konsenji	金泉寺	Shakuson	Shingon
4	Dainichiji	大日寺	Dainichi	Shingon
5	Jizōji	地蔵寺	Jizō	Shingon
6	Anrakuji	安楽寺	Yakushi	Shingon
7	Jūrakuji	十楽寺	Amida	Shingon
8	Kumadaniji	熊谷寺	Kannon	Shingon

continued

Number	Name	Ideograms	Main image	Sect
9	Hōrinji	法輪寺	Shakuson	Shingon
10	Kirihataji	切幡寺	Kannon	Shingon
11	Fujiidera	藤井寺	Yakushi	Rinzai Zen
12	Shōsanji	焼山寺	Kokūzō	Shingon
13	Dainichiji	大日寺	Dainichi and Kannon	Shingon
14	Jōrakuji	常楽寺	Miroku	Shingon
15	Kokubunji	国分寺	Yakushi	Sōtō Zen
16	Kannonji	観音寺	Kannon	Shingon
17	Idoji	井戸寺	Yakushi	Shingon
18	Onzanji	恩山寺	Yakushi	Shingon
19	Tatsueji	立江寺	Jizō	Shingon
20	Kakurinji	鶴林寺	Jizō	Shingon
21	Tairyūji	太龍寺	Kokūzō	Shingon
22	Byōdōji	平等寺	Yakushi	Shingon
23	Yakuōji	薬王寺	Yakushi	Shingon

Temples in Kōchi (formerly Tosa, the *shugyō* temples, 24–39)

Number	Name	Ideograms	Main image	Sect
24	Hotsumisakiji (Higashi-dera)	最御崎寺 (東寺)	Kokūzō	Shingon
25	Shinshōji (Tsudera)	津照寺 (津寺)	Jizō	Shingon
26	Kongōchōji (Nishidera)	金剛頂寺 (西寺)	Yakushi	Shingon
27	Kōnimineji	神峰寺	Kannon	Shingon
28	Dainichiji	大日寺	Dainichi	Shingon
29	Kokubunji	国分寺	Kannon	Shingon
30	Zenrakuji	善楽寺	Amida	Shingon
31	Chikurinji	竹林寺	Monju	Shingon
32	Zenjibuji	禅師峰寺	Kannon	Shingon
33	Sekkeiji	雪蹊寺	Yakushi	Rinzai Zen
34	Tanemaji	種間寺	Yakushi	Shingon
35	Kiyotakiji	清滝寺	Yakushi	Shingon
36	Shōryūji	青龍寺	Fudō	Shingon
37	Iwamotoji	岩本寺	Fudō, Kannon, Yakushi, Jizō, Amida	Shingon
38	Kongōfukuji	金剛福寺	Kannon	Shingon
39	Enkōji	延光寺	Kannon	Shingon

Temples in Ehime (formerly Iyo, the *bodai* temples, 40–65)

Number	Name	Ideograms	Main image	Sect
40	Kanjizaiji	観自在寺	Yakushi	Shingon
41	Ryūkōji	龍光寺	Kannon	Shingon
42	Butsumokuji	仏木寺	Dainichi	Shingon
43	Meisekiji	明石寺	Kannon	Tendai
44	Taihōji	大宝寺	Kannon	Shingon
45	Iwayaji	岩屋寺	Fudō	Shingon
46	Jōruriji	浄瑠璃寺	Yakushi	Shingon
47	Yasakaji	八坂寺	Amida	Shingon
48	Sairinji	西林寺	Kannon	Shingon
49	Jōdoji	浄土寺	Shakuson	Shingon
50	Hantaji	繁多寺	Yakushi	Shingon
51	Ishiteji	石手寺	Yakushi	Shingon
52	Taisanji	太山寺	Kannon	Shingon
53	Enmyōji	円明寺	Amida	Shingon
54	Enmeiji	延命寺	Fudō	Shingon
55	Nankōbō	南光坊	Daitsūchishō	Shingon
56	Taisanji	泰山寺	Jizō	Shingon
57	Eifukuji	栄福寺	Amida	Shingon
58	Senyūji	仙遊寺	Kannon	Shingon
59	Kokubunji	国分寺	Yakushi	Shingon
60	Yokomineji	横峰寺	Dainichi	Shingon
61	Kōonji	香園寺	Dainichi	Shingon
62	Hōjuin	宝寿寺	Kannon	Shingon
63	Kichijōji	吉祥寺	Bishamonten	Shingon
64	Maegamiji	前神寺	Amida	Shingon
65	Sankakuji	三角寺	Kannon	Shingon

Temples in Kagawa (formerly Sanuki, the *nehan* temples, 66–88)

Number	Name	Ideograms	Main image	Sect
66	Unpenji	雲辺寺	Kannon	Shingon
67	Daikōji	大興寺	Yakushi	Shingon
	(Komatsuoji)	(小松尾寺)		
68	Jinnein	神恵院	Amida	Shingon
69	Kannonji	観音寺	Kannon	Shingon
70	Motoyamaji	本山寺	Kannon	Shingon
71	Iyataniji	弥谷寺	Kannon	Shingon
72	Mandaraji	曼荼羅寺	Dainichi	Shingon
73	Shusshakaji	出釈迦寺	Shakuson	Shingon

continued

Number	Name	Ideograms	Main image	Sect
74	Kōyamaji	甲山寺	Yakushi	Shingon
75	Zentsūji	善通寺	Yakushi	Shingon
76	Konzōji	金倉寺	Yakushi	Shingon
77	Dōryūji	道隆寺	Yakushi	Shingon
78	Gōshōji	郷照寺	Amida	Jishū
79	Kōshōji (Tennōji)	高照寺 (天皇寺)	Kannon	Shingon
80	Kokubunji	国分寺	Kannon	Shingon
81	Shiramineji	白峰寺	Kannon	Shingon
82	Negoroji	根香寺	Kannon	Shingon
83	Ichinomiyaji	一宮寺	Kannon	Shingon
84	Yashimaji	屋島寺	Kannon	Shingon
85	Yakuriji	八栗寺	Kannon	Shingon
86	Shidoji	志度寺	Kannon	Shingon
87	Nagaoji	長尾寺	Kannon	Shingon
88	Ōkuboji	大窪寺	Yakushi	Shingon

Appendix 2

Explanations for the Number of Temples on the *Henro*

There is no clear evidence as to why there are 88 temples on the pilgrimage. Nor is there any authoritative source to indicate when the *henro* became fixed as an 88-stage pilgrimage. There are a number of popular theories and ideas that can be found in pilgrimage literature and that people associated with the pilgrimage may well express when asked about origins. I have heard most of the theories set out below from at least one, and often many, priests, pilgrims, or other participants during the course of my research.

All these theories start from the assumption that the number 88 must have some significance (in the same way the number 33, with its allusions to the Lotus Sutra, does in the context of Kannon pilgrimages) and that this was not a random but a deliberate number chosen for the *henro*. The guidebook produced by Yamashita Hirotaka gives four standard explanations for the number while emphasizing that he has no idea which, if any, is correct (1984, 11). The four explanations are as follows.

- It is the combination of the *yakudoshi* (dangerous year/age) of a man (42), woman (33), and child (13) added together.
- It represents 88 evil passions *(bonnō)* that are to be eradicated before one can attain enlightenment; hence each temple represents the eradication of one passion.
- In China, Kūkai/Kōbō Daishi learned that the remains of the historical Buddha Shakyamuni had been placed in eight stupas. In Buddhist thought there are ten directions or realms, and Kūkai/Kōbō Daishi took the notion of these ten realms, in each of which he visualized eight such stupas, and added to them the original eight stupas of the historical Buddha to come to the figure 88, which he then designated as the correct figure for the number of temples on the pilgrimage.

- The number 88 derives from the ideogram for rice (*mai, kome* 米), whose constituent elements can be seen to produce the three ideograms 八十八 —i.e., 88.

Murakami Mamoru (1986, 136) suggests both the combination of *yakudoshi* ages and the number of stupas as possible explanations. He also argues that one early school of Buddhism in Japan (the Kūsha school, which was extant during Kūkai's life) spoke of there being 88 delusions (which equate to the evil passions mentioned by Yamashita)—32 in the *yokukai* (world of desires), 28 in the *shikikai* (phenomenal world, the world of form), and 28 in the *mūshikikai* (world of nonform). Thus the pilgrimage was constructed to provide a means of getting rid of these 88 delusions.

Kondō Yoshihiro, whose argument that the *henro* in effect was developed by Kumano ascetics and emanated out of the Kumano pilgrimage was introduced in chapter 4, suggests that while there were supposedly 99 *ōji* (stages of worship) along the Kumano pilgrim's way, in reality the number was less and might have been only 88; he cites text about Kumano that mentions just 88 such *ōji*. Thus Kondō suggests that the number itself might have been transplanted from Kumano (1982, 150–180)—a suggestion that remains speculative rather than grounded in the available evidence.

More recently, Matsuo Gōji (2002, 111–113, 130) has suggested—basing his comments mainly on inscriptions from the Kōya priest Kōhan contained in Hosoda Shūei's 1763 map, the earliest pilgrimage map of Shikoku—that esoteric Buddhism might provide the most plausible explanation for the number 88. Kōhan's inscription affirms that the number 88 stands for 88 evil passions and for the places through which these may be eradicated and also speaks of the *henro* as incorporating the ten Buddhist realms, each represented by the eight petals of the lotus on which sits a Buddha figure. This combination (ten lotuses with eight petals each plus eight buddhas) makes 88.

It seems most likely to me that the explanations that focus on Buddhist cosmology and the eradication of evil passions are the most likely—and that they probably emerged due to influences from Kōyasan and esoteric Buddhism. The number 88 became a part of the *henro* landscape in the seventeenth century, at a period (see chapter 4) when Shingon priests and others with connections to Kōyasan played a significant role in developing the pilgrimage. It would probably need some form of authority (in the guise of temple or sect priests) to be able to establish a fixed number and framework to the temple, and I find it hard to conceive that a "folk" explanation, such as the combination of *yakudoshi* numbers, could be so authoritative as to be widely adopted and accepted in this way. Hence my inclination is to consider that explanations centered on esoteric Buddhist ideas, and on the evil passions, are the most likely—although they remain unproven in empirical terms.

Appendix 3

Ways of Doing the Pilgrimage: Average Duration and Costs

The costs given here are in Japanese yen. To give an approximate idea of these prices in other currencies, as of January 2004 there were approximately 191 Japanese yen to the British pound and 106 yen to a U.S. dollar. Costs of lodging vary, but I base my estimates on *shukubō*, whose price in 2000 was fixed by the Reijō-kai at 5,500 yen per night (including evening meal and breakfast). In addition, at minimum one would require lunch, drinks, and other additional items; I am assuming that the average pilgrim is not going to do it as an austerity, beg, and sleep out. I would thus assume a general figure of 10,000 yen a day for all-in costs, although one could keep it lower by being parsimonious about food and other expenditures during the day.

Walking

This generally takes around forty to fifty days if walked at a reasonable pace— although many pilgrims now appear to get round more quickly still (see chapter 6). An average estimate of costs for walkers is around 400,000 yen (approximately 10,000 yen per day for forty days), although according to the Waseda Daigaku survey, close to 30 percent of walkers spent more than this (1997, 73). The same source indicates that only 2.4 percent of those going by car or bus spend anything like as much. This is because, of course, walkers spend far longer on the pilgrimage and hence their costs are incurred over almost four times as many days as bus or car pilgrims.

Bus

Bus pilgrimages usually take about ten to twelve days for an all-in-one tour of the sort Iyo Tetsu and others organize, or four shorter *ikkoku mairi* journeys. In *ikkoku mairi* bus pilgrimages, the pattern is usually to take around three to four full days per region, although Kōchi (Tosa) on some tours takes four to five days because of the greater distance that has to be covered.

It would cost, in 2000 terms, around 200,000–240,000 yen to do it by bus. Standard Iyo Tetsu all-in-one tours cost 218,000 yen, while their *ikkoku mairi* tours were around 60,000 yen each. To this the pilgrims would need to expend a small amount extra for additional snacks and foodstuffs and so on beyond the food provided at mealtimes.

Taxi and private car

Taxi tours depend on a quotation from the taxi company concerned, but firms I have spoken to consider that they can take a group of five pilgrims on a seven-to eight-day pilgrimage for less than the 218,000 yen per person quoted for Iyo Tetsu tours. The costs include the hire and overnight accommodation of a driver.

By private car, the amount varies depending on the number of passengers. A full carload of four or five people would travel most cheaply by this means. It would take around eight days or so by private car (taxis tend to be quicker because the drivers are usually well versed in the route), and I would estimate that each person would spend 10,000 yen or so a day on accommodation and basic foodstuffs, plus a share of petrol costs and occasional toll-road fees. In such terms, a figure of just over 100,000 yen per person would be likely.

Helicopter tours

Information gleaned in 2000 indicated that helicopter pilgrimage tours cost just over 1,000,000 yen in all and took three to four days (some time is spent in cars because helicopters are not allowed to fly over a number of the built-up areas where some of the temples are located).

For all these types of pilgrimage, one has to add the costs of getting to and from Shikoku—a cost that will escalate if one breaks the journey up into several trips, as *ikkoku mairi* bus pilgrims or walkers who do the *henro* in a series of stages would do.

NOTES

Introduction

1. The best times for travel in Japan are spring and early autumn, when the weather is generally warm and comfortable. By contrast, the period from June to early September is first extremely wet and then excessively hot and muggy, while winter is cold, with snow making the paths to temples in mountainous areas impassable. In earlier times, when Japan was largely agricultural, people found it difficult to get away from the land in early autumn because of the harvest; hence spring became the peak time for pilgrimage. Studies of pilgrimage in the present day indicate that the March–May period remains the main time for pilgrims to travel in Shikoku (see Satō Hisamitsu 1990a and 1990b).

2. As will be seen later, my choice of the words "cacophony" and "chaos" is influenced by their use by Susan Naquin and Chün Fang Yü in the introduction to their edited book on pilgrimage in China (Naquin and Yü 1992, 7).

3. This information came from Tanaka-san, an official of Iyo Tetsu, in an interview in Matsuyama, April 10, 2000.

1. Pilgrimage, Practice, Meanings: Making Pilgrimages in Shikoku

1. See Shinno (1980, 1991a, and 1991b; esp. 1991a, 19), who argues that pilgrimage is one of the great pillars of Japanese religion. Similar emphases on pilgrimage as a core theme in Japanese religious structure can be found in the works of Gorai (e.g., 1975, 1984, and 1989) and in Miyake 1980.

2. Of course, pilgrimages that may ostensibly focus on a single goal or center frequently have other sacred sites associated with them, which may be visited by pilgrims en route to the sacred goal. Along the Camino or Pilgrim's Way to Santiago de Compostela in Spain there are found numerous holy sites such as the

shrine of St. Foy at Conques, which pilgrims commonly visit (see Mullins 1974; Tate and Tate 1987). However, these sites are not obligatory calling places for pilgrims, unlike the designated sites on such Japanese routes.

3. E.g., one finds multiple site pilgrimages also in India (Bhardwaj 1973). However, the sheer numbers of such multiple-site pilgrimages in Japan make this a phenomenon that is perhaps unequaled anywhere else; see, e.g., the extensive lists in compendia such as Tsukuda 1981; Tahara et al. 1980; Daihōrinkaku henshūbu 1997; and Shiragi 1994, 206–271.

4. Shinto and Buddhism have a long history of interrelationship and interaction, and this has been manifest in pilgrimages, with certain types of route (e.g., the highly popular *shichifukujin meguri*, or pilgrimages associated with the Seven Gods of Good Fortune) combining sites from both traditions (see Reader and Tanabe 1998, 156–163; Ōzeki Chikayasu 1993; and Satō and Kaneko 1989).

5. See Tsukuda 1981 and Daihōrinkaku henshūbu 1997.

6. The number 33 is assumed to be symbolic, standing for infinite.

7. Jakuhon 1689 [1981], 120; see also Hoshino 1997, 298.

8. By contrast, the Saikoku pilgrimage is regarded as a *honzon junrei*, or pilgrimage in which all the temples visited enshrine the same figure of worship—in this case Kannon. The edited series by Shinno (1996) is based on a standard Japanese typology into *honzon* (main image), *seiseki*, and regional pilgrimages. Kitagawa 1967 uses a threefold typology, *honzon, seiseki,* and single-site places. For further discussions and definitions of terms and types see Kojima 1987 and Hoshino 2001, 57. See also Reader and Swanson 1997 for further discussion of Japanese classifications of pilgrimage.

9. On Santiago and miracles along the way see Ward 1982, 115–117, and Frey 1998, 105–106.

10. See, e.g., the prints in texts and guidebooks from the late seventeenth century such as Shinnen 1687 and Jakuhon 1689, reproduced in Iyoshi Dankai 1981.

11. For instance, Kagita Chūsaburō, who made the pilgrimage with a companion from Nara Prefecture in 1961, records that they were dressed as priests because, for the duration of the pilgrimage, they had taken priestly vows and had been given a priestly title and temporary ordination and blessing by their local Buddhist priest (Kagita 1962, 10–11, 21–22, and 90).

12. This is the term I use in Reader 1993a.

13. See Reader 1987b for further discussion.

14. Clockwise circumambulation is the classically prescribed way of going round temples and pilgrimages in Buddhist terms; it is a process widely followed, for instance, in Tibetan Buddhist pilgrimages, while standard Tibetan terms for pilgrimage contain within them the notion of "going around" (Huber 1999, 13).

15. The earliest pilgrim accounts by Kenmyō (1638) and Chōzen (1653) make no mention of *orei mairi* or returning to the first temple they had visited. See Reader (forthcoming) for fuller discussion of this issue.

16. This last interpretation is suggested by Shinno 1991a, 2.

17. On *yakudoshi* see Reader and Tanabe 1998, 62–63.

18. Thus, e.g., Kagita is impressed with temples such as Zentsūji but is highly critical of some of the smaller temples, including Temple 15 near Tokushima, which he describes as run-down, in need of repair, and unworthy of the status of a pilgrimage temple (1962, 51).

19. At present most of the evidence I have for this comment is anecdotal and based on comments to me by priests I know in the Reijōkai and their observations about the impact of the three bridges on the ways in which pilgrims perform the *henro*.

20. See Takamure 1939, 1983, 1987. *Gyaku uchi* is supposedly more arduous not just because (since all the directions for the *henro* point one in a clockwise direction) it is harder to navigate one's way around, but because if one does it this way one has more sharp ascents to make on the route.

21. Osada, Sakata, and Seki 2003, 248–251.

22. Hoshino 1986b, 261ff.

23. Miyazaki Tateki 1991, 34–77.

24. The history of Saba Daishi is outlined in Yanagimoto 1990 and is supplemented by an interview with Rev. Yanagimoto Myōzen in March 1991.

25. Matsuo 2002, 115.

26. See, e.g., Hirahata 1982, 1:243.

27. Gold 1989, 263; Eck 1983, 21.

28. See, e.g., Statler 1984, 298, in which he dismisses bus pilgrimages as "sense numbing" and claims that they make a travesty of the pilgrimage and cause its central meaning to be lost. Miyazaki Tateki, who will be encountered in later chapters as the founder of a modern-day pilgrimage support society, has stated to me that in his view those who go by bus are not real pilgrims (interview with Matsuyama, April 8, 2000). Osada, Sakata, and Seki (2003, 409) show that just over 20 percent of pilgrims disapproved of doing the pilgrimage by bus or car.

29. See, e.g., Childs 1999, in which she shows how English pilgrims often preferred the dangerous sea journey across the Bay of Biscay to northern Spain to get to Santiago de Compostela over the land route through France, because it was quicker and thus cheaper.

30. These helicopter tours were set up by the Shikoku Kūkaisha (Shikoku Air and Sea Company—a name that uses the same ideograms as for Kūkai) in 1998, require three to five people to be viable, cost over one million yen, take three to four days, and cover one prefecture per day. The tours start at Temple 1 (Ryōzenji), with a sermon from its priest, after which the pilgrims go by taxi to the Tokushima helicopter port. The helicopter has an offertory box in it for offerings and *osame-fuda*—and hovers over each temple visited as the passengers pray. There are twenty-four temples that the helicopters cannot fly over because they are in no-fly zones in towns, and for these pilgrims have to use taxis. See Yūraku Shuppansha 1998, 19–21, for details.

31. The longest period I have come across this far in this connection was not in Shikoku but on the Saikoku pilgrimage, where I met a man who intended to complete this pilgrimage on the thirteenth anniversary of his father's death (thirteen being a significant death anniversary memorial date in Japanese Buddhist terms).

32. Frey 1998, 215.

33. Even walkers can find a variety of paths to choose from: when walking in April 2000 between Temples 44 and 45 I came across a place where the path split into two, with signs indicating that each path was the *henro michi* (pilgrimage path) to Temple 45.

34. On the meanings of this invocation see Reader and Tanabe 1998, 169–170.

35. See Shimizutani 1992 for a discussion of *go-eika* in the context of pilgrimage.

36. For a discussion of the role of amulets and talismans in Japanese religion see Reader and Tanabe 1998.

37. See Shinjō 1971, 1982; Miyamoto 1987; and Vaporis 1994 for further discussion of travel policies in the Tokugawa, especially in relation to pilgrimages.

38. In the mid-nineteenth century, one feudal authority (Tosa) in Shikoku, often considered the toughest of all four fiefdoms in Shikoku, instituted a law demanding that travelers produce a *nōkyōchō* as proof that they were genuine pilgrims (see chapter 4).

39. Shinno 1980, 52, discusses how the stamp was initially an indication that the pilgrim had performed an act of sutra copying at the temple concerned, but that later this changed to an acknowledgment that s/he had chanted prayers there, and later to simple recognition of having been there.

40. Such an advertisement appeared in the *Asahi shinbun* on March 24, 1984, for example. Officials of the Reijōkai told me that they quickly cracked down on this and informed the company concerned that they would not stamp any scrolls from them in future. I have very recently heard (admittedly only as gossip from a Japanese colleague who has done some work on the *henro*) that a new venture of this sort has started up, thus far without attracting opprobrium from the Reijōkai.

41. Frey (1998, 201) is here speaking about the various objects Santiago pilgrims take home from their pilgrimages and that serve as reminders of their journeys.

42. Although very recent statistics are unavailable to compare Shikoku with the Saikoku pilgrimage (along with Shikoku the most prominent multiple-site pilgrimage in Japan), preliminary evidence suggests that the former has been growing more than the latter. While Satō Hisamitsu's studies (1989, 1990a, and 1990b) of both routes in the 1980s indicate that both had relatively similar numbers of pilgrims, word-of-mouth testimonies from temple priests and others indicate to me that, while Shikoku has been experiencing a growth in numbers, Saikoku has experienced something of a downturn in recent years. However, the reasons for

this are beyond the scope of the present study and must await a more extended general survey of Japanese pilgrimages.

43. See Miyoshi 1996, 16–17; and Satō Hisamitsu 1989, 205. Matsubara Tetsumyō, a Buddhist priest who did both the Saikoku and Shikoku pilgrimages, makes it clear in his account of these two that the former was more of a cultural tour and the latter far more of an ascetic endeavor (Matsubara 1987, 172).

44. For further comments on these issues, on their nostalgic connotations, and on what in Japan is often referred to as the "nostalgia boom," see Robertson 1991; Ivy 1995; and, in the context of religious discourse, Reader 1987a.

45. This series focused on a weekly basis on a section of the route and on the temples along that section of the route, covering all eighty-eight temples, and has since been followed up with a series of videos of the same, plus accompanying guidebooks and the like (see, e.g., NHK Shikoku hachijūhakkasho purojekuto 1999–2000). In chapter 5 I discuss further such media depictions of the pilgrimage in recent years.

46. See, e.g., *Ehime keizai repōto* no. 1200 (2000, 3, 24–25).

47. Waseda Daigaku Dōkūkan Kenkyūkai 1997, 63; and Osada, Sakata, and Seki 2003, 228–229.

48. As Satō Hisamitsu 1989, 192, shows, most Saikoku pilgrims come from the areas immediately around that part of Japan, and few if any at all come from distant prefectures.

49. Bhardwaj 1973.

50. Statler 1984 mentions several earlier Western pilgrims; his book has helped arouse interest in the pilgrimage among Westerners. MacGregor 2002 is a master's thesis focusing on the attitudes of Western pilgrims, while there are a small number of web sites produced by Westerners who have done the pilgrimage.

51. This view is implicit in definitions, such as that by Barber of pilgrimage as a "journey to a distant goal" (1991, 1). This assumption has been challenged by Eade and Sallnow, who comment that it is "a commonplace in the literature (on pilgrimage) that people who live in the vicinity of an important shrine rarely visit it, preferring instead to make pilgrimage to shrines further afield" (1991, 12), a fact that they suggest is normally attributed to "the devotional necessity of arduous travel as a form of penance in order to make the invocation of divine power effective" (1991, 12). Eade and Sallnow challenge such ideas, suggesting that they are superficial.

52. Hoshino 2001, 264. This number may be high because, as Hoshino recognizes, the temple concerned was also on a shorter local pilgrimage commonly done by people from the area. Maeda 1971, 160–161, shows that a sizable proportion of Tokugawa-period pilgrims were from Shikoku.

53. Satō Hisamitsu 1990a, 442.

54. Waseda Daigaku Dōkūkan Kenkyūkai 1997, 17.

55. Kaneko 1991. Kaneko's study is especially striking since it focuses on adherents of the Jōdo Shin (Pure Land) sect in Shikoku. Since Jōdo Shin tradi-

tionally emphasizes faith in and veneration of the Buddha Amida and in theory refutes other forms of worship, the emphasis placed by Jōdo Shin members in Shikoku on Kōbō Daishi and the pilgrimage is highly illustrative of their importance as intrinsic elements in local religious culture.

56. Ehime-ken Shōgaigakushū Sentā 2001, frontispiece.

57. Eade and Sallnow 1991, 12. See also McKevitt 1991 in the same book for an example of the ambivalent attitudes of local people to the pilgrims who visit the shrine of Padre Pio in Italy.

58. Frey 1998, 148

59. In Reader 1993a I suggested that only two hundred to three hundred people a year were walking the pilgrimage in the 1980s. Numerical estimates are, to say the least, imprecise, but recent estimates from priests I know in Shikoku are that around two thousand to three thousand pilgrims per year now walk most of the route, while the head priest at Taisanji (Temple 52) put it as high as five thousand. Hoshino 2001, 354, suggests perhaps one thousand walkers, while the findings of the Waseda University survey, which found that 10.8 percent of all their survey respondents were doing it on foot (Osada, Sakata, and Seki 2003, 354; Waseda Daigaku Dōkūkan Kenkyūkai 1997, 54), indicate possibly a higher figure.

60. Osada, Sakata, and Seki also refer to *risutora* as a modern category of pilgrim (2003, 264).

61. See, e.g., the pilgrims cited in Hoshino 1999 and 2001, 353–378. Similar themes came through in my interviews with pilgrims in 2000.

62. Baba 2000, 105. I heard similar complaints during my last visit to Shikoku.

63. Eade and Sallnow 1991, 5; their italics.

64. This issue is set out in Eade and Sallnow 1991 and discussed further in the various essays in their edited book.

65. Takamure 1987, 62–64. Elsewhere in her account Takamure draws attention to the problems young women pilgrims such as herself faced and to the dangers and divisions in the pilgrimage.

66. Turner's theory (which he developed first in single-authored works and then in conjunction with his wife Edith) is set out and discussed in Turner 1974, 1979 and Turner and Turner 1978.

67. See, e.g., Pfaffenberger's study (1979) of the Kataragama pilgrimage in Sri Lanka, which, he argues, heightens ethnic differences between the Tamil Hindus and Singhalese Buddhists who both visit the site, and Sallnow's study (1981) of Peruvian Indian pilgrimages in the Andes, which provides a critique of *communitas*.

68. Aziz 1987, 248, 253–254.

69. Aoki 1985, 174.

70. Naquin and Yü 1992, 7.

71. Ibid., 22.

72. Eade 2000, xx.

73. See Tanaka Hiroshi 1983; Oda 1996; and Reader 1988 for discussions of replicated eighty-eight-stage pilgrimages in Japan.

74. On the various terms that are usually translated by "pilgrimage," see Reader and Swanson 1997, 232–237.

75. See, e.g., the comments along these lines by Fritz Graf (2002, 195–196) in a review of Dillon's book (1997) on Greek pilgrimages.

76. Dubisch 1995, 46.

77. Ibid., 46.

78. Crumrine and Morinis 1991, 2. See also Morinis 1984, 2, where he refers to pilgrimage as the "full composite of relevant features . . . [and] . . . total set of symbols, history, rituals, legends, behaviour, deities, locations, specialists or whatever" that center on pilgrimage sites.

79. Dubisch 1995, 7.

80. Ibid., 7.

81. Ibid.

82. Gold 1989; see also Sax 1991 for analysis of another (Hindu) pilgrimage as it relates to social structure and is embedded in the communities that participate in it.

83. Frey 1998, 18, 26–27. Frey (perhaps because she did her fieldwork primarily among walkers) appears to support this attitude in that her study of pilgrims is limited to those who go by foot, cycle, and horse, and because the data she uses for numbers of pilgrims includes only these categories (29).

84. See Reader 1993a.

85. I have spent long periods in the courtyards of Shikoku temples timing and calculating the average time spent at the site by walkers and bus groups; on average, bus groups tended to spend thirty to forty-five minutes at each site, while those on foot often spent under ten.

86. Shinno 2002, 469.

87. In both Europe and Japan pilgrimage provided an early stimulus to concepts of tourism and helped shape the idea of organized tourism. In Europe it is thought that some of the earliest "package tours" were developed by the Venetian merchants who controlled the eastern Mediterranean and who took pilgrims to the Holy Land for an "all-in" price, and by the English sea captains who provided similar services to British pilgrims headed for Santiago de Compostela (see, e.g., Childs 1999). In Japan, the origins of the tourism and package tours can be traced to the services such as those provided by the *Ise oshi* (pilgrimage guides of Ise), who took care of the visits of pilgrims to that sacred location in earlier centuries and arranged their lodgings as well as their visits to the shrines. On such issues see Kanzaki 1990.

88. Turner and Turner 1978, 27; Davies and Davies 1982, passim.

89. See Reader 1991, 134–167; and also Graburn 1983.

90. Naquin and Yü 1992, 22.

91. Dupront 1987, 413.

2. Making Landscapes: Geography, Symbol, Legend, and Traces

1. I take this term from John Nelson's discussion (1999, 25) of Shinto shrines in Japan.

2. This idea of pilgrimage as text is found also in Dubisch's study (1995, 173–174) of Greek pilgrimage.

3. See Coleman and Elsner 1995, 196–220, esp. 209; and 1999, in which they critique Eade and Sallnow's (1991) failure to take heed of such issues in their studies of pilgrimage.

4. Coleman and Elsner 1995, 83–88.

5. Frey 1998, 75, and 265, note 7.

6. See Slater 1986.

7. Huber 1999, 58–77.

8. For fuller details on Kūkai and his life and works, see Abe 1999 and Hakeda 1972, from which works I have drawn the biographical data given here.

9. Kūkai wrote about such experiences in his *Sangō shiki* (Indications of the goals of the three teachings), which he drafted in 797 (Hakeda 1972, 16–17).

10. See Goodwin 1994 for further discussion of this dynamic.

11. D. and A. Matsunaga 1974, 197.

12. Ibid.

13. See Kitamura 1988 for discussion of subsequent stories and texts emanating from Kōyasan that embellished the legends. In the Miroku cult it was believed that all whose remains were placed at Kōyasan in the company of Kōbō Daishi would be able to rise again when Miroku came to this world (according to popular belief, in 567 million years' time), and hence it became a popular custom to have part of one's ashes interred at Kōyasan, which has developed one of the greatest and most extensive graveyards in Japan. See Miyata Noboru 1988 [1975], 112–114; and Shinno 1991a, 91–113.

14. On the activities of holy mendicants associated with Kōyasan and the legends of Kōbō Daishi, see Gorai 1975.

15. Saitō Akitoshi (1988) has collected 3,282 such Kōbō Daishi miracle tales from throughout Japan. On this issue see also Watanabe Akiyuki 1988.

16. In Reader and Tanabe 1998, 170, we describe him in these terms as both human and divine. I use the terms "savior" and "saint" here, too, because they convey many of the attributes—the ability to aid people in their search for salvation and the capacity to perform miracles and intercede between the human and other realms—that are characteristics of saints in various religious traditions. The terms "saint-like" and "saint" provide a succinct and indicative way of referring to a figure who, while associated with Buddhism, does not fit into other normative categories (Buddha, bodhisattva) normally associated with the tradition. Abe 1999, 2, also uses the term "saint" in this context. I thank Robert Sharf, Ryuichi Abe, George J. Tanabe Jr., and Clark Chilson for assisting in discussions on this matter.

For a fuller discussion of the various elements incorporated into *Daishi shinkō* (the cult of worship of Kōbō Daishi), see Hinonishi 1988; Miyata Noboru 1988 [1975], 97–137, esp. 120–127; and Hoshino 1986a, 89–103, esp. 91, where Hoshino identifies five main strands to this faith, some of which are clearly associated with the Shingon sect, others more evidently linked to a wider and commonly held religious belief structure that goes beyond sectarian boundaries. The five strands are founder veneration, veneration of the spirits of the dead (who may be entrusted to his care after death), beliefs linked to his entry into eternal meditation, faith in his ability to bring salvation (associated with faith in Miroku, the Future Buddha), and the miracle-making capacities manifest in folk legends and stories related to Daishi.

17. Yoritomi and Shiragi 2001,14.

18. On *hijiri*, see Shinno 1991a and b; and Gorai 1975.

19. Yamamoto 1995, 58–59. Among the well-known wandering ascetic figures of Japanese Buddhism whose stories and miraculous deeds Kōbō Daishi has absorbed she cites Gyōgi, En no Gyōja, Kūya, and Ippen.

20. See Reader and Tanabe 1998, 167–169, for discussion of how Kōbō Daishi is thus promoted in Shingon; and Saitō 1984 for an extensive survey of how Shingon priests regard Kōbō Daishi as the core of their faith.

21. Waseda Daigaku Dōkūkan Kenkyūkai 1997, 23. See also Reader 1996a, 281–282, which discusses a pilgrimage association in Shiga Prefecture whose members are mostly of the Jōdo Shin Buddhist sect but who have built a hall of worship to Kōbō Daishi. Kaneko's study (1991) of Pure Land devotees in Shikoku indicates the extent to which Kōbō Daishi is a figure of devotion for Pure Land sect members in Shikoku as well.

22. Ōzeki Gyōō 1936, 18.

23. The most prevalent female *yakudoshi* is thirty-three, and it is not uncommon to meet females doing the pilgrimage at this age.

24. See, e.g., Hakeda 1972. Kūkai also left fairly clear writings of his activities and did not mention the *henro*.

25. Hasuo 1931, 342–351.

26. See, e.g., Hatada Shuhō n.d.-a, written by his son and successor as head of Anrakuji.

27. Yamashita 1984, 22–23.

28. One should note that in stating that St. James travels as a pilgrim along his own route, Frey (1998, 11) errs (perhaps because of a rather narrow focus on Western European Catholic pilgrimages) by asserting, "Uniquely, Santiago appears in the iconography as a pilgrim to his own shrine." Rather than being unique, I would assert that, as the Kōbō Daishi case suggests, this need not be an uncommon element in pilgrimage.

29. See, e.g., Shinnen 1690 and Shikoku Hachijūhakkasho Reijōkai 1984 as examples of early and modern miracle tale collections of this ilk, which are full of encounters with Kōbō Daishi.

30. Kino 1985, 65.

31. The main exception here is Matsuyama, one of the four main towns and regional capitals of the island. While the *henro* skirts every other major population center, it passes close to the center of Matsuyama.

32. Dubisch 1995, 120–130. The term "different place" is from the title of her book.

33. This, of course, is a theme in the Heart Sutra (with its images of the "other shore"), which is widely chanted by Shikoku pilgrims, and of the equinoctial rituals of *higan*.

34. See Itamura 1989, 20–21, where he uses the term "sacred island" *(sei naru shima)* to describe Shikoku.

35. On our first visit to Shikoku in 1984 my wife and I encountered in the southeastern part of the island a young man in his early twenties who informed us he was the only one left of his age-set in the region who still lived there. The rest had either left to go to university in cities such as Osaka and Tokyo—and would not come back—or had migrated for work reasons.

36. Preston 1992, 33.

37. This practice effectively was a form of ritual suicide as ascetics were encased in boats and pushed off from the shore heading south—the direction in which Fudaraku was believed to be. On this issue see ten Grotenhuis 1999, 173–175, where she discusses the practice in Kumano; and Kondō 1982, 14, where he mentions these promontories in Shikoku as settings for the cult. See also Hirota 1999, 198.

38. Yoritomi and Shiragi give the figure as 21 (2001, 50).

39. There is an immense literature on the significance of mountains in religious terms in Japan; see Reader and Swanson 1997, 248–250, for a brief overview of this literature.

40. On Ishizuchisan and its religious significance, see Nishigai 1984.

41. Takeda 1972, 110–111. The ten temples in Shikoku most closely associated with *reizan*, according to Takeda, are 10 (Kirihataji), 12 (Shōsanji), 20 (Kakurinji), 21 (Tairyūji), 24 (Higashideranji), 32 (Zenjibuji), 45 (Iwayaji), 60 (Yokomineji), 71 (Iyataniji), and 88 (Ōkuboji). However, there are several other temples on the fringes of the Shikoku *reizan* that are linked to this cult of death (e.g., all the temples between 59 and 64 are in the environs of Ishizuchi-san and can be seen as gateways to or protective temples surrounding this mountain).

42. Maeda 1971, 122.

43. See ibid., 17–18; and Shinno 1991a, 105, for the cult of Iyataniji in Tokugawa times.

44. Dubisch 1995, 36–37, makes the same point about Tinos, which, she notes, may be exotic to those coming from the mainland but is also home to the locals who make pilgrimages to its sacred site.

45. See Reader 1987a for a discussion of this issue in religious contexts.

46. Coleman 2000, 156.

47. See Grapard 1982, which discuses how wandering ascetics were involved in the establishment of a sacred geography in Japan; and Grapard 1989.

48. Grapard 1989, 171; his italics.

49. Ibid., 172.

50. Ibid., 172–173.

51. Grapard 1982, 210.

52. Shinno 1991a, 82ff. One should stress that this envisioning process in which place is transformed into mandala and in which the existence of a mandala is perceived within the physical terrain is not limited to Japan: as Huber 1999, 26, discusses, in Tibetan Buddhism too—where ascetic wanderers played a role in creating mountain pilgrimage routes—mountains were envisioned as mandalas.

53. Iwamura 1973, 3; and Tanaka Tomohiko 1989, 245.

54. Hoshino 2001, 29.

55. Interview with Hatada Zenpō, Anrakuji, November 6, 1990. See also Hatada Zenpō 1989, 35; and Hatada Shuhō n.d.-a. Sermons I have heard while staying at this temple over many years have also emphasized this imagery.

56. Based on several visits to Gokurakuji between October 1990 and April 2000.

57. Murakami 1986.

58. Hirota 1999, 199.

59. Howard 1980, 6–13.

60. Morinis 1984, 298.

61. Hoshino 2001, 329–331.

62. See, e.g., Watanabe Yasuhiro 1999, which describes his thirty-day foot pilgrimage in this way through the framework of *hosshin-nehan*.

63. See, e.g., NHK Shikoku hachijūhakkasho purojekuto 1999–2000.

64. Hoshino 2001, 369.

65. This story of a female figure ceding ownership of a sacred location to Kūkai-Kōbō Daishi has parallels in the founding stories of Kōyasan, where a female deity cedes land to Kūkai, and can be seen to represent, inter alia, a gender bias in which a female figure yields power and authority to a male.

66. Hirahata 1982, 1:85.

67. See, e.g., Shinnen 1690 and the translation and commentary by Reader 1999, as well as Shikoku Hachijūhakkasho Reijōkai 1984 and Kōbō Daishi Kūkai Kankōkai 1985.

68. Ogasawara 1984, 89–91.

69. Sada 1984, 194–195.

70. The white clothing particularly resembles that of the *yamabushi* (mountain ascetics), who have played a prominent role in traditional Japanese religion and who are closely associated also with many of the mountain religious centers in Shikoku.

71. Shinnen 1690; for a commentary and translation of some of the tales in the collection, see Reader 1999.

72. Kondō Yoshihiro 1982, 26–28; and Hoshino 2001, 177. Chōzen 1653 [1981], 44–46, mentions the story in the context of pilgrimage foundation.

73. Hashimoto 1984 [1950], 221.

74. Ibid.

75. Interview with Tanaka-san of Iyo Tetsu, October 16, 1990, at Ishiteji.

76. Tosa 1972, 123–126.

77. Statler 1984, 191–192.

78. Takeda 1972, 6.

79. Interviews with members of the Arita Settaikō, February 14, 1991; see also Hoshino 2001, 348–349. Such acts of giving protective amulets to pilgrims and others who make donations so that they can be taken home as a means of protection for members of the pilgrims' community has traditionally been a common practice at pilgrimage temples and shrines in Japan.

80. In traditional Japanese beliefs associated with death, the spirit undergoes a journey that transforms it into an ancestor who is revered by (and cares for) its bereaved family members. Part of this process involves obtaining a *kaimyō* (posthumous name or Buddhist preceptual name), which is usually given to the person by a Buddhist temple and priest and which identifies the deceased as an ancestor.

81. I first learned about this custom when I lived in Kobe from a Japanese academic colleague who told me that when his father-in-law, a member of the Shingon sect who had done the *henro*, died, he was placed in his casket dressed as a pilgrim. Imai Misako 1981, 171, states that pilgrims she spoke to said they were going to have their pilgrims' books put in their coffins at death.

82. See, e.g., Arai 1819 [1966], 104.

83. See Miyazaki Ninshō 1985, 46; and Hoshino 2001, 110.

84. Araki 1990, 66–67.

85. Yamamoto 1995, 13.

86. Shikoku Hachijūhakkasho Reijōkai 1984, 1–2.

87. Starkie 1957, 1.

88. Hoinacki 1997, 147.

89. Frey 1998, 82.

90. See, for instance, Takamure 1983, 109–110; and Kagita 1962, 40–41.

91. See, e.g., Harada 1999, 20.

92. Hoshino 1999, 51; MacGregor 2002, 26–27, also has similar findings.

93. Interview with Miyazaki, April 10, 2000.

94. Interview with Yamaguchi-san at Beppu, Kyushu, December 15–16, 1990.

95. See, e.g., Miyazaki Ninshō 1981.

96. Other temples that have similar collections of such items include Temple 16 (Taisen Miyata 1984, 59).

97. On *henro ishi* in general, see Kiyoyoshi 1984 and 1999.

98. See Kiyoyoshi 1999, 76–81. One of the most accessible of these is just off the current *henro* route, not far from Anrakuji (Temple 6), at the edge of rice fields alongside a small road; one can get a map of its location from Anrakuji.

99. See Kiyoyoshi 1999 for further information on these pilgrims; see also Mori Masayasu 1986, 110, for discussion of Takeda's stones and activities; and Yoritomi and Shiragi 2001, 142–143, for details of Takeda and Shōren.

100. Kiyoyoshi 1999, 241, provides a chart of Nakatsuka's stones, giving the years when they were erected, while in Kiyoyoshi 1984 he gives a full account of the locations and history of Nakatsuka's stones.

101. Kiyoyoshi 1999, 241.

102. Takada Shinkai 1985, 63.

103. See also Hoshino 2001, 368, for an interview with another pilgrim who comments on how Miyazaki's signs helped encourage her.

3. Making Pilgrimages: Pilgrims, Motives, and Meanings

1. See, e.g., Imai Misako 1981, 131–144.

2. Waseda Daigaku Dōkūkan Kenkyūkai 1997, 78–80.

3. Ibid., 33–38.

4. Hoshino 2001, 276.

5. Waseda Daigaku Dōkūkan Kenkyūkai 1997, 15–17, gives the number at 50.2 percent.

6. *Henro* 13 (1985):8.

7. Satō Hisamitsu 1990a, 449.

8. Waseda Daigaku Dōkūkan Kenkyūkai 1997, 15–17. Satō Hisamitsu 1990a, 451, states that in the mid-1960s the number of those over sixty was higher at around 45 percent, but then declined to approximately 33 percent in the mid-1980s.

9. Waseda Daigaku Dōkūkan Kenkyūkai 1997, 29; *Henro* 13 (1985):8

10. Waseda Daigaku Dōkūkan Kenkyūkai 1997, 50.

11. Maeda 1971, 160–161.

12. See Satō Hisamitsu 1990a and b. Satō Hisamitsu 1990a, 442, indicates that during the 1980s, Shikoku pilgrims came from all over Japan (even if the Shikoku and adjacent regions still provided the bulk of them). The 1997 Waseda survey shows that 14.6 percent of the pilgrims surveyed came from the Kantō area, while an official from the Iyo Tetsu Company told me that their main growth area in terms of pilgrims in the late 1990s was the Kantō region, along with Tōhoku and Hokkaidō.

13. E.g., many pilgrims I have interviewed on the Saikoku and Shōdoshima pilgrimages have indicated that they are doing it as a *kuyō* for their departed kin. See also Maeda 1971, 206, where he shows that this is an important motive for Saikoku pilgrims.

14. Waseda Daigaku Dōkūkan Kenkyūkai 1997, 24–26; for fuller discussion of these survey results, see also Osada, Sakata, and Seki 2003, 329–332.

15. Imai Misako 1981, 74–78.

16. Miyazaki Ninshō 1985, 44–46.

17. On *ihai* and dealing with the dead in Japan, see Reader 1991, 90–96.

18. Iwanami Shashin Bunko 1956, 12, 35.

19. *Henro* 38 (1987):1

20. *Henro* 33 (1986):3

21. *Henro* 43 (1987):1

22. I am grateful to the temple concerned, which is one of the most popular temples for pilgrims to stay at and one that maintains very close relations especially with foot pilgrims, for allowing me to read through this book (which is openly available to all who stay there), for providing me with photocopies of entries from the period between spring 1999 and April 2000, and for giving me permission to cite cases from this book with the proviso that all pilgrims will be cited in ways that preserve their anonymity. I have therefore cited from this book, but do not give the names of the pilgrims concerned or of the temple.

23. *Yomiuri shinbun*, April 11, 1989, and April 18, 1989.

24. See, e.g., Kobayashi's account of his 1988 pilgrimage, titled *Teinen kara dōgyōninin* (1990; *teinen kara* meaning "after reaching retirement age"), which is an example of this genre, its cover adorned with a drawing of elderly pilgrims on foot and its text drawing attention to his position as a retired person intent on walking the *henro*.

25. Imai Misako 1981, 131–144.

26. During this interview in Beppu, Kyushu, on December 15–16, 1990, he showed me photographs of himself in the snow, barefoot, on this pilgrimage.

27. Hoshino 2001, 361 ff. See also Waseda Daigaku Dōkūkan Kenkyūkai 1997, 142–170, for comments by pilgrims about their motivations, which often emphasize the importance of challenge.

28. This diary is by a young Tokyo woman who walked the pilgrimage in 1975 and who wrote that she was driven to quit university and set off for Shikoku because of "anguish and personal setback" (see Reader 1993a, 128).

29. Takamure 1983, 46.

30. Satō Ken 1989, 15–17.

31. Tsukioka 2002. The word "Heisei" refers to the modern (1989–) era in Japan.

32. Araki 1990, 67–75.

33. Nakatsuka will be discussed further in later chapters; on his life, see Tsurumura 1978 and 1979; Mori 1986; and Kiyoyoshi 1999.

34. See also Hoshino 1999, 53, for an account of a sixty-year-old male pilgrim who felt his entire life had been full of spiritual pollution and evil passions and for whom the *henro* was a chance to repent and to purify himself of such feelings.

35. My interview with Tabuchi is supplemented by his reminiscences about the pilgrimage in Tabuchi 1984.

36. Tabuchi 1984, 55–57.

37. Kagayama 2000, 60.

38. *Asahi shinbun*, June 4, 2001 (evening edition), 3.

39. I have not met him since, but on my visit to Shikoku in April 2000 a tem-

ple priest who knows him told me he was still doing the pilgrimage and was still keeping well.

40. This opinion is partially borne out by my own studies of pilgrimages in Japan; most pilgrims on the Saikoku pilgrimage, e.g., tend to be first-timers, and there is relatively little evidence of repeated pilgrimages there (Leavell and Reader 1988; Satō Hisamitsu 1989). However, studies I have done on some of the smaller-scale pilgrimages in Japan, such as the eighty-eight-stage Shōdoshima pilgrimage, indicate that many people do these shorter pilgrimages many times as well.

41. Information from officials of the Reijōkai in April 2000.

42. Interviews with officials of Iyo Tetsu in October 1990 and April 2000, and with officials from the Kotosan Bus Company (Takamatsu), November 1990, and Setouchi Bus Company (Imabari), October 1990.

43. Tabuchi 1984, 60.

44. I would like to thank Professor Timothy Barrett of SOAS in London for drawing my attention to this issue and suggesting it as one reason why people may do the pilgrimage repeatedly.

45. The term "Shikoku byō" was mentioned to me, for instance, by the head priest at Temple 52 during an interview, April 8, 2000. Satō Takako 1999b, 3–4, writing about walking the pilgrimage, also uses this term to describe the captivating allure of the henro for all who become involved in it.

46. Kinpō is a religious name acquired after undergoing a lay Buddhist ordination.

47. I have given a fuller account of Naitō in Reader 1996a. This account is based on interviews with Naitō Hirozō, the widow of Naitō Kinpō, and other members of the Shingyōkai on March 16, 1991, along with reminiscences from a temple priest in Shikoku who knows the association well, plus the account in Shingyōkai Honbu 1981.

48. For a full list of the Shiga Shingyōkai's annual events, see Shingyōkai Honbu 1981, 315.

49. Waseda Daigaku Dōkūkan Kenkyūkai 1997, 23.

50. My knowledge of this association came initially from Maeda 1971, 239–244, followed by a visit to the association and interview with members in December 1990. See also Hoshino 2001, 338.

51. Kondō Tō 1989, 3.

52. Henro 70 (1990):4.

53. Matsuura Harutake 1988, 8.

54. Matsuura Tadatoshi 1988.

55. Waseda Daigaku Dōkūkan Kenkyūkai 1997, 55.

56. It has become increasingly common in recent years for people to do memorial services (petto kuyō) for deceased animals in Japan.

57. This interview was carried out in October 1990 at the end of one of Iyo Tetsu's pilgrimage tours. I am grateful to the company for enabling me to meet with parties of their pilgrims so that I could conduct such interviews.

58. Shinjō 1960, i, comments that for premodern Japanese, virtually all travel consisted of going to shrines and temples, and that pilgrimage and travel were thus virtually synonymous.

59. See Waseda Daigaku Dōkūkan Kenkyūkai 1997, 64–68, which indicates that around 20 percent of all pilgrims travel with a spouse. Shikoku may actually have a lower rate of husband-wife pilgrimage than other routes in Japan. In a survey of the Saikoku pilgrimage in 1988, for instance, a colleague and I found that about 55 percent of pilgrims on this route were doing it with their husband or wife (Leavell and Reader 1988, 116–118).

60. See Reader and Tanabe 1998 for a comprehensive discussion of these issues.

61. One could argue that all *osamefuda* contain requests for worldly benefits, since they generally have a couple of printed prayer requests (often for good crops, family safety, or peace on earth) on them. However, many pilgrims also write in their own requests as well.

62. The full list of requests on the *osamefuda* I analyzed are given in Reader and Tanabe 1998, 200–201.

63. Tanaka's findings, which are set out in his doctoral dissertation (Tanaka Hiroshi 1975, 26), are reported in the unpublished master's thesis by Fiona Mac-Gregor (2002, 28).

64. Interview with Nakayama Mamoru (pseudonym), whom I initially met in Kōchi on March 4, 1991, and subsequently in Osaka on March 20, 1991.

4. History, Footsteps, and Customs: Making the Premodern Pilgrimage

1. The work of scholars such as Shinjō Tsunezō (1982) Kondō Yoshihiro (1971, 1982), Maeda Takashi (1971), Miyazaki Ninshō (1985), and Kiyoyoshi Eitoku (1984, 1999) provides a broad understanding of the historical background of the pilgrimage and of the historical and economic underpinnings to religious travel and pilgrimage. In European languages I have especially relied on Nathalie Kouamé's works (1998, 2001) on laws and almsgiving in Tokugawa-era Shikoku.

2. In Shikoku much material has been brought into the public domain by such sources as e.g., Hiroe 1966 (a valuable collation of pilgrimage diaries, legal decrees, and other records from the seventeenth to nineteenth centuries), Tsurumura 1978 and 1979, Iyoshi Dankai 1981 (which is a collection of pilgrimage texts and journals, including those of Chōzen, Shinnen, and Jakuhon cited in this chapter), and Ehime-ken Shōgaigakushū Sentā 2001.

3. See especially Shinno 1991a and 1991b, as well as Gorai 1984, 206–217, and Imai Masaharu 1986.

4. On the Kumano pilgrimage, see Moerman 1997, and on Saikoku, its development, and links to other aspects of Japanese religious faith in the late Heian and early Kamakura periods, see Hayami 1983, 222–316.

5. Hayami 1983, 317–336.

6. See Shinjō 1982 for a comprehensive account of the social and economic conditions that contributed to the development of pilgrimage in Japan through the early, medieval, and early-modern periods.

7. For further discussion of these texts and their links to the *henro*, see Shinjō 1982, 481; and Shinno 1980, 71; 1991a, 82.

8. Shinjō 1982, 479–485. Yoritomi and Shiragi 2001, 37–38, also suggests that the focus on Shikoku came about because there were a number of ascetics from Sanuki, Kūkai's home province in Shikoku, among his disciples at Kōyasan.

9. Shinjō 1982, 480.

10. Kondō Yoshihiro 1982, 8.

11. Ibid., 163

12. See Kondō Yoshihiro 1971 and 1982. Others who see a close link between the Kumano cult and the *henro* include the folklorist Takeda Akira (e.g., 1987, 172–202) and Miyazaki Ninshō 1985, whose work closely follows Kondō's.

13. See Gorai 1975, 1989, 1996, in the latter of which he argues that a significant element of mountain ascetic centers was that they provided a setting from which one could perform austerities while viewing the sea.

14. Yoritomi and Shiragi 2001, 49–55.

15. Ibid., 63.

16. Ibid., 43.

17. Shinno 1991a, 110–112, argues that the *henro* fuses two originally disparate elements: faith in Miroku the Future Buddha and faith in the Buddha of the Pure Land, Amida, into whose land the faithful will be reborn at death. By the Muromachi period, Pure Land beliefs had become widespread at Kōyasan (see Gorai 1975, 65–73), and these merged with earlier aspects of faith in Kōbō Daishi that centered on his association with Miroku.

18. Kenmyō 1638 [1981], 17, and Shinnen 1687 [1981], 82–83, both call it Saba Gyōgi. By the early eighteenth century, however, it had become Saba Daishi (Takeda 1972, 47–48).

19. Yoritomi and Shiragi 2001, 74.

20. On Ippen and Shikoku, see Kondō Yoshihiro 1982, 9; and Yoritomi and Shiragi 2001, 71.

21. Yoritomi and Shiragi 2001, 71–72.

22. This legend appears, e.g., in a text dating from 1739, the *Yoyō seisuiki*, according to Miyazaki Ninshō 1985, 157.

23. See Shinjō 1982, 482–484, for a discussion of the different ideograms used to write *"hen"* over the centuries.

24. Shinjō 1982, 485, quotes Yūkai's statement from this text.

25. Yoritomi and Shiragi 2001, 76.

26. See Shinjō 1982, 482–484, for further discussion of this point.

27. Yoritomi and Shiragi 2001, 161; Shinjō 1982, 486.

28. Matsuo 2002, 125. The problem occurs because Japanese dates use the era names of emperors. The inscription appears to be Bunmei 3, i.e., 1471. How-

ever, Matsuo notes that the inscription is unclear and suggests that the first ideogram *(bun)* may in fact be the (somewhat similar) *ten,* giving the date as Tenmei 3, i.e., 1783.

29. See Reader 1988 for a more detailed discussion of the development of replicated pilgrimages in Japan, and Yoritomi and Shiragi 2001, 161, on the Mikawa route.

30. Chōzen 1653 [1981], 67.

31. See Hoshino 2001, 181.

32. Maeda 1971, 61.

33. Hoshino 2001, 264.

34. Yoritomi and Shiragi 2001, 78.

35. Shinjō 1982, 489.

36. Ibid., 489. Shinjō is able to tell that such people are from the masses because they do not have surnames, as was the norm for such classes until the Meiji era.

37. On the impact of this warfare on the *henro,* see Tanimura 1973, 16–23.

38. Yoritomi and Shiragi 2001, 80.

39. Kondō Yoshihiro 1982, 28.

40. Shinjō 1982, 1072–1074.

41. Ibid., 1074–1078.

42. Kiyoyoshi 1999, 33.

43. Yoritomi and Shiragi 2001, 83.

44. Ibid., 84.

45. Kenmyō 1638 [1981], 10–20.

46. The following section is taken from Chōzen (1653) [1981]; discussions of Chōzen's diary and travels can be found also in Miyazaki Ninshō 1977; Yamamoto 1995, 92–102; and Yoritomi and Shiragi 2001, 84–102.

47. Chōzen 1653 [1981], 67.

48. Yoritomi and Shiragi 2001, 133–134.

49. See, e.g., Chōzen 1653 [1981], 28.

50. Ibid., 22.

51. Ibid., 40. In all, Chōzen spent more than half his nights at temples and just over a quarter in ordinary people's homes (Kiyoyoshi 1998, 6).

52. Chōzen 1653 [1981], 45–46.

53. Ibid., 27.

54. Yoritomi and Shiragi 2001, 89.

55. Chōzen 1653 [1981], 24, 26.

56. Ibid., 37–38.

57. Ibid., 46–48.

58. Shinnen 1687 [1981], 113–114. Dōkyū's age and death are recorded on his grave according to Kiyoyoshi 1999, 36.

59. Ōishi 1999, 6.

60. Hoshino 2001, 180.

61. Yoritomi and Shiragi 2001, 107–108. Details about Shinnen's life are primarily taken from Kiyoyoshi 1984, 35–58; and 1999, 65–81; Yoritomi and Shiragi 2001, 105–131; and Murakami 1987, 28–33; and from the three texts he is associated with (Shinnen 1687 [1981], 1690 [1981]; and Jakuhon 1689 [1981].

62. Kenmyō 1638 [1981], 19. When I visited Shinnen-an in 1991, it no longer provided lodging and was merely a small hall enshrining Jizō and looked after by local people. However, I have been told recently that a former pilgrim has taken up residence there and is now looking after the place. There is some doubt as to whether this Shinnen-an and the Shinnen-an of Kenmyō's text are the same: Kiyoyoshi 1999, 72, thinks Shinnen established his lodge in 1682, although Yoritomi and Shiragi 2001, 109–110, argues that the Shinnen-an of Kenmyō's text was the one founded by Shinnen and that he therefore had fifty-three years of association with the *henro*.

63. In Shinnen 1690 [1981], 230–232, it is stated that he had made around twenty pilgrimage circuits, while the text also provides a list of donors, including several from Terashima in Osaka, who had supported publication of the text.

64. Mori Masayasu 1986, 108.

65. Shinnen 1690 [1981], 232, states that he put up around two hundred stones, although Yoritomi and Shiragi 2001, 113–115, thinks this may be an exaggeration. Kiyoyoshi 1984 lists twenty-four extant stones erected by Shinnen.

66. Shinnen 1687 [1981], 115.

67. Yoritomi and Shiragi 2001, 123; Yamamoto 1995, 118.

68. Yoritomi and Shiragi 2001, 123–129.

69. As Yoritomi and Shiragi 2001, 127, comments, Jakuhon's work contains scholastic detail that was beyond the ken of Shinnen, who was effectively an ascetic and proselytizer, not an academically oriented monk.

70. Jakuhon 1689 [1981], 120.

71. Yoritomi and Shiragi 2001, 134–135.

72. Shinnen 1690 [1981]. In Tale 16, the fisherman repents of his sins and gains spiritual awakening as a result. The tale in which water gushes out of the ground is one of the most ubiquitous folk tales in Japan, known as *Kōbō shimizu* (Kōbō's pure water), and is found throughout the country (Saitō 1988).

73. Jakuhon 1689 [1981], 213–214.

74. Ibid., 214.

75. Shinjō 1982, 1025.

76. Matsuo 2002, 111–113.

77. Hirahata Ryōyū's guidebook to the Shikoku pilgrimages (Hirahata 1982), one of the most widely used in the modern era, is a good example of this interplay of the pragmatic, the historical, and the magical.

78. See Hashizume 1926 for a collection of Tatsueji's miracle tales. I am grateful to David Moreton for this reference.

79. Such ascetics were especially prominent in the seventeenth and eighteenth centuries and, living on a diet mainly of pine nuts, performed severe aus-

terities and preached salvation to the masses. Yoritomi and Shiragi 2001, 145, refers to several other *mokujiki* ascetics in Shikoku at this period, although Bukkai was the best known.

80. Ibid., 144–145.

81. Mori Masayasu 1986, 110.

82. Personal communication, Niihima, Shikoku, April 7, 2000.

83. Yoritomi and Shiragi 2001, 142; Mori Masayasu 1986, 110.

84. Kiyoyoshi 1999, 36–38.

85. On Nakatsuka, see Tsurumura 1978 and 1979; Kiyoyoshi 1984 and 1999, 237–288; Mori Masayasu 1986; and Yoritomi and Shiragi 2001, 196–197.

86. This is the view of Mori Masayasu 1986, 112.

87. Yoritomi and Shiragi 2001, 196.

88. Shinjō 1982, 1079–1081.

89. Hayasaka 1992, 248.

90. Shinjō 1982, 754; Hoshino 2001, 117.

91. Kojima 1989.

92. Arai 1819, 89. See also Shinjō 1982, 1079–1080, for further discussion of *settai* in early nineteenth-century pilgrims' diaries.

93. Shinjō 1982, 1080–1082.

94. See Maeda 1971, 222–223.

95. Hoshino 2001, 197.

96. Kouamé 2001, 161–175; and also Yamamoto 1995, 159–171.

97. Shinjō 1982, 1086.

98. Ibid., 1087. Under Tokugawa laws, everyone had to register as a member of a Buddhist temple. Such registration, which determined one's official religious orientation, tended to be contingent on local circumstances (i.e., what sect the nearest temple to one's home belonged to).

99. Ibid., 1096–1097.

100. The account is given in Iyoshi Dankai 1981, 234–316, with the account of receiving *settai* from this group being on 282–283.

101. Shinjō 1982, 1080–1091.

102. Yoritomi and Shiragi 2001, 171, records several *settai* groups that probably date from the late eighteenth or early nineteenth century. When I interviewed members of the Arita group in December 1990, they thought the association had started in 1818—a date also given by Yoritomi and Shiragi (171), although probably from the same oral source.

103. Maeda 1971, 182–183.

104. Hoshino 2001, 151.

105. The ideograms for *hendo* are the same as for *henro*, but the ideograms were pronounced differently in this context and contained an implicit scurrilous nuance; see Yamamoto 1995, 146; and Takeda 1972, 164.

106. Yamamoto 1995, 146.

107. Miyazaki Ninshō 1985, 184; and Maeda 1971, 39.

108. Hoshino 2001, 87, discusses the impact of the indigo and salt trades on links between Osaka and Tokushima. Maeda 1971, 248, argues that regional authorities in Shikoku encouraged the pilgrimage because of its economic impact.

109. Ehime-ken Shōgaigakushū Sentā 2001, 131.

110. Shinjō 1982, 754.

111. Foard 1982.

112. See Vaporis 1994, passim, but esp. 5.

113. Shinjō 1982, 1023–1025.

114. Yoritomi and Shiragi 2001, 157.

115. Kouamé 2001, 52; and Shinjō 1982, 1023–1028.

116. Miyazaki Ninshō 1985, 185. This appears to be a large number—comparable to the 1970s and 1980s, when bus travel and a much larger population boosted the pilgrimage considerably—but it must also be remembered that pilgrimages to the shrines of Ise during the Tokugawa era often produced much larger numbers—often several hundred thousand a year and several million during major cyclical peak periods (see Nishigaki 1983).

117. Kouamé 1998, 187; 2001, 112–114.

118. Vaporis 1994, 198–199, 217–242. Foard 1982 also discusses the increasingly tourist nature of Saikoku through showing how guidebooks in Tokugawa and beyond became progressively more focused on what to see and what to eat, rather than on the sacred sites themselves.

119. Vaporis 1994, 247.

120. Maeda 1971, 52, 72–127, demonstrates that from the Tokugawa right up to the late 1960s, pilgrims in Saikoku considerably outnumbered those in Shikoku.

121. Shinjō 1982, 1066; and Maeda 1971, 251, both indicate that Shikoku pilgrims were poor and marginalized, while Miyazaki Ninshō 1985, 76–77, considers Shikoku to be more of a pilgrimage for the common people than was Saikoku.

122. Shinjō 1982, 1019–1022.

123. Maeda 1971, 122.

124. Takamure 1983, passim.

125. Kouamé 2001, 212–228.

126. Ibid., 216–228.

127. This text is given in Iyoshi Dankai 1981, 234–316; see also Yoritomi and Shiragi 2001, 139–141, for a brief summary of its themes.

128. Arai 1819, 88–111.

129. See Maeda 1971, 160–161, for fuller details of where the pilgrims came from.

130. Kouamé 2001, 70; and Shinjō 1982, 1048.

131. Hoshino 2001, 151. There were two sites on the *henro* (Temples 24 and 26) that, until the Meiji reforms, prohibited females from entering their precincts, but otherwise women were able to pursue the pilgrimage in the same manner as males.

132. Arai 1819, 104.

133. Maeda 1971, 99–103; see also Yamamoto 1995, 180–183. One should note, too, that Maeda is speaking here only of graves at the temples, not those found along the route as well.

134. These details are taken from the *Gokurakuji kakōchō*, examined at the temple on November 5, 1990.

135. This was the opinion of Rev. Aki Shōgen, head priest of Gokurakuji. I spent several days at Gokurakuji in November 1990 and in January and March 1991, during which time I had access to the *kakochō*. Hoshino 2001, 111–112, also considers that many pilgrims came on a "meritorious death or cure" pilgrimage.

136. This is the suggestion of Maeda 1971, 126, to account for a clear drop in pilgrim deaths in Meiji Japan.

137. Takamure 1987, 60.

138. See Hoshino 2001, 95, 117–121.

139. The biblical prejudices about leprosy are well known, of course, but similarly problematic views are evident in many other cultures and religious traditions. In some Buddhist and folk contexts, leprosy has been seen as the result of karmic sins, and even in some modern Japanese religions it remains anathema as a disease: the new Japanese religion Mahikari, e.g., while claiming that its spiritual healing techniques can cure virtually anything, regards leprosy as something that cannot be cured because it is the result of such deep karmic impediments (see Davis 1980, 37).

140. Shinjō 1982, 754; and Hoshino 2001, 117–121.

141. Maeda 1971, 261.

142. Ibid., 259.

143. Ibid., 258. Hoshino 2001, 120, mentions different routes for sufferers.

144. Interview October 1990; he was keen not to have the temple identified, and hence I have just given an approximate location for it.

145. Information from Rev. Aki Shōgen of Gokurakuji, November 5, 1990.

146. Dubisch 1995, 97.

147. Kouamé 2001, 40, gives a general overview plus French translation of this text.

148. See Maeda 1971, 254–259, 266–270, for further discussion and examples of the pejorative meanings of being a Shikoku pilgrim in Tokugawa times.

149. Imai Misako 1981, 88.

150. Kannuchi 1963, 1–2.

151. This is the title of an unpublished paper I gave at the University of Stirling in May 1993.

152. Maeda 1971, 265.

153. The text of this decree is given in Hiroe 1966, 22.

154. Kouamé 2001, 105.

155. Vaporis 1994, 153, 198–210.

156. This regulation is cited in Kouamé 1998, 61.

157. Shinjō 1982, 1023.

158. Kouamé 1998, 212.

159. Ibid., 188.

160. Ibid., 153.

161. Kouamé 2001, 115–119.

162. Ibid., 116–118

163. Ibid., 115–124.

164. Ibid., 119–124.

165. Yamamoto 1995, 154–156.

166. Kouamé 2001, 229–249.

167. See Kouamé 1997, 413.

168. For a comprehensive discussion of this period and the policies and their results on Buddhism, see, in particular, Ketelaar 1990.

169. Ehime-ken Shōgaigakushū Sentā 2001, 101.

170. This edict is given in Hiroe 1966, 13.

171. On the Anrakuji-Zenrakuji issue, see Ehime-ken Shōgaigakushū Sentā 2001, 101–102.

172. Shinno 1991a, 33, outlines this ban on *takuhatsu.*

173. I would like to thank an anonymous manuscript reviewer for alerting me to the nationwide push toward improving hygiene at this period and for suggesting that this also formed part of the context in which the antipilgrim invectives of the period should be considered.

174. The text of this editorial opinion piece is given in Hiroe 1966, 14–20. See also Yoritomi and Shiragi 2001, 188–191; and Ehime-ken Shōgaigakushū Sentā 2001, 112–114, for further comments.

175. Shinno 1991a, 27.

176. Ehime-ken Shōgaigakushū Sentā 2001, 113–114; and Shinno 1991a, 29.

177. See, e.g., the account in Takamure 1983, 217–220, of her encounter with two policemen and rumors of a pilgrim roundup at the lodge where she was staying. It should be noted that such roundups were not limited just to Tosa, although, as with so much of the antipilgrim hostility of the period, it was there that the most draconian manifestations of this activity appear to have occurred.

178. Maeda 1971, 109–112.

179. Shinno 1991a, 34.

180. Maeda 1971, 126; and Ehime-ken Shōgaigakushū Sentā 2001, 117.

181. These are (in sequence) Takamure 1983, 1987, 1939.

182. See, e.g., the description of one such lodge and its occupants in Takamure 1983, 95–98.

183. Yamamoto 1995, 225.

184. Takamure 1987, 56.

185. Ibid., 63.

186. Ibid., 64.

187. In April 2000 Kiyoyoshi Eitoku took me around Ehime Prefecture, pointing out the courses of different pilgrimage routes near Temple 65 and showing me

where new roads had developed in the mid-nineteenth century to accommodate horses and carts.

188. Kobayashi's pilgrimage is described in Hoshino 2001, 193.

189. Tanaka Hiroshi 1983, 33.

190. Hoshino 2001, 190–191, 262.

191. Shinno 1980, 56.

192. Ehime-ken Shōgaigakushū Sentā 2001, 130.

193. The title of this book was *Shikoku henro no hanashi,* and it was published in 1928 (according to Ehime-ken Shōgaigakushū Sentā 2001, 133). Unfortunately, I have not as yet been able to locate a copy of this book.

194. Shimomura and Iijima 1934.

195. Hoshino 2001, 193.

196. Shima 1930, 66.

197. Ibid., 1.

198. Ibid, 79.

199. Adachi 1934; see also Yoritomi and Shiragi 2001, 209–211, for details of its success as a guidebook.

200. Miyao 1943; see also Hoshino 2001, 195–200.

201. Ōzeki 1936, 60.

202. Ibid., 104

203. Ogihara 1941, 3–7, 123–124.

204. See Hoshino 2001, 203–204, for further discussion of Tomita and his magazine.

205. Ibid., 258–310.

206. Hayasaka 1992a, 248.

207. Hoshino 2001, 264–284.

208. This information came from officials of the Shikoku Reijōkai during interviews in January and February 1991, and their informal comments suggested that a certain amount of feuding over influence and power hindered the development of a formal organization prior to the war. However, I have not been able to verify this point via written sources.

209. Hoshino 2001, 203.

210. Ibid., 330–331. See Reader (forthcoming) for a fuller discussion of Shingon sectarian attempts to impose or assert Shingon interpretations and images onto the pilgrimage and to transform it into a Shingon pilgrimage with close ties to Kōyasan.

211. Ehime-ken Shōgaigakushū Sentā 2001, 132.

5. Shaping the Pilgrimage: From Poverty to the Package Tour in Postwar Japan

1. Information from the son, now head priest of Gokurakuji, November 1990.

2. This testimony came from our next-door neighbor in Hirakata, Osaka

Prefecture, where we lived from 1987–1989, who was born and brought up in Shikoku.

3. Interview, Nagahama, March 1991. See also Hoshino 1986b, 231, where he cites an old, now deceased Shikoku priest saying the same to him.

4. Tezuka 1988, 48.

5. Interview, Tokyo, January 8, 1991.

6. Yoritomi and Shiragi 2001, 216.

7. Waseda Daigaku Dōkūkan Kenkyūkai 1994, 76. My interviews with various officials at the Iyo Tetsu Company in October 1990 and April 2000 confirm this point: according to my interviewees at the company, the person who first saw the potential for pilgrimage tours was a young office worker named Nagano Hiroshi, who later became the company president.

8. Shikoku Reijō Sanpai Hōsankai 1953, 1 and frontispiece.

9. Waseda Daigaku Dōkūkan Kenkyūkai 1994, 76, gives the date as April 26, but Iyo Tetsu officials insisted to me that it was April 28, and this date is always used in *Henro* and Iyo Tetsu literature and is also the date I use. There is some dispute about the number of pilgrims involved: Osada, Sakata, and Seki 2003, 452, states that there were twelve, while Iyo Tetsu officials have told me that they think around twenty-five were involved.

10. Some information on this tour is found in Waseda Daigaku Dōkūkan Kenkyūkai 1994, 76, and additional material was provided by Tanaka-san of the Iyo Tetsu Company in an interview in April 2000. See also Yoritomi and Shiragi 2001, 217, for a brief account of the tour's problems.

11. Shikoku Reijō Sanpai Hōsankai 1954–1956 (2d and 3d eds.)

12. Seki 1999, 70.

13. Maeda 1971, 67.

14. Seki 1999, 70, gives the earlier figures; the later figures come from officials at Iyo Tetsu in April 2000.

15. Information about these companies was gathered during a number of interviews with company officials in Imabari and Takamatsu during October and November 1990.

16. Information from Reijōkai officials, temple priests, and officials from Iyo Tetsu, April 2000.

17. Information from the Bandō Taxi Company, Itano, Tokushima, January 30, 1991.

18. Maeda 1971, 47–54.

19. *Shikoku shinbun*, July 14, 1987, 20.

20. Satō Hisamitsu 1990a, 33–35. It should be noted, however, that not all pilgrims carry books or get them stamped and that temples may not always report every pilgrim who pays for the stamp.

21. Osada, Sakata, and Seki 2003, 456.

22. Ibid., 227.

23. Ibid., and Hoshino 2001, 264–284.

24. These statistics come from Satō Ken 1989. It should be noted that, as Foard 1982 has amply demonstrated, Saikoku was very much seen as a "national" pilgrimage in Tokugawa times.

25. Satō Hisamitsu 1990b; Hoshino 1981, 180–193; and 2001, 316.

26. See Ivy 1995, 34–35.

27. See Reader 1987a for further discussion of such issues, and Hoshino 2001, 320, for further discussion of why the *henro* retains this image of "tradition" in the present.

28. This information emerged during discussions with officials of the Reijōkai in April 2000. See also Osada, Sakata, and Seki 2003, 132–165. The Ehime government has especially put a lot of resources into the study of the pilgrimage because it regards it as one of the prefecture's great cultural resources.

29. When we stayed overnight at this temple in 1984, the road up to Yokomineji had opened only a month before, and the priest and his wife had already noted a decrease in the numbers of their visitors.

30. Interview with temple priest, Sankakuji (Temple 65), April 7, 2000.

31. I base these comments on interviews with officials from Kotosan, Iyo Tetsu, and an Osaka-based company, Tōyō Kankō, whose tour will be described in chapter 7.

32. *Chūgai Nippō* (May 28, 1995).

33. See also Reader 1991, 161–167, for further examples and discussion.

34. Iwanami Shashin Bunko 1956, 46.

35. Seki 1999, 61.

36. Kagita 1962, 85.

37. Hoshino 2001, 261.

38. Interview, Chōchinya, October 16, 1990.

39. Indeed, a temple priest (for diplomatic reasons left unnamed here) told me that the owners of this lodge had been more than just astute in their business dealings with bus companies and in ensuring that they flourished while their rivals closed down.

40. Interview, Sankakuji (Temple 65), April 7, 2000.

41. Interview at a shop near Tatsueji, April 12, 2000.

42. I develop this term from Marion Bowman's discussion (1993, 49) of the "service industry" around the English pilgrimage center of Glastonbury.

43. See Reader 1987a, 134–135, for a discussion of commercial pilgrimage advertisements, including those of Iyo Tetsu.

44. Interview, February 8, 1991, Takamatsu, Shikoku.

45. This idea of Shikoku as the "most traditional" pilgrimage in Japan has been cited as a reason for its popularity by many people such as Hoshino (e.g., 1981, 2001) and Matsubara (1987). My observations at Saikoku, too, are that the numbers of people who wear other than everyday clothes when they visit is very small in comparison with Shikoku.

46. Interview with a temple official at Temple 5, November 6, 1990, and observations at Temple 10, November 7, 1990.

47. Information from Tanaka-san, April 2000, and corroborated by officials from the Reijōkai.

48. Information is somewhat scarce as to exact dates: Waseda Daigaku Dōkū-kan Kenkyūkai 1994, 21, gives 1956 as the formal starting date, while my interviews with Reijōkai officials in 1990–1991 indicate that a more informal structure developed in 1955 and became formalized in 1956.

49. I am grateful to various temple priests for explaining to me the workings of the Reijōkai. Osada, Sakata, and Seki 2003, 116–117, gives the formal structures of the organization.

50. This does not mean that it regulates each temple's individual spending and tax affairs, which are the concern of each individual temple and priest, but all collective financial matters.

51. I am grateful to officials of the Reijōkai for information about their activities; see also Osada, Sakata, and Seki 2003, 118–129, for an extended discussion of these roles.

52. Hoshino 2001, 380, note 31, suggests that a Reijōkai guidebook from 1974 was especially important in this context.

53. I am aware of some unease about the emphasis that gets placed on Shingon doctrinal issues by some people in the Reijōkai. Such unease has been expressed to me by temple priests who are themselves Shingon but who feel that the *henro* should retain a nonsectarian ambience. I have not been able to say much about such tensions partly because while some priests have spoken to me about them, they have also wished that such matters remain largely off the record.

54. Matsuura Harutake 1988, 8.

55. See Hatada Zenpō 1989, 1990; and Hatada Shuhō n.d-b. I should note that the Hatada family in general has been generous in assisting this researcher as well.

56. *Henro* 190 (2000):2.

57. Much of the information in the following sections comes from Reader 1993d, supplemented by interviews with Reijōkai officials.

58. See Shinjō 1982, 200–220, for a general discussion of *sendatsu* in Japanese religious culture.

59. Swanson 1981, 57, 62–63.

60. Chōzen 1653 [1981], 24, 26.

61. Shikoku Reijōkai Honbu 1983 [1967].

62. See, e.g., the comments of Fujita Kendō (1986, 4), the priest of Kichijōji (Temple 63), as reported in *Henro*.

63. *Henro* 64 (1989):8.

64. Kotosan, based in Takamatsu, is relatively local to Zentsūji, where the meetings are held, and I believe its assistance is a result of this close link.

65. Osada, Sakata, and Seki 2003, 458, states that Suzuki Fūei was awarded this rank at the 1997 Sendatsukai meeting. In 2000, however, Reijōkai officials told me that there were no *genro daisendatsu,* and Osada and Sakata confirmed to me that this was so in November 2002. It may be that Suzuki died and that no one else has yet attained the rank.

66. These figures were given to me in 1990, and I was informed in April 2000 that they still pertained then.

67. These numbers were given to me by Reijōkai officials in 1991 and 2000. Osada, Sakata, and Seki 2003, 127, gives figures for promotions and new *sendatsu* in the 1990s.

68. This point came out in interviews conducted with priests from Anrakuji, Gokurakuji, Taisanji, and others in interviews during October–November 1990 and March 1991 and April 2000.

69. See Reader 1993d for examples of this phenomenon.

70. Mizutani 1984, 49–54.

71. See also *Henro* 28 (1986):3, and 49 (1988):3, for further examples of this story.

72. The first time I heard this story was from members of the Kansai Sendatsukai at the aforementioned exhibition in Osaka in December 1990.

73. Mori Harumi 1999, 10–11.

74. Interview with Miyazaki, Matsuyama, April 8, 2000.

75. In 1986, e.g., there were seven people at this rank, three of whom were female (*Henro* 28 [1986]:3).

76. Shinno 1991a, 91.

77. This issue of the unmediated nature of pilgrimage and the importance of the rumor of miracles is central to the work of Victor and Edith Turner (1978, 25).

78. This book is Shikoku Hachijūhakkasho Reijōkai 1989; the photograph in question is on 27.

79. See NHK 1990.

80. I discuss in fuller detail how nostalgia and tradition are transformed into symbols of cultural heritage and discuss the significance of the notion of "spiritual homeland" *(kokoro no furusato)* in Reader 1987a, where I also provide examples of such imagery and advertisements used by Iyo Tetsu and others (291–292).

81. The priests at Ryōzenji make a list each year of those who start their pilgrimages on foot there: in 1989 the number was 136 (information from Ryōzenji, November 5, 1990), although the priest conceded that there were probably others who did not sign or start there.

82. See *Henro* 49 (1988):2–3 for further details of this exhibition.

83. See the report and photographs in *Henro* 50 (1988):4–5.

84. See *Henro* 48–50 (1988) for various articles on the bridge and the walk across it.

85. The Reijōkai video is titled *Shikoku henro: Ima wo ikiru michishirube.* Its web site is www.henro.org. Colleagues have informed me that a CD-ROM has

recently been issued in Japan containing material similar to the video and other Reijōkai productions.

86. Fujita 1996; this image of a journey through nature is highlighted on the book's dust jacket.

87. Miyazaki 1995.

88. Kagita 1962, 31.

89. Noda 1983, 173.

90. *Shikoku shinbun*, July 14, 1987, 20.

91. Interview conducted in Kagawa Prefecture, February 7, 1991.

92. Hoshino 2001, 355.

93. The Kagawa government, e.g., began a scheme in 1993 to emphasize Shikoku as a "walking island" (Osada, Sakata, and Seki 2003, 457).

94. Even as early as 1991 this was the case in one village in Kōchi where my wife and I had stayed in 1984. At the time there was nowhere in the area for pilgrims to stay, but the family running a local grocery store offered us lodgings, stating that they had for generations lodged pilgrims as *settai*. In 1991, when we returned to the area to visit this family, we noticed a small pilgrims' lodge in the village, which had, we were told, been opened by a local priest who wanted to help pilgrims.

95. Among such sites are www.kushima.com/henro, www.henshubu.org, and www.happy.or.jp/96082900/henro/henro.htm. Osada, Sakata, and Seki 2003, 461, notes that in 2001 the Japanese version of the Yahoo search engine had recognized the term "*Shikoku henro*" as a valid search category item.

6. Walking Pilgrimages: Meaning and Experience on the Pilgrim's Way

1. I have been given one unpublished journal that records the one hundredth pilgrimage circuit of Matsuura Harutake (see chapter 3), compiled by his son (Matsuura Tadatoshi [1988]), which focuses largely on practical details of where they went and what they did, but I have not come across much other writing about bus pilgrimages. There is one book that I know of by a cyclist-pilgrim describing his experiences (Kita 2000), but as yet I have come across none by taxi, car, or helicopter pilgrims

2. Frey 1998, 160.

3. See, e.g., Harada 1999, 107–109, which tells us about the route and scenery on the way to Temple 39 but then deals with the temple in one line, with a single comment on an interesting bronze turtle statue at the temple. Elsewhere, when walking through Imabari, where a number of temples are close together, he covers four temples in the space of twelve lines.

4. See, e.g., ibid., 86–87.

5. E.g., ibid, 25.

6. Ibid, 156.

7. Ibid, 34.

8. Ibid. 34, 196.

9. Ibid., 141.

10. See, e.g., Satō Takako 1999b, 61–68; Harada 1999, 81–85; and Kagayama 2000, 170–176. Barbara Aziz (1987), in critiquing socially/group-based theories of pilgrimage, has argued for an individual interpretation of pilgrimage and has suggested, based on her fieldwork interviews, that pilgrims may not care about the motives, feelings, or experiences of other pilgrims. This is not, however, my view, based on Shikoku pilgrims' accounts and on interviews with many pilgrims along the way; pilgrims very often are concerned about the feelings and interests of other pilgrims—a point I will discuss more fully in the next chapter, where I look more closely at Aziz's comments in the context of the views of bus pilgrims in Shikoku.

11. E.g., see Harada 1999, 72, 184.

12. Ibid., 81–85.

13. Ibid., 72.

14. Ikeda's comments are in his foreword to Kagita 1962, 1–2, in which he states his illness (I believe it was a skin complaint or infection) was cured through doing a *henro*. Although Ikeda does not state which pilgrimage this was, I have heard through various sources that it was a small-scale, eighty-eight-stage pilgrimage in the Inland Sea region.

15. Kagita 1962, 51–52, 136, expresses various criticisms of temple priests and makes unfavorable comments about innkeepers (99–100).

16. Kagayama 2000, 325.

17. Miyazaki Tateki, cited in Hoshino 2001, 364.

18. Harada 1999, 164–166. See also Kagayama 2000 and Shiraga 1997 for similarly worried accounts. The journals my wife and I kept of our 1984 pilgrimage contain similar themes, and I remember vividly the daily unease on this matter, often involving long discussions with the people whose lodge we had stayed at overnight to work out where we would probably be the next night and what accommodations might be available.

19. Harada 1999, 69–70, 165–167.

20. Ibid., 167.

21. Watanabe Yasuhiro 1999; see also Zaitsu 2000, 249–254, which also gives a chart of the itinerary that he and his wife followed and the distances they covered every day.

22. Shiraga 1997.

23. Nishikawa 1999.

24. Harada 1999, 79–80.

25. Ibid., 139.

26. Tsukioka 2002, 56.

27. Interview with male pilgrim near Temple 3, April 11, 2000.

28. Frey 1998, 30.

29. Satō Takako 1999b; Mori Harumi 1999, whose title, *Onna henro genki*

tabi, translates as the "Healthy travels of a female pilgrim"; Takamure 1983; and Tsukioka 2000.

30. See, e.g., Zaitsu 2000, 31, for a description of the Shōsanji *henro korogashi*, and Kagayama 2000, 306, for comments on the *henro korogashi* leading to Yokomineji.

31. Kagayama 2000, 258–259.

32. Harada 1999, 11, 64–65, 107, respectively.

33. Ibid., 49; and Hirota 1999, 226. Hirota estimates that about 80 percent of the henro is along roads.

34. Takada Shinkai 1985, 14, 42.

35. Hirota 1999, 225–226; and Imai Misako 1981, 37.

36. Harada 1999, 45–46.

37. This, e.g., was the course of action taken by Tosa (1972, 132–133) in the early 1970s and by Itō (1985, 23–24).

38. Hirota 1999, 226.

39. Tsukioka 2002, 117–119.

40. See, e.g., Kagita 1962, 53.

41. Takada Shinkai 1985, 21. See also MacGregor 2002, 46, for further pilgrim complaints about *shukubō* not being helpful to single pilgrims (and also the fact that many are not open outside of the peak pilgrimage season).

42. Kobayashi 1990, 216–225.

43. Harada 1999, 128.

44. This point surfaced, e.g., in the comments of respondents to the Waseda survey (Waseda Daigaku Dōkūkan Kenkyūkai 1997, 157), where respondents complained about the delay when group representatives produced piles of books to be stamped and also said that individual foot pilgrims ought to be given precedence over group pilgrims.

45. See Osada, Sakata, and Seki 2003, 407–409, which shows that while 20 percent of those surveyed disapproved of pilgrimages using vehicles, 27 percent fully approved, and 48 percent to some extent approved of them.

46. These comments were made to me while visiting Matsuyama in October 1990 and are representative of general comments made to me over the years during my visits to Shikoku. See also Waseda Daigaku Dōkūkan Kenkyūkai 1997, 151, for a series of comments by pilgrims about office opening hours and related issues. Opinion columns in the newsletter *Henro* also often contain comments along similar lines.

47. Tsukioka 2002, 126.

48. Harada 1999, 171–172.

49. Ibid., 172.

50. Tsukioka 2002, 126.

51. Satō Ken 1989, 13.

52. Hoshino 2001, 335.

53. Shiraga 1997, 131.
54. Tsukioka 2002, 24–27, 114.
55. See Takada Kyōko 2000, 172–179.
56. Satō Takako 1999b, 94.
57. Harada 1999, 37–41.
58. Satō Takako 1999b, 92–94.
59. Kagayama 2000, 225–226.
60. Harada 1999, 26.
61. Ibid., 31–32.
62. Takada Kyōko 2000, 11, 34.
63. Watanabe Yasuhiro 1999, 110.
64. Hosoya 1999; and Satō Takako 1999b, 136.
65. Satō Ken 1989, 27–30; and Harada 1999, 149–152.
66. See, e.g., Hoshino 2001, 368.
67. See, e.g., Shiraga 1997, 127–136.
68. See, e.g., Mori Harumi 1999, 38.
69. Harada 1999, 86–87. See also Hoshino 2001, 371, for the account of a female pilgrim in such contexts.
70. Harada 1999, 71–74.
71. Ibid., 115–116.
72. Ibid., 118–120.
73. Satō Takako 1999b, 198–201.
74. Ibid., 95–96.
75. Harada 1999, 121–125; and Kagita 1962, 64.
76. Satō Takako 1999b, 136.
77. Harada 1999, 25–26.
78. Watanabe Yasuhiro 1999, 28–43.
79. Kagita 1962, 57, 89.
80. Harada 1999, 214.
81. Kagita 1962, 216.
82. Ibid., esp. 223.
83. Ibid., 216.
84. Harada 1999, 192–193.
85. Watanabe 1999, 141.
86. Satō Takako 1999b, 134–138.
87. Hoshino 2001, 375–377.
88. Nishikawa 1999, 12.
89. Harada 1999, 207–208. See also Nishikawa 1999, 220–226, for similar comments.
90. Harada 1999, 215–218.
91. Kobayashi 1990, 237.
92. Harada 1999, 215–219.
93. Ibid., 220.

94. Kobayashi 1990, 14–15.

95. Ibid., 223.

96. Nishikawa 1999, 221.

97. Kagita 1962, 215.

98. Kagita 1962, 51–52, raises this issue because he felt one temple was badly maintained and that he could help improve it; later, on page 97, he speaks again of his wish to work for his country and society and again returns to this idea of going back to Shikoku to help at this temple.

99. Among such sites I have come across are www.kushima.com/henro and www.henshubu.org.

7. Making Bus Pilgrimages: Practice and Experience on the Package Tour

1. For a discussion of how I joined this tour and the role of chance in research, see Reader 2003.

2. Gold 1989, 271–277.

3. Christine King (1993, 92) has commented also on how the idea of "next year in Graceland" (Elvis Presley's home and the focus of an annual pilgrimage by fans during Elvis Memorial Week in August each year) is found among fans who make that pilgrimage.

4. Aziz 1987, 254.

5. See Osada, Sakata, and Seki 2003, 329–332, and Reader and Tanabe 1998, 200–201.

6. I have discussed these issues, and specifically the notion of pilgrimages in the context of prayers for preventing senility, in Reader 1995, 12–15.

7. In my field notebook I failed to record who did this, but I think it was the Matsudas.

8. Sallnow 1981, 173.

9. Gold 1989, 263, 291–292.

8. A Way of Life: Pilgrimage, Transformation, and Permanence

1. Frey 1998, 177.

2. Critiques of Turner tend to focus on his discussion of *communitas*, while his liminal paradigm remains widely accepted as a standard mode of interpretation, and this emphasizes the idea of an "out there" disjunction from the norm. I also think that the paradigm proposed by Eade and Sallnow 1991 and others of pilgrimage as a setting for contest, coupled with their views of sacred sites as largely "empty" arenas in which such contests can be enacted, also places immense emphasis on the site and the transitory activities that occur there and fails to give adequate consideration to what happens before and after engagement with the sacred center.

3. See Gold 1988, 1; and Frey 1998, 178–179, for their comments on these problematic issues in the methodological study of pilgrimage.

4. Sax 1991 also shows similar themes in his study of Himalayan pilgrimages.

5. Frey 1998, 177–231.

6. Kawano 1977, 15.

7. Takamure and Hashimoto 1965, 159.

8. Hoshino 2001, 12.

9. Ibid., 233.

10. *Yomiuri shinbun,* February 27, 1990.

11. Tattebe 1985, 9–17.

12. Two short accounts of Tsujita's experiences can be found in pilgrimage miracle collections: Tsujita 1984, 162–169; and 1985, 218–220.

13. Tsujita 1984, 162–169, largely narrates the same story he told me, albeit with occasional differences: in his oral account he told me that no one apart from him had seen the monk who entered his house, while in his written account his father shows the monk in.

14. Conversation with Statler after a seminar presentation by him in October 1992 at the University of Hawai'i at Mānoa, Honolulu.

15. Frey 1998, 179–180, comments on the shock many Santiago pilgrims feel when they use such means to return and how the speed of trains and planes causes a severely disjunctive feeling. I recall being similarly disturbed when, after forty days on foot in Shikoku in 1984, I got back on a train again.

16. For further details and a full discussion of Yamamoto's life, see Obigane 2002. Yamamoto has been discussed in a rather different context by Brian Victoria (2003) because of his nationalism in the war period, although this aspect of his activities is outside the scope of my current study of the *henro.*

17. The most widely used guidebook at this period was Hirahata 1982, vols. 1 and 2, which we used when we walked in 1984 because there was little else available but which is mainly focused on road transport and is not always accurate about footpaths.

18. The three books, respectively, are Miyazaki Tateki 1993 and 1995 and Henro Michi Hozon Kyōryokukai 1995.

19. I base this comment on interviews conducted with priests at temples in Sasaguri in October 1988 and on information gathered in Shōdoshima during over a dozen visits there from 1985–1997.

20. Eck 1983, 28.

21. Frey 1998, 87ff.

22. Ibid., 211.

23. Ibid., 211–212.

24. This was the basic assumption about pilgrimage as devised by participants in a conference on pilgrimage at the University of Pittsburgh in 1981, as reported by Morinis 1981.

Conclusion

1. See the comments on this point in Reader and Swanson 1997, 226–227.

2. See John Eade's new introduction to *Contesting the Sacred* in which he recognizes the problem of grand narratives and theories in the study of pilgrimage—even as he speaks of the influence such narratives and theories have had on his work (2000, xx–xxi).

3. A similar point has been made by Toni Huber about Tibetan pilgrimage, which, Huber says, has no single discourse, for different people from different perspectives (e.g., high lamas and illiterate nomads) have both different experiences and different competing interpretations of the same pilgrimage (1999, 20).

Glossary

The terms below are widely used in the context of the Shikoku pilgrimage. I give a general definition of each term along with the kanji (ideograms) normally used to write them and, where applicable, the hiragana (Japanese syllabary), which is often also used to write them in Shikoku. Many of these terms may be commonly used with Japanese honorific expressions (e.g., the prefix 'o-' or 'go-').

aibeya 相部屋 communal rooms (found in old pilgrimage lodges).

akazue 赤杖 red pilgrim's staff; carried by senior *sendatsu*. Such a staff has been given by the Reijōkai to the Iyo Tetsu Company for its services to the pilgrimage.

atodōri 後通り "coming along after"; when company officials follow behind a pilgrimage party carrying their scrolls and getting them stamped, so as to not slow down the journey of the pilgrims.

bangai 番外 pilgrimage site not on the official list of eighty-eight temples but often visited by pilgrims and considered to have a special link to the route.

bodai 菩提 state of enlightenment; also the third stage (the Iyo temples) of the pilgrimage in Shingon orthodox interpretations.

bonnō 煩悩 evil passions; in Buddhism, hindrances on the path to enlightenment.

chaya 茶屋 teahouse.

chū sendatsu 中先達 third-level rank in the *sendatsu* system.

daisan 代参 performing the pilgrimage on behalf of someone else.

daisendatsu 大先達 fifth-level rank in the *sendatsu* system.

Daishi 大師 "Great Teacher"; title bestowed on various famous Japanese Buddhist leaders, but when used just in this form, always referring to Kōbō Daishi.

Daishi shinkō 大師信仰 faith in Kōbō Daishi.

daishidō 大師堂 hall of worship to Kōbō Daishi.

degaichō 出開帳 exhibiting Buddhist images (at a site away from the temple where they are normally housed).

dōgyō 同行 someone doing the practice as oneself; a fellow pilgrim.

dōgyōninin 同行二人 "two people doing the same practice together"; concept that Kōbō Daishi is doing the pilgrimage with the pilgrim.

dōgyōsan (sha) 同行さん（者） a fellow pilgrim.

eika 詠歌 pilgrimage song; each temple has its own one, which contains special references to events or characteristics of the temple concerned.

ekiroji 駅路寺 temple established as a lodging facility for pilgrims.

engi 縁起 foundation legend/story (of a temple).

fuda 札 (also often written in hiragana ふだ) pilgrim's name slip and offering, formerly made of wood or metal, now usually of paper, containing pilgrim's name and prayers; also an amulet received at temples and shrines.

fudasho 札所 pilgrimage site/temple (literally "the place where one leaves one's *fuda*").

fudasho hachijūhachi 札所八十八 eighty-eight pilgrimage sites; first reference to the number eighty-eight in connection with the pilgrimage, from Chōzen's 1653 journal.

furusato ふるさと (usually nowadays written in hiragana); "one's native village" —term used in nostalgic discourse to refer to the notion of a traditional homeland.

genro daisendatsu 元老大先達 seventh and highest-level rank in the *sendatsu* system.

gokasho 五か所 five-site pilgrimage route.

gonchū sendatsu 権中先達 second-level of the *sendatsu* system.

gondai sendatsu 権大先達 fourth-level rank in the *sendatsu* system.

goriyaku ご利益 benefits (primarily this worldly and practical).

gyaku uchi 逆うち doing the pilgrimage "in reverse order" (i.e., going around the island anticlockwise).

hachijūhakkasho 八十八か所 the Shikoku pilgrimage (literally "eighty-eight places"—a term referring to the number of sites on the route).

haibutsu kishaku 廃仏棄釈 "destroying Buddhism and driving out the buddhas" —the campaign launched by the Meiji government to eradicate Buddhism.

hakui 白衣 pilgrim's white shirt/shroud.

hannyatō 般若湯 "wisdom water"; Buddhist euphemism for *sake*.

hashiri hendo 走り遍路 running pilgrims; term used for poor local pilgrims, usually on initiatory pilgrimages, who ran *(hashiri)* to save time and money. The ideograms read here as *hendo* are usually read as *henro*, but in this context the alternative (pejorative) reading was used.

heji 辺地 early term used for the route and practice of going around the island; believed to be the precursor of the term *"henro."*

henro 遍路 (also often written in hiragana へんろ) the Shikoku pilgrimage. Also used to refer to the pilgrims who are *henro* (normally with an honorific such as *o-henro* or *o-henro-san*). When referring to pilgrims, the term is normally written in hiragana, not in kanji.

henro ai 遍路愛 "pilgrims' love"; term used by Tomita Gakuun and Takamure Itsue in the 1930s to suggest communal feelings between pilgrims.

henro boke 遍路ぼけ pilgrimage senility/immersion (state of becoming wholly absorbed in the process of walking the pilgrimage).

henro ishi 遍路石 (also often written in hiragana へんろいし) pilgrimage stones erected as markers of distances and directions on the pilgrimage route.

henro korogashi 遍路ころがし "pilgrimage falling place"; term used for very steep paths on the pilgrimage route in the mountains, usually leading up to mountain temples such as Temple 60.

henro michi 遍路道 or へんろ道 the pilgrimage route/path in Shikoku.

henrogari 遍路狩り "pilgrim roundups" conducted by the police from the 1870s until the 1930s to keep pilgrims in check and arrest miscreants and those suspected of having no funds.

henroya 遍路屋 pilgrimage lodge, usually wayside huts for overnight free lodgings.

higaeri 日帰り day return visits—a contemporary way of doing the pilgrimage by day return visits to the sites.

higan 彼岸 "the other shore"; Buddhist festival for the dead at the spring and autumn equinoxes.

hijiri 聖 wandering holy persons and ascetic practitioners, usually with Buddhist connections, active in medieval and premodern Japan.

honzon 本尊 main image of a temple.

honzon junrei 本尊巡礼 pilgrimage whose core theme is visiting a number of temples, all of which have the same sacred figure (e.g., Kannon) as their main image of worship.

hosshin 発心 "awakening the Buddha mind"; term used to refer to the first stage of the pilgrimage (the Awa temples) in Shingon Buddhist orthodox terms.

Ichinomiya 一の宮 (also 一宮) state Shinto shrines established by the Imperial Court in each province for the defense of the realm; four such were pilgrimage sites on the *henro* until the 1870s, and all remain locations of modern-day pilgrimage temples.

ihai 位牌 Buddhist memorial tablet for the ancestors.

ikkoku mairi 一国まいり "one province pilgrimage"; visiting the temples in one prefecture of Shikoku.

Ise oshi 伊勢御師 Pilgrimage guides linked to the sacred shrines of Ise.

jūkasho 十か所 ten-site pilgrimage route.

junrei 巡礼 pilgrimage; standard Japanese term for multiple-site pilgrimages.

juzu 数珠 Buddhist rosary, usually worn around the wrist.

kaichō 開帳 publicly exhibiting the normally hidden Buddhist image of a temple.

kaimyō 戒名 Buddhist posthumous name.

kakejiku 掛け軸 hanging scroll (on which pilgrims get the stamps of the temples).

kakochō 過去帳 death register.

kami 神 (Shinto) deity.

kasa 笠 pilgrim's hat (normally of sedge/bamboo).

kechiganjo 結願所 place where one's vow is complete (i.e., the last pilgrimage on one's journey).

kinen shashin 記念写真 commemorative photograph.

Kōbō Daishi 弘法大師 sacred figure at the center of the pilgrimage; also posthumous title of Kūkai.

Kokubunji 国分寺 state Buddhist temples established for the protection of the realm in each province in the eighth century; four such temples are on the *henro*.

Kōyasan 高野山 sacred center of the Shingon sect, in Wakayama Prefecture, founded by Kūkai.

Kūkai 空海 Buddhist monk (774–835) born in Shikoku, founder of the Shingon sect and Kōyasan and founder, in legend, of the *henro*.

Kumano mōde 熊野詣で Kumano pilgrimage.

kuyō 供養 memorial service/ritual for the spirits of the dead.

mairi 参り (also often written in hiragana まいり) pilgrimage, visit to a sacred center.

mandala 曼陀羅 spiritual/ritual representation of the cosmos in esoteric Buddhism.

michishirube 道しるべ pilgrimage route marker.

mizuko 水子 fetus that has died in the womb (commonly via abortion).

mōde 詣で pilgrimage, visit to a sacred site/place.

mokujiki 木食 tree eating; term of reference for ascetics (especially in the seventeenth–eighteenth centuries) who lived on wild food, such as bark, nuts, and pine needles, from trees.

muga 無我 selflessness (Buddhist concept).

mūshikai 無色界 world of nonform, formless realm.

mushinkō 無信仰 without faith, having no faith.

musume 娘 young woman (term used in titles of various pilgrimage accounts by young female pilgrims, e.g., by Takamure Itsue).

namu daishi henjō kongō 南無大師遍照金剛 "hail to Daishi the universally resplendent diamond"; the consecration name given to Kūkai by his Chinese Buddhist teacher master, Hui-kuo (746–805), and used as an invocation of praise to Kōbō Daishi by pilgrims.

nanakasho 七か所 seven-site pilgrimage route.

nehan 涅槃 absolute enlightenment; also the final stage in the journey to enlightenment in Shingon terms, and the fourth stage of the pilgrimage.

nojuku 野宿 sleeping out, sleeping rough.

nōkyō 納経 receiving the stamps or seals of each temple one visits.

nōkyōchō 納経帳 pilgrim's book in which the temple seals are affixed.

nōkyōjo 納経所 temple office where pilgrims' scrolls and books are stamped.

ōji 王子 sacred places along the Kumano pilgrimage route.

okashi お菓子 Japanese sweet cakes.

okunoin 奥の院 inner sanctum; also refers to a subsidiary temple linked to a main temple.

omamori お守り amulet.

ōraitegata 往来手形 Tokugawa-era pilgrim's passport/travel document.

orei mairi お礼参り "thanks visit"; the visit made by pilgrims after completing the pilgrimage to the temple where they started, to give thanks for a safe trip.

osamefuda 納め札 the pilgrim's *fuda* that is stored or left at temples as a sign of a pilgrim's visit.

petto kuyō ペット供養 memorial service for deceased pets.

reigen 霊験 miracle.

reijō 霊場 pilgrimage site/temple (literally "spirit place").

Reijōkai 霊場会 abbreviated name of the Shikoku Pilgrimage Temples' Association, the organization representing the eighty-eight Shikoku temples and administering aspects of the *henro*.

reizan 霊山 "spirit mountain"; mountain where the souls of the dead congregate and are venerated.

risutora リストラ "restructuring"; capitalist weasel word relating to maximizing profits and reducing workforces; used also to indicate people who, as a result, have been thrown out of work.

Saikoku sanjūsankasho junrei 西国三十三か所巡礼 pilgrimage to the thirty-three sacred temples of Saikoku/the thirty-three-stage Saikoku pilgrimage.

sakidōri 先通り "going along ahead"; when company officials go ahead of a pilgrimage party carrying their scrolls and getting them stamped in advance, so that the scrolls are waiting when the pilgrims end their journey.

satori 悟り spiritual awakening, enlightenment.

seichi 聖地 sacred territory, holy land.

seiseki 聖跡 holy traces (of a figure of worship).

seiseki junrei 聖跡巡礼 "holy traces pilgrimage"; pilgrimage route that visits a series of temples/sites associated with the travels or presence of a holy figure.

sekihan 赤飯 dish of red beans and rice; a common Japanese celebratory meal.

sekisho 関所 barrier gate; also in pilgrimage lore, a temple on the route beyond which one cannot pass unless pure in spirit.

sendatsu 先達 pilgrimage guide/leader; also title conferred by the Shikoku Reijōkai on pilgrims who do the *henro* multiple times.

sendatsu kenshūkai 先達研修会 training meeting for *sendatsu*.

sendatsu seido 先達制度 sendatsu system operated by the Shikoku Reijōkai.

sendatsu taikai 先達大会 annual general meeting for *sendatsu*.

settai 接待 alms given to pilgrims.

settaisho 接待所 place where alms are distributed to pilgrims.

shakyō 写経 making copies of Buddhist sutras (for offering at temples).

shikikai 色界 phenomenal world, world of form.

Shikoku byō 四国病 "Shikoku sickness"; term used by some in Shikoku to refer to the "addictive" nature of the *henro* and the tendency of some to do it repeatedly.

Shikoku Reijōkai 四国霊場会 Shikoku Pilgrimage Temples' Association.

Shikoku shugyō 四国修行 "Shikoku austerity"; early term referring to ascetic travels around Shikoku.

shinbutsu bunri 神仏分離 "separating the *kami* from the buddhas"; Meiji campaign to enforce the institutional separation of Shinto shrines from Buddhist temples.

Shingon 真言 name of the Buddhist tradition established in Japan by Kūkai; Shingon means "true word" or mantra.

Shugendō 修験道 mountain ascetic tradition in Japan that influenced the development of pilgrimages such as Shikoku.

shugyō 修行 ascetic practice, austerities.

shuin 朱印 red ink seal stamped onto pilgrims' books and scrolls by temples.

shukubō 宿坊 pilgrims' lodge located at a temple.

sunafumi 砂踏み "walking on the soil"; small-scale pilgrimage route made by taking soil from each temple on a pilgrimage and placing it (usually in front of small statues representing each temple) in a circuit.

takuhatsu 托鉢 begging for alms by Buddhist monks and pilgrims.

tokunin daisendatsu 特任大先達 sixth-level rank in the *sendatsu* system.

tsue 杖 pilgrim's staff.

wagesa 輪袈裟 surplice worn by lay Buddhists (often worn by pilgrims in Shikoku, especially when traveling as part of a group or pilgrimage association).

yakudoshi 厄年 dangerous or unlucky year; in Japanese popular/folk beliefs, certain years are unlucky or dangerous: the most common of these are the forty-second year for males, the thirty-third for females, and the thirteenth for children.

yamabushi 山伏 mountain ascetics, usually associated with the Shugendō tradition, who were associated with the development of the pilgrimage.

yokukai 欲海 realm/world of desires.

zenkonyado 善根宿 "good deed/charity lodging"; free lodging and lodges for pilgrims.

References

Abe, Ryūichi. 1999. *The weaving of mantra: Kūkai and the construction of esoteric Buddhist discourse* (New York: Columbia University Press).

Adachi Chūichi. 1934. *Dōgyō ninin Shikoku henro tayori* (Osaka: Kineidō Shuppan).

Aoki Tamotsu. 1985. *Ontake junrei—gendai kami to hito* (Tokyo: Chikuma Shobō).

Arai Raisuke. 1819. *Shikoku junpai nikki.* Text in Hiroe Kiyoshi, ed. 1966. *Kinsei Tosa henro shiryō* (Kōchi: Tosa Minzoku Gakkai), 88–111.

Araki Michio. 1990. Junrei no genshō. *Bukkyō* 12 (July 1990):65–75.

Aziz, Barbara. 1987. Personal dimensions of the sacred journey: What pilgrims say. *Religious Studies* 23.2:247–261.

Baba, Junko. 2000. *Settai* practice in the Shikoku pilgrimage: Maintenance and change of tradition in the modern context. *Virginia Review of Asian Studies* 2:91–110.

Barber, Richard. 1991. *Pilgrimages* (Woodbridge, U.K.: The Boydell Press).

Bhardwaj, Surinder. 1973. *Hindu places of pilgrimage in India: A study in cultural geography* (Berkeley: University of California Press).

Blacker, Carmen. 1975. *The catalpa bow: A study of shamanistic practices in Japan* (London: George Allen and Unwin).

Bowman, Glenn. 1988. Pilgrimage conference report. *Anthropology Today* 4.6: 20–23.

Bowman, Marion. 1993. Drawn to Glastonbury. In Reader and Walter, eds., *Pilgrimage in popular culture*, 29–62.

Childs, Wendy R. 1999. The perils, or otherwise, of maritime pilgrimage to Santiago de Compostela in the fifteenth century. In J. Stopford, ed., *Pilgrimage explored* (York: York Medieval Press), 123–143.

Chōzen. 1653. *Shikoku henro nikki.* Text in Iyoshi Dankai, ed. 1981. *Shikoku henro kishū*, 21–67.

Coleman, Simon. 2000. Meanings of movement, place and home at Walsingham. *Culture and Religion* 1.2:153–170.

Coleman, Simon, and John Elsner.1995. *Pilgrimage past and present in the world religions* (Cambridge, Mass: Harvard University Press).

———. 1999. Pilgrimage to Walsingham and the re-invention of the Middle Ages. In J. Stopford, ed., *Pilgrimage explored* (York: York Medieval Press), 189–214.

Crumrine, N. Ross, and Alan Morinis. 1991. La Peregrinacion: The Latin American pilgrimage. In Crumrine and Morinis, eds., *Latin American pilgrimage* (Connecticut: Greenwood Press), 1–17.

Daihōrinkaku henshūbu, ed. 1997. *Nihon zenkoku junrei jiten* (Tokyo: Daihōrinkaku).

Davies, Horton, and Marie-Hélène Davies. 1982. *Holy days and holidays: The medieval pilgrimage to Compostela* (London: Associated University Presses).

Davis, Winston B. 1980. *Dojo: Magic and exorcism in modern Japan* (Stanford, Calif.: Stanford University Press).

Dillon, Matthew. 1997. *Pilgrims and pilgrimage in ancient Greece* (London: Routledge).

Dubisch, Jill. 1995. *In a different place: Pilgrimage, gender, and practice at a Greek island shrine* (Princeton, N.J.: Princeton University Press).

Dupront, Alphonse. 1987. *Du Sacré: Croisades et pèlerinages, Images et langages* (Paris: Gallimard).

Eade, John. 2000. Introduction to the Illinois paperback. In Eade and Sallnow, eds., *Contesting the sacred* (new edition), ix–xxvii.

Eade, John, and Michael Sallnow, eds. 1991a. *Contesting the sacred: The anthropology of Christian pilgrimage* (London: Routledge).

———. 1991b. Introduction. In Eade and Sallnow, eds., *Contesting the sacred*, 1–29.

Eck, Diane. 1983. *Banares: City of light* (London: Routledge and Kegan Paul).

Ehime-ken Shōgaigakushū Sentā, ed. 2001. *Shikoku henro no ayumi* (Matsuyama: Ehime-ken Shōgaigakushū Sentā).

Finucane, Ronald. 1977. *Miracles and pilgrims: Popular beliefs in medieval England* (London: J. M. Dent).

Foard, James. 1982. The boundaries of compassion: Buddhism and national tradition in Japanese pilgrimage. *Journal of Asian Studies* 16.2:231–251.

Frey, Nancy Louise. 1998. *Pilgrim stories: On and off the road to Santiago* (Berkeley: University of California Press).

Fujita Kendō. 1986. Sendatsu-san o-negai. *Henro* 24:4.

Fuller, Christopher. 1992. *The camphor flame: Popular Hinduism and society in India* (Princeton, N.J.: Princeton University Press).

Gokurakuji, ed. 1976. *Gokurakuji* (Tokushima: Gokurakuji).

Gold, Anne Grodzins. 1988. *Fruitful journeys: The ways of Rajashtani pilgrims* (Berkeley: University of California Press).

Goodwin, Janet. 1994. *Alms and vagabonds: Buddhist temples and popular patronage in medieval Japan* (Honolulu: University of Hawai'i Press).

Gorai Shigeru. 1975. *Kōya hijiri* (Tokyo: Kadokawa Sensho).

———. 1984. *Bukkyō to minzoku* (Tokyo: Kadokawa Sensho).

———. 1989. *Yugyō to junrei* (Tokyo: Kadokawa Sensho).

———. 1996. *Shikoku henro no tera* (2 vols.) (Tokyo: Kadokawa Shoten).

Graburn, Nelson H. H. 1978. Tourism: The sacred journey. In V. Smith, ed., *Hosts and guests: The anthropology of tourism* (Oxford: Blackwell).

———. 1983. *To pray, pay and play: The cultural structure of Japanese tourism* (Aix-en-Provence: Centre des Hautes Études Touristiques).

Graf, Fritz. 2002. Review of Matthew Dillon, *Pilgrims and pilgrimage in ancient Greece*. In *History of Religions* 42.2:193–196.

Grapard, Allan G. 1982. Flying mountains and walkers of emptiness: Toward a definition of sacred space in Japanese religions. *History of Religions* 21.2: 195–221.

———. 1989. The textualized mountain-enmountained text: The Lotus Sutra in Kunisaki. In George J. Tanabe, Jr., and Willa Jane Tanabe, eds., *The Lotus Sutra in Japanese culture* (Honolulu: University of Hawai'i Press), 159–189.

Hagiwara Tatsuo and Shinno Toshikazu, eds. 1986. *Bukkyō minzokugaku taikei*, vol. 2: *Hijiri to minshū* (Tokyo: Meicho Shuppan).

Hakeda, Y. S. 1972. *Kūkai: Major works* (New York: Columbia University Press).

Harada Nobuo. 1999. *Kanreki no niwaka ohenro: 35 nichi.1200 kiro wo aruite watashi ga mitsuketa mono* (Takarazuka: Shinfū Shobō).

Hashimoto Tetsuma. 1984 [1950]. *Shikoku henroki* (Tokyo: Shiunsō).

Hashizume Rinsui. 1926. *Tatsueji reigenki* (Tokushima: Matuso Shuppansha).

Hasuo Kanzen. 1931. *Kōbō Daishiden* (Koyasan: Konogobuji).

Hatada Shuhō. n.d-a. *Jinsei wa henro nari* (Tokushima: Anrakuji) (undated pilgrimage pamphlet).

———. n.d-b. *Shikoku henro shunjū* (Tokushima: Anrakuji) (undated historical timeline of the pilgrimage).

Hatada Zenpō. 1989. Awa no kuni: Hosshin no dōjō. In Shikoku Hachijūhakkasho Reijōkai, ed., *Henro: Shikoku hachijūhakkasho*, 35.

———. 1990. *Dōgyō nininai jissen Bukkyō toshite on Shikoku henro* (Ehime-ken Bandōbu: Anrakuji).

Hayami Tasuku. 1983. *Kannon shinkō* (Tokyo: Hanawa Shobō).

Hayasaka Akira. 1992a. Atogaki. In Hayasaka Akira, ed., *Junrei*, 248–249.

———, ed. 1992b. *Junrei* (Tokyo: Sakuhinsha).

Henro Michi Hozon Kyōryokukai, ed. 1995. *Shikoku hachijū hakkasho o aruku: 1100 kiro 53 nichikan kokoro no tabi* (Osaka: Yama to Keikokusha).

Hinonishi Shinjō, ed. 1988. *Kōbō Daishi shinkō* (Tokyo: Yūzankaku).

Hirahata Ryōyū, ed. 1980. *Yasuragi: Junpai hikkei* (Chōshi, Chiba: Manganji Kyōkabu).

———. 1982. *Shikoku hachijūhakkasho*. 2 vols. (Chōshi, Chiba: Manganji Kyōkabu).

———. 1983. *Shōdoshima henro* (Chōshi, Chiba: Manganji Kyōkabu).

———. 1988. Gendaijin to henro. In Shikoku Hachijūhakkasho Reijōkai, ed., *Henro: Shikoku hachijūhakkasho*, 136–138.

———. 1990. *Shōdoshima henro* (new edition) (Chōshi, Chiba: Manganji Kyōkabu).

Hiroe Kiyoshi, ed. 1966. *Kinsei Tosa henro shiryō* (Kōchi: Tosa Minzoku Gakkai).

Hirota Mio. 1999. *Shikoku ohenro nazo toki sanpo* (Tokyo: Hōzaidō Shuppan).

Hoinacki, Lee. 1997. *El Camino: Walking to Santiago de Compostela* (University Park: Pennsylvania State University Press).

Hori, Ichirō. 1968. *Folk religion in Japan* (Chicago: University of Chicago Press).

Hoshino Eiki. 1979. Shikoku henro to sangakushinkō. In Miyake Hitoshi, ed., *Daisen Ishizuchi to Saikoku shugendō* (vol. 12 of the Sanshūkyōshi kenkyū series) (Meicho Shuppan, Tokyo), 310–328.

———. 1980. Shikoku henro ni okeru seichisei no tokushitsu. In Sasaki Kōkan et al., eds., *Gendai shūkyō—3 Seichi* (Tokyo: Shunjūsha), 89–102.

———. 1981. *Junrei: Sei to zoku no genshōgaku* (Tokyo: Kōdansha Gendaishinsho).

———. 1986a. Kisei bukkyō kyōdan no kōzō to minshū bukkyō. *Tōyō gakujitsu kenkyū* 25.1:89–103.

———. 1986b. Aruki to mawari no shūkyōsei. In Yamaori Tetsuo, ed., *Yugyō to hyōhaku*, 231–271.

———. 1989. Junrei to seichi. In Kanaoka Shūyū and Yanagawa Keiichi, eds., *Bukkyō bunka jiten* (Tokyo: Kōsensha), 731–740.

———. 1997. Pilgrimage and peregrination: Contextualising the Saikoku *junrei* and the Shikoku *henro*. In *Japanese Journal of Religious Studies* 24.3–4:271–300 (trans. of Hoshino 1986b, by Ian Reader).

———. 1999. Shikoku henro ni nyū eiji? Gendai aruki henro no taiken bunseki. In *Shakaigaku Nenshi* (Waseda Shakaigakkai) 40.3:47–64.

———. 2001. *Shikoku henro no shūkyōgakuteki kenkyū* (Kyoto: Hōzōkan).

Hosokawa Jun, ed. 1998. *Shikoku hachijū hakkasho no tabi: Inori no michi, iyashi no michi* (Tokyo: Ars Books).

Hosoya Masako. 1999. *Jikoku henroki* (Tokyo: Shinhyōron).

Howard, Donald R. 1980. *Writers and pilgrims: Medieval pilgrimage narratives and their posterity* (Berkeley: University of California Press).

Huber, Toni. 1999. *The cult of pure Crystal Mountain* (New York: Oxford University Press).

Imai Masaharu. 1986. Yugyō no shūkyōsha. In Yamaori Tetsuo, ed., *Yugyō to hyōhaku*, 153–190.

Imai Misako. 1981. *Oyako henro tabi nikki* (Tokyo: Tōhō Shuppan).

Itamura Shinmin. 1989. Sei naru shite nite. In Shikoku hachijūhakkasho Reijōkai, ed., *Henro: Shikoku hachijūhakkasho*, 20–21.

Itō Enichi. 1985. *Shikoku henroki* (Tokyo: Furukawa Shobō).

Ivy, Marilyn. 1995. *Discourses of the vanishing: Modernity, phantasm, Japan* (Chicago: University of Chicago Press).

Iwamura Takeo, ed. 1973. *Shikoku henro no furuchizu* (Tokyo: KK Shuppan).

Iwanami Shashin Bunko, ed. 1956. *Shikoku henro* (Tokyo: Iwanami Shoten).

Iyoshi Dankai, ed. 1981. *Shikoku henro kishū* (Matsuyama: Ehimeken Kyōka Tosho).

Jakuhon. 1689. *Shikoku henro reijōki*. Text in Iyoshi Dankai, ed. 1981. *Shikoku henro kishū*, 117–207.

Kagayama Kōichi. 2000. *Saa, junrei da—tenki toshite no Shikoku hachijūhakksho* (Tokyo: Sangokan).

Kagita Chūsaburō. 1962. *Henro nikki: Mokujiki angya sanbyakuri* (Tokyo: Kyōdō Shuppan).

Kaneko Satoru. 1991. *Shinshū shinkō to minzoku shinkō* (Kyoto: Nagata Bunshōdō).

Kannuchi Shinzō. 1963. *Henro nikki* (Osaka: Kannuchi Shinzō) (Private publication).

Kanzaki Noritake. 1990. *Kankō minzokugaku e no tabi* (Tokyo: Kawade Shobō).

Kawano Nobuko. 1977. *Hi no kuni no onna: Takamure Itsue* (Tokyo: Shinhyōron).

Kenmyō. 1638. *Kūshō Hōshinō Shikoku reijō gojungyōki*. Text in Iyoshi Dankai, ed. 1981. *Shikoku henro kishū*, 9–20.

Ketelaar, James Edward. 1990. *Of heretics and martyrs in Meiji Japan: Buddhism and its persecution* (Princeton, N.J.: Princeton University Press).

Kimizuka Mikio. 2001. *Shikoku hachijū hakkasho burabura tabi: Nanajūsai no junrei kikō* (Tokyo: Inpakuto Shuppan).

King, Christine. 1993. His truth goes marching on: Elvis Presley and the pilgrimage to Graceland. In Reader and Walter, eds., *Pilgrimage in popular culture*, 92–104.

Kino Kazuyoshi. 1985. *Kokoro no furusato: Tabi to Nihonjin* (Tokyo: Kōsei Shuppansha).

Kita Isao. 2000. *Kūkai no kaze ni notte: Chūnen jitensha henro no susume* (Tokyo: Kyūryūsha).

Kitagawa, Joseph. 1967. Three types of pilgrimage in Japan. In E. E. Urbach, et al., eds., *Studies in mysticism and history* (Jerusalem: Magnes Press, Hebrew University), 155–164.

Kitamura, Satoshi. 1988. Daishi nyūjō shinkō. In Kanaoka Shūyū, et al., eds., *Nihon bukkyō no sekai* (Tokyo: Shūeisha), 4:128–145.

Kiyoyoshi Eitoku. 1984. *Michi shirube—tsuke Nakatsuka Mohei nikki* (Shin Niihama: Kaiōsha).

———. 1998. Henro yado moyō. In *Shikoku Henro Kenkyū* 16:1–20 (private journal published from Kaiōsha, Niihama, Shikoku).

———. 1999. *Henrobito retsuden: Gyōgi bosatsu kara Nakatsuka Mōhei made* (Shin Niihama: Kaiōsha).

Kobayashi Atsuhiro. 1990. *Teinen kara wa dōgyōninin: Shikoku aruki henro ni nani wo mita* (Tokyo: PHP Kenkyūjo).

Kōbō Daishi Kūkai Kankōkai, eds. 1985. *Nihon junrei kishūsei* (Takamatsu: Kōbō Daishi Kūkai Kankōkai).

Kōdansha, ed. 1989. *Henro: Shikoku hachijūhakkasho* (Tokyo: Kōdansha).

Kojima Hiromi. 1987. Junrei henro. In Tamamuro Fumio et al., eds., *Minkan shinkō chōsa seiri handobukku* (Tokyo: Yuzankaku), 1:158–169.

———. 1989. Junrei: "Meguri" to "morai" to. In Setouchi Jakuchō, Fujii Masao, and Miyata Noboru, eds., *Bukkyō gyōji saijiki: Gogatsu yamairi* (Tokyo: Dai-ichi Hōkan), 168–179.

Kondō Tō. 1989. Watakushi no nōkyōchō. *Henro* 60 (March):3.

Kondō Yoshihiro. 1971. *Shikoku henro* (Tokyo: Ofūsha).

———. 1982. *Shikoku henro kenkyū* (Tokyo: Miyai Shoten).

Kouamé, Nathalie. 1997. Shikoku's local authorities and *henro* during the golden age of the pilgrimage. *Japanese Journal of Religious Studies* 24.3–4:413–425.

———. 1998. Le pèlerinage de Shikoku pendat l'epoque Edo: Pèlerins at sociétés locales. Unpublished Ph.D. dissertation. (Paris: Institut National Des Langues et Civilisations Orientales).

———. 2001. *Pèlerinage et société dans le Japon des Tokugawa: Le pèlerinage de Shikoku entre 1598 et 1868* (Paris: École Française d'Extrème-Orient).

Kubota Nobuhiro. 1985. *Sangaku reijō junrei* (Tokyo: Shinchōsha).

Lafleur, William. 1979. Points of departure: Comments on religious pilgrimage in Sri Lanka and Japan. *Journal of Asian Studies* 38.2:271–281.

Leavell, James, and Ian Reader. 1988. Research report on the Saikoku pilgrimage. *Studies in Central and East Asian Religions* 1.1:116–118.

MacCannell, D. 1976. *The tourist: A new theory of the leisure class* (London: Macmillan).

MacGregor, Fiona. 2002. Shikoku *henro*: A study of Japanese and Western pilgrims on the Shikoku eighty-eight sacred places pilgrimage. Unpublished master's dissertation, University of Sheffield.

Maeda Takashi. 1971. *Junrei no shakaigaku* (Kyoto: Mineruba Shobō).

McKevitt, Christopher. 1991. San Giovanni Rotondo and the shrine of Padre Pio. In Eade and Sallnow, eds., *Contesting the sacred*, 77–97.

Matsubara Tetsumyō. 1987. *Junrei henro: Tomo ni ayumu* (Tokyo: Shūeisha).

Matsunaga, D., and A. Matsunaga. 1974. *Foundations of Japanese Buddhism*, vol. 1 (Los Angeles: Buddhist Books International).

Matsuo Gōji. 2002. Shikoku hachijūhachi fudasho no seiritsu: Shikoku ezu wo tegakari toshite. *Shūkyō Kenkyū* no. 333, 76/2:107–134.

Matsuura Harutake. 1988. Tsui ni junpai hyakkai mangan. *Henro* 51:8.

Matsuura Tadatoshi. 1988. *Henroki: Hon Shikoku hachijūhakkasho* (Komaki, Aichi: privately produced and distributed by Matsuura Tadatoshi).

Matsuzaki Kenzō. 1985. *Mawari no fo-kuroa* (Tokyo: Meicho Shuppan).

Miyake Hitoshi. 1980. Seikatsu no naka no shūkyō (Tokyo: Nihon Hōsō Shuppan).

Miyamoto Tsuneichi, ed. 1987. *Shōmin no tabi* (Tokyo: Yasaka Shobō).

Miyao Shigeo. 1943. *Shikoku henro* (Tokyo: Tsuru Shobō).

Miyata Noboru. 1988 [1975]. *Miroku shinkō no kenkyū* (Tokyo: Miraisha).

———. 1988. Daishi shinkō to Nihonjin. In Hinonishi Shinjō, ed., *Kōbō Daishi shinkō,* 19–48.

Miyata, Taisen. 1984. A henro *pilgrimage guide to the 88 temples of Shikoku Island, Japan* (Sacramento: North California Koyasan Temple).

Miyazaki Ninshō.1972. *Henro: Sono kokoro to rekishi* (Tokyo: Shogakkan).

———. 1977. *Chōzen: Shikoku henro nikki* (Tokyo: Daitō Shuppansha).

———. 1981. *Shakyō to Hannya Shingyō* (Osaka: Toki Shobō).

———. 1985. *Shikoku henro: Rekishi to kokoro* (Tokyo: Toki Shobō).

Miyazaki Tateki. 1991. *Shikoku henro hitori aruki dōgyōninin* (Matsuyama: Henro Michi Hozon Kyōryokukai).

———. 1993. *Shikoku reijō sendatsu: JR.shitetsu.rosen basu noritsugi junpai gaido* (Matsuyama: Henro Michi Hozon Kyōryokukai).

———. 1995. *Shikoku hachijū hakkasho meguri: Daishi no toku wo motomete kokoro no tabi e* (Tokyo: Nihon Kōtsū Kōsha).

Miyoshi Shōichirō. 1996. Shikoku henroshi kenkyū yosetsu: Henro no minshūka to shohan no henro seisaku. In Shinno Toshikazu, ed., *Nihon no junrei,* 3:3–21.

Mizutani Shigeji. 1984. Kumo no ue ni wa taiyō ga kagayaite iru. In Shikoku Hachijūhakkasho Reijōkai, ed., *Shikoku hachijūhakksho reigenki,* 49–54.

Moerman, David. 1997. The ideology of landscape and the theater of state: Insei pilgrimage to Kumano (1090–1220). *Japanese Journal of Religious Studies* 24.3–4:347–374.

Mori Harumi. 1999. *Onna henro genki tabi: Shikoku hachijū hakkasho* (Osaka: JDC).

Mori Masayasu. 1986. Shikoku henro no hijiri: Nakatsuka Mōhei. In Hagiwara and Shinno, eds., *Bukkyō minzokugaku taikei,* 2:99–116.

Morinis, Alan. 1981. Pilgrimage: The human quest. *Numen* 28.2:280–285.

———. 1984. *Pilgrimage in the Hindu tradition: A case study of West Bengal* (New Delhi: Oxford University Press).

Mullins, Edwin. 1974. *The pilgrimage to Santiago* (London: Secker and Warburg).

Murakami Mamoru. 1986. *Henro mandara* (Tokyo: Kōsei Shuppan).

———. 1987. *Shikoku henro reijōki no sekai* (Tokyo: Kyōikusha).

Murayama Shūichi. 1972. *Yamabushi no rekishi* (Tokyo: Hanawa Shobō).

Naquin, Susan, and Chün-Fang Yü. 1992. Introduction. In Naquin and Yü, eds., *Pilgrims and sacred sites in China* (Berkeley: University of California Press), 1–38.

Nelson, John. 1999. *Enduring identities: The guise of Shinto in contemporary Japan* (Honolulu: University of Hawai'i Press).

NHK, ed. 1990. *Shikoku hachijūhakkasho: Kandō taiken* (Tokyo: Nihon Hōsō Shuppan).

NHK Shikoku hachijūhakkasho purojekuto, ed. 1999–2000. *Shikoku hachijūhakkasho kokoro no tabi.* 4 vols. (Tokyo: NHK Shuppan).

Nii Hiromasa and Nakajima Yoshimine. 1982. *Odaishisama* (Kōyasan: Kōyasan Shuppan).

Nishibata Sakae. 1964. *Shikoku hachijūhakkasho henroki* (Tokyo: Daihōrinkaku).

Nishigai Kenji. 1984. *Ishizuchisan to shugendō* (Tokyo: Meicho Shuppan).

Nishigaki Haruji. 1983. *O-Ise Mairi* (Tokyo: Iwanami Shinsho).

Nishikawa Arao. 1999. *Aruku Shikoku henro sennihyaku kiro* (Tokyo: Gendai Shokan).

Noda, Kesaya. 1983. A pilgrimage in Shikoku. In Intercultural Association of Kyoto, ed., *Essays on Japanology 1978–1982* (Kyoto: Bunrikaku), 171–184.

Obigane Mitsutoshi. 2002. *Sairai Yamamoto Genpōden* (Tokyo: Daihōrinkaku).

Oda Masayuki. 1996. Shōdoshima ni okeru utsushi reijō no seiritsu. In Shinno Toshikazu, ed., *Nihon no junrei*, 3:169–193.

Ogasawara Shōichi. 1984. Odaishi-sama ni yotte sukuwareta taikendan. In Shikoku Hachijūhakkasho Reijōkai, ed., *Shikoku hachijūhakkasho reigenki*, 89–95.

Ogihara Seisensui. 1941. *Henro nikki* (Tokyo: Fujokaisha).

Ōishi Mitsuzen. 1999. Shinnen hōshi: O-Shikoku henro no chichi. *Henro* 181: 6–7.

Okamoto Yukiko. 2002. *Heisei musume junreiki* (Tokyo: Bungei Shunjū).

Osada Seiichi, Sakata Masaaki, and Seki Mitsuo. 2003. *Gendai no Shikoku henro: Michi no shakaigaku no shiten kara* (Tokyo: Gakubunsha).

Ōzeki Chikayasu. 1993. *Shichifukujin meguri: Omairi no reishiki to kokoroe* (Tokyo: Sanshindō).

Ōzeki Gyōō. 1936. *Shikoku reijō junpai nisshi* (Kyoto: Ritsumeikan).

Pfaffenberger, Brian. 1979. The Kataragama pilgrimage: Hindu-Buddhist interaction and its significance in Sri Lanka's polyethnic social system. *Journal of Asian Studies* 38.2:253–270.

Preston, James. 1992. Spiritual magnetism: An organizing principle for the study of pilgrimage. In Alan Morinis, ed., *Sacred journeys* (Westport, Conn: Greenwood Press), 31–46.

Reader, Ian. 1984. Only *gakusei* and *gaijin*: An account of the Shikoku pilgrimage. *Kansai Time Out* (June):8–11.

———. 1987a. Back to the future: Images of nostalgia and renewal in a Japanese religious context. *Japanese Journal of Religious Studies* 14.4:287–303.

———. 1987b. From asceticism to the package tour: The pilgrim's progress in Japan. *Religion* 17. 2:133–148.

———. 1988. Miniaturization and proliferation: A study of small-scale pilgrimages in Japan. *Studies in Central and East Asian Religions* 1.1:50–66.

———. 1991. *Religion in contemporary Japan* (Basingstoke: Macmillans).

———. 1992. Pilgrim, miracle worker, and wandering saint: Kōbō Daishi in Japanese popular lore. Paper delivered at the Folklore Society Conference on Saintlore and Popular Religion. Glasgow, April 10–12.

———. 1993a. Dead to the world: Pilgrims in Shikoku. In Ian Reader and Tony Walter (eds.) *Pilgrimage in popular culture* (Basingstoke: Macmillans). pp. 107-136.

———. 1993b. Introduction. In Reader and Walter, eds., *Pilgrimage in popular culture*, 1–25.

———. 1993c. Conclusions. In Reader and Walter, eds., *Pilgrimage in popular culture*, 220–246.

———. 1993d. Sendatsu *and the development of contemporary Japanese pilgrimage.* Nissan Occasional Papers on Japan no. 17 (Oxford: Nissan Institute for Japanese Studies).

———. 1995. Social action and personal benefits in contemporary Buddhism in Japan. *Buddhist-Christian Studies* 15:3–17.

———. 1996a. Pilgrimage as cult: The Shikoku pilgrimage as a window on Japanese religion. In P. F. Kornicki and I. J. McMullen, eds., *Religion in Japan: Arrows to heaven and earth* (Cambridge: Cambridge University Press), 267–286.

———. 1996b. Creating pilgrimages: Buddhist priests and popular religion in contemporary Japan. *Proceedings of the Kyoto Conference on Japanese Studies* (Kyoto: International Research Center for Japanese Studies), 3:311–324.

———. 1999. Legends, miracles, and faith in Kobo Daishi and the Shikoku pilgrimage: A commentary and selected translations from Shinnen's *Shikoku henro kudokuki* of 1690. In George J. Tanabe, Jr., ed., *Religions of Japanese in practice* (Princeton, N.J.: Princeton University Press), 360–369.

———. 2001. Reflected meanings: Underlying themes in the experiences of two Japanese pilgrims to Europe. In Adriana Boscaro and Maurizio Bozzi, eds., *Firenze, il Giappone e l'Asia Orientale* (Florence: Leo S. Olschi), 121–139.

———. 2003. Chance, fate, and undisciplined meanderings: A pilgrimage through the fieldwork maze. In Theodore C. Bestor, Patricia G. Steinhoff, and Victoria Lyon Bestor, eds., *Doing fieldwork in Japan* (Honolulu: University of Hawai'i Press), 89–105.

———. forthcoming. Weaving the landscape: The Shikoku pilgrimage, Kōbō Daishi and Shingon Buddhism. *Bulletin of the Research Institute of Esoteric Buddhist Culture.*

Reader, Ian, and Paul L. Swanson. 1997. Editors' introduction: Pilgrimage in the Japanese religious tradition. *Japanese Journal of Religious Studies* 24.3–4: 225–270.

Reader, Ian, and George J. Tanabe, Jr. 1998. *Practically religious: Worldly benefits and the common religion of Japan* (Honolulu: University of Hawai'i Press).

Reader, Ian, and Tony Walter, eds. 1993. *Pilgrimage in popular culture* (Basingstoke: Macmillans).

Robertson, Jennifer. 1991. *Native and newcomer: Making and remaking a Japanese city* (Berkeley: University of California Press).

Sada Itsue. 1984. Odaishi-sama ni watakushi wa sukuwareta. In Shikoku Hachijūhakkasho Reijōkai, ed., *Shikoku hachijūhakkasho reigenki*, 194–195.

Saitō Akitoshi. 1975. *Bukkyō junreishū* (Tokyo: Bukkyō Minzoku Gakkai).

———. 1984. Kōbō Daishi shinkō ni kansuru jittai chōsa. In *Bukkyō bunka ronshū* no. 4, 400–479.

———. 1988. Kōbō Daishi densetsu. In Hinonishi Shinjō, ed., *Kōbō Daishi shinkō*, 49–61.

Sallnow, Michael J. 1981. Communitas revisited: The sociology of Andean pilgrimage. *Man* 16:163–182.

———. 1987. *Pilgrims of the Andes: Regional cults in Cusco* (Washington, D.C.: Smithsonian Institution Press).

Satō Hisamitsu. 1989. Gendai no junrei: Saikoku junrei ni tsuite. In Maeda Takashi, ed., *Kazoku shakaigaku nōto* (Kyoto: Kansai Daigaku), 183–222.

———. 1990a. Osamefuda ni miru Shikoku henro. In Nakao Shunpaku Sensei Koki Kinenkai, ed., *Bukkyō to shakai: Nakao Shunpaku sensei koki kinen* (Kyoto: Nagata Bunshōdō), 437–459.

———. 1990b. Shikoku henro no shakaigakuteki kōsatsu. *Mikkyōgaku* 26:29–47.

Satō Ken. 1989. Ohenro kisha no 43 nichi. In Mainichi Shinbunsha, ed., *Shūkyō wa kokoro wo mitasu ka* (Tokyo: Mainichi Shinbun), 2:10–78.

Satō Takako. 1999a. *Shikoku ohenro gaidobukku* (Tokyo: Tōhō Shuppan).

———. 1999b. *O henro no saku hana tōru kaze: Genki obasan o Shikoku wo aruku* (Tokyo: Ryonsha).

Satō Tatsugen and Kaneko Wakō. 1989. *Shichifukujin* (Tokyo: Mokujisha).

Sax, William S. 1991. *Mountain goddess: Gender and politics in a Himalayan pilgrimage* (New York: Oxford University Press).

Seki Mitsuo. 1999. Shikoku henro to idō media no tayōka. *Shakagaku Nenshi* (Waseda Shakagakkai) no. 40, 65–80.

Shikoku Hachijūhakkasho Reijōkai, ed. n.d. (probably ca. 1965). *Shikoku hachijūhakkasho reijōkai kōnin sendatsu bangikai kisoku* (Shikoku: Shikoku Hachijūhakkasho Reijōkai Jimusho).

———, ed. 1984. *Shikoku hachijūhakkasho reigenki* (Sakaide: Shikoku Hachijūhakkasho Reijōkai Honbu Jimusho).

———, ed. 1989. *Henro: Shikoku hachijūhakkasho* (Tokyo: Kōdansha).

Shikoku Reijō Sanpai Hōsankai, ed. 1953–1956 (1st-3rd eds.). *Namu Daishi: Shikoku junpai* (Wakayama: Shikoku Reijō Sanpai Hōsankai).

Shikoku Reijōkai Honbu, ed. 1983 [1967]. *Sendatsu hikkei* (Nishijō, Ehime: Shikoku Reijōkai Honbu Jimusho).

Shima Namio. 1930. *Fudasho to meisho: Shikoku henro* (Tokyo: Hōbunkan).

Shimizutani Kōshō. 1986. *Junrei no kokoro* (Tokyo: Daizō Shuppan).

———. 1992. *Junrei to goeika: Kannon shinkō e no hitotsu no dōhyō* (Osaka: Toki Shobō).

Shimomura Kainan and Iijima Hiroshi. 1934. *Henro* (Osaka: Asahi Shinbunsha).

Shingyōkai Honbu, ed. 1981. *Henro* (Nagahama: Shingyōkai Honbu) (private publication).

Shinjō Tsunezō. 1960. *Shaji to kōtsū* (Tokyo: Shibundō).

———. 1971. *Shomin no tabi no rekishi* (Tokyo: Nihon Hōsō Shuppan).

———. 1982. *Shaji sankei no shakai keizaishiteki kenkyū* (Tokyo: Hanawa Shobō).

Shinnen. 1687. *Shikoku henro michishirube*. Text in Iyoshi Dankai, ed. 1981. *Shikoku henro kishū*, 69–116.

———. 1690. *Shikoku henro kudokuki*. Text in Iyoshi Dankai, ed. 1981. *Shikoku henro kishū*, 209–232.

Shinno Toshikazu. 1978. Shikoku henro no hijiri to sono shūkyō katsudō. In Sakurai Tokutarō, ed., *Nihon shūkyō no fukugōteki kōzō* (Tokyo: Kōbundō), 83–108.

———. 1980. *Tabi no naka no shūkyō* (Tokyo: NHK Books).

———. 1991a. *Nihon yugyō shūkyōron* (Tokyo: Yoshikawa Kōbunkan).

———. 1991b. *Sei naru tabi* (Tokyo: Tōkyōdō).

———, ed. 1996. *Nihon no junrei*. 3 vols. 1: *Honzon junrei*. 2: *Seiseki junrei*. 3: *Junrei no kōzō to chihō junrei* (Tokyo: Yūzankaku).

———. 2002. Journeys, pilgrimages, excursions. Trans. Laura Nenzi. In *Monumenta Nipponica* 57.4:448–471.

Shiraga Tadashi. 1997. *O-henro: Aruita Shikoku hachijūhakkasho 42 nichi no kiroku* (Tokyo: Yōyōsha).

Shiragi Toshiyuki. 1994. *Junrei.sanpaiyōgo jiten* (Osaka: Toki Shobō).

Shūkyō Shakagaku no Kai, eds. 1985. *Ikoma no kamigami: Gendai toshi no minzoku shūkyō* (Osaka: Sōgensha).

Slater, Candace. 1986. *Trail of miracles: Stories from a pilgrimage in northeast Brazil* (Berkeley: University of California Press).

Starkie, Walter. 1957. *The road to Santiago: Pilgrims of St. James* (Berkeley: University of California Press).

Statler, Oliver. 1984. *Japanese pilgrimage* (London: Picador).

Sumption, Jonathan. 1975. *Pilgrimage: An image of medieval religion* (London: Faber and Faber).

Swanson, Paul. 1981. Shugendō and the Yoshino-Kumano pilgrimage: An example of mountain pilgrimage. *Monumenta Nipponica* 36.1:55–79.

Tabuchi Yoshio. 1984. Junpai no omoide. In Shikoku Hachijūhakkasho Reijōkai, ed., *Shikoku hachijūhakkasho reigenki*, 55–67.

Tahara Hisashi et al., eds. 1980. *Nihon sairei chizu*, vol. 5 (Tokyo: Kokudo Chiri Kyōkai).

Takada Kyōko. 2000. *Aru hi totsuzen, o-henrosan: Shikoku hachijūhakkasho meguri* (Tokyo: JTB).

Takada Shinkai. 1985. *Sutete aruke* (Tokyo: Yamanote Shobō).

Takamure Itsue. 1939. *Henro to jinsei* (Tokyo: Kōseikaku).

———. 1983. *Musume junreiki* (Tokyo: Asahi Shinbunsha).

———. 1987. *Ohenro* (Tokyo: Chūō Bunko) (originally published in 1936 by Kōseikaku).

Takamure Itsue and Hashimoto Kenzō. 1965. *Hi no kuni no onna no nikki* (Tokyo: Rironsha).

Takeda Akira. 1972. *Junrei no minzoku* (Tokyo: Iwasaki Bijitsusha).

———. 1987. *Nihonjin no shireikan: Shikoku minzokushi* (Tokyo: Sanichi Shobō).

Tanabe, George J. Jr. n.d. Legends and legitimacy: The founding of Mount Koya and its cult. Unpublished manuscript.

Tanaka, Hiroshi. 1975. Pilgrim places: A study of the eighty-eight sacred precincts of the Shikoku pilgrimage, Japan. Unpublished Ph.D. dissertation, Simon Fraser University.

———. 1983. *Junreichi no sekai* (Tokyo: Kokon Shoin).

Tanaka Tomohiko. 1989. Shikoku henro ezu to Kōbō Daishi zuzō. In Katsuragikawa Kenkyūkai, ed., *Ezu no kosumorojii* (Kyoto: Chinin Shobō), 2:239–256.

Taniguchi Hiroyuki. 1997. *Denshō no ishibumi: Henro to iu shūkyō* (Tokyo: Kanrin Shobō).

Tanimura Shunrō. 1973. *Fudasho no tabi: Shikoku hachijūhakkasho* (Tokyo: Kōdansha).

Tate, Brian, and Marcus Tate. 1987. *The Pilgrim route to Santiago* (Oxford: Phaidon).

Tattebe Zuiyū.1985. *Kokoro no ryoji* (Kyoto: Hōzōkan).

ten Grotenhuis, Elizabeth. 1999. *Japanese mandalas: Representations of sacred geography* (Honolulu: University of Hawai'i Press).

Tezuka Myōken. 1988. *Ohenro de meguri atta hitobito* (Tokyo: Ryonsha).

Tosa Fumio. 1972. *Dōgyō ninin* (Kōchi: Kōchi Shinbunsha).

Tsujita Shōyū. 1984. Shi no sunzenryosō ni keshin no odaishisama ni sukuwareta. In Shikoku Hachijūhakkasho Reijōkai, ed., *Shikoku hachijūhakkasho reigenki*, 162–169.

———. 1985. Takuhatsushugyō no Shikoku reijō oreimairi. In Kōbō Daishi Kūkai Kankōkai, ed., *Nihon junrei kishūsei*, 218–220.

Tsukioka Yukiko. 2002. *Heisei musume junreiki: Shikoku hachijūhakkasho aruki henro* (Tokyo: Bungei Shunjū).

Tsukuda Yoshio. 1981. *Nihon zenkoku sanjūsankasho, hachijūhakkasho shūran* (Tokyo: Tsukuda (private publication).

Tsurumura Shōichi. 1978. *Shikoku henro: 282 kai Nakatsuka Mohei gikyō* (Matsuyama: Matsuyama Furusatoshi Bungaku Kenkyūkai).

———, ed. 1979. *Dōchūki taisei* (Matsuyama: Matsuyama Furusato Shibunka Kenkyūkai).

Turner, Victor. 1974. *Dramas, fields and metaphors* (Ithaca, N.Y.: Cornell University Press).

———. 1979. *Process, performance and pilgrimage* (New Delhi: Concept).

Turner, Victor, and Edith Turner. 1978. *Image and pilgrimage in Christian culture* (Oxford: Blackwell).

Urry, John. 1990. *The tourist gaze* (London: Sage).

Vaporis, Constantine Nomikos. 1994. *Breaking barriers: Travel and the state in early modern Japan* (Cambridge, Mass.: Harvard University Press).

Victoria, Brian Daizen. 2003. *Zen war stories* (London: Routledge Curzon).

Ward, Benedicta. 1982. *Miracles and the medieval mind: Theory, record and event 1000–1215* (London: Scholar Press).

Waseda Daigaku Dōkūkan Kenkyūkai, ed. 1994. *Gendai shakai to Shikoku henro michi* (Tokyo: Waseda Daigaku Dōkūkan Kenkyūkai).

———, ed. 1997. *Shikoku henro to henro michi ni kansuru ishikichōsa* (Tokyo: Waseda Daigaku Dōkūkan Kenkyūkai).

Watanabe Akiyuki. 1988. Daishi no denki densetsu to minkan kōhi. In Hinonishi Shinjō, ed., *Kōbō Daishi shinkō*, 183–233.

Watanabe Yasuhiro. 1999. *Shikoku hachijūhakksho reijō meguri* (Tokyo: Bungei-sha).

Yamaori Tetsuo, ed. 1986. *Yugyō to hyōhaku*, vol. 6 (Tokyo: Shunjūsha).

Yamamoto Wakako. 1995. *Shikoku henro no minshūshi* (Tokyo: Shinjinbutsu Ōraisha).

Yamashita Hirotaka. 1984. *Shikoku hachijūhachi fudasho: Densetsu to shinkō no tabi* (Tokyo: Kyōrakusha).

Yanagimoto Myōzen. 1990. Saba daishi no shinkō to rekishi. *Shūkyō to Gendai* no.12, 14–17.

Yoritomi Motohiro and Shiragi Toshiyuki. 2001. *Shikoku henro no kenkyū*. Nichi-bunken Sōsho no. 23 (Kyoto: Kokusai Nihon Bunka Kenkyū Sentā)

Yūraku Shuppansha, ed. 1998. *Shikoku hachijūhakksho yasuragi no tabi: Atarashi ohenro no arukikata* (Tokyo: Jitsugyō no Nihonsha).

Zaitsu Sadayuki. 2000. *Ohenro ha daishi sama to sannin tabi: Aruite mitsuketa fufu no kizuna* (Tokyo: Ryonsha).

Journals and newspapers

Asahi shinbun
Chūgai Nippō
Ehime keizai repōto
Henro (monthly newsletter published by Iyo Tetsu)
Shikoku shinbun
Tosa shinbun
Yomiuri shinbun

Web sites

www.happy.or.jp/96082900/henro/henro.htm
www.henro.org
www.henshubu.org
www.kushima.com/henro

Index

absolution, 60, 120; granted by Kōbō
Daishi to pilgrims, 59–60
addictive nature of pilgrimage, 91,
255–257, 262, 264–265
alcohol, abstinence from and enjoyment
of by pilgrims, 17–18, 191, 209–210;
214–215, 233–235, 247
alms *(settai)* and almsgiving, 21, 59, 113,
115, 122–126, 129, 200–208; and
ancestors, 125; Buddhist aspects of 83,
122–123; contemporary walkers and,
200–206; dilemmas created by,
206–208; as embedded in Shikoku
social structures,124–126; as energizing walkers, 205–206; as form of protest, 125; free lodgings as, 113, 115,
122, 205, 212–213; and link to *dōgyō*,
125; manipulative aspects of, 60–61,
123; organized dimensions of, 114,
122, 124–126; as part of Shikoku pilgrimage culture, 122–123; within pilgrimage parties, 232–233; preoccupa-
tion of pilgrims with, 123; reasons for
seeking and giving, 123–125; as
restricted by Shikoku authorities
140–141; reward and retribution and,
60–61, 118; Shikoku residents and,
60–61, 122–126, 203–206; soliciting
of, 28, 60–61, 83, 113, 123, 204. *See
also* Arita Settaikō, Emon Saburō,
fuda, Nakatsuka Mōhei, reward and
retribution; Shinnen
ambivalence: as theme of pilgrimage, 6, 9,
12, 27, 29, 32, 50, 126, 148–149,

211–213, 263–264, 269–271. *See also*
common bonds among pilgrims;
hierarchy and status; Kōbō Daishi;
pilgrimage; pilgrims in Shikoku
Amida, 14
ancestors, 102–103, 125, 229, 245. *See
also* dead, the; death; memorializing
the dead
Arai Raisuke, 131–132
Arita Settaikō (pilgrimage association), 62,
69, 95–96, 126, 203, 251, 300n.102;
links with Ryōzenji (Temple 1), 69, 96,
169. *See also* alms
ascetic practices, 67, 83–85, 108–110,
113, 115–116, 121, 171, 299n.79;
pilgrimage as asceticism/austerity,
202, 209. *See also* hardship
authenticity: problematic notions of in
pilgrimage, 18, 36, 146
Aziz, Barbara, 30, 227, 310n.10

bangai, 16–17, 118. *See also* Ikiki Jizō,
Kaiganji, Saba Daishi
barrier gate temples, 120
begging for alms *(takuhatsu)*, 28, 60–61,
83, 113, 123, 204. *See also* alms
bicycle, pilgrimage by, 18, 104, 309n.1
books, scrolls, and stamps, 14, 22, 92;
cost of stamps, 23; inheriting from
ancestors, 96; as motive for doing the
pilgrimage, 23–24, 101; as objects of
beauty, 23, 101; as passport to the
Pure Land, 23; photographs of, 24,
244; pilgrims carrying multiple copies

of, 23, 230–231; practical reasons for, 22–23, 136, 284n.39; as protective talismans, 100; as reminders of pilgrimage, 23, 104; use in funerals and death ceremonies, 23–24, 247
Buddhist ordinations, 13, 17, 192, 256–257, 282n.11
Bukkai, 121
bus package tours, 7, 99–101, 152–154, 163–167, 181–182, 217–248; advent and growth of, 152–154; arduous nature and intensity of, 222–223, 231; as combining individual themes and group consciousness, 237–238; common bonds and identity in, 217–221, 224–225, 232–236; contest between groups, 236–237; development of as start of modern era, 152; devotional aspects of, 219–220; as differing from tourist package tours, 163; dissolution of common bonds in, 248; harmonious interactions between, 219–220, 236–238; individualized themes within, 219, 222, 224–225, 236; internal hierarchies within, 218–219; as main mode of travel in Shikoku, 99, 155; as means of accessing the 'traditional,' 182; as pilgrimages, 36–37; as reinforcing customs and devotion, 166–167, 218, 230; reinvigorating nature of, 222; as temporary/transitory communities, 99–101, 217–218, 224–226; temporary escape from, 238–239; varieties and variable dynamics of, 217; as widening the scope of participation, 155–157, 233. See also bus pilgrims; Iyo Tetsu Company; Kotosan Bus Company; Setouchi Bus Company; temporary communities
bus pilgrims, 99–101, 220–248; celebrations on completion, 246–247; costs incurred by, 279; criticisms by, 222; criticisms of, 27, 183–184, 262, 283n.28; devotional orientations of, 18, 37, 230–231; as focused on temples more than route, 9, 188–189; giving alms to walkers, 204; as happy with service provided, 165; individual volition of, 219, 222, 235–236; interactions with other bus pilgrims, 232, 234, 236–238; interactions with walkers, 188, 204, 245–246; interest in motives of others, 227; as likely to repeat the pilgrimage with same firm, 90, 165, 224; as meeting up again on package tours, 224; as more focused on worship than walkers, 18, 37, 189, 287n.85; motives of, 224–229; sharing alms (settai) amongst, 232–233; as sharing experiences and miracle stories, 234, 237–238

Cape Ashizuri, 48–49, 51–52, 109
Cape Muroto, 41, 48–49, 51–52, 109
car pilgrimages, 18, 143–144, 154
Chichibu pilgrimage (Japan), 265
Chōzen, 112, 114–115, 171; hardships endured by, 114–115
Coleman, Simon, and John Elsner, 39–40
commemorating pilgrimages, 70–71, 114, 122, 231
commercial developments and infrastructures, 6–7, 17, 23, 48, 114, 145, 152–167, 238–240; and connections to temples, 148, 158, 164, 179; earliest indications of in Shikoku, 114; as facilitating post-war growth, 152–154; impact on visual structure of pilgrimage, 183–184; as intrinsic to Shikoku pilgrimage, 25; and links of commercial and spiritual themes in, 164–166, 220–221; as source of innovation and development, 162–163. See also bus package tours; Iyo Tetsu Company; Kotosan Bus Company; pilgrims' lodges; Setouchi Bus Company; Shikoku Reijōkai
common bonds among pilgrims, 29–30, 59, 64–65, 76, 142–143, 237–238; within groups, 217–221, 224–225, 232–237; and temporary dimensions of, 76. See also dōgyō, equality among pilgrims; hierarchy and status; pilgrims' love; temporary communities
communitas, 30, 263; problems with theories of, 30, 268, 313n.3. See also contest; dōgyō; equality among pilgrims; hierarchy and status; liminality; Turner, Victor
contest, 29, 236–237; problems with theories of, 29–30, 40, 237–238, 249,

268, 313n.3. *See also* Eade, John, and Michael Sallnow
cultural heritage and identity: as motive for pilgrims, 82, 156, 228

Dainichi, 93
daishidō, 11, 114, 118
day trip pilgrimages, 20, 102, 157–158
dead pilgrims: corpses dealt with by feudal and local authorities, 137; given funerals by temples, 133, 137
dead, the, 80–82; as accompanying pilgrims, 80–82; memories of afflicting pilgrims, 209–210; merit created for, 125; spirits of as linked to pilgrimage sites, 14. *See also* ancestors; death; graves; memorializing the dead
death, 10–11, 14, 133, 292n.80; decrease in, 133; landscape of Shikoku as setting for, 48–49; pilgrimage as a way of dealing with grief of, 81–82, 151; and pilgrims' clothing, 13, 63–64, 292n.81; of pilgrims on route, 64, 132–133, 137; and rebirth, 63–64; symbolic imagery of, 13, 47–48, 63–64; as visual element in landscape, 64. *See also* ancestors; dead, the; graves of pilgrims on route; memorializing the dead; rebirth
Dōgō hot springs, 37, 47, 115, 131, 165
dōgyō, 12, 30, 52, 57–59, 64–65, 76, 200, 219–220, 237, 270; and almsgiving, 125; and death symbolism of, 80; first use of term, 113; as providing individual meaning for pilgrims, 59; as reducing tensions and contest, 237; as shared journey, 64–65; and unity among pilgrims and with Kōbō Daishi, 13, 57–59, 76. *See also* common bonds among pilgrims; hierarchy and status; Kōbō Daishi; pilgrims in Shikoku
dōgyōninin. See *dōgyō*
Dubisch, Jill, 32–35, 134–135, 268, 290n.32
Dupront, Alphonse, 38

Eade, John, and Michael Sallnow, 26–27, 29–30, 285n.51, 313n.3
Eck, Diana, 264
economic factors influencing pilgrimage, 79, 123, 128–131, 151–152, 301n.108
eighty-eight: earliest usage of, 112, 114;

suggested reasons for, 10, 112, 118–119, 277–278; unclear origins of, 10, 111–112
Emon Saburō, 60–61, 110, 113; legends and traces of, 61, 113; as permanent pilgrim, 256
emotional landscape/terrain, 5–6, 13, 38, 39–41, 46, 50, 64, 74. *See also* landscape
enlightenment, 52–53
entertainment and leisure, 91, 100–101; criticisms of, 146; early examples of, 115, 127; growth of in Tokugawa period Shikoku, 129–131; growth of in twentieth century, 145; as motive of pilgrims, 91, 100–101, 227–230; relatively low levels of in Tokugawa era Shikoku, 129–130. *See also* Dōgō hot springs; tourism
equality among pilgrims, 59, 263; tensions with hierarchy and status, 59, 177, 200, 263–264, 269. *See also* common bonds among pilgrims; *dōgyō*; hierarchy and status
evil passions *(bonnō)*: temples as representing eradication of, 119, 277–278

family pilgrimages, 97, 102; pilgrimage customs as inherited through, 93, 96–97. *See also* generational influences
female pilgrims, 77, 85, 131; as benefiting from modern developments, 159, 177; high proportion of in Tokugawa pilgrimage, 131–132; as most numerous in modern period, 77–78; as *sendatsu*, 177–178; as suffering discrimination and sexual harassment in pre-modern period, 130, 286n.65, 301n.131; as walkers, 196–197. *See also* loss of love; Satō Takako; Takamure Itsue; Tsukioka Yukiko
feudal authorities, 114, 123, 135–138; and ambivalent views of pilgrims, 126, 135–136; as assisting, caring for, and repatriating pilgrims, 114, 137–138; as regulating and punishing pilgrims, 114, 126, 135–137
foot pilgrims. *See* walkers
footsteps: continued creation of, 262; of influential pilgrims, 121–122; of

Kōbō Daishi, 12, 57; pilgrimage as lineage and trail of, 41, 92; as pilgrimage motif, 12, 83; of *sendatsu*, 179; of Takamure Itsue, 86; of teachers, 83–85

fragmented pilgrimages, 20, 76–77. *See also* day trip *(higaeri)* pilgrimages; *ikkoku mairi*

Frey, Nancy Louise, 20, 27, 36, 39, 65, 196, 237, 249–250, 255–256, 264–265, 287n.83, 314n.15. *See also* Santiago de Compostela Pilgrimage

fuda, 21, 62, 66, 97, 112, 132, 241; earliest examples of, 114; and local customs, 62; as sacred, 62, 92, 177; as signifying pilgrimage experience, 21. *See also* alms *(settai)* and almsgiving

generational influences: and inherited family traditions, 96–99; as motive for becoming pilgrims, 92–99, 170

goals: pilgrims as goal-centered while on route, 187, 249; studies of pilgrimage as tending to be focused on, 187, 249–250, 313n.3

Gold, Anne, 35, 223, 240, 250

Gorai Shigeru, 109, 297n.13

Grapard, Allan, 50–51

graves of pilgrims on route, 63, 65, 116, 121, 132–133. *See also* dead, the; death

Greek pilgrimages, 32, 35, 134

group pilgrimages, 18; devotional orientations of, 18, 37; earliest evidence of, 114; and individualized dimensions of, 30–31, 219, 237–238, 248; as normative, 99, 155. *See also* bus package tours; bus pilgrims; family pilgrimages

guidebooks, 17, 114–119, 145, 153, 162–163, 180–183, 314n.17; appearance of with tourist themes, 131, 145; as combining the miraculous and the practical, 119; earliest examples, 114; modern publishing industry in, 162–163; traditional images in, 180–182; for walkers, 185, 261. *See also* commercial developments and infrastructures; Iyo Tetsu Company; NHK; nostalgia; Shikoku Reijōkai

gyaku uchi, 16, 60, 257, 283n.20.

Gyōgi, 44, 110

hakui (pilgrim's shirt), 1, 12, 57, 230. *See also* pilgrims' clothing/garb

Hannya Shingyō, 21, 102, 230, 290n.33

Harada Nobuo, 65, 189–190, 191–194, 196–200, 206–207, 211–214, 309n.3

hardship, 141–142, 202, 209–210; as integral to benefits of pilgrimage, 202–203, 211; in package tours, 223; as trial set by Kōbō Daishi, 213. *See also* ascetic practices; walkers

Hatada family (at Anrakuji, Temple 6), 94, 170, 259, 307n.55; Hatada Shūhō, 94, 170, 307n.55; Hatada Zenpō, 52, 93–94, 170

health: as motivation for pilgrims, 82, 183–184, 192, 196, 228–229, 259–260. *See also* miracles; motives of pilgrims; pilgrims in Shikoku

helicopter pilgrimages, 18, 29, 279, 283n.30

henro: etymology and meanings in Japanese, 33; first use of in Shikoku, 111; significance of term, 9; translated by 'pilgrimage,' 32. *See also* pilgrimage; pilgrims in Shikoku; Shikoku pilgrimage

Henro (monthly pilgrimage newsletter), 81, 96, 162, 179, 255

henro boke. See walkers

henro ishi. See pilgrimage stones/markers

Henro Michi Hozon Kyōryokukai, 65, 71, 117, 185, 259–262. *See also* Miyazaki Tateki

hierarchy and status, 21, 29, 59, 88, 177–178, 262–264; as acquired through multiple performance, 91, 262–264; as emerging within tour groups, 218–219; as manifest in the *sendatsu* system, 177–178, 263; as passed from generation to generation, 92–97; tensions with notions of equality, 59, 177, 200, 263–264, 269. *See also* common bonds among pilgrims; communitas; *dōgyō*; equality among pilgrims; *sendatsu*

hijiri, 44, 108

Hirahata Ryōyū, 56, 314n.17

hobby: pilgrimage as, 102, 228

home, 34–35, 50, 251, 265; as being on pilgrimage route, 257–262; as integral to the pilgrimage process, 35, 265–266,

268–269; and problematic contrast with movement, 266, 268–269; problems experienced on return to, 255–256. *See also* pilgrimage
honeymoon pilgrimages, 93
Hoshino Eiki, 17, 26, 51, 53, 85, 112, 125–127, 132, 146–147, 160, 214, 253, 289n.16

Ichinomiya (regional state shrines), 112; as pilgrimage sites, 112; secession from route in Meiji period, 138, 139
Ikeda Hayato, 192, 310n.14
Ikiki Jizō, 93; and loss of pilgrims due to route changes, 157, 306n.29
ikkoku mairi, 19–20, 100; as initiatory pilgrimages, 127
images of tradition, 12, 24–25, 49–50, 152, 180–183; as central to Shikoku pilgrimage's appeal, 12, 152; and fusion with the modern, 182–183; Shikoku as symbol of cultural tradition, 29, 144, 152, 180–183; used to promote pilgrimage, 24–25, 49–50, 180–183. *See also* guidebooks; NHK; Shikoku Reijōkai
Imai Misako, 80, 135, 197
income, temple sources of, 150
initiation through pilgrimage, 81–82, 97, 122, 126–127, 146
inscriptions: as early evidence of pilgrimage, 111–114; left by pilgrims, 66–67
Internet: and cyberspace pilgrim communities, 183–184, 309n.95
Ippen Shōnin, 110
Ise pilgrimage, 129, 301n.116
Iwaki-kai (pilgrimage association), pilgrimage tour of, 220–248
Iyo Tetsu Company, 3, 61, 99, 152–155, 163–167, 219, 224–225; costs of pilgrimages run by, 279–280; honored for its services by Shikoku Reijōkai, 167; relationship between commerce and piety in, 163–167; staff as *sendatsu*, 164, 173. *See also* bus package tours; bus pilgrims; commercial developments and infrastructures; *Henro*; *sendatsu* system; Shikoku Reijōkai

Jakuhon, 117–119; promotes Shingon focus to the pilgrimage, 118–119

Jishū (Buddhist sect), 14, 110
Jōdo Shin (Pure Land) Buddhism: members of as Shikoku pilgrims, 95, 285n.55, 289n.21
journalists, 80, 144–145. *See also* Imai Misako; mass media; NHK (Japan Broadcasting Corporation); Satō Ken
Junrei no Kai (pilgrimage association), 56, 225

Kagayama Kōichi, 191–193
Kagita Chūsaburō, 65, 159, 192–193, 198, 211, 213, 216, 252–253; 282n.11, 313n.98
Kaiganji, 17
kakejiku. See books, scrolls, and stamps
Kannon, 10, 14, 108
Kansai Sendatsukai (pilgrimage association), 89, 174
kasa (pilgrim's hat), 1, 12, 57
Kenmyō, 114, 116
Kiyoyoshi Eitoku, 70–72, 121, 257, 303n.187
Kōbō Daishi, 10–12, 41–47; as ambivalent figure, 12, 59, 169; as architect of pilgrimage/as sacralizing the landscape, 39, 54–57; as being with and protecting pilgrims, 12, 45, 56–59, 214, 254–255; bestows reward and retribution, 56–57, 118; as central organizing focus of pilgrimage, 30, 109–111, 270; creates hardships to test pilgrims, 56, 213–214; faith in, legends and cult of, 11, 42–46, 54–57, 88, 90–91, 254–255, 262–263, 288n.16; feet washed by pilgrims, 57–58; footsteps of, 45, 57; legends and miracles of, 41, 54–57, 88, 92, 118, 213, 254–255, 299n.72; parallels with St. James, 11–12, 44, 289n.28; as permanent pilgrim and wanderer, 11, 43, 46, 256; pilgrim invocations to, 20–21; and pilgrimage foundation legends, 45–47, 56; presence permeates route, 12, 44, 119; presence symbolized by pilgrim's clothing 57; relationship with Shikoku, 12; as role model for ascetics, 110–111; and Shingon Buddhism, 10, 41–44; as source of practical benefits, 45, 102–103; as transcendent miracle worker, 10–12; venerated by Jōdo Shin

(Pure Land) Buddhists, 95, 285n.55, 289n.21. See also *dōgyō;* footsteps; Kōyasan; miracles; pilgrims in Shikoku; reward and retribution
Kokubunji (regional state temples), 112
Kondō Yoshihiro, 108–109, 278
Konjaku Monogatari, 108
Konpira Shrine, 17, 131, 238–240
Kotosan Bus Company, 153–154, 158; and *sendatsu,* 172–174; service and piety in, 164
Kouamé, Nathalie, 125–126, 129–131, 137–138
Kōyasan (Mount Kōya), 10, 13–14, 42–43, 51, 257, 288n.13; barred to women until 1873, 132; influences/ attempted influences on pilgrimage, 108–111, 117–119, 147–148, 278, 304n.210
Kūkai, 10–11, 21, 41–43, 45. *See also* Kōbō Daishi
Kumano pilgrimage, 108–109, 278; and influences on Saikoku and Shikoku, 108
Kunisaki, 50–51

landscape, 5–6, 20, 36–38, 39–41, 73–74, 109, 186; as constantly changing text, 74, 186; importance of in studying pilgrimages, 36–38, 267; as infused with miracles and sacred narratives, 39–41, 56–57; as interweaving of physical and emotional, 38, 41, 73–74. *See also* emotional landscape/terrain; pilgrimage community; Shikoku, island of; Shikoku pilgrimage *(henro)*
legends, 6, 56–57, 60; as 'historical realities,' 45–46, 54–56, 61–62; moral meanings in, 60–61; as shaping pilgrims' understandings, 61
leprosy, 118, 123, 133–134, 142, 302n.139; miraculous cure from, 118; as reason for becoming pilgrims, 133
liminality, 30, 125, 134–135, 249–250; problems of viewing pilgrimage in the context of, 188, 249–250, 313n.3. *See also* marginality
local communities: as shaping pilgrimage traditions, 26, 92–97, 122–127, 267–268. *See also* Shikoku residents
local pilgrimages, 10, 14–15, 112; as

absorbed into Shikoku route, 14–15, 112; as performed by Shikoku residents, 112
lodgings. *See* pilgrims' lodges; temple lodges
loss of love *(shitsuren):* as motive for pilgrimage, 85–87. *See also* Nakatsuka Mōhei; Takamure Itsue

MacGregor, Fiona, 296n.63
Maeda Takashi, 112, 124, 126, 130–134
Maitreya (Miroku), 42–43
mandala, pilgrimage as, 51–52, 153; Shikoku landscape as, 51–52
marginality: as an attraction for pilgrims, 134; and death, 63–64; marginal nature of pilgrims 27, 125, 134, 301n.121; marginal nature of route, 47–48, 134. *See also* ambivalence; liminality
married couples as pilgrims together, 101–103, 258–259
mass media, 24–25; attacks by against pilgrims, 140–141; develop and portray positive views of pilgrimage from 1920s, 144–145; portray Shikoku pilgrimage as symbol of Japanese tradition, 144–145, 156–157, 180–183. *See also* cultural heritage and identity; images of tradition; journalists; nostalgia; NHK (Japan Broadcasting Corporation)
Meiji Restoration, 138–141; impact of anti-Buddhist campaigns in Shikoku, 138–139
memorializing the dead, 64, 80–82, 102–103, 227–229, 245. *See also* ancestors; dead, the; death; motives of pilgrims
michishirube. See pilgrimage stones/ markers
miracles, miracle stories, 6, 14, 54–62, 67–68, 83–84, 88, 93–95, 118, 120–121, 175–176, 253–255; as central to the construction of pilgrimage, 119; collections of, 56–57, 289n.29; narration of by *sendatsu,* 175–176; occurring along the route, 14, 56–57; occurring at temples, 14, 67–68, 120–121; as passed on/shared among pilgrims, 54–56, 76, 84, 237–238. *See*

also Kōbō Daishi; pilgrims in Shikoku; *Shikoku henro kudokuki;* temples on Shikoku pilgrimage

misfortune, as motivation for pilgrimage, 27–28, 84, 85, 92, 256

Miyazaki Tateki, 65, 71–72, 117, 194, 259–264, 265, 270; criticizes temples and *sendatsu,* 177, 261–262; erects pilgrimage markers, 71, 260–261; produces guidebooks for walkers, 185, 261; promotes walking, 185, 261, relationship with Shikoku Reijōkai, 262, 270. *See also* Henro Michi Hozon Kyōryokukai

modernization: as facilitating pilgrimage growth, 143–146; pilgrims as reacting against, 156; as transforming pilgrimage and temples, 150–157. *See also* commercial developments and infrastructures; transport developments

modes of travel in Shikoku, 18–19; different modes of as creating different perceptions of pilgrimage, 188–189; different modes of travel combined in, 88–89; doing pilgrimage in sections, 19–20, 77. *See also* bicycle, pilgrimage by; bus package tours; bus pilgrims; car pilgrimages; helicopter pilgrimages; walkers

money: and costs, 279–280; readiness of pilgrims to spend, 238–240

moral landscapes, 60–61, 119–120

Moreton, David, 299n.78

motives of pilgrims, 27–28, 90–92, 156, 226–229; challenging oneself as, 85; enjoyment as, 91; as multiple, 80, 82, 102, 106; not necessarily connected to faith, 85; as not necessarily known prior to departure, 103–106; as retirement hobby, 82, 102, 294n.24; scenery and environment as, 79–80, 100–102, 197, 228, 231; seeking solace as, 28. *See also* books, scrolls, and stamps; cultural heritage and identity; death; entertainment and leisure; generational influences; health; Kōbō Daishi; loss of love; memorializing the dead; miracles, miracle stories; misfortune; pilgrims in Shikoku; practical benefits; salvation; tourism; *yakudoshi*

mountains, 49; mountain temples as

prevalent on route, 16; as *reizan* associated with death, 49, 290n.41

movement: interrelationship with home, 265–266. *See also* home

multiple performances of pilgrimage, 87–92, 249–266; competitive aspects of, 91, 263; early evidence of, 114; as means of acquiring status, 91; as posing a challenge to normative understandings of pilgrimage, 268; reasons for, 262–265. *See also* addictive nature of pilgrimage; permanent pilgrims; *sendatsu;* way of life, pilgrimage as

multiple site pilgrimages, 9–10

Naitō Hirozō, 92–95, 151; inherits leadership of Shiga Shingyōkai, 93; recalls poor state of temples after World War II, 151; walks pilgrimage in 1946, 93–94; walks pilgrimage with father aged nine, 93. *See also* Naitō Kinpō; Shiga Shingyōkai

Naitō Kinpō, 92–93; founds Shiga Shingyōkai, 93; healed by Kōbō Daishi, 92; miracles associated with, 93; widow's recollections of pilgrimages with, 142–143. *See also* Naitō Hirozō; Shiga Shingyōkai

Nakatsuka Mōhei, 53, 70, 86–87, 91, 121–122, 256, 263, 265; commemorates own pilgrimages, 70, 122; does 282 circuits of island, 121; erects 237 pilgrimage stones, 70, 122, 293n.100; as permanent pilgrim, 121–122, 256; as sacred figure through pilgrimage, 122, 262; unhappiness as initial motivation for, 86–87

Naquin, Susan and Chün Fang Yü, 31, 37, 268, 281n.2

NHK (Japan Broadcasting Corporation): and documentaries and publications about the pilgrimage, 25, 53, 82, 180–181, 285n.45; and images of tradition, 180–181

nōkyōchō. See books, scrolls, and stamps

nostalgia, 24–25, 142–143, 156, 181, 184; as factor in modern pilgrimage growth, 24–25, 156–157; in pilgrimage publicity, 181, 308n.80. *See also* images of tradition

numerical order of temples, 13; becomes

settled by eighteenth century, 127; development of, 116–117; as matter of convenience and historical circumstance, 13

Ontake pilgrimage (Japan), 30–31
ōraitegata, 136
orei mairi, 13–14, 214, 247, 249, 251; as not integral to pilgrimage, 214–215, 247, 282n.11
Osada Seiichi and Sakata Masaaki, 16, 25, 26, 265. *See also* Waseda University research studies of Shikoku pilgrimage
Osaka region: economic links to Shikoku, 127–128; as focus of promotional activities by temples, 128, 148; influence in pilgrimage development, 128

permanent pilgrims, 36, 255–266. *See also* Nakatsuka Mōhei; *sendatsu;* way of life
photographs: of the dead, 80–81; left by pilgrims, 66; of missing pilgrims, 67
pilgrim numbers, 1, 3–4, 129, 154–155; contemporary growth and reasons for, 4, 25, 155–157, 284n. 42; fluctuations due to economic and other circumstances, 4, 128–129, 141; growth of in early twentieth century, 141; in Tokugawa period, 129
pilgrim profiles and statistics: age, gender, and provenance, 25–26, 77–79, 130–132, 146–147, 155, 293n.12, 296n.59; with whom pilgrims travel, 101–102. *See also* multiple performances of pilgrimage; pilgrims in Shikoku; Shikoku pilgrimage; Shikoku residents
pilgrim round-ups, 140–141, 303n.177
pilgrimage: ambivalent nature of, 6, 9, 29, 32, 148, 263–264, 269–271; as being constantly remade, 5, 36–38, 271; cacophony, chaos, and unbounded/unruly nature of, 3, 31–32, 34–36, 268, 270; capacity to incorporate conflicting themes, 28–29, 148–149, 267–271; as continuing after completion, 251–266; contribution of Shikoku to studies of, 267–271; convenience as factor in, 18; cumulative nature of, 31–32, 37–38; as embedded in notions

of home and community, 35, 250, 265–266, 268–269; as encompassing phenomenon and process, 33–34, 269–270; and home, 34–35, 50, 92–96, 265–266, 268–269; importance of geography and landscape in, 4–5; importance of the 'local' in, 267–268; as individual process, 18, 224–225, 248; as influenced by local communities and practices, 26–27, 96–97, 126–127, 132, 267–268; Japanese terms translated as, 32–33; as lacking single theoretical narrative, 31, 315n.3; and landscape, 20, 183; as made by combination of influences and participants, 4–5, 36–38; as means of escape, 27, 100–101, 227–230; need for multidisciplinary approach to the study of, 34–35, 270; as not just transitory/marginal, 8, 96, 250; as point of departure, 216, 253; and ready assimilation of new modes of transport, 18; studies of as tending to focus on goals and transience, 7, 31, 187, 249–250, 313n.3; as symbolic journey to enlightenment, 52–53; as text and narrative, 39–41, 64, 73–74; as 'trail of miracles,' 41, 253–255; and tourism, 36, 287n.87; uses and validity of the term in cross-cultural contexts, 32–33; as way of life and central organizing principle in pilgrims' lives, 8, 187–188, 249–266. *See also* ambivalence; common bonds among pilgrims; communitas; contest; emotional landscape/ terrain; goals; hierarchy and status; home; landscape; multiple performances of pilgrimage; permanent pilgrims; Shikoku pilgrimage
pilgrimage associations. *See* Arita Settaikō; Iwaki-kai; Junrei no Kai; Kansai Sendatsukai; Shiga Shingyōkai; Toho no Kai
pilgrimage community. *See* common bonds among pilgrims; *dōgyō*
pilgrimage guides/leaders. See *sendatsu*
pilgrimage songs, 21
pilgrimage stones/markers, 66, 69–73, 121–122, 260–261, 292n.98; earliest examples of, 114; as encouragement for and creation of bonds between

pilgrims, 71–72; and meanings/uses, 70–71; used to commemorate pilgrimages, 70–71, 114
pilgrimage typologies in Japan, 9–10
pilgrims' books. *See* books, scrolls, and stamps
pilgrims' clothing/garb, 1, 12–13, 63–64, 57, 230; left behind at temples, 68; as mixture of traditional and convenient, 77; modern amendments to, 12–13; symbolism of, 12, 63–64. See also *hakui; kasa; tsue*
pilgrims in Shikoku: as ambivalent/dangerous figures, 13, 126, 135; accompanied and protected by Kōbō Daishi, 12, 45, 56–59, 254–255; becoming pilgrims through performance, 105–106; as challenged by other pilgrims, 242–243; change in post-war image of, 152; as 'dead to the world,' 63–64; as determining own ways of making pilgrimages, 16–17, 20, 235; diversity of in Tokugawa times, 131; as having individual relationship with Kōbō Daishi, 59, 254–255; increasing demands of in modern day, 159; and interest in other pilgrimages, 226; as Kōbō Daishi, 59–62, 123–124; leaving traces of themselves behind at temples/along the route, 66–73; offerings made by, 67, 230–231; as outsiders/marginal, dangerous, poor, and diseased, 27–28, 123–126, 130, 132–133, 134–135, 140, 159; passing on legends and miracles to other pilgrims, 54–56, 76, 84, 237–238; practices and activities at pilgrimage temples, 3, 20–24, 64–69, 230–231; rights and obligations of in feudal times, 137; as sacred and dangerous, 123, 125, 134–138, 149; as sacred/empowered/healing figures, 59–62, 123–124, 263; seek to retain links with pilgrimage community after completion, 216, 264–266; sexual activities among, 130; as shaping the pilgrimage and emotional landscape, 6, 54–56, 64–73; and shared historical consciousness, 64–69; as simultaneously exotic and familiar, 75, 269; as symbolically equal, 59, 263; as travelling with the dead, 80–82;

treated as equal by temple, 189. *See also* bus pilgrims; common bonds; *dōgyō;* equality; hierarchy and status; miracles; motives; permanent pilgrims; pilgrim numbers; pilgrim profiles; Shikoku residents; walkers
pilgrims' lodge owners, 57–58; commercial acumen of, 160–161; and maintenance of pilgrimage customs, 57–58, 160–161, 259
pilgrims' lodges, 25, 144; decline of old-style and rise of large modern lodges, 159–160; impact of modern developments on, 158–161; recent appearance of new lodges for walkers, 185, 309n.94; role of in preserving pilgrimage customs, 58–59, 161; uncomfortable nature of in earlier times, 142, 159. *See also* pilgrims' lodge owners; temple lodges *(shukubō)*
pilgrims' love *(henro ai)*, 30, 142–143. *See also* common bonds among pilgrims; *dōgyō;* equality; Takamure Itsue
practical benefits, 45, 102–103, 228–229
preparing for death and afterlife, pilgrimage as means of, 228–229
priests: criticisms of walkers, 37, 189, 208; as having different views from pilgrims, 12, 94–95; as knowing frequent pilgrims, 241–242; as pilgrims 13; as promoting faith and enthusiasm among pilgrims, 46; as rarely mentioned in early historical accounts, 111; relationships with pilgrims and pilgrimage associations, 93–94, 199–201, 241–242. *See also* Shikoku Reijōkai; Temple numbers; temples
professional pilgrims, 123
promontories, 48–49, 51–52, 109. *See also* Cape Ashizuri; Cape Muroto
Pure Land/Pure Land beliefs and influences in Shikoku, 23, 80, 110, 113, 221. *See also* Jōdo Shin (Pure Land) Buddhism

Rajashthani pilgrims, 35, 223, 250
rebirth, 47, 63–64, 213; and funerals of pilgrims, 23
regional governments and support for

pilgrimage, 48, 157, 161–162, 184, 306n.28, 309n.93

Reijōkai. *See* Shikoku Reijōkai

reintegration and return, 215–216

repentance, 87, 120

reward and retribution, 56–57, 118, 120; and almsgiving, 59–61; as theme of pilgrimage stories, 56–61, 119–120. *See also* alms; Kōbō Daishi; miracles, miracle stories

Rinzai Zen Buddhist sect, 14

Ryōjin Hishō, 108

Saba Daishi, 17, 44, 72, 157

Saikoku pilgrimage, 10, 15, 32, 108, 129, 155, 226, 282n.8, 284n.42, 295n.40

salvation, 23, 83–84, 100, 110, 120; linked to Kōbō Daishi, 43. *See also* absolution; rebirth; transformation

Santiago de Compostela pilgrimage (Camino), 11–12, 20, 27, 36, 65, 77, 189, 237, 250, 255–256, 281n.2; addictive aspects of, 264–265; historical traces of pilgrims on, 65; pilgrims' focus on speed and distances in, 196; walkers and, 83–85, 189. *See also* St. James

Sasaguri pilgrimage (Japan), 265

Satō Hisamitsu, 26, 77, 155–156, 284n.42, 293n.12

Satō Ken, 203, 209

Satō Takako, 192, 196, 206–207, 209–210, 211, 214

sendatsu, 3, 90, 167–172, 251; as ambivalent figures, 178–179; and commercial enterprise, 220–221; criticisms of, 176–177; *female* sendatsu, 96–97, 177–178; first mention of, 171; and hierarchy and status in, 177–178, 263; and miracle stories, 175–177; numbers and regional distribution of, 90, 174–175; ranks, fees, and means of promotion, 172–174; roles in promoting pilgrimage, 171, 175. *See also* bus package tours; hierarchy and status; multiple performances of pilgrimage; permanent pilgrims; *sendatsu* system; way of life, pilgrimage as

sendatsu system, 3, 171–174; assistance of bus companies in, 172. See also *sendatsu*; Shikoku Reijōkai

Seto Ōhashi (bridge), 157, 182; impact on route, 157–158; and use in pilgrimage publicity, 182–183

Setouchi Bus Company, 153–154, 163, 166–167; and *sendatsu*, 173

settai. *See* alms

shakyō (copying Buddhist sutras), 20, 67, 102, 230. See also *Hannya Shingyō*

Shiga Shingyōkai (pilgrimage association), 92–96, 217, 251; and Anrakuji (Temple 6), 93–94; children's pilgrimages of, 92–95; and creation of pilgrimage traditions in local communities, 95–96; reminiscences of members of, 142–143. *See also* Naitō Hirozō; Naitō Kinpō; Temple 6 (Anrakuji)

Shikoku henro kudokuki (1690), 59, 118–119

Shikoku henro michishirube (1687), 116–117, 122

Shikoku henro reijōki (1689), 117

Shikoku, island of: administrative regions of in feudal and modern times, 53; as 'country of death,' 63–64, 133; economic benefits of pilgrimage to, 161–162; folk traditions in, 12; geography and location of, 47–48; landscape of as ambivalent, 50; landscape of as mandala, 51–52; local pilgrimage routes in, 14–15; as marginal and 'other,' 47–50; as sacred island, 48; scenery and environment of as attracting pilgrims, 79–80, 100–102, 157, 181–182, 197, 228, 231; as second home for pilgrims, 50; as simultaneously familiar and other, 49–50; as symbolizing 'traditional' Japan, 49–50, 82; as synonymous with the pilgrimage, 47

Shikoku pilgrimage *(henro)*, 9–10; Buddhist orientations in, 10, 35, 139, 191, 278; as central organizing feature in pilgrims' lives, 99, 187–188, 249–266; costs of, 279–280; development of as mass practice, 113–115, 127–148; emergence of infrastructure and numerical order in, 113–119, 127–148; as encompassing Shikoku's landscape, geography, and religious traditions, 10, 15, 33–34, 109–113; foundation legends of, 45–47, 60; history of post-World War II, 150–186; history of, pre-World War II, 107–149; importance of to Shikoku's economy, 25; Japanese academic theories about origins of, 108–110; Japanese terms for, 9; as journey with Kōbō Daishi, 12, 52, 56–59; lack of early documentary evidence of origins, 107–108; as local, national, and international, 25–27, 29, 35, 155, 267; marginal dimensions of, 27, 47–48; maps of, 119, 278; moral rules and pilgrim choice in, 17–18, 235; as moving text, 66–74; multiple ways of performing, 18–20, 89; multiplicity of participants in, 36–38; no fixed order or route to, 20; as part of the cultural tradition of Shikoku, 26; as performed on behalf of others, 23, 68, 102–103, 234, 284n.40; probable ascetic origins of, 107–111; publicity and promotion of, 127–128, 148, 180–183; role of interest groups in post-war development of, 152–174; route and structure of, 9–10, 13–15, 52; as shaped by historical contexts, 107; spatial location of temples in, 15; structure as facilitating repeated pilgrimages, 255–256; as symbolic journey between death and rebirth, 64; as symbolic map of enlightenment, 52–53; tense relationship of Shingon Buddhist and folk religious themes in, 12, 178; time taken to perform, 19, 114–115, 279–280; as transcending sectarian barriers, 95; variety of temples on route, 14–15. *See also* images of tradition; Kōbō Daishi; pilgrims; Shikoku, island of; Shikoku Reijōkai; temples on Shikoku pilgrimage

Shikoku Pilgrimage Temples' Association. *See* Shikoku Reijōkai

Shikoku Reijōkai (Shikoku Pilgrimage Temples' Association), 7, 152; and commercial firms, 164, 167–168, 172, 179; development, organization, and roles of, 167–169; mediates in Temple 30 dispute, 139–140; and NHK (Japan Broadcasting Corporation), 180–183; organizes pilgrimage publicity, 169; organizes *sendatsu* system, 171–172; and pilgrimage promotion, 49–50,

180–183; produces videos and CD-ROMs, 183, 308n.85; publishes/ promotes miracle tales, 56, 64; seeks to regulate temple and pilgrim activities, 168–169; and Shingon influences/ teachings, 53, 169–170, 172. *See also* images of tradition; *sendatsu* system; temples

Shikoku residents, 25–26, 259; almsgiving and moral support to pilgrims, 60–62, 124–126, 203–206; ambivalent attitudes to pilgrims, 26–27, 125–126, 135; care for sick pilgrims, 137–138; criticize modern pilgrimage, 27, 183; generational influences among, 97; influence in shaping pilgrimage, 26, 259–262, 267–268; and maintenance and passing on of pilgrimage customs, 26, 58–59, 62, 259–262; as pilgrims in Shikoku, 26–27, 49, 97, 126–127, 132, 146. *See also* alms; generational influences; pilgrim profiles

Shimada Taiichirō, 220–226, 234, 244–245; combining commercial and spiritual activities, 220–221; commercial links in Shikoku, 238–240; criticism of 'false pilgrim,' 241–243; duties as leader of pilgrimage tours, 220–221; interactions with pilgrims in party, 220–226, 234, 241–243; miracle narratives by, 221; and pilgrimage etiquette, 235, 244–245; promotion of pilgrimage tours by, 221, 226, 234

Shingon Buddhism, 10, 12, 41–44, 51–52, 170; and influences on pilgrimage, 51–53, 117–119, 147, 153, 278, 307n.53; tensions with folk tradition, 12, 178. *See also* Kōbō Daishi; Kōyasan; Kūkai

Shinjō Tsunezō, 108, 130

Shinnen, 59–61, 115–121; establishes first pilgrimage stones and pilgrims' lodge, 116, 299n.62, 299n.65; as 'father of the pilgrimage,' 116; as inspirational figure for later pilgrims, 65, 121, 262; links with Kōyasan, 116; and pilgrimage stones, 70; produces early guidebook and collection of miracle tales, 116–118; role in developing the pilgrimage, 115–119. *See also* Jakuhon; *Shikoku henro kudokuki; Shikoku henro michishirube*

Shinno Toshikazu, 9, 51, 178, 281n.1, 297n.17
Shinto shrines: as pilgrimage sites in Shikoku, 10, 112, 138–139. *See also* Konpira Shrine; Meiji Restoration
Shōdoshima pilgrimage (Japan), 265, 295n.40
Shōren, 70, 121
Shugendō, 14, 171
shukubō. See temple lodges
Sōtō Zen Buddhist sect, 14
souvenirs, 22, 37, 238–240, 246–247
St. James, 11–12, 289n.28; parallels with Kōbō Daishi, 11–12, 44. *See also* Santiago de Compostela
Statler, Oliver, 62, 255

Tabuchi Yoshio, 88–92, 262–263, 265; activities on behalf of the pilgrimage, 89, 175; pilgrim's book of, 92; as *sendatsu*, 174–175. *See also* miracles; *sendatsu*; way of life
Tada Emon, 70, 256; does pilgrimage, 136, times, 70, 121, 256; grave of, 121
Takada Shinkai, 71, 197–198, 201
Takamure Itsue, 16, 20, 85–87, 133, 141–143, 251–253; does pilgrimage in reverse order, 16; fears of pilgrim round-ups, 141; hardships experienced by, 141–142; nostalgic themes of, 141–142, 252; and pilgrims' love, 30, 142; as role model for young female pilgrims, 86, 252; suffers sexual harassment, 130; transformation and, 251–253; writings of, 141, 252. *See also* female pilgrims; Tsukioka Yukiko
Takeda Tokuemon, 70, 121
Tattebe Zuiyū, 253
taxi, pilgrimage by, 18, 143–144, 154; costs of, 279
Temple 1 (Ryōzenji), 13, 44, 69, 96, 213–214; designated as Number 1 by Shinnen, 116, 127; links to Arita Settaikō, 69, 96, 169.
Temple 2 (Gokurakuji), 52, 134, 150–151; death register at, 133
Temple 6 (Anrakuji), 71–72; links with pilgrimage associations, 93–94; interactions with pilgrims, 169–171, 259. *See also* Hatada family; Shiga Shingyōkai

Temple 19 (Tatsueji), 15, 120
Temple 20 (Tairyūji), 14
Temple 23 (Yakuōji), 15
Temple 24 (Higashidera), 14, 41
Temple 27 (Kōnomineji), 120, 177; destroyed and rebuilt during Meiji period, 139
Temple 30 (Zenrakuji and Anrakuji), dispute over rightful position as, 139–140
Temple 38 (Kongōbuji), 15
Temple 41 (Ryūkōji), 1–3, 75–76
Temple 42 (Butsumokuji), 2
Temple 43 (Meisekiji), 2, 16
Temple 45 (Iwayaji), 14, 54, 110; Kōbō Daishi legends and, 54, 110; landscape of, 54
Temple 49 (Jōdoji), early graffiti and inscriptions at, 113
Temple 51 (Ishiteji), 60–61, 113, 165
Temple 52 (Taisanji), 97
Temple 60 (Yokomineji), 14, 15, 120, 197; and new road, 157
Temple 61 (Kōonji), temple lodge at, 144, 155, 252
Temple 66 (Unpenji), 14, 120; as highest temple on route, 20; now reached by ropeway, 158; setting of enhances pilgrims' interactions, 232
Temple 71 (Iyataniji), 14; and death, 49; impact of atmosphere of on pilgrims, 16, 68, 232; landscape of, 49; miracles at, 67–68, 120; and Pure Land, 221
Temple 75 (Zentsūji), 14, 41, 118; as birthplace of Kūkai, 14, 110; grandeur of affects pilgrims, 15–16, 235; suggested as starting point by Jakuhon, 118
Temple 80 (Kokubunji), evidence of early inscriptions and graffiti at, 113
Temple 84 (Yashimaji), 15
Temple 86 (Shidoji), holds exhibition in Osaka to promote pilgrimage, 128
Temple 88 (Ōkuboji), 13, 68, 208, 216, 227, 249; excitement of pilgrims at reaching, 214–215, 246–247; souvenir stalls at 22, 246–247
temple lodges *(shukubō)*, 77, 144, 150, 161, 205
temple offices *(nōkyōjo)*, 22, 243; and books, scrolls, and stamps, 22–23; and kindness to pilgrims, 201; as

sources of frustration for pilgrims, 199–200, 243–244, 311n.44, 311n.46
temples on Shikoku pilgrimage: as affording special treatment to walkers, 199–201; connections to and relationships with pilgrims, 17, 93–96, 169–171; death registers at, 133; destruction of, 113, 138–139; development of cooperation between, 147–149, 168; as focus of miracle stories, 67–68, 120–121; foundation stories of, 14, 44; as having different orientations from pilgrims, 170–171; impoverished state of post-World War II, 150–151; income and modern opulence of, 150; numbers assigned to, 2, 118; numbers, names, and sectarian affiliations of, 273–276; pilgrim activities at, 20–24, 64–69, 230–231; as *reijō*, 14; as theoretically all equal, 15; as 'unequal' in pilgrims' minds, 15–16, 234–235. *See also* priests; Shikoku Reijōkai; Temple numbers
temporary communities: pilgrimage groups as, 99–101, 217–218, 220–248; as providing identity and purpose for individual pilgrims, 248; transient nature and rapid dissolution of, 248. *See also* bus package tours; bus pilgrims; group pilgrimages
Tendai Buddhist sect, 14
Tibetan pilgrimages, 41, 291n.52, 315n.3
Tinos (Greek pilgrimage site), 35, 47, 134–135
Toho no Kai (pilgrimage association), 70–71, 170
Tokugawa period: as facilitating pilgrimage development, 122–123, 128–129; growth of tourism during, 129–131; transport improvements in, 128
Tomita Gakujun, 146–148; promotes Shingon themes, 148. *See also* pilgrims' love
tourism, 100–101, 129–131, 145, 149, 183, 238–240; problems with distinctions between tourists and pilgrims 36–37. *See also* entertainment and leisure
transformation: as motif of pilgrimage experiences, 27, 64, 86, 213–215, 251–253

transport developments, 6–7, 16, 18, 143–146, 155–158; criticisms of, 27, 146; and decline in numbers of walkers, 181; impact on route and patterns of pilgrimage, 6–7, 157–158; improvements in Tokugawa Japan, 128–129; and increasing use of modern forms of, 143–146, 155–158; as making pilgrimage accessible to wider community, 79, 155–158; as making pilgrimage quicker for walkers, 128, 131; as providing increasing choice for pilgrims, 79. *See also* bus package tours; helicopter tours; Iyo Tetsu Company; Kotosan Bus Company; Setouchi Bus Company; Seto Ōhashi
tsue (pilgrim's staff), 1, 12, 57; death symbolism of, 63; as representing Kōbō Daishi, 12, 57–59, 63. *See also* pilgrims' clothing/garb
Tsujita Shōyū, 253–255, 265. *See also* miracles; way of life
Tsukioka Yukiko, 86, 196–197, 198–199, 205; as following in the footsteps of Takamure Itsue, 86. *See also* female pilgrims; Takamure Itsue
Turner, Victor, 30, 249, 263, 313n.2. *See also* communitas; liminality

unemployment, 27–28;

walkers, 7, 187–216; alms and support received by, 200–208; and cathartic experiences, 211–213; challenge as motivating factor for, 85, 195; complaints about temples, 199–200; complaints about the route, 197–198; complaints over accommodation, 161, 195, 198–199, 310n.18, 311n.41; concerns with health and fitness, 183–184, 192, 196; costs incurred by, 279; criticisms of, 37, 189, 208; decline in numbers of in 1980s, 183–184, 308n.81; dilemmas faced over offers of lifts, 206–208; emotions and problems faced on completion, 214–216, 255–256, 314n.115; as expecting special treatment and precedence, 191–192, 199–201, 311n.44; focus on basic practicalities, 191–195; focus on route and spaces between temples, 189–190, 261,

309n.3; hardships endured by, 141–142, 202, 209–213; as having different perceptions from bus pilgrims, 9, 188–190, 194; improving facilities for, 185–186; interactions with bus pilgrims, 188, 204, 245–246; interactions with other walkers, 191–192; and memories of the dead, 209–210; obsession with speed and distances, 194–197; and pilgrimage immersion/self-absorption, 76, 191–194; problems caused by loss of old paths, 181, 260; rapid mood changes of, 211–213; revival in numbers of, 184–186, 286n.59; and senses of transformation and rebirth, 213–216, 251–253; tensions and insecurities of, 194; written accounts by, 187–216. *See also* Harada Nobuo; Imai Misako; Kagita Chūsaburō; Satō Ken; Satō Takako; Takada Shinkai; Takamure Itsue; Tsukioka Yukiko

Waseda University research studies of Shikoku pilgrimage, 16, 77–78, 80, 95, 99, 229, 279. *See also* Osada Seiichi and Sakata Masaaki

way of life, pilgrimage as, 8, 99, 187–188, 249–266. *See also* generational influences, permanent pilgrims; *sendatsu;* Shiga Shingyōkai; Tabuchi Yoshio; Tsujita Shōyū

World War II: impact on pilgrimage, 148; returnee soldiers as pilgrims, 150

yakudoshi, 15, 45, 70, 100, 122, 289n.23
Yakushi, 14, 177
Yamamoto Genpō, 256–257, 314n.16
Yoritomi Motohiro and Shiragi Toshiyuki, 109, 112, 115, 297n.8
Yoshino River, 14, 15
zenkonyado (free lodgings for pilgrims). *See* alms

About the Author

Ian Reader has written widely on aspects of Japanese social and religious life. Among his book publications are *Japanese Religions: Past and Present; A Poisonous Cocktail: Aum Shinrikyo's Path to Violence; Religious Violence in Contemporary Japan;* and (with George J. Tanabe, Jr.) *Practically Religious: Worldly Benefits and the Common Religion of Japan.* He is currently professor of religious studies at Lancaster University, England.